Cancún, Cozumel & the Yucatán

THIS EDITION WRITTEN AND RESEARCHED BY

John Hecht, Lucas Vidgen

PLAN YOUR TRIP

SAM CAMP / GETTY IMAGES ©
LAGUNA BACALAR P133

JOSE IGNACIO SOTO / GETTY IMAGES ©
X'KEKÉN P192

ON THE ROAD

WITOLD SKRYPCZAK / GETTY IMAGES ©
COBÁ P121

Contents

UNDERSTAND

SURVIVAL GUIDE

SPECIAL FEATURES

Welcome to Cancún, Cozumel & the Yucatán

Few Mexican destinations can dazzle you with ancient Maya ruins, azure Caribbean waters and colonial cities all in one fell swoop. Actually, there's only one – the Yucatán.

Life's a Beach

Without a doubt, this corner of Mexico boasts some of the most beautiful stretches of coastline you'll ever see – which explains in large part why beaches get top billing on the peninsula. On the east coast you have the famous coral-crushed white sands and turquoise waters of the Mexican Caribbean, while up north you'll find sleepy fishing villages with sandy streets and wildlife-rich surroundings. For the ultimate beach-bumming experience you can always hit one of several low-key islands off the Caribbean coast, where life moves at a refreshingly slow pace.

Maya Ruins Galore

You can't help but feel awestruck when standing before the pyramids, temples and ball courts of one of the most brilliant pre-Hispanic civilizations of all time. Yes, those Maya certainly knew a thing or two about architecture and they were no slouchers when it came to astronomy, science and mathematics either. Witnessing their remarkable achievements firsthand leaves a lasting impression on even the most jaded traveler. The peninsula is chock-full of these mind-blowing Maya archaeological sites, several of which were built right on the coast.

Nature's Playground

The Yucatán always keeps nature enthusiasts thoroughly entertained. With colorful underwater scenery like no other, it offers some of the best diving and snorkeling sites in the world. Then you have the many biosphere reserves and national parks that are home to a wide array of animal and plant life. Just to give you an idea of what's in store: you can swim with whale sharks, observe crocodiles and monkeys, help liberate newborn sea turtles, and spy hundreds upon hundreds of bird species in mangroves and jungles.

Culture & Fun

Those who need more than just pretty beaches and ancient ruins will be glad to know that cultural and recreational activities are plentiful in the Yucatán. On any given day you may come across soulful dance performances, free concerts, interesting museums and art shows – especially in Mérida, the peninsula's colonial cultural capital. For some fun in the sun, the Yucatán is one big splash fest after another, with thousands of underground natural pools, parks with subterranean rivers and all kinds of thrilling boat tours.

Why I Love Cancún, Cozumel & the Yucatán

By John Hecht, Writer

Above all, I love the colors. Maybe I've been living in smog-choked Mexico City *waaay* too long, but every time I visit the peninsula I find myself asking: can an ocean or lake really have that many shades of blue, and can jungles and mangroves really look so chlorophyll green? Also, it's just great to be in a place with so many outdoorsy things to do. Had your fill of Maya ruins? No problem, have a dip in a limestone sinkhole or explore coral reefs. And don't even get me started about the Yucatán's wonderful regional cuisine.

For more about our writers, see page 320

Above: Ek' Balam (p195)

Cancún, Cozumel & the Yucatán

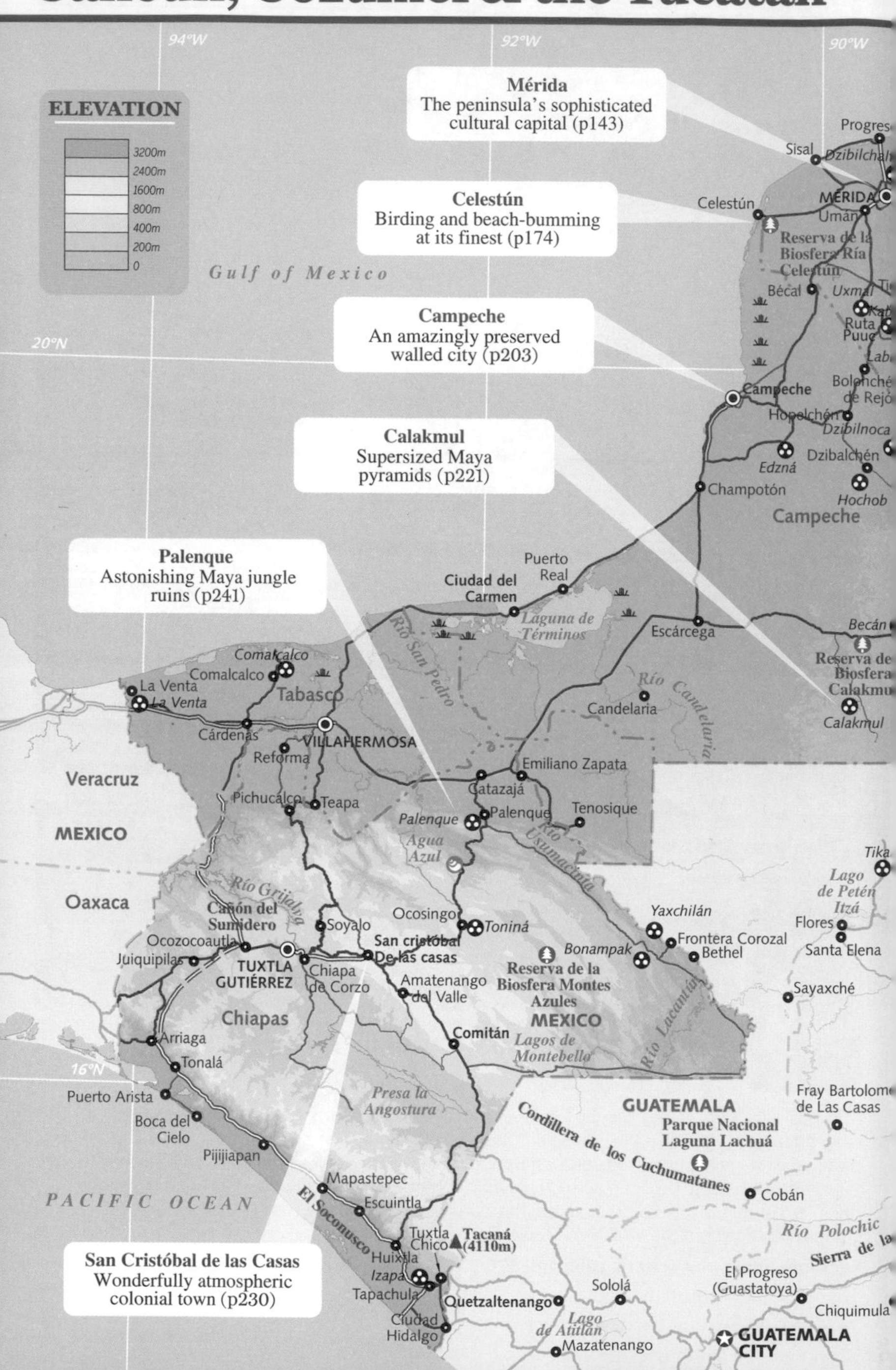

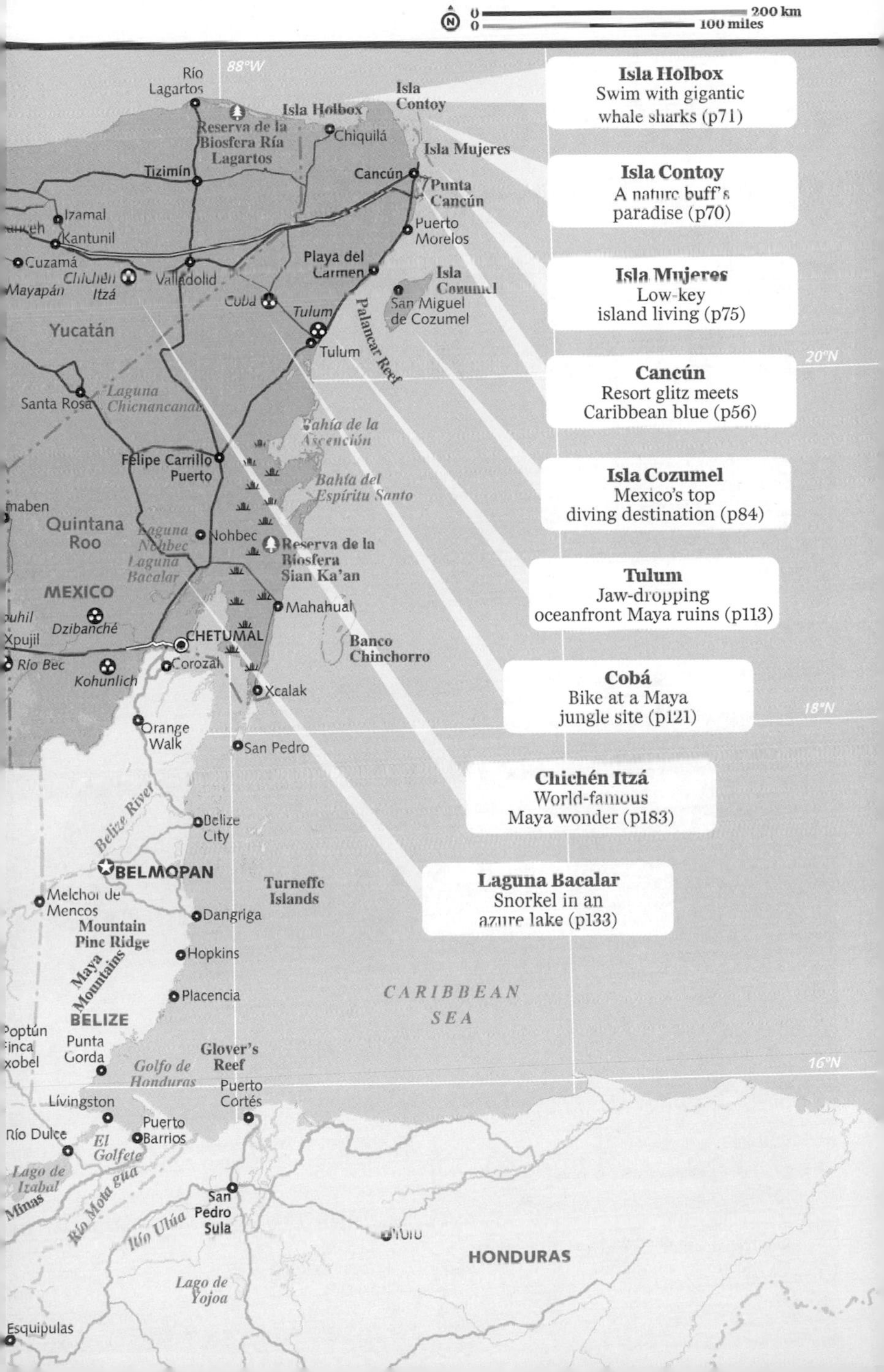

0 — 200 km
0 — 100 miles

Isla Holbox
Swim with gigantic whale sharks (p71)

Isla Contoy
A nature buff's paradise (p70)

Isla Mujeres
Low-key island living (p75)

Cancún
Resort glitz meets Caribbean blue (p56)

Isla Cozumel
Mexico's top diving destination (p84)

Tulum
Jaw-dropping oceanfront Maya ruins (p113)

Cobá
Bike at a Maya jungle site (p121)

Chichén Itzá
World-famous Maya wonder (p183)

Laguna Bacalar
Snorkel in an azure lake (p133)

88°W
20°N
18°N
16°N
Río Lagartos
Isla Holbox
Isla Contoy
Reserva de la Biosfera Ría Lagartos
Chiquilá
Isla Mujeres
Tizimín
Cancún
Punta Cancún
Izamal
Kantunil
Puerto Morelos
Cuzamá
Playa del Carmen
Chichén Itzá
Valladolid
Isla Cozumel
Mayapán
Cobá
Tulum
San Miguel de Cozumel
Yucatán
Palancar Reef
Tulum
Santa Rosa
Laguna Chichancanab
Bahía de la Ascención
Felipe Carrillo Puerto
Bahía del Espíritu Santo
Quintana Roo
Laguna Nohbec
Nohbec
Reserva de la Biosfera Sian Ka'an
Laguna Bacalar
MEXICO
Dzibanché
Mahahual
Xpujil
CHETUMAL
Banco Chinchorro
Río Bec
Corozal
Kohunlich
Xcalak
Orange Walk
San Pedro
Belize River
Belize City
BELMOPAN
Turneffe Islands
Melchor de Mencos
Mountain Pine Ridge
Dangriga
Maya Mountains
Hopkins
Placencia
CARIBBEAN SEA
BELIZE
Punta Gorda
Glover's Reef
Golfo de Honduras
Puerto Cortés
Lívingston
Puerto Barrios
Río Dulce
El Golfete
Lago de Izabal
Río Motagua
San Pedro Sula
Río Ulúa
HONDURAS
Lago de Yojoa
Esquipulas

Cancún, Cozumel & the Yucatán's Top 17

1

Peerless Palenque

1 Gather all your senses and dive headfirst into the amazing Palenque ruins (p241), one of the Maya world's finest. Here pyramids rise above jungle treetops and howler monkeys sound off like monsters in the dense canopy. Wander the mazelike palace, gazing up at its iconic tower. Scale the stone staircases of the Templo de las Inscripciones, the lavish mausoleum of Pakal (Palenque's mightiest ruler). Then head downhill, following the Otulum river and its pretty waterfalls, and end by visiting Palenque's excellent museum.

Below: Templo de las Inscripciones (p242)

Swimming in Cenotes

2 The Maya considered them sacred gateways to the underworld. OK, so maybe they had a flair for the dramatic, but once you visit a cenote (a limestone sinkhole) you'll better understand where the Maya were coming from. More than 7000 cenotes dot the peninsula; some, such as the spectacular pair of caverns at X'Kekén Jungle Park (Dzitnup), make for refreshing, fun-filled swimming holes, while others, such as the underground cave system at Parque Dos Ojos (p112), draw divers from far and wide.

Below: Swimming at Cenote X'Kekén (p192)

FER GREGORY / SHUTTERSTOCK ©

JOSE IGNACIO SOTO / SHUTTERSTOCK ©

Savor the Flavors

3 If you've never tried regional Yucatecan cuisine (p45), you're in for a real treat. Even by Mexican standards, with its strong culinary tradition, the Yucatán is without a doubt a foodie's haven. Yucatecans are famous for their fiery salsas and marinated *pibiles*. Often wrapped in banana leaves and cooked underground, this meaty traditional dish is a classic on the peninsula. And a visit wouldn't be complete without sampling a delicious home-style *sopa de lima* (a brothy lime soup) or *salbutes* (stuffed tortillas). *¡Buen provecho!*
Below: *Cochinita pibil* (slow-roasted pork; p266)

Isla Holbox

4 You gotta love a place with no cars and zero streetlights. Granted, you may see some golf carts humming up and down Holbox's sandy streets for the dinner-hour rush, but that's about as hectic as it gets on this low-key fisherfolks' island (p71). Snorkeling with 15-ton whale sharks is all the rage in Holbox nowadays. Even if you miss whale-shark season, boat tours go to a freshwater spring and nearby islands for some excellent bird-watching.

BRIAN LASENBY / SHUTTERSTOCK ©

GUMBAO / SHUTTERSTOCK ©

Tulum, Scenic Ruins

5 Talk about your prime beachfront real estate. The dramatically situated Tulum ruins (p114) sit pretty atop a high cliff overlooking a spectacular white-sand beach. After marveling at the sun-baked Maya ruins, and dodging iguanas and distracted tourists, you can cap off your history lesson with a refreshing dip in the azure waters of the Mexican Caribbean. Come nighttime, join soulful fiestas at bars in Tulum Pueblo or escape to the Zona Hotelera for a quiet oceanfront dinner.

Diving in Cozumel

6 Don't miss the opportunity to plunge into the colorful waters surrounding Isla Cozumel (p84), one of the world's best diving and snorkeling destinations. While the spectacular coral reefs are undeniably the main draw, the island's beautiful beaches and pleasant town square keep nondiver types sufficiently entertained. If you're planning to visit in February, don't miss the annual Carnaval, a street celebration with lively music, dancing and plenty of partying.

Magical San Cristóbal

7 Wander through the cobblestone streets of San Cristóbal de las Casas (p230), the high-altitude colonial city in the heart of indigenous Chiapas. A heady mix of modern and Maya, with cosmopolitan cafes and traditional culture, it's also a jumping-off point for fascinating Tzotzil and Tzeltal villages. Spend sunny days exploring captivating churches and shopping at markets for amber or chocolate, then dine at one of many gourmet restaurants in town. Late nights are best whiled away by the fireplace of a cozy watering hole.

DC_APERTURE /SHUTTERSTOCK ©

Scenic Laguna Bacalar

8 Known as 'the lake of seven colors' for its varied shades of blue and aqua-green, it doesn't get any more scenic for an afternoon swim than sparkling Laguna Bacalar (p133). Resort hotel Rancho Encantado has quite possibly the best view on the shore, and at the lake's south end you can take a plunge into the 90m-deep Cenote Azul.

Mérida, Cultural Capital

9 Everyone who goes to Cancún or Playa del Carmen should carve off a couple of days to get to Mérida (p143), a city with awesome Spanish colonial architecture unlike anything you'll find by the sea. The weekends see great parties in steamy Caribbean cantinas and on Sunday morning the city center closes to cars and you can munch on Yucatecan street eats as you watch all sorts of spirited song and dance around the city's main square, Plaza Grande. And living up to its fame as the peninsula's cultural capital, museums and art abound in Mérida.

Isla Mujeres

10 Isla Mujeres (p75) generally shuns the megaresort mindset of nearby Cancún across the bay, and therein lies its appeal. Even though it's a fairly small island, you should have no problem finding things to do. Scuba diving and snorkeling are big and it has some of the most swimmable beaches on the Yucatán, making it perfect for kids. The island's also home to the Isla Mujeres Turtle Farm, which releases tens of thousands of turtles each year and has a nice little aquarium.

Above: Green sea turtle

Calakmul, Jungle Ruins

11 The 'Kingdom of the Serpent's Head' was one of the most powerful Maya cities that ever existed. What has survived the ravages of time here is very impressive – some of the Maya's largest and tallest pyramids, with awesome views of expansive surrounding jungle alive with birds, monkeys and jaguars. And relatively recent excavations at Calakmul (p221) have unearthed an amazing rarity in the Maya world – incredibly well-preserved painted murals and a spectacular stucco frieze. Below: Estructura II, Calakmul

Isla Contoy

12 Parque Nacional Isla Contoy (p70), an uninhabited island just a short distance from Cancún and Isla Mujeres, accepts only 200 visitors a day in order to retain its mostly pristine environment. Home to more than 170 bird species and nesting sea turtles during the summer months, a day trip to the island will definitely appeal to nature lovers – or even to those simply looking to get in a little hiking and snorkeling.

11

12

Celestún

13 Most people head to Celestún (p174) to observe an impressive colony of flamingos, and impressive it is when the brilliant orange-red birds are out in full force. Bird-watching tours take you to a mangrove tunnel and a freshwater spring, and you can get in some nighttime crocodile-watching, too. But what makes this place truly special are its quiet beaches, calm waters and pleasant little town square. It just feels more relaxed than many of the popular Caribbean coast beaches.

Below: Reserva de la Biosfera Ría Celestún (p174)

Wonderful Chichén Itzá

14 Ever since Chichén Itzá (p183) was named one of the new seven wonders of the world, for better or worse, it has become the Yucatan's hottest bucket-list item. The massive El Castillo pyramid, Chichén Itzá's most iconic structure, will knock your socks off, especially at vernal and autumnal equinoxes, when morning and afternoon sunlight cast a shadow of a feathered serpent on the staircase.

Below: El Castillo pyramid (p184)

13

14

WITOLD SKRYPCZAK / GETTY IMAGES ©

POLA DAMONTE / GETTY IMAGES ©

Campeche's Walled City

15 This lovely colonial city (p203) is a pleasant antidote to the larger, more bustling tourist-filled destinations in other parts of the Yucatán. And since relatively few tourists make it here you'll get more of that real Mexican experience. Campeche's Unesco-listed historic center is like a pastel wonderland, surrounded by high stone walls and home to narrow cobbled streets with well preserved buildings. Nearby, the kilometers-long *malecón* (beachside promenade) provides a fine place to stroll, people-watch and say goodnight to the setting sun.

Morning in Cobá

16 Everyone will tell you to get to the ruins of the Yucatán early to beat the crowds, but at the ruins of Cobá (p121) it really makes a difference. To be there as the jungle awakens – with bird calls and the morning light filtering through the canopy – is magical. The experience of climbing the massive Nohoch Mul pyramid and looking out over the surrounding jungle on your own is unbeatable. Make it even more memorable and explore the ruins on a rented bike.

Above: View from the top of Nohoch Mul (p122)

Cancún

17 Cancún (p56) may not appeal to everyone, but the resort city certainly has its charms. The Zona Hotelera, for instance, straddles some of the most precious Caribbean coastline in all of the Yucatán and it boasts the new Museo Maya de Cancún and adjoining Maya ruins. For local flavor, stay in downtown Cancún, where most hotels are within walking distance of low-key bars and a slew of restaurants serving Yucatecan and international cuisine. About 10km north of downtown lie the sublime beaches of Isla Blanca, where you can see the Cancún that once was.

Need to Know

For more information, see Survival Guide (p283)

Currency
Mexican peso (M$)

Languages
Spanish, Maya

Visas
Tourist permit required; some nationalities also need visas.

Money
ATMs widely available in medium-size and large cities. Credit cards accepted in some hotels and restaurants, most often in midrange and top-end establishments.

Cell Phones
Many US cell-phone companies offer Mexico roaming deals. Local SIM cards can only be used on phones that have been unlocked.

Time
Central Standard Time (GMC/UTC minus six hours) in states of Yucatán, Campeche and Chiapas; Eastern Standard Time (GMC/UTC minus five hours) in Quintana Roo.

When to Go

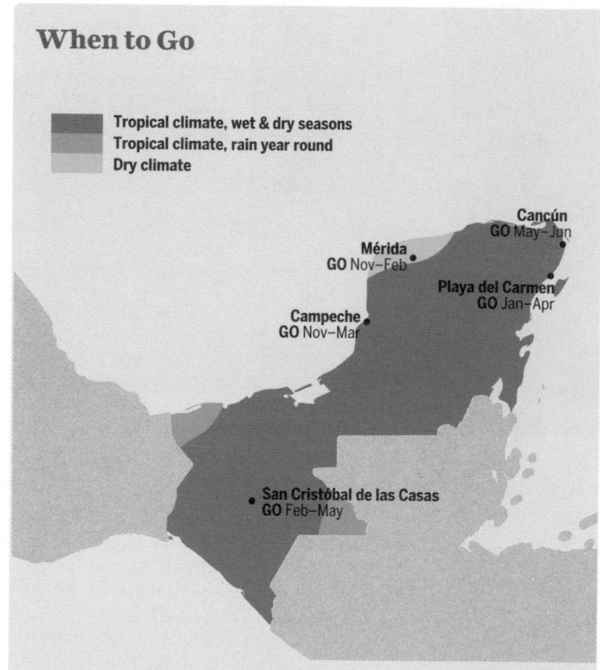

High Season
(Dec–Apr)

➡ Mostly dry, but so-called *'nortes'* bring northerly winds.

➡ Hotel rates increase, some more than double around Christmas and Easter.

➡ Mérida Fest is held in January; the weather is much cooler.

Shoulder Season
(Jul & Aug)

➡ Very hot and humid throughout the peninsula. Hurricane season begins.

➡ Vacationing Mexicans flock to the beaches to beat the heat; hotel rates rise.

Low Season
(May–Jun & Sep–Nov)

➡ Weather cools down from September to November. Hurricane and rainy seasons end in December.

➡ Great hotel deals. Crowds thin out at ruins and other popular attractions.

Useful Websites

Grand Costa Maya (www.grandcostamaya.com) Maps, events listings and diving info.

Loco Gringo (www.locogringo.com) Book homes and hotels in Riviera Maya.

Lonely Planet (lonelyplanet.com/mexico) Lonely Planet's Mexico web page.

Riviera Maya (www.rivieramaya.com) For sights and activities.

Yucatán Today (www.yucatantoday.com) All things Yucatán.

Yucatán Tierra de Maravillas (www.yucatan.travel) Yucatán state tourism site.

Important Numbers

Dial ☎1 before toll-free or long-distance calls. To call cell phones, dial ☎044 and the city code before the cell number; do the same for long-distance cell phone calls, but use ☎045.

Country code	☎52
Directory assistance	☎040
Emergencies	☎066
International access code	☎00; ☎011 from USA and Canada
Roadside assistance	☎078

Exchange Rates

Australia	A$1	M$13.30
Belize	BZ$1	M$9.32
Canada	C$1	M$14.09
Euro zone	€1	M$20.58
Guatemala	Q$1	M$2.41
Japan	¥100	M$16.77
New Zealand	NZ$1	M$12.47
UK	UK£1	M$20.95
USA	US$1	M$18.45

For current exchange rates, see www.xe.com.

Daily Costs

Budget: Less than M$700

- Dorm bed: M$150-220
- Double room in budget hotel: M$400-500
- Street eats or economical set menu: M$20-60
- City bus: M$4-10

Midrange: M$700-1500

- Double room in comfortable hotel: M$600-1200
- Lunch or dinner in restaurant: M$80-160
- Short taxi trip: M$20-50
- Sightseeing, activities: M$100-200

Top End: More than M$1500

- Double room in upscale hotel: from M$1200
- Dining in fine restaurant: M$250-500
- Car rental including liability insurance: from M$500 per day
- Tours: M$1000-2500

Opening Hours

Hours at some places may decrease during shoulder and low seasons. Some shops, restaurants and hotels may close for several weeks – or several months – during low season.

Archaeological sites 8am-5pm

Banks 9am-5pm Monday to Friday, some open 10am-2pm Saturday (hours may vary)

Cafes 8am-9pm

Cenotes 9am-5pm

Museums 9am-6pm Tuesday to Sunday

Arriving in Cancún, Cozumel & the Yucatán

Aeropuerto Internacional de Cancún (p295) Green Line shuttles and Super Shuttle charge M$160 per person to Ciudad Cancún or the Zona Hotelera. ADO buses (M$64) go to the downtown bus station. Regular taxis charge M$500.

Aeropuerto Internacional de Mérida (p295) Curbside taxis charge M$200 per carload to downtown. Buses (M$7) do not enter the airport; catch one on the main road if you don't mind walking.

Cozumel International Airport (p95) Shared shuttles from the airport into town cost M$57. For hotels on the island's north and south ends, they charge M$97 to M$140.

Aeropuerto Ángel Albino Corzo International (p295) Minibuses run between Tuxtla Gutiérrez's airport and San Cristobal de las Casas' bus terminal.

Getting Around

Shared Van *Colectivos* (shared vans) are quicker and cheaper than buses. Most have frequent departures.

Bus 1st- and 2nd-class buses go pretty much everywhere in the Yucatán.

Car Great option for traveling outside big cities. Expect to pay about M$750 a day for rental and gas.

Ferry Frequent boats depart from Playa del Carmen to Cozumel, Chiquilá to Isla Holbox and Cancún to Isla Mujeres.

For much more on **getting around**, see p297.

First Time
Cancún, Cozumel & the Yucatán

For more information, see Survival Guide (p283)

Checklist

- ➡ Ensure your passport is valid
- ➡ Check if you need a visa
- ➡ Inform your debit/credit card company of your travels
- ➡ Get necessary vaccinations
- ➡ Book hotels in advance
- ➡ Get travel insurance
- ➡ Check whether you can use your cell phone
- ➡ Confirm your airline's baggage restrictions

What to Pack

- ➡ Passport
- ➡ Credit or debit card
- ➡ Driver's license (if driving)
- ➡ Cell phone and charger
- ➡ Sunscreen
- ➡ Insect repellent
- ➡ Swim suit
- ➡ Phrasebook
- ➡ Camera
- ➡ Pocketknife
- ➡ Snorkel gear
- ➡ Toiletries
- ➡ Flashlight

Top Tips for Your Trip

- ➡ For beaches and scuba diving, visit the peninsula's Caribbean side. For culture, Maya ruins and nature experiences, go west. Cancún and Riviera Maya are very touristy.
- ➡ Avoid staying in mosquito-infested accommodations. If you're unfortunate enough to get pricked by one carrying dengue or chikungunya, it's usually not life-threatening but expect to spend several days in bed.
- ➡ Visiting Maya communities brings money into local economies and the experience leaves you with a lasting impression.
- ➡ Driving at night can be dangerous. If you must do it, toll highways have better lighting and fewer potholes than the *libre* (free) roads.

What to Wear

Keep in mind that the Yucatán, particularly Mérida, gets very hot from April through August, so bring light and loose-fitting clothes to stay cool. If you're staying on the coast or in cool inland areas, bring a light sweater or jacket for evenings. Take long-sleeve shirts and long pants/skirts for protection against mosquitoes, especially if you plan to be near mangroves or jungles; this attire is also good for formal restaurants and for visiting nonbeach towns, where you'll see fewer people wearing shorts and tank tops.

Sleeping

If you're visiting between mid-December to April, it's a good idea to book your accommodation in advance. Many places are booked solid in July and August.

B&Bs Usually more intimate and more upscale than guesthouses.

Bungalows Anything from cheap rustic cabins to boutique setups.

Guesthouses Family-run houses (often called *posadas* in Spanish) that usually provide good value and more personable service.

Hostels The most affordable option and a great way to meet other travelers.

Hotels Range from budget digs to expensive all-inclusive resorts.

Discounts & Peso-Pinching

Discounts Many museums and archaeological sites have discounts for kids, while some hotels and bus lines offer good savings for online reservations.

Colectivos Shared vans are a very affordable and efficient way to move around the peninsula.

Hammocks Some hotels will allow you to hang a hammock on their property for a fraction of what it would cost to get a room.

Bargaining

Most stores and shops have set prices. You can do some friendly haggling in some arts and crafts markets, but don't get carried away most of the artisans are just trying to make a living. Some hotels are willing to negotiate rates with walk-ins, especially during low season.

Tipping

Hotels About 5% to 10% of room costs for staff.

Restaurants Leave 15% if service is not included in check.

Supermarket baggers/gas station attendants Usually get M$3 to M$5.

Porters Tip M$25 per bag.

Taxis Drivers don't expect tips unless they provide an extra service.

Bars Bartenders usually don't get tipped so anything is appreciated.

Language

English is widely spoken in Cancún and the Riviera Maya. Elsewhere on the peninsula, you can get by with English in the main tourist centers, but outside of these Spanish is useful. Any effort to speak Spanish is appreciated and Yucatecans are generally very patient and helpful when they see that you're trying to speak their language. Most Maya speakers also speak Spanish. See Language (p302) for more.

Where can I buy handicrafts?
¿Dónde se puede comprar artesanías?
don·de se pwe·de kom·prar ar·te·sa·nee·as

Star buys in Mexico are the regional handicrafts produced all over the country, mainly by the indigenous people.

Which *antojitos* do you have?
¿Qué antojitos tiene? *an·to·khee·tos tye·ne*

'Little whimsies' (snacks) can encompass anything – have an entire meal of them, eat a few as appetisers, or get one on the street for a quick bite.

Not too spicy, please.
No muy picoso, por favor. *no mooy pee·ko·so por fa·vor*

Not all food in Mexico is spicy, but beware – many dishes can be fierce indeed, so it may be a good idea to play it safe.

Where can I find a *cantina* nearby?
¿Dónde hay una cantina cerca de aquí?
don·de ai oo·na kan·tee·na ser·ka de a·kee

Ask locals about the classical Mexican venue for endless snacks, and often dancing as well.

5 **How do you say ... in your language?**
¿Cómo se dice ... en su lengua?
ko·mo se dee·se ... en su len·gwa

Numerous indigenous languages are spoken around Mexico, primarily Mayan languages and Náhuatl. People will appreciate it if you try to use their local language.

Etiquette

Greetings A handshake is standard when meeting people for the first time. Among friends, men usually exchange back-slapping hugs; for women it's usually an (air) kiss on the cheek.

Conversation Yucatecans are generally warm and entertaining conversationalists. As a rule, they express disagreement more by nuance than by open contradiction. The Maya can be slightly more reserved in conversation.

Getting directions Mexicans are very cordial and eager to please, so much so that some folks will steer you in the wrong direction rather than saying they don't know where a particular place is. It can be frustrating at times, but keep in mind that it's done with good intentions.

If You Like...

Maya Ruins

The peninsula boasts some of the best-preserved and most remarkable ruins in all of Mexico.

Uxmal Set in the hilly Puuc region, this site contains some of the most fascinating structures you'll ever see. (p160)

Palenque Exquisite Maya temples backed by steamy, jungle-covered hills. (p241)

Chichén Itzá Recently named one of the 'new seven wonders of the world.' Enough said. (p183)

Tulum Maya ruins perched atop a cliff with jaw-dropping views of the Caribbean blue down below. (p114)

Cobá A sprawling site in a jungle setting that's best explored on a bicycle. (p121)

Calakmul High pyramids sitting pretty in a huge Maya city tucked away in a rainforest. (p221)

Dzibilchaltún Ruins, a Maya museum and an onsite swimmable cenote. What's not to like? (p177)

Beach Resorts

There's more to the resort experience than white sands and turquoise waters. Each destination has its own unique vibe.

Puerto Morelos A comforting small-town feel, plus some mighty fine diving and snorkeling. (p99)

Tulum The action shifts between a jungly hotel zone on the coast and an inland town jam-packed with bars and restaurants. (p113)

Isla Mujeres People get around in golf carts and scooters, and the island's sole public bus always seems to be running late. (p75)

Isla Cozumel A hugely popular divers' destination with a pleasant town square and surprisingly quiet beaches. (p84)

Cancún An oddball mix of glitzy hotel zone, local downtown scene and secluded beaches up north. (p56)

Playa del Carmen A hip beach town on the coast where European chic meets the Mexican Caribbean. (p103)

Diving & Snorkeling

Not only does this region have some of the best reef diving in the world, it also offers fascinating dives in cave systems.

Isla Cozumel The famed reefs of this island draw diving aficionados from all over the world. (p84)

Banco Chinchorro The largest coral atoll in the western hemisphere; known for its colorful underwater scenery and sunken ships. (p129)

Isla Mujeres Boasts excellent reef diving and a very cool underwater sculpture museum. (p75)

Tulum Nearby cenotes (limestone sinkholes) provide wonderful opportunities to snorkel and dive in caverns and caves. (p113)

Puerto Morelos Get in some wreck diving here; the barrier reef is just 600m offshore. (p99)

Nature Experiences

The peninsula spoils nature lovers with its wide array of wildlife in biosphere reserves and national parks.

Reserva de la Biosfera Ría Celestún Head out to the mangroves to observe flamingos and crocs. (p174)

Reserva de la Biosfera Ría Lagartos Experienced guides lead bird-watching and snorkeling tours in this magnificent reserve. (p197)

Parque Nacional Isla Contoy An uninhabited island that's

Top: Puerto Morelos (p99)
Bottom: Gran Cenote (p120) near Tulum

home to more than 170 bird species and provides nesting grounds for sea turtles as well. (p70)

Sian Ka'an Biosphere Reserve A sprawling jungle with a pristine coastline and camping sites for intrepid travelers. (p124)

Isla Mujeres Turtle Farm Liberates more than 100,000 of these little flippered guys each year. (p78)

Swimming

Between cenotes, Caribbean beaches and spectacular waterfalls you can enjoy a perfectly amphibious existence here.

Cenote X'Kekén Near Valladolid, this spot has a lovely cavern pool with *álamo* (poplar) roots stretching down many meters. (p192)

Playa Norte The shallow turquoise waters of this Isla Mujeres beach are like nothing you've ever seen. (p77)

Isla Holbox During summer months you can snorkel with whale sharks off the coast of this low-key island. (p71)

Cristalino Cenote A quiet spot with mangroves on one side and a large open section you can dive into. (p106)

Agua Azul/Misol-Ha These thundering cascades south of Palenque are downright amazing water attractions. (p244)

Colonial Towns

The 300-year period of Spanish rule left behind awesome plazas and opulent mansions and haciendas.

Mérida Even if you're not big on architecture, the stately mansions in the peninsula's cultural capital never cease to impress. (p143)

Campeche The protective walls once used to fend off pirate attacks still stand tall today. (p203)

Valladolid Think Mérida without the grandeur. Colonial flavor here comes on a smaller, more intimate scale. (p191)

San Cristóbal de las Casas The cobbled streets of San Cristóbal lead to splendid colonial-era churches. (p230)

Izamal Smack in the middle of town rises the imposing Convento de San Antonio de Padua. (p181)

Regional Cuisine

The Yucatán is unquestionably one of Mexico's most remarkable culinary destinations.

Yerba Buena del Sisal Vegetarians can delight in delicious, healthy Yucatecan fare at this Valladolid establishment. (p194)

Restaurante LUM A swanky San Cristóbal de las Casas restaurant serving excellent dishes from Chiapas, Veracruz and Yucatán. (p236)

Kinich Exquisitely prepared traditional dishes in Izamal – try the *papadzules* (egg enchiladas) and you'll understand why. (p182)

La Chaya Maya A trip to Mérida wouldn't be complete without a meal at the Chaya. (p153)

La Fuente Well-known in Ciudad del Carmen for its *pibipollo* (chicken tamales cooked underground). (p220)

Arts & Crafts

Buying crafts is a good way to support local economies.

Hamacas El Aguacate Who doesn't like to catch a siesta on a quality hammock? Buy one here, then it's sweet dreams baby. (p156)

Artisans Market A main attraction in Puerto Morelos, this market sells authentic Tixkokob hammocks and fine jewelry at fair prices. (p102)

Tierra Huichol Intricate bead and yarn art made by indigenous Huichol artists is sold at this Playa del Carmen shop. (p108)

Bazar Artesanal Campeche's Folk Art Bazaar is a one-stop shop for regional crafts. (p211)

Los Cinco Soles Pick up black ceramics from Oaxaca and Talavera pottery at this Isla Cozumel crafts store. (p95)

Centro Cultural y Artesanal Crafts purchases made here in Izamal help support rural indigenous families. (p181)

Nightlife & Dancing

The peninsula has no shortage of places to shake your hips.

Grand Mambo Café Groove to live Cuban salsa sounds at this downtown Cancún nightclub. (p66)

T&T Tropical Paradise Forget about all the lame touristy bars in Isla Mujeres – this sand-floor bar has got soul. (p82)

La Fundación Mezcalería Sip smoky mezcals while watching live bands at this happening Mérida bar. (p155)

Fusion The beach becomes a stage for fire dancers at this open-air Playa del Carmen bar. (p108)

Salón Rincón Colonial An atmospheric Cuban-style drinking establishment that served as a location for the Antonio Banderas flick *Original Sin*. (p211)

Getaway Destinations

Hit these quiet beach towns for some prime R&R.

Xcalak No streetlights, no banks, no problem. This is the Caribbean coast as it once was. (p131)

Río Lagartos Nature tours and whiling away the time in a sleepy fishing village on the northern coast. (p197)

Punta Allen The road to this remote beach community ain't pretty but the village sure is. (p125)

Dzilam de Bravo It's just you, a breezy white-sand beach and some rustic cabins – the ultimate escapist's retreat. (p180)

Celestún Aside from nature tours, not much happens in this small coastal community, and we mean that in a good way. (p174)

Family-Friendly Trips

The Yucatán is one of Mexico's friendliest family destinations.

Riviera Maya The land of nature parks, various swimming sites and excellent snorkeling. (p97)

Cancún Plenty of water-related activities, hotels with kids clubs, and tours geared toward children. (p56)

Casa del Adivino (p162), Uxmal

Valladolid Nearby cenotes make a big splash with the little ones and the town's pyramids are fun to climb. (p191)

Campeche Pirate-themed cruises and a walled city full of swashbuckler legends makes for good family entertainment. (p203)

Progreso A popular family beach destination, first and foremost because you can do it on the cheap here. (p178)

Studying Spanish

Learning *español* allows for a deeper understanding of the culture.

Instituto Benjamín Franklin Take classes in the Yucatán's cultural capital of Mérida at this non-profit organization. (p149)

La Casa en el Árbol Head down to the lovely San Cristóbal de las Casas and brush up on your skills. (p234)

Puerto Morelos Language Center Between beach-bumming and scuba diving, squeeze in a few hours of Spanish classes at this place. (p100)

International House Ask about very affordable homestays in Playa del Carmen. (p105)

Playalingua del Caribe Once you've mastered Spanish, take a Maya language course in the Riviera Maya. (p105)

Month by Month

TOP EVENTS

Mérida Fest, January

Carnaval, February

Vernal Equinox, March

Swimming with Whale Sharks, July

Día de Muertos, November

January

The first week of January is one of the busiest times of the year, meaning hotel rates spike. Weather-wise, it's relatively cool.

Mérida Fest

This cultural event, running most of January across the city, celebrates the founding of Mérida with art exhibits, concerts, plays and book presentations. (p151)

Día de los Reyes Magos

(Three Kings' Day) January 6 is the day Mexican children traditionally receive gifts, rather than at Christmas. Weeklong celebrations take place in Tizimín.

February

Temperatures rise slightly and it remains fairly dry. It's still considered high season but most destinations have quietened down significantly.

Carnaval

A big street bash preceding the 40-day penance of Lent, Carnaval usually falls in February or early March. It's festively celebrated in Mérida, Campeche, Chetumal and Isla Cozumel with parades, music, dancing and lots of partying.

Cruzando Fronteras

A weeklong cultural festival in Mahahual featuring concerts, art exhibits and food stalls along the boardwalk. Usually held in late February or early March. (p130)

March

The thermometer rises a few notches in more ways than one as US spring breakers flock to the peninsula for tequila-fueled revelry.

Spring Break

Beer bong, anyone? Most US university students get midterm break in March and many descend on Cancún – so either join the party or head for the hills.

Vernal Equinox

On the day of the spring equinox (usually around March 20) and for about a week thereafter, thousands head to Chichén Itzá to witness the shadow formation of a serpent appear on the staircase of the El Castillo pyramid. Dzibilchaltún shines on this day with glowing temple doors. (p183 and p177)

April

One of the hottest and driest months of the year on the peninsula. Semana Santa brings out Mexican tourists in droves as they look to cool off at the beach.

Semana Santa

Held throughout Holy Week (starting on Palm Sunday, in March or April), solemn processions move through the streets. On Good Friday (Viernes Santo) there are dramatic re-enactments of the Passion Play.

Feria de San Cristóbal

Starting on Easter Sunday, the weeklong Feria de la Primavera y de la Paz in San Cristóbal de las Casas features art shows, song and dance, amusement rides, bullfights, fireworks and, of course, lots of food.

May

A scorcher of a month, especially in Mérida where the daily high averages around 36°C. Not surprisingly, great hotel deals can be found.

Feria del Cedral

On Isla Cozumel, the entertaining Feria del Cedral honors a group of Caste War refugees who settled on the island in 1848. The fairgrounds have rides and rodeo events, and you can see the time-honored 'Dance of the Pigs' Heads.' (p91)

June

It's still very hot and June 1 marks the beginning of hurricane season, which runs to November 30. Tourism slows down a lot.

Día de la Marina

On June 1 in Río Lagartos a crown of flowers is taken out to the water as an offering to fishermen who have perished at sea.

July

Expect warm, wet and humid weather. This is a summer holiday month for Mexicans and North Americans so book hotels in advance.

Swimming with Whale Sharks

A good time to spot these gentle giants off the coasts of Isla Holbox and Isla Mujeres. (p72)

Fiesta de la Virgen del Carmen

For the last two weeks of July, the patron saint of Ciudad del Carmen, Campeche, is taken on a journey over land and across the harbor. The fiesta features artistic and cultural events and craft shows.

August

Summer holiday season continues, as do the rains. Inland spots tend to be sticky at this time of year.

Festival Jats'á Já

Held in Mahahual, this festival is a prayer offering of sorts to the hurricane gods. Traditional Maya dancing, art exhibits and culinary events take place. (p130)

September

The height of the hurricane season, though it shouldn't present a problem if you keep an eye out for alerts. It's also Mexico's most patriotic month of the year.

Día de la Independencia

(Independence Day; September 16) The anniversary of the start of Mexico's War of Independence in 1810. On the evening of the 15th, the famous call to rebellion is repeated from the balcony of every town hall in the land.

October

Cooler climes and slightly less rainfall. If you visit during the last days of October and the first days of November it's always interesting to compare Halloween with Day of the Dead celebrations.

Halloween

Playa del Carmen is the scene of a wild, all-night costume party that draws a sizable crowd of inebriated zombies.

November

The rainy season has passed and temperatures are subsiding. Some accommodations drop prices by as much as 50%.

Día de Muertos

(Day of the Dead; November 1) Families build altars in their homes and visit graveyards to commune with their dead, taking garlands and gifts. Many cities place giant altars in their main squares.

December

Hurricane season ends. *Nortes* (northerly winds that bring showers) are prevalent along the coast from November to January. The first two weeks of December are quiet on the peninsula ahead of Christmas.

Plan Your Trip
Itineraries

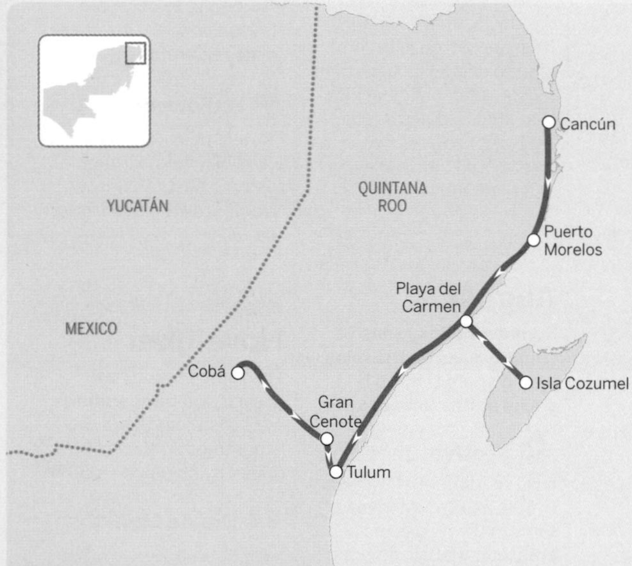

Cancún & the Riviera Maya

The road from Cancún to Cobá is chock full of surprises. Along the way you'll find fun-filled cenotes (limestone sinkholes), astonishing Maya ruins and sweet little beach towns with sugar-white sands.

Get things started with a dip in the sapphire waters along the Zona Hotelera (hotel zone) of **Cancún** (p56) or hit the secluded beaches north of downtown on Isla Blanca, then return to town for dinner, drinks and perhaps some salsa dancing.

After a day or two in Cancún, make your way south about 30km and stop in **Puerto Morelos** (p99) to duck out to the beach, browse for handmade crafts and get in some snorkeling or diving.

Next, spend a little time beach-bumming and partying in uberchic **Playa del Carmen** (p103), a large city with a dizzying array of restaurants, bars and discos.

Playa, as it's called, is a good jumping-off point for **Isla Cozumel** (p84), where you can enjoy some of the best diving in the world, quiet beaches on the island's windswept side and a pleasant town plaza.

Tulum ruins (p114)

Frequent ferries run between Playa and Cozumel.

Back on the mainland, you'll definitely want to make time for **Tulum** (p113), where Maya ruins are perched atop a spectacular cliff overlooking the Mexican Caribbean. While at the site, take the stairs down to the beach and have a refreshing swim to cool off. Stay the night in Tulum's town, where the main drag is lined with happening bars and restaurants, or head 3km south to the coast and get a quiet bungalow in Tulum's Zona Hotelera.

With an early start, take off for the Maya ruins of **Cobá** (p121; find the road to Cobá at Tulum's north end). Once inside this archaeological site, rent a bicycle and marvel at jungle ruins connected by ancient paths. Stop for lunch at a lakeside restaurant in Cobá, then on the way back to Tulum, drop by the **Gran Cenote** (p120) for a swim or snorkel in a large sinkhole with small fish.

This easy 170km trip stays close to Cancún and there's frequent transport to all of these destinations, or you can just rent a car.

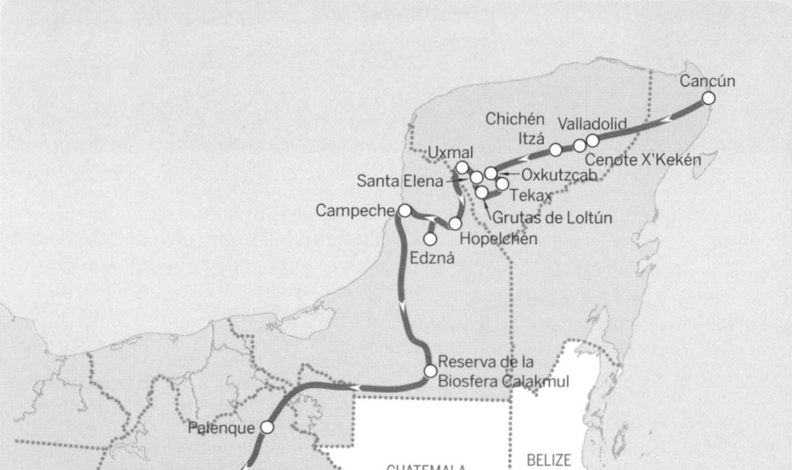

Cancún
Chichén Itzá
Valladolid
Cenote X'Kekén
Uxmal
Oxkutzcab
Santa Elena
Tekax
Grutas de Loltún
Campeche
Hopelchén
Edzná
Reserva de la Biosfera Calakmul
Palenque
San Cristóbal de las Casas
MEXICO
GUATEMALA
BELIZE

JLAZOUPHOTO / GETTY IMAGES ©

GERARD SIDANER / GETTY IMAGES ©

Top: Grutas de Loltún (p168)
Bottom: Edzná (p216)

Maya Country

The architectural and artistic achievements of the Maya are prominently displayed across the peninsula. Though the ancient cities are long abandoned, the Maya people and their traditions are still very much present.

For background, visit the shiny new Museo Maya de Cancún in the heart of Zona Hotelera in **Cancún** (p56), where the price of admission includes access to adjoining Maya ruins.

Hit the road the next day and spend a day or two in the colonial town of **Valladolid** (p191), a former Maya ceremonial center with a climbable pyramid near the center of town. For some respite from your Maya itinerary, drop by **Cenote X'Kekén** (p192) on your way out of town and take a plunge into a spectacular limestone cavern pool.

Next up you'll want to set aside a day for **Chichén Itzá** (p183), a Maya archaeological site that was named none other than one of the 'new seven wonders of the world.'

A route then leads to **Oxkutzcab** (p171) and **Tekax** (p172), offering glimpses of traditional Maya life. While in Oxkutzcab, check out the nearby **Grutas de Loltún** (p168), the peninsula's largest cave system.

The following day move on to **Santa Elena** (p163), which makes a fine base for exploring the impressive ruins of **Uxmal** (p160), Kabah and several other archaeological sites tucked away in the rolling Puuc hills.

After crossing the Yucatán-Campeche border, stop at **Hopelchén** (p214), where you can witness the ancient arts of beekeeping and herbal medicine.

Then make your way to the walled city of **Campeche** (p203), a good base for visiting **Edzná** (p216), a formidable Maya site with a five-story temple. The peninsula's south harbors numerous fascinating remnants of classic Maya civilization ensconced in the vast **Reserva de la Biosfera Calakmul** (p222).

Extend your explorations for several days to the ruins of **Palenque** (p241) and the contemporary Maya domain of **San Cristóbal de las Casas** (p230), both in Chiapas.

Most destinations on this route are reachable by bus or shared transport vehicles, but for some you'll need to hire a car or taxi, or go with a tour operator.

Off the Beaten Track: Cancún, Cozumel & Yucatán

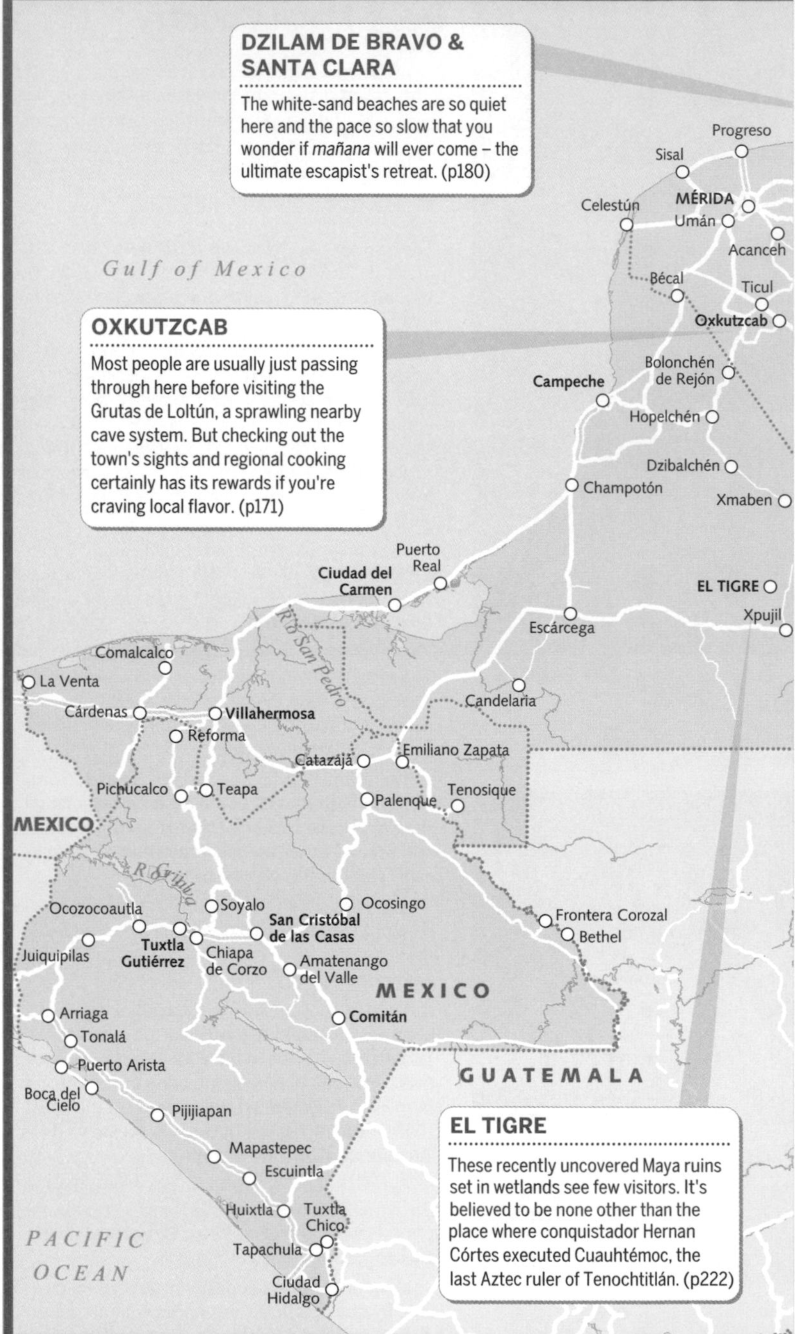

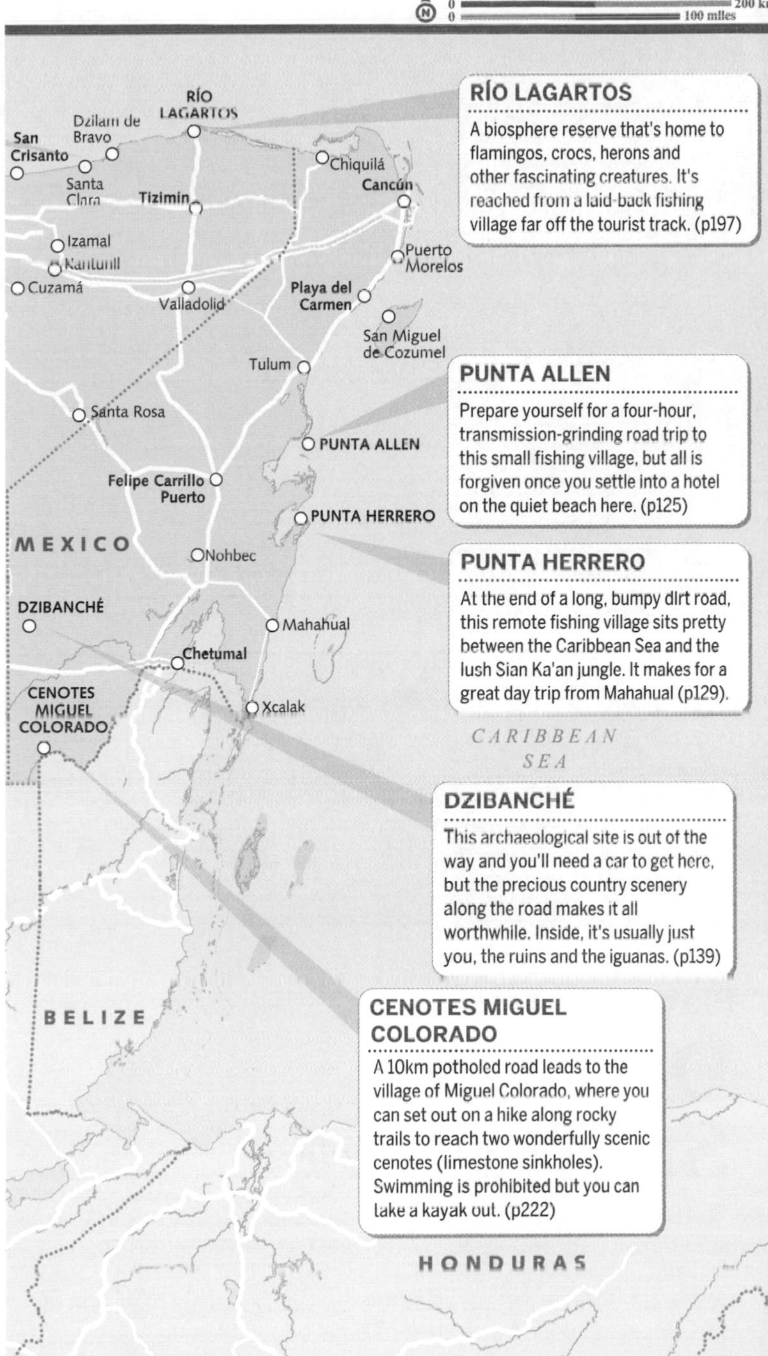

RÍO LAGARTOS

A biosphere reserve that's home to flamingos, crocs, herons and other fascinating creatures. It's reached from a laid-back fishing village far off the tourist track. (p197)

PUNTA ALLEN

Prepare yourself for a four-hour, transmission-grinding road trip to this small fishing village, but all is forgiven once you settle into a hotel on the quiet beach here. (p125)

PUNTA HERRERO

At the end of a long, bumpy dirt road, this remote fishing village sits pretty between the Caribbean Sea and the lush Sian Ka'an jungle. It makes for a great day trip from Mahahual (p129).

DZIBANCHÉ

This archaeological site is out of the way and you'll need a car to get here, but the precious country scenery along the road makes it all worthwhile. Inside, it's usually just you, the ruins and the iguanas. (p139)

CENOTES MIGUEL COLORADO

A 10km potholed road leads to the village of Miguel Colorado, where you can set out on a hike along rocky trails to reach two wonderfully scenic cenotes (limestone sinkholes). Swimming is prohibited but you can take a kayak out. (p222)

Diving, Isla Cozumel (p8

Plan Your Trip

Diving & Snorkeling

The Mexican Caribbean is world famous for its colorful coral reefs and translucent waters full of tropical fish so, not surprisingly, diving and snorkeling are the area's top activity draw. Add cenote (limestone sinkhole) dives to the mix and you truly have one of the most intriguing dive destinations on the planet.

Best Dives

Isla Cozumel (p89)

Hands down Mexico's most popular scuba-diving location, Cozumel gets high praise for its excellent visibility and wide variety of marine life. The amazing sights are sure to keep even the most experienced diver in a constant state of awe.

Banco Chinchorro (p129)

The largest coral atoll in the northern hemisphere, Banco Chinchorro boasts a glorious underwater fantasy world of wrecked ships and vivid reefs. Best of all, rarely will you find crowded dive sites at Chinchorro.

Isla Mujeres (p77)

With snorkeler-friendly shallow reefs, shark caves and an underwater sculpture museum, Isla Mujeres' sites appeal to both novice and advanced divers. From June to September you can snorkel with 15-ton whale sharks.

Cenote Dos Ojos (p112)

Belonging to one of the largest underwater cave systems in the world, divers have the unforgettable experience of exploring the mysteries of the deep at this cenote.

Diving

Isla Cozumel

If you can visit only one dive destination in Mexico, the wonderful underwater world of Isla Cozumel (p88) is your best bet. Once a pilgrimage site of the Maya and little more than a small fishing community up until the late 1950s, today Cozumel and its astoundingly rich reefs draw divers from far and wide.

Drift diving is the norm in Cozumel – local divers say there's nothing like the sensation of gliding through the water as you're carried by the strong currents. So what can you see? Imposing drop-off wall reefs, sea turtles, moray eels, black grouper, barracuda, rainbow parrotfish, large coral and giant Caribbean anemones.

Although Cozumel was hammered by two hurricanes (Emily and Wilma) in 2005, most of the island's diveable reefs, and all of the deeper ones, remained unharmed. Unsurprisingly, it was the snorkeling sites that were hardest hit; yet, thanks to the tireless efforts of the local diving community (whose livelihood depends on the health of the reefs), and to the resilience of this amazing ecosystem, things have now returned to normal.

If you're a diver heading to this area, Cozumel's Punta Sur and Palancar Gardens are well worth visiting. Snorkelers will want to check out Dzul-Há, near the town of San Miguel de Cozumel, and Colombia Shallows on the island's south side. For background on the island's marine ecosystem, hit the Museo de la Isla de Cozumel (p86) before diving.

Other Diving Spots

Recreational and serious divers alike will be happy to know that there are great dive sites to be enjoyed all along the eastern coast of the Yucatán Peninsula. Cancún, Isla Mujeres, Puerto Morelos, Playa del Carmen, Mahahual and Xcalak are all prime places to plan a vacation around diving and snorkeling.

The Banco Chinchorro (p129), a sprawling coral atoll off the southern Quintana Roo coast, was pounded by Hurricane Dean in 2007, but the government designated new dive sites so that the hardest-hit areas could recover, which they have. Home to more than 90 coral species, the biosphere reserve of Chinchorro gets fewer visitors than the reefs of Cozumel and Isla Mujeres, making it a very attractive option. Here you can see rays, eels, conch and giant sponges.

In and around Cancún there's an interesting snorkeling and diving attraction called the Museo Subacuático de Arte (p57), aka MUSA, an underwater sculpture museum created by British artist and diving aficionado Jason deCaires Taylor. Built to divert divers away from deteriorating coral reefs, this one-of-a-kind aquatic museum features some 500 life-size sculptures in the waters of Cancún and Isla Mujeres. The artificial reefs are submerged at a depth of 28ft, making them ideal for snorkelers and first-time divers.

Cenote Dives

When you find yourself yawning at the green morays, eagle rays, dolphins, sea turtles, nurse sharks and multitudinous tropical fish, you're ready to dive a cenote (a deep limestone sinkhole containing water). Hook up with a reputable dive shop and prepare for (in the immortal words of Monty Python) 'something completely different.' The Maya saw cenotes as gateways to the underworld.

You won't see many fish on a typical cenote dive. You'll be trading brilliance for darkness and blue for black. Check that your regulator is working flawlessly and enter a world unlike anything you've ever dived before. Soar around stalactites and stalagmites, hover above cake-frosting-like formations and glide around tunnels that will make you think you're in outer space. Some of the best cenote dives include Cenote Manatí (p113), Cenote Angelita (p114) and those run by **Dos Ojos** (www.cenotedosojos.com; admission M$100; ⏲8am-5pm).

Swimming in Dos Ojos (p167)

Keep in mind that these are fragile environments. Avoid applying sunscreen or insect repellent before entering. Use care when approaching, entering or exiting, as the rocks are often slippery. Loud noises such as yelling disturb bats and other creatures – though most people find themselves subdued by the presence in these caverns. In rare cases, tourists have been seriously injured or killed by climbing on the roots or stalactites.

Be very careful when cenote diving; it can be an extremely dangerous activity, especially when done in caves. A good rule of thumb is to go with local dive shops that have knowledge of the cave system. And above all, do not attempt cave diving without proper certification.

WHEN TO GO

Generally you can dive year-round in the Yucatán: however, before you leave for Mexico you should take into account several considerations.

➡ From November through January the peninsula gets northerly winds and showers known as *nortes*. In Cozumel they can blow so strongly that the harbormaster closes ports – sometimes for days. While this won't affect the ferry between Cozumel and Playa del Carmen, it could alter diving plans.

➡ If you're planning to visit from June through November, you'll want to keep a watchful eye out for hurricane alerts.

➡ The best time to see whale sharks is between mid-June and late August but be aware that the water will be crowded with tour boats at this time of year. See page 72 for more information.

Snorkeling

Many spots on the Yucatán's Caribbean side make for some fine snorkeling. The best sites are generally reached by boat,

Green sea turtle below snorkelers, Akumal (p110)

but areas near Akumal, Isla Mujeres and Cozumel all offer pretty decent beach-accessed spots. In Cozumel, you'll find some of the most popular snorkeling sites along the western shore.

Inland you can snorkel in some of the Yucatán's famed cenotes. Some places rent gear, but, when in doubt, take your own.

Snorkeling with whale sharks (p25) has become very popular in recent years... too popular some might say. Just about all of the dive shops in Isla Mujeres and Isla Holbox offer whale shark tours. Just make sure before signing up that the tour operator abides by responsible practices recommended by the World Wildlife Fund. Only three swimmers (including your guide) are allowed in the water at a time. Also, you are not allowed to touch these giant fish, and you must wear either a life jacket or wetsuit to ensure you do not dive below the shark.

Keep in mind that tour operators can never fully guarantee that they'll actually track down a whale shark – sometimes nature has her own plans.

Responsible Diving & Snorkeling

Remember that coral reefs and other marine ecosystems are particularly fragile environments. Consider the following tips when diving to help preserve the ecology and beauty of the reefs.

- Avoid touching or standing on living marine organisms or dragging equipment across the reef. Polyps can be damaged by even the gentlest contact. If you must hold on to the reef, only touch exposed rock or dead coral.
- Be conscious of your fins. Even without contact, the surge from fin strokes near the reef can damage delicate organisms. Take care not to kick up clouds of sand, which can smother them.
- Practice and maintain proper buoyancy control and avoid over-weighting. Major damage can be done by divers descending too fast and colliding with the reef.
- Take great care in underwater caves. Spend as little time in them as possible as your air bubbles may be caught within the roof and

KAREN DOODY/STOCKTREK IMAGES / GETTY IMAGES ©

Shipwreck diving

thereby leave organisms high and dry. Take turns to inspect the interior of a small cave.

➡ Resist the temptation to collect or buy corals or shells or to loot marine archaeological sites (mainly shipwrecks).

➡ Ensure that you take home all your rubbish and any litter you may find. Plastics in particular are a serious threat to marine life.

➡ Do not feed the fish. In doing so you may be encouraging aggressive behavior or giving them food that may be harmful to their health.

➡ Minimize your disturbance of marine animals. Never ride on the backs of turtles.

Safety

Most dive shops rent equipment. If you do rent diving equipment, make sure that it's up to standard. Before embarking on a scuba-diving or snorkeling trip, consider the following tips to ensure a safe and enjoyable experience:

➡ If scuba diving, carry a current diving-certification card from a recognized instruction agency.

➡ Regardless of skill level, you should be in good condition and know your physical limitations.

➡ If you don't have your own equipment, ask to see the dive shop's before you commit. Also, make sure you feel comfortable with your dive master.

➡ Obtain reliable information about physical and environmental conditions at the dive site from a reputable local dive operation, and ask how locally trained divers deal with these considerations.

➡ Be aware of local laws, regulations and etiquette about marine life and the environment.

➡ Dive only at sites within your level of experience: if available, engage the services of a competent, professionally trained dive instructor or dive master.

➡ Avoid decompression sickness by diving no less than 18 hours prior to a high-altitude flight.

➡ Know the locations of the nearest decompression chambers and emergency numbers.

➡ Find out if your dive shop has up-to-date certification from PADI (www.padi.com), NAUI (www.naui.org) or the internationally recognized Mexican diving organization FMAS (www.fmas.com.mx).

➡ Always put safety above cost considerations – in the spirit of competition, some dive shops offer great deals, but as the old saying goes, sometimes you get what you pay for.

Casa del Adivino (p162), Uxmal

Plan Your Trip

Exploring Maya Ruins

When you stop and think about it, the Maya accomplished some downright remarkable feats. Not only did they pull off very sophisticated architecture, but they also made mind-blowing contributions to mathematics, astronomy and art. The cities they left behind remind us of this brilliant legacy.

Planning Your Trip

When to Go

The best time of year to visit archaeological sites is from November to mid-December, when the peninsula has cooler climes and is generally dry. If you visit during high season, from Christmas to April and the months of July and August, you'll be dealing with large crowds unless you arrive early in the morning.

Where to Stay

Tulum makes a great base for visiting both the Tulum archaeological site and Cobá. For the ruins of Chichén Itzá and Ek' Balam, consider staying in colonial Valladolid. In Chiapas, Palenque has many nice accommodations nearby. An overnight in Campeche is convenient for getting an early start at Edzná, and the tranquil town of Santa Elena is the perfect hub for exploring the Ruta Puuc, Kabah and Uxmal.

What to See

So many interesting sites, so little time. Definite must-sees include Chichén Itzá, Palenque, Tulum, Uxmal and Edzná.

What to Take

Ensure you have comfortable walking shoes, a hat, sunscreen and plenty of water.

Amazing Maya

Classic Maya (AD 250–900), seen by many experts as the most glorious civilization of pre-Hispanic America, flourished in three areas:

North The low-lying Yucatán Peninsula.

Central The Petén forest of Guatemala, and the adjacent lowlands in Chiapas and Tabasco in Mexico (to the west) and Belize (to the east).

South Highland Guatemala and a small section of Honduras.

It was in the northern and central areas that the Maya blossomed most brilliantly, attaining groundbreaking heights of artistic and architectural expression.

Among the Maya's many accomplishments, they developed a complex writing system, partly pictorial, partly phonetic, with 300 to 500 symbols. They also refined a calendar used by other pre-Hispanic peoples into a tool for the exact recording and forecasting of earthly and heavenly events. Temples were aligned to enhance observation of the heavens, helping the Maya predict solar eclipses of the sun and movements of the moon and Venus.

They also believed in predestination and developed a complex astrology. To win the gods' favor they carried out elaborate rituals involving dances, feasts, sacrifices, consumption of the alcoholic drink *balché* and bloodletting.

They believed the current world to be just one of a succession of worlds, and the cyclical nature of their calendrical system enabled them to predict the future by looking at the past.

Top Museums

All of the following museums provide interesting background information that's often missing from some of the archaeological sites.

Gran Museo del Mundo Maya (p147) Adding to Mérida's rich cultural tradition, this world-class museum showcases more than 1100 Maya pieces with permanent and temporary exhibits focusing on culture, art, science and Maya worldview. There's a free nightly light-and-sound show here as well.

Museo Maya de Cancún (p56) This relatively new museum houses an important collection of Maya artifacts. The adjoining San Miguelito archaeological site contains more than a dozen restored Maya structures and an 8m-high pyramid. The entrance fee for the museum includes access to San Miguelito.

Museo Arqueológico de Campeche (p206) Set in an old fortress, this museum exhibits pieces from the Maya sites of Calakmul and Edzná. Stunning jade jewelry and exquisite vases, masks and plates are thematically arranged in 10 halls; the star attractions are the jade burial masks from Calakmul.

Museo de la Cultura Maya (p135) Chetumal's pride and joy illustrates the Maya's calendrical system, among other intriguing exhibits. It's organized into three levels, mirroring Maya cosmology. The main floor represents this world; the upper floor the heavens; and the lower floor Xibalbá, the underworld. Go here before visiting the nearby sites of Kohunlich and Dzibanché. It's short on artifacts, but interesting nonetheless.

ANGELA ARENAL / GETTY IMAGES ©

Detail, Cuadrángulo de las Monjas (p162), Uxmal

Practicalities

- Admission to the Yucatán's archaeological sites ranges from free to M$220; children under 13 often cost a fraction of the adult entrance fee. Both Chichén Itzá and Uxmal project nightly light-and-sound shows.
- Opening hours at most major sites are from 8am to 5pm.
- Drink lots of water and bring protection against the sun. Insect repellent keeps the mosquitoes away when visiting jungle sites.
- Explanatory signs may be in Spanish only, or both Spanish and English. Audio translators are available at Chichén Itzá and Uxmal (M$39).
- Multilingual guides offer one-hour tours (from M$500 to M$750). Official tour-guide rates are posted at the entrances of some sites; legit guides carry government-issued badges.
- Avoid midday visits when the sun is beating down and tourists are out in full force.
- Seldom-visited sites have no food or water available; pack a lunch or stop off for a meal or supplies along the way.

SITE HIGHLIGHTS AT A GLANCE

SITE	PERIOD	HIGHLIGHTS
Becán	550 BC-AD 1000	towered temples
Calakmul	approx AD 1-900	high pyramids with views over rainforest
Chichén Itzá	approx AD 100-1400	El Castillo pyramid, Mexico's biggest ball court, El Caracol observatory, Cenote Sagrado
Cobá	AD 600-1100	colossal pyramids in jungle setting
Dzinbanché	approx 200 BC-AD1200	semi-wild site with palaces & pyramids
Edzná	600 BC-AD 1500	five-story pyramid palace, Temple of the Masks
Ek' Balam	approx AD 600-800	huge Acrópolis & high pyramid with unusual carving
Kabah	AD 750-950	Palace of the Masks with 300 Chaac masks
Kohunlich	AD 100-600	Temple of the Masks
Ruta Puuc	AD 750-950	three sites (Sayil, Xlapak, Labná), palaces with elaborate columns & sculpture, including Chaac masks
Tulum	AD 1200-1600	temples and towers overlooking the Caribbean Sea
Uxmal	AD 600-900	pyramids, palaces, riotous sculpture featuring masks of rain god Chaac
Xpujil	flourished AD 700-800	three-towered ancient 'skyscraper'

El Castillo (p184), Chichén Itzá

Resources

The following books and organizations provide a wealth of information on Maya history and culture.

➡ *An Archaeological Guide to Central and Southern Mexico* Joyce Kelly's book was published in 2001 and is still very useful, with coverage of 70 sites.

➡ *Archaeology of Ancient Mexico and Central America: An Encyclopedia* An excellent reference book by Susan Toby Evans and David L Webster incorporating recent discoveries and scholarship.

➡ *Chronicle of the Maya Kings and Queens* Looks at the dynasties and rulers of the most important ancient Maya kingdoms, by Simon Martin and Nikolai Grube.

➡ *Incidents of Travel in Yucatán* A travelogue written by American explorer John Lloyd Stephens documenting the Maya sites he visited with English artist Frederick Catherwood in the mid-19th century.

➡ Instituto Nacional de Antropología e Historia (INAH; www.inah.gob.mx) The website of Mexico's National Institute of Anthropology and History offers virtual tours of its sites and museums, practical information for visiting the ruins, and details of the historical significance of each site, mostly in Spanish.

➡ Maya Exploration Center (www.mayaexploration.org) A Maya-specific nonprofit offering education programs, tours and study abroad courses.

➡ Mesoweb (www.mesoweb.com) A great, diverse resource that focuses on the ancient cultures of Mexico and Central America.

Behind the Names

Calakmul (Adjacent Mounds) Dubbed as such by US botanist Cyrus Lundell when he first come across the hidden jungle ruins in the 1930s.

Chichén Itzá (Mouth of the Well of the Itzá) The ancient Maya city was built around a well known today as the 'sacred cenote.'

Palenque (Palisade) The Spanish name has no relation to the city's ancient name, Lakamha, which translates as 'big water' and probably refers to the area's springs, streams and waterfalls.

Palenque ruins (p241)

Tulum (Wall) Refers to the stone walls that once protected the city. The original Maya name, Zamá, means 'dawn' or 'sunrise.'

Uxmal (Thrice Built) Alludes to how many times the city was built, though it was actually constructed five times.

LIFE AFTER THE APOCALYPSE

As you probably heard, some folks were predicting the end of the world on December 21, 2012, when the Maya long-count calendrical cycle came to an end, yet the date actually signaled the beginning of a new *bak'tun* (about a 400-year period).

Despite all the media hype focusing on doomsday scenarios, some good came out of all the attention: in the year leading up to that December day, federal and state governments poured some serious money into new Maya museums and into restoring existing archaeological sites. Some say the renewed interest in Maya culture was short-lived, but at the very least we can report that research and excavations do continue in the post-apocalypse era.

Tours

If you don't have a car, tours are especially convenient when you're pressed for time or find that a site is difficult to reach by bus. Youth hostels throughout the Yucatán often provide affordable outings and they welcome non-guests. Here are some of the better tour operators:

Community Tours Sian Ka'an (p114) This Maya-run ecotourism outfit will take you on a guided walk of the interpretive trail at the Muyil archaeological site, south of Tulum.

Ecoturismo Yucatán (p151) One-day excursions to Chichén Itzá and Uxmal include entrance fees, transportation, guide and lunch. The owners of this tour company are passionate about both sharing and protecting the state's natural treasures.

Hostel Mundo Joven (p59) This Cancún hostel/travel agency runs day trips to Chichén Itzá and Tulum. Tours include guide, transport, entrance fee and a meal.

Nómadas Hostel (p150) Does day trips from Mérida to Uxmal, Chichén Itzá and Kabah. Tours include transportation and guide, but you pay for the sites' entrance fees.

Turitransmérida (p151) This Mérida-based operator goes to the hard-to-reach Ruta Puuc, Dzibilchaltún, Chichén Itzá, Kabah and Uxmal; includes transportation, lunch and guide. A four-person minimum is required for Ruta Puuc.

Plan Your Trip

Travel with Children

Snorkeling in caves, playing on the beach, running amok in the jungle...kids will find plenty of ways to keep busy in the Yucatán. And as elsewhere in Mexico, children take center stage – with few exceptions, they're welcome at all kinds of hotels and in virtually every cafe and restaurant.

Best Regions for Kids

Riviera Maya

Kids can splash themselves silly in the Riviera at family-friendly beaches and cenotes. The area also has many theme parks, which will burn a hole in your pocket, but they'll keep the little ones entertained for hours on end.

Cancún

Cancún was made with children in mind. From pirate-ship cruises and hotels with kids clubs to a wide offering of water-related activities and tours, boredom is simply not an option (especially if mom and dad are willing spenders).

Isla Mujeres

With its shallow and swimmable beaches and a great little turtle farm, Isla Mujeres is a big hit with kids. Nearby is Isla Contoy, which offers the thrill of visiting an uninhabited island, and the kids can do some snorkeling there as well.

The Yucatán for Kids

Getting Around

Watching scenery go by doesn't go over too well with most kids, so try to do your traveling between towns in smallish chunks. Distance between towns in the Riviera Maya is short and sweet.

Most 1st-class Mexican buses show nonstop movies on video screens, which diverts kids above toddler age, and most of the movies are pretty family-friendly. Children under 13 pay half-price on many long-distances buses, and if they're small enough to sit on your lap, they usually go for free.

Car rental is a practical alternative to buses. If you need a child safety seat, the major international car-rental firms are the most reliable providers. You will probably have to pay a few dollars extra per day. Car seats are compulsory for children under five.

Of course, some forms of traveling are fun – there are boat trips of many kinds to be had, plus you'll find bicycles, ATVs (all-terrain vehicles) and horses for rent.

Health & Safety

Children are more easily affected than adults by heat, disrupted sleeping patterns and strange food. Be particularly careful that they don't drink tap water or consume any questionable food or beverage. Take care to avoid sunburn, cover them up against insect bites, and ensure you replace fluids if a child gets diarrhea.

See a doctor about vaccinations at least one month – preferably two – before your trip. Once there, don't hesitate to go to a doctor if you think it may be necessary. In general, privately run hospitals and clinics offer better facilities and care than the public ones. Make sure you have adequate travel insurance that will cover the cost of private medical care.

Child safety provisions in Mexico may be less strict than what you're accustomed to. Check out things like toddler pools, cribs, guardrails and even toys so that you're aware of any potential hazards.

Facilities for changing diapers can be found in some shopping centers and restaurants. Breast-feeding in public is not common in the Yucatán.

Sleeping

The peninsula has an exciting variety of different places to stay that should please most kids – anything beachside is usually a good start, and rustic *cabañas* (cabins) provide a sense of adventure (but choose one with good screens and mosquito nets).

Many hotels have a rambling layout and a good amount of open-air space – courtyards, pool areas, gardens – allowing for some light exploring by kids. The most family-oriented hotels, with expansive grounds and facilities such as shallow pools, playgrounds and kids clubs, tend to be found in the big resorts.

Family rooms are widely available, and many hotels will put an extra bed or two in a room at little or no extra cost. You can find a room with air-conditioning nearly everywhere, and most midrange and top-end hotels have wi-fi access and child-friendly channels on the TV and/or DVD players for when your kids just need to flop down in front of something entertaining.

Eating

In most restaurants in Mexico you will see entire families and their kids eating together, especially on weekends. Waiters are used to accommodating children and will promptly help you with high chairs (*silla para niños* or *silla periquera*), and in some places they will bring crayons or some other toys to keep them entertained.

The Yucatán has plenty of eateries serving up international comfort food should Mexican fare not sit well with your children. Along the Riviera Maya you'll find many Italian-owned establishments preparing pizzas and pastas, while in gringo-friendly Cancún, there are so many restaurants doing burgers and the like that it'll seem like you never left home. Yucatecan *antojitos* (snacks) such as *sopa de lima* (which tastes like chicken soup) and *salbutes* (lightly fried tortillas topped with shredded poultry and other fixings) are fairly neutral options for experimenting with local flavors.

The closer you are to tourist centers, the better chance you have of finding more diverse and child-friendly menus. If your kid is a finicky eater, consider packing a lunch when visiting small towns where menu options may be more limited.

The spacious open-air character of many Yucatán eateries conveniently means that children aren't compelled to sit nicely at the table all the time. Some restaurants even have play areas or small pools to keep kids busy while the grown-ups have a drink.

PLANNING

- Cots for hotel rooms and high chairs for restaurants are available mainly in midrange and top-end establishments.
- It's usually not hard to find an inexpensive babysitter – ask at your hotel. Some top-end hotels provide the service at an additional cost.
- It's a good idea to book some accommodations for at least the first couple of nights, even if you plan to be flexible once you've arrived.
- Make sure when reserving a room that the establishment accepts children – some are adults-only.
- Lonely Planet's *Travel with Children* has lots of practical advice on the subject, drawn from firsthand experience.

UNDER-18 AIR TRAVELERS

To conform with regulations to prevent international child abduction, minors (people aged under 18) traveling to Mexico without one or both of their parents may need to carry a notarized consent form signed by the absent parent or parents, giving permission for the young traveler to make the international journey. Though Mexico does not specifically require this documentation, airlines flying to Mexico may refuse to board passengers without it. In the case of divorced parents, a custody document may be required. If one or both parents are dead, or the traveler has only one legal parent, a notarized document may be required.

Children's Highlights

Apart from the ruins, beaches and swimming pools, you'll find excellent kid-friendly attractions such as amusement and water parks, zoos, aquariums and other fun places on the peninsula. Kids can also enjoy activities such as snorkeling, riding bikes and observing wildlife. Archaeological sites can be fun if your kids are into climbing pyramids and exploring tunnels. The Tulum site has a pretty beach.

Water Worlds

Spot crocodiles and whale sharks Boat tours at **Río Lagartos** (p197) and **Isla Holbox** (p25) offer unique animal-spotting opportunities.

Sail on a pirate ship A replica Spanish galleon stages nightly swashbuckler battles off the waters of Cancún (p65). Pirate ships sail in Campeche, too.

Snorkel in the Caribbean Many beaches on the Yucatán's Caribbean coast provide calm waters and colorful marine life for beginners.

Swim and explore Visitors can make their way through underground rivers and caves at Riviera Maya theme parks (p101).

Cruise the jungle Reach the ancient cities of Yaxchilán (p247) by an adventurous river boat trip.

Inland Fun

Selvática (p101) An award-winning zip-line circuit through the jungle near Puerto Morelos, with its own cenote (limestone sinkhole) for swimming.

Cobá (p121) This jungle-surrounded ancient Maya site near Tulum has pyramids, a zip-line, and bicycles for pedaling around the network of dirt trails.

Aktun Chen (p101) This park near Akumal features a 60m-long cave, a 12m-deep cenote, 10 zip-lines and a small zoo.

Boca del Puma (p99) Near Puerto Morelos, Boca del Puma has zip-lining, horseback riding, wall climbing and a cenote to dip into.

Animal Encounters

Isla Mujeres Turtle Farm (p78) Has hundreds of sea turtles, both big and small, and there's an aquarium, too. The staff is very friendly and will take the time to explain how and why the farm protects the turtles.

Parque Zoológico del Centenario (p146) This park/zoo in Mérida has lions, bears, an aviary, playground, bumper boats and much more.

Reserva de la Biosfera Ría Celestún (p174) Take a boat tour through the mangroves of Ría Celestún, home to flamingos and harpy eagles.

Crococun Zoo (p65) Visitors can interact with the animals at this zoo near Puerto Morelos. You get an up-close look at crocodiles and wild spider monkeys.

Pan de muerto is traditionally eaten on Día de Muertos

Plan Your Trip

Eat & Drink Like a Local

The Yucatán is an endless feast of traditional regional flavors, fresh fish and seafood, and an eclectic mix of international cuisine. The wonderfully unique recipes you'll encounter on the peninsula leave no doubt: folks in this corner of Mexico are passionate about food.

The Year in Food

Spring (Apr–May)

Celebrity chefs from Mexico and abroad descend on the Yucatán for the Cancún-Riviera Maya Wine & Food Festival (www.crmfest.com) from late April to early May; a good chance to sample Mexican wines and gourmet dishes.

Summer (Jun–Aug)

Oh yeah, lobster season begins in July! Trapping season for lobster actually runs through February. In small fishing villages, that usually means you're getting the fresh catch of the day. The Jats'a Já Festival in Mahahual celebrates the town's fishing tradition with food stands in August.

Autumn (Sep–Nov)

Pibes (chicken tamales) are cooked underground for Day of the Dead in many cities throughout the peninsula, while bakeries make *pan de muerto* (colorful seasonal bread).

Winter (Dec–Mar)

The Mérida Fest in January brings food vendors to the main plaza; in late February or early March you'll find tasty street eats during Carnaval festivities in Cozumel, Chetumal and Campeche.

Food Experiences

Meals of a Lifetime

Kiosco Verde, Cancún (p63) Quite possibly Cancún's most underrated fish and seafood restaurant.

La Socorrito (p154) Standing the test of time, La Socorrito has been slow-cooking *cochinita* in underground pits for more than six decades.

Nohoch Kay, Mahahual (p131) Try the fried whole fish in wine and garlic sauce and you'll understand why this place is called 'The Big Fish.'

El Mirador, Ticul (p170) It's hard to imagine a better *recado blanco* (hearty turkey stew) than the one you get at this lookout restaurant.

La Fuente, Ciudad del Carmen (p220) A waterfront cafe famous for its *pibipollo* (chicken tamales cooked underground).

Cheap Treats

You'll find the best cheap eats at market stalls, street stands, cafes and *cocinas económicas* (economical eateries). Keep in mind that some budget options have sketchy hygiene standards, so it can be a bit of a crapshoot (no pun intended).

Wayan'e, Mérida (p153) Greet the new day with the greasy goodness of a *castacan* (pork belly) sandwich or taco.

Lonchería Doña Mary, Playa del Carmen (p107) Yucatecan comfort food at its best with a very local ambience.

Christian's Tacos, Laguna Bacalar (p134) These guys can hold their own against the best of Mexico's *al pastor* (spit-roasted pork) *taquerías*.

TierrAdentro, San Cristóbal de las Casas (p236) Run by Zapatista supporters, this cafe keeps it real with an affordable and delicious set menu.

Dare to Try

- Pickled pigs feet, snout and ears in Mérida's sprawling Mercado Municipal Lucas de Gálvez (p153).
- The four-alarm habanero chili salsas at Marisquería El Taco Loco (p137) in Chetumal.
- Lionfish at Sulumar (p131) in the Costa Maya beach town of Mahahual – hold the venom please!

Local Specialties

Food is a tremendous source of pride on the peninsula and the origins of some of the most popular dishes can easily become a topic of hot debate. We've broken down what's on offer in each state, but you'll definitely find variations of the most popular local dishes across state lines.

Yucatán State

Cochinita/pollo pibil Pork (often suckling pig) or chicken marinated in citrus juices and *achiote* (a spice made from annatto seed). When done properly, *cochinita* is slow-cooked in an underground pit.

Papadzules Diced hard-boiled eggs wrapped in corn tortilla and topped with pumpkin seed and tomato sauces.

Queso relleno A hollowed-out ball of Edam cheese stuffed with ground pork and smothered in tomato sauce and gravy.

Sopa de lima Soup with shredded turkey or chicken, lime and tortilla strips.

Panuchos Fried tortilla filled with beans and topped with chicken, lettuce, tomato and pickled red onion.

Quintana Roo

Lobster A popular menu item in Cancún and other coastal towns. Some restaurants prepare it with chili and tamarind sauces, giving it a very distinct Mexican taste.

Fish and shrimp tacos Beer-battered fish and shrimp are topped with shredded cabbage and the salsas of your choice. They're fast, cheap and highly addictive.

Ceviche Raw fish or seafood marinated in lime juice and spices and served with *tostadas*. Ceviche and *cerveza* (beer) go down great together on a warm day.

Fusion With so many Americans, Italians and other transplants living in these parts, you get some interesting blends of international and Mexican cuisine.

Campeche

Pibipollo Chicken tamales cooked underground and usually wrapped in banana leaves.

Chocolomo A hearty stew made of beef, kidneys, brain, tongue, liver, etc. You get the point – nothing goes to waste.

Pan de Cazón Stewed shark placed between corn tortillas and bathed in a tomato sauce.

DABBLE IN THE CULINARY ARTS

Take a cooking course to find out about the ingredients and techniques that go into Mexican cooking. Some recommended schools:

Los Dos (p149) Located in Mérida, Los Dos focuses on Yucatecan cuisine. Take a cooking course with a market tour or go for a multiday, all-inclusive culinary workshop.

Little Mexican Cooking School (p100) In Puerto Morelos, classes here provide a general overview of regional Mexican cuisine. You'll learn how to prepare seven to eight dishes and get background information on local culinary traditions.

Cochinita pibil

Chiapas

Coffee Optimal growing conditions (high altitude, good climate, rich soil) produce some of the finest coffee in the country.

Tamales If you haven't tried a tamale with the aromatic *hoja santa* herb, wrapped in a banana leaf, you're missing something truly special.

How to Eat & Drink

When to Eat

Desayuno (breakfast) Usually consists of fresh fruit, *pan dulce* (sweet bread) or egg dishes; served between 7am and 11am in restaurants and cafes.

Almuerzo (light lunch) Locals usually take a light lunch when they've missed breakfast or want something to hold them over until *la comida*, the big meal of the day.

La comida (heavy lunch) From 2pm to 5pm. Many establishments offer gut-busting four-course meals. Shops can close between these hours, especially in smaller towns.

Sopa de lima

La cena (supper) Some people like to grab a light dinner, between 7pm and 11pm, before hitting the bars and clubs; it's also a popular time for taco stands.

Where to Eat

Restaurante Restaurants offer the widest variety in terms of menu items, price ranges and hours; most are family-friendly establishments and they're usually your best shot at finding vegetarian options.

Cocina Económica/Fonda These affordable eateries specialize in home-style cooking and they're great spots to mingle with locals.

EATING PRICE INDICATORS

The following price ranges refer to the cost of a main dish for lunch or dinner:

$ Less than M$80

$$ M$80 to M$160

$$$ More than M$160

Taquería Taco shops are a perfect late-night option and the food's cheap if you're looking to pinch some pesos.

Mercado Many markets have a cluster of food stalls preparing decent, reasonably priced local dishes.

Cafe Coffee shops are a good breakfast option when you have an early start.

Puesto Street stalls whip up everything from tacos to ceviche cocktails. Opening hours vary considerably; some work mornings, others keep night hours.

Menu Decoder

Menú del día/comida corrida Affordable set menu with three or four courses.

Menú degustación A menu normally consisting of six to eight tasting-size courses.

Entradas/antojitos Appetizers or snacks; common in the Yucatán, especially in bars.

Plato fuerte Main course or main dish.

Postre Dessert.

Bebida Drink.

Panuchos

A FEW TIPS

- When sharing a table with Mexicans or dining in close quarters with them, it's customary to wish them '*buen provecho*' (enjoy your meal) before you leave.
- Waiters will not bring you the check until you ask for it. In Mexico it is considered rude to leave a check on a table while customers are still eating.
- The standard tip in Mexico is 10% of the bill. If you like the service, bump it up to 15% or 20%.

Where to Drink

Cantinas All cantinas serve *cerveza* and some, but not all, have licenses to pour tequila and other spirits. Some may even have *xtabentún*, a regional anise-flavored liqueur made from fermented honey. Cantinas usually open at high noon and close around 11pm or midnight. The cantina experience varies considerably from one watering hole to the next. Some are festive, family-friendly establishments offering live music and complimentary snacks, others have a down-and-dirty barfly vibe that's best avoided, especially if you're a woman traveling alone.

Nightclubs Some nightclubs in the region charge hefty covers (that means you, Cancún) with open bar included in the price of admission. So, of course you're gonna try to get your money's worth – just don't say we didn't warn you about the nasty hangover. The party usually gets started around 11pm and thumps well into the wee hours of the morning.

Mezcalerías Essentially small bars that specialize in mezcal, a distilled alcoholic drink made from the agave plant. Though mezcal is not actually made in the Yucatán, *mezcalerías* have grown very popular in recent years, especially in larger cities such as Mérida, Tulum and Playa del Carmen. Mezcal has a higher alcohol content than tequila, so expect the unexpected after knockin' a few back.

Juice Bars Usually found in markets, *juguerías* sell freshly squeezed juices, *liquados* (fruits blended with milk) and *aguas frescas* (water flavored with local ingredients such as chia seed and chaya greens). Water used to prepare drinks at juice bars is purified.

Cafes There's no shortage of cafes in the Yucatán serving quality organic coffee from Chiapas, Oaxaca and Veracruz, Mexico's top coffee-producing regions. Most cafes open early and close around 10pm.

Regions at a Glance

Cancún & Around

Beaches
Nature
Activities

Beach-Bumming

Cancún was built as a resort city with its scenic beaches in mind, so whether you like what's become of it today or not, the one constant is the fine white sands and turquoise blue waters, especially along the northern coast of Isla Blanca, where the coast remains relatively undeveloped.

Wildlife Watching

Several islands near Cancún offer unforgettable encounters with nature. Off the coasts of Islas Mujeres and Holbox, you can swim with ginormous whale sharks, while national park Isla Contoy provides excellent bird-watching opportunities. Just don't miss the boat back from uninhabited Contoy or you'll be sleeping with the turtles!

Water Sports

Name your water activity, Cancún has it: snorkeling, kayaking, wakeboarding, fishing – there's even a unique underwater sculpture museum for beginner divers. If you have kids and visit the area's water parks, the biggest problem will be convincing them that it's time to leave.

p54

Isla Mujeres

Conservation
Beaches
Activities

Wildlife Conservation

At the Isla Mujeres Turtle Farm, more than 100,000 of the little guys are released into the great big sea each year from July through November. Turtle eggs are gathered and secured in safe sands during peak nesting season from May to October.

Calm Beaches

The waters on Isla Mujeres' north shore, known as Playa Norte, are calm, shallow, warm and remarkably blue. On the island's south side, you'll come across some sweet snorkeling sites.

Great Outdoors

Snorkel with whale sharks, hook big game fish on a sportfishing excursion, or go diving and spot manta rays, barracuda and sea turtles. There's also the option of renting a golf cart and visiting beach clubs on the island's quieter south side.

p75

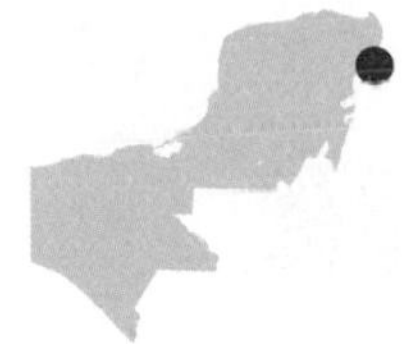

Isla Cozumel

Activities
Scenery
Food

Divine Diving

Isla Cozumel is a must-visit if you're into diving – in fact, some rank the island's sites among the world's best. Cozumel is known for its drift diving, year-round visibility, spectacular walls and impressive variety of colorful marine life.

Island Escape

A road trip on a scooter or convertible VW to the island's less-visited side is a moving picture of windswept beaches and scrubby jungle scenery. There are even small Maya ruins along the way. It all makes a nice escape from the cruise-ship crowds back in town.

Wining & Dining

Cozumel certainly has no shortage of quality restaurants serving fine local and international cuisine. The highest concentration of restaurants and bars is near the main plaza, but many hidden gems lie outside the tourist center.

p84

Riviera Maya

Beaches
Nightlife
Activities

Beach Life

The Riviera Maya sits on prime beach real estate. In Tulum, Maya ruins are perched atop a cliff tower above the beach in dramatic fashion. In tranquil Paamul, it's just you and the sea urchins, while up north in Puerto Morelos, a colorful reef awaits you just 600m offshore.

Party Central

With beachside discos featuring fire-dancer shows and cool 'inland' salsa clubs, Playa del Carmen still rules as the Riviera's top party town. But in recent years Tulum has gained ground on Playa in its bid to claim *pueblo*-that-never-sleeps status.

Cenote Diving

Take a plunge into a cenote (limestone sinkhole) and explore an intriguing underwater world of caverns and caves. Cenotes also make great swimming holes for nondivers. The Maya referred to these intricate river systems as gateways to the underworld.

p97

Costa Maya & Southern Caribbean Coast

Scenery
Activities
Beaches

Shades of Blue

Dubbed the 'lake of seven colors,' the crystalline waters of Laguna Bacalar have shades of blue that you never even knew existed. The glorious colors are on full display at Cenote Azul.

Take the Plunge

Divers won't want to miss out on the opportunity to explore Banco Chinchorro, the largest coral atoll in the northern hemisphere and a ship graveyard. There's fantastic snorkeling here as well.

Sleepy Beach Towns

Once tiny fishing villages, Mahahual and Xcalak are seeing more tourism these days, but fortunately they're still very chill – a far cry from the megaresort madness of Cancún.

p126

Yucatán State & the Maya Heartland

Archaeology
Nature
Food

Maya Ruins

Yucatán has so many Maya ruins that you'd probably need a leave of absence to visit them all. The most famous of them all, Chichén Itzá, draws more than a million visitors a year and has been declared one of the 'new seven wonders of the world.'

Birdies & Crocs

The Yucatán's two largest biosphere reserves, Celestún and Ría Lagartos, are always a hit with nature buffs. Tour boats take you out to observe crocodiles, flamingos and other bird species.

Food, Glorious Food

Yucatán state is one of Mexico's most exciting culinary destinations. In state capital Mérida, you get an interesting mix of traditional Yucatecan fare such as *cochinita pibil* (slow-cooked pork) and quality international cuisine.

p142

Campeche & Around

History
Nature
Archaeology

Pirates Ahoy

Campeche's most unique feature is its pretty historical center surrounded by stone walls built to fend off pirate attacks. It's a serene destination with few tourists, where a beachside boardwalk creates an atmosphere more romantic than ravaged.

Fins & Flippers

Laguna de Terminos' collection of estuaries and mangroves provides a rich coastal habitat for many critters. Keep a lookout for migratory birds or spot playful dolphins from a boat.

Lofty Pyramids

Deep in a jungle full of toucans and monkeys lies Calakmul, a significant Maya site. Originally a huge city, it covered 72 sq km and supported over 50,000 people – and it boasts one of the tallest Maya pyramids in Mexico.

p201

Chiapas & Tabasco

Architecture
Archaeology
Nature

Colonial Grace

San Cristóbal's cobbled streets and colonial architecture are charming enough, but add a dash of Zapatista history and colorful indigenous people and you've hit something special. Visit the church in nearby San Juan Chamula – it's almost magical.

Exquisite Temples

Unique in the Maya world is Palenque's four-story, stone tower – perhaps an old observatory? And the Templo de las Inscripciones once held the skeleton of Pakal the Great, draped with jewels and a priceless jade mask.

Riverside Adventure

It takes a long bus trip, plus a half-hour boat ride, but a visit to the Maya city of Yaxchilán is indelible. Note the hieroglyphics and interesting facades on buildings, and listen for howler monkeys in the jungle. Did we mention the croc-infested waters?

p227

On the Road

Cancún & Around

☎998 / POP 630,000

Includes ➡

Best Places to Eat

- Kiosco Verde (p63)
- Los Peleones (p73)
- El Tigre y El Toro (p64)
- El Chapulím (p73)
- Checándole (p63)

Best Places to Stay

- Hotel El Rey del Caribe (p59)
- Mezcal Hostel (p59)
- Casa Takywara (p73)
- Casa Lupita (p72)

Why Go?

Cancún is a tale of two cities. There's the glitzy hotel zone with its famous white-sand beaches, unabashed party scene and sophisticated seafood restaurants. Then there's the actual city itself, which gives you a taste of local flavor at, say, a neighborhood taco joint or a nearby, undeveloped beach.

That's what keeps Cancún interesting. Had your fill of raucous discos in the hotel zone? Escape to a downtown salsa club. Tired of lounging around the pool in Ciudad Cancún? Simply hop on a bus and head for the sapphire waters of the hotel zone.

Or even better, venture out and explore more of Quintana Roo state. Just a day trip away from Cancún, the pristine national park of Isla Contoy beckons with a fascinating variety of bird and plant species. And up north awaits low-key Isla Holbox, where swimming with massive whale sharks has become all the rage.

When to Go

- A visit to Cancún in late April or early May, following spring break madness, shows you a relatively quiet side of the resort city and many accommodations offer great online deals at that time of year.
- Don't miss the thrilling opportunity to snorkel with whale sharks off the coast of Isla Holbox; the gentle giants congregate around the island from May through September, but the best time to go is from mid-June to late August.
- Three species of sea turtles flock to the shores of Parque Nacional Isla Contoy for nesting season from April to October; the uninhabited island is also home to more than 170 bird species.

Cancún & Around Highlights

1 Dive among the fish and life-size sculptures at the **Museo Subacuático de Arte** (p57), a one-of-a kind underwater museum.

2 Swim with massive whale sharks, kayak through wildlife-rich mangroves and enjoy laid-back island living on **Isla Holbox** (p71).

3 Snorkel and get in some birdwatching on the uninhabited **Isla Contoy** (p70), a wildlife refuge that receives only 200 visitors a day.

4 Visit the quiet beaches of undeveloped **Isla Blanca** (p68), near Ciudad Cancún, then shake your booty to live salsa music at a downtown club.

5 Chill on the soft sands of the **Zona Hotelera** (p66), take a dip in the Caribbean blue, then check out the city's new Maya museum (p56) and adjoining ruins.

CANCÚN

History

When you look around at the giant hotels and supermalls it's hard to imagine that 40 years ago there was nothing here but sand and fishing boats. In the 1970s Mexico's ambitious planners decided to outdo Acapulco with a brand-new, world-class resort located on the Yucatán Peninsula. The place they chose was a deserted sandspit located offshore from the little fishing village of Puerto Juárez, on the peninsula's eastern shore, known as Isla Cancún (Cancún Island). Vast sums were sunk into landscaping and infrastructure, yielding straight, well-paved roads, potable tap water and great swaths of sandy beach. As the Zona Hotelera (Hotel Zone) mushroomed, Ciudad Cancún cropped up on the mainland and became one of the fastest growing cities in Mexico – today it's Quintana Roo's most populated city.

Hurricanes Wilma and Emily whipped into town in 2005, destroying area hotels, flooding much of the city and carrying off tons of Cancún's precious beach sand. The hotels have been rebuilt and the sands have since been replaced. That's right, the sands have been replaced. Much to the ire of environmentalists, this involved a massive undertaking of dredging sand from the ocean floor and then moving it ashore. Those in favor call it 'beach nourishing,' those opposed warn that it causes serious environmental damage to the marine ecosystem. But it's not just the storms that are washing Cancun's sand away. Making matters even more complicated, beaches are eroding because of sea-level rise. It certainly appears that mother nature will have the final say on the future of Cancun's beaches.

Sights

Most of Cancun's star attractions – namely its beaches, museum, ruins and water-related activities – are in the Zona Hotelera. If you're staying in Ciudad Cancún, any 'R-1', 'R-2,' or 'Zona Hotelera' bus will drop you off at any point along the coast.

★Museo Maya de Cancún MUSEUM
(Maya Museum; Map p58; www.inah.gob.mx; Blvd Kukulcán Km 16.5; M$64; 9am-6pm Tue-Sun; R-1) Holding one of the Yucatán's most important collections of Maya artifacts, this modern museum is a welcome sight in a city known more for its party scene than cultural attractions. On display are some 400 pieces found at key sites in and around the peninsula, ranging from sculptures to ceramics and jewelry. One of the three halls shows temporary Maya-themed exhibits.

Cancún's original anthropology museum shut down in 2006 due to structural damage from hurricanes. The new museum features hurricane-resistant reinforced glass. The price of admission includes access to the adjoining San Miguelito archaeological site.

San Miguelito ARCHAEOLOGICAL SITE
(Map p58; 998-885-38-43; www.inah.gob.mx; Blvd Kukulcán Km 16.5; M$64; 9am-4:30pm; R-1) Cancún's newest archaeological site opened in 2012 and contains more than a dozen restored Maya structures inhabited between AD 1200 and 1550, prior to the arrival of the conquistadors. A path from the Museo Maya leads to remains of houses, a palace with 17 columns and the site's tallest structure: the 8m-high Pirámide (Pyramid), which was rebuilt three times. Access to the ruins is included in the entrance fee to the Museo Maya.

Zona Arqueológica El Rey ARCHAEOLOGICAL SITE
(Map p58; Blvd Kukulcán Km 18; M$47; 8am-4:30pm; R-1) In the Zona Arqueológica El Rey, on the west side of Blvd Kukulcán, there's a small temple and several ceremonial platforms. The site gets its name from a sculpture excavated here of a noble, possibly a *rey* (king), wearing an elaborate headdress. El Rey, which flourished from AD 1200 to 1500, and nearby San Miguelito were communities dedicated to maritime trade and fishing.

Yamil Lu'um ARCHAEOLOGICAL SITE
(Map p58; off Blvd Kukulcán Km 12.5; R-1) FREE Also known as the Templo del Alácran (Scorpion's Temple), Yamil Lu'um was used between AD 1200 and 1550, and sits atop a beachside knoll in the parklike grounds between the Park Royal and Westin Lagunamar hotels. The ruin makes a pleasant venture for its lovely setting more than anything else. Only the outward-sloping remains of the weathered temple's walls still stand. To reach the site visitors must discreetly pass through either of the hotels flanking it.

Beaches

Starting from Ciudad Cancún in the northwest, all of Isla Cancún's beaches are on the left-hand side of the road (the lagoon is on your right). The first beaches are Playas Las Perlas, Juventud, Linda, Langosta, Tortugas and Caracol. With the exception of Playa Caracol, these are Cancún's most swimmable beaches.

When you round Punta Cancún the water gets rougher (though it's still swimmable) and the beaches become more scenic as white sands meet the turquoise-blue Caribbean, from Playa Gaviota Azul, all the way down south to Punta Nizuc at Km 24. Playa Delfines, at Km 18, is about the only beach with a public parking lot big enough to be useful; unfortunately, its sand is coarser and darker than the exquisite, fine sand of the more northerly beaches.

Access

Under Mexican law you have the right to walk and swim on every beach in the country except those within military compounds. In practice, it is difficult to approach many stretches of beach without walking through the lobby of a hotel, particularly in the Zona Hotelera. However, as long as you look like a tourist (this shouldn't be hard, right?), you'll usually be permitted to cross the lobby and proceed to the beach.

Safety

Avoid swimming along the shores of Laguna de Nichupté. The lagoon is a crocodile habitat and, although attacks are very rare, you're better off at the beach. In April 2015, a reportedly inebriated man ignored signposts warning that the lagoon was not safe for swimming and died in a crocodile attack.

Cancún's ambulance services respond to as many as a dozen near-drownings per week. The most dangerous beaches with the strongest undercurrents line the eastern shore, from Playa Chac-Mool at Km 10 to Playa Delfines at Km 18.

Though the surf is usually gentle, undertow is a possibility, and sudden storms can blacken the sky and sweep in at any time without warning. A system of colored pennants warns beachgoers of any potential danger:

- Blue: Normal, safe conditions.
- Yellow: Use caution, changeable conditions.
- Red: Unsafe conditions; use a swimming pool instead.

Activities

For decent snorkeling, you need to travel to one of the nearby reefs. Several dive shops now offer diving and snorkeling outings to Museo Subacuático de Arte (MUSA), a unique underwater attraction.

Most of the major resorts rent kayaks and the usual water toys; a few make them available to guests free of charge.

Cancún has pretty weak surf, but a core group of locals still heads out to Playa Chac-Mool and Playa Marlin to hit the little rollers. 'Surf season' runs from October to March. There's no place in town to rent boards, but there's a downtown surf shop where you can buy one.

★Museo Subacuático de Arte DIVING, SNORKELING

(MUSA Underwater Museum; www.musacancun.com; snorkeling tour US$41.50, 1-tank dive US$65) Built to divert divers away from deteriorating coral reefs, this one-of-a-kind aquatic museum features more than 500 life-size sculptures in the waters of Cancún and Isla Mujeres. The artificial reefs are submerged at depths of 4m and 8m, making them ideal for snorkelers and first-time divers. Organize dives through diving outfits; Scuba Cancún is recommended.

The underwater museum is a creation of British-born sculptor Jason deCaires Taylor.

Scuba Cancún DIVING

(Map p58; ☎998 849-75-08; www.scubacancun.com.mx; Blvd Kukulcán Km 5.2; 1-/2-tank dives US$62/77, equipment rental extra) A family-owned and PADI-certified dive operation with many years of experience, Scuba Cancún was the city's first dive shop. It offers a variety of snorkeling, fishing and diving expeditions (including cenote and night dives). It also runs snorkeling and diving trips to the underwater sculpture museum, aka MUSA.

Koko Dog'z Surf Shop WATER SPORTS

(Map p62; ☎998-887-36-35; www.kokodogz.com; Av Náder 42; noon-8pm Mon-Fri, to 4pm Sat; R-1) Sells all sorts of boards – surf, kite, boogie and skim.

Bike Around BICYCLE RENTAL

(Map p58; www.bikearoundcancun.com; Blvd Kukulcán Km 9.5, Forum Mall; per hour M$120-190; 11am-11pm) Rent a city, mountain or racing bike and pedal south down the coast or head west along a bike trail to Ciudad Cancún.

Cancún

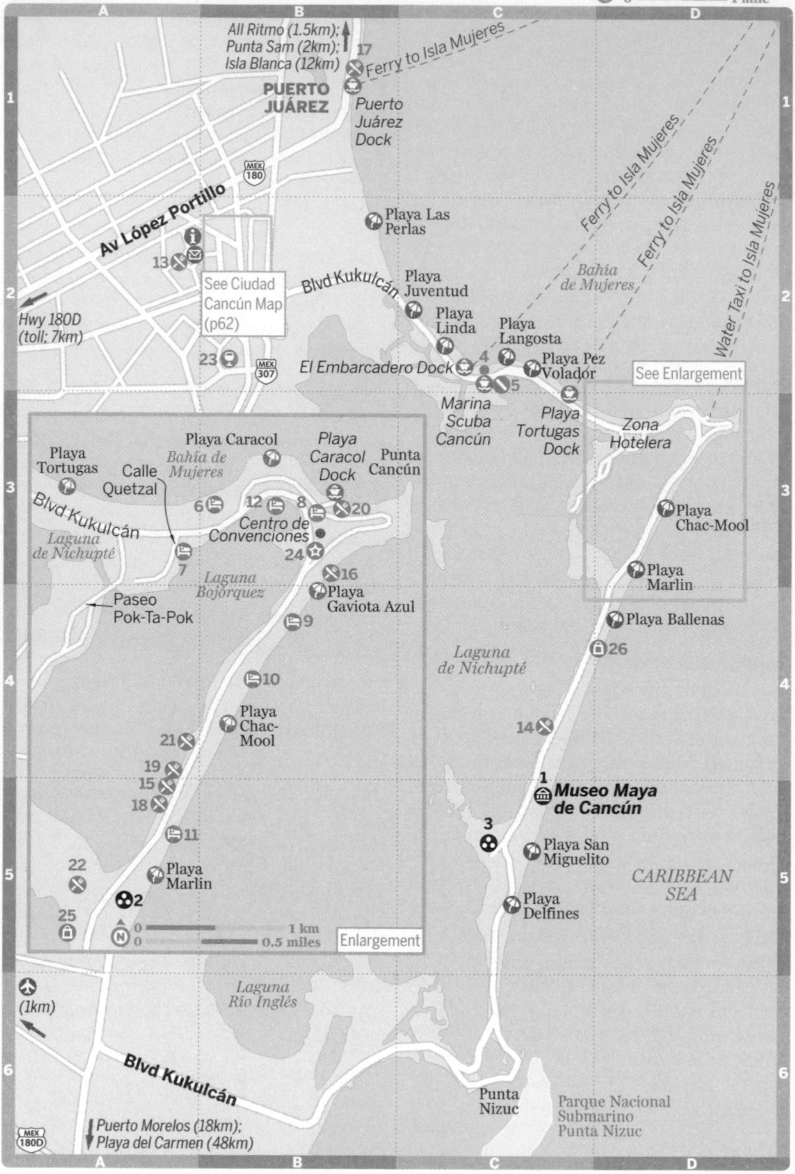

0 2 km
0 1 mile

All Ritmo (1.5km); Punta Sam (2km); Isla Blanca (12km)
17
Ferry to Isla Mujeres
PUERTO JUÁREZ
Puerto Juárez Dock
MEX 180
Av López Portillo
13
Playa Las Perlas
Ferry to Isla Mujeres
Ferry to Isla Mujeres
Water Taxi to Isla Mujeres
Bahía de Mujeres
See Ciudad Cancún Map (p62)
Hwy 180D (toll; 7km)
Blvd Kukulcán
Playa Juventud
Playa Linda
Playa Langosta
Playa Pez Volador
23
MEX 307
El Embarcadero Dock
4
5
Marina Scuba Cancún
Playa Tortugas Dock
See Enlargement
Zona Hotelera
Playa Chac-Mool
Playa Marlin
Playa Ballenas
26
Laguna de Nichupté
14
1
Museo Maya de Cancún
3
Playa San Miguelito
CARIBBEAN SEA
Playa Delfines
Punta Nizuc
Parque Nacional Submarino Punta Nizuc
(1km)
Laguna Río Inglés
Blvd Kukulcán
MEX 180D
Puerto Morelos (18km); Playa del Carmen (48km)

Enlargement
Playa Tortugas
Calle Quetzal
Bahía de Mujeres
Playa Caracol
Playa Caracol Dock
Punta Cancún
6
12
8
20
Blvd Kukulcán
Centro de Convenciones
Laguna de Nichupté
7
24
Laguna Bojórquez
16
Playa Gaviota Azul
Paseo Pok-Ta-Pok
9
10
Playa Chac-Mool
21
19
15
18
11
22
Playa Marlin
2
25
0 1 km
0 0.5 miles

Teatro Xbalamqué COURSE

(Map p62; ☎998-204-10-28, cell 998-1228084; www.teatroxbalamque.com/; cnr Jazmines & Av Yaxchilán; dance class M$50; ⏲6-10pm Mon-Sat) A salsa class here will help you avoid those embarrassing moments on the dance floor.

Tours

Most hotels and travel agencies work with companies that offer tours to surrounding attractions.

Cancún

Top Sights
1 Museo Maya de Cancún C5

Sights
San Miguelito .... (see 1)
2 Yamil Lu'um A5
3 Zona Arqueológica El Rey C5

Activities, Courses & Tours
Asterix .... (see 5)
Bike Around .... (see 16)
4 Captain Hook C2
5 Scuba Cancún C2

Sleeping
6 Beachscape Kin Ha Villas & Suites B3
7 Grand Royal Lagoon A3
8 Hostal Mayapan B3
9 Hostel Natura B4
10 Le Blanc B4
11 Me by Melia A5
12 Suites Costa Blanca B3

Eating
13 Chooándole A2
14 Crab House C4
15 El Fish Fritanga A5
16 Forum Mall B3
17 Kiosco Verde B1
18 La Habichuela Sunset A5
19 Lorenzillo's A4
20 Mocambo B3
21 Plaza Flamingo A4
Restaurante Natura .... (see 9)
Surfin' Burrito .... (see 9)
22 Thai Lounge A5

Drinking & Nightlife
23 Marakame Café B2
Rose Bar .... (see 11)

Entertainment
Cinemex .... (see 22)
Coco Bongo .... (see 16)
24 Dady'O B3

Shopping
25 La Europea A5
La Isla Shopping Village .... (see 22)
Mercado 28 .... (see 13)
26 Plaza Kukulcán D4

Hostel Mundo Joven TOUR
(Map p62; 998-271-47-40; www.mundojoven.com; Av Uxmal 25; 10am-7pm Mon-Fri, to 2pm Sat; R-1) Drop by this excellent downtown travel agency to hook up tours to uninhabited Isla Contoy or for excursions to the Maya ruins of Chichén Itzá and Tulum.

Sleeping

Almost all hotels offer discounts during the 'low' season, but at many places there are up to five different rate periods: Christmas and New Year are always at a premium, and there are high rates from late February to early March for US spring break, Easter, and even during July and August (when locals have their holidays). Many places have great online promotions.

Ciudad Cancún

'Budget' is a relative term; prices in Cancún are higher for what you get than most anywhere else in Mexico. There are many cheap lodging options within several blocks of the bus terminal, northwest on Avenida Uxmal. The area around Parque de las Palapas has numerous hostels and budget digs as well.

Midrange in Cancún is a two-tiered category; the Ciudad Cancún area is much cheaper than the Zona Hotelera and only a short bus ride away from the Zona's beaches.

Mezcal Hostel HOSTEL $
(Map p62; cell 998-1259502; www.mezcalhostel.com; Mero 12; dm/r incl breakfast US$14/45; ; R-1) Any place with mezcal in its name must be good, or so the logic goes. In this case, it is indeed all good at the Mezcal Hostel, which occupies a beautiful two-story house in a quiet residential area. Private rooms and dorms are kept very clean and weekly Sunday BBQ parties are perfect for sipping smoky mezcal.

Hostel Ka'beh HOSTEL $
(Map p62; 988-892-79-02; www.cancunhostel.hostel.com; Alcatraces 45; dm from M$250, r M$700, incl breakfast; ; R-1) A good central option just off the buzzing Parque de las Palapas, this small hostel has a lived-in feel that goes hand in hand with the relaxed vibe. Expect many social activities at night, most organized around food and drink.

★ **Hotel El Rey del Caribe** HOTEL $$
(Map p62; 998-884-20-28; www.elreydelcaribe.com; Av Uxmal 24; s/d incl breakfast M$900/983; ; R-1) El Rey is a true ecotel – it recycles, employs solar collectors and cisterns, uses gray water on the

LIVING LARGE IN THE MEXICAN CARIBBEAN

Cancún and its surrounding areas have many establishments selling the 'resort' experience, but only some are truly worth the splurge. Non-negotiable is a prime beachfront location; after that, it's really just a question of what best suits your needs: some hotels put a premium on over-the-top comfort and elegance, others specialize in family-friendly getaways with around-the-clock activities. When booking a room, keep in mind that some resorts do not accept children and most, though not all, offer all-inclusive plans with an endless banquet of food and drink.

Grand Velas (toll-free 800-831-11-65; www.rivieramaya.grandvelas.com; Hwy 307 Km 62; all-inclusive d from US$894, child 4-15yr US$100; P) The mother of all beach resorts, the sprawling Grand Velas boasts one of the best spas on the coast; an azure, free-form infinity pool; marble-floored rooms that put other so-called luxury accommodations to shame; loads of activities for kids and grown-ups; and the list goes on. It's 6km north of Playa del Carmen.

Le Blanc (Map p58; in USA 877-883-3696, toll-free 800-272-02-15; www.leblancsparesort.com; Blvd Kukulcán Km 10; d US$806 all-inclusive; P; R-1) You can't miss the glaring white exterior of the aptly-named Le Blanc, arguably Cancun's most sophisticated resort. This adults-only retreat comes with all the amenities you'd expect in this category – there's even butler service should life in Cancún become too complicated.

Petit Lafitte (984-877-40-00; www.petitlafitte.com; Carretera Cancún-Chetumal Km 296, Playa Xcalacoco, 6km north of Playa del Carmen; d/bungalow incl breakfast & dinner from US$230/280, child 3-11yr additional US$50; P) Occupying a quiet beach far removed from the Playa del Carmen party scene, Petit Lafitte is an excellent family vacation spot. Stay in a room or a 'bungalow' (essentially a wood cabin with tasteful rustic furnishings, some of which sleep up to five guests). Kids stay entertained with the large pool, small zoo, game room and various water activities.

See website for directions.

gardens, and has some rooms with composting toilets. This beautiful spot has a swimming pool and Jacuzzi in a jungly courtyard that's home to a small family of *tlacuaches* (opossums). All rooms have a fully equipped kitchenette, comfortable beds and fridges.

Offers good online deals.

Náder Hotel & Suites HOTEL $$
(Map p62; 998-884-15-84; www.suitesnadercancun.com; Av Náder 5; d/ste incl breakfast US$54/75; ; R-1) The Náder caters to business travelers but it's also a hit with families thanks to its ample rooms and suites with large common areas and kitchens. Even the 'standard' setup here gets you digs with some serious elbow room.

Cancún International Suites HOTEL $$
(Map p62; 998-884-17-71; www.cancuninternationalsuites.com; Gladiolas 16, cnr Alcatraces; r/ste M$1100/2000; ; R-1) Colonial-style rooms and suites in this remodeled hotel are comfortable and quiet and the location is great – right off Parque de las Palapas and conveniently close to downtown's restaurant and bar zone.

Soberanis Hotel HOTEL $$
(Map p62; 998-884-45-64; www.hotelsoberanis.com; Av Cobá 5 s/n; d incl breakfast M$1000; @; R-1) Location, location, location. The Soberanis sits right on a corner where buses stop before continuing on to the Zona Hotelera, plus there's a supermarket right next door. The remodeled rooms recently got comfortable new beds and wood furnishings.

Colonial Cancún HOTEL $$
(Map p62; 998-884-15-35; www.hotelcolonialcancun.com/; Tulipanes 22; d incl breakfast M$850; ; R-1) Rooms are anything but colonial, but they're pleasant enough and they overlook a leafy central courtyard with a gurgling fountain. The hotel has a small pool area.

Hotel Bonampak HOTEL $$
(Map p62; 998-884-02-80; www.hotelbonampak.com; Av Bonampak 225; r incl breakfast M$880; P@; R-27) Good value by Cancún standards, rooms at this business-style hotel have been spruced up with comfy new mattresses, dark-wood furnishings and flat-

screen TVs. Ask for one overlooking the sunny pool area.

Hotel Plaza Caribe HOTEL $$

(Map p62; ☎998-884-13-77; www.hotelplazacaribe.com; Pinos s/n; r M$900-1100; P ⊖ ❄ 🛜 ≋; 🚌R-1) Directly across from the bus terminal, this hotel offers comfortable rooms, a pool, restaurant and gardens with peacocks roaming about. The remodeled 'executive' rooms sport a more modern look than the 'standard' digs.

Hotel Antillano HOTEL $$$

(Map p62; ☎998-884-11-32; www.hotelantillano.com; Claveles 1; s/d incl breakfast M$1120/1270; ⊖ ❄ 🛜 ≋; 🚌R-1) Just off Avenida Tulum is this very pleasant and quiet place with a relaxing lobby, nice pool, good central air-con and cable TV. Rooms on the Avenida catch more street noise. Rates drop considerably during low season.

Zona Hotelera

With few exceptions, most hotels lining Blvd Kukulcán are of the top-end variety. Many offer all-inclusive packages, often at reasonable rates if you're willing to forgo eating elsewhere. Often the best room rates are available through hotel-and-airfare packages, so shop around.

Hostal Mayapan HOSTEL $

(Map p58; ☎998-883-32-27; www.hostalmayapan.com; Blvd Kukulcán Km 8.5; incl breakfast dm M$180-235, r M$850; ⊖ ❄ @ 🛜; 🚌R-1) Located in an abandoned mall, this is a great budget spot in the Zona Hotelera. Thanks to its location just 30m from the beach, it's one of our favorite hostels in town. The rooms are superclean and there's a little hangout area in an atrium upstairs (the old food court?).

Hostel Natura HOSTEL $$

(Map p58; ☎998-883-08-87; www.hostelnaturacancun.com; Blvd Kukulcán Km 9.5; dm US$26-27, r US$60; ⊖ ❄ 🛜; 🚌R-1) Up above a health-food restaurant of the same name, this new hostel offers private rooms with lagoon views and somewhat cramped dorms, offset by the airy rooftop common area. The party zone is close by.

Suites Costa Blanca HOTEL $$

(Map p58; ☎998-883-08-88; www.suitescostablanca.com; Blvd Kukulcán Km 8.5; r from M$950; ⊖ ❄ 🛜; 🚌R-1) A rare midrange option in the Zona Hotelera, which in and of itself makes this a great find. The hotel claims to offer 'Mediterranean-style' suites, but they're really just large (somewhat outdated) rooms with sitting areas and small balconies.

Grand Royal Lagoon HOTEL $$

(Map p58; ☎998-883-27-49, toll-free 800 522 46-66; www.gr-lagoon.com; Quetzal 8A; r M$1100; P ⊖ ❄ 🛜 ≋; 🚌R-1) A breezy place, and relatively affordable for the Zona Hotelera, the Grand Royal offers cable TV, safes and a small pool. Most rooms have two double beds, while some have kings, lagoon views and balconies. It's 100m off Blvd Kukulcán Km 7.5.

Beachscape Kin Ha Villas & Suites HOTEL $$$

(Map p58; ☎998-891-54-00; www.beachscape.com.mx; Blvd Kukulcán Km 8.5; r from US$138; P ⊖ ❄ @ 🛜 ≋ 👶; 🚌R-1) A good family spot, Beachscape offers a babysitting service, a play area for kids and a swimmable beach with calm waters. You'll never need to leave the hotel's grounds (though we think you should), as there are bars, markets, travel agencies and more on the premises. All rooms feature a balcony and two double beds or one king-sized bed. The price listed is for the European plan, but you can arrange an all-inclusive stay.

Me by Melia LUXURY HOTEL $$$

(Map p58; ☎998-881-25-00; www.mebymelia.com; Blvd Kukulcán Km 12; d all inclusive from M$6550; P ⊖ ❄ @ 🛜 ≋; 🚌R-1) 'Enough about you, let's talk about me!' That's the philosophy at this ubermodern, expressionist-inspired hotel. It won't suit everyone, but if you prefer clean lines over standard Cancún baroque, it's the place for you. Only half the rooms have ocean views, and it just ain't worth it to pay this much and not have a view of the Caribbean blue.

Eating

Ciudad Cancún

Eating options in Ciudad Cancún range from your standard-issue taco joints to upscale seafood restaurants. You'll find many restaurants near Parque de las Palapas and along Avenida Yaxchilán. Mercados 23 (p67) and 28 (p67) serve up good market food, and there are some **food stands** (Map p62; Parque de las Palapas; ⏰7:30am-midnight) right on the Palapas plaza. For groceries, try **Comercial Mexicana** (Map p62; cnr Avs Tulum & Uxmal; ⏰7am-11pm), close to the bus station, or **Chedraui Supermarket** (Map p62; cnr Avs Tulum & Cobá; ⏰7am-11pm; 🚌R-1).

Ciudad Cancún

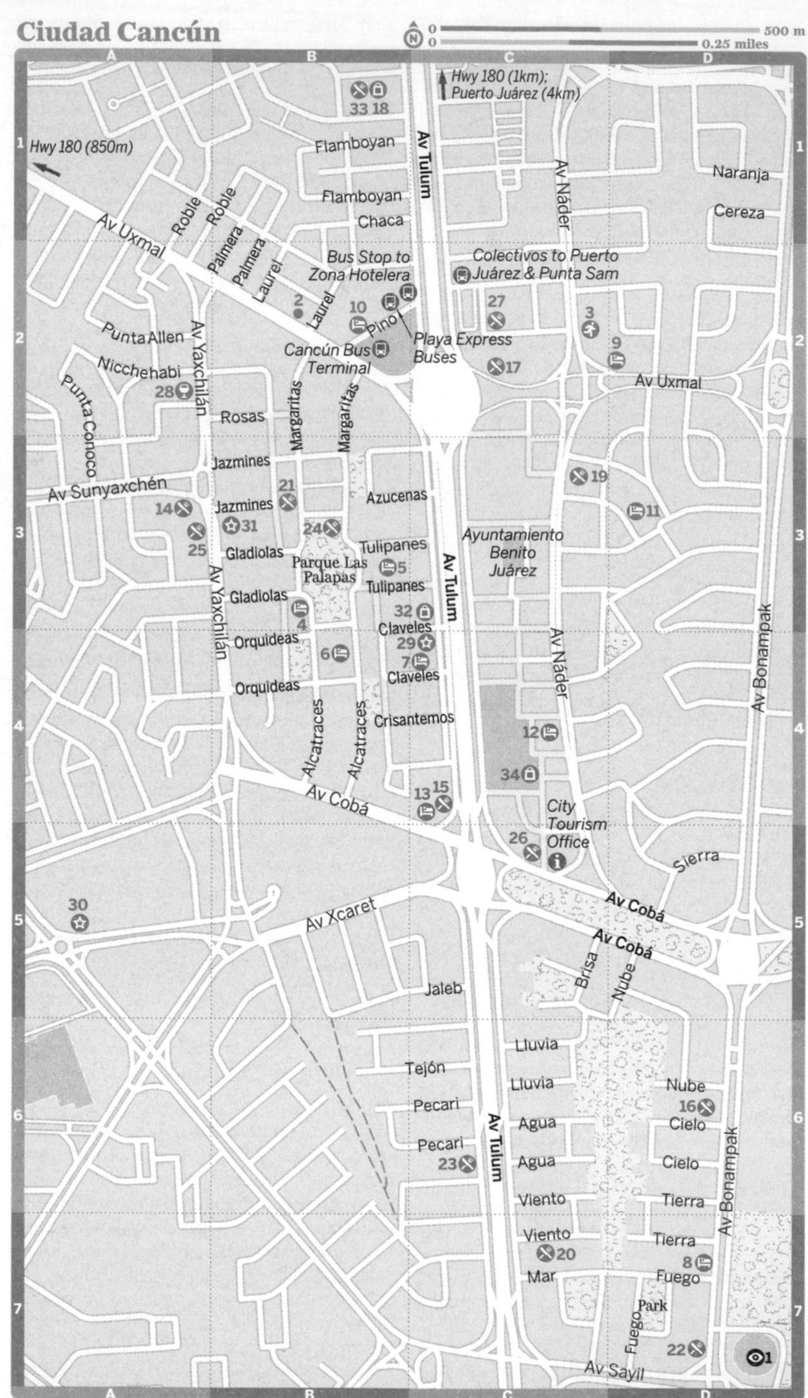

Ciudad Cancún

Sights
1 Plaza de Toros D7

Activities, Courses & Tours
2 Hostel Mundo Joven B2
3 Koko Dog'z Surf Shop C2
Teatro Xbalamqué .... (see 31)

Sleeping
4 Cancún International Suites B3
5 Colonial Cancún B3
6 Hostel Ka'beh B4
7 Hotel Antillano C4
8 Hotel Bonampak D7
9 Hotel El Rey del Caribe D2
10 Hotel Plaza Caribe B2
11 Mezcal Hostel D3
12 Náder Hotel & Suites C4
13 Soberanis Hotel C4

Eating
14 100% Natural A3
15 Chedraui Supermarket C4
16 Cocina Jalisco D6
17 Comercial Mexicana C2
18 El Paisano del 23 .... B1
19 El Tigre y El Toro C3
20 Irori C7
La Barbacoa de la Tulum .... (see 1)
21 La Habichuela B3
22 La Playita D7
23 Los de Pescado C6
24 Mexican Food Stalls B3
25 Pescaditos A3
26 Rolandi's Restaurant & Pizzeria C5
27 Ty-Coz C2

Drinking & Nightlife
28 La Taberna A2

Entertainment
29 11:11 .... C4
30 Grand Mambo Café A5
31 Teatro Xbalamqué B3

Shopping
32 Colormax C3
33 Mercado 23 .... B1
34 Mercado Municipal Ki-Huic C4

Los de Pescado SEAFOOD $
(Map p62; www.losdepescado.com; Av Tulum 32; tacos & tostadas M$27-29, ceviche M$86-129, burritos M$39-43; 10am-6pm; ; R-27) It's easy to order at a place where you have only four choices: ceviche (seafood marinated in lemon or lime juice, garlic and seasonings), tacos, *tostadas* (fried tortilla) or burritos. Try the fish and shrimp tacos with fixings from the salad station and you'll understand why locals dig this spot.

El Paisano del 23 MEXICAN $
(Map p62; cnr Cedro & Cericote, Mercado 23; tortas M$35; 6am-4pm; R-1) A local favorite for more than 40 years, the *paisano* ('fellow countryman' – it's the owner's nickname) marinates *pierna* (pork leg) in red wine and then slow cooks it. The *tortas* (sandwiches) go fast, especially on weekends.

La Barbacoa de la Tulum MEXICAN $
(Map p62; cnr Avs Sayil & Bonampak, Plaza de Toros; tacos M$20-31; 24hr; ; R-27) If you love tacos, head to this 24-hour restaurant/bar, where the specialties are *barbacoa* (mutton) and *cochinita* (slow-cooked pork).

Cocina Jalisco MEXICAN $
(Map p62; Av Bonampak 193; quesadillas M$20, set meals M$70; 8am-5pm Mon-Sat; R-1) For a cheap lunch on this side of town, head over to this small sidewalk restaurant where the friendly owner, Javier, serves up affordable lunches and quesadillas.

Ty-Coz SANDWICHES $
(Map p62; 998-884-60-60; Av Tulum s/n; sandwiches M$38-80; 8am-10pm Mon-Sat; ; R-1) This little deli serves sandwiches on croissants and baguettes with a variety of meats and cheeses, and there's a vegetarian option as well.

★**Kiosco Verde** SEAFOOD $$
(Map p58; www.restaurant-kiosco-verde.blogspot.mx; Av López Portillo s/n, Puerto Juárez; mains M$80-140; noon-7pm Wed-Mon;) The Green Kiosk just might be the most underrated seafood restaurant in all of Cancún. It began in 1974 as a grocery store and now it serves elaborate fresh fish and seafood dishes, such as coconut-encrusted shrimp and succulent grilled whole fish. Don't leave without trying the Mexican craft beers or mezcal.

To get here, catch a northbound 'Puerto Juárez' *colectivo* along Avenida Tulum, opposite the bus station.

Checándole MEXICAN $$
(Map p58; 998-884-71-47; Av Xpujil 27, cnr Calle Coral; set menu M$65, mains M$67-144; noon-8pm Mon-Sat; ; R-6) Specializes in regional Mexican cuisine, offering great value in

its *menú del día* (fixed three-course meal). If *pollo en mole poblano* (chicken smothered in a handmade chocolate and chili sauce) is an option, you should definitely go for it.

Va q' Va SEAFOOD $$

(www.vaqva.com.mx; Calle 107, btwn Av Leona Vicario & Niños Héroes; mains M$80-160; ⏲10am-7pm; ⊜) The fish and seafood are pretty good here but the real draw is the festive atmosphere, plus you get to enjoy a meal in a working-class neighborhood far removed from the tourist center. It's worth the trip just for the marimba music and *Clamato micheladas* (beer with Clamato juice – a tomato and clam cocktail mix – lime and salt).

It's best reached by taxi.

La Playita SEAFOOD $$

(Map p62; Av Bonampak 60; mains M$90-170; ⏲11am-2am; ⊜ⓦ; 🚌R-27) Beat the heat with refreshing, light dishes such as seafood cocktails and ceviche *tostadas*. To drink, try the 'frozen *miche*,' a beer-based cocktail best described as a brain freeze waiting to happen. The daily drink specials and outdoor seating make this one of downtown's most popular bars.

Pescaditos SEAFOOD $$

(Map p62; Av Yaxchilán 69; snacks & mains M$44-169; ⏲11am-midnight Mon-Thu, to 1am Fri & Sat; ⓦ) The namesake *pescaditos* (fried fish sticks served with a mayo-*chipotle* sauce) are the star attraction here, but the menu features plenty of other fresh fish and seafood dishes that are well worth trying.

100% Natural MEXICAN $$

(Cien Por Ciento Natural; Map p62; ☎998-884-01-02; www.100natural.com.mx; Av Sunyaxchén 62; mains M$60-188; ⏲7am-11pm; ⊜ⓦ🖉) Vegetarians and health-food nuts delight at this health-food chain near Avenida Yaxchilán, which serves juice blends, a wide selection of yogurt-fruit-vegetable combinations, brown rice, pasta, fish and chicken dishes. The on-site bakery turns out whole-wheat products, and the entire place is very nicely decorated and landscaped.

El Tigre y El Toro ITALIAN $$$

(Map p62; Av Náder 64; mains M$105-180; ⏲6pm-midnight; ⊜ⓦ🖉; 🚌R-1) Gourmet thin-crust pizza and homemade pastas are served in a pebbly candlelit garden at El Tigre y El Toro ('tiger' and 'bull' are the owners' nicknames). Many locals rank this as Cancún's *numero uno* pizza joint.

La Habichuela FUSION $$$

(Map p62; ☎998-884-31-58; www.lahabichuela.com; Margaritas 25; mains M$190-315, cocobichuela M$525; ⏲1pm-midnight; ⊜ⓦ; 🚌R-1) This elegant restaurant has a lovely courtyard dining area, just off Parque de las Palapas. The specialty is the *cocobichuela* (shrimp and lobster in curry sauce served inside a coconut with tropical fruit), but almost anything on the menu is delicious. The seafood ceviche and *tapas al ajillo* (assorted seafood accented with garlic) are mouthwatering.

La Habichuela Sunset (Map p58; ☎998-840-62-80; Blvd Kukulcán Km 12.6; mains M$250-400; ⏲noon-midnight; ⓦ; 🚌R-1), the restaurant's slightly pricier Zona Hotelera branch, affords a gorgeous lagoon view.

Rolandi's Restaurant & Pizzeria ITALIAN $$$

(Map p62; ☎998-884-40-47; www.rolandirestaurants.com; Av Cobá 10; mains M$131-226; ⏲12:30pm-midnight; ⊜🖉; 🚌R-1) A longtime Cancún favorite, Italian eatery Rolandi's serves wood-fired pizzas, calzones, homemade pasta plates, and a range of meat and seafood dishes.

Irori JAPANESE $$$

(Map p62; ☎998-892-30-72; www.iroricancun.com.mx; Av Tulum 226; mains M$85-220; ⏲1-11pm Mon-Sat, to 10pm Sun; ⊜ⓦ👪; 🚌R-27) Enjoy the show as the chef slices and dices the night away at this Japanese-run restaurant serving sushi and many other Japanese favorites in an intimate setting. There's even a kids menu and playroom if you've got little sushi-scoffers in tow. You'll find the entrance on Calle Viento.

Zona Hotelera

'Pay-per-view' takes on a whole different meaning in the Zona Hotelera. Prices sometimes reflect the location of the restaurant and what's outside the window more than the quality of food. That being said, there are a fair number of excellent seafood restaurants along the strip too.

For budget eats in the Zona Hotelera, you can always hit the food courts at any large mall. La Isla Shopping Village (p67), **Plaza Flamingo** (Map p58) and the **Forum Mall** (Map p58) have other options to get a bite.

Surfin' Burrito MEXICAN $$

(Map p58; www.facebook.com/thesurfinburrito; Blvd Kukulcán Km 9.5; burritos M$62-119; ⏲24hr; ⊜; 🚌R-1) Always a crowd-pleaser on the strip, where cheap eats come few and far

CANCÚN FOR CHILDREN

With such easy access to sand, sea and swimming pools, most kids will have a blast in Cancún. Some hotels offer babysitting or day-care services – be sure to check in advance if these are needed. Remember that the sun, strong enough to scald even the thickest of tourist hides, can be even more damaging for kids and babies.

If you want a change of scenery, check out the numerous theme parks south of town. For a bit more culture, head over to the Maya ruins at Tulum (p113), which has a great beach, or to the Cobá archaeological site (p121), where you can pedal around on a bike.

When all else fails, you can never go wrong with a day at the zoo or a nighttime swashbuckling outing.

Captain Hook (Map p58; ☎998 849 40 31; www.capitanhook.com; Blvd Kukulcán Km 5, Marina Capitán Hook; adult US$77-114, child under 13 free; ⊙tour 7-10:30pm) There's nothing like a swashbuckling adventure with sword fights and cannon battles to get kids' imaginations running wild. The 3½-hour tour aboard a Spanish galleon replica includes dinner service, and it costs a pretty doubloon if you opt for the steak and lobster option, but children under 13 are free if they eat from the complimentary kids buffet.

Boats depart from Marina Capitán Hook.

Crococun Zoo (☎998-850 37 19; www.crococunzoo.com; Hwy 307 Km 31, 3km north of Puerto Morelos; adult/child 6-12yr US$30/20; ⊙9am-5pm) About 23km south of the Cancún airport, this former crocodile farm now calls itself a conservationist zoo that protects some of the area's endangered species. The price of admission includes a guided tour in which visitors are allowed to interact with some of the animals, such as white-tailed deer, boa constrictors, macaws, crocs and wild spider monkeys.

All Ritmo (www.allritmocancun.com/en/waterpark; Puerto Juárez-Punta Sam Hwy Km 1.5; adult M$295-310, child 5-12yr M$247-260; ⊙10am-7pm Wed-Mon) Little ones can splish and splash to their heart's content at this water park, which also has mini-golf and shuffleboard. The turnoff is 2km north of the Ultramar ferry terminal. 'Punta Sam' *colectivos* on Avenida Tulum (opposite the bus terminal) will drop you at the turnoff, and it's a short walk from there.

between, this small joint prepares beef, shrimp, fish and vegetarian burritos with your choice of tasty fixings. It's open 24/7 and makes jumbo margaritas, making it a popular late-night haunt.

Restaurante Natura VEGETARIAN $$
(Map p58; Blvd Kukulcán Km 9.8; breakfast M$69-85, lunch & dinner M$95-189; ⊙7:30am-10:30pm; ; R-1) This little bistro offers up a good mix of natural and vegetarian Mexican cuisine – think giant natural juices, and quesadillas with Chihuahua cheese, spinach, mushrooms and whole-wheat tortillas. There's also a vegan menu.

El Fish Fritanga SEAFOOD $$
(Map p58; www.elfishfritanga.com; Blvd Kukulcán Km 12.6; mains M$132-265, tacos M$23-28; ⊙11am-11pm; ; R-1) With plastic tables set under little *palapa* huts (shelter with a thatched, palm-leaf roof and open sides) on a sandy floor, this is one of the Zona Hotelera's back-to-basics places. Good-value seafood, killer one-liter mojitos and a great place for sunset drinks overlooking the lagoon. If you need to go even further back to basics, they run a cut-price taco stand out front.

Mocambo SEAFOOD $$$
(Map p58; ☎998-883-03-98; www.mocambocancun.mx; Blvd Kukulcán Km 9.5; mains M$150-355; ⊙noon-11pm; ; R-1) Definitely one of the best spots in the Zona Hotelera, the *palapa*-covered Mocambo sits right on the ocean and serves up excellent seafood dishes such as grouper and a savory seafood paella. There's live music Tuesday through Sunday nights.

Lorenzillo's SEAFOOD $$$
(Map p58; ☎998-883-12-54; www.lorenzillos.com.mx; Blvd Kukulcán Km 10.5; mains M$325-670, lobster M$700; ⊙1pm-12:30am; ; R-1) Reputed by locals to be Cancún's best seafood restaurant, Lorenzillo's gives you 20 separate choices for your lobster presentation, including a taste bud-popping *chipotle*,

plum and tamarind sauce. Facing the lagoon, it's a wonderful sunset joint.

Thai Lounge THAI $$$

(Map p58; ☎988-176-80-70; www.thai.com.mx; La Isla Shopping Village, Blvd Kukulcán Km 12.5; M$265-510; ⏲6pm-11:30pm; ⊜; 🚌R-1) Tucked away in the rear of La Isla Shopping Village, this place serves Thai food under your own private, stilted *palapa,* either with a garden or lagoon view. The Pla de Phuket, a crunchy fish fillet in tamarind chili sauce, is especially good.

Crab House SEAFOOD $$$

(Map p58; ☎998-193-03-50; www.crabhousecancun.com; Blvd Kukulcán Km 14.7; dishes M$250-480; ⏲noon-11:30pm; ⊜📶; 🚌R-1) Offering a lovely view of the lagoon that complements the seafood, the long menu here includes many shrimp and fish-fillet dishes. Crab and lobster are priced by the pound.

Drinking & Nightlife

Ciudad Cancún

Ciudad Cancún's clubs and bars are generally mellower than those in the rowdy Zona Hotelera. Stroll along Avenida Yaxchilán down to Parque de las Palapas and you are sure to run into something (or somebody) you like.

Built into the **Plaza de Toros** (Bullring; Map p62; cnr Avs Bonampak & Sayil) are several bars, some with music, that draw a largely local crowd.

★**Grand Mambo Café** CLUB

(Map p62; ☎998-884-45-36; www.mambocafe.com.mx; Plaza Hong Kong, cnr Avs Xcaret & Tankah; ⏲10:30pm-5am Wed-Sat; 🚌R-2) The large floor at this happening club is the perfect place to practice those Latin dance steps you've been working on. Live groups play Cuban salsa and other tropical styles.

Marakame Café BAR

(Map p58; ☎998-887-10-10; www.marakamecafe.com; Av Circuito Copán 19, near Av Nichupté; ⏲8am-1am Mon-Wed, 8am-2am Thu & Fri, 9am-2am Sat, 9am-midnight Sun; 📶) An excellent open-air breakfast and lunch spot by day, and a popular bar with live music by night. The bartenders, or mixologists if you will, prepare interesting concoctions such as kiwi-flavored mojitos and margaritas blended with *chaya* (tree spinach), cucumber and lime. It's a short taxi ride from downtown.

La Taberna SPORTS BAR

(Map p62; www.lataberna.com.mx; Av Yaxchilán 23; ⏲1pm-5am; 📶) A popular kid-friendly bar and grill with pool tables, and a sports book in the back for you die-hard gamblers.

11:11 GAY

(Once Once; Map p62; cnr Av Tulum & Claveles; ⏲10:30pm-6am Thu-Sat; 🚌R-1) The main room in this large house stages drag shows, go-go dancers and the like, while DJs in smaller rooms spin electronica and pop tunes till the sun comes up.

Zona Hotelera

The club scene in the Zona Hotelera is young, loud and booze-oriented – the kind that often has an MC urging women to display body parts to hooting and hollering crowds. The big dance clubs charge around M$1100 to M$1300 admission, which includes open-bar privileges (ie drink all you want). Most don't get hopping much before midnight.

A number of clubs are clustered along the northwest-bound side of Blvd Kukulcán, all within easy stumbling distance of each other. Be careful crossing the street.

Rose Bar BAR

(Map p58; Me by Melia, Blvd Kukulcán Km 12; ⏲4pm-midnight Sun-Fri, to 3am Sat; 📶; 🚌R-1) In hipster hotel Me by Melia, Rose Bar has a more sophisticated, chilled-out vibe than some of the raucous clubs in the party zone. DJs spin tunes on the bar's open-air deck on Saturday and on Thursday at 9pm there's a short burlesque show.

Coco Bongo CLUB

(Map p58; ☎998-883-50-61; www.cocobongo.com.mx; Forum Mall, Blvd Kukulcán Km 9.5; ⏲10pm-5am; 🚌R-1) This is the spot where spring-breakers go wild, and it tends to be happening just about any day of the year. Dancing is interspersed with live acts featuring celebrity impersonators and acrobats throughout the night.

Dady'O CLUB

(Map p58; ☎998-883-33-33; www.dadyo.com; Blvd Kukulcán Km 9.5; ⏲10:30pm-4am; 🚌R-1) One of Cancún's classic dance clubs. The setting is a five-level, black-walled faux cave with a two-level dance floor and what seems like zillions of laser beams and strobes. The predominant beats are Latin, house, techno and pop, and the crowd is mainly 20-something.

Entertainment

Cinemex CINEMA
(Map p58; toll-free 800-710-88-88; www.cinemex.com; Blvd Kukulcán Km 12.5, in La Isla Shopping Village; R-1) Screens mostly Hollywood movies. Some are shown in English with Spanish subtitles, others are dubbed in Spanish.

Teatro Xbalamqué THEATER
(Map p62; 998-204-10-28; www.teatroxbalamque.com; Av Yaxchilán 31, cnr Jazmines) Stages musicals, comedies and monologues.

Shopping

Shopaholics will enjoy the city's colorful markets, which offer jewelry, handicrafts and souvenirs, as well as a variety of inexpensive Mexican food. Locals head to either **Mercado 28** (Mercado Veintiocho; Map p58; cnr Avs Xel-Há & Sunyaxchén; 6am-7pm) or **Mercado 23** (Map p62; Av Tulum s/n; 6am-7pm; R-1) for clothes, shoes, inexpensive food stalls and so on. Of the two, Mercado 23 is the least frequented by tourists. If you're looking for a place without corny T-shirts, this is the place to go.

There's definitely no shortage of modern malls in Cancún.

La Europea DRINK
(Map p58; www.laeuropea.com.mx; Blvd Kukulcán Km 12.5; 10am-9pm Mon-Sat, 11am-7pm Sun; R-1) A gourmet liquor store with reasonable prices, knowledgeable staff and the best booze selection in town, including top-shelf tequilas and mezcals. Most airlines allow you to travel with up to 3L of alcohol, but check first. Salud!

La Isla Shopping Village MALL
(Map p58; www.laislacancun.com.mx; Blvd Kukulcán, Km 12.5; ; R-1) Unique among the island's malls, this is an indoor-outdoor place with canals, an aquarium, a movie theater and enough distractions to keep even the most inveterate hater of shopping amused. Consider picking up a bottle of *xtabentún*, a Yucatecan anise-flavored liqueur.

Plaza Kukulcán MALL
(Map p58; www.kukulcanplaza.mx; Blvd Kukulcán Km 13; 10am-10pm; ; R-1) The largest of the indoor malls is Plaza Kukulcán. Of note here are the temporary art exhibits, the many stores selling silverwork and La Ruta de las Indias, a shop featuring wooden models of Spanish galleons and replicas of conquistadors' weaponry and body armor.

Mercado Municipal Ki-Huic MARKET
(Map p62; Av Tulum s/n; 9am-9pm; R-1) This warren of stalls and shops carries a wide variety of souvenirs and handicrafts.

Colormax ACCESSORIES
(Map p62; Av Tulum 22; 9am-8pm Mon-Fri, 10am-5pm Sat; R-1) Sells GoPro and disposable waterproof cameras and memory cards.

Orientation

Cancún consists of two very distinct areas: Ciudad Cancún (downtown) and Isla Cancún (the Zona Hotelera).

The Zona Hotelera is what most people think of when they say 'Cancún': the sandy spit that encloses a scenic lagoon on one side and has the Caribbean's azure-greens on the other. Its main road, Blvd Kukulcán, is a four-lane, divided avenue that leaves Ciudad Cancún and heads eastward for 9km, passing condominium developments, hotels and shopping complexes, to Punta Cancún (Cancún Point) and the **Centro de Convenciones** (Convention Center; Map p58).

From Punta Cancún, the boulevard heads south for about 15km to Punta Nizuc, flanked on both sides for much of the way by huge hotels, shopping centers, dance clubs and many restaurants and bars. Here it turns westward and then rejoins the mainland, cutting through light tropical forest for several more kilometers to its southern terminus at Cancún's international airport.

Addresses in the Zona Hotelera are refreshingly simple: instead of a street name (usually Blvd Kukulcán anyway) a kilometer distance from the 'Km 0' roadside marker at the boulevard's northern terminus in Ciudad Cancún is given. Each kilometer is similarly marked. Most bus drivers will know the location you're heading but, if in doubt, you can just ask to be dropped off at the appropriate kilometer marker.

Information

DANGERS & ANNOYANCES

The biggest safety danger in Cancún isn't street crime – it's the streets themselves. Vehicles speed by along narrow roads and pedestrians (often drunk) sometimes get injured. A night spent clubbing is more likely to lead to a poked eye or twisted ankle than a mugging; however, if anyone *does* demand money, don't argue with them. Most violent incidents have involved fights where tourists or locals have actively put themselves in danger.

DAY-TRIPPER: FIVE GREAT EXCURSIONS FROM CANCÚN

What are you waiting for? There's a whole world beyond Cancún.

And here's a quick sustainable travel tip: skip the group tour and use that extra dough to hire a local guide and buy some crafts. Staying the night in your destination will bring even more money into the local community.

Chichén Itzá (p183) Rent a car so you can take the old highway through Valladolid. Stop in the small Maya communities along the way for out-of-sight *panuchos* (small corn tortillas stuffed with mashed beans and topped with shredded turkey or chicken).

Isla Mujeres (p75) Take the ferry from Puerto Juárez. Check out the turtle farm in the morning, then swing up north for a swim in the stunningly beautiful turquoise waters of Playa Norte.

Tulum (p113) Get up early and rent a car to make your way down to Tulum. Along the way, you'll want to stop at Akumal's Laguna Yal-Kú for a dip. On the way back, stop at one of the numerous cenotes clearly marked from the highway.

Puerto Morelos (p99) Just a half-hour ride heading south of Cancún, you'll find this quiet beach town with a small plaza, an excellent crafts market and surprisingly good restaurants. Playa Express buses depart frequently from in front of the bus terminal.

Isla Blanca See what Cancún used to look like before the development boom! A dirt road north of Punta Sam leads to Isla Blanca, where you'll find a gorgeous stretch of secluded white-sand beach. About 10km from Punta Sam you'll reach the beach club and cabins of **Cabañas Playa Blanca** (cell 998-2139131; Isla Blanca; beach club admission M$30, cabins M$500-1000; P), which has a sublime coast overlooking Isla Mujeres.

Theft of valuables left unattended is a possibility, but no more so than in other parts of the world. Use prudence, keeping vital items with you or leaving them in a hotel safe, and you'll avoid problems. Napping sunbathers may wake up to find cameras, phones or wallets gone; don't leave anything unattended on the beach.

Hawkers can be quite irritating but are not dangerous. The best way to avoid them is to just keep walking. As frustrating as this may be, remember that these vendors are just trying to make a living.

EMERGENCY

Cruz Roja (Red Cross; 065)

Fire (998-884-12-02)

Police (066; Blvd Kukulcán Km 12.5; R-1)

Tourist Police (998-885-22-77)

IMMIGRATION

To replace lost immigration forms, go to the **Instituto Nacional de Migración** (Immigration Office; 998-881-35-60; cnr Av Náder 1 & Av Uxmal; 9am-1pm Mon-Fri).

MEDICAL SERVICES

Hospital Playa Med (998-140-52-58; Av Náder 13, cnr Av Uxmal; 24hr; R-1) is a modern facility with 24-hour assistance.

MONEY

There are several banks with ATMs throughout the Zona Hotelera and downtown on Avenida Tulum (between Avenidas Cobá and Uxmal). Cancún's airport also has ATMs and money exchange.

American Express (Av Tulum 208, cnr Agua)

Banamex ATM (Blvd Kukulcán Km 8.5; 24hr)

BBVA Bancomer (Av Tulum 150) Next to Mercado Municipal Ki-Huic.

Scotiabank (La Isla Shopping Village, Zona Hotelera; 24hr)

POST

There is no post office in the Zona Hotelera, but most hotels' reception desks sell stamps and will mail letters.

The **Main Post Office** (Map p58; cnr Avs Xel-Há & Sunyaxchén; 8am-4pm Mon-Fri, 9am-12:30pm Sat) is downtown at the edge of Mercado 28. You can also post mail in the red postal boxes sprinkled around town.

TOURIST INFORMATION

Cancún Visitors Bureau (www.cancun.travel) An informative website, but no tourist office.

City Tourism Office (Map p62; 998-887-33-79; cnr Avs Cobá & Náder; 9am-4pm Mon-Fri) City tourist office with ample supplies of printed material and knowledgeable staff.

Getting There & Away

AIR

Aeropuerto Internacional de Cancún (998-848-72-00; www.asur.com.mx; Hwy 307 Km 22) is the busiest airport in southeast Mexico. It has all the services you would expect from a major international airport: ATMs, money exchange, car-rental agencies. It's served by many direct international flights and by connecting flights from Mexico City. Low-cost Mexican carriers VivaAerobus, Interjet and Volaris have service from Mexico City.

There are direct flights to Cancún from Guatemala City and Flores (Guatemala), Havana (Cuba), Panama City and São Paulo (Brazil). The Havana–Cancún flights continue to Mérida. At the time of writing, it was still illegal for US nationals to visit Cuba for tourism purposes – but many do, traveling via Cancún. Those who do, get a Cuba entry stamp on a piece of paper (and not in their passport), to avoid getting fined.

The following carriers run flights to Cancún. For a more complete list, see the airport website.

Aeroméxico (998-193-18-68; www.aeromexico.com; Av Cobá 80; R-1) Direct flights from Mexico City and New York. Office just west of Avenida Bonampak.

Interjet (998-892-02-78; www.interjet.com; Av Xcaret 35, Plaza Hollywood) Flies direct to Miami and Havana.

Magnicharters (998-884-06-00, toll-free 800-201-14-04; www.magnicharters.com.mx; Av Náder 93, cnr Av Cobá; R-1) To Mexico City.

VivaAerobus (81-8215-0150; www.vivaaerobus.com; Cancún airport, Hwy 307 Km 22) Non-stop to Houston.

Volaris (55-1102-8000; www.volaris.com; Cancún airport, Hwy 307 Km 22) Service to Mexico City.

BOAT

There are several points of embarkation to reach Isla Mujeres from Cancún by boat. From Puerto Juárez (Map p58) it costs M$80; leaving from the Zona Hotelera it runs about M$235. If you want to transport a vehicle you'll need to head to Punta Sam, 8km north of Ciudad Cancún.

For Isla Holbox, ferries leave from Chiquilá, and for Isla Contoy boats depart from the Marina Scuba Cancún (Map p58). For more on hours and departure points to Isla Mujeres, see www.granpuerto.com.mx.

BUS

Cancún's modern **bus terminal** (Map p62; cnr Avs Uxmal & Tulum) occupies the wedge formed where Avenidas Uxmal and Tulum meet. It's a safe area and you'll be fine walking around. Across Pino from the bus terminal, a few doors from Avenida Tulum, is the ticket office and miniterminal of **Playa Express** (Map p62; Calle Pino), which runs air-conditioned buses down the coast to Playa del Carmen every 10 minutes until early evening, stopping at major towns and points of interest. **ADO** (800-009-90-90; www.ado.com.mx) covers the same ground and beyond with its 1st-class service.

BUSES FROM CANCÚN

DESTINATION	COST (M$)	DURATION (HRS)	FREQUENCY (DAILY)
Chetumal	235-456	5½-6	frequent
Chichén Itzá	135-258	3-4	14
Chiquilá	114	3-3½	3 (Mayab)
Felipe Carrillo Puerto	186-248	3½-4	3
Mérida	198-578	4-4½	frequent
Mexico City	1928	27	1 to Terminal Norte; 6:30pm
Mexico City (TAPO)	1904-2160	24½-28	4
Palenque	876-1040	13-13½	3
Playa del Carmen	34-60	1-1½	frequent ADO & Playa Express
Puerto Morelos	22-24	½-¾	frequent ADO & Playa Express
Ticul	220-296	8½	frequent
Tizimín	130-280	3	3
Tulum	92-130	2½	frequent
Valladolid	150-158	2-2¼	8
Villahermosa	550-1480	12¾-14½	frequent

ADO sets the 1st-class standard, while **ADO Platino** (☎ toll-free 800-737-58-56; www.adoplatino.com.mx), **ADO GL** (☎ toll-free 800-900-01-05; www.adogl.com.mx) and **OCC** (☎ 800-900-0105; www.occbus.com.mx) provide luxury services. Mayab provides good 'intermediate class' (tending to make more stops than 1st class) to many points, while Oriente's 2nd-class air-con buses often depart and arrive late.

CAR

You're better off leaving the rental car parked inside Cancún and walking or catching a bus to most places till you're ready to get out of town. Be warned that Hwy 180D, the *cuota* (toll road) running much of the way between Cancún and Mérida, costs M$414. An economy size rental car with liability insurance runs about M$500 per day.

National (☎ 998-881-87-60; www.nationalcar.com; Cancún airport)

Hertz (☎ 800-709-50-00; www.hertz.com; Cancún airport)

Getting Around

If you're staying in Ciudad Cancún, the Zona Hotelera is just a 15-minute ride away. The main north–south thoroughfare, Avenida Tulum, is the easiest street to catch city buses and taxis.

TO/FROM THE AIRPORT

Frequent ADO buses go to Ciudad Cancún (M$64) between 7:40am and 12:30am. They depart from outside the terminals. Once in town, the buses travel up Avenida Tulum to the bus terminal on the corner of Avenida Uxmal. Going to the airport from Ciudad Cancún, the same ADO airport buses (Aeropuerto Centro) leave regularly from the bus station. ADO also offers bus services out of the airport to Playa del Carmen and Mérida.

Airport shuttle vans Green Line and Super Shuttle run to and from Ciudad Cancún and the Zona Hotelera for about M$160 per person.

Regular taxis into town or to the Zona Hotelera cost up to M$500 (up to four people).

Expect to pay about M$200 for a city cab when returning to the airport.

BUS

To reach the Zona Hotelera from Ciudad Cancún, catch any bus with 'R-1' 'Hoteles' or 'Zona Hotelera' displayed on the windshield as it travels along Avenida Tulum toward Avenida Cobá then eastward on Avenida Cobá. South of Avenida Cobá, along Avenida Tulum, you can also catch the 'R-27' to the Zona Hotelera.

To reach Puerto Juárez and the Isla Mujeres ferries, you can either take a northbound 'Punta Sam' or 'Puerto Juárez' **colectivo** (Map p62) from a bus stop on Avenida Tulum (across from the ADO terminal), or you can wait on Avenida Tulum for an R-1 'Puerto Juárez' bus.

TAXI

Cancún's taxis do not have meters. Fares are set, but you should always agree on a price before getting in; otherwise you could end up paying for a 'misunderstanding.' From Ciudad Cancún to Punta Cancún it's usually M$100 to M$130, to Puerto Juárez M$50 to M$70. Trips within the Zona Hotelera or downtown zones cost around M$30 to M$50. Hourly and daily rates should run about M$240 and M$2000, respectively.

NORTH OF CANCÚN

Isla Contoy

Spectacular **Parque Nacional Isla Contoy** (☎ 998-234-99-05; contoy@conanp.gob.mx) is a bird-lover's delight: an uninhabited national park and sanctuary that is an easy day trip from Cancún and from Isla Mujeres. About 800m at its widest point and more than 8.5km long, it has dense foliage that provides ideal shelter for more than 170 bird species, including brown pelicans, olive cormorants, turkey birds, brown boobies and frigates, and is also being a good place to see red flamingos, snowy egrets and white herons.

Whale sharks are often sighted north of Contoy between June and September. In an effort to preserve the park's pristine natural areas, only 200 visitors are allowed access each day. Bring binoculars, mosquito repellent and sunblock.

Tours

Guided tours to Isla Contoy give you several hours of free time to explore the island's interpretive trails, climb a 27m-high observation tower and get in a little snorkeling.

For more information on the island, **Amigos de Isla Contoy** (Map p58; ☎ 998-884-74-83; www.islacontoy.org; Plaza Bonita Mall) has a website with detailed information on the island's ecology.

Tours to Contoy are offered by The **fisherman's cooperative** (p77) on Isla Mujeres and **Asterix** (Map p58; ☎ 998-886-42-70; www.contoytours.com; Blvd Kukulcán Km 5.2; adult/child 5-12yr US$109/63; ⏲ tours 9am-5pm Tue, Thu

& Sat) in Cancún. The latter departs from Marina Scuba Cancún (Map p58) and includes guide, breakfast, lunch, open bar and snorkeling gear.

Isla Holbox

984 / POP 1500

Isn't life great when it's low-fi and low-rise? That's the attitude on friendly Isla Holbox (hol-bosh), with its sandy streets, colorful Caribbean buildings, and lazing, sun-drunk dogs. Holbox is a welcome refuge for anyone looking to just get away from it all ('all' likely meaning the hubbub of Cancún).

The island is about 30km long and from 500m to 2km wide, with seemingly endless beaches, tranquil waters and a galaxy of shells in various shapes and colors. Lying within the Yum Balam reserve, Holbox is home to more than 150 bird species, including roseate spoonbills, pelicans, herons, ibis and flamingos. In summer, whale sharks congregate nearby.

Golf carts are big here, but walking to the town square from the dock takes less than 10 minutes and the beach is just a few blocks away from the square. Nobody uses street names, but just so you know, it's Avenida Tiburón Ballena that connects the town with the ferry dock.

The water is not the translucent turquoise common to Quintana Roo beach sites, because here the Caribbean mingles with the darker Gulf of Mexico. The island's darkwater lagoon on the south side inspired the Maya to name it Holbox or 'black hole.' During the rainy season there are clouds of mosquitoes: bring repellent and be prepared to stay inside for a couple of hours after dusk.

Beaches

Most people come here for the whale sharks and to lounge on the beach. But you can also head out to observe birds and other wildlife around the island.

Punta Coco BEACH
On the western edge of the island, about 2.5km from downtown, Punta Coco is a great sunset beach.

Punta Mosquito BEACH
On the eastern side of the island, Punta Mosquito is about 2.5km east of the downtown area. It has a large sandbar and is a good place to spot flamingos.

Activities

Abarrotes Addy BICYCLE RENTAL
(Av Damero; per hour/day M$20/150; 9am-9pm) To get around the island, consider renting a bike here. It's 1½ blocks east of the plaza.

Tours

★ **Turística Moguel** TOUR
(984-875-20-28, cell 984-1149921; www.holboxislandtours.com; cnr Avs Tiburón Ballena & Damero; per person M$1200) Operating out of the minimarket on the plaza, this is considered one of the best outfits running whale-shark tours. The expedition includes a stop at a beautiful spring (where you can go swimming) and a visit to Isla Pasión, an island that provides great bird-watching.

Willy's Tours BOAT TOUR
(cell 984-7430827; loveme_forever10@hotmail.com; Av Tiburón Ballena s/n, cnr Gerónimo de Aguilar; whale shark/birding/fishing & snorkeling tours M$1500/350/800) Willy's Tours, south of the plaza, offers whale shark, birding, fishing and snorkeling tours.

OFF THE MAP: ALTERNATIVE TOURISM ON THE RISE

Many Maya communities are beginning to welcome tourism – it may be the only way to maintain their language and culture as mass migration to boom towns such as Cancún draws away the best and brightest, and children ask to study English rather than Maya.

Ecoturismo Certificado (www.ecoturismocertificado.mx) supports ecotourism in numerous communities throughout Mexico, including two projects that can be found on the road to Chiquilá, in the towns of Solferino and San Ángel. Ecotourism center **El Corchal** (cell 998-1657105; pepecorcho05@gmail.com; tour M$500), in Solferino, has an orchid garden, jungle camping sites and kayak tours, while at San Ángel you can go kayaking, bicycling or learn about medicinal plants. **Alfonso Tuz** (984-1830111 cell), whose family owns a small grocery store west of the town square, is a good source of information in San Ángel.

GAME OF DOMINOES: SWIM WITH THE WHALE SHARKS

Between mid-May and late August, massive whale sharks congregate around Isla Holbox to feed on plankton. They are the largest fish in the world, weighing up to 15 tons and extending as long as 15m from gaping mouth to arching tail. Locals call them dominoes because of their speckled skin.

The best time to track these gentle giants is in July and August, but that also happens to be shoulder season, when you can get up to two dozen boats rotating around a single whale shark. It's unpleasant for both shark and swimmer, so think twice about taking a tour during this season. The alternative is going in June, but you risk not spotting any whale sharks.

The World Wildlife Fund has been working with the local community since 2003 to develop responsible practices for visiting the whale sharks, trying to balance the economic boon of these tours with the environmental imperatives of protecting a threatened species.

When swimming with the whale shark only three swimmers (including your guide) are allowed in the water at a time. You are not allowed to touch the fish, and are required to wear either a life jacket or wetsuit to ensure you do not dive below the shark.

Villas HM Paraíso del Mar TOUR
(☎984-875-20-62; www.hmhotels.net/destinos_holbox.php; Av Plutarco Elías s/n, Zona Hotelera; per person M$450) Beachfront hotel Villas HM Paraíso del Mar arranges a '*tres islas*' (three islands) tour, which goes to Isla Pájaros and Isla Pasión for bird-watching and to the Yalahau spring for swimming.

Explora Holbox KAYAKING
(☎cell 984-1387793; www.carlosveracruz71.wix.com/kayakholbox; Sierra s/n; tour per person M$550) Guide Carlos Brassel does beginner- to advanced-level kayak tours through the mangroves, providing excellent bird-watching opportunities.

Los Potrillos HORSEBACK RIDING
(☎cell 984-1299995; dorymar16@hotmail.com; tours M$600) Bilingual guides offer horseback-riding tours along a beach that leads to a remote lagoon. You'll find Los Potrillos on the beach about 500m west of Avenida Tiburón Ballena.

Sleeping

Not surprisingly, *cabañas* (cabins) and bungalows are everywhere along the beach. Some of the most upscale places can be found east of town, out along the island's northern shore in what locals call the Zona Hotelera. Budget and midrange hotels are clustered around the plaza.

Hostel Tribu HOSTEL $
(☎984-875-25-07; www.tribuhostel.com; Av Pedro Joaquín Coldwell; dm/r from M$170/550;) With so many activities available here (from salsa lessons to yoga and kayaking), it doesn't take long to settle in with the tribe. Six-bed dorms and private rooms are clean, colorful and cheerful. Tribu also has a book exchange and a bar that stages weekly jam sessions. From the plaza, it's one block north and two blocks west.

Hostel Ida y Vuelta HOSTEL $
(☎984-875-23-58; www.holboxhostel.com; Av Paseo Kuka; campsites & hammocks M$100, dm M$155, bungalow with/without bathroom M$460/390, house M$860;) A great spot for modern primitives, the basic dorm room sleeps eight, or you can stay in a bungalow with a private bathroom. There's also a very affordable house with a kitchen – an ideal setup for small groups. From the plaza, head two blocks north, then walk about six blocks east (the hostel is near Hotel Xaloc). Bring insect repellent.

Casa Lupita HOTEL $$
(☎984-875-20-17; casalupita@sihoteles.net; Calle Palomino; r/ste M$800/1500;) A great midrange option on the east side of the plaza, the spacious rooms catch good breezes and the suites have private balconies overlooking the action on the square.

Hotel Casa Barbara HOTEL $$
(☎984-875-23-02; reservas@hotelcasabarbara.mx; Av Tiburón Ballena s/n; r incl breakfast M$1092;) A very comfortable hotel with a swimming pool surrounded by a verdant garden. Rooms are decked out with rustic

furnishings and cushy beds, and most have porches overlooking the garden. It's halfway between the ferry dock and the beach.

Hotel Arena HOTEL $$

(☎984-875-21-69; www.hotelarenaholbox.com; Tiburón Ballena s/n; r from M$900;) A straight shoot from the ferry dock, all of the pleasant rooms here are furnished in minimalist style and some have balconies overlooking the plaza. There's not much of a lobby but who needs one when you have a rooftop bar and Jacuzzi upstairs?

Hotel Holmar HOTEL $$

(☎984-875 21-00; www.hotelholmar.com; Calle Carito s/n; r M$1000;) Design-wise rooms at the Holmar are nothing out of this world, unless you have a thing for towel animals, but the price is fair for what you get and it's only 50m from the beach and a block east of the square.

★Casa Takywara HOTEL $$$

(☎984-875-22-55; www.casatakywara.com; Paseo Carey s/n; r incl breakfast US$132-165;) Out on the quiet western end of town, this beautiful waterfront hotel stands out for its striking architecture and stylishly decorated rooms with kitchenettes and sea-view balconies. It's built next to a patch of protected wetland where you'll hear the song of chirping cicadas. Rates drop considerably during the low season. It's 1km west of Avenida Tiburón Ballena.

Posada Mawimbi HOTEL $$$

(☎984-875-20-03; www.mawimbi.net; Av Damero s/n; r from US$115, bungalow US$175, ste US$197 incl breakfast;) Mosquito nets are a welcome luxury in this pleasant two-story place just off the beach and about three blocks east of the plaza. On offer are standard rooms with comfortable beds, bungalows and oceanview suites. Conch lamps light the walkways after dark – a beautiful finishing touch.

Hotel La Palapa HOTEL $$$

(☎984-875-21-21; www.hotellapalapa.com; Morelos; r US$150;) La Palapa offers cozy beachfront rooms, some with balconies overlooking the sea, and a cloistered beach area complete with an outdoor bar that serves scrumptious Italian food. The ocean view from the rooftop terrace is simply awesome. It's 100m east of Avenida Tiburón Ballena along the beach.

Eating

Holbox has a surprising number of good restaurants for such a small island. Remember that some places close early, especially during the low season. For cheap Yucatecan eats, hit the market on the plaza's southwest end.

Taco Cueto MEXICAN $

(Av Pedro Joaquín Coldwell, btwn Av Tiburón Ballena & Esmedregal; tacos M$14-23, burritos M$79-115; 6pm-12:30am;) Tired of seafood? Head to this taco joint for good *arrachera* (flank steak) and *al pastor* (marinated pork) tacos and burritos. There's even a few vegetarian options for non-carnivores. It's northeast of the plaza.

Limoncito BREAKFAST $

(Av Damero s/n; breakfast M$60-80; 8:30am-9pm;) This colorful little *palapa*-covered restaurant on the square slings excellent Mexican breakfasts. The *motuleños* (eggs in tomato sauce served with fried plantain, ham and peas) is a local favorite, as are the enchiladas

Las Panchas MEXICAN $$

(Morelos s/n, btwn Avs Damero & Pedro Joaquín Coldwell; antojitos M$24-36, mains M$90-150; 7:30am-11:30am & 1-6pm;) Ask just about anyone in town where to go for good, cheap eats and they'll probably point to Las Panchas, where you can get delicious Yucatecan *antojitos* (snacks) such as *chaya* (tree spinach) tamales, *panuchos* and *salbutes* (fried tortillas with tasty toppings).

Edelyn Pizzería & Restaurant PIZZA $$

(Plaza Principal; pizzas M$100-190, pizzas with lobster topping M$300-450; noon-11:30pm;) We would be remiss if we didn't mention the self-proclaimed creators of Holbox's famous lobster pizza, but locals say you can find much better pies with the coveted lobster topping elsewhere in town (hint: one is right across the square).

Los Peleones FUSION $$$

(Av Tiburón Ballena s/n; mains M$140-250; 4-11pm;) Mexico meets Argentina at this small, wrestling-themed restaurant overlooking the town square. The homemade pasta is excellent – try the portobello raviolis in Gorgonzola sauce.

El Chapulím MEXICAN $$$

(Tiburón Ballena s/n; mains M$220-250; 7pm till the food runs out Mon-Sat;) 'No menu, always fresh' is the motto at this Mexican bistro. El Chapulím doesn't take reservations and the kitchen closes when the food runs out, usually around 10pm or so. Since fresh is the operative word here, chef Erik Winckelmann comes to your table usually offering some type of fish or seafood creation.

Viva Zapata SEAFOOD $$$
(Av Damero s/n, just off plaza's northwest end; mains M$100-270; ⏲11am-11:30pm;) You really shouldn't leave the island without trying the mixed seafood platter here (order for two or ask for a single portion if traveling solo). It's a wonderful feast usually consisting of grilled lobster tail, fish, crab and other fresh shell fish, or you can opt for the surf-and-turf option.

Drinking & Nightlife

Nightlife on Holbox is pretty tame but there's just enough action to keep you entertained.

Carioca's BAR, DISCO
(⏲bar noon-3am, disco midnight-6am Fri & Sat) Located beachside just northeast of 'downtown', this little *palapa* beach bar is a great chill-out spot. There's a disco here as well.

Raices Beach Club BAR
(⏲noon-9pm) This *palapa* bar on the beach has good ceviche, hammocks and occasionally live music. It's northeast of the square.

Entertainment

Tribu Bar LIVE MUSIC
(Av Coldwell s/n; ⏲7pm-2am Tue-Sun) Drop by the *palapa* bar at Hostel Tribu for live music, the occasional salsa class and weekly pub quizzes.

El Cine CINEMA
(Av Tiburón Ballena s/n, Plaza Pueblito; tickets M$27; ⏲8pm Sat & Sun) Screens mostly second-run Hollywood movies dubbed in Spanish and subtitled in English.

Information

Holbox has no banks. There's an ATM on the plaza above the police station, but it often runs out of money so bring lots of cash.

Emergency (☎066) Police, fire or medical assistance.

Getting There & Around

Ferries run to Holbox from the port town of Chiquilá, usually from 6am to 9pm (M$80 one-way). It takes about 25 minutes to reach the island. Smaller, faster and wetter *lanchas* (motorboats) make the crossing after dark for M$750.

Buses from the terminal in Cancún (M$86, 3½ hours) leave for Chiquilá at 7:50am, 10:10am and 12:50pm. Alternatively, you have the option of taking a taxi from Cancún for about US$100.

If you're driving, your vehicle will be safe in the Chiquilá parking lot for M$50 per 12 hours. You definitely won't need a car on the island.

Holbox's sand streets see few autos, but golf carts have become ubiquitous – still, consider using your walking shoes instead. Golf-cart taxis cost M$30 in town and M$80 out to Punta Coco.

See **Rentadora El Brother** (☎984-875-20-18; Av Tiburón Ballena s/n, north of plaza; cart per hr/day M$150/800; ⏲9am-5pm) if you want to rent a golf cart.

BUSES FROM CHIQUILÁ

DESTINATION	FARE (M$)	DURATION (HRS)	FREQUENCY (DAILY)
Cancún	114	3-3½	4
Mérida	205	6	1; 5:45am
Playa del Carmen	180	1½	1; 5pm Thursday to Sunday, daily in high season
Tulum	210	2	1; 5pm Thursday to Sunday, daily in high season
Tizimín	85	3	3

Isla Mujeres

☎998 / POP 16,000

Includes ➡

Best Places to Eat

- Olivia (p81)
- Mango Café (p81)
- Mininos (p81)
- Lola Valentina (p81)
- Pita Amore (p79)

Best Places to Stay

- Poc-Na Hostel (p78)
- Casa El Pío (p79)
- Hotel Villa Kiin (p79)
- Xbulu-Ha Hotel (p79)
- Hotel Kinich (p79)

Why Go?

Some people plan their vacation around Cancún and pencil in Isla Mujeres as a side trip. But Isla Mujeres is a destination in its own right, and it's generally quieter and more affordable than the options you get across the bay.

Sure, there are quite a few ticky tacky tourist shops, but folks still get around by golf cart and the crushed-coral beaches are even better than those of Cozumel and Holbox. As for the calm turquoise water of Isla Mujeres, well, you really just have to see it for yourself.

There's just enough here to keep you entertained: snorkel or scuba dive, visit a turtle farm or put on your sunglasses and settle in with that book you've been dying to finish. Come sunset, there are plenty of dining options, and the nightlife scene moves at a relaxed island pace.

When to Go

- For the experience of a lifetime, go from mid-June through August to snorkel with 15-ton whale sharks in nearby waters.
- It's quite a sight to watch sea turtles come ashore for nesting season around August and September, and if you want to get a closer look at the little fellas you can always drop by the island's turtle farm.
- Hotels tend to get booked up during the winter high season (December to April), so you're better off visiting in November, when you'll find vacancies and low-season discounts.

Isla Mujeres Highlights

1. Drop by the **Isla Mujeres Turtle Farm** (p78) and say hello to your new flippered friends.

2. Relax on the white sands of **Playa Norte** (p77) and have a swim in the shallow crystalline waters.

3. Rent a golf cart or scooter and feel the warm wind in your face as you explore **Punta Sur** (p77) and other parts of the island.

4. Head out on a boat from the **Fisherman's Cooperative** (p77) to go snorkeling with whale sharks.

5. Dive into the deep Caribbean blue and explore a sunken ship at **Ultrafreeze** (p77).

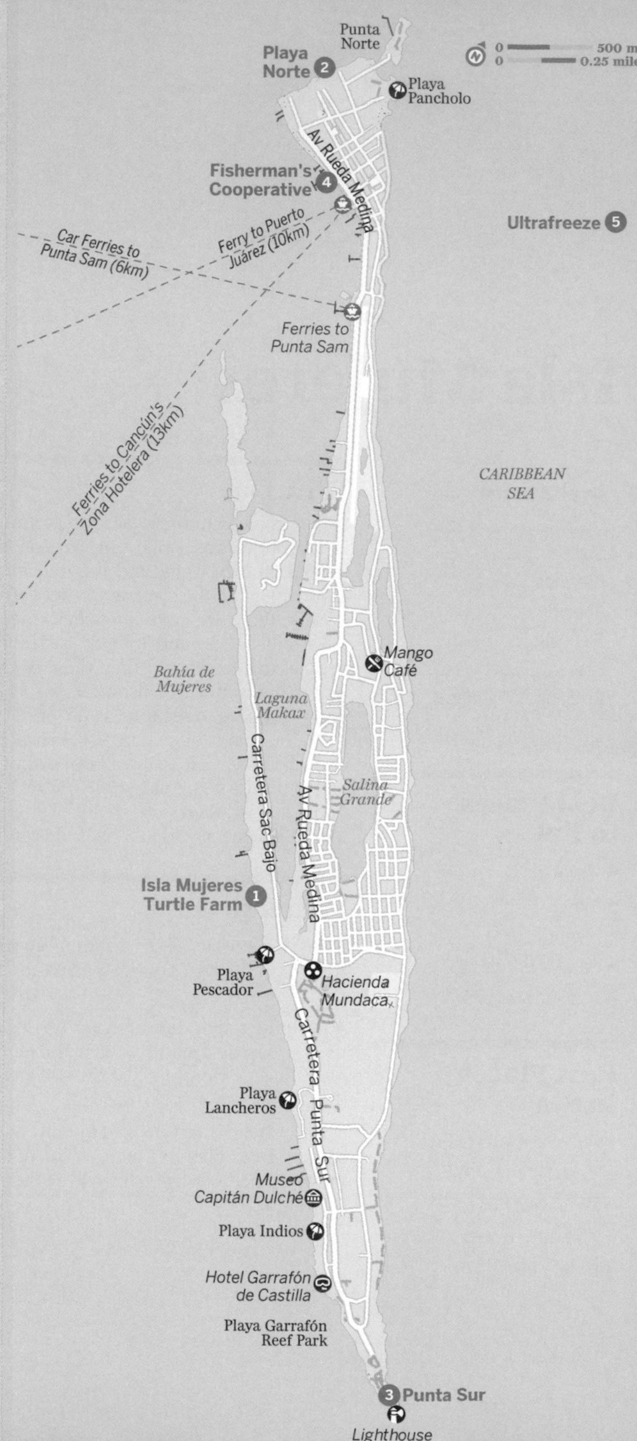

History

A glimpse of the sunbathers on the beach may have you thinking that the moniker 'Island of Women' comes from the bikini-clad tourists; however, the name Isla Mujeres goes at least as far back as Spanish buccaneers, who (legend has it) kept their lovers in safe seclusion here while they plundered galleons and pillaged ports on the mainland. An alternative theory suggests that in 1517, when Francisco Hernández de Córdoba sailed from Cuba and arrived here to procure slaves, the expedition discovered a stone temple containing clay figurines of Maya goddesses; it is thought that Córdoba named the island after the icons.

Today some archaeologists believe that the island was a stopover for the Maya en route to worship their goddess of fertility, Ixchel, on Isla Cozumel. The clay idols are thought to have represented the goddess. The island may also have figured in the extensive Maya salt trade, which extended for hundreds of kilometers along the coastline.

Sights

Museo Capitán Dulché MUSEUM, BEACH

(www.capitandulche.com; Carretera a Garrafón Km 4.5; M$65; 10:30am-6:30pm; P) And you thought Isla Mujeres had no culture. Here you get not only a maritime museum detailing the island's naval history but also one of the best beach clubs in town – and we're not just saying that because of the cool boat bar.

Punta Sur VIEWPOINT, GARDENS

(ruins M$30) At the island's southernmost point you'll find a lighthouse, a sculpture garden and the worn remains of a temple dedicated to Ixchel, Maya goddess of the moon and fertility. Various hurricanes have pummeled the ruins over time and there's now little to see other than the sculpture garden, the sea and Cancún in the distance. Taxis from town cost about M$105.

Beaches

Playa Norte BEACH

(Map p80) Once you reach Playa Norte, the island's main beach, you won't want to leave. Its warm, shallow waters are the color of blue raspberry syrup and the beach is crushed coral. Unlike most of the island's east coast, Playa Norte is safe for swimming and the water is only chest deep even far from shore.

Playa Garrafón BEACH

Head to this beach for excellent snorkeling. It's 6.5km from the tourist center. A cab costs M$100.

Playa Secreto BEACH

(Map p80;) The lagoon separating a large hotel complex from the rest of the island has a shallow swimming spot that's ideal for kids.

Playa Lancheros BEACH

About 5km south of town and the southernmost point served by local buses, this beach is less attractive than Playa Norte, but it sometimes has free music festivities at night. A taxi ride from town costs about M$75.

Activities

Within a short boat ride of the island there's a handful of lovely dives, such as **La Bandera**, **Arrecife Manchones** and **Ultrafreeze** (El Frío), where you'll see the intact hull of a 60m-long cargo ship, thought to have been deliberately sunk in 30m of water. Expect to see sea turtles, rays and barracuda, along with a wide array of hard and soft corals.

There's good shore-snorkeling near **Playa Garrafón** and at **Yunque Reef**. As always, watch for boat traffic when you head out snorkeling.

Snorkeling with whale sharks (around M$2000) is the latest craze on the island. The peak season runs from mid-June through August. It can get downright crazy, with up to a dozen boats circling one whale shark, but they limit the number of swimmers in the water to three people (including one guide). Most dive shops offer whale-shark excursions.

The fisherman's cooperative offers deep-sea fishing trips to catch marlin, sailfish and dorado, including bait, tackle and drinks, or you can opt for a half-day outing around the bay to hook barracuda and snapper. You'll find the cooperative next to the ferry docks. Ask for Captain Blacky.

Sea Hawk Divers DIVING

(Map p80; 998-877-02-96; www.seahawkislamujeres.com; Carlos Lazo s/n; 1-/2 tank dives incl equipment US$70/85, resort course US$95, whale-shark tour US$125) Offers reef dives, resort courses, fishing trips and whale-shark snorkeling tours. Rents rooms, too.

Fisherman's Cooperative TOUR

(Map p80; cell 998-1534883; cnr Av Rueda Medina & Madero; snorkeling incl lunch M$350, Isla

DREAM GREEN AT ISLA MUJERES TURTLE FARM

Although they're endangered, sea turtles are still killed throughout Latin America for their eggs and meat. In the 1980s, efforts by a local fisherman led to the founding of **Isla Mujeres Turtle Farm** (Isla Mujeres Tortugranja; ☎998-888-07-05; Carretera Sac Bajo Km 5; M$30; ⌚9am-5pm; 👪), a *tortugranja* (turtle farm) 5km south of town, which safeguards breeding grounds and protects eggs.

If you're coming from the bus stop, bear right at the 'Y' just beyond Hacienda Mundaca's parking lot (the turn is marked by a tiny sign). The farm is easily reached from town by taxi (M$60).

Hatchlings are liberated immediately. The turtles that leave this secure beach return each year, which means their offspring receive the same protection. The sanctuary releases about 125,000 turtles each year, but only one of every 1000 will survive.

The farm provides refuge for loggerhead, hawksbill and green turtles ranging in weight from 150g to more than 300kg. It also has a small but interesting aquarium, displays on marine life and a pen that holds large nurse sharks. Tours are conducted in Spanish and English. If you'd like to see the turtles get released, you can ask the staff if they plan on doing so that day. The farm usually releases turtles around 7pm from July through November. It's quite a sight to see the tiny creatures scurry into the great big sea.

Contoy tours M$1000, whale-shark tour M$1400; ⌚office 8am-8pm) The local fisherman's cooperative offers snorkeling tours to various sites, including Isla Contoy and the reef off Playa Garrafón, and it does whale-shark outings as well.

Aqua Adventures Eco Divers DIVING
(Map p80; ☎998-236-43-16; www.diveislamujeres.com; Juárez 1, cnr Morelos; 2-tank dives incl equipment US$90, whale-shark tour US$125; ⌚8:30am-7pm Mon-Sat, 10am-6pm Sun) Great option for snorkeling with whale sharks and goes to 15 sites for reef dives.

Mundaca Divers DIVING
(Map p80; ☎cell 998-1212228; www.mundacadiversisla.com; Madero s/n; 2-tank dives US$80-95, snorkeling US$47, fishing US$450) Does everything from shark-cave dives and fishing expeditions to snorkeling trips to a one-of-a-kind underwater sculpture museum known as MUSA.

Hotel Garrafón de Castilla SNORKELING
(☎998-877-01-07; Carretera Punta Sur Km 6; admission M$50, snorkel-gear rental M$80; ⌚10am-6pm) Avoid the overpriced Playa Garrafón Reef Park and visit instead Hotel Garrafón de Castilla's beach club for a day of snorkeling.

Felipez Water Sports Center WATER SPORTS
(Map p80; ☎cell 998-5933403; nachankan@aol.com; Playa Norte, off Av Hidalgo; kayak/paddle boat/sailboat per hour M$250/350/400, fishing M$6000) Hit the water in a sailboat, kayak or paddle boat. Felipez also does fishing expeditions.

Sleeping

Many hotels on the island are booked solid during high season, which runs roughly from mid-December through April.

★**Poc-Na Hostel** HOSTEL $
(Map p80; ☎998-877-00-90; www.pocna.com; Matamoros 15; dm with fan/air-con M$155/195, d with/without bathroom M$430/370, incl breakfast, camping per person M$110; 🚭❄📶) You can't beat this hostel's common areas. For starters, it's right on a lovely palm-shaded beach, home to one of the town's most happening beach bars at night – and you can also pitch a tent if you bring your own. Guests can chill in a cool *palapa* lobby bar, where breakfast is served and local bands play nightly.

If at some point you get bored with all the lazing around, Poc-Na keeps things interesting by offering activities ranging from salsa and Spanish classes to snorkeling tours and bike rental.

Apartments Trinchan APARTMENT $
(Map p80; ☎998-877-08-56, cell 998-1666967; atrinchan@prodigy.net.mx; Carlos Lazo 46; r with fan/air-con M$400/450, apt with fan/air-con M$450/500; 🚭❄📶) Since it has no website, you'll have to take our word for it when we say this is one of the best budget deals in town – and the beach is right around the corner. If it's available, opt for one of the large apartments with full kitchen.

Xbulu-Ha Hotel HOTEL $$
(Map p80; ☎998-877-17-83; www.islamujeres.biz; Guerrero 4; d/tr/ste from M$700/820/980;) Quite a bargain, especially if you're traveling with a small group or family. Some of the standard and deluxe rooms here can accommodate three to four people, as can the larger suites, which come with kitchenette.

Hotel Kinich BOUTIQUE HOTEL $$
(Map p80; ☎998-888-09 09; www.islamujeres kinich.com; Juárez 20; r/ste incl breakfast M$1200/1800;) Boutique Hotel Kinich gives you plenty of bang for your buck in low season, when rates drop by about 40%, and even in high season the huge rooms with balconies are still a pretty good deal, especially the family-friendly suites.

Hotel Belmar HOTEL $$
(Map p80; ☎998-877-04-30; www.hotelbelmar isla.com; Av Hidalgo 110; d/ste M$1100/1600;) Run by the same friendly family that owns the pizza joint downstairs, Belmar offers comfy, well-kept rooms with tiled floors and (some) balconies. Prices span four distinct seasons.

Hotel Francis Arlene HOTEL $$
(Map p80; ☎998-877-03-10; www.francisarlene.com; Guerrero 7; r with fan/air-con from US$67/78;) This place offers comfortable, good-size rooms with fan (or air-con) and fridge. Most have a king-size bed or two doubles, and many have balconies and partial sea views. The lounging frog sculptures will either seem hokey or cute, but either way they kinda fit right in. Good low-season rates.

Hotel Villa Kiin HOTEL $$$
(Map p80; ☎998-877-10-24; www.villakiin.com; Zazil-Ha 129; r from M$1530, bungalows from M$1955, incl breakfast;) With one of the safest beaches for swimming, and recently remodeled rooms, Villa Kiin remains one of the island's premier hotels. You can opt for a room with new furniture, rocking chairs and ocean views (from some), or you can stay in a bungalow. The bungalows sit right on a beach with hammocks.

Casa El Pío BOUTIQUE HOTEL $$$
(Map p80; www.casaelpio.com; Hidalgo 3; r US$95-113;) Book a room well in advance if you want to stay at this small – and very popular – boutique hotel. One of the five rooms has an ocean view, as does the rooftop terrace, and all rooms have handcrafted wood furnishings, fantastic photographs of the island and many other interesting design details. Online reservations only (there's no phone).

Hotel Na Balam BOUTIQUE HOTEL $$$
(Map p80; ☎998-881-47-70; www.nabalam.com; Zazil-Ha 118; r/ste incl breakfast from US$196/283;) Iguanas roam the beautiful hibiscus and palm gardens at this beachfront hotel on Playa Norte. All rooms are decorated with simple elegance and have safes, hammocks, private balconies or patios...and some come with TVs. The hotel offers yoga and meditation classes as well as massage services and a swimming pool.

Su Casa COTTAGE $$$
(☎998-877-01-80, cell 998-1901375; www.sucasa mexico.com; Carretera Sac Bajo s/n; r from US$81; P) Want to get away from the tourist center? Head south to these oceanfront cottages on a gorgeous stretch of white beach. There's no room service and no TV here, but once you get a look at the azure water you won't miss the boob tube. It's adults only from December through April and there's a two-night minimum stay.

You'll need a vehicle or taxi to get here. It's about 800m south of the Isla Mujeres Turtle Farm, along Carretera Sac Bajo.

Hotel Rocamar HOTEL $$$
(Map p80; ☎998-877-01-01; www.rocamar-hotel.com; cnr Bravo & Guerrero; r from M$1809; P) Almost achingly modern rooms (the goldfish-bowl bathrooms in some may not appeal if you're sharing with a casual acquaintance) feature private balconies with sea views. The view from the pool ain't too shabby either. Prices drop considerably in low season.

Eating

Súper Xpress, a supermarket on the plaza, has a solid selection of groceries, baked goods and snacks.

Pita Amore MEDITERRANEAN $
(Map p80; Guerrero s/n, btwn Morelos & Madero; sandwiches M$35-45; 12:30-10pm Mon-Sat, 6-10pm Sun;) This unassuming shack does just three varieties of pita sandwiches and does them extremely well. The chicken, beef and vegetarian pitas are the creation of a New York Culinary Institute alum. The secret lies in the homemade sauces and outstanding pita bread, which comes from a Lebanese bakery in Mérida.

Isla Mujeres Town

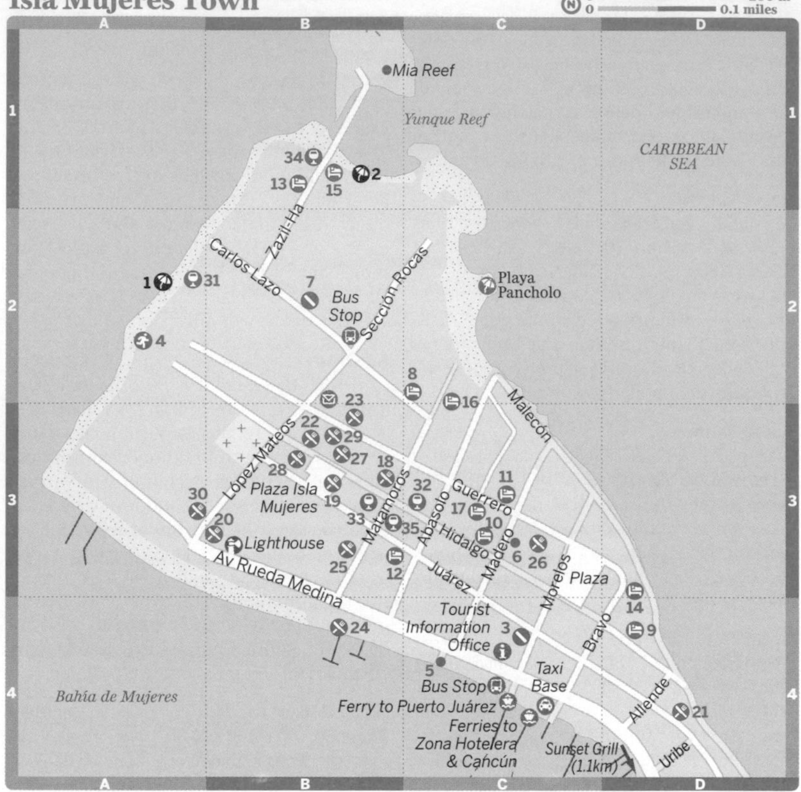

Isla Mujeres Town

Sights

1 Playa Norte A2
2 Playa Secreto B1

Activities, Courses & Tours

3 Aqua Adventures Eco Divers C4
4 Felipez Water Sports Center A2
5 Fisherman's Cooperative C4
6 Mundaca Divers C3
7 Sea Hawk Divers B2

Sleeping

8 Apartments Trinchan C2
9 Casa El Pío D4
10 Hotel Belmar C3
11 Hotel Francis Arlene C3
12 Hotel Kinich B3
13 Hotel Na Balam B1
14 Hotel Rocamar D3
15 Hotel Villa Kiin B1
16 Poc-Na Hostel C2
17 Xbulu-Ha Hotel C3

Eating

18 Aluxes Coffee Shop B3
19 Angelo B3
20 Jax Bar & Grill B3
21 La Lomita D4
22 Lola Valentina B3
23 Mercado Municipal B3
24 Mininos B4
25 Olivia B3
26 Pita Amore C3
27 Qubano B3
Rolandi's .... (see 10)
28 Rooster Café B3
29 Ruben's Restaurant B3
30 Satay A3

Drinking & Nightlife

31 Buho's A2
32 El Patio C3
33 Fayne's B3
34 Fenix Lounge B1
Poc-Na Hostel .... (see 16)
35 T&T Tropical Paradise B3

Mercado Municipal MARKET $

(Map p80; Guerrero s/n, btwn López Mateos & Matamoros; mains M$35-100; ⏲7am-5pm) Inside the remodeled market are several stalls selling cheap hot food, while other vendors offer a variety of produce and fresh juices. Outside the market, four open-air restaurants prepare simple regional fare like *sopa de lima* (lime soup) at decent prices.

Aluxes Coffee Shop CAFE $

(Map p80; Matamoros s/n; mains M$30-85; ⏲7am-11pm Wed-Mon;) Aluxes serves bagels, baguettes and mighty fine banana bread, and it's one of the friendliest joints in town.

Ruben's Restaurant MEXICAN $

(Map p80; Guerrero 18; breakfast M$40-80, lunch & dinner M$70-120; ⏲9am-8pm Mon-Sat;) There's nothing fancy about this little diner, but homemade Mexican food and great service are guaranteed. Regulars usually go for the daily set menu, which includes a choice of soup or salad and a main dish. There are also a few gringo-friendly items on the menu, for example the 'super burrito'.

Mango Café BREAKFAST $$

(Payo Obispo 725, Colonia Meterológico; mains M$85-125; ⏲7am-3pm;) See the south side of town and drop by Mango Café for some self-serve coffee and a hearty Caribbean-inspired breakfast. The hot items here are coconut French toast and eggs Benedict in a curry hollandaise sauce. It's a short bike or cab ride away, about 3km south of the ferry terminal.

La Lomita MEXICAN $$

(Map p80; Juárez s/n; mains M$70-230; ⏲9am-10pm;) The 'Little Hill' serves good, cheap Mexican food in a small, colorful setting. Seafood and chicken dishes predominate. Try the fantastic bean and avocado soup, or the ceviche (seafood marinated in lemon or lime juice, garlic and seasonings).

Mininos SEAFOOD $$

(Map p80; Av Rueda Medina s/n; mains M$90-170; ⏲10am-9pm) A colorfully painted *palapa* restaurant with a sand floor, Mininos dishes up tasty garlic shrimp, fried whole fish and octopus, as well as delicious seafood soups. It's popular with locals and tourists alike.

Rooster Café CAFE $$

(Map p80; Hidalgo s/n; breakfasts M$77-125; ⏲7am-3pm;) The undeniable king of the breakfast providers on the island is this cute little cafe with a couple of tables out front and blasting air-con inside. The menu covers the classics and throws in a couple of inventive twists, all served up with excellent coffee and attentive service.

Rolandi's ITALIAN $$

(Map p80; ☎998-877-04-30; www.rolandirestaurants.com; Av Hidalgo 110; mains M$131-226; ⏲7am-midnight;) Bakes very good thin-crust pizzas and calzones in a wood-fired oven. The menu also includes pasta, fresh salads, fish and some Italian specialties – don't come here looking for Mexican.

Qubano CUBAN $$

(Map p80; www.facebook.com/qubanoIsla; Av Hidalgo s/n; mains M$80-190; ⏲noon-midnight Mon-Fri, 4pm-midnight Sat;) It competes for decibel levels with neighboring restaurants, but really, we all like Cuban *son* (a type of dance) more than bad disco remixes, don't we? Apart from that, you get a change from Mexican fare with *ropa vieja* (slow-cooked shredded beef), Cuban lobster and mojitos.

Jax Bar & Grill BREAKFAST $$

(Map p80; www.facebook.com/jaxislamujeres; López Mateos 1; breakfast M$65-100, lunch & dinner M$110-320; ⏲8am-10pm;) Aside from the hearty breakfasts here, you get a birds-eye view of the boardwalk scene from the restaurant's upper deck. And Jax probably has the biggest TV screens on the island if you need your sports fix.

★ **Olivia** MEDITERRANEAN $$$

(Map p80; ☎998-877-17-65; www.olivia-islamujeres.com; Matamoros; mains M$120-235; ⏲5-9:30pm Tue-Sat;) This delightful Israeli-run restaurant makes everything from scratch, from Moroccan-style fish served on a bed of couscous to chicken shawarmas wrapped in fresh-baked pita bread. Ask for a candlelit table out back in the garden. Olivia closes from mid-September to mid-October. Reservations recommended.

Lola Valentina FUSION $$$

(Map p80; Av Hidalgo s/n; mains M$125-275; ⏲8am-1pm & 5-10pm;) Overlooking the quieter north side of the restaurant strip, Lola does excellent Mexican fusion with dishes along the line of Thai-style shrimp tacos. Also on the menu are several vegan, gluten-free items such as a quinoa, rice and potato burrito wrap.

Angelo ITALIAN $$$

(Map p80; ☎998-877-12-73; www.restauranteangelo.com; Hidalgo, btwn López Mateos & Matamoros; M$139-359; ⏲4pm-midnight;) Pretty much everything on the menu is good at this sidewalk steakhouse, especially the black grouper fillet, the baked mussels and the Angus beef cuts. When he's around, Italian owner Angelo is a great source of information.

Sunset Grill INTERNATIONAL **$$$**
(998-877-07-85; www.sunsetgrill.com.mx; Av Rueda Medina s/n; mains M$170-270; 2-10pm Wed-Mon;) A romantic spot for sunset cocktails and a waterfront meal, the Sunset Grill prepares dishes that run the gamut from seafood to pasta; the fried whole fish is especially tasty. There's a smattering of vegetarian options too, like black rice with Mexican truffle and grilled veggies.

You'll find the restaurant on Isla Mujeres Bay, about 800m south of the car ferry terminal.

Satay ASIAN **$$$**
(Map p80; 998-848-84-84; López Mateos s/n; mains M$155-192; 6-10pm;) Mix things up a little with some beef in shiitake-mushroom sauce at this Asian-fusion restaurant. It's not beachfront, but the modern, cool ambience is pleasant.

Drinking & Nightlife

Isla Mujeres' highest concentration of nightlife is along Avenida Hidalgo, and hot spots on or near the beach form an arc around the northern edge of town.

★T&T Tropical Paradise LOUNGE
(Map p80; www.facebook.com/tropicalparadiseislamujeres; Matamoros 20; 5am-2pm) You gotta love a place with sand floors – and unlike some of the nearby bars, T&T dares to play music from the 21st century!

Poc-Na Hostel BAR
(Map p80; www.pocna.com; Matamoros 26; 7pm-3am;) Has a lobby bar with nightly live music and a beachfront bar with bonfires and more hippies than all the magic buses in the world. It's a scene, and an entertaining one at that.

Fenix Lounge BAR
(Map p80; 998-274-00-73; www.fenixisla.com; Zazil-Ha 118; 11:30am-10pm Tue-Sat, to 8pm Sun;) A waterfront *palapa* bar where you can go for a swim in calm waters, enjoy excellent cocktails like the spicy mango margarita and groove to live music on weekends.

Buho's BAR
(Map p80; Playa Norte; 9:30am-11pm;) The quintessential swing-bar experience right on the beach. You can also take morning and afternoon yoga classes here. It's near Calle Carlos Lazo.

El Patio BAR
(Map p80; Av Hidalgo 17; 7:30-11:30pm;) The self-proclaimed 'house of music' has an open-air patio and rooftop terrace where on a good night you can catch blues or jazz acts and on a bad night mediocre '80s cover bands.

Fayne's BAR
(Map p80; www.faynesbarandgrill.com; Av Hidalgo 12; 11am-midnight) This disco-bar and grill often features live reggae, salsa and other Caribbean sounds.

Orientation

The island is 8km long, 150m to 800m wide. You'll find most restaurants and hotels in the town of Isla Mujeres, with the pedestrian corridor on Hidalgo the focal point. The ferry arrives in the town proper on the island's northern side. On the southern tip are the lighthouse and vestiges of the Maya temple. The two are linked by Avenida Rueda Medina, a loop road that follows the coast. Between them are a handful of small fishing villages, several saltwater lakes, a string of westward-facing beaches, a large lagoon and a small airstrip.

The eastern shore is washed by the open sea, and the surf there is dangerous. The most popular sand beach (Playa Norte) is at the northern tip of the island.

Information

Several banks are directly across from the ferry dock. Most exchange currency and all have ATMs.

Hospital Integral Isla Mujeres (998-877-17-92; Guerrero, btwn Madero & Morelos) Doctors available 24/7.

HSBC (cnr Av Rueda Medina & Morelos)

Hyperbaric Chamber (998-877-17-92; Morelos s/n) Next to Hospital Integral Isla Mujeres. It's often closed; inquire at the hospital.

Internet Café (cnr Matamoros & Guerrero; per hour M$10; 9am-9:30pm Mon-Sat) As yet unnamed.

Police (066)

Post Office (Map p80; 998-877-00-85; cnr Guerrero & López Mateos; 9am-5pm Mon-Fri, to noon Sat)

Tourist Information Office (Map p80; 998-877-03-07; direcciondeturismo@hotmail.com; Av Rueda Medina 130, btwn Madero & Morelos; 9am-4pm Mon-Fri) Offers a

THE MYSTERY OF HACIENDA MUNDACA

A 19th-century slave trader and reputed pirate, Fermín Antonio Mundaca de Marechaja, fell in love with a local woman known as La Trigueña (The Brunette). To win her, Mundaca built **Hacienda Mundaca** (Av Rueda Medina; admission M$20; ⏲9am-4pm), a two-story mansion complete with gardens and graceful archways. But while Mundaca was building the house, La Trigueña married another islander. Brokenhearted, Mundaca died, and the hacienda fell into disrepair.

Some documents indicate that Mundaca died during a visit to Mérida and was buried there. Others say he died on the island, and indeed there's a grave in the town cemetery that supposedly contains his remains. Despite the skull and crossbones on his headstone (a common memento mori), there's no evidence that Mundaca was ever a pirate. Instead, it is said he accumulated his wealth by transporting slaves from Africa to Cuba, where they were forced to work in mines and sugar-cane fields.

Today the complex has some walls and foundations, a large central pond, some rusting cannons and a partially rebuilt house. At the southern end stands a gateway with an impressive stone arch. The shady grounds make for pleasant strolling, but watch out for the droppings of spiny-tailed iguanas. The ruins are about 4km south of town; they're easily reached by bike, taxi, or bus if you don't mind waiting.

number of brochures. Some staff members speak English.

Getting There & Away

There are several points of embarkation from Cancún to reach Isla Mujeres. Most people cross on Ultramar passenger ferries. The R-1 'Puerto Juárez' city bus in Cancún serves all Zona Hotelera departure points and Puerto Juárez, in Ciudad Cancún. If you arrive by car, daily parking fees in and around the terminals cost between M$50 and M$100.

Fares for ferries departing from the Zona Hotelera are in US dollars. If you're on a tight budget, it's much cheaper to leave from Puerto Juárez. Ferries (www.granpuerto.com.mx) depart from the following docks:

El Embarcadero (Blvd Kukulcán Km 4) Six daily departures; one way US$14.

Playa Caracol (Blvd Kukulcán Km 9.5) Six daily departures; one way US$14.

Playa Tortugas (Blvd Kukulcán Km 6.5) Eight daily departures; one way US$14.

Puerto Juárez (4km north of Ciudad Cancún) Leave every 30 minutes; one way M$78.

Punta Sam, 8km north of Ciudad Cancún, is the only ferry that transports vehicles and bikes. From Punta Sam, drivers are included in prices for the following one-way fares: cars (M$292), motorcycles (M$99), bicycles (M$93); additional passengers pay M$40. Get there an hour before if you're transporting a vehicle. See www.maritimaislamujeres.com for departure times. To reach Punta Sam, take a taxi or northbound 'Punta Sam' *colectivo* along Avenida Tulum.

Getting Around

With all rented transportation it's best to deal directly with the shop supplying it, as opposed to going through a middle person.

BICYCLE

Bicycling is a great way to get around on the island's narrow streets and to explore outlying areas.

Rentadora Fiesta (Av Rueda Medina s/n, btwn Morelos & Bravo; per hr/day M$50/150; ⏲8am-5pm) rents mountain bikes and beach cruisers.

BUS & TAXI

A local bus (there's just one) departs from behind the market or from the ferry dock and heads along Avenida Rueda Medina, stopping along the way. You can get to the entrance of Hacienda Mundaca, within 300m of the Turtle Farm (Tortugranja), and as far south as Playa Lancheros (1.5km north of Playa Garrafón). It's a cheap ride at M$5, but expect long waits.

Taxi rates are set by the municipal government and posted at the taxi base just south of the passenger-ferry dock.

MOTORCYCLE & GOLF CART

Inspect all scooters carefully before renting. Costs vary, and are sometimes jacked up in high season, but generally start at about M$250 per day (9am to 5pm).

Many people find golf carts to be a good way to get around the island, and caravans of them can be seen tooling down the roads. The average cost is M$550 per day (9am to 5pm).

Scooters and golf carts get good maintenance at **Mega Ciro's** (☎998-877-05-68; Av Guerrero 11; incl gas & insurance scooter per 8hr M$250, golf cart per 24hr M$650; ⏲9am-5pm).

Isla Cozumel

☎987 / POP 80,000

Includes ➡

Best Places to Eat

- ➡ Kinta (p94)
- ➡ La Cocay (p94)
- ➡ Guido's Restaurant (p94)
- ➡ La Choza (p93)
- ➡ Camarón Dorado (p93)

Best Places to Stay

- ➡ Hotel B Cozumel (p92)
- ➡ Hostelito (p91)
- ➡ Hotel Villas Las Anclas (p92)
- ➡ Ventanas al Mar (p92)
- ➡ Hotel Mary Carmen (p92)

Why Go?

Cozumel is too resilient, too proud to let itself become just another cheesy cruise-ship destination. Leaving the tourist area – and the gringo-friendly souvenir shops – behind, you see an island of quiet cool and genuine authenticity. Garages still have shrines to the Virgin, there's a spirited Caribbean energy, and of course there are some holiday things to do, such as diving some of the best reefs in the world.

While diving and snorkeling are the main draws, the town square is a pleasant place to spend the afternoon, and it's highly gratifying to explore the less-visited parts of the island on a rented scooter or convertible bug. The coastal road leads to small Maya ruins, a marine park and captivating scenery along the unforgettable windswept shore.

When to Go

➡ The festive Carnaval celebration in February brings live music acts and dancers festooned with feathers out into the streets. It's not Rio de Janeiro, but it sure is a hoot.

➡ In late April and early May folks in the town of El Cedral pay tribute to Caste War refugees with a fun-filled fair featuring rides, rodeos and traditional dance, including the time-honored Dance of the Pigs' Heads.

➡ If you're planning a trip around diving and snorkeling you might want to visit March through May, when you don't have to worry about hurricanes or strong winter winds.

History

Maya settlement here dates from AD 300. During the post-Classic period, Cozumel flourished as a trade center and, more importantly, a ceremonial site. Every Maya woman living on the Yucatán Peninsula and beyond was expected to make at least one pilgrimage here to pay tribute to Ixchel, the goddess of fertility and the moon, at a temple erected in her honor. Archaeologists believe this temple was at San Gervasio, a bit north of the island's geographical center.

At the time of the first Spanish contact with Cozumel (in 1518, by Juan de Grijalva and his men), there were at least 32 Maya building groups on the island. According to Spanish chronicler Diego de Landa, a year later Hernán Cortés sacked one of the Maya

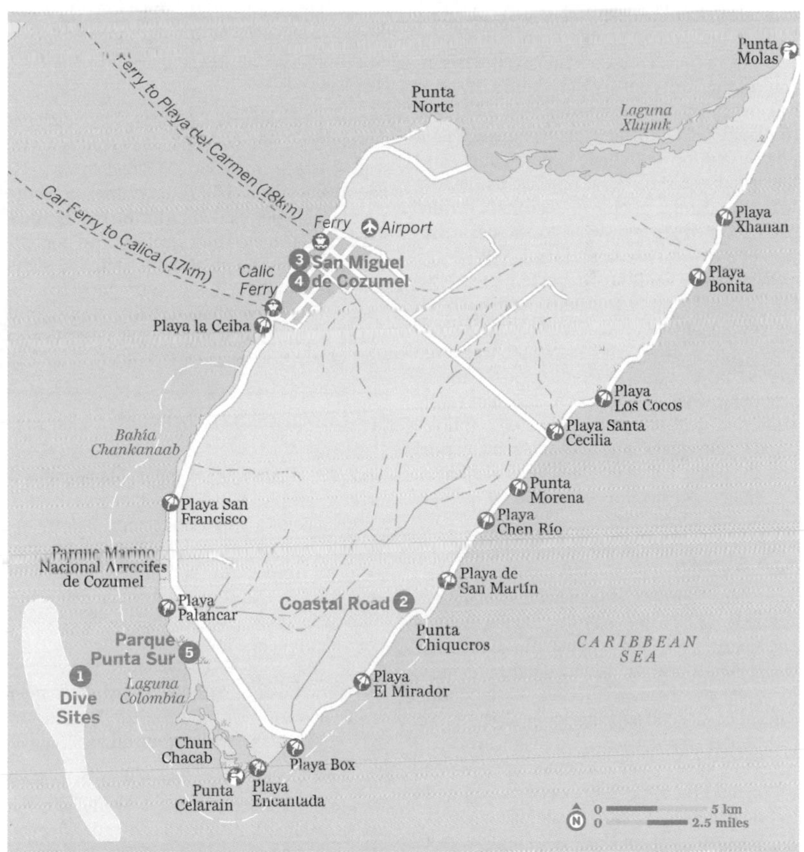

Isla Cozumel Highlights

1 Plunge into the deep blue and explore some of the world's best **dive sites** (p89), offering the likes of drift diving and imposing underwater walls that descend into the Caribbean.

2 Rent a scooter, bike or car to cruise the **coastal road** (p88) to Maya ruins and beaches along Cozumel's wild, windswept southeastern side.

3 Spend an evening hanging out at a bar or sidewalk restaurant in the buzzing town plaza of **San Miguel de Cozumel** (p86).

4 Learn all kinds of interesting tidbits about the island's geology and Maya history at the **Museo de la Isla de Cozumel** (p86).

5 Visit ecopark **Parque Punta Sur** (p86), where you can swim at a beach with a shallow reef and take a boat tour of a lagoon with migratory birds and crocs.

centers but left the others intact, apparently satisfied with converting the island's population to Christianity. Smallpox introduced by the Spanish wiped out half the 8000 Maya and, of the survivors, only about 200 escaped genocidal attacks by conquistadors in the late 1540s.

The island remained virtually deserted into the late 17th century, its coves providing sanctuary for several notorious pirates, including Jean Lafitte and Henry Morgan. In 1848 indigenous people fleeing the Caste War began to resettle Cozumel. At the beginning of the 20th century the island's (by then mostly mestizo) population grew, thanks to the craze for chewing gum. Cozumel was a port of call on the chicle-export route, and locals harvested the gum base on the island. After the demise of chicle, Cozumel's economy remained strong owing to the construction of a US air base here during WWII.

When the US military departed, the island fell into an economic slump, and many of its people moved away. Those who stayed fished for a living and it wasn't until the 1960s that Cozumel started to gain fame as a popular diving destination. Tourism really started taking off in the early 1980s following the construction of a commercial airport and the island's first cruise-ship dock. Today, Cozumel is Mexico's most important cruise-ship destination.

Sights

The route encompassing El Cedral, Playa Palancar and Parque Punta Sur will take you south from San Miguel, then counterclockwise around the island. There are some places along the way to stop for food and drink, but it's good to bring water all the same.

In order to see most of the island you will need to rent a vehicle or take a taxi (M$700 to M$1000 for a day trip); cyclists will need to brave the regular strong winds.

Access to many of Cozumel's best stretches of beach has become limited. Resorts and residential developments with gated roads create the most difficulties. Pay-for-use beach clubs occupy some other prime spots, but you can park and walk through or around them and enjoy adjacent parts of the beach without obligation. Sitting under their umbrellas or otherwise using the facilities requires you to fork out some money, either a straight fee or a *consumo mínimo* (minimum consumption of food and drink), which can add up in some places. It's not always strictly applied, especially when business is slow.

San Miguel de Cozumel

It's easy to make your way on foot around the island's main town, San Miguel de Cozumel. The waterfront boulevard is Avenida Melgar; along Melgar south of the main ferry dock *(muelle fiscal)* is a narrow sand beach. The main plaza, opposite the ferry dock, has an entertaining light-and-dancing-fountains show at 8:30pm, accompanied by classical music.

Museo de la Isla de Cozumel MUSEUM

(Map p90; ☎987-872-14-34; www.cozumelparks.com; Av Melgar s/n; M$60; ⏲9am-4pm Mon-Sat) The Museo de la Isla de Cozumel presents a clear and detailed picture of the island's flora, fauna, geography, geology and ancient Maya history. Thoughtful and detailed signs in English and Spanish accompany the exhibits. It's a good place to learn about coral before hitting the water, and it's one not to miss before you leave the island.

South of San Miguel

El Cedral ARCHAEOLOGICAL SITE

(Map p87; ⏲24hr) FREE This Maya ruin, a fertility temple, is the oldest on the island. It's the size of a small house and has no ornamentation. El Cedral is thought to have been an important ceremonial site; the small church standing next to the tiny ruin today is evidence that the site still has religious significance for locals.

The village of El Cedral is 3km west of Carretera Costera Sur. The turnoff is near Km 17, across from the Alberto's Restaurant sign. Look for the white-and-red arch.

Playa Palancar BEACH

(Map p87; Carretera Costera Sur Km 19; snorkel-gear rental M$130) About 17km south of town, Palancar is a great beach to visit during the week when the crowds thin out. It has a beach club renting snorkel gear and there's a restaurant. Near the beach, Arrecife Palancar (Palancar Reef) has some excellent diving (it's known as Palancar Gardens), as well as fine snorkeling (Palancar Shallows).

Parque Punta Sur NATURE RESERVE

(Map p87; ☎987-872-40-14; www.cozumelparks.com; Carretera Costera Sur Km 27; adult/child 3-11yr M$210/120; ⏲9am-4pm Mon-Sat) For the price of admission to this ecotouristic park,

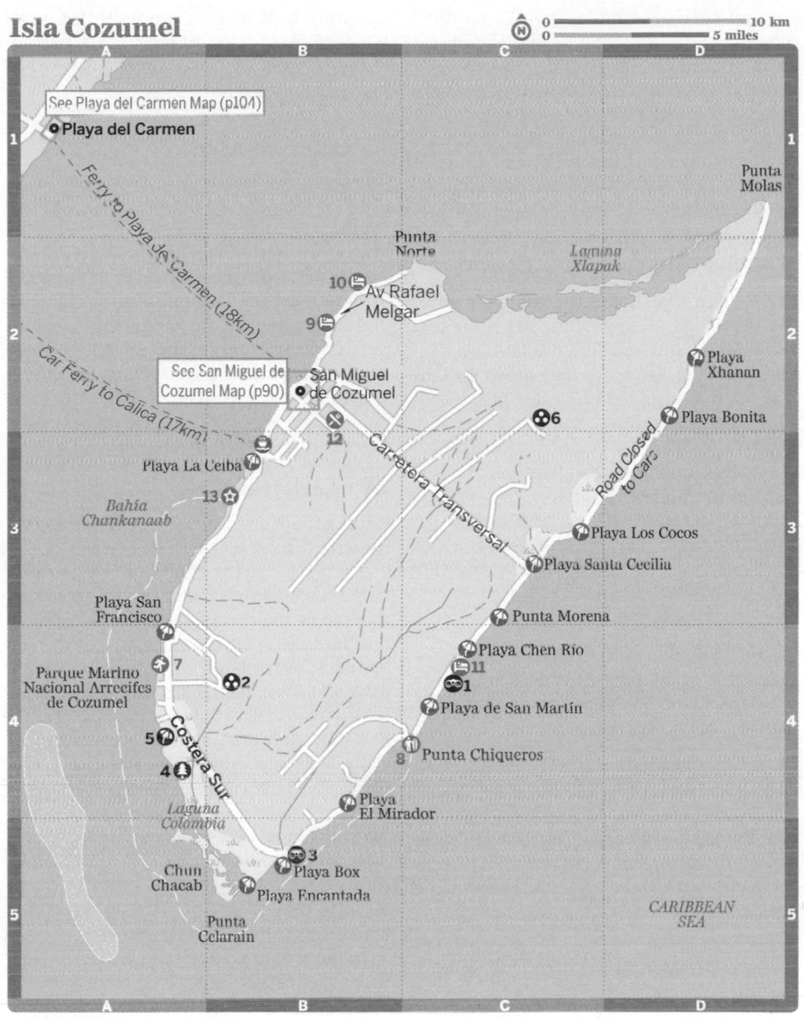

Isla Cozumel

Sights
1 Coconuts Bar & Grill.............................C4
2 El Cedral..D4
3 Freedom in Paradise.............................B5
4 Parque Punta Sur..................................A4
5 Playa Palancar......................................A4
6 San Gervasio Ruins...............................C2

Activities, Courses & Tours
7 Mr. Sancho's...A4
8 Playa Bonita Surfboard Rental..............C4

Sleeping
9 Hotel B Cozumel....................................B2
10 Hotel Playa Azul...................................B2
11 Ventanas al Mar....................................C4

Eating
12 Camarón Dorado...................................B2

Entertainment
13 La Hach...B3

you can visit a lighthouse, a small nautical museum and a Maya ruin. About 10 minutes away by car is an observation tower where you can see migratory birds and possibly crocodiles. The park area offers a beach with a shallow reef, a restaurant and three midday boat tours to Laguna Colombia. You'll need your own vehicle or a taxi (M$300 one way) to get here.

East Coast

The eastern shoreline is the wildest part of the island and presents some beautiful seascapes and many small blowholes (there's a bunch around Km 30.5). Swimming is dangerous on most of the east coast because of riptides and undertows. At Playa Chen Río, just past El Pescador restaurant at Km 42, there's a swimmable saltwater pool.

At Punta Chiqueros, at Km 37, a restaurant rents bodyboards and longboards.

As you travel along the coast, consider stopping at one of several restaurant-bars with great lookout points.

Freedom in Paradise VIEWPOINT
(Map p87; www.bobmarleybar.com; Carretera Coastal Oriente Km 29.5; 10am-5:30pm) Someone here, and at sister bar Rasta's across the highway, really digs reggae. Long live Bob!

Coconuts Bar & Grill VIEWPOINT
(Map p87; www.coconutscozumel.com; Carretera Coastal Oriente Km 43.5; 10am-7pm) It's over-the-top touristy, but what would you expect from a cliffside bar serving tropical drinks with Jimmy Buffett tunes in the background?

Punta Molas

Beyond where the east-coast highway meets the Carretera Transversal, intrepid travelers may take a poorly maintained, infrequently traveled and almost impossible to find track toward Punta Molas, the island's northeast point, accessible only by all-terrain vehicles (ATV) or on foot. A sign at the entrance reads 'Enter at your own risk. Irregular path even for 4x4 vehicles.'

If you head up the road, be aware that you can't count on flagging down another motorist for help in the event of a breakdown or accident, and most car-rental agencies' insurance policies don't cover any mishaps on unpaved roads. About 17km up the road are the Maya ruins known as **El Castillo Real**, and a few kilometers further is **Aguada Grande**. Both sites are quite far gone, their significance lost to time. In the vicinity of Punta Molas are some fairly good beaches and a few more minor ruins.

San Gervasio

San Gervasio Ruins ARCHAEOLOGICAL SITE
(Map p87; www.cozumelparks.com; Carretera Traversal Km 7; M$125; 8am-3:45pm; P) This overpriced Maya complex is Cozumel's only preserved ruin. San Gervasio is thought to have been the location of the sanctuary of Ixchel, goddess of fertility, and thus an important pilgrimage site at which Maya women – in particular prospective mothers – worshipped. But its structures are small and crude, and the clay idols of Ixchel were long ago destroyed by the Spaniards.

Activities

Cozumel and its surrounding reefs are among the world's most popular diving spots.

The sites have fantastic year-round visibility (commonly 30m or more) and a jaw-droppingly impressive variety of marine life that includes spotted eagle rays, moray eels, groupers, barracudas, turtles, sharks, brain coral and some huge sponges. The island can have strong currents (sometimes around 3 knots), making drift dives the standard, especially along the many walls. Even when diving or snorkeling from the beach you should evaluate conditions and plan your route, selecting an exit point down-current beforehand, then staying alert for shifts in currents. Always keep an eye out (and your ears open) for boat traffic as well. It's best not to snorkel alone away from the beach area.

Prices are usually quoted in US dollars. In general expect to pay anywhere between US$80 and US$100 for a two-tank dive (equipment included) or an introductory 'resort' course. PADI open-water certification costs US$350 to US$400.

Multiple-dive packages and discounts for groups or those paying in cash can bring rates down significantly.

If you encounter a decompression emergency, head immediately to the hyperbaric chamber at Cozumel International Clinic (p95).

There are scores of dive operators on Cozumel. All limit the size of their groups to six or eight divers, and the good ones take pains to match up divers of similar skill levels. Some offer snorkeling and deep-sea fishing trips as well as diving instruction.

SNORKELING & DIVING

The best snorkeling sites are reached by boat. Most snorkeling-only outfits in downtown go to one of three stretches of reef nearby, all accessible from the beach. If you go with a dive outfit instead, you can often get to better spots, such as Palancar Reef or the adjacent Colombia Shallows, near the island's southern end.

You can save on boat fares (and see fewer fish) by walking into the gentle surf north of town. One good spot is a beach club next to Hotel Playa Azul, 4km north of the turnoff to the airport; its *palapas* offer shade, and it has a swimming area with a sheltering wharf and a small artificial reef.

But your best option for snorkeling is heading out on a diving boat with **Deep Blue**, which will take you to three of the best snorkeling sites on the island.

Ask any dive operator in Cozumel to name the best dive sites in the area and the following names will come up time and again.

Santa Rosa Wall

This is the biggest of the famous sites. The wall is so large most people are able to see only a third of it on one tank. Regardless of where you're dropped, expect to find enormous overhangs and tunnels covered with corals and sponges. Stoplight parrotfish, black grouper and barracuda hang out here. The average visibility is 30m and minimum depth 10m, with an average closer to 25m. Carry a flashlight with you, even if you're diving at noon, as it will help to bring out the color of the coral at depth and illuminate the critters hiding in crevices. Hurricane Wilma in 2005 left shallower spots with uncovered coral, but for the most part it is unharmed.

Punta Sur Reef

Unforgettable for its coral caverns, each of which is named, this reef is for very experienced divers only. Before you dive be sure to ask your divemaster to point out the Devil's Throat. This cave opens into a cathedral room with four tunnels, all of which make for some pretty hairy exploration. Only certified cave divers should consider entering the Devil's Throat. Butterfly fish, angelfish and whip corals abound at the reef.

Colombia Shallows

Also known as Colombia Gardens, Colombia Shallows lends itself equally well to snorkeling and scuba diving. Because it's a shallow dive (maximum depth 10m, average 2m to 4m), its massive coral buttresses covered with sponges and other resplendent life forms are well illuminated. The current at Colombia Gardens is generally light to moderate. This and the shallow water allows you to spend hours at the site if you want, and you'll never get bored spying all the elkhorn coral, pillar coral and anemones that live here.

Palancar Gardens

This dive consists of a strip reef about 25m wide and very long, riddled with fissures and tunnels. The major features here are enormous stovepipe sponges and vivid yellow tube sponges, and you can always find damselfish, parrotfish and angelfish around you. In the deeper parts of the reef, divers will want to keep an eye out for the lovely black corals. The Gardens can be appreciated by snorkelers in the area known as Palancar Shallows, due to the slight current usually found in it and its modest maximum depth (20m).

A bike can be a great way to get to the northern and southern beaches on the western side of flat Cozumel. A full day's rental typically costs M$150. The completely separate bicycle and scooter lane on the Carretera Costera Sur sees a good deal of car traffic from confused tourists and impatient cab drivers, so be careful.

Deep Blue DIVING

(Map p90; ☎987-872-56-53; www.deepbluecozumel.com; Calle Salas 200; 2-tank dives incl equipment US$100, snorkeling incl gear US$57; ⊙7am-9pm) This PADI and National Association of Underwater Instructors (NAUI) operation has knowledgeable staff, state-of-the-art gear and fast boats that give you a chance

San Miguel de Cozumel

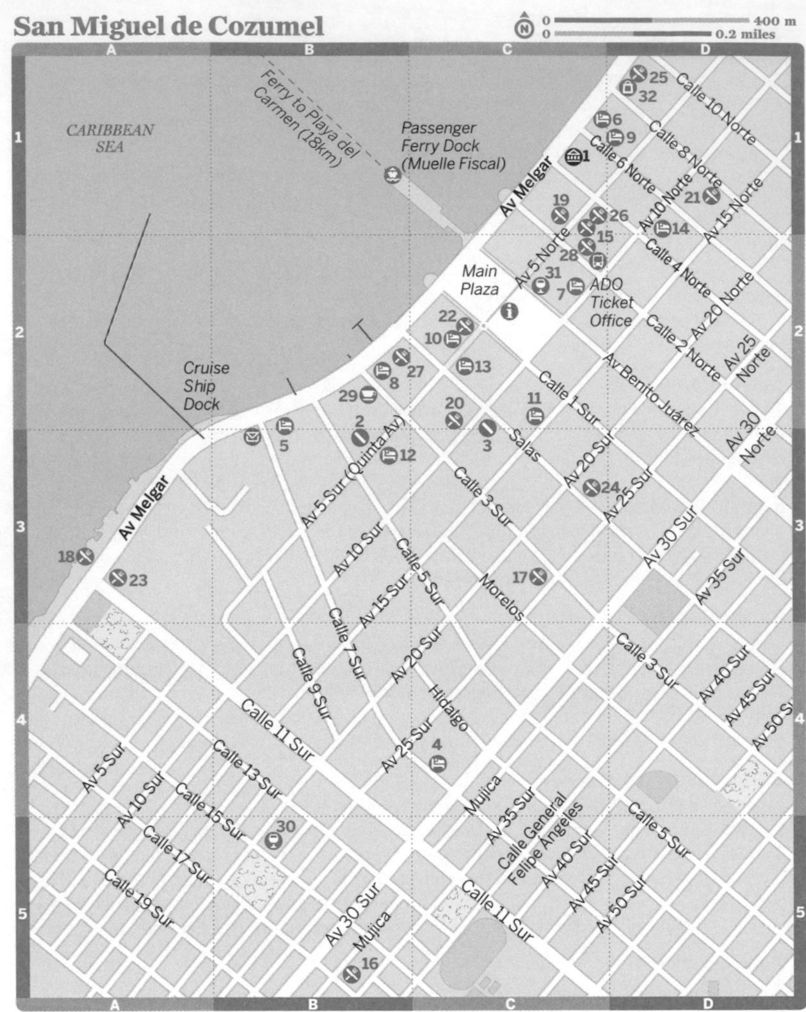

to get more dives out of a day. A snorkeling outing visits three sites.

Aldora Divers DIVING
(Map p90; ☎987-872-33-97; www.aldora.com; Calle 5 Sur 37; 1-/2-tank dives incl equipment US$88/126, 3-tank shark-cave dives US$200; ⏰7am-3pm & 6-8pm) One of the best dive shops in Cozumel, Aldora will take divers to the windward side of the island when weather is bad on the western side. It also does full-day excursions to caves with sleeping sharks; these trips include a stop at a lagoon with Maya ruins.

Shark Rider BICYCLE RENTAL
(☎987-120-02-31; Av 5 Norte s/n, btwn Av Juárez & Calle 2 Norte; per day bikes M$100-150, scooters M$250; ⏰8am-7pm) You can rent beach cruisers, mountain bikes and racing bikes, as well as scooters, here. It's on an alley off Avenida 5 Norte.

Mr. Sancho's HORSEBACK RIDING
(Map p87; Carretera Costera Sur Km 15.5; 1hr tours US$45; ⏰8am-3:30pm Mon-Sat) Saddle up at Mr. Sancho's for guided horseback rides along the coast and into the surrounding jungle, where you can see deer and pintail ducks.

San Miguel de Cozumel

Sights
1 Museo de la Isla de Cozumel....C1

Activities, Courses & Tours
2 Aldora Divers....B3
3 Deep Blue....C2

Sleeping
4 Amigo's Hostel....C4
5 Casa Mexicana....B2
6 Guido's Boutique Hotel....C1
7 Hostelito....C2
8 Hotel Bahía....B2
9 Hotel Flamingo....D1
10 Hotel Mary Carmen....C2
11 Hotel Pepita....C2
12 Hotel Villas Las Anclas....B3
13 Suites Colonial Cozumel....C2
14 Suites Vima....D1

Eating
15 Burritos Gorditos....C1
16 Cha Cha's Kitchen....B5
17 Cocina Económica Las Palmas....C3
Guido's Restaurant....(see 6)
18 Jeanie's....A3
19 Kinta....C1
20 La Choza....C2
21 La Cocay....D1
22 Los Dorados de Villa....C2
23 Mega....A3
24 Mercado Municipal....C3
25 Pancho's Backyard....D1
26 Pastelería y Panadería Zermatt....C1
27 Pepe's Grill....B2
28 Taquería El Sitio....C2

Drinking & Nightlife
Aqua....(see 9)
29 El Coffee Cozumel....B2
30 El Volado....B5
La Cocay....(see 21)
31 Woody's Bar & Grill....C2

Shopping
32 Los Cinco Soles....D1

Playa Bonita Surfboard Rental SURFING
(Map p87; Carretera Coastal Oriente Km 37; per day bodyboard/surfboard M$120/480) Hit the surf on a bodyboard or longboard at Punta Chiqueros. Playa Bonita restaurant, at Km 37, rents them with proof of ID.

Festivals & Events

Carnaval RELIGIOUS
(Feb) We know, it's not the wild Carnaval of Rio de Janeiro, but don't underestimate a century-old tradition along the waterfront. The five-day celebration brings dancers festooned with feathers out into the streets, along with colorful floats, live-music acts, food stalls and impromptu fiestas just about everywhere you turn.

Feria del Cedral RELIGIOUS
(late Apr & early May) Held in Cozumel's southern town of El Cedral, this annual celebration honors a group of Caste War refugees forced to flee the mainland and settle in Cozumel in 1848. The fair features rides, food stands, rodeos and traditional dance, including the time-honored Baile de las Cabezas de Cochino (Dance of the Pigs' Heads).

May 3 marks the Day of the Holy Cross (a religious procession paying tribute to a wooden cross carried over by the settlers).

Sleeping

'High season' is mid-December to mid-April, but whatever the season, if business is slow, most places are open to negotiation. Almost all places raise their rates at Christmas and Easter.

Many budget and midrange places are in San Miguel de Cozumel. Several kilometers north and south of town are a few big, luxury resort hotels.

★ Hostelito HOSTEL $
(Map p90; 987-869-81-57; www.hostelcozumel.com; Av 10 Norte s/n, btwn Av Juárez & Calle 2 Norte; dm with/without air-con M$195/180, d M$550, ste from M$600;) Stay in a fan-cooled or air-conditioned dorm room, or check out the recently remodeled rooms and suites, which have been significantly improved with new beds and furnishings. Hostelito's pleasant open-air kitchen and rooftop sundeck are great spaces for hanging out and exchanging diving stories.

Hotel Pepita HOTEL $
(Map p90; 987-872-00-98; www.hotelpepitacozumel.com; Av 15 Sur 120; r M$450;) The HP's owner, Maria Teresa, takes pride in her work and it shows, as this is one of the best economical hotels in the city. It's friendly, with well-maintained rooms grouped around a garden. All have two double beds, refrigerators and air-con. There's

free morning coffee and wi-fi in the common area.

Amigo's Hostel HOSTEL $

(Map p90; ☎987-872-38-68; www.cozumelhostel.com; Calle 7 Sur 57, btwn Avs 25 Sur & 30 Sur; dm/r M$185/600;) Unlike some cramped budget digs, here you get a large garden, an inviting pool and a good lounge area stocked with reading material. Some guests say it's too far removed from the tourist center; others like it that way. Bike and snorkel-gear rentals available.

Suites Vima HOTEL $

(Map p90; ☎987-872-51-18; suitesvima@hotmail.com; Av 10 Norte s/n; s/d M$450/550;) Has spotless and spacious modern rooms with tiled floors, Barney Rubble–hard beds, good air-con, and fridges, tables and chairs. A small swimming pool lies in a green area in the back of this family-run hotel.

Hotel Mary Carmen HOTEL $$

(Map p90; ☎987-872-05-81; www.hotelmarycarmen.com.mx; Av 5 Sur 132; d M$790;) Mary Carmen's lobby seems a bit odd in a design sense with its mix of antiques and mismatched modern furnishings, but it definitely ain't boring. Clean, colorful rooms overlook a central courtyard where the owner keeps more than a dozen turtles, so watch your step! It's just a short walk from the ferry terminal.

Hotel Bahía HOTEL $$

(Map p90; ☎987-872-90-90, USA 877-228-6747; www.suitesbahia.com; cnr Av Melgar & Calle 3 Sur; d incl breakfast US$59-68, r with ocean view US$96;) Opt for a standard room with a street-facing balcony or a more expensive one with balcony and ocean view. You can save some pesos by staying in one of the smaller, interior rooms, but it's not worth it.

Suites Colonial Cozumel HOTEL $$

(Map p90; ☎USA 877-228-6747, toll-free 800-227-26-39; www.suitescolonial.com; Av 5 Sur, btwn Calles 1 Sur & Salas; r/ste incl breakfast US$59/68;) Down a passageway off Avenida 5 Sur, this place has lovely 'studios' (rooms with cable TV, fridge and lots of varnished-wood touches) and nice, spacious one-bedroom suites with kitchenettes. A complimentary breakfast buffet is served around the corner at sister property Casa Mexicana.

★ **Hotel B Cozumel** BOUTIQUE HOTEL $$$

(Map p87; ☎987-872-03-00; www.hotelbcozumel.com; Carretera Playa San Juan Km 2.5; r US$120-160, ste US$170;) The place to B and B seen, this hip hotel on the north shore may not have that sand beach you're after, but just wait till you get a look at the azure infinity pool, saltwater pool and oceanfront hot tub. Rooms here are fashioned with recycled objects, and bikes are available to hit the town.

It's about 3km north of the ferry terminal.

Hotel Villas Las Anclas VILLA $$$

(Map p90; ☎987-872-54-76, USA 305-771-8176; www.hotelvillalasanclas.com; Av 5 Sur 325; d US$131;) If you like having space, check out these two-story villas. A spiral staircase ascends to a snug loft bedroom, while downstairs you get a full kitchen and living room with a garden view. In the leafy patio there's a shady pool with a waterfall and a large outdoor kitchen with an integrated BBQ grill.

Ventanas al Mar HOTEL $$$

(Map p87; ☎984-267-22-37; www.ventanasalmarcozumel.com; Carretera Costera Oriente Km 43.5; r/ste incl breakfast from US$115/175;) Notable as it's the only windward hotel on the island, Ventanas al Mar might be right for you if you are looking to get away from it all (*way* away from it all). The rooms have great ocean views and the constant wind will lull you to sleep – or drive you crazy if you're a light sleeper.

If you don't want to have dinner at the hotel's restaurant every day, you'll need to go into town after dark as nearby restaurants close early. There are bikes and a swimming pool here, too.

Guido's Boutique Hotel BOUTIQUE HOTEL $$$

(Map p90; ☎987-872-09-46; www.guidosboutiquehotel.com; Av Melgar 23; ste US$130-154;) Right on the main strip with an ocean view, Guido's has four chic suites with full kitchens, large common areas and private balconies, making them ideal for families or small groups. The same owners run a great Italian restaurant downstairs.

Hotel Flamingo BOUTIQUE HOTEL $$$

(Map p90; ☎987-872-12-64; www.hotelflamingo.com; Calle 6 Norte 81; r incl breakfast from US$93, apt US$230;) The colorful Hotel Flamingo is a nicely decorated place offering spacious rooms loaded with amenities. There's a large penthouse apartment here, too. Common areas include a leafy courtyard, a pool-table room, a popular bar and a rooftop sundeck with a hot tub. The hotel can arrange various activities for you, such as bicycling, horseback riding, windsurfing and fishing.

Casa Mexicana HOTEL $$$
(Map p90; USA 877-228-6747, toll-free 800-227-26-39; www.casamexicanacozumel.com; Av Melgar 457; d incl breakfast with/without ocean view from US$125/86;) The breezy open-air lobby with swimming pool and ocean view is pretty awesome here. Rooms are standard issue for the most part, but all in all Casa Mexicana offers a good deal given its prime location and free breakfast buffet.

Hotel Playa Azul HOTEL $$$
(Map p87; 987-869-51-60; www.playa-azul.com; Carretera a San Juan Km 4; d incl breakfast & green fee from US$238;) This is in the sedate area north of town on a pretty little stretch of beach, and there's good snorkeling. All rooms have a sea view, a balcony or terrace, and one king or two queen beds. The hotel has a gorgeous pool, and guests can play free golf at a nearby Jack Nicklaus–designed course.

Eating

Cozumel pretty much has it all, from cheap market eats and taco joints to candlelit restaurants serving seafood and gourmet fare. In an effort to appease the cruise-ship crowd, international cuisine abounds. The *comida corrida* (a set meal of several courses, usually offered at lunchtime) is always filling and is reasonably priced in most places.

Camarón Dorado SEAFOOD $
(Map p87; www.facebook.com/camaron.dorado; cnr Av Juárez & Calle 105 Sur; tortas M$33-38, tacos M$17-28; 7am-3pm Tue-Sun;) If you're headed to the windward side of the island or just want to see a different aspect of Cozumel, drop by the Camarón Dorado for a superb *torta de camaron capeado* (battered shrimp on a roll). Be warned: these bad boys are highly addictive. It's 2.5km southeast of the ferry terminal.

Mercado Municipal MARKET $
(Map p90; Calle Salas s/n, btwn Avs 20 & 25 Sur; snacks & mains M$25-80; 8am-5pm) Visit this downtown market for your daily supply of fruits and veggies; it's also a good spot to munch on cheap eats.

Taquería El Sitio TAQUERÍA $
(Map p90; Calle 2 Norte; tacos & tortas M$12-37; 7:30am-12:30pm) For something quick, cheap and scrumdiddlyumptious, head over to El Sitio for breaded shrimp and fish tacos or a *huevo con chaya torta* (egg and tree spinach sandwich).

Pastelería y Panadería Zermatt BAKERY $
(Map p90; cnr Av 5 Norte & Calle 4 Norte; bread M$7-12; 7am-3pm & 6-9pm Mon-Sat;) Bakes pastries, cakes and wholewheat bread. Unlike many Mexican bakeries, it does its cooking in the early morning.

Cocina Económica Las Palmas MEXICAN $
(Map p90; cnr Calle 3 Sur & Av 25 Sur; mains M$65-130, set menu M$65; 9am-7pm Mon-Sat;) This place really packs 'em in at lunchtime. And though it gets hotter than Hades, you'll love the *chicharrones* (fried pork rinds) and Maya favorites such as *poc-chuc* (grilled pork).

La Choza MEXICAN $$
(Map p90; 987-872-09-58; Av 10 Sur 216; breakfast M$52-70, lunch & dinner M$96-180, set menu M$115; 7am-10pm;) An excellent and popular restaurant specializing in regional Mexican cuisine, with classics like chicken in *mole poblano* (a sauce of chilies, fruits, nuts, spices and chocolate). All mains come with soup. La Choza also offers a *comida corrida* (set menu) for the lunch crowd.

Cha Cha's Kitchen INTERNATIONAL $$
(Map p90; cell 987-5642525; www.facebook.com/chachaskitchen; Calle Mujíca s/n, btwn Calles 15 Sur & 17 Sur; soups & salads M$35-100, mains M$95-110; noon-4pm Mon-Thu;) A mom-and-daughter team from Minnesota whip up everything from gringo comfort food to Mexican fusion and vegan dishes out of their Cozumel home-turned-restaurant. The changing menu usually features a main dish, soup, salad and dessert, and believe us when we say you shouldn't skip dessert.

Burritos Gorditos FAST FOOD $$
(Map p90; www.facebook.com/burritosgorditos; Av 5 Norte s/n; burritos US$5-8; 9am-3pm Mon-Sat;) This friendly little burrito joint prepares the typical vegetarian, chicken and beef variety, or you can experiment with Yucatán-inspired *cochinita* (slow-cooked pork) or apple-cinnamon-flavored burritos.

Jeanie's MEXICAN $$
(Map p90; 987-878-46-47; www.jeaniescozumel.com; Av Melgar 790; breakfasts M$79-110,

mains M$110-230; 7am-10pm;) The views of the water are great from the outdoor patio here. Jeanie's serves waffles, plus hash-brown potatoes, eggs, sandwiches and other tidbits like vegetarian fajitas. Frozen coffees beat the midday heat.

Los Dorados de Villa MEXICAN **$$**
(Map p90; 987-872-01-96; Calle 1 Sur; mains M$70-130; 8am-11pm;) Near the edge of the plaza, this place has a wide variety of Mexican dishes, including Yucatecan snacks, various seafood items and the signature enchilada dishes. There's a vegetarian menu as well.

★ **Kinta** MEXICAN **$$$**
(Map p90; 987-869-05-44; www.kintarestaurante.com; Av 5 Norte; mains M$170-215; 5:30-11pm Tue-Sun;) Putting a gourmet twist on Mexican classics, this chic bistro is one of the best restaurants on the island. The shrimp-and-scallop enchiladas dish is a tried-and-true favorite, and for dessert treat yourself to a *budín de la abuelita*, aka granny's pudding.

La Cocay MEDITERRANEAN **$$$**
(Map p90; 987-872-55-33; www.lacocay.com; Calle 8 Norte 208; mains M$150-340; 5:30-11pm;) The intimate atmosphere makes this smart restaurant a very enjoyable night out. Sit at the bar sipping a good single malt or find a quiet table in the back garden to chat with someone special. The menu changes seasonally but focuses on light, Mediterranean-influenced fare. The welcoming owners, Gary and Kathy Klein, seem to know every guest by name.

Guido's Restaurant ITALIAN **$$$**
(Map p90; www.guidoscozumel.com; Av Melgar 23; mains M$205-305, pizzas M$180-225; 11am-11pm Mon-Sat, 3-11pm Sun;) Drawing on recipes from her father, Guido, chef Yvonne Villiger has created a menu ranging from wood-fired pizzas and homemade pastas to prosciutto-wrapped scallops. To accompany the meal, order a pitcher of sangria, the house specialty.

Pancho's Backyard MEXICAN **$$$**
(Map p90; 987-872-21-41; www.panchosbackyard.com; Av Melgar 27; mains M$149-212; 9am-11pm Mon-Sat, 4-11pm Sun;) Atmospheric Pancho's is set in an early-20th-century building with a beautifully decorated courtyard. The food's not bad, either, focusing on Mexican dishes, international favorites and seafood.

Pepe's Grill STEAK **$$$**
(Map p90; 987-872-02-13; www.pepescozumel.com; Av Melgar; mains M$165-360; 10am-11pm Mon-Thu, to midnight Fri & Sat, noon-11pm Sun;) This is traditionally considered Cozumel's finest restaurant and the prices reflect its reputation. It's mostly Angus steaks, pastas, fresh fish and charbroiled lobster (available at market prices).

Mega SUPERMARKET
(Map p90; cnr Av Melgar & Calle 11 Sur; 7am-11pm;) Head to this mega-market to sort out your picnic lunch.

Drinking & Nightlife

San Miguel de Cozumel's nightlife is quiet and subdued. Most restaurants are open for drinks, but by 11pm things wind down, though several places around the plaza keep later hours.

El Coffee Cozumel CAFE
(Map p90; cnr Calle 3 Sur & Av Melgar; mains M$63-89; 7am-11pm) A tempting array of fresh-baked goods and organic coffee from the Mexican highlands make this place popular with locals and visitors alike. Pies are baked fresh daily.

La Cocay BAR
(Map p90; 987-872-55-33; www.lacocay.com; Calle 8 Norte 208; 5:30-11pm;) A great place for an after-dinner drink, La Cocay has a good wine list and serves Mexican craft beers.

Woody's Bar & Grill BAR
(Map p90; Av Juárez s/n, btwn Avs 5 & 10; 9am-midnight Mon-Fri, to 1am Sat & Sun;) This easygoing shotgun bar is about as festive as you can get.

Aqua BAR
(Map p90; www.hotelflamingo.com; Calle 6 Norte 81;) The Hotel Flamingo's lobby bar is an attractive lounge drawing mostly an older, margarita-drinking expat crowd.

El Volado BAR
(Map p90; cnr Av 20 Sur & Calle 15 Sur; 6:30pm-2am Tue & Wed, 7:30pm-3am Thu-Sun) Rarely visited by foreigners, this two-story Mexican pub is a good spot to brush up on your Spanish. If you can't muster up the courage to converse, order a beer tower and see how that works for you.

☆ Entertainment

La Hach LIVE MUSIC

(Map p87; www.lahachcozumel.com; Av Melgar Km 2.9; ⌚8am-1am Mon, to 11pm Tue-Thu, to 3am Fri & Sat, 4pm-1am Sun) Cozumel has a limited live-music scene and what you get at La Hach (meaning 'one for the road' in Maya) are usually cover bands playing Friday and Saturday nights. That being said, the ocean view here rocks and the restaurant whips up decent pub grub in a friendly cantina setting. It's a 10-minute cab ride from the town center.

Shopping

Los Cinco Soles ARTS, CRAFTS

(Map p90; www.loscincosoles.com; Av Melgar 27; ⌚9am-7pm Mon-Sat, 11am-5pm Sun) Like many shops along Avenida Melgar, this large store sells its fair share of junk, but there are some keepers on the shelves if you take the time to look, such as black ceramics from Oaxaca, Talavera pottery, and yarn and bead art made by indigenous Huichol artists.

Information

EMERGENCY

Police (☎066)

INTERNET ACCESS

Cyber-fon (Av 10 Norte s/n; per hour M$10; ⌚8am-11pm) offers internet services and cheap calls to the US and Europe (M$4 and M$5 per minute, respectively).

MEDICAL SERVICES

Cozumel International Clinic (Hyperbaric Chamber; ☎987-872-14-30; Calle 5 Sur, btwn Avs Melgar & 5 Sur; ⌚24hr) has a hyperbaric chamber.

MONEY

ATMs are the most convenient way to get quick cash, though expect to get hit with international transaction fees. For currency exchange, try any of the banks near the main plaza.

Banorte (Av 5 Norte s/n, btwn Av Juárez & Calle 2 Norte; ⌚9am-5pm Mon-Fri, to 2pm Sat)

HSBC (cnr Av 5 Sur & Calle 1 Sur; ⌚9am-5pm Mon-Fri)

POST

Post Office (Map p90; cnr Calle 7 Sur & Av Melgar; ⌚9am-4:30pm Mon-Sat)

TELEPHONE

Telmex card phones are abundant around town and are often cheaper than making calls at internet cafes.

The **Telecomm Office** (cnr Calle 7 Sur & Av Melgar; ⌚8am-7:30pm Mon-Fri) handles faxes and money orders.

TOURIST INFORMATION

Pick up maps and travel brochures at the **Tourist Information Office** (Map p90; ☎987-869-02-11; 2nd fl, Av 5 Sur s/n, Plaza del Sol; ⌚8am-3pm Mon-Fri).

Getting There & Away

AIR

Cozumel International Airport (☎987-872-20-81; www.asur.com.mx; Blvd Aeropuerto Cozumel s/n) Cozumel's small airport is about 3km northeast of the ferry terminal; follow the signs along Avenida Melgar. Some airlines fly direct from the US; European flights are usually routed via the US or Mexico City. Mexican carriers Interjet and MayAir serve Cozumel.

Interjet (☎800-011-23-45, USA 866-285-95-25; www.interjet.com) Flies direct to Mexico City.

MayAir (☎987-872-36-09; www.mayair.com.mx) Service to Cancún with continuing flight to Mérida.

BOAT

Passenger ferries operated by **México Waterjets** (www.mexicowaterjets.com) and **Ultramar** (www.granpuerto.com.mx) run to Cozumel from Playa del Carmen (one way M$155, hourly 6am to 9pm). See websites for schedules.

To transport a vehicle to Cozumel, go to the Calica car-ferry terminal (officially known as the Terminal Marítima Punta Venado), about 7km south of Playa del Carmen. There are four daily departures Tuesday to Saturday and two on Sunday. See www.transcaribe.net for the schedule. You'll need to line up at least one hour before departure, two hours beforehand in high season. Fares are M$500 to M$1153, depending on the size of the vehicle.

BUS

At the **ADO Ticket Office** (Map p90; ☎987-869-25-53; cnr Av 10 Norte & Calle 2 Norte; ⌚8:30am-8:30pm), you can buy tickets in advance for buses departing from Playa del Carmen to all over the Yucatán.

Getting Around

TO/FROM THE AIRPORT

The airport is about 3km northeast of the ferrry terminal. Frequent, shared shuttle vans run from the airport into town (M$57), to hotels on the island's north end (M$96) and to the south side (M$97 to M$140). To return to the airport in a taxi, expect to pay M$85 from town.

CAR

A car is the best way to get to the island's farther reaches, and you'll get plenty of offers to rent one. All rental contracts should automatically include liability insurance *(daños a terceros)*. Check that taxes are included in the price you're quoted: they often are not. Collision insurance is usually about M$150 extra, with a M$5000 deductible for the cheapest vehicles.

Rates start at around M$500 all-inclusive, though you'll pay more during late December and January. There are plenty of agencies around the main plaza, but prices are about 50% lower from the dock to the fringes of the tourist zone.

When renting, check with your hotel to see if it has an agreement with any agencies, as you can often get discounts. Some agencies will deduct tire damage (repair or replacement) from your deposit, even if tires are old and worn. Be particularly careful about this if you're renting a 4WD for use on unpaved roads; straighten out the details before you sign. And always check your car's brakes before driving off.

If you rent, observe the law on vehicle occupancy. Usually only five people are allowed in a vehicle. If you carry more, the police will fine you. You'll need to return your vehicle with the amount of gas it had when you signed it out or pay a premium. There's a gas station on Avenida Juárez, five blocks east of the main square.

Rentadora Isis (☎987-872-33-67; www.rentadoraisis.com.mx; Av 5 Norte, btwn Calles 2 Norte & 4 Norte; scooter/car per day incl liability insurance US$20/35; ⏰8am-6:30pm) is a fairly no-nonsense place with cars in good shape. Rentadora Isis' Cozumel branch rents convertible VW Beetles and scooters with little seasonal variation in prices.

SCOOTER & BICYCLE

Solo touring of the island by scooter is a blast, provided you have experience with them and with driving in Mexico. Two people on a bike is asking for trouble, though, as the machines' suspension will be barely adequate for one. Riders are injured in crashes on a regular basis, so always wear a helmet and stay alert. Collision insurance is not usually available for scooters: you break, you pay. Be sure to carefully inspect the scooter for damage before driving off or you may get hit with a repair bill.

To rent, you must have a valid driver's license and leave a credit-card slip or put down a cash deposit. There is a helmet law, and it is enforced.

Rentadora Isis is a good rental place; Shark Rider (p90) rents bikes as well.

TAXI

As in some other towns on the Yucatán Peninsula, the taxi syndicate on Cozumel wields a good bit of power. Fares are around M$35 (in town), M$80 (to the Zona Hotelera) and M$1000 for a day trip around the island. Fares are posted just outside the ferry terminal.

Riviera Maya

Includes ➡

Best Places to Eat

- ➡ Posada Margherita (p118)
- ➡ Taquería Honorio (p118)
- ➡ Al Chimichurri (p102)
- ➡ Los Aguachiles (p107)

Best Beaches

- ➡ Punta Allen (p124)
- ➡ Puerto Morelos (p99)
- ➡ Tulum (p113)
- ➡ Xcacel (p111)
- ➡ Playa del Carmen (p103)

Why Go?

The Riviera Maya, a tourist corridor of white-sand beaches, scenic ruins and fun-filled cenotes (limestone sinkholes), was made for road-tripping. Yes, it's growing fast, too fast some will say, but despite all the development, you can still find that small fishing town or head inland to catch a glimpse of the Mexico that tourism forgot.

If it's partying you want, you'll find serious hedonism in boomtown Playa del Carmen. Playa still trumps fast-growing Tulum as the Riviera's wildest city, but it's got nothing on Tulum's spectacular Maya ruins perched high above the beach.

Whether traveling by car or bus, getting from one town to the next is a breeze – after all, the Riviera is basically 135km of coastline that stretches south from Puerto Morelos to Tulum. Everything's so close that you can go diving in Puerto Morelos by day and still have time for a candlelit dinner in Tulum.

When to Go

- ➡ The Riviera Maya Film Festival in April screens local and international films on the beaches of Playa del Carmen; several weeks thereafter the fest tours to nearby Tulum, Puerto Morelos, Isla Mujeres and Cancún.
- ➡ Playa del Carmen hosts a wild Halloween street bash, then you can stick around for colorful Day of the Dead festivities in and around the Riviera Maya.
- ➡ The Riviera Maya Jazz Festival in Playa del Carmen features beachside performances from Mexico and abroad. The annual event is usually held in November, so good hotel deals can be found

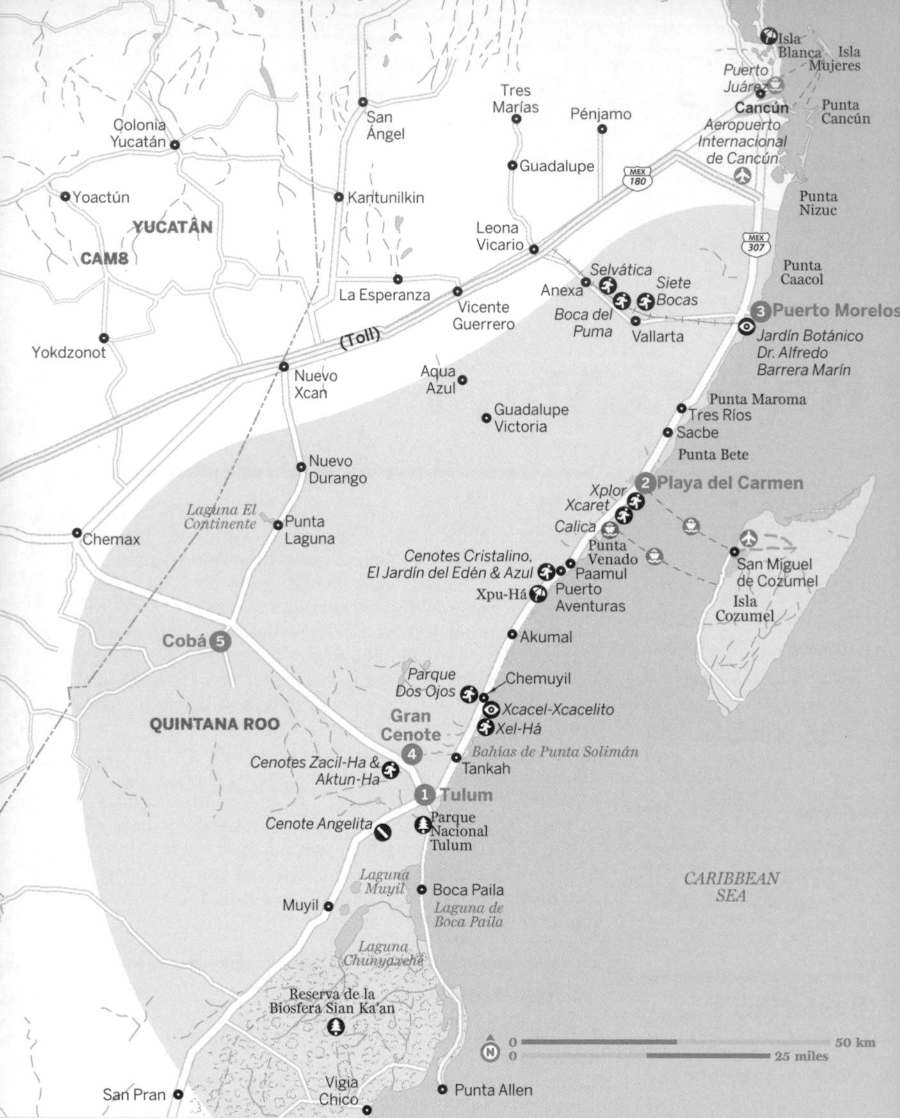

Riviera Maya Highlights

1 Marvel at **Maya ruins** (p114) dramatically situated on a rugged cliff in Tulum, then go for a swim down below.

2 Hang out at chic sidewalk restaurants and beachside bars in **Playa del Carmen** (p103), or if you're feeling inspired, take a Spanish course.

3 Dive into the waters of **Puerto Morelos** (p99) and explore a colorful barrier reef.

4 Splash around or do some serious diving at impressive **cenotes** (p120) in Tulum's surrounding areas.

5 Rent a bike at **Cobá** (p121) and follow trails that lead to amazing Maya ruins, then go for a dip in nearby swimming holes.

Puerto Morelos

998 / POP 9200

Halfway between Cancún and Playa del Carmen, Puerto Morelos retains its quiet, small-town feel despite the building boom north and south of town. While it offers enough restaurants and bars to keep you entertained by night, it's really the shallow Caribbean waters that draw visitors here. Brilliantly contrasted stripes of bright green and dark blue separate the shore from the barrier reef – a tantalizing sight for divers and snorkelers – while inland a series of excellent cenotes beckon the adventurous. There's a nice market just a few minutes' walk from the plaza with a good selection of crafts and hammocks.

Sights

Jardín Botánico Dr Alfredo Barrera Marín GARDENS
(Jardín Botánico Yaax Che; 998-206-92-33; Hwy 307 Km 320; adult/child 3-10yr M$120/50; 8am-4pm Mon-Sat;) One of the largest botanical gardens in Mexico, this 65-hectare reserve has about 2km of trails and sections dedicated to epiphytes (orchids and bromeliads), palms, ferns, succulents (cacti and their relatives) and plants used in traditional Maya medicine. The garden also holds a large animal population, including the only coastal troops of spider monkeys left in the region.

It's 1.3km south of the Puerto Morelos turnoff.

Activities

The barrier reef that runs along most of the coast of Quintana Roo is only 600m offshore here, providing both divers and snorkelers with views of sea turtles, sharks, stingrays, moray eels, lobsters and loads of colorful tropical fish. Several sunken ships make great wreck diving, and the dive centers have cenote trips as well.

Wet Set DIVING
(998-206-92-04; www.wetset.com; Hotel Ojo de Agua, Av Rojo Gómez s/n; 2-tank dive incl equipment US$99, snorkeling US$35-69; 8am-4pm) Operates trips to more than 30 dive sites, including nearby reefs, an underwater sculpture museum and Parque Dos Ojos. Also has snorkeling outings to reefs and cenotes.

Aquanauts DIVING
(998-206-93-65; www.aquanautsdiveadventures.com; Hotel Hacienda Morelos, Av Melgar s/n; 1-/2-tank reef dives US$70/90, snorkeling US$30; office 8am-4pm Mon-Sat) Runs many interesting tours, including drift diving, cenote and shipwreck dives, and lionfish hunting. The dive shop is one block south of the plaza, in Hotel Hacienda Morelos.

Boca del Puma SWIMMING
(cell 998-2412855; www.bocadelpuma.com; Ruta de los Cenotes Km 16; cenote admission adult/child 5-14yr US$12/7; 9am-5pm;) For chilling cenote action, check out the ecopark Boca del Puma, 16km west of Puerto Morelos. Other activities available include zip-lining, horseback riding and ATVs.

SEAWEED SURGE

By the time you're reading this we certainly hope that you'll no longer be seeing (and smelling) mounds of brown seaweed piling up on the white sands of the Yucatán's Caribbean shore.

At last visit, a massive influx of free-floating algae known as sargassum seaweed, which gets its name from the Sargasso Sea in the Atlantic Ocean, was washing up like never before on beaches from Cancún in the north all the way down to the Costa Maya in the south.

No one knows for sure how long the blooms will last, and the exact cause of the historic increase has elicited much debate. Some experts blame climate change and shifting ocean currents, others believe that nutrient-rich pollutants that are spilled into the ocean over time are acting as fertilizers for the seaweed.

The government has invested millions of dollars in clean-up efforts and many hotels are raking their sands daily, but it's a Herculean task and a tricky one at that, as many beaches are turtle nesting grounds.

If the seaweed invasion continues, keep in mind that sea algae plays a crucial role in marine ecosystems and also remember that the surge is not your hotel's fault.

Siete Bocas SWIMMING
(998-208-91-99; Ruta de los Cenotes Km 15; admission incl life jacket M$350; 7:30am-6:30pm;) Seldom-visited Siete Bocas, 15km west of Puerto Morelos, has seven 'mouths' (openings) in a jungle setting.

La Bici Roja BICYCLE RENTAL
(Av Niños Héroes s/n; per day incl helmet & lock M$130; 9am-2pm & 4-7pm Wed-Mon) Rent a mountain bike, beach cruiser or tandem bike here and pedal to the less touristy side of town across the highway. It's one block west and two blocks north of the plaza. Bring ID.

Courses

Little Mexican Cooking School COOKING COURSE
(998-251-80-60; www.thelittlemexicancookingschool.com; Av Rojo Gómez 768, cnr Lázaro Cárdenas; per class US$128; 10am-3:30pm Tue-Fri) Ever wonder how to cook delicious regional Mexican cuisine? Here's your chance. During this six-hour course you'll learn all about ingredients used in Mexican cooking and how to prepare at least seven dishes. See website to book a class.

Puerto Morelos Language Center LANGUAGE COURSE
(998-871-01-62; www.puertomorelosspanishcenter.com; Niños Héroes 46; classes per hour/week US$25/200, homestay per day US$45-60) In addition to hourly and weekly classes of 20 hours, the language center also offers an immersion program with the option of living with a Mexican host family. The school doubles as a travel agency if you're looking to hook up tours and activities.

Sleeping

Hotels can be surprisingly full even at non-peak times, so call or book ahead if at all possible.

Hotel Sevilla HOTEL $
(998-206-90-81; pm.h.sevilla@gmail.com; Av Niños Héroes 29; d from M$500;) The Spanish-run Sevilla is really nothing special but it's one of the only budget options in town during high season. The best bet are the rooftop rooms, which get good natural light and afford partial views of Puerto Morelos.

★ **Posada El Moro** HOTEL $$
(998-206-90-05; www.posadaelmoro.com; Av Rojo Gómez s/n; r incl breakfast US$69-79, ste US$105-117;) A well-run property, with cheery geraniums in the halls and courtyard. Some rooms have kitchenettes, all have couches that fold out into futons, and there's a small pool in a tropical garden. Prices drop substantially in low season. It's northwest of the plaza.

Hotel Ojo de Agua HOTEL $$
(998-871-02-02; www.hotelojodeagua.com; Av Rojo Gómez s/n; r M$900-1100, ste M$1500;) Offers 36 rooms on a nice stretch of beach. You can get a fairly basic 'standard' room, but it's well worth a few hundred pesos more for one with an ocean view. The 'studio' suite, which sleeps five, is good value for families. You'll find the hotel about three blocks north of the plaza.

Posada Amor HOTEL $$
(998-871-00-33; www.posada-amor.wix.com/puertom; Av Rojo Gómez s/n; s/d M$600/750;) About 100m southwest of the plaza, Posada Amor has been in operation for many years. The simple white-walled rooms have some creative touches. There's a shady back area with tables and plenty of plants, the restaurant offers good meals, and there's a friendly expat bar.

Casitas Kinsol GUESTHOUSE $$
(998-206-91-52; www.casitas-kinsol.com; Av Zetina Gazca Lote 18; r from US$49;) Great for people who want to see what life's like on the other side of town (yes, there are signs of life west of the highway!). Kinsol offers eight *palapa*-style huts with beautiful design details such as Talavera tile sinks and handcrafted furnishings. It's a peaceful spot where even the dogs and cats get along. It's 3km west of town.

Abbey del Sol APARTMENT $$$
(998-871-01-27, cell 998-1152244; www.abbeydelsol.com; Av Niñoes Héroes s/n; apt from US$142;) No need to hole up in a stuffy hotel room when you have this spacious option eight blocks north of the plaza. Studio and one-bedroom apartments with full kitchens overlook a well-manicured garden and pool area. Some units come with sleeper sofas to accommodate small families and groups. Other perks: free bikes and a DVD library.

Casa Caribe B&B $$$
(998-251-80-60; www.casacaribepuertomorelos.com; Av Rojo Goméz 768; r incl breakfast M$1610;) Just follow your nose to Casa Caribe, an elegantly decorated B&B that shares its

RIVIERA THEME PARKS

Always a big hit with children, there are several theme parks between Cancún and Tulum, many of which have fantastic scenery – truly some of the most beautiful lagoons, cenotes and natural areas on the coast. Sure, some will find these places too cheesy, but the kids couldn't care less.

It's worth mentioning that some parks offer an optional swim with dolphins activity, and though it may seem like a lovely idea, animal welfare groups suggest interaction with dolphins and other sea mammals held in captivity creates stress for these creatures.

Here are some of the most popular parks.

Aktun Chen (toll-free 800-099-07-58; www.aktun-chen.com; Hwy 307 Km 107; full tour incl lunch adult/child US$110/88; 9:30am-5:30pm Mon-Sat;) Forty kilometers south of Playa del Carmen, this small park features a 585m-long cave, a 12m-deep cenote, 10 zip lines and a small zoo.

Xplor (984-803 44-03; www.xplor.travel; all-inclusive adult/child 5-11yr M$1904/952; 9am-5pm;) This large park 6km south of Playa del Carmen features circuits that take you zip-lining, rafting, driving amphibious jeeps, swimming in an underground river and hiking through caverns.

Xel-Há (984-803-44-03, toll-free 855-326-26-96; www.xelha.com; Hwy Chetumal-Puerto Juárez Km 240; adult/child 5-11yr from M$1424/712; 9am-6pm;) Billing itself as a natural outdoor aquarium, it's built around an inlet 13km north of Tulum. There are lots of water-based activities on offer, including a river tour and snorkeling.

Xcaret (984-206-00-38; www.xcaret.com; Hwy Chetumal-Puerto Juárez Km 282; adult/child 5-12yr from M$1584/792; 9am-9pm;) One of the originals in the area, with loads of nature-based activities and stuff for grown-ups like a Mexican wine cellar and day spa. It's 6km south of Playa del Carmen.

Selvática (998-847-45-81; www.selvatica.com.mx; Ruta de los Cenotes Km 19; canopy tour incl hotel pick-up adult/child 3-11yr US$99/49; tour times 9am, 10:30am, noon & 1:30pm;) Inland from Puerto Morelos, this adventure outfit only runs prearranged tours. Come for adrenaline-pumping zip-lining, swimming in a cenote and more. Check the website for age restrictions for each tour.

lovely grounds with the Little Mexican Cooking School. Rooms have sweeping beach views from private balconies, and though only one comes with air-con, all five get fantastic sea breezes. Breakfast is a creation of the culinary school, so you know it will be good. There's a three-night minimum stay.

Hacienda Morelos HOTEL $$$
(998-871-04-48, toll-free 800-972-02-10; www.haciendamorelos.com; Av Melgar s/n; d from M$1500;) With a fantastic location right on the beach and a short walk from the plaza, the large, rather plain rooms here are a good bet and the on-site dive shop is among the best in town. Ground-level rooms have a pool and beach at the doorstep.

Eating

Le Café d'Amancia CAFE $
(Av Rojo Gómez s/n; sandwiches & bagels M$35-85; 7am-2pm & 5-10pm Tue-Sun;) Right on the plaza, this is a spotlessly clean place with pleasing ambience. It serves bagels, sandwiches, pies, good strong coffee, and fruit and veggie *licuados* (milkshakes).

El Nicho BREAKFAST $$
(www.elnicho.com.mx; cnr Avs Tulum & Rojo Gómez; breakfast M$55-105, lunch M$75-150; 7am-2pm Fri-Wed;) Puerto Morelos' best and most popular breakfast spot, El Nicho serves organic egg dishes, eggs Benedict, *chilaquiles* (fried tortilla strips in salsa) with chicken, and organic coffee from Chiapas. Vegetarians will find many good options here.

El Merkadito SEAFOOD $$
(www.elmerkadito.mx; Av Melgar s/n, north of the lighthouse; snacks M$48-58, mains M$115-190; noon-9pm;) You gotta love a place that serves tortilla chips in a '*Hecho en Mexico*' (Made in Mexico) paper bag, even more so when you're sitting in a delightful beachside *palapa* restaurant. The shrimp *aguachile*

THOSE MYSTERIOUS ALUXES

Aluxes (a-loosh-es) are Yucatecan forest sprites, and many of the Maya still believe they can bring good or bad luck, even death, to those around them. Therefore, when forests are cleared, whether to make a field or build a house, offerings of food, alcohol and even cigarettes are made to placate them.

ceviche is excellent, as are the green mussels in white-wine broth. Top it off with a refreshing ice cream served in a hollowed-out orange peel.

El Pirata MEXICAN **$$**
(Av Rojo Gómez s/n, north of the plaza; breakfast M$80-85, lunch & dinner M$110-250; ⏲7am-11pm Thu-Tue;) Known for its varied menu and casual atmosphere, this place does everything from tacos and classic Mexican dishes to gringo comfort food such as burgers.

★ **Al Chimichurri** STEAK **$$$**
(☎998-252-46-66; Av Rojo Gómez s/n; mains M$115-320; ⏲5-11pm Tue-Sun;) You definitely can't go wrong with the fresh pasta and wood-fired pizza here, but this Uruguayan grill is best known for its steaks. The star cuts are a *Flintstones*-size rib eye, tender flank steak and filet mignon in homemade beef gravy. It's just south of the plaza.

John Gray's Kitchen INTERNATIONAL **$$$**
(☎998-871-06-65; Av Niños Héroes 6; breakfast M$65-100, dinner M$200-355; ⏲8am-3pm Wed-Sat & 5-10pm Mon-Sat;) One block west and two blocks north of the plaza, this 'kitchen' turns out some truly fabulous food. The chef's specialty, though not listed on the regularly changing menu, is the duck in chipotle, tequila and honey sauce. John Gray's opens for breakfast, too.

Drinking & Entertainment

Puerto Morelos' nightlife scene is pretty chill. If you can't stand the quiet, you can always hop in a taxi or bus for some raunchy fun in nearby Playa del Carmen.

Bara Bara BAR
(Av Rojo Gómez s/n; ⏲8pm-4am Tue-Sun) The party usually spills out onto the street at this popular bar just south of the plaza. Bara Bara spins the best tunes in town, prepares martinis that would have made Sinatra proud and has a foosball table!

Que Hora Es DANCING
(Av Rojo Gómez s/n; ⏲11am-1:30am) Posada Amor has a happening bar where you can practice salsa steps with a live band on Friday. If tropical sounds don't get you excited, a rock group plays on Saturday night. This is one of the few places that stays open relatively late. It located southwest of the plaza.

Shopping

One of the best reasons to come to Puerto Morelos is to hit the artisans market, one block south of the plaza.

Artisans Market ARTS & CRAFTS
(Av Rojo Gómez s/n; ⏲9am-6pm) Find high-quality hammocks, *alebrijes* (colorful, hand-carved wooden animals), handbags, masks, jewelry and more. It's refreshingly low-key and you can often see the craftspeople at work.

Alma Libre Books & Gifts BOOKS, CRAFTS
(www.almalibrebooks.com; Av Tulum; ⏲10am-6pm mid-Nov–late Apr) Has more than 20,000 new and used books. The friendly owners are a great resource for information about the area, as is the website, which has vacation rental listings and a monthly newsletter. The store also carries art from the Yucatán, gift items and local gourmet food products.

Information

Puerto Morelos' central plaza is 2km east of Hwy 307 nearly at the end of the main road into town (the main dock is the true end of the road). The town, all of three streets wide from east to west, stretches several blocks to the north of the plaza and about three long blocks south.

Locals refer to the neighborhood west of the highway as 'la colonia,' where you'll find more affordable eateries and several lodging options. You can catch a *colectivo* to *la colonia* from the plaza.

An ATM is on the northeast corner of the plaza.

Getting There & Away

Playa Express and ADO buses that travel between Cancún and Playa del Carmen drop you on the highway. Buses and Playa Express vans from Cancún's ADO terminal cost M$22 to M$24. If you're arriving at the Cancún airport, there are frequent bus departures from there to Puerto Morelos for M$90.

Taxis are usually waiting at the turnoff to shuttle people into town; cabs parked at the plaza will take you back to the highway. Some drivers will tell you the fare is per person or overcharge in some other manner; strive for M$25 for the 2km ride, for as many people as you can stuff in.

Punta Bete

A rocky, reef-hugged point 65km south of Cancún, Punta Bete is reached by a dirt road that runs past a large new housing development and weaves 2.5km from Hwy 307 (turn at the sign for Xcalacoco) before reaching the sea. North and south of the point there are beautiful and occasionally wide stretches of beach upon which sit a few low-profile hotels and restaurants. The hotels and restaurants are within walking distance of each other, but you're best off getting here by car or taxi.

Sleeping

Coco's Cabanas BUNGALOW **$$$**
(cell 994-1337598; www.cocoscabanas.com; r/ste from US$107/167;) Offers six nicely decorated *cabañas* with good beds, hammocks, iPod docks and TVs with DVD players. It's a short walk from the beach and has a bar, a small pool, a pleasant garden and a restaurant.

Playa del Carmen

984 / POP 150,000

Playa del Carmen, now the third largest city in Quintana Roo, ranks up there with Tulum as the Riviera's trendiest cities. Sitting coolly on the lee side of Cozumel, the town's beaches are jammed with super-fit Europeans. The waters aren't as clear as those of Cancún or Cozumel, and the beach sands aren't quite as champagne-powder-perfect as they are further north, but still Playa (as it's locally known) grows and grows.

Strolling down Playa del Carmen's pedestrian corridor, Quinta Avenida (*keen*-ta; 5 Avenida), is a fabulous game of see-and-be-seen.

The town is ideally located: close to Cancún's international airport, but far enough south to allow easy access to Cozumel, Tulum, Cobá and other worthy destinations. The reefs here are excellent, and offer diving and snorkeling close by. Look for rays, moray eels, sea turtles and a huge variety of corals. The lavender sea fans make for very picturesque vistas.

With daily cruise-ship visitors, Playa's tourist center now feels like a mass-tourism destination, but it manages to retain its European chic, and one need just head several blocks west of the main strip to catch glimpses of the nontouristic side of things.

Beaches

Avid beachgoers won't be disappointed here. Playa's lovely white-sand beaches are much more accessible than Cancún's: just head down to the ocean, stretch out and enjoy. Numerous restaurants front the beach in the tourist zone and many hotels in the area offer an array of water-sport activities.

If crowds aren't your thing, go north of Calle 38, where a few scrawny palms serve for shade. Here the beach extends for uncrowded kilometers, making for good camping, but you need to be extra careful with your belongings, as thefts are a possibility.

Some women go topless in Playa (though it's not a common practice in most of Mexico, and is generally frowned upon by locals – except the young bucks, of course). **Mamita's Beach**, north of Calle 28, is considered the best place to let loose.

About 3km south of the ferry terminal, past a group of all-inclusives, you'll find a refreshingly quiet stretch of beach that sees relatively few visitors.

Activities

In addition to great ocean diving, many outfits offer cenote dives. Prices are similar at most shops: two-tank dives (M$1700), cenote dives (M$2500), snorkeling (M$750), whale-shark tour (M$2700) and open-water certification (M$7200).

Playa used to be a fishing village, and you can still go out on small skiffs in search of kingfish, tarpon, barracuda and maybe even a sailfish. April to July is the best time.

A bike outing is a great way to discover outlying neighborhoods or visit a nearby cenote.

Scuba Playa DIVING
(984-803-31-23; www.scubaplaya.com; Calle 10 s/n; 7:30am-9pm) A PADI five-star instructor development dive resort, with technical diving courses available.

Phocea Mexico DIVING
(984-873-12-10; www.phocea-mexico.com; Calle 10 s/n; 8am-6pm) French, English and Spanish are spoken at Phocea Mexico. The shop does dives with bull sharks from November to March.

Playa del Carmen

0 200 m
0 0.1 miles

Loncheria Doña Mary (600m); Los Aguachiles (700m)

La Fé (400m); El Diez (500m); La Bodeguita del Medio (600m); La Semilla (850m); Tierra Huichol (900m); La Cueva del Chango (1km);

Calle 16 Bis
Calle 14 Bis
Calle 14
Calle 12 Bis
Calle 12
Calle 10 Bis
Calle 10
Calle 8
Calle 6 Norte Bis
Calle 6
Calle 4
Calle 2
Av Juárez
Calle 1 Sur
25 Av
20 Av
15 Av
10 Av
Quinta Av (5 Av)
1 Av
1 Av Bis

Terminal ADO
Parque 28 de Julio
Playa Express
Parque Turístico Leona Vicario
Terminal del Centro
Plaza Mayor
CARIBBEAN SEA
Cozumel Ferry Ticket Booths

To Gas Station (400m); Hwy 307 (450m); Cozumel (10km)

Ferries to Cozumel (19km)

1 2 3 4 5 6 7 8 9 10 11 12 13 14 15 16 17 18 19 20 21 22 23 24 25 26 27

Playa del Carmen

Activities, Courses & Tours
1 Arrendadora Turística Noa B4
2 Fisherman's Cooperative D1
3 International House C1
4 Phocea Mexico D2
5 Scuba Playa C3
6 Yucatek Divers B5

Sleeping
7 Casa de las Flores A4
8 Hostel Playa A3
9 Hostel Quinta Playa D5
10 Hostel Río Playa C3
11 Hotel Barrio Latino B5
12 Hotel Casa Tucán B5
13 Hotel Playa del Karma B1
14 Kinbé Hotel C3
15 Playa Palms D2
16 Sahara Hotel B3

Eating
17 100% Natural C2
18 Babe's C3
19 Club Náutico Tarraya D5
20 Don Sirloin B2
21 Kaxapa Factory B3
22 La Famiglia B2
23 Market B4
24 Mercado Nuestra Señora del Carmen C3

Drinking & Nightlife
25 Blue Parrot Club D2
26 Playa 69 ..... C4

Entertainment
27 Fusion D4

Yucatek Divers DIVING
(984-803-28-36; www.yucatek-divers.com; 15 Av s/n; 8am-5pm) Yucatek Divers has pretty good deals that include diving and lodging at the nearby Paraiso Azul hotel.

Fisherman's Cooperative FISHING
(cell 984-8795161, cell 984-1276230; coopturmarcaribe@hotmail.com; Calle 16 bis s/n; up to 4 people US$200) Support the locals and head to the fisherman's cooperative at this beachfront kiosk. They do four-hour fishing or snorkeling trips, or you can combine both activities.

Arrendadora Turística Noa BICYCLE RENTAL
(984-803-34-94; 10 Av s/n; per day M$150, cenote tour M$650; 8am-7pm Mon-Sat) Rent bikes here to explore the city on your own, or go on a three-hour tour to the Chaak Tun cenote, about 6.5km west of town.

Courses

Playa has a couple of good language schools and you'll find plenty of folks to practice Spanish with, especially if you venture out beyond the tourist center.

International House LANGUAGE COURSE
(984-803-33-88; www.ihrivieramaya.com; Calle 14 No 141; per week US$230, r US$36, homestay incl breakfast US$33) Offers 20 hours of Spanish class per week. You can stay in residence-hall rooms (even if you're not taking classes), but the best way to learn a language is to take advantage of the school's homestays with Mexican host families.

Playalingua del Caribe LANGUAGE COURSE
(984-873-38-76; www.playalingua.com; Calle 20 s/n; 1 week without/with homestay US$245/455, hourly class US$23) Offers 20-hour-per-week classes as well as homestays. It also has optional classes in Maya language, Mexican cooking and salsa dancing.

Tours

Alltournative ADVENTURE TOUR
(984-803-99-99; www.alltournative.com; Hwy 307 Km 287) Alltournative's packages include zip lining, rappelling and kayaking, often combined with visits to archaeological sites. It also takes you to nearby Maya villages for an 'authentic' experience that could easily be had on your own. The office is out of the way; you're better off calling or reserving online.

Sleeping

Affordable midrange hotels can be found within several blocks of the beach, and a number of hostels offer dorm-style lodging and private rooms. Regular high season runs from January to April, while prices spike by as much as M$1000 for the 'super high season' around Christmas.

Hostel Playa HOSTEL $
(984-803-32 77; www.hostelplaya.com.mx; Calle 8 s/n; dm/d/tr incl breakfast M$200/490/735; P) This place was made for mingling with its central common area, a cool garden spot and a rooftop terrace. The private rooms are simple but decent enough, and

WORTH A TRIP

CRISTALINO CENOTE

On the west side of the highway, 23km south of Playa del Carmen, is a series of wonderful cenotes. Among these is **Cristalino Cenote** (Hwy 307 s/n; adult/child 3-10yr M$100/60; ⏲8am-6pm) , just south of the Barceló Maya Resort. It's easily accessible, only about 70m from the entrance gate, which is just off the highway. Two more sinkholes, **Azul** and **El Jardín del Edén**, sit just south of Cristalino along the highway. But Cristalino is the best of the three, as you can dive there (or just launch yourself off the rocks into the water below).

the staff is extremely helpful and has great suggestions on what to see and do.

Hostel Río Playa HOSTEL **$**
(☎984-803-01-45; hostelrios@gmail.com; Calle 8 s/n; incl breakfast dm M$220-270, r without bathroom M$500-600;) A good budget buy, the Río offers easy beach access, a women's-only dorm, two large dorms sleeping 14 and several six-person dorms. It also has a shared kitchen, a nice rooftop bar and hangout area – with a remarkably shallow pool – and air-con in all the rooms. Did we mention it's close to the beach?

Hostel Quinta Playa HOSTEL **$**
(☎984-147-04-28; www.quintaplaya.com; Calle 2, btwn Quinta Av & beach; dm with/without air-con M$200/180;) It's all about the location here. Just 30m from the beach, one block from the bus station and two blocks from the ferry terminal. The hostel runs a simple operation: six rooms each with six clean beds, a small pool and a full kitchen for guests. The lobby bar is the domain of Elvis, a Yucatán parrot.

★ **Hotel Playa del Karma** BOUTIQUE HOTEL **$$**
(☎984-803-02-72; www.hotelplayadelkarma.com; 15 Av, btwn Calles 12 & 14; r from M$1084;) The closest you're going to get to the jungle in this town; rooms here face a lush courtyard with a small pool. All rooms have air-con and TV, and some come with kitchenette, sitting area and sweet little porches with hammocks. The hotel arranges tours to nearby ruins and diving sites.

Hotel Barrio Latino HOTEL **$$**
(☎984-873-23-84; www.hotelbarriolatino.com; Calle 4 s/n; r incl breakfast M$1200;) Offers 18 clean, colorful rooms with good ventilation, ceiling fans or air-con, tiled floors, bathrooms and hammocks (in addition to beds). The place is often full and the front gate often locked. Discounted rates are available for extended stays, and the prices drop precipitously in low season. Guests get to make free international calls.

Hotel Casa Tucán HOTEL **$$**
(☎984-873-02-83; www.casatucan.de; Calle 4 s/n; r with fan/air-con US$60/80, ste US$100;) This German-run hotel is a warren of 30 rooms of several types. Rooms have fans or air-con, a couple have kitchenettes, and some come with a minibar. The Casa has a pleasant tropical garden (that draws in a lot of mosquitoes) and a cafe serving good, affordable food.

Sahara Hotel HOTEL **$$**
(☎984-873-22-36; www.tucasaenplaya.com/en; 15 Av s/n; r/ste incl breakfast M$950/1500;) An Italian-owned establishment with 25 comfortable rooms (most with balconies), the Sahara is centrally located across from a park and it's one of the rare hotels near the tourist center with a parking lot. The wi-fi is often spotty and the hotel could probably do without piping pop music through the lobby.

Kinbé Hotel HOTEL **$$$**
(☎984-873-04-41; www.kinbe.com; Calle 10 s/n; r incl breakfast M$2500;) An Italian owned and operated hotel, it has 29 clean, simple but elegant rooms with lovely aesthetic touches and a breezy rooftop terrace with fab views from the 3rd floor. Choose a room in the soothing 'water' section, which has an indoor pool and waterfall, or opt for the 'land' side and surround yourself with lush vegetation.

La Semilla B&B **$$$**
(☎984-147-32-34; www.hotellasemilla.com; Calle 38 Norte s/n; r incl breakfast from US$238;) Smallish rustic-chic rooms here are attractively adorned with vintage objects purchased from flea markets and haciendas. At night guests mingle in a lush candlelit garden over complimentary wine or beer, and upstairs breakfast is served in an open-air loft space decorated with antique furniture.

Playa Palms BOUTIQUE HOTEL $$$
(984-803-39-08, toll-free USA 888-676-4431; www.playapalms.com; 1 Av Bis s/n; incl breakfast r US$170-265, ste US$225;) A rip-roaring deal in low season (get the best price online), Playa Palms is right on the beach. The shell-shaped rooms have balconies that look out to the ocean past the curly-whirly pool, or you can opt for the cheaper garden-view studio. Continental breakfast is delivered to your room.

Casa de las Flores HOTEL $$$
(984-873-28-98; www.hotelcasadelasflores.com; 20 Av No 150, btwn Calles 4 & 6; r from M$1425;) With a good mix of colonial charm and modern comfort, this sizable but intimate family-run hotel offers cheerful, colorful rooms set around a delightful plant-filled patio.

Eating

For cheap eats, head away from the tourist center, or try the small **market** (Av 10 s/n, btwn Calles 6 & 8; mains M$30-70; 7:30am-11pm) for some homestyle regional cooking.

Lonchería Doña Mary YUCATECAN $
(Calle 28 s/n, cnr 30 Av; snacks M$10-35, soups M$30-50; 6pm-1:30am;) You'll probably have to wait for a table at this popular eatery and service can be slow. But it's worth the wait when you try Mary's Yucatecan comfort food. All dishes are prepared with chicken: tamales, *panuchos* (fried tortilla with refried beans and toppings), *salbutes* (same as *panuchos* sans beans) and a hearty chicken soup, just like Ma used to make.

Kaxapa Factory SOUTH AMERICAN $
(www.kaxapafactory.com; Calle 10 s/n; mains M$50-90; 10am-10pm Tue-Sun;) The specialty at this Venezuelan restaurant on the park is *arepa*, a delicious corn flatbread stuffed with your choice of shredded beef, chicken or beans and plantains. There are many vegetarian and gluten free options here and the refreshing fresh-made juices go nicely with just about everything on the menu.

Don Sirloin MEXICAN $
(www.donsirloin.com; 10 Av s/n; tacos M$12-21; 2pm-6am;) *Al pastor* (marinated pork) and sirloin beef are sliced right off the spit at this popular late-night taco joint, which now has three branches in Playa.

Los Aguachiles SEAFOOD $$
(Calle 34 s/n, btwn Avs 25 & 30; tostadas M$39-43, mains M$99-160; noon-7:30pm;) Done up in Mexican cantina style yet with one big difference: the menu – consisting of tacos, *tostadas* and the like – was designed by a chef. So yeah, good luck finding artfully prepared tuna *tostadas* in any of the neighborhood watering holes.

La Cueva del Chango MEXICAN $$
(www.lacuevadelchango.com; Calle 38 s/n, btwn Quinta Av & beach; breakfast M$76-90, lunch & dinner M$136-172; 8am-11pm Mon-Sat, to 2pm Sun;) You're in for a real treat when you visit the 'Monkey's Cave,' a Mexican restaurant known for its fresh and natural ingredients. Grab a table in a jungly *palapa* setting or enjoy the verdant garden out back. For breakfast, try the *chilaquiles* with *xcatic* chili; for dinner, go for the shrimp in chili *pasilla* with cacao and fried plantain.

Club Náutico Tarraya SEAFOOD $$
(Calle 2, on the beach; mains M$60-165; noon-9pm;) One of the few restaurants in Playa del Carmen that dates from the 1960s. It continues to offer good seafood at decent prices in a casual place on the beach with a nice view.

Mercado Nuestra Señora del Carmen MARKET $$
(10 Av s/n; mains M$60-150; 9am-9pm;) An upscale take on traditional market food courts, eateries here offer an array of *mercado* fare such as *chilaquiles* (fried tortilla strips in salsa), tacos and *tortas* (sandwiches) and ceviche, as well as international food.

Babe's FUSION $$
(www.babesnoodlesandbar.com; Calle 10 s/n; mains M$130-200; 1pm-midnight Tue-Sun;) Babe's serves some excellent Asian food, including a yummy homestyle *tom kha gai* (chicken and coconut-milk soup) brimming with veggies. Vietnamese shrimp and rice noodles is another good one. Most dishes can be done vegetarian, and to mix things up a bit the Swedish cook has some tasty Korean and Indian items on the menu.

100% Natural VEGETARIAN $$
(Cien Por Ciento Natural; www.100natural.com; Quinta Av s/n, cnr Calle 10; mains M$85-177; 7am-11pm;) The trademark offerings of this quickly establishing chain – vegetable- and fruit-juice blends, salads, various vegetable and chicken dishes and other healthy foods – are delicious and filling.

La Famiglia ITALIAN $$$
(www.facebook.com/lafamigliapdc; 10 Av s/n; mains M$140-250; ⌚4-11:30pm Tue-Sun;) Pay a visit to the family and enjoy superb wood-fired pizza and handmade pastas, raviolis and gnocchi. Playa is a magnet for Italian restaurants, but this definitely ranks among the best of them.

El Diez ARGENTINE $$$
(www.eldiez.com.mx; Quinta Av s/n, cnr Calle 30; pizzas M$148-171, mains M$85-210; ⌚1pm-midnight;) In a loving nod to soccer legend Diego Maradona, who wore the number *diez* (10), El Diez serves up pizzas and *parrilladas* (Argentine-style barbecues) just the way the Diego likes them. The outside seating on La Nueva Quinta makes for some great people-watching.

Drinking & Entertainment

You'll find everything from mellow, tranced-out lounge bars to thumping beachfront discos here. The party generally starts on Quinta Avenida then heads down toward the beach on Calle 12.

La Bodeguita del Medio DANCING
(www.labodeguitadelmedio.com.mx; Quinta Av s/n; ⌚1:30pm-2am;) The writing is literally on the walls, and on the lampshades, and pretty much everywhere at this Cuban restaurant-bar. After a few mojitos you'll be dancing the night away to live *cubana* music. Get here at 7:30pm for free salsa lessons.

La Fé BAR
(cnr Quinta Av & Calle 26; ⌚10am-2pm;) Caters to a young hipster crowd with its affordable *cubetazos* (bottled beer served in buckets) and DJ nights Wednesday through Sunday.

Playa 69 GAY
(www.rivieramayagay.com; alley off Quinta Av, btwn Calles 4 & 6; ⌚9pm-5am Tue-Sun) This gay dance club proudly features foreign strippers from such far-flung places as Australia and Brazil, and it stages weekend drag-queen shows.

Blue Parrot Club DANCE
(cell 984-1862515; www.facebook.com/blueparrotplaya; Calle 12 s/n; ⌚10am-5am) This is the Blue Parrot Suites' immensely popular open-sided *palapa* beachfront bar with swing chairs, a giant outdoor dance floor and lots of sand. The bar stages live music or DJs and features a nightly fire-dancing show.

★**Fusion** LIVE MUSIC
(Calle 6 s/n; ⌚7am-1am) This beachside bar and grill stages live music, belly dancing and a fire-dancing show every night. Now that's entertainment!

Shopping

Tierra Huichol CRAFTS
(984-803-59-54; www.tierrahuichol.com; 5 Av s/n, btwn Calles 38 & 40; ⌚10am-10pm) Tierra Huichol's new Playa del Carmen store sells intricate yarn art and colorful beaded animal figurines crafted by indigenous Huichol artists from the Pacific coast states of Jalisco and Nayarit. International delivery service available.

BUSES FROM PLAYA DEL CARMEN

DESTINATION	FARE (M$)	DURATION (HRS)	FREQUENCY (DAILY)
Cancún	48-60	1¼	frequent
Cancún International Airport	156	1	frequent
Chetumal	266-382	4¼-5	13
Chichén Itzá	135-282	4	7:30am (2nd-class), 8am, 2:30pm (2nd-class)
Cobá	84-120	2	11 (1st and 2nd class)
Mérida	408-450	4¼-5¾	frequent
Palenque	812-972	11½-12	3
San Cristóbal de las Casas	1010-1218	17-17½	3
Tulum	54-62	1	frequent
Valladolid	186	2¾	6

Information

DANGERS & ANNOYANCES

Playa is generally safe: you are very unlikely to experience street crime or muggings. However, pickpockets do circulate, especially in crowded dance clubs. Never leave valuables unattended on the beach. Run-and-grab thefts while victims are swimming or sleeping, especially on the isolated beaches to the north, are a common occurrence (the jungle has eyes).

EMERGENCY

Ambulance, Fire & Police (066)

MEDICAL SERVICES

Hospiten (984-803-10-02; www.hospiten.com; Hwy 307, in front of Centro Maya; 24hr) A private hospital south on Hwy 307, just past Sam's Club.

Playa International Clinic (984-873-13-65; 10 Av s/n, cnr Calle 28; 24hr) Excellent medical clinic with on-site hyberbaric chamber.

MONEY

There are many ATMs around town.

Banamex (cnr Calle 12 & 10 Av)

Bancomer (Av Juárez s/n, cnr 25 Av)

Scotiabank (Quinta Av s/n, cnr Av Juárez)

POST

Post Office (cnr 20 Av & Calle 2; 9am-4pm Mon-Fri, to noon Sat)

Getting There & Around

BOAT

Ferries depart frequently to Cozumel from Calle 1 Sur, where you'll find three companies with **ticket booths.** Barcos Caribe is the cheapest of the bunch. Prices are subject to change. Transcaribe, south of Playa, runs car ferries to Cozumel.

Barcos Caribe (www.barcoscaribe.com; one-way fare adult/child 5-12yr M$135/70)

Mexico Waterjets (www.mexicowaterjets.com; one-way fare adult/child 6-11yr M$162/96)

Ultramar (www.granpuerto.com.mx; one-way fare adult/child 6-11yr M$163/97)

Transcaribe (www.transcaribe.net; Hwy 307 Km 282, Calica-Punta Venado; one-way fare M$500; departures 8am, 1:30pm & 6pm Mon-Sat, 6am & 6pm Sun) Runs daily ferries to Cozumel if you want to cross with your vehicle. One-way fare includes the driver's passage; each additional person costs M$68 and children under 12 years are free. The terminal is 7km south of Playa del Carmen.

BUS

Playa has two bus terminals; each sells tickets and provides information for at least some of the other's departures. You can save money by buying a 2nd-class bus ticket, but remember that it's often stop-and-go along the way. A taxi from Terminal ADO to the Plaza Mayor runs about M$25.

Playa Express shuttle buses are a much quicker way to get around the Riviera Maya, or to Cancún.

Terminal ADO (www.ado.com.mx; 20 Av s/n, cnr Calle 12) The Terminal ADO is where most 1st-class bus lines arrive and depart.

Terminal del Centro (Quinta Av s/n, cnr Av Juárez) All 2nd-class bus lines (including Mayab) are serviced at the old bus station, Terminal del Centro.

Playa Express (Calle 2 Norte) Offers quick, frequent service to Puerto Morelos for M$22 and downtown Cancún for M$34 .

COLECTIVO

Colectivos are a great option for cheap travel southward to Tulum and north to Cancún.

Colectivos to Tulum & Cancún (Calle 2, cnr 20 Av) depart from Calle 2 as soon as they fill (about every 15 minutes) from 4am to midnight. They will stop anywhere along the highway between Playa and Tulum, charging a minimum of M$20. Luggage space is somewhat limited, but they're great for day trips. From the same spot, you can grab a *colectivo* to Cancún (M$34).

Punta Venado

A nice spot for horseback riding and swimming, Punta Venado lies about 15km south of Playa del Carmen and 2km further east of the highway.

Activities

Punta Venado Eco-Park HORSEBACK RIDING

(984 870 39 98; www.puntavenadoadventures.com; Hwy 307 Km 278, Punta Venado; horseback riding per person US$90; 9am-5pm) In addition to guided horseback riding tours through mostly virgin jungle terrain, you can book excursions to a cenote and snorkeling site reached by ATVs or wave runners. In the course of the horse ride, you're likely to see a variety of birds, snakes and possibly monkeys and deer.

Paamul

Paamul, 87km south of Cancún, is a de facto private beach on a sheltered bay. Like many other spots along the Caribbean coast, it has signs prohibiting entry to nonguests, and parking is limited.

The attractions here are great diving and a sandy, palm-fringed beach, which, though lovely, has many small rocks, shells and spiked sea urchins in the shallows offshore; take appropriate measures. A large recreational vehicle (RV) park here is greatly favored by snowbirds; the 'BC' license plates you see are from British Columbia, not Baja California. An attractive alabaster sand beach lies about 2km north.

Giant sea turtles come ashore here at night in July and August to lay their eggs. If you run across one during an evening stroll along the beach, keep your distance and don't turn your flashlight on – or take flash photography – or you might scare it away.

If you come by bus, it's a 500m walk from the highway to the hotel and beach.

Activities

Scuba-Mex DIVING
(cell 984-8751066, toll-free USA 888-871-6255; www.scubamex.com; Hwy 307 Km 85; 1-tank reef dive incl gear US$45, 1-/2-tank cenote dive US$80/140) Offers trips to any of 30 superb sites, including reef and cenote dives.

Sleeping

Paamul Hotel HOTEL $$$
(984-875-10-50; www.paamul.com; Hwy 307 Km 85; ste from US$175, cabañas from US$120, campsites per person US$13; P) Choose between gorgeous, modern beachfront suites or rustic *cabañas* built on stilts. Each *cabaña* has two beds, air-con, bathroom with hot water, and a veranda. Gaps in the wooden floors provide additional ventilation. A serene atmosphere prevails in both accommodations. There are also campsites available.

Xpu-Há

Xpu-Há (shpoo-*ha*) is a beach area about 95km south of Cancún that extends for several kilometers. It's reached by numbered access roads (most of them private). They are building all-inclusive resorts here faster than you can say 'cultural degradation,' but it's still worth your trip if you are looking to get away from it all.

Sleeping

Al Cielo Hotel BOUTIQUE HOTEL $$$
(984-840-91-81; www.alcielohotel.com; Hwy 307 Km 264.6; r incl breakfast from US$516; P) Right on the beach, El Cielo stands out in this land of giant all-inclusives for its intimacy, but that intimacy comes with a hefty price tag. On offer are four smallish, upscale suites and four larger villas, a spa and an excellent on-site restaurant. Reservations are recommended for both the hotel and the restaurant.

Akumal

984 / POP 1400

Famous for its beautiful beach and large, swimmable lagoon, Akumal (Place of the Turtles) does indeed see turtles come ashore to lay their eggs from May to November, even though resort development has encroached on some of their nesting grounds. Akumal is one of the Yucatán Peninsula's oldest resort areas and consists primarily of pricey hotels, condominiums and residential developments (occupied mostly by Americans and Canadians) on nearly 5km of wide beach bordering four consecutive bays. Most sights and facilities are reached by taking the first turnoff, Playa Akumal, as you come south on the highway. It's about 500m from the highway to the entrance.

Sights & Activities

Although increasing population is taking its toll on the reefs that parallel Akumal, diving remains the area's primary attraction.

You can also simply find a place to park and snorkel or swim on your own, as the shallow waters are pretty and fun. Close to the shore you will not have problems with currents, though at times the surf can be rough.

Centro Ecológico Akumal MUSEUM
(984-875-90-95; www.facebook.com/cea.akumal; 4-week volunteer program incl lodging from US$360; P) FREE To learn more about the area's ecology, check out this center's small museum on the east side of the road at the town's entrance, where there are several exhibits on reef and turtle ecology. And for those aged over 21, it offers a four-week volunteer program focused on protection, conservation and research of female sea turtles, their nests and hatchlings.

For more information, its office is across the street in Plaza Ukana.

Laguna Yal-Kú SWIMMING
(adult/child 4-12yr M$218/155, snorkel gear M$78; 9am-5pm;) Laguna Yal-Kú is a beautiful lagoon 2km north of the Playa Akumal en-

trance. The rocky lagoon, without a doubt one of the region's highlights, runs about 500m from its beginning to the sea. It is home to large schools of brightly colored fish, and the occasional visiting turtle.

Showers, parking and bathrooms are included in the admission price, and you can rent snorkel gear. Taxis from the Playa Akumal entrance charge about M$100 to the lagoon. In an effort to protect the lagoon's fragile environment, sunblock is prohibited.

Akumal Dive Shop DIVING
(984-875-90-32; www.akumaldiveshop.com; 1-/2-tank dive M$700/1120, fishing per boat M$2520-3800, snorkeling M$300, catamaran M$630-1330; 8am-5pm) Dive trips and deep-sea fishing excursions are offered by Akumal Dive Shop, at the town entrance. It also does snorkeling trips to the reef and remote beaches, and it rents catamarans.

Sleeping & Eating

You'll find a bunch of houses for rent on www.akumalvacations.com, or you can check out one of the area's hotels, which are generally quite expensive.

Just outside the entrance to Playa Akumal are two minimarkets that stock a good selection of food.

Hotel Maria José HOTEL $
(cell 984-1194530; r M$500;) There's not much joy for budget travelers in Akumal, but across the highway in Akumal Pueblo (about a 10-minute walk or short taxi ride from the beach), this family-run place offers rather sparse but clean rooms.

★ **Que Onda** HOTEL $$$
(984-875-91-01; www.facebook.com/queondaakumal; Caleta Yalkú Lote 97; s/d/q US$90/110/150;) Relatively affordable by Akumal standards, Que Onda has quiet, pleasant rooms overlooking a lush garden with a large pool and one of the best restaurants in town. A large two-story room sleeps four people.

Villa Las Brisas HOTEL $$$
(984-874-92-63, cell 984-8762110; www.aventuras-akumal.com; 2.5km south of Akumal, off Hwy 307; r US$114, apt US$137-228;) On the beach in Aventuras Akumal, this is an attractive, modern place with two hotel-type rooms, some one- and two-bedroom condos and a studio apartment – all under two roofs. Room prices vary greatly by category and season. The friendly owners Horacio and Kersten speak five languages! The turnoff is 3km south of the turnoff for Playa Akumal.

Del Sol Beachfront HOTEL $$$
(984-875-90-60, USA toll-free 888-425-8625; www.akumalinfo.com; r/apt from US$131/202, bike rental per hr US$8;) This place looks more like Del Taco headquarters with its bright new paint job. The compact rooms come with beach-view patios or balconies, or you can opt for more spacious studios and two-bedroom condos. The hotel rents bikes as well.

Eating & Drinking

Lonchería Akumalito MEXICAN $
(sandwiches M$30-55, mains M$70-135; 7am-9pm) A good spot to pick up *tortas* (sandwiches) for a picnic on the beach. It's at the town's entrance.

Turtle Bay Café & Bakery CAFE $$
(www.turtlebaycafe.com; Plaza Ukana 1; mains M$85-165; 7am-9pm;) A popular breakfast spot, this appealing cafe slings a wide variety of gringo comfort food ranging from breakfast burritos to eggs Benedict. The lunch and dinner menu include sourdough flat-bread pizzas, burgers and tasty fish and seafood options, such as blackened grouper tacos. It's near the town entrance.

La Cueva del Pescador SEAFOOD $$
(mains M$80-170; noon-9pm;) Near the town's entrance, this popular foreigners hangout does good grilled fish dishes and shrimp tacos in a casual atmosphere with outdoor seating and a pool table inside.

La Buena Vida BAR
(www.labuenavidarestaurant.com; coast road Lote 35; 11am-11pm;) A popular beachside restaurant-bar with sand floors, roaming musicians, swings and a drink menu with gimmicky cocktail names such as 'The Viagra,' which offers you 'a stiff one.' The **restaurant** (mains M$100 to M$240) is very good here.

Xcacel-Xcacelito

At Km 112 on the Cancún–Tulum Hwy (between the Chemuyil and Xel-Há exits) is a tiny sign on the east side of the highway marking the short dirt road that leads to the two arching bays Xcacel and Xcacelito. Also here you'll find a cenote, good snorkeling and, most notably, Quintana Roo's most important loggerhead and white sea turtle nesting site.

About 500m south of the parking area, there's a lovely cenote, while the northern edge of the beach has a protected coastal reef perfect for snorkeling.

There's no food or lodging on this protected beach and it's open to the public from 9am to 5pm (the guard booth accepts donations on a voluntary basis for beach upkeep).

Tours

Turtle-Watching Tour ECOTOUR
(☎984-871-52-44; www.florafaunaycultura.org; turtle observation tour US$25, volunteer program incl room & board M$1500) Sign up online or make a telephone reservation with the Flora, Fauna y Cultura office to watch turtles come ashore to lay their eggs. The guided tours in Xcacel are in July and August. You can also arrange one-month volunteer stays through the organization, which includes room and board at an oceanside campsite.

Parque Dos Ojos

South of Xcacel-Xcacelito, you'll find one of the world's largest cave systems and some of the finest stretches of beach along the Riviera.

About 4km south of Xcacel-Xcacelito – and 1km south of amusement park Xel-Há – is the turnoff to the enormous Dos Ojos cave system. Operating as a sustainable tourism project by the local Maya community, **Parque Dos Ojos** (www.parquedosojos.com; Hwy 307 Km 124; admission M$200, snorkel gear M$50, guided snorkel tour M$500,1/2-tank dive incl guide & equipment US$1335/2000; ⏲8am-5pm) offers guided snorkeling and diving tours of some amazing underwater caverns, where you float past illuminated stalactites and stalagmites in an eerie wonderland.

With an extent of about 83km and some 30 cenotes, it's one of the largest underwater cave systems in the world. One of the most popular sites for experienced divers is the Pit, a 110m-deep cenote in which you can see ancient human and animal remains. If you are not a certified diver, you can pay the price of admission and go swimming or snorkeling.

Bahías de Punta Solimán

These two beautiful, protected bays are separated by a narrow point, 123km south of Cancún and 11km north of Tulum. To get here, head east (toward the sound of the ocean) on an unmarked road directly opposite Hwy 307's Oscar y Lalo's Restaurant. When you get to the ocean, you'll need to pass through a guarded gate to gain access to the bays.

You can rent a kayak here and paddle out to the reef that shelters the mouth of the bay. You could probably snorkel out, too, if you are a good swimmer. There's a dense mangrove forest here, and the mosquitoes and sand flies on the powder-white beach can get a bit rough.

Birds of interest here include Yucatán vireos, Yucatán woodpeckers, rose-throated tanagers, black catbirds and orange orioles. If you're very lucky, you may spot one of the pumas seen in the area from time to time.

Turning right (south) at the beachfront intersection takes you to **Bahía Solimán** (though some call it Bahía de San Francisco). Currently the only spot to find lodging in the area – they are redeveloping the areas north of here – it has terrific coral heads, tons of colorful fish, plenty of grouper and reef sharks, and the occasional sea turtle and even tuna.

A number of beach houses, some quite luxurious, line the dirt road. Most of them rent by the week, some at well over M$20,000. A good website for house rentals in the area is www.locogringo.com.

Most people get to Punta Solimán by car, or by taking a bus to Tulum and a taxi from there.

Sleeping & Eating

Nah Uxibal APARTMENT $$$
(☎USA 707-407-8033; www.nahuxibal.com; 500m south of entrance; studio/villa/ste US$196/252/448; P) It's rare to find a place in these parts offering nightly (as opposed to weekly) stays, and this one is relatively affordable for the area. The 'studios' and beachside casitas here are spacious spreads with fully equipped kitchens, lovely tilework and private porches with hammocks. The enormous suite upstairs can accommodate a small army, but only six are allowed.

Chamicos SEAFOOD $$
(southern end of town; mains M$150-250) At the south end of the road, Chamicos is the budget traveler's friend. The restaurant prepares good fried fish and seafood dishes, the oceanfront campsites (M$100) sit on a palm-shaded beach and there are kayak rentals (per hour M$100). If you'd like to camp, you'll need to bring your own tent and insect repellent. If not, the beach makes a nice lunch stop.

Tankah

A few kilometers south of the Hwy 307 turnoff for Punta Solimán is the exit for Tankah, which has a picturesque stretch of beach and top-end accommodations that have the sea for a front yard and mangroves out back.

Cenote Manatí SWIMMING

(admission M$50, snorkel gear M$30, kayak M$75; ⏲8am-5pm) Besides the attractions of beach and reef, Tankah offers Cenote Manatí, named for the gentle 'sea cows' that used to frequent it. It's actually a series of seven cenotes connected by a channel that winds through the mangrove a short distance before heading back underground briefly to reach the sea. The swimming, snorkeling and kayaking are great.

Sleeping

Casa Cenote HOTEL $$$

(☎USA 361-993-2462, cell 984-1156996; www.casacenote.com; r incl breakfast US$140; P❄≋) Across the road from a gorgeous cenote, the beachside bungalows are lovingly done up with Maya touches, each with a screened sliding glass door leading to its own little terrace with hammock. The Casa offers rustic cabins and an on-site restaurant as well. To get here, turn east at the 'Casa Cenote' sign and it's about 2km from the highway.

Tankah Inn HOTEL $$$

(☎USA 918-582-3743, cell 984-1000703; www.tankah.com; Tankah 3, Lote 16; d incl breakfast US$149; P❄ᯤ) Tankah Inn has five comfortable rooms with tiled floors, all with private terraces, good beds and nice cross-ventilation. A large upstairs kitchen, dining room and common area afford splendid views. A slew of activities are offered here, including diving, fishing and kayaking. It's less than 2km east of the highway.

Tulum

☎984 / POP 18,000

Tulum's spectacular coastline – with all its confectioner-sugar sands, jade-green water and balmy breezes – makes it one of the top beaches in Mexico. Where else can you get all that *and* a dramatically situated Maya ruin? There's also excellent cave and cavern diving, fun cenotes, and a variety of lodgings and restaurants to fit every budget.

Some may be put off by the fact that the town center, where the really cheap eats and sleeps are found, sits right on the highway, making the main drag feel more like a truck stop than a tropical paradise. But rest assured that if Tulum Pueblo isn't to your liking, you can always head to the coast and find that tranquil beachside bungalow.

Exploring Tulum's surrounding areas pays big rewards: there's the massive Reserva de la Biosfera Sian Ka'an, the secluded fishing village of Punta Allen and the ruins of Cobá.

History

Most archaeologists believe that Tulum was occupied during the late post-Classic period (AD 1200–1521) and that it was an important port town during its heyday. The Maya sailed up and down this coast, maintaining trading routes all the way down into Belize. When Juan de Grijalva sailed past in 1518, he was amazed by the sight of the walled city, its buildings painted a gleaming red, blue and yellow and a ceremonial fire flaming atop its seaside watchtower.

The ramparts that surround three sides of Tulum (the fourth side being the sea) leave little question as to its strategic function as a fortress. Several meters thick and 3m to 5m high, the walls protected the city during a period of considerable strife between Maya city-states. Not all of Tulum was situated within the walls. The vast majority of the city's residents lived outside them; the civic-ceremonial buildings and palaces likely housed Tulum's ruling class.

The city was abandoned about 75 years after the Spanish conquest. It was one of the last of the ancient cities to be abandoned; most others had been given back to nature long before the arrival of the Spanish. But Maya pilgrims continued to visit over the years, and indigenous refugees from the Caste War took shelter here from time to time.

'Tulum' is Maya for 'wall,' though its residents called it Zama (Dawn). The name Tulum was apparently applied by explorers during the early 20th century.

Present-day Tulum is growing fast: since 2006 the population has more than doubled and there are no signs of it slowing down.

Sights

Tulum Ruins ARCHAEOLOGICAL SITE

(www.inah.gob.mx; Hwy 307 Km 230; M$64, parking M$50-100, tours from M$644; ⏰8am-5pm; P) The ruins of Tulum preside over a rugged coastline, a strip of brilliant beach and green-and-turquoise waters that'll leave you floored. It's true the extents and structures are of a modest scale and the late post-Classic design is inferior to those of earlier, more grandiose projects – but, wow, those Maya occupants must have felt pretty smug each sunrise.

Tulum is a prime destination for large tour groups. To best enjoy the ruins without feeling like part of the herd, you should visit them early in the morning. A M$20 train takes you to the ticket booth from the entrance, or just hoof the 500m. You'll find cheaper parking just east of the main parking lot, along the old entrance road. There's a less-used southern foot entrance from the beach road.

Activities

You'll find many shops offering their services for reef dives, as well as cavern and cave dives (a big draw in Tulum's surrounding areas). Keep in mind that cave diving can be very dangerous and should only be attempted with proper certification. Even with certification, always dive with professionals who are well familiar with the cave systems.

The spectacular **Cenote Angelita** is most notable to divers for the unique, curious, even eerie layer of hydrogen sulfide that 'fogs' the water about halfway through the descent. Look up and see the sunlight filtering down through ancient submerged tree branches that are wonderfully creepy – like outstretched witches' arms. The dive is deep and should only be done by experienced divers; make arrangements through a dive center.

Snorkeling or swimming from the beach is possible and fun, but be extra careful of boat traffic (a dive flag is a good idea), as the strip between the beach and reef offshore is traveled by dive boats and fishers. If there's a heavy wind onshore, strong currents can develop on the lee side of the reef. Inexperienced swimmers should stay close to shore.

Xibalba Dive Center DIVING

(☎984-871-29-53; www.xibalbadivecenter.com; Andromeda 7, btwn Libra Sur & Geminis Sur; 1-/2-tank dive US$85/140) One of the best dive shops in Tulum, Xibalba is known for its safety-first approach to diving. The center specializes in cave and cavern diving, but it also does ocean dives. Xibalba doubles as a hotel and offers attractive packages combining lodging, diving and cave-diving classes.

I Bike Tulum BICYCLE RENTAL

(☎984-802-55-18; www.ibiketulum.com; Av Cobá Sur s/n, cnr Venus; bicycle per day M$100, scooter per day incl insurance M$500; ⏰9am-5:30pm Mon-Sat) Rents a bike with lock and helmet, or if you prefer, a scooter.

Tours

Community Tours Sian Ka'an ECOTOUR

(☎984-871-22-02, cell 984-1140750; Osiris Sur s/n, cnr Sol Oriente; tours per person US$75-129; ⏰7am-8pm) Runs various excursions to the magnificent Reserva de la Biosfera Sian Ka'an, which include kayaking in canals, birdwatching or visiting Maya ruins. Community Tours is a sustainable tourism project run by locals from Maya communities.

Sleeping

The biggest decision, aside from budget, is whether to stay in the town center or out along the beach. Both have their advantages: most of the daytime action is at the beach or ruins, while at night people tend to hit the restaurants and bars in town.

You'll find better deals in town, where clean hostels and midrange options abound. Affordable is a relative term on the beach; some of the so-called 'budget' places are overpriced, fairly basic and of questionable hygiene in a few cases. On the high end, some of the accomodations advertising themselves as 'eco-chic' might as well just say ridiculously expensive.

Tulum Pueblo

Unless you're up for a long walk, you'll have to take a taxi, bike or *colectivo* to the beach. If you crave sand and surf, consider staying along the Zona Hotelera.

El Jardín de Frida HOSTEL $
(☎984-871-28-16; www.fridastulum.com; Av Tulum s/n, btwn Av Kukulcán & Chemuyil; dm/r/ste incl breakfast M$200/650/1200; P⊖🛜) 🌿 The

EXPLORING TULUM RUINS

Visitors are required to follow a prescribed route around the ruins. From the ticket booth, head north along nearly half the length of Tulum's enormous **wall**, which measures approximately 380m south to north and 170m along its sides. The **tower** at the corner, once thought to be a guard post, is now believed by some to have been a type of shrine. Rounding the corner, you enter the site through a breach in the north wall.

Once inside, head east toward the **Casa del Cenote**, named for the small pool at its southern base, where you can sometimes see the glitter of little silvery fish as they turn sideways in the murky water. A small tomb was found in the casa. Walk south toward the bluff holding the **Templo del Dios del Viento** (Temple of the Wind God), which provides the best views of El Castillo juxtaposed with the sea below.

Below the Wind God's hangout is a lovely little stretch of **beach** (roped off at last visit). Next, head west to **Estructura 25**, which has some interesting columns on its raised platform and, above the main doorway (on the south side), a beautiful stucco frieze of the Descending God. Also known as the Diving God, this upside-down, part-human figure appears elsewhere at Tulum, as well as at several other east-coast sites and Cobá. It may be related to the Maya's reverence for bees (and honey), perhaps a stylized representation of a bee sipping nectar from a flower.

South of Estructura 25 is **El Palacio**, notable for its X-figure ornamentation. From here, head east back toward the water and skirt the outside edge of the central temple complex (keeping it to your right). Along the back are some good views of the sea. Heading inland again on the south side, you can enter the complex through a corbeled archway past the restored **Templo de la Estela** (Temple of the Stela), also known as the Temple of the Initial Series. Stela 1, now in the British Museum, was found here. It was inscribed with the Maya date corresponding to AD 564 (the 'initial series' of Maya hieroglyphs in an inscription gives its date). At first this confused archaeologists, who believed Tulum had been settled several hundred years later than this date. It's now thought that Stela 1 was brought to Tulum from Tankah, a settlement 4km to the north dating from the Classic period.

At the heart of the complex you can admire Tulum's tallest building, a watchtower appropriately named **El Castillo** (The Castle) by the Spaniards. Note the Descending God in the middle of its facade, and the Toltec-style 'Kukulcánes' (plumed serpents) at the corners, echoing those at Chichén Itzá. To the Castillo's north is the small, lopsided **Templo del Dios Descendente**, named for the relief figure above the door. South of the Castillo you'll find steps leading down to a (usually very crowded) beach, where you can go for a swim.

After some beach time, heading west toward the exit will take you to the two-story **Templo de las Pinturas**, constructed in several stages around AD 1400 to 1450. Its decoration was among the most elaborate at Tulum and included relief masks and colored murals on an inner wall. The murals have been partially restored, but are nearly impossible to make out. This monument might have been the last built by the Maya before the Spanish conquest and, with its columns, carvings and two-story construction, it's probably the most interesting structure at the site.

Tulum

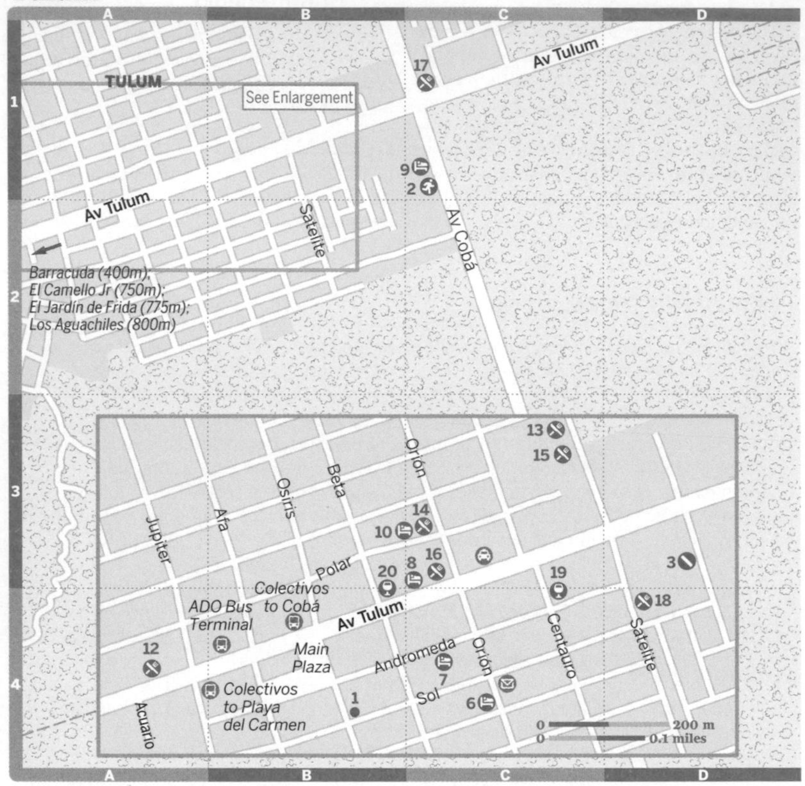

main house, dorms and private rooms are painted in colorful Mexican pop-art style at this ecohostel. All rooms are fan-cooled with the exception of the suites, which come with optional air-con. The mixed dorms are clean and cheerful, and the hostel has a fun little bar area.

Weary Traveler HOSTEL $
(☎984-106-71-92; www.wearytravelerhostel.com; Polar s/n, btwn Orión Norte & Beta Norte; dm without/with air-con M$180/200, r without/with air-con M$500/550;) A great place to meet friends, the Weary Traveler has moved into a new location with a swimming pool and pebbly dining area and bar with picnic tables. Guests prepare their own breakfast provided free of charge by the hostel. For your entertainment needs, there's a foosbal table in the lobby.

★**L'Hotelito** HOTEL $$
(☎984-160-02-29; www.hotelitotulum.com; Av Tulum s/n; d incl breakfast US$60;) Wooden boardwalks pass through a jungle-like side patio to generous, breezy rooms at this character-packed, Italian-run hotel. The attached restaurant does good breakfasts, too. Two rooms upstairs come with wide balconies, but they also catch more street noise from the main strip down below.

Hotel Kin-Ha HOTEL $$
(☎984-871-23-21; www.hotelkinha.com; Orión Sur s/n, btwn Sol & Venus; d with fan/air-con US$70/83; P) A small Italian-run hotel with pleasant rooms surrounding a small courtyard with hammocks. The location is ideal – the bus stop for *colectivos* going to the beach and ruins is right around the corner. Guests are allowed to use Kin-Ha's sister property facilities on the beach.

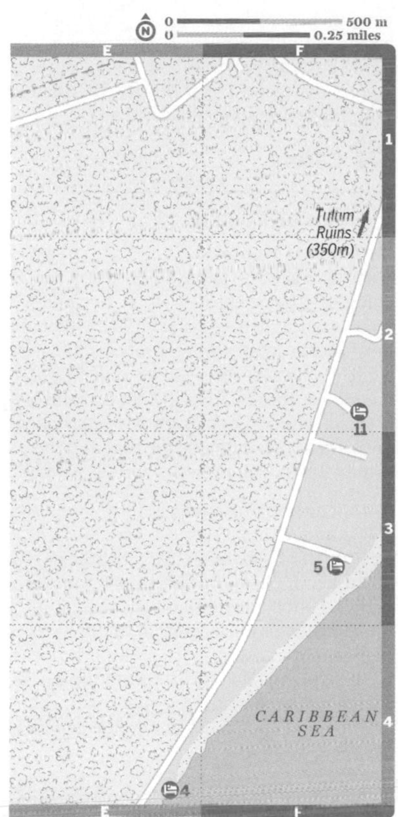

Tulum

Activities, Courses & Tours

1 Community Tours Sian Ka'an B4
2 I Bike Tulum C1
3 Xibalba Dive Center D3

Sleeping

4 Diamante K E4
5 El Paraiso F3
6 Hotel Kin Ha C4
7 Hotel Latino C4
8 L'Hotelito C3
9 Teetotum C1
10 Weary Traveler B3
11 Zazil-Kin F2

Eating

12 Antojitos la Chiapaneca A4
13 Azafran C3
14 Cetli C3
15 El Asadero C3
16 La Nave C3
17 Súper San Francisco de Asis C1
18 Taquería Honorio D4

Drinking & Nightlife

19 Batey C4
20 Curandero B4

Hotel Latino HOTEL **$$**

(☎984-871-26-74; www.hotellatinotulum.com; Andromeda Oriente 2103; r/ste from US$65/80;) The tiny televisions and petite plunge pool must be part of the whole minimalist concept here. If available, request one of the rooms upstairs that come with balconies and hammocks. On-site bike rentals are useful for pedaling to the beach.

Teetotum BOUTIQUE HOTEL **$$$**

(☎984-143-89-56; www.hotelteetotum.com; Av Cobá Sur 2; r incl breakfast US$161;) There are just four stylish rooms in this hip boutique hotel. Common areas include a sundeck upstairs, a dip pool just below and an excellent restaurant. It's a bit overpriced for not being on the beach, but a nice place to stay all the same. It's 200m south of Avenida Tulum.

Zona Hotelera

Quality and price are so varied here that it's best to look before you decide. Accommodations range from rustic *cabañas* with sand floors to pricey bungalows with pricier restaurants. Some places have no electricity, or shut their generators off at night; some have no phone, or lines that rarely work.

Bedbugs, sand fleas and mosquitoes are all a possibility. Bring repellent or consider burning a noxious mosquito coil near your door. Nights can be cold if there's a breeze blowing.

Places along the coastal road are either north or south of the T-junction.

Cenote Encantado CAMPGROUND **$**

(☎cell 984-1425930; www.cenoteencantado.com; Carretera Tulum-Boca Paila Km 10.5; tents per person M$290;) A rare budget option near the beach, this new-agey spot gets its name from a pretty cenote right in the campground's backyard. Guests here stay in large furnished tents with beds, rugs and nightstands. It's not in front of the beach, but you can walk or bike there.

You can swim or snorkel in the cenote, but watch out for crocs! It's 6.5km south of the T-junction, near the Reserva de la Biosfera Sian Ka'an entrance.

Diamante K CABAÑAS **$$**
(cell 984-8762115; www.diamantek.com; Carretera Tulum-Boca Paila Km 2.5; cabin from US$69;) At last visit, Diamante K had just five affordable cabins remaining as it gradually transitions into a high-end beach hotel, so be sure to check what you're getting beforehand or you may be in for a costly surprise.

Zazil-Kin CABAÑAS **$$**
(984-124-00-82; www.hotelzazilkintulum.com; Carretera Tulum-Boca Paila Km 0.47; cabañas with/without bathroom M$1050/750, r from M$1550; P) About a 10-minute walk from the ruins, this popular place resembles a little Smurf village with its dozens of painted *cabañas*. Zazil-Kin also has more expensive air-conditioned, double-occupancy rooms, some of which can be a bit musty. If you opt for the bare bones *cabañas,* electricity is available from 7am to 7pm. Bring insect repellent, you'll need it!

★Hotel La Posada Del Sol BOUTIQUE HOTEL **$$$**
(cell 984-1348874; www.laposadadelsol.com; Carretera Tulum-Boca Paila Km 3.5; r incl breakfast US$179;) Employing recycled objects found on the property after a hurricane, Posada Del Sol stands out for its naturally beautiful architecture. The solar- and wind-powered hotel has no air-con, but rooms catch a nice ocean breeze and just wait till you see the many wonderful design details. The beach here is pretty darn sweet, too.

Posada Margherita HOTEL **$$$**
(cell 984-8018493; www.posadamargherita.com; Carretera Tulum-Boca Paila Km 7; d from M$2200; noon-9:30pm;) Unlike many so-called 'ecotels,' everything here is totally solar- or wind-powered – even the kitchen, which makes amazing food using mainly organic ingredients. All rooms have good bug screening, 24-hour lights and a terrace or balcony with hammock. The beach here is wide and lovely.

El Paraíso HOTEL **$$$**
(USA 310-295-9491, cell 984-1137089; www.elparaisohoteltulum.com; Carretera Tulum-Boca Paila Km 1.5; r US$188; P) Has 10 rooms in a one-story hotel-style block, each with two good beds, private hot-water bathroom, fine cross-ventilation and 24-hour electricity. The restaurant is very presentable, and the level beach, with its palm trees, *palapa* parasols, swing-chaired bar and soft white sand, is among the nicest you'll find on the Riviera Maya. Bike rentals available.

Eating

Tulum Pueblo

★Taquería Honorio TAQUERÍA **$**
(Satélite Sur s/n; tacos M$13, tortas M$28; 5:30pm-1:30am Tue-Sun;) It began as a street stall and became such a hit that it's now a taco joint with a proper roof overhead. Yucatecan classics like *relleno negro* (shredded turkey in dark sauce) and *cochinita* (pulled pork in annatto marinade) are served on handmade tortillas and *tortas* (sandwiches). You should definitely eat here.

Antojitos la Chiapaneca TAQUERÍA **$**
(Av Tulum s/n, btwn Júpiter & Acuario; tacos & antojitos M$7-10, tortas M$15-20; 5:30pm-1am;) A good, cheap option to get your late-night taco fix. You'll often have to wait for a table at this popular spot. In addition to *al pastor* (spit-roasted marinated pork) tacos, the Chiapaneca does tasty Yucatecan snacks, such as *panuchos* (fried tortillas with beans and toppings) and *salbutes* (same as *panuchos* sans beans).

Los Aguachiles SEAFOOD **$$**
(984-802-54-82; Av Tulum s/n, cnr Palenque; tostadas M$40-43, mains M$70-175; noon-7:30pm;) If you skipped this place while in Playa del Carmen, here's another chance. Fish tacos and tuna *tostadas* go down oh-so-nicely with a *michelada* (beer, lime and Clamato juice) in this airy cantina-style restaurant at the south end of town.

La Nave ITALIAN **$$**
(984-871-25-92; Av Tulum s/n; mains M$120-190, pizzas M$80-190; 8am-midnight Mon-Sat;) This open-air Italian joint is perpetually packed. There are delicious pasta dishes, such as shrimp or lobster raviolis, brick-oven pizzas, and an assortment of meat and fish dishes on offer.

Barracuda SEAFOOD **$$**
(www.facebook.com/barracudatulum1; Av Tulum; mains M$80-180; noon-9:30pm Tue-Sun;) A very popular seafood eatery known for its *parillada de mariscos,* a large platter (for two people) with grilled fish, shrimp, lobster, octopus and squid.

Azafran BREAKFAST $$
(Av Satélite s/n, cnr Calle 2; mains $65-105; 8am-3pm Wed-Mon;) A great little German-owned breakfast spot in a shady rear garden, the favorite dish is the 'hangover breakfast,' a hearty portion of homemade sausage, mashed potatoes, eggs, rye toast, bacon and you might even have a lettuce sighting. There are lighter items on the menu, too, such as freshly baked bagels topped with brined salmon.

El Camello Jr SEAFOOD $$
(Av Tulum s/n, cnr Av Kukulcán; mains M$80-160; 10:30am-9pm Mon-Sat, to 9pm Sun;) Immensely popular with locals, this roadside eatery guarantees fresh fish and seafood. Regulars don't even need to look at the menu – it's all about the fish and seafood ceviches.

El Asadero STEAK $$$
(984-157-89-98; Satélite 23; mains M$110-265; 5-11pm;) The house specialty, grilled *arrachera* (flank steak) served with sides of potato, *nopal* (cactus paddle) and sausage, pairs nicely with the Mexican craft beers on offer.

Cetli MEXICAN $$$
(cell 984-1080861; Polar; mains M$230-290; 5-10pm Thu-Tue;) If you're looking for traditional Mexican food such as *mole* (a chili sauce) dishes or *chile en nogada* (stuffed chilies in walnut sauce), hit this homey restaurant on a quiet Tulum backstreet.

Zona Hotelera

Most hotel restaurants welcome nonguests.

Súper San Francisco de Asis SUPERMARKET $
(Av Tulum s/n, cnr Av Cobá; 7am-10pm) A large supermarket at the town's north end.

Posada Margherita ITALIAN $$$
(cell 984-8018493; www.posadamargherita.com; Carretera Tulum-Boca Paila Km 7; mains M$80-250; 7am-9:30pm;) This hotel's restaurant is candlelit at night, making it a beautiful, romantic place to dine. The fantastic food, including pasta, is made fresh daily and consists mostly of organic ingredients. The wines and house mezcal are excellent. It's 3km south of the T-junction.

Puro Corazón MEXICAN $$$
(cell 984-1151197; www.purocorazontulum.wordpress.com; Carretera Tulum-Boca Paila Km 5.5; appetizers M$95-150, mains M$195-250; 10:30am-10pm Tue-Sun;) Reasonably priced by Zona Hotelera standards, and with its nightly live music and excellent cocktails, Puro Corazón is an inviting spot to spend an evening. Everything on the menu is prepared with a gourmet twist.

Hartwood FUSION $$$
(www.hartwoodtulum.com; Carretera Tulum-Boca Paila Km 7.5; set menu M$500; 6-11pm Wed-Sun;) Take a break from all the Italian food in the area at this sweet 'n' simple nouveau cuisine restaurant down on the beach road. Ingredients are fresh and local, flavors and techniques are international. The set menu changes daily, and the solar-powered open kitchen and wood-burning oven serve to accentuate the delicious dishes. It's about 4.5km south of the T-junction.

Reservations are recommended and only accepted in person at Hartwood between 3pm and 6pm. Cash only.

Drinking & Nightlife

Curandero BAR
(www.curanderotulum.com; Av Tulum s/n, cnr Beta; 7am-2pm) This cool space fashioned almost entirely from recycled materials has bands playing several nights a week, as well as DJ sets and the occasional film screening. At last visit, electronica and afro-funk sounds were in the air.

Batey BAR
(Centauro Sur s/n, btwn Av Tulum & Andrómeda; noon-2am Mon-Sat, 5pm-2am Sun) Mojitos are a bit overpriced at this popular Cuban bar, but you can catch fun music acts in the rear garden.

Papaya Playa Project BAR
(www.facebook.com/papayaplayaproject; Carretera Tulum-Boca Paila Km 4.5; from 10pm) Hipster hotel Papaya Playa Project hosts monthly full-moon parties and Saturday night resident DJ sessions at its beachside bar. It's 500m south of the T-junction.

Shopping

Avenida Tulum is lined with shops offering many items, including hammocks, blankets and handicrafts.

Orientation

Tulum lies 131km south of Cancún and is spread out over quite a large area. Approaching from the north on Hwy 307, the first thing you reach is Crucero Ruinas, where the old access road heads in a straight line about 800m to the ruins' ticket booth. About 400m further south on Hwy 307 (past the gas station) is the new entrance for vehicles going to the ruins; it leads to a parking lot. Another 1.5km south on the highway brings you to the Cobá junction; turning right (west) takes you to Cobá, and turning east leads about 3km to the north–south road (or T-junction) servicing the Zona Hotelera, the string of waterfront lodgings extending for more than 10km south from the ruins. This road eventually enters the Reserva de la Biosfera Sian Ka'an, continuing some 50km past Boca Paila to Punta Allen.

The town center, referred to as Tulum Pueblo, straddles the highway (Avenida Tulum through town) south of the Cobá junction.

Information

EMERGENCY

Police (☎066)

MONEY

Tulum has numerous currency-exchange offices and a bank along Avenida Tulum. There's also an ATM in the ADO bus terminal.

There is a bank and ATM at **HSBC Bank** (Av Tulum, btwn Alfa Sur & Osiris Sur; 9am-5pm Mon-Fri).

DANGERS & ANNOYANCES

Tulum is generally safe and locals welcome tourists. However, if you nod off on the beach, your valuables (and even nonvaluables) may disappear. And bring your own lock if you plan on staying in the cheap, no-frills beachfront *cabañas*.

Getting There & Away

If you're headed for Valladolid, be sure your bus is traveling the short route through Chemax, not via Cancún. *Colectivos* leave from Avenida Tulum for Playa del Carmen (M$40, 45 minutes). Colectivos for Felipe Carrillo Puerto (Av Tulum s/n; M$50, one hour) depart from a block south of the ADO bus terminal.

The ADO Bus Terminal (www.ado.com.mx; Av Tulum s/n) is between Calles Alfa & Júpiter.

Getting Around

Colectivos to the beach (M$10) run frequently from a bus stop on the corner of Venus and Orión from 6am to 7:30pm. You can also catch *colectivos* from there to the ruins.

Bicycles and scooters can be a good way to go back and forth between the town and beach. Many hotels have free bikes for guests. **I Bike Tulum** (p114) has a good selection of bike and scooter rentals.

Taxi fares are fixed, from either of the two taxi stands in Tulum Pueblo (one south of the ADO bus terminal, which has fares posted; the other, four blocks north). They charge M$70 to the ruins and M$70 to M$150 from town to the Zona Hotelera.

Around Tulum

There's much to be explored around Tulum. Head inland to visit cenotes, the ruins at Cobá and the grass-roots tourism project at Punta Laguna. Or cruise down the coast to Punta Allen and the wild Reserva de la Biosfera Sian Ka'an.

Activities

Gran Cenote SWIMMING

(Hwy 109 s/n; M$150, snorkeling gear M$80, diving M$200; 8am-5pm) About 4km west of Tulum is Gran (Grand) Cenote, a worthwhile stop on the highway between Tulum and the Cobá ruins, especially if it's a hot day. You

BUSES FROM TULUM

DESTINATION	COST (M$)	DURATION (HRS)	FREQUENCY (DAILY)
Cancún	92-130	2	frequent
Chetumal	174-268	3¼-4	frequent
Chichén Itzá	190	2½-2¾	2; 9am, 2:45pm
Cobá	66	1	1; 10:10am
Felipe Carrillo Puerto	54-92	1¼	frequent, consider taking a *colectivo*
Laguna Bacalar	180	3	1; 8:30pm
Mahahual	240	2½	2; 9am, 5:45pm
Mérida	206-298	4-5	frequent
Playa del Carmen	38-62	1	frequent
Valladolid	84-108	2	frequent

can snorkel among small fish and see underwater formations in the caverns if you bring your own scuba gear. A cab from Tulum costs M$60 one way, or it's an easy bike ride.

Aktun-Ha SWIMMING

(Hwy 109 s/n; admission M$50, diving M$150, snorkel gear M$20; ⏲8am-6pm) In the 1970s taxi drivers used to wash their cabs here and to this day Aktun-Ha is still referred to as Car Wash. It's a good swimming spot and several dive shops teach cave and cavern diving classes here. It's 7.5km west of Tulum heading toward Cobá.

Zacil-Ha SWIMMING

(Hwy 109 s/n; admission M$50, snorkel gear M$20, zip line M$10; ⏲10am-6pm; 📶) At this cenote you can combine swimming, snorkeling and zip-lining. It's 8km west of Avenida Tulum on the road to Cobá.

Cobá

☎984 / POP 1300

Though not as large as some of the more famous ruins, Cobá is cool because you feel like you're in an Indiana Jones flick. It's set deep in the jungle and many of the ruins are yet to be excavated. Walk along ancient *sacbés* (ceremonial limestone avenues or paths between great Maya cities), climb up vine-covered mounds, and ascend to the top of Nohoch Mul for a spectacular view of the surrounding jungle.

From a sustainable-tourism perspective, it's great to stay the night in small communities like Cobá.

History

Cobá was settled earlier than Chichén Itzá or Tulum, and construction reached its peak between AD 800 and 1000. Archaeologists believe that this city once covered 70 sq km and held some 40,000 Maya.

Cobá's architecture is a mystery; its towering pyramids and stelae resemble the architecture of Tikal, which is several hundred kilometers away, rather than the much nearer sites of Chichén Itzá and the northern Yucatán Peninsula.

Archaeologists say they now know that between AD 200 and 600, when Cobá had control over a vast territory of the peninsula, alliances with Tikal were made through military and marriage arrangements in order to facilitate trade between the Guatemalan and Yucatecan Maya. Stelae appear to depict female rulers from Tikal holding ceremonial bars and flaunting their power by standing on captives. These Tikal royal females, when married to Cobá's royalty, may have brought architects and artisans with them.

Archaeologists are still baffled by the extensive network of *sacbés* in this region, with Cobá as the hub. The longest runs nearly 100km from the base of Cobá's great Nohoch Mul pyramid to the Maya settlement of Yaxuna. In all, some 40 *sacbés* passed through Cobá, parts of the huge astronomical 'time machine' that was evident in every Maya city.

The first excavation at Cobá was led by the Austrian archaeologist Teobert Maler in 1891. There was little subsequent investigation until 1926, when the Carnegie Institute financed the first of two expeditions led by Sir J Eric S Thompson and Harry Pollock. After their 1930 expedition, not much happened until 1973, when the Mexican government began to finance excavation. Archaeologists now estimate that Cobá contains more than 6500 structures, of which just a few have been excavated and restored, though work is ongoing.

Sights

Cobá Ruins ARCHAEOLOGICAL SITE

(www.inah.gob.mx; M$64, guides M$500, bike rentals M$45, parking M$50; ⏲8am-5pm; Ⓟ) The archaeological site entrance, at the end of the road on the southeast corner of Laguna Cobá, has a parking lot with surrounding eateries and snack stands. Be prepared to walk several kilometers on paths, depending on how much you want to see. If you arrive after 11am, you'll feel a bit like a sheep in a flock.

A short distance inside, at the Grupo Cobá, there is a concession renting bicycles. These can only be ridden within the site, and are useful if you really want to get around the further reaches; also they're a great way to catch a breeze and cool off. If the site is crowded, however, it's probably best to walk. Pedicabs are another popular option for those who are tired or have limited mobility. Bring insect repellent.

➡ Grupo Cobá

The most prominent structure in the Grupo Cobá is **La Iglesia** (the Church). It's an enormous pyramid; if you were allowed to climb it, you could see the surrounding lakes (which look lovely on a clear day) and the Nohoch Mul pyramid. To reach it walk just under 100m along the main path from the entrance and turn right.

Cobá

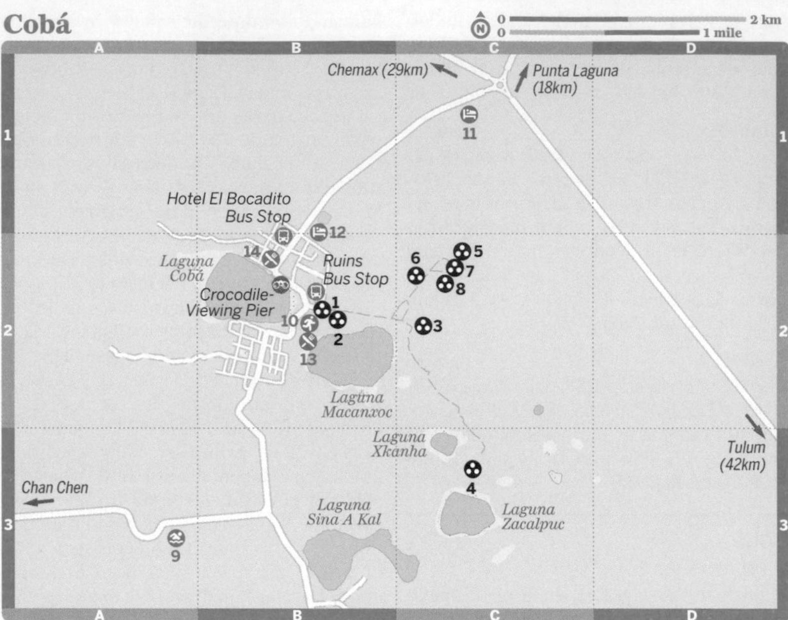

Cobá

Sights

1 Cobá Ruins....B2
2 Grupo Cobá....B2
3 Grupo de las Pinturas....C2
4 Grupo Macanxoc....C3
5 Grupo Nohoch Mul....C2
6 Juego de Pelota....C2
7 Templo 10....C2
8 Xaibé....C2

Activities, Courses & Tours

Bicycle Rental....(see 14)
9 Cenotes Choo-Ha, Tamcach-Ha & Multún-Ha....A3
10 Zipline....B2

Sleeping

11 Hacienda Cobá....C1
12 Hotel Sac-Be....B1

Eating

Chile Picante....(see 12)
13 Restaurant Ki-Jamal....B2
14 Restaurant La Pirámide....B2

Take the time to explore Grupo Cobá; it has a couple of corbeled-vault passages you can walk through. Near its northern edge, on the way back to the main path and the bicycle concession, is a very well-restored *juego de pelota* (ball court).

➡ Grupo Macanxoc

As you head for Grupo Macanxoc you'll see interesting flora along the 1km-long trail. At the end of the path stands a group of restored stelae that bore reliefs of royal women who are thought to have come from Tikal. You'll find the path to Macanxoc about 200m beyond the *juego de pelota*.

➡ Grupo de las Pinturas

The temple at Grupo de las Pinturas (Paintings Group) bears traces of glyphs and frescoes above its door and remnants of richly colored plaster inside. You approach the temple from the southeast. Leave by the trail at the northwest (opposite the temple steps) to see two stelae. The first of these is 20m along, beneath a *palapa*. Here, a regal figure stands over two others, one of them kneeling with his hands bound behind him.

Sacrificial captives lie beneath the feet of a ruler at the base. You'll need to use your imagination, as this and most of the other stelae here are quite worn. Continue along the path past another badly weathered stela and a small temple to rejoin a path leading to the next group of structures.

➡ Grupo Nohoch Mul

Nohoch Mul (Big Mound) is also known as the Great Pyramid, which sounds a lot better than Big Mound. It reaches a height of 42m, making it the second-tallest Maya structure on the Yucatán Peninsula (Calakmul's Estructura II, at 45m, is the tallest). Climbing the old steps can be scary for some. Two diving gods are carved over the doorway of the temple at the top (built in the post-Classic period, AD 1100–1450), similar to sculptures at Tulum.

The view from up top is over many square kilometers of flat scrubby forest, with peeks of lake. The trail to Grupo Nohoch Mul takes you past several interesting sights along the way. Northeast of the Grupo de las Pinturas turnoff you'll reach one of Cobá's two **juego de pelota** courts. Look at the ground in the center of the court to spot a carved stone skull (the winner or loser of the ball game?) and the carved relief of a jaguar.

After the ball court, the track bends between piles of stones – a ruined temple – and you reach a junction of sorts. Turn right (east) and head to the structure called **Xaibé**. This is a tidy, semicircular stepped building, almost fully restored. Its name means 'the Crossroads,' as it marks the juncture of four separate *sacbés*. Going north from here takes you past **Templo 10** and **Stela 20**. The exquisitely carved stela – worn, but not nearly so badly as the others – bears the date AD 730 and a familiar theme: a ruler standing imperiously over two captives. In front of it is a modern line drawing depicting the original details.

Activities

If you want to hit the cenotes south of town, **bicycle rental** (per day M$50; 8am-5pm) is available on the main drag, next to Restaurant La Pirámide. Hotel Sac-Be rents bicycles, too.

Cenotes Choo-Ha, Tamcach-Ha & Multún-Ha SWIMMING
(admission per cenote M$55; 8am-6pm) About 6km south of the town of Cobá, on the road to Chan Chen, you'll find a series of three locally administered cenotes: Choo-Ha, Tamcach-Ha and Multún-Ha. These cavern-like cenotes are nice spots to cool off with a swim, or a snorkel if you bring your own gear.

Zipline ADVENTURE SPORTS
(Zip-line M$130, lookout M$30; 10am-6pm) In the Cobá ruins parking lot a high tower doubles as a lookout point and zip-line. Don't fall…there are large crocs in the waters below.

Sleeping & Eating

Cobá has several decent sleeping options, even though most people usually use Tulum or Valladolid as bases for day trips here.

Hotel Sac-Be HOTEL $
(cell 984-1443006; www.hotelsacbe.com; dm M$150, d/tr M$550/650; P) The best budget digs in town. Clean and friendly, the Sac-Be is actually two sister properties on the main strip heading into Cobá. It offers air-conditioned dorms with in-room bathrooms and private rooms that sleep up to four people.

Hacienda Cobá HOTEL $$$
(cell 998-2270168; www.haciendacoba.com; Av 1 Principal Lote 114; d incl breakfast US$75; P) Hacienda-style rooms with rustic furniture sit in a pleasant jungle setting with lots of chirping birdies and the occasional spider-monkey sightings. It's about 200m south of the Hwy 109 turnoff to Cobá and 2.5km from the ruins, so you'll either need a car or be willing to walk or cab it into town.

Restaurant Ki-Jamal MEXICAN $$
(mains M$70-160, lunch buffet M$170; 8am-5pm) Owned by the local Maya community, Ki-Jamal (which means 'tasty food' in Maya) does indeed do some tasty traditional dishes and there's a daily lunch buffet as well. It's a pleasant spot for a meal when there are no tour buses around. It's in the ruins parking lot.

Chile Picante MEXICAN $$
(Hotel Sac-Be; mains M$85-180; 7:30am-11pm) Located at Hotel Sac-Be, Chile Picante does

TINY TRAILBLAZERS

The small trails you'll see crisscrossing the cleared areas in many of the Cobá ruins baffle observant visitors. What made them? A rodent? To get the answer right you have to think tiny: ants.

Leaf-cutter ants, to be specific. Sometimes marching up to several kilometers from their colony, leaf-cutter ants walk in single file along predetermined routes, often wearing down a pathway over a period of months or years. Patient observers can often see the tiny landscapers at work, carrying fingernail-sized clippings back home. Though they can bite if molested, these ants are generally harmless and should be left in peace to do their work.

everything from vegetarian omelets with *chaya* (Mexican tree spinach) and fresh fruit plates to panuchos (handmade fried tortillas with beans and toppings).

Restaurant La Pirámide MEXICAN **$$**
(mains M$70-150; ⏲8am-5pm;) At the end of the town's main drag, by the lake, this restaurant is pretty touristy but does decent Yucatecan fare like *cochinita* and *pollo pibil* (achiote-flavored chicken or pork). The open-air setup allows for nice views.

Information

You may want to buy a book on Cobá before coming. On-site signage and maps are minimal and cryptic. Tours in English run about M$500 to M$750. The Nohoch Mul pyramid is the only structure the public is allowed to climb.

Be careful not to picnic beside the lake outside the entrance, as it has large crocodiles. Bring plenty of cash.

Getting There & Away

Most buses serving Cobá swing down to the ruins to drop off passengers at a small bus stop; some only go as far as Hotel El Bocadito, which also serves as a bus stop. Buses run six times daily between Tulum and Cobá (M$50 to M$68, 45 minutes). Buses also go to Valladolid (M$60 to M$70, 45 minutes) and Chichén Itzá (M$120, 1½ hours).

Day-trippers from Tulum can reach Cobá by taking *colectivos* (M$50) that depart from Av Tulum and Calle Osiris.

The road from Cobá to Chemax is arrow-straight and in good shape. If you're driving to Valladolid or Chichén Itzá, this is the way to go.

Punta Laguna

Punta Laguna is a fair-sized lake with a small Maya community nearby, 20km northeast of Cobá on the road to Nuevo Xcan. The forest around the lake supports populations of spider and howler monkeys, as well as a variety of birds, and contains small, unexcavated ruins and a cenote. A surprising jaguar population was recently discovered, though chances of seeing one are very slim. Toucans sometimes flit across the road.

Intrepid travelers can bring a tent and camp out near the lake, but you'll need to pack your own food, water and insect repellent.

Public transportation is so sparse as to be nonexistent. In a car, you can reach Punta Laguna by turning south off Hwy 180 at Nuevo Xcan and driving 26km, or by heading 18km north from the Cobá junction.

The best time to see the monkeys is at noon.

Tours

Punta Laguna Tourist Cooperative TOUR
(Najil Tucha; cell 985-11148630; www.puntalaguna.com.mx; admission M$70, tour M$400, camping M$150; ⏲6am-5pm) A guided tour includes canoeing on the lagoon, zip-lining, a shamanic ceremony, rapelling into a pitch-black cenote and visiting a nearby monkey cave.

Tulum to Punta Allen

Punta Allen sits at the end of a narrow spit of land that stretches south about 40km from its start below Tulum. There are some alluring beaches along the way, with plenty of privacy, and most of the spit is within the protected, wildlife-rich Reserva de la Biosfera Sian Ka'an, aka Sian Ka'an Biosphere Reserve.

The road can be a real muffler-buster between gradings, especially when holes are filled with water from recent rains, making it difficult to gauge their depth. The southern half, south of the bridge beyond Boca Paila, is the worst stretch – some spots require experienced off-road handling or you'll sink into the mud. It is doable even in a non-4WD vehicle, but bring along a shovel and boards just in case – you can always stuff palm fronds under the wheels to gain traction – and plan on returning that rental with a lot more play in the steering wheel.

There's an **entrance gate** to the reserve about 10km south of Tulum. At the gate, there's a short nature trail taking you to a rather nondescript **cenote** (Ben Ha). The trail's short, so go ahead and take a second to have a look.

For remote **coastal camping**, this is where intrepid adventuring really takes off. Bring a tent, a couple of hammocks, lots of water, mosquito nets and food supplies. Around 30km from the entrance gate is an excellent camping spot with the lagoon on one side and glorious blue ocean on the other.

Sights

Reserva de la Biosfera Sian Ka'an NATURE RESERVE
(Sian Ka'an Biosphere Reserve) More than 5200 sq km of tropical jungle, marsh, mangroves and islands on Quintana Roo's coast have been set aside by the Mexican government as a large biosphere reserve. In 1987 the UN classified it as a World Heritage site – an irreplaceable natural treasure.

Sian Ka'an (Where the Sky Begins) is home to a small population of spider and howler monkeys, American crocodiles, Central American tapirs, four turtle species, giant land crabs, more than 330 bird species (including roseate spoonbills and some flamingos), manatees and some 400 fish species, plus a wide array of plant life.

About 10km south of the reserve entrance is the visitors center, where you'll find a watchtower that provides tremendous bird's-eye views of the lagoon.

There are no hiking trails through the heart of the reserve; it's best explored with a professional guide.

Tours

If you'd like to see more of Sian Ka'an, Maya-run Community Tours Sian Ka'an (p114) runs various expeditions into the sprawling biosphere reserve.

Punta Allen

984 / POP 470

The town of Javier Rojo Gómez is more commonly called by the name of the point 2km south, Punta Allen. Hurricane Gilbert nearly destroyed the town in 1988, and there was some damage and a lot of wind-scrubbed palms after Hurricane Dean. But Punta Allen is still standing. The village, which is truly the end of the road, exudes a laid-back ambience reminiscent of the Belizean cays. There's also a healthy reef 400m from shore that offers snorkelers and divers wonderful sights.

The area is known primarily for its catch-and-release bonefishing; tarpon and snook are very popular sportfish as well.

There are no ATMs or internet cafes in town. Electricity generally works between 10am to 2pm, and 7pm to midnight.

Tours

Cooperativa Punta Allen TOUR

(984-801-15-64; toursallen@hotmail.com; Calle Punta Nizuc s/n, north of the dock; per boat fishing/snorkeling & dolphin-watching M$3350/2200) The Punta Allen cooperative runs various boat tours in the area, such as fly-fishing, dolphin- and turtle-watching, and snorkeling.

Sleeping & Eating

Vigía Grande and Galletanes are among several of the town's dining choices, both close to the water and both owned by co-ops that run snorkeling and fishing trips.

Casa de Ascensión HOTEL $

(cell 984-8010034; www.facebook.com/casadeascension; r with fan/air-con M$500/600;) This budget hotel is three blocks inland. Fairly simple rooms surround a breezy lobby area with a large TV. There's 24-hour electricity and wi-fi at an additional cost.

Hotel Costa del Sol BUNGALOW $$

(cell 984-8025387; caribejew@gmail.com; campsites per person M$125, r M$900-1200; P) At the entrance to town, this laid-back spot has quaint fan-cooled bungalows and rooms right on the beach. If you bring your own tent, you can camp on the sand.

Cuzán BUNGALOW $$

(cell 984-1640322; www.flyfishmx.com; r from US$50; P) Just south of the town's center along the main road, Cuzán has rustic ocean-front *cabañas* – one set on the remains of an old boat.

Grand Slam Fishing Lodge HOTEL $$$

(984-139-2930, 998-800-10-47; www.grandslamfishinglodge.com; at town entrance; r US$350; P) If you've got money to burn, this place is for you. The upscale lodge boasts 12 oceanfront rooms with Jaccuzi, iPod docks, large balconies and around-the-clock electricity (a true luxury in Punta Allen). Fly-fishing enthusiasts can request lodging and fishing packages.

Muelle Viejo SEAFOOD $$

(mains M$70-150; noon-9pm Tue-Sun; P) Overlooking a dock where fishermen bring in the daily catch, this colorful beach house serves fresh seafood cocktails, decent fried fish dishes and lobster when it's in season.

Fisherman Fishing Lodge SEAFOOD $$

(984-107-35-02; www.fishermanlodge.net; south of the dock; mains M$120-195, lobster M$250; 8am-10pm;) Serves breakfast meals fit for a hearty angler's appetite and a varied lunch and dinner menu featuring pizza and fresh lobster. Offers good lodging-and-fishing package deals (rooms from M$800) and welcomes non-fisherfolk, too.

Getting There & Away

The best way to reach Punta Allen is by rental car or scooter, but prepare for 5km/h to 10km/h speeds and more than a few transmission-grinding bumps. The ride can take three to four hours, depending on the condition of the road.

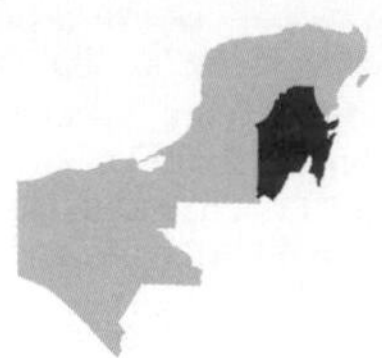

Costa Maya & Southern Caribbean Coast

Includes ➡

Why Go?

The Southern Caribbean Coast, or the Costa Maya as the tourist brochures call it, is the latest region to be hit by the development boom. But if you're looking for a quiet escape on the Mexican Caribbean, it's still the best place to be.

Streching about 100km south of Sian Ka'an biosphere reserve down to the small town of Xcalak, you'll find many surprises along the way, such as the mesmerizing Laguna Bacalar, aka the 'lake of seven colors.' East of Bacalar, the tranquil fishing towns of Mahahual and Xcalak offer great beach-bumming, bird-watching and diving opportunities – residents in both spots put a premium on sustainable development, and it shows.

In the interior, the seldom-visited ruins of Dzibanché and Kohunlich seem all the more mysterious without the tour vans. For both the ruins and trips down south to Belize, Quintana Roo's state capital Chetumal is a great jumping-off point.

When to Go

➡ Don't miss the Caribbean-flavored Carnaval (p135) street festival in February in the Quintana Roo state capital, Chetumal. It's definitely one of the best fiestas of the year on the southern coast.

➡ The weeklong cultural festival Cruzando Fronteras (p130) is held in late February and/or early March in the town of Mahahual; it's still low season and early enough to avoid spring-break crowds.

➡ A visit from early- to mid-December has several advantages: hurricane season has passed, the weather has cooled considerably and many great hotel deals can be found ahead of the holiday season.

Off the Beaten Track

- Xcalak (p131)
- Dzibanché (p139)
- Kohunlich (p140)
- Kinich-Ná (p140)
- Corozal (p140)

Best Places to Eat

- Nohoch Kay (p131)
- Restaurante Xel-Ha (p137)
- Luna de Plata (p131)
- Christian's Tacos (p134)
- La Playita (p134)

Costa Maya & Southern Caribbean Coast Highlights

1. Dive at **Banco Chinchorro** (p129), the largest coral atoll in the western hemisphere and a fascinating ship graveyard.
2. Take a refreshing dip in the 90m-deep **Cenote Azul** (p133), then bask on **Laguna Bacalar** (p133), one of the most beautiful lakes that you'll ever set your eyes on.
3. Go snorkeling, fishing or bird-watching in **Mahahual** (p129), or simply chill at a boardwalk bar or restaurant in this laid-back coastal town.
4. Escape to the remote beach village of **Xcalak** (p131) for quality R&R, diving and fishing.
5. Beat your own path to a series of seldom-visited **Maya ruins** (p139) west of the Quintana Roo capital Chetumal.

Felipe Carrillo Puerto

☎983 / POP 26,000

Now named for a progressive governor of Yucatán, this crossroads town 95km south of Tulum was once known as Chan Santa Cruz, the rebel headquarters during the Caste War. Besides its historical and cultural significance, Carrillo Puerto has few points of interest other than an attractive ecotourism park about 11km southwest of town. There's a main square with a clock tower, church and cultural center; the plaza takes center stage in late April and early May when the town celebrates its patron saint, Santa Cruz.

History

In 1849, when the Caste War turned against them, the Maya of the northern Yucatán Peninsula made their way to this town seeking refuge. Regrouping, they were ready to sally forth again in 1850 when a 'miracle' occurred. A wooden cross erected at a cenote on the western edge of the town began to 'talk,' telling the Maya they were the chosen people, exhorting them to continue the struggle against the government and promising victory. The talking was most likely done by a ventriloquist who used sound chambers, but the people looked upon it as the authentic voice of their aspirations.

The 'oracle' guided the Maya in battle for more than eight years, until their great victory conquering the fortress at Bacalar. For the latter part of the 19th century, the Maya in and around Chan Santa Cruz were virtually independent of governments in Mexico City and Mérida.

A military campaign by the Mexican government retook the city and the surrounding area at the beginning of the 20th century, and the talking-cross shrine was desecrated. Many of the Maya fled to small villages in the jungle and kept up the fight into the 1930s; some resisted even into the 1950s.

Carrillo Puerto today remains a center of Maya pride. The talking cross, hidden away in the jungle for many years following the Mexican takeover, has been returned to its shrine, and Maya from around the region still come to visit it, especially on May 3, the day of the Holy Cross.

Sights & Activities

Centro Cultural Chan Santa Cruz ARTS CENTER
(cnr Calles 67 & 68; ⏲8am-8pm Mon-Fri) FREE On the plaza, the cultural center has art exhibitions, workshops and the occasional exhibit on the Caste War. Be sure to check out the mural outside, which highlights accomplishments of Maya culture.

Santuario de la Cruz Parlante SHRINE
(cnr Calles 69 & 60; ⏲5:30am-9pm) Folks come from all over to pray before this shrine dedicated to the talking cross, a symbol of the Maya people's struggle against inequality and injustice. You'll find the thatched-roof sanctuary next to a dried-up cenote in a small park about five blocks west of Hwy 307. The cross is on the right side of the altar. No one may enter wearing hats or shoes.

Síijil Noh Há SWIMMING
(☎984-834-05-25; siijilnohhankp@gmail.com; off Hwy 307, Laguna Ocom turnoff; admission M$15, kayaks M$50, cabañas M$250; ⏲7am-7pm) About 8km south of Felipe Carrillo Puerto, off Hwy 307, you'll find a 3km dirt road leading to this sublime, solar-powered ecotourism center. Run by the local Maya community, the wooded grounds overlook a quiet lake shore. You can rent a kayak, take a dip in a freshwater spring and go hiking or biking along nature trails.

BUSES FROM FELIPE CARRILLO PUERTO

DESTINATION	FARE (M$)	DURATION (HRS)	FREQUENCY (DAILY)
Cancún	154-248	3½-4	frequent
Chetumal	88-168	2-3	frequent
Laguna Bacalar	66	2	frequent
Mérida	200-260	5-6	3
Playa del Carmen	88-174	2½	frequent
Ticul (for Uxmal)	150	4	2
Tulum	60-116	1¼	frequent

If you like what you see, you can stay in a rustic cabin here. Taxis from town charge M$120 to Síijil, or catch a southbound *colectivo* to the turnoff and walk the 3km.

Sleeping & Eating

Hotel Esquivel HOTEL $
(☎983-834-03-44; www.hotelesquivel.blogspot.com; Calle 63 s/n, btwn Calles 66 & 68; d with fan/air-con M$500/570, ste M$670; P) Around the corner from the plaza and bus terminal, the Esquivel offers the best deal in town with its spacious remodeled rooms. Across the street it has family-friendly suites with kitchenettes and fridges.

Mercado Público MARKET $
(cnr Calles 70 & 71; snacks & mains M$20-50; 6am-3pm) A decent spot to fuel up and do a bit of people-watching.

Hotel El Faisán y El Venado MEXICAN $$
(☎983-834-07-02; Av Juárez 781, cnr Calle 69; mains M$95-140; restaurant 7:30am-10:30pm;) Come here for the best eats in town. The house specialty (not listed on the menu) is grilled *venado* (deer) steaks prepared *poc-chuc* style (marinated and grilled). They do a good liver and onions dish here as well. It's also one of the better hotels in town, with clean, though somewhat darkish, rooms (double M$450)

Information

HSBC (Calle 69 s/n, btwn Calle 68 & Av Juárez; 9am-5pm Mon-Fri) Has an ATM.

Post Office (cnr Calles 68 & 69; 9am-5:30pm Mon-Fri, to 1pm Sat)

Getting There & Away

Most buses serving Carrillo Puerto are *de paso* (they don't originate there).

Frequent *colectivos* (shared vans) leave for Playa del Carmen (M$85, two hours) and Tulum (M$60, one hour) from Hwy 307, just south of Calle 73.

At Calles 66 and 63 you'll find *colectivos* for Chetumal (M$70, two hours).

Mahahual

☎983 / POP 920

Some locals weren't exactly crying the blues after Hurricane Dean rolled into town in 2007 and badly damaged the town's new cruise-ship dock. But the dock has been rebuilt and despite ongoing concerns about encroaching development, Mahahual has managed to retain a pretty laid-back Caribbean vibe.

Sure, cruise-ship tourism has brought quite a few tacky shops and gringo-friendly bars to the north side of town, but head south in the direction of Xcalak and you'll have no problem finding your own private beach with sugary white sand.

What's more, there's great diving and snorkeling here, and there's just enough nightlife along the beachfront *malecón* (waterfront promenade) to keep you entertained.

Sights & Activities

Banco Chinchorro DIVE SITE
Divers won't want to miss the reefs and underwater fantasy worlds of the Banco Chinchorro, the largest coral atoll in the northern hemisphere. Some 45km long and up to 14km wide, Chinchorro's western edge lies about 30km off the coast, and dozens of ships have fallen victim to its barely submerged ring of coral.

The atoll and its surrounding waters were made a biosphere reserve (Reserva de la Biosfera Banco Chinchorro) to protect them from depredation. But the reserve lacks the personnel and equipment needed to patrol such a large area, and many abuses go undetected.

Most dives here go to a maximum of 30m, as there are no decompression chambers for miles. And with a ban on wreck dives recently lifted, there are plenty of shipwreck sites worth exploring. Along the way you'll also spot coral walls and canyons, rays, turtles, giant sponges, grouper, tangs, eels and, in some spots, reef, tiger and hammerhead sharks.

There's good snorkeling as well, including *40 Cannons*, a wooden ship in 5m to 6m of water. Looters have taken all but about 25 of the cannons, and it can only be visited in ideal conditions.

Mahahual Beach BEACH
The beach right off Mahahual's beautiful *malecón* has great sand, plus water so shallow you can swim out a good 100m.

Mahahual Dive Centre DIVING
(☎983-102-09-92, cell 983-1367693; www.mahahualdivecentre.com; Huachinango Km 0.7, cnr Cazón; 2-/3-tank dives M$2450/2850, snorkeling M$1650) Does trips to nearby sites as well as Banco Chinchorro and the fishing village of Punta Herrero.

Doctor Dive DIVING

(☎ cell 983-1036013; www.doctordive.com; Av Mahahual s/n, cnr Coronado; 2-tank dive/snorkeling incl equipment US$100/30; ⏰ 8am-9pm) In addition to scuba and snorkeling excursions, the Doctor runs spearfishing outings for lionfish, an invasive species with no known predators in the Caribbean region. Lionfish ceviche, anyone? It's actually quite good.

Las Cabañas del Doctor KAYAKING

(☎ 983-832-21-02; www.lascabanasdeldoctor.com; Av Mahahual 6 Km 2; per hr M$50) You can rent kayaks here for some fun in the sun.

Festivals & Events

Cruzando Fronteras FESTIVAL

(www.mahahualcruzandofronteras.com) A week-long cultural festival featuring concerts, art exhibits, movie screenings, food stands and more. It's usually held around late February or early March.

Jats'a Já Festival FESTIVAL

This festival in August is a prayer offering of sorts to the hurricane gods. Activities include pre-Hispanic dancing, art shows and culinary events.

Sleeping

Some addresses are given with distances from the military checkpoint at the northern entrance to town.

Hostal Jardín Mahahual HOTEL $

(☎ 983-834-57-22; www.facebook.com/hostal.jardin; Sardina s/n, cnr Rubia; dm M$130, r with/without air-con M$620/450;) For the price, this is a surprisingly stylish little hostel with five private rooms and an eight-bed coed dorm. Rooms are spotless and the dorms are the best in town by far. It's set back two blocks from the beach, near Calle Rubia.

★ **Posada Pachamama** HOTEL $$

(☎ 983-834-57-62; www.posadapachamama.net; Huachinango s/n; r from M$700, q M$1200;) Rooms at the Pachamama (which means Mother Earth in Inca) range from small interior singles and doubles with ocean views to more ample digs that sleep four. The posada has a good on-site restaurant and the staff are very knowledgeable about local activities.

Travel In' GUESTHOUSE $$

(☎ 983-110-94-96; www.travel-in.com.mx; Coast road Km 6; camping M$75, r M$650;) About 4km south of town, this solar-powered guesthouse is ideal for nature lovers. There are just two accommodations: a rustic cabin-like room beside a mangrove, or a more modern guesthouse with its own library. You can also camp on the beach. Even if you're not staying at Travel In', its restaurant and quiet beach are worth visiting.

Unless you're up for the walk, you'll need a car or taxi to get here. Online reservations are recommended.

Ko'ox Matan Ka'an HOTEL $$

(☎ 983-834-56-79; www.kooxmatankaanhotel.com; Calle Huachinango s/n, cnr Coronado; r/ste from M$1100/1600;) On the south side of the soccer field, this large whitewashed hotel has a relaxed resort feel, plenty of common areas and large, clean rooms. We only wish 'the gift from the heavens' – that's what Matan Ka'an means in Maya – included beach access, but hey, the ocean is only 100m away.

Las Cabañas del Doctor HOTEL $$

(☎ 983-832-21-02, cell 983-1025676; www.lascabanasdeldoctor.com; Av Mahahual 6 Km 2; camping per person M$100, cabañas s/d M$400/600, room with air-con M$850;) Across the street from the beach and about 200m south of the end of the *malecón,* this spot offers several simple *palapa* (palm-leaf roofed) bungalows, as well as more modern hotel-style rooms. There's also the option of camping right on the beach with use of the hotel's shared bathroom, but you'll need to bring a tent.

40 Cañones HOTEL $$$

(☎ 983-834-57-30; www.40canones.com; Malecón Mahahual Km 1.5, cnr Huachinango; r M$1368-1606, ste M$2368-2677, apt M$2618-3094;) This stylish Italian-owned hotel on the *malecón* is clean and comfortable. Only a few of the rooms have ocean views, but you're right on the boardwalk, so you can always get your fix. Across the street, the hotel offers daily apartment rentals, the largest of which sleeps six.

Ko'ox Quinto Sole BOUTIQUE HOTEL $$$

(☎ 983-834-59-42; www.kooxquintosoleboutiquehotel.com; Carretera Mahahual-Xcalak Km 0.35; r M$1775-2500, ste M$3200-3500;) One of the fanciest hotels in town, the spacious rooms here have heavenly beds and private balconies (some with Jacuzzi). It's on a quiet beach north of the boardwalk and 350m south of the lighthouse at town's entrance.

Eating

There are about a dozen restaurants along the *malecón*, each offering an assortment of seafood, Mexican favorites and pub grub.

★Nohoch Kay SEAFOOD $$

(Big Fish; cnr Malecón & Cazón; mains M$125-160, platter per person M$300; ⏲1-9:30pm; ⊜📶) Nohoch Kay, aka the Big Fish, definitely lives up to its name. Don't miss this beachfront Mexican-owned restaurant, where they prepare succulent whole fish in a garlic and white-wine sauce, or opt for the surf-and-turf platter for two, which includes lobster, steak, octopus and shrimp.

Fernando's 100% Agave MEXICAN $$

(Malecón, btwn Calles Martillo & Coronado; mains M$110-180; ⏲2-10pm Tue-Sun; ⊜) With its new smaller boardwalk location, Fernando's feels more intimate now. The restaurant-bar offers up various fish and seafood dishes prepared with sauces ranging from sweet coconut-mango to spicy red. After dinner – or before – try a smooth-tasting Siete Leguas tequila.

Sulumar SEAFOOD $$

(Mahahual beach; mains M$80-180; ⏲9am-7pm; ⊜📶) Lobster, lionfish, octopus, you name it – this fishermen's cooperative cooks up the fresh catch of the day and serves it to you right on the beach at the south end of the boardwalk. Locals love this place.

Luna de Plata ITALIAN $$$

(☎983-119-22-73; www.lunadeplata.info; Av Mahahual Km 2; mains M$85-230; ⊜📶) The 'ristorante' of this Italian-owned hotel prepares fresh bread and pasta, pizzas and seafood dishes. Try the scrumptious lobster-filled raviolis in shrimp sauce. Rooms here aren't too shabby either.

Information

You'll find an ATM on Calle Coronado, between Calle Huachinango and the *malecón*, but bring plenty of cash in case the machine runs out of money.

Ambar Hill (Cherna s/n, btwn Huachinango & Malecón; ⏲11am-7pm) is a currency-exchange office.

Getting There & Around

Mahahual is 127km south of Felipe Carrillo Puerto, and approximately 100km northeast of Bacalar.

There's no official bus terminal in Mahahual. At last visit, liquor store **Solo Chelas** (at Calles Huachinango and Cherna) was selling tickets for a daily ADO northbound bus, which departs Mahahual at 5pm for Tulum (M$240, three hours), Playa del Carmen (M$310, four hours) and Cancún (M$370, five hours). A Xcalak-bound Caribe bus (M$50, 1¼ hours) passes through town along Calle Huachinango, usually between 7am and 8am.

Shuttle vans leave hourly from 5:45am to 6:45pm to Chetumal (M$88, 2½ hours), Laguna Bacalar (M$55, two hours) and Limones (M$50, one hour), where you can catch frequent northbound buses. The terminal is on the corner of Calles Sardina and Cherna, on the soccer field's north end.

There's a Pemex gas station in Mahahual if you need to fill your tank. The Xcalak turnoff is about 100m west of the gas station.

Xcalak

☎983 / POP 380

The rickety wooden houses, beached fishing launches and lazy gliding pelicans make this tiny town plopped in the middle of nowhere a perfect escape. And by virtue of its remoteness and the Chinchorro atoll, Xcalak may yet escape the development boom.

If diving isn't your thing, there's still plenty to do. Come here to walk along dusty streets and sip frozen drinks while frigate birds soar above translucent green lagoons. Explore a mangrove swamp by kayak, or just doze in a hammock and soak up some sun. And, though tiny, Xcalak has a few nice restaurants and an easygoing mix of foreigners and local fishers.

The mangrove swamps stretching inland from the coastal road hide some large lagoons and form tunnels that invite kayakers to explore. They and the drier forest teem with wildlife; in addition to the usual herons, egrets and other waterfowl, you can see agoutis, jabirus (storks), iguanas, javelinas (peccaries), parakeets, kingfishers, alligators and more. Unfortunately, the mangrove also breeds mosquitoes and some vicious *chaquistes* (sand flies).

Xcalak was an important port during the Caste War, and the town even had a cinema until a series of hurricanes wiped everything away. Today, the town shows no signs of getting a bank, grocery store or gas station anytime soon, so stock up before you come.

Activities

XTC Dive Center DIVING

(www.xtcdivecenter.com; Coast road Km 0.3; 2-tank dives to Banco Chinchorro US$110, snorkeling trips US$45-75, PADI certification US$529, r US$45-60) XTC is the one-stop shop for all your needs. It offers dive and snorkel trips to the wondrous barrier reef offshore, and to Banco Chinchorro. It also rents diving equipment, provides PADI open-water certification, and operates fishing and bird-watching tours. Additionally, XTC rents three nice, affordable rooms and has a good restaurant-bar.

It's 300m north of town.

Sleeping

There are bargain-basement cabins at the entrance to town, but they are pretty dirty, so we'd suggest going to one of the places on the old coastal road leading north from town. All have purified drinking water, ceiling fan, hot-water bathroom, 24-hour electricity (from solar or wind with generator backup), and bikes and/or kayaks for guest use.

Most places don't accept credit cards without prior arrangements, and are best contacted through their websites or via email. Addresses are given in kilometers north along the coast from town.

Hotel Tierra Maya HOTEL $$$

(USA 330-735-3072; www.tierramaya.net; Coast road Km 2; r US$107-119, ste US$179; P) This modern beachfront hotel has six lovely rooms (three quite large), each tastefully appointed with many architectural details. Each of the rooms has a balcony facing the sea; the bigger rooms even have small refrigerators.

Casa Carolina HOTEL $$$

(USA 678-630-7080; www.casacarolina.net; Coast road Km 2.5; r incl breakfast US$120;) Bright, cheery yellow Casa has four guest rooms with large, hammock-equipped balconies facing the sea. Each room has a kitchen with fridge, and the bathrooms try to outdo one another with their beautiful Talavera tilework. Free use of kayaks, snorkel gear and bicycles is included.

Eating & Drinking

Food in Xcalak tends to be tourist-grade seafood or Mexican.

Gringo Dave's JAPANESE $

(at town entrance; M$60-80; 7am-10pm Nov-Apr, 4-6pm Mon-Thu & noon-9pm Fri-Sun May-Oct;) Gringo Dave is actually a Japanese guy named Go (long story). Anywho, the menu consists of curry dishes, Japanese-style fried chicken or you can simply tell Go to 'give you his best shot' and he'll gladly improvise. At last visit, Go was building bungalows next door.

Toby's SEAFOOD $$

(mains M$85-165; 11am-8:30pm Mon-Sat;) On the main drag in town, the friendly chitchat and well-prepared fish and seafood dishes make this a popular expat spot. Try the coconut shrimp or lionfish and you'll know why.

Costa de Cocos INTERNATIONAL $$

(www.costadecocos.com; Coast road Km 1; breakfast US$5-6, lunch & dinner US$5-19; 7am-8:30pm;) This fishing lodge's restaurant-bar is one of the better options in town for eating and drinking. It serves both American- and Mexican-style breakfasts and does fish tacos for the lunch and dinner crowd. The bar produces its own craft whiskey and has pale ale on tap.

Lonchería Silvia's SEAFOOD $$

(mains M$90-130, lobster M$180; 9am-10pm;) About three blocks south of the plaza and a block in from the coast, Silvia's serves mostly fish fillets and *ceviche*. The long menu doesn't mean that everything is available...you'll likely end up having the fish.

Getting There & Around

Buses to Chetumal (and Limones, a stop where you can grab northbound buses) leave at 5am and 2pm; they stop on the coast road behind the lighthouse.

Cabs from Limones, on Hwy 307, cost about M$700 (including to the northern hotels). Driving from Limones, turn right (south) after 55km and follow the signs to Xcalak (another 60km). Keep an eye out for the diverse wildlife that frequents the forest and mangrove; a lot of it runs out onto the road.

You can take a coastal road from Xcalak to Mahahual, but don't be surprised if it's closed during the rainy season.

You can charter a boat at XTC Dive Center for US$300 (minimum five people) to San Pedro, Belize.

Laguna Bacalar

☎983 / POP 11,000

Laguna Bacalar comes as a surprise in this region of scrubby jungle. More than 60km long with a bottom of sparkling white sand, this crystal-clear lake offers opportunities for camping, swimming, kayaking and simply lazing around.

The small, sleepy, lakeside town of Bacalar lies east of the highway, 125km south of Felipe Carrillo Puerto. It's noted mostly for its old Spanish fortress and popular *balnearios* (swimming grounds). There's not a lot else going on, but that's why people like it here. Around the town plaza, you'll find an ATM, a small grocery store, a taxi stand and tourist information office.

Sights & Activities

Fortress FORTRESS

(cnr Av 3 & Calle 22; M$67; 9am-7pm Tue-Sun) The fortress above the lagoon was built to protect citizens from raids by pirates and the local indigenous population. It also served as an important outpost for the Spanish in the War of the Castes. In 1859 it was seized by Maya rebels, who held the fort until Quintana Roo was finally conquered by Mexican troops in 1901.

Today, with formidable cannons still on its ramparts, the fortress remains an imposing sight. It houses a museum exhibiting colonial armaments and uniforms from the 17th and 18th centuries.

Cenote Azul SWIMMING

(Hwy 307 Km 34; adult/child under 10yr M$10/free; 10am-6pm;) Just shy of the south end of the *costera* (coast highway) and about 3km south of Bacalar's city center is this cenote, a 90m-deep natural pool with an onsite bar and restaurant. It's 200m east of Hwy 307, so many buses will drop you nearby. You can rent kayaks here.

Cuco's Tours BOAT TOUR

(☎cell 983-1079980; Av Costera 479; per boat M$1400) Boat tours departing from Hotel Laguna Bacalar visit freshwater springs, a shallow white-sand beach, cenotes and a gorgeous canal. Don't forget your swim suit.

Balneario SWIMMING

(Av Costera s/n, cnr Calle 14; 9am-5pm) FREE This beautiful public swimming spot lies several blocks south of the fort, along Avenida Costera. Parking costs M$10.

Sleeping

Bacalar

Hostal Pata de Perro HOSTEL $

(☎983-834-20-62; www.patadeperrobacalar.com; Calle 22 No 63; d from M$510, ste M$750-1560;) This adults-only hostel on the square houses immaculate rooms, ranging from three-bed setups with shared bathrooms to ample suites with kitchenettes and private bathrooms. Your detail-oriented hosts, Veronica and Alejandro, go out of their way to make sure you have a pleasant stay. Curiously, the 'dog's paw' doesn't accept pets.

Casita Carolina GUESTHOUSE $

(☎983-834-23-34; www.casitacarolina.com; Av Costera 15, btwn Calles 16 & 18; campsites M$250, trailers M$300-350, d M$400-500, q M$700-800; P) A delightful place about 1½ blocks south of the fort, the Casita has a large lawn leading down to the lake, five fan-cooled rooms and a deluxe *palapa* that sleeps up to four. Guests can explore the lake in kayaks. For those on a tight budget, there's a camping ground and two small funky trailers parked on the lawn.

Amigo's Hotel Bacalar HOTEL $$

(☎983-107-92-34; www.bacalar.net; Av Costera s/n; d M$900; P@) Right on the lake and about 500m south of the fort, this ideally located property has five spacious guest rooms with king-size beds, hammocks, satellite TV, terraces and a *palapa*-covered common area with a lake view.

Hotel Laguna Bacalar HOTEL $$$

(☎983-834-22-05; www.hotellagunabacalar.com; Av Costera 479; d with fan/air-con M$1368/1548, bungalow from M$2280; P) This breezy place boasts a small swimming pool, a restaurant and excellent views of the lagoon, which you can explore by way of kayak or boat tours. It's 2km south of Bacalar town and only 150m east of Hwy 307, so if you're traveling by bus you can ask the driver to stop at the turnoff.

At last visit, the hotel was remodeling its rather plain rooms and bungalows.

Casa Caracol HOTEL $$$

(☎983-834-30-14; www.hotel-caracol.com; Av Costera 609; r US$136; P) If you're looking for creature comforts such as air-con and TV, this place isn't for you. If, on the other hand, you want a sublime place to relax, Casa Caracol delivers big time. Five *'cabañas'* overlook a lush garden and a lakeshore full of stromatolites (rock formations with ancient fossil remains) that date back more than 3 billion years.

Kayaks, paddle boards and bicycles are available. It's 3km south of town. There's a three-night minimum stay during high season.

Villas Bakalar APARTMENT $$$
(983-834-20-49; www.villasbakalar.com; Av 3 No 981, btwn Calles 28 & 30; ste incl breakfast M$1869;) Villas Bakalar offers a little bit of everything: a pool area with an excellent lake view, lush gardens and large suites with full kitchens.

Around Bacalar

★Rancho Encantado CABIN $$$
(998-884-20-71; www.encantado.com; Hwy 307 Km 24; d/ste incl breakfast from $2053/2761;) Laguna Bacalar is absolutely beautiful in and of itself, so imagine what it's like to stay at one of the most striking locations along the shore. A typical day on the *rancho* goes something like this: wake up in comfy thatch-roof cabin, have breakfast with lagoon view, snorkel in crystalline waters. The ranch is 3km north of Bacalar.

Eating & Drinking

Christian's Tacos TAQUERÍA $
(Calle 18, btwn Calles 7 & 9; tacos M$10-25, nachos M$45-70; 6:30pm-1am) If Christian's were in the *al pastor* (spit-roasted marinated pork) capital, Mexico City, it would compete with the best of them. The gooey *pastor nachos*, topped with slices of pork, beans and cheese, go just a little too far though.

Orizaba MEXICAN $
(Av 7, btwn Calles 24 & 26; breakfast M$30-50, set menu M$60; 8am-4pm;) Highly recommended by locals and expats alike, this place prepares breakfast and a set menu of homestyle Mexican favorites such as *poc-chuc* (grilled pork) in a casual setting.

Tacos de Cochinita Chepe's MEXICAN $
(Av 7 s/n, btwn Calles 20 & 22; tacos M$10, tortas M$20; 6am-noon Tue-Sun) There's no sign outside this mornings-only taco joint, so just follow your nose to the sweet smell of *cochinita* (slow-cooked pork).

★La Playita SEAFOOD $$
(www.laplayitabacalar.com; Av Costera 765, cnr Calle 26; mains M$104-159; 2-10pm Tue-Sun;) A sign outside reads, 'Eat, drink and swim' – and that pretty much sums it up. Fish and seafood dishes are tasty, albeit on the smallish side, but the Alipús mezcal and fine swimming certainly make up for that. A large rubber tree, which provides shade in the pebbly garden, was nearly uprooted in 2007 when Hurricane Dean pummeled the coast.

Los Aluxes MEXICAN $$$
(Av Costera 69; mains M$90-210; 1pm-9pm;) An open-air *palapa* restaurant serving Yucatecan and fusion dishes, this waterfront restaurant prepares interesting creations such as a rum-flambéed *filete de pescado en salsa de aluxes* (fish fillet in a creamy garlic-butter sauce). It's 1km south of town.

Entertainment

Galeón Pirata LIVE MUSIC
(www.facebook.com/galeonpirata.bacalar.1; Av Costera s/n, btwn Calles 30 & 32; 4pm-11pm Tue-Thu, 7pm-3am Fri & Sat) This indie cultural center stages live music, art exhibits, movie screenings and plays. It doubles as a restaurant-bar.

Information

Tourist Office (983-834-28-86; Av 3 s/n, btwn Calles 22 & 24; 8am-4pm Mon-Fri) Has useful info about local activities.

Getting There & Away

Buses don't enter town, but taxis and most combis will drop you at the town square. Buses arrive at the Bacalar's ADO terminal on Hwy 307, near Calle 30. From there it's about a 10-block walk southeast to the main square or you can grab a local taxi for M$15.

From the ADO station, buses go to Cancún, Mahahual, Xcalak and Tulum, to name just some of the destinations.

If you're driving from the north and want to reach the town and fort, take the first Bacalar exit and continue several blocks before turning left (east) down the hill. From Chetumal, head west to catch Hwy 307 north; after 25km on the highway you'll reach the signed right turn for Cenote Azul and Avenida Costera, aka Avenida 1.

Chetumal

983 / POP 150,000

The capital of Quintana Roo, Chetumal is a relatively quiet city going about its daily paces. The bayside esplanade hosts carnivals and events, and the modern Maya museum is impressive (though a bit short on artifacts). Excellent Maya ruins, amazing jungle

BODY ARTISTS: CRANIAL DEFORMATION, PIERCING & TATTOOS

Take a second to imagine what the Maya at the height of the Classic period must have looked like. Their heads were sloped back; their ears, noses, cheeks and sometimes even genitals were pierced; and their bodies were tattooed. These were, indeed, some of the first body artists.

Cranial deformation was one of the Maya's most unusual forms of body art, and was most often performed to indicate social status. Mothers would bind the head of their infant (male or female) tightly to a board while the skull was still soft. By positioning the board either on top of or behind the head, the mother could shape the skull in many ways – either long and pointy (known as 'elongated') or long and narrow, extending back rather than up (known as 'oblique'). As the infant grew older and the bones calcified, the headboard was no longer needed: the skull would retain its modified shape for life. Apparently, compressing the skull did not affect the intelligence or capabilities of the child. Both practices became less and less common after the Spanish arrived.

and the border to neighboring Belize are all close by. Though sightings are rare (there are no tours), manatees can sometimes be seen in the rather muddy bay or nearby mangrove shores.

History

Before the Spanish conquest, Chetumal was a Maya port used for shipping gold, feathers, cacao and copper to the northern Yucatán Peninsula. After the conquest, the town was not actually settled until 1898, when it was founded by the Mexican government to put a stop to the arms and lumber trade carried on by descendants of the Maya who fought in the Caste War. Dubbed Payo Obispo, the town changed its name to Chetumal in 1936. In 1955, Hurricane Janet virtually obliterated it, and 2007's Hurricane Dean did a bit of damage to the town's infrastructure.

Sights & Activities

Museo de la Cultura Maya MUSEUM
(☎983-832-68-38; Av de los Héroes 68, cnr Av Gandhi; M$69; ⊙9am-7pm Tue-Sun) The Museo de la Cultura Maya is the city's claim to cultural fame – a bold showpiece beautifully conceived and executed, though regrettably short on artifacts. It's organized into three levels, mirroring Maya cosmology. The main floor represents this world; the upper floor the heavens; and the lower floor Xibalbá, the underworld. The various exhibits cover all of the Mayab (lands of the Maya).

Scale models show the great Maya buildings as they may have appeared, including a temple complex set below Plexiglas you can walk over. Though original pieces are in short supply, there are replicas of stelae and a burial chamber from Honduras' Copán, reproductions of the murals found in Room 1 at Bonampak, and much more. Mechanical and computer displays illustrate the Maya's complex calendrical, numerical and writing systems.

The museum's courtyard, which you can enter for free, has salons for temporary exhibitions of modern artists. In the middle of the courtyard is a *na* (thatched hut) with implements of daily Maya life on display: gourds and grinding stones.

Museo de la Ciudad MUSEUM
(Local History Museum; Héroes de Chapultepec, cnr Av de los Héroes; adult/child under 13yr M$26/13; ⊙9am-7pm Tue-Sun) This museum is small but neatly done, displaying historic photos, military artifacts and old-time household items (even some vintage telephones and a TV). At last visit, the museum was adding two new rooms and interactive exhibits to bring it up to speed with the 21st century.

Ikadventure BICYCLE RENTAL
(www.ikadventures.blogspot.mx; Blvd Bahía s/n, cnr Emiliano Zapata; bike/inline skates per hour M$20/15; ⊙10am-10pm) This outfit rents bikes and skates, and runs an array of tours, including kayaking and fishing. For an enjoyable bike ride, pedal north along Boulevard Bahía to Calderitas, a pleasant fishing town about 8km away.

Festivals & Events

Carnaval RELIGIOUS
Carnaval in February is particularly lively in Chetumal. Colorful nightly parades bring locals into the streets to watch floats and plumed dancers pass by.

Chetumal

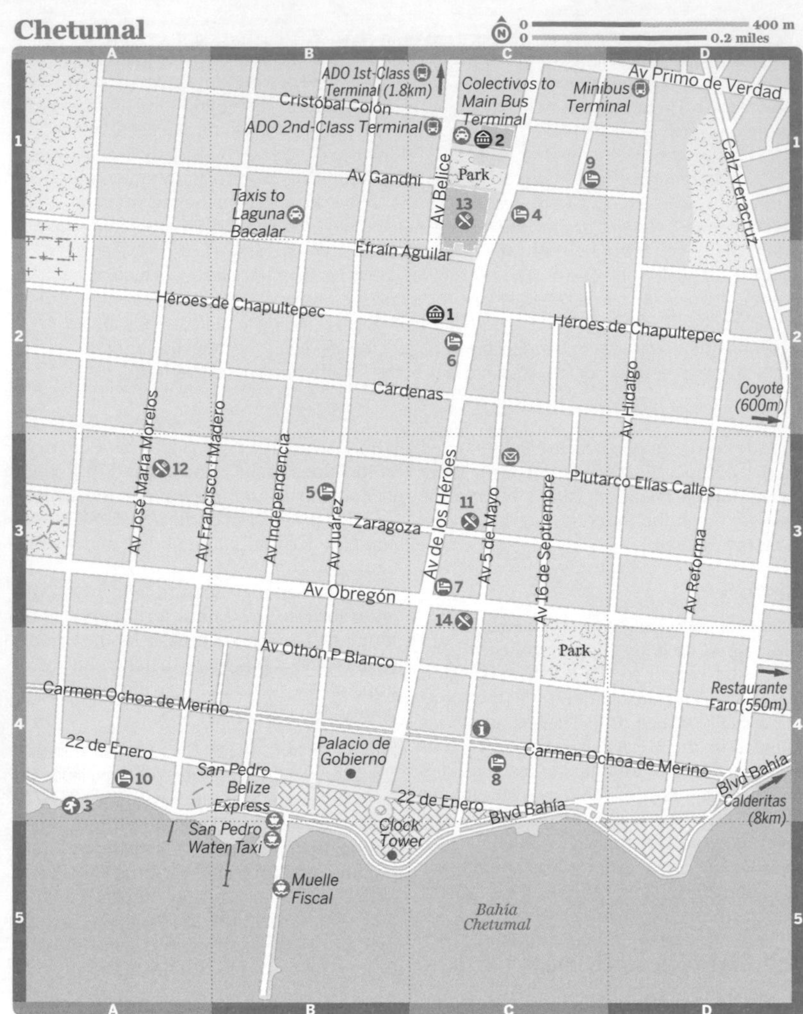

Sleeping

Hotel Palma Real HOTEL $

(983-833-09-63; www.palmarealchetumal.com; Av Obregón 193; d M$500; P) Unlike many of the budget hotels in town, rooms here get plenty of natural light and they're spacious, too. The only drawback is that it straddles a busy intersection, but traffic usually quiets down at a reasonable hour.

Hotel Xcalak HOTEL $

(983-129-17-08; www.hotelxcalak.com.mx; Av Gandhi, cnr 16 de Septiembre; r M$400;) That rare Chetumal budget hotel that doesn't look like it's trapped in the '70s. It's near the city's best museum and transport to Laguna Bacalar, and there's a good restaurant downstairs.

Hotel Villanueva HOTEL $$

(983-267-33-70; www.hotel-villanueva.com; Ochoa de Merino 166; d/ste M$800/1050; P) A good central option for the price, Villanueva's minimalist-designed rooms overlook an Astroturf courtyard with palm trees, a decent-sized pool and a tiny gym. The larger suites get you a more spacious bathroom and a microwave, and some have balconies.

Chetumal

Sights

1 Museo de la Ciudad C2
2 Museo de la Cultura Maya C1

Activities, Courses & Tours

3 Ikadventure A4

Sleeping

4 Capital Plaza C1
5 Hotel Grand Marlon B3
6 Hotel Los Cocos C2
7 Hotel Palma Real C3
8 Hotel Villanueva C4
9 Hotel Xcalak C1
10 Noor Hotel A4

Eating

11 Café Los Milagros C3
12 Marisquería El Taco Loco A3
13 Mercado Ignacio Manuel Altamirano C1
Restaurant Pantoja .... (see 9)
14 Sergio's Pizzas C3

Hotel Grand Marlon HOTEL **$$**
(☎983-285-32-79; www.hotelesmarlon.com; Av Juárez 88, btwn Zaragoza & Plutarco Elías Calles; r/ste from M$700/930; P) With modern facilities and a pool area complete with Astroturf and a lukewarm Jacuzzi, the 'Grand' almost achieves 'hip boutique' status. The simple, stylish rooms are an excellent deal. Or, save a few hundred pesos by heading across the street to the plain ol' Marlon, its sister hotel, but don't say we didn't warn you about the noisy air-con units.

Hotel Los Cocos HOTEL **$$**
(☎983-835-04-30; www.hotelloscocos.com.mx; Av de los Héroes 134, cnr Héroes de Chapultepec; d/ste with air-con from M$912/1824; P@) With a great location, Hotel Los Cocos has a seriously mirrored lobby that gets your inner disco-dancer rising. There's also a nice swimming pool, Jacuzzi, gym and a popular restaurant. All rooms have small fridges and balconies. Los Cocos runs 'promotions' pretty much year-round, so it's likely you'll pay at least a couple of hundred pesos less than the fares listed here.

Noor Hotel HOTEL **$$**
(☎983-835-13-00; Blvd Bahía 3, cnr Av Morelos; r M$1065; P) Right on the bay, the Noor will appeal to those looking to get away from the bustling *centro*. Bayview rooms are your best bet here, as the interior rooms tend to get poor ventilation. There's a decent pool and the restaurant prepares international cuisine. The boardwalk across the way is sweet for afternoon strolls.

Capital Plaza HOTEL **$$$**
(☎983-835-04-00; www.capitalplaza.mx; Av de los Héroes 171, cnr Av Gandhi; d M$1200, ste M$1600-2600; P) One of the fanciest hotels in town, comfortable rooms overlook a courtyard with a swimming pool surrounded by tropical gardens, a restaurant and bar.

Eating & Drinking

There is a row of small, simple eateries serving inexpensive Yucatecan food at **Mercado Ignacio Manuel Altamirano** (cnr Avenida de los Héroes & Efraín Aguilar).

A fun six-block strip of bars lines Boulevard Bahía, north of Avenida Othón Blanco.

Café Los Milagros CAFE **$**
(☎983-832-44-33; Zaragoza s/n; breakfast M$45-110, lunch M$26-92; ⏰7am-6pm Mon-Fri, 7am-1pm Sat & Sun;) Serves great espresso and food outdoors. A favorite with Chetumal's student and intellectual set, it's a good spot to chat with locals or while away the time with a game of dominoes.

Restaurant Pantoja MEXICAN **$**
(☎983-832-39-57; cnr Avs Gandhi & 16 de Septiembre; mains M$35-70, menu del día M$65; ⏰7am-6pm Mon-Sat;) A popular, family-run restaurant serving breakfasts, enchiladas and a variety of meat dishes, or you can opt for the set meal *(menu del día)*. Although fan-cooled, it gets a bit warm in the afternoon.

★ **Restaurante Xel-Ha** SEAFOOD **$$**
(☎983-285-02-87; Av Yucatán s/n, Calderitas; mains M$120-200; ⏰11am-8pm;) For some of the best fresh fish around, head about 8km north of Chetumal to the fishing village of Calderitas, where you'll find this classic bayside seafood restaurant. The fried whole fish, usually *boquinete* (hogfish), is cooked just right and deftly plated.

To get here, head north on Boulevard Bahía to Avenida Yucatán. Or take a 'Calderitas' bus from the Museo de la Cultura Maya. You can also cycle here.

Marisquería El Taco Loco SEAFOOD **$$**
(www.tacolocochetumal.com; Av Morelos 87; tacos M$15-20, mains M$85-138; ⏰8am-6pm;) A Chetumal favorite for more than three decades. Try the house specialty, *camaron empanizado* (breaded shrimp), or the fish taco *a la mantequila* (sautéed in butter),

both of which are served on handmade tortillas and come with creamy garlic sauce and spicy habanero salsa on the side.

Sergio's Pizzas PIZZA **$$**
(☎983-832-29-91; Av Obregón 182, cnr Av 5 de Mayo; mains M$80-190; ⏰7am-midnight; 🚭📶) This well air-conditioned place serves pizzas and cold beer in frosted mugs, plus Mexican dishes, steaks and seafood.

Restaurante Faro STEAK **$$$**
(www.facebook.com/rest.faro; Blvd Bahía 54, btwn Av Othón Blanco & Heróico Colegio Militar; breakfast M$65-79, lunch & dinner M$175-229; ⏰8am-1pm Mon, to 11:30pm Tue-Thu & Sun, to 12:30am Fri & Sat; 🚭📶) With indoor and outdoor seating overlooking the bay, the Faro offers reasonably priced breakfasts and a bay view. The steakhouse's lunch and dinner menu includes choice beef cuts, fish, seafood dishes and an array of salads.

Coyote LIVE MUSIC
(Blvd Bahía s/n, cnr Cádenas; ⏰10pm-5am Thu-Sun) Local and national *banda* (*norteña* music) groups take the stage around midnight at the open-air Coyote – in no time they'll have you howling at the moon.

ℹ Orientation

Chetumal is laid out on a grand plan with a grid of wide boulevards. The southern edge is bordered by the water. The main street, Avenida de los Héroes, divides the city into east and west sides, ending at the waterfront. Avenida Obregón parallels the bay and leads, heading westward, first to a *glorieta* (traffic circle), then to the airport and nearby immigration office, then to the turn for Belize.

ℹ Information

There are numerous banks and ATMs around town, including an ATM inside the 1st-class bus terminal.

Arba (☎983-832-25-81; Efraín Aguilar s/n, btwn Avs de los Héroes & Juárez; per hr M$13; ⏰7am-10:30pm) Internet cafe with several similar cafes nearby.

Banorte (Av de los Héroes, btwn Plutarco Elías Calles & Cárdenas; ⏰9am-5pm Mon-Sat, to 2pm Sat) For ATM and bank services.

Cruz Roja (Red Cross; ☎065; cnr Avs Independencia & Héroes de Chapultepec; ⏰24hr) For medical emergencies.

Emergency (☎066)

Instituto Nacional de Migración (Immigration Office; www.inm.gob.mx; Hwy 186, across from

BUSES FROM CHETUMAL

DESTINATION	FARE (M$)	DURATION (HRS)	FREQUENCY (DAILY)
Bacalar	30-32	¾	frequent; from 2nd-class terminal, minibus terminal
Belize City, Belize	150	4-4½	frequent; from Nuevo Mercado Lázaro Cárdenas
Campeche	283-440	6-7	3; from 1st- and 2nd-class terminals
Cancún	235-354	5½-6½	frequent
Corozal, Belize	30-50	1	frequent; from Nuevo Mercado Lázaro Cárdenas
Escárcega	232-288	4	9
Felipe Carrillo Puerto	128	2½-3	5; from 1st- and 2nd-class terminals
Flores, Guatemala (for Tikal)	450	7½-8	7am
Mahahual	80-128	2½-3½	3; from 1st- and 2nd-class terminals
Mérida	444	5½-6	4
Orange Walk, Belize	75	2¼	frequent; from Nuevo Mercado Lázaro Cárdenas
Palenque	356-602	6½-7½	5
Tulum	179-268	3¼-4	11
Valladolid	202	5½	3; from 2nd-class terminal
Veracruz	1070	17	1 at 6:30pm
Villahermosa	580	8¼-9	7
Xcalak	100	4-4½	2 at 5:40am and 4:10pm; from 2nd-class terminal
Xpujil	118-140	2-3	5

airport; 9am-1pm Mon-Fri) Head here to replace lost tourist permits.

Post Office (983-832-98-47; cnr Plutarco Elías Calles & Av 5 de Mayo; 8am-7pm Mon-Fri, to 2pm Sat)

Tourist Information Office (983-833-24-65; Av 5 de Mayo 21, cnr Ochoa de Merino; 8:30am-4:30pm Mon-Fri) Has brochures and a well-meaning staff.

Getting There & Away

AIR

Chetumal's small airport is roughly 2km northwest of the city center along Avenida Obregón.

Interjet (800-011-23-45; www.interjet.com) runs direct flights from Mexico City.

BOAT

Belize-bound ferries depart from the **muelle fiscal dock** (Dock; Blvd Bahía) on Boulevard Bahía.

San Pedro Belize Express (983-832-16-48; www.belizewatertaxi.com; Av Blvd Bahía s/n, Muelle Fiscal) Boat transportation to Belize City, Caye Caulker and San Pedro.

San Pedro Water Taxi (www.sanpedrowatertaxi.com; Blvd Bahía s/n, Muelle Fiscal; one-way to San Pedro/Caye Caulker US$60/65) Runs water taxis to San Pedro and Caye Caulker, in Belize.

BUS

The ADO 1st-class bus terminal is about 2km north of the center, just west of the intersection of Avenidas Insurgentes and Belice. Services are provided by ADO and OCC (1st class) and Mayab (2nd class), among other bus lines.

The ADO 2nd-class terminal, just west of the Museo de la Cultura Maya, is a good place to get info. Caribe, Sur and Mayab buses leave from here.

Beilze-bound buses depart from the Nuevo Mercado Lázaro Cárdenas, on Calzada Veracruz at Confederación Nacional Campesina Campeche (also called Segundo Circuito), about 10 blocks north of Avenida Primo de Verdad. Bus line San Juan departs from the Ist-class terminal to Flores, Guatemala for Tikal. Tickets can be purchased at the Mi Escape booth.

Double-check bus details before departure as buses leave from multiple locations and this information is subject to change. Departures leave from the 1st-class terminal, unless noted otherwise.

ADO 1st-Class Terminal (983-832-51 10; www.ado.com.mx; Salvador Novo 179, off Av Insurgentes) Services to Cancún, Mérida, Valladolid, Xcalak and other destinations.

ADO 2nd-Class Terminal (Av Belice s/n; 6am-10pm) Buses to Mahahual, Xcalak, Campeche, Cancún and Riviera Maya

Minibus Terminal (cnr Avs Primo de Verdad & Hidalgo) Minibuses serve Laguna Bacalar (M$30) from 8am to 2pm.

TAXI

City cabs charge about M$20 for short trips. **Taxis** on Avenida Independencia (between Efraín Aguilar and Avenida Gandhi) charge M$40 per person for Laguna Bacalar.

Getting Around

Most places in Chetumal's tourist zone are within walking distance. To reach the main bus terminal from the center, catch a **colectivo** from the corner of Avenidas Belice and Cristóbal Colón, in front of the 2nd-class bus station. Ask to be left at the *glorieta* at Avenida Insurgentes. Head left (west) to reach the terminal.

You'll also find Calderitas buses departing from the same corner.

Corredor Arqucológico

The Corredor Arqueológico comprises the archaeological sites of Dzibanché and Kohunlich, two intriguing and seldom-visited Maya ruins that can be visited on a day trip from Chetumal.

Sights

Dzibanché ARCHAEOLOGICAL SITE

(admission incl entry to Kinich-Ná M$52; 8am-5pm) Though it's a chore to get to, this site is definitely worth a visit for its secluded, semi-wild nature. Dzibanché (meaning 'writing on wood') was a major city extending more than 40 sq km and there are a number of excavated palaces and pyramids, though the site itself is not completely excavated. On the way there you'll pass beautiful countryside

The first restored structure you will come to is Edificio 6, the **Palacio de los Dinteles** (Palace of the Lintels), which gave the site its name. This is a perfect spot to orient yourself for the rest of the site: facing Edificio 6's steps, you are looking east. It's a pyramid topped by a temple with two vaulted galleries; the base dates from the early Classic period (AD 300–600), while the temple is from the late Classic period (AD 600–900). Climb the steps and stand directly under the original lintel on the right (south) side of the temple. Looking up you can see a Maya calendrical inscription with the date working out to AD 733. This is some old wood

On descending, head to your left (south) and thread between a mound on the right and a low, mostly restored, stepped structure on the left. This structure is Edificio 16, **Palacio de los Tucanes**; in the center from the side you first approach are the visible remains of posts that bore a mask. The path then brings you into **Plaza Gann**. Circling it counterclockwise takes you past Edificio 14 (stuck onto the north side of a larger building), decorated at the base with *tamborcillos* (little drums), in late Classic Río Bec style – look up the dirt hill to see them. The larger building to the south is Edificio 13, **Templo de los Cautivos**, so named for the carvings in its steps of captives submitting to whatever captives submitted to in those days. This seems to be the dominant (if you'll pardon the pun) theme in most Maya stelae.

On the east side of the plaza is Dzibanché's highest structure, the **Templo de los Cormoranes** (Temple of the Cormorants; Edificio 2), whose upper structure has been restored.

Exit the plaza by climbing the stone steps to the north of Edificio 2. At the top of the stairs is **Plaza del Xibalbá** (Plaza of the Underworld), though it's higher than Plaza Gann.

Opposite Palacio Norte is, of course, Palacio Sur, and from here you can see more of Edificio 2, but the most notable building is across the plaza: Edificio 1, the recently restored **Templo del Buho** (Temple of the Owl). It had an inner chamber with a stairway leading down to another chamber, in which were found the remains of a VIP and burial offerings. The nearly 360-degree views from the very top of the temple (it's a bit dicey, so be careful) are quite impressive. You can see Grupo Lamay to the west and you may spot Kinich-Ná, more than 2km to the northwest.

Part of Dzibanché but well removed from the main site, **Kinich-Ná** consists of one building. But what a building: the megalithic **Acrópolis** held at least five temples on three levels, and a couple more dead VIPs with offerings. The site's name derives from the frieze of the Maya sun god once found at the top of the structure. It's an easy drive of 2km along a narrow but good road leading north from near Dzibanché's visitors center.

Kohunlich ARCHAEOLOGICAL SITE
(off Hwy 186; adult/child under 13yr M$62/free; ⌚8am-5pm) This archaeological site sits on a carpeted green. The ruins, dating from both the late pre-Classic (AD 100–200) and the early Classic (AD 300–600) periods, are famous for the great **Templo de los Mascarones** (Temple of the Masks), a pyramid-like structure with a central stairway flanked by huge, 3m-high stucco masks of the sun god.

The thick lips and prominent features are reminiscent of Olmec sculptures. Of the eight original masks, only five remain relatively intact following the ravages of archaeological looters. Large thatch coverings have been erected to protect the masks from weathering, but you can still get a good look at them. Try to imagine what the pyramid and its red masks must have looked like in the old days as the Maya approached them across the sunken courtyard at the front.

A few hundred meters southwest of Plaza Merwin are the **27 Escalones** (27 Steps), the remains of an extensive residential area.

The hydraulic engineering used at Kohunlich was a great achievement; 90,000 of the site's 210,000 sq meters were cut to channel rainwater into Kohunlich's once-enormous reservoir.

Getting There & Away

The turnoff for Dzibanché from Hwy 186 is about 44km west of Chetumal, on the right just after the Zona Arqueológico sign. From there it's another 24km north and east along a narrow road. About 2km after the tiny town of Morocoy you'll need to turn right again. It's easy to miss the sign unless you're looking for it.

Kohunlich's turnoff is 3km west along Hwy 186 from the Dzibanché turnoff, and the site lies at the end of a 9km road. It's a straight shot from the highway.

There's no public transportation running directly to either of the sites. They're best visited by car, though Kohunlich could conceivably be reached by taking an early bus to the village of Francisco Villa near the turnoff, then either hitchhiking or walking the 9km to the site. To return by bus to Chetumal or head west to Xpujil or Escárcega you'll have to flag down a bus on the highway; not all buses will stop.

Taxis can be rented in Chetumal for as little as M$200 per hour; to visit both sites you'd need at least five hours, or roughly M$1000. A group could pile in and split the cost.

Corozal

☎501 / POP 9100

This fairly laid-back town, 18km south of the Mexico-Belize border, is an appropriate introduction to English-speaking Belize. There's a simple plaza in the center, a waterfront, some small ruins and a warm Caribbean vibe. You'll find an ATM at the plaza.

Sights

Santa Rita RUIN
(admission BZ$10; ⌚8am-6pm) Santa Rita was an ancient Maya coastal town that once occupied the same strategic trading position as

CROSSING THE MEXICO-BELIZE BORDER

If you want to do a day trip or extended stay in Belize, or perhaps continue on to Guatemala, here are some helpful tips about crossing the Mexico–Belize border.

- If you enter Mexico by air, a fee called the *derecho de no residente* (DNR, no resident fee) is usually included in the ticket price and you will not be required to pay an 'exit fee,' as the occasional unscrupulous Mexican border offical may suggest.
- Those entering by land and who have been in the country for more than seven days must pay M$332 at the border before leaving Mexico. Keep in mind that an itemized receipt of the airline ticket detailing payment of the DNR is the only form of proof that you did fork out the fee.
- The Belizean embassy says tourists entering the country for less than 24 hours are not required to show proof of a hotel reservation, however, if you plan on staying longer you'll be asked to do so (there's a terminal for booking reservations at the border station).
- Cabs waiting on the Belize side charge US$20 to Corazal.
- Visitors who have been in Belize for less than 24 hours must pay a US$15 departure fee; it's US$19 for stays longer than 24 hours.

present-day Corozal Town, namely the spot between two rivers – the Río Hondo (which now forms the Belize–Mexico border) and the New River (which enters Corozal Bay south of town). Much of Santa Rita remains unexcavated, but it's worth a short excursion out of town to explore the site.

To reach the Maya site, head out of town on Santa Rita Rd. Continuing north on the main highway toward Mexico, turn left at the Super Santa Rita store. Some 320yd past the store you'll find a wooded area on the right and in its midst a partially restored pyramid offering an amazing view across the surrounding town to the bay. Apply liberal amounts of bug spray before making the trip. A taxi from downtown costs BZ$5.

Sleeping & Eating

★Serenity Sands B&B $$
(☎669-2394; www.serenitysands.com; Consejo Rd; d BZ$190-200, house BZ$220; P❄@📶) 🍃 Located about 3 miles north of Corozal Town, this B&B is off the beaten track, off the grid and out of this world. The remote beachside setting offers the perfect combination of isolation and accessibility (though you'll need a vehicle to get here), and the four spacious tiled rooms are decorated with locally crafted furniture and boast private balconies.

★Almond Tree Resort RESORT $$$
(☎422-0006; www.almondtreeresort.com; 425 Bayshore Dr; r BZ$196-338; P❄📶) The town's most luxurious lodging, this gorgeous seaside inn offers spacious, stylish rooms with wonderful sea views, Caribbean-style furniture and tempurpedic beds. Deluxe suites have full kitchenettes. The whole place is centered on lush grounds and a glorious swimming pool.

The 1 MEXICAN $
(4th Ave; tacos BZ$2; ⏰8am-8pm) Right on the corner of Central Park, this popular little shop serves authentic Mexican-style tacos and *tortas* (Mexican pressed sandwiches) with a great variety of sauces.

Venky's Kabab Corner INDIAN $
(☎402-0546; 5th St South; dishes BZ$10-15; ⏰9am-9:30pm) Chef Venky is the premier – and, as far as we know, only – Hindu chef in Corozal, cooking excellent Indian meals, both meat and vegetarian. The place is not much to look at on the inside, in fact there is just one table that is usually covered in assorted clutter, but the food is excellent and filling.

Getting There & Away

Buses to Belize (M$30 to M$50) depart from Chetumal's Nuevo Mercado Lázaro Cárdenas. The same buses return to Chetumal, departing from the Corozal bus station. You can also catch Guatemala-bound buses from Corozal to Tikal.

Yucatán State & the Maya Heartland

POP 2 MILLION

Includes ➡

Best Places to Eat

- Kinich (p182)
- Yerba Buena del Sisal (p194)
- El Mirador (p170)
- Wayan'e (p153)

Best Places to Stay

- Luz en Yucatán (p152)
- Casa Isabel (p153)
- Pickled Onion (p164)
- Casa de Celeste Vida (p176)

Why Go?

Sitting regally on the northern tip of the peninsula, Yucatán state sees less mass tourism than its flashy neighbor, Quintana Roo. It is sophisticated and savvy, and the perfect spot for travelers more interested in cultural exploration than beach life. Sure, there are a few nice beaches in Celestún and Progreso, but most people come to this area to explore the ancient Maya sites peppered throughout the region, like the Ruta Puuc, which will take you to four or five ruins in just a day.

Visitors also come to experience the past and present in the cloistered corners of colonial cities, to visit *henequén* haciendas (vast estates that produced agave plant fibers, used to make rope) lost to time or restored by caring hands to old glory, and to discover the energy, spirit and subtle contrasts of this authentic corner of southeastern Mexico.

When to Go

- The region's cultural mecca hosts the month-long Mérida fest in January, which celebrates the founding of the city. It's also the coolest time of the year – an important consideration when visiting the capital.
- Every vernal and autumnal equinox visitors at Chichén Itzá can witness the appearance of a shadow serpent figure on the stairs of the site's iconic pyramid, El Castillo.
- Beat the heat from November to March, especially if you're planning on visiting inland cities, plus they're ideal months for flamingo-watching in Celestún.

MÉRIDA

999 / POP 780,000

Since the Spanish conquest, Mérida has been the cultural capital of the entire Yucatán Peninsula. At times provincial, at others *'muy cosmopolitano,'* it is a town steeped in colonial history, with narrow streets, broad central plazas and the region's best museums. It's also a perfect place from which to kick off your adventure into the rest of Yucatán state. There are cheap eats, good hostels and hotels, thriving markets and events happening just about every night somewhere in the downtown area.

Long popular with European travelers looking to go beyond the hubbub of Quintana Roo's resort towns, Mérida is not an 'undiscovered Mexican gem' like some of the tourist brochures claim. Simply put, it's a tourist town, but a tourist town too big to feel like a tourist trap. And as the capital of Yucatán state, Mérida is also the cultural crossroads of the region, and there's something just a smidge elitist about Mérida: the people who live here have a beautiful town, and they know it.

History

Francisco de Montejo (the Younger) founded a Spanish colony at Campeche, about 160km to the southwest, in 1540. From this base he took advantage of political dissension among the Maya, conquering T'ho (now Mérida) in 1542. By decade's end Yucatán was mostly under Spanish colonial rule.

When Montejo's conquistadors entered T'ho, they found a major Maya settlement of lime-mortared stone that reminded them of the Roman architecture in Mérida, Spain. They promptly renamed the city and proceeded to build it into the regional capital, dismantling the Maya structures and using the materials to construct a cathedral and other stately buildings. Mérida took its colonial orders directly from Spain, not from Mexico City, and Yucatán has had a distinct cultural and political identity ever since.

During the Caste War, only Mérida and Campeche were able to hold out against the rebel forces. On the brink of surrender, the ruling class in Mérida was saved by reinforcements sent from central Mexico in exchange for Mérida's agreement to take orders from Mexico City.

Mérida today is the peninsula's center of commerce, a bustling city that has been growing rapidly ever since *maquiladoras* (low-paying, for-export factories) started cropping up in the 1980s and '90s, and as the tourism industry picked up during those decades as well. The growth has drawn migrant workers from all around Mexico and there's a large Lebanese community in town.

Sights

Plaza Grande & Around

Plaza Grande is one of the nicest plazas in Mexico, and huge laurel trees shade the park's benches and wide sidewalks. It was the religious and social center of ancient T'ho; under the Spanish it was the Plaza de Armas, the parade ground, laid out by Francisco de Montejo (the Younger). There's a crafts market on Sunday and dance or live music nearly every night.

★**Casa de Montejo** MUSEUM

(Museo Casa Montejo; www.casasdeculturabanamex.com/museocasamontejo; Calle 63 No 506, Palacio de Montejo; 10am-7pm Mon-Sat, to 2pm Sun) FREE Casa de Montejo is on the south side of the Plaza Grande and dates from 1549. It originally housed soldiers but was soon converted into a mansion that served members of the Montejo family until 1970. Today it houses a bank and museum with a permanent exhibition of renovated Victorian, neorococo and neorenaissance furnishings of the historic building.

Outside, take a close look at the facade, where triumphant halberd-bearing conquistadors stand on the heads of generic barbarians (though they're not Maya, the association is inescapable). Typical of the symbolism in colonial statuary, the vanquished are rendered much smaller than the victors; works on various churches throughout the region feature big priests towering over or in front of small indigenous people. Also gazing across the plaza from the facade are busts of Montejo the Elder, his wife and his daughter.

Museo de Arte Contemporáneo MUSEUM

(Macay; 999-928-32-36; www.macay.org; Pasaje de la Revolución s/n, btwn Calles 58 & 60; 10am-6pm Wed-Mon) FREE Housed in the former archbishop's palace, the attractive Museo de Arte Contemporáneo holds permanent exhibitions of Yucatán's most famous painters and sculptors, as well as revolving exhibitions of contemporary art from Mexico and abroad.

Yucatán State & the Maya Heartland Highlights

1 Marvel at colonial architecture or enjoy a free concert in the cultural capital of **Mérida** (p143).

2 Find out why they named **Chichén Itzá** (p183) one of the 'new seven wonders of the world,' and why **Ek' Balam** (p195) should have made the short list.

3 Scan the salty horizon for flamingos at the **Reserva de la Biosfera Ría Celestún** (p174) or **Reserva de la Biosfera Ría Lagartos** (p197).

4 Cool off at low-key beach town **Progreso** (p178) and explore even quieter coastal communities to the east.

5 Spin off the tourist track to the less-visited areas and cenotes around **Valladolid** (p191) and the archaeological sites of the **Ruta Puuc** (p165).

Las Coloradas
Estero Río Lagartos
Río Lagartos
Isla Cerritos
El Cuyo
San Felipe
3 Reserva de la Biosfera Ría Lagartos
Parque Natural San Felipe
Solferino
Reserva Estatal Dzilam de Bravo
Loche
Dzilam de Bravo
Santa Clara
Colonia Yucatán
Panabá
Dzilam de Gonzalez
Yoactún
Kantunilkin
Dzidzantun
Sucilá
Tizimín
Buctzotz
Popolnah
Temax
Calotmul
Chancenote
Cansahcab
Yokdzonot
Tepakán
Espita
Genesis Eco-Oasis
Xcan
Nuevo Xcan
Tekanto
Cenotillo
2 Ek' Balam
Izamal
Tunkas
Dzitás
Yaxche
Hoctún
Kantunil
5 Valladolid
Chemax
Zocchel
Holca
(Toll)
Pisté
Chichimilá
Huhí
Yodznot
2 Chichén Itzá
Tekom
Cobá
Tixcalpupu
Sotuta
Yaxcabá
Cantamayec
Chan Chimila
Chumayel
Teabo
Chiquindzonal
Tepich
Muyil
Tihosuco
Yucatan Peninsula
Ichmul
Tekax
Peto
Saban
La Ruta de los Conventos
Tzucacab
QUINTANA ROO
Santa Rosa
Dzuiché
Senor
Laguna Chicnancanab
José María Morelos
Felipe Carrillo Puerto
Polyuc
Reserva de la Biosfera Sian Ka'an
Laguna Kaná
Kantemo

Palacio de Gobierno MURALS
(Calle 61 s/n; ⏲8am-8pm) FREE Built in 1892, the Palacio de Gobierno houses the state of Yucatán's executive government offices (and a tourist office). Have a look inside at the murals and oil paintings by local artist Fernando Castro Pacheco. Completed in the late 1970s, they portray a symbolic history of the Maya and their interaction with the Spaniards.

Catedral de San Ildefonso CATHEDRAL
(Calle 60 s/n; ⏲6am-7pm) On the site of a former Maya temple is Mérida's hulking, severe cathedral, begun in 1561 and completed in 1598. Some of the stone from the Maya temple was used in its construction. The massive crucifix behind the altar is **Cristo de la Unidad** (Christ of Unity), a symbol of reconciliation between those of Spanish and Maya heritage.

To the right over the south door is a painting of Tutul Xiu, *cacique* (indigenous chief) of the town of Maní paying his respects to his ally Francisco de Montejo at T'ho. (De Montejo and Xiu jointly defeated the Cocomes; Xiu converted to Christianity, and his descendants still live in Mérida.)

In the small chapel to the left of the altar is Mérida's most famous religious artifact, a statue called **Cristo de las Ampollas** (Christ of the Blisters). Local legend says the statue was carved from a tree that was hit by lightning and burned for an entire night without charring. It is also said to be the only object to have survived the fiery destruction of the church in the town of Ichmul (though it was blackened and blistered from the heat). The statue was moved to the Mérida cathedral in 1645.

Other than these items, the cathedral's interior is largely plain, its rich decoration having been stripped away by angry peasants at the height of anticlerical fervor during the Mexican Revolution.

Museo de la Ciudad MUSEUM
(City Museum; ☎999-924-42-64; Calle 56 No 529A, btwn Calles 65 & 65A; ⏲9am-6pm Tue-Fri, to 2pm Sat & Sun) FREE The Museo de la Ciudad is housed in the old post office and offers a great reprieve from the hustle, honks and exhaust of this market neighborhood. There are exhibits tracing the city's history back to pre-Conquest days up through the belle epoque period, when *henequén* (sisal) brought riches to the region, and into the 20th century.

Palacio Municipal HISTORIC BUILDING
(City Hall; Calle 62 s/n) FREE Originally built in 1542, Mérida's Palacio Municipal was twice refurbished, in the 1730s and the 1850s.

Centro Cultural Olimpo BUILDING
(☎999-942-00-00, ext 80125; www.merida.gob.mx/capitalcultural; cnr Calles 61 & 62) Attempts to create a modern exterior for Mérida's municipal cultural center were halted by government order to preserve the colonial character of the plaza. The ultramodern interior serves as a venue for music and dance performances, as well as other exhibitions.

Mercado Municipal Lucas de Gálvez MARKET
(cnr Calles 56A & 67; ⏲6am-5pm) Mérida's main market is an ever-evolving mass of commerce, with stalls selling everything from *panuchos* (fried tortillas stuffed with beans and topped with meat and veggies) to ceviche. The chaotic surrounding streets are all part of the large market district.

Parque Zoológico del Centenario ZOO
(www.merida.gob.mx/centenario/php/index.phpx; Av Itzáes s/n, cnr Calle 59; ⏲6am-6pm Tue-Sun; 👪; 🚌R-2 Herradura) FREE The large, verdant Parque Centenario, bordered by Avenida Itzáes, features lions, bears, an aviary, a playground and bumper boats. It's about 12 blocks west of the main square. To get here take a 'R-2 Herradura' bus from the corner of Calles 64 and 65.

Calle 60

Lined with many of the city's most emblematic sights, Calle 60 cuts through the heart of the Centro, and further north it runs parallel to Paseo de Montejo, a wide main avenue known for its elegant mansions.

★ **Parque Santa Lucía** PARK
(cnr Calles 60 & 55) The pretty little Parque Santa Lucía has arcades on the north and west sides; this was where travelers would get on or off the stagecoaches that linked towns and villages with the provincial capital. Today it's a popular restaurant area and venue for **Serentas Yucatecas** (Yucatacen Serenades), a free weekly concert on Thursday at 9pm.

Teatro Peón Contreras THEATER
(www.sinfonicadeyucatan.com.mx; cnr Calles 60 & 57) The enormous Teatro Peón Contreras was built between 1900 and 1908, during

Mérida's *henequén* heyday. It boasts a main staircase of Carrara marble, a dome with faded frescoes by Italian artists, and various paintings and murals throughout the building. The **Yucatán Symphony Orchestra** performs here Friday at 9pm and Sunday at noon throughout most of the year. See the website for more information.

Iglesia de Jesús CHURCH
(Calle 60 s/n) The 17th-century Iglesia de Jesús is also called Iglesia de la Tercera Orden. Built by Jesuits in 1618, this is the sole surviving edifice from a complex of buildings that once filled the entire city block. The church was built from the stones of a destroyed Maya temple that once occupied the same site. On the west wall facing Parque Hidalgo, look closely and you can see two stones still bearing Maya carvings.

Universidad Autónoma de Yucatán UNIVERSITY
(www.cultura.uady.mx; Calle 60 s/n) The modern Universidad Autónoma de Yucatán was established in the 19th century by Governor Felipe Carrillo Puerto and General Manuel Cepeda Peraza. Inside you'll find the university cultural center, which stages dance, music and theater performances.

Parque de la Mejorada

Head six blocks east of Calle 60 and you'll find this pleasant square flanked by a pretty colonial-era monastery and a small pop-art museum.

Museo de Arte Popular de Yucatán MUSEUM
(Yucatán Museum of Popular Art; Calle 50A No 487; 10am-5pm Tue-Sat, to 3pm Sun) FREE In a building built in 1906, the Museo de Arte Popular de Yucatán has a small rotating exhibition downstairs that features popular art from around Mexico. The permanent exhibition upstairs gives you an idea of how locals embroider *huipiles* (long, woven, white sleeveless tunics with intricate, colorful embroidery) and it explains traditional techniques used to make ceramics. Watch out for jaguars drinking toilet water!

Iglesia La Mejorada CHURCH
(Calle 50 s/n) Across from Parque de la Mejorada stands Iglesia La Mejorada, a large 17th-century church. The building just north of it was a monastery (el Convento de La Mejorada) until the late 19th century. It now houses an academic building, but visitors are sometimes allowed to view the grounds.

Paseo de Montejo

Paseo de Montejo, which runs parallel to Calles 56 and 58, was an attempt by Mérida's 19th-century city planners to create a wide boulevard similar to the Paseo de la Reforma in Mexico City or the Champs-Élysées in Paris. Though more modest than its predecessors, the Paseo de Montejo is still a beautiful swath of green, relatively open space in an urban conglomeration of stone and concrete. There are occasional sculpture exhibits along the *paseo* (promenade).

Europe's architectural and social influence can be seen along the *paseo* in the fine mansions built by wealthy families around the end of the 19th century. The greatest concentrations of surviving mansions are north of Calle 37, and on the first block of Avenida Colón west of Paseo de Montejo.

★ **Gran Museo del Mundo Maya** MUSEUM
(Calle 60 Nte No 299E; M$150; 8am-5pm Wed-Mon, light & sound show 8:30pm; P; R-2) A world-class museum celebrating Maya culture, the Gran Museo houses a permanent collection of more than 1100 remarkably well-preserved artifacts, including a reclining chac-mool sculpture from Chichén Itzá and a cool underworld figure unearthed at Ek' Balam (check out homeboy's punk-rock skull belt and reptile headdress). If you're planning on visiting the area's ruins, drop by here first for some context and an up-close look at some of the fascinating pieces found at the sites.

Inaugurated in 2012, the contemporary building was designed in the form of a ceiba, a sacred tree believed by the Maya to connect the living with the underworld and the heavens above. On a wall outside, the museum offers a free light-and-sound show at night.

You'll find it about 12km north of downtown on the road to Progreso. Public transportation running along Calle 60 will leave you at the museum's entrance.

★ **Museo Regional de Antropología** MUSEUM
(Regional Anthropology Museum; 999-923-05-57; www.palaciocanton.inah.gob.mx; Paseo de Montejo No 485; adult/child under 13yr M$52/free; 8am-5pm Tue-Sun) The massive Palacio

Mérida

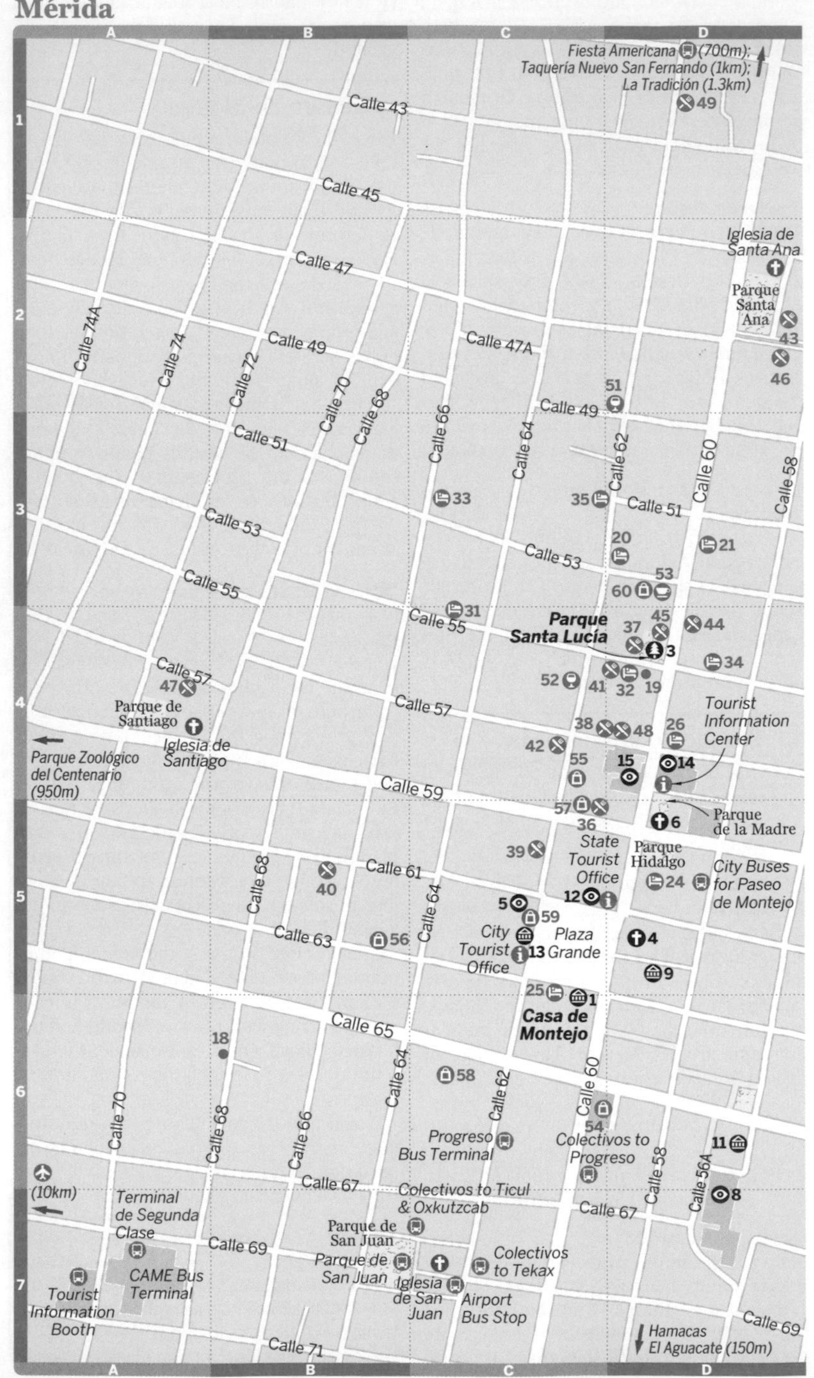
Fiesta Americana (700m); Taquería Nuevo San Fernando (1km); La Tradición (1.3km)
Calle 43
Calle 45
Calle 47
Calle 47A
Calle 49
Calle 51
Calle 53
Calle 55
Calle 57
Calle 59
Calle 61
Calle 63
Calle 65
Calle 67
Calle 69
Calle 71
Calle 74A
Calle 74
Calle 72
Calle 70
Calle 68
Calle 66
Calle 64
Calle 62
Calle 60
Calle 58
Calle 56A
Iglesia de Santa Ana
Parque Santa Ana
Parque Santa Lucía
Parque de Santiago
Iglesia de Santiago
Parque Zoológico del Centenario (950m)
Tourist Information Center
Parque de la Madre
State Tourist Office
Parque Hidalgo
City Buses for Paseo de Montejo
City Tourist Office
Plaza Grande
Casa de Montejo
Progreso Bus Terminal
Colectivos to Progreso
Colectivos to Ticul & Oxkutzcab
(10km)
Terminal de Segunda Clase
CAME Bus Terminal
Tourist Information Booth
Parque de San Juan
Iglesia de San Juan
Colectivos to Tekax
Airport Bus Stop
Hamacas El Aguacate (150m)

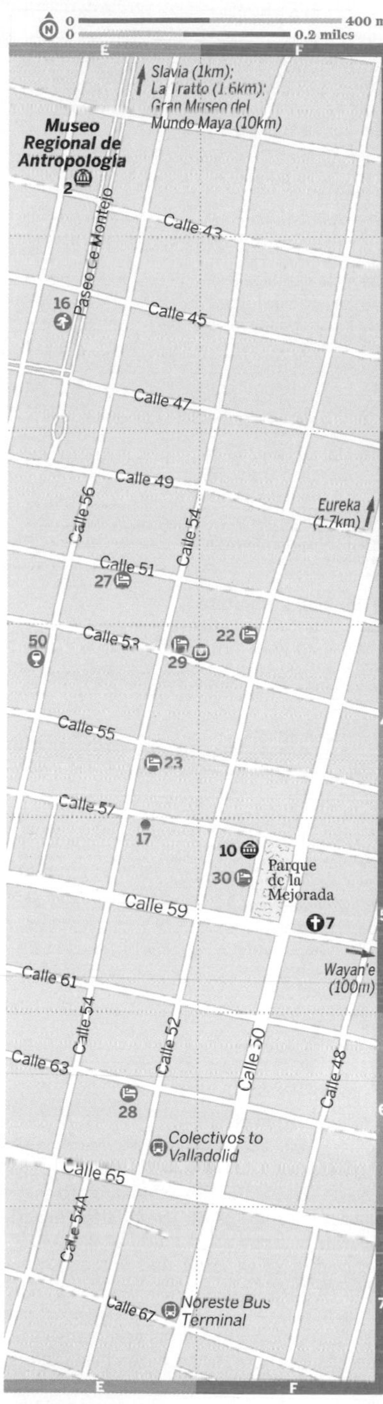

Cantón houses the Museo Regional de Antropología, an anthropology museum with temporary exhibits focusing primarily on culture and history in the Yucatán (ie Maya customs), although some exhibits will occasionally offer a broader look at other regions of Mexico. Construction of the mansion lasted from 1909 to 1911.

Its owner, General Francisco Cantón Rosado (1833–1917), lived here for only six years before his death. The Palacio's splendor and pretension make it a fitting symbol of the grand aspirations of Mérida's elite during the last years of the Porfiriato – the period from 1876 to 1911 when Porfirio Díaz held despotic sway over Mexico.

Activities

In an effort to make the city more bike-friendly, Mérida closes down stretches of Paseo de Montejo and Calle 60 to traffic on Sunday morning. For night tours, the bicycle activist group **Cicloturixes** (www.cicloturixes.org) gathers at Parque Santa Ana on Wednesday at around 8:30pm. See its blog for times.

Bici Mérida BICYCLE RENTAL
(cell 999-2873538; Paseo de Montejo s/n, btwn Calles 45 & 47; per hr M$30; 8am-9pm Mon-Fri, to 6pm Sat, 7am-2pm Sun; R-2) Rents mountain bikes, tandems, bicycles for kids and other cool rides.

Courses

Los Dos COOKING COURSE
(www.los-dos.com; Calle 68 No 517; 1-day courses & tours US$185-210) Run by US-educated chef David Sterling, this cooking school offers a wide variety of courses and tours with a focus on flavors of the Yucatán. A morning street-eats tour visits popular stalls and markets.

Instituto Benjamín Franklin LANGUAGE COURSE
(999-928-00-97; www.benjaminfranklin.com.mx; Calle 57 No 474A; per hr/4-week course US$12/720) This nonprofit teaches intensive Spanish-language courses and content courses on Mexican history for advanced students.

Tours

City

Historic Center Tours WALKING TOUR
(999-942-00-00; www.merida.gob.mx/turismo; Calle 62 s/n, Plaza Grande; walking tours 9:30am

Mérida

Top Sights
1 Casa de Montejo C6
2 Museo Regional de Antropología E1
3 Parque Santa Lucía D4

Sights
4 Catedral de San Ildefonso D5
5 Centro Cultural Olimpo C5
6 Iglesia de Jesús D5
7 Iglesia La Mejorada F5
8 Mercado Municipal Lucas de Gálvez D7
9 Museo de Arte Contemporáneo D5
10 Museo de Arte Popular de Yucatán F5
11 Museo de la Ciudad D6
12 Palacio de Gobierno C5
13 Palacio Municipal C5
14 Teatro Peón Contreras D4
15 Universidad Autónoma de Yucatán D4

Activities, Courses & Tours
16 Bici Mérida E2
Historic Center Tours .... (see 13)
17 Instituto Benjamín Franklin E5
18 Los Dos B6
Nómadas Hostel .... (see 35)
Transportadora Turística Carnaval .... (see 19)
19 Turitransmérida D4

Sleeping
20 62 St Guesthouse D3
21 Art Apart Hostel D3
22 Casa Ana B&B F4
23 Casa Isabel E4
24 Gran Hotel D5
25 Hostal Zócalo C5
26 Hotel Casa del Balam D4
27 Hotel del Peregrino E3
28 Hotel Dolores Alba E6
29 Hotel Julamis E4
30 Hotel La Piazzetta F5
31 Hotel Medio Mundo C4
32 Hotel Santa Lucía D4
33 Los Arcos Bed & Breakfast C3
34 Luz en Yucatán D4
35 Nómadas Hostel C3

Eating
36 Amaro C5
37 Apoala D4
38 Cafetería Pop C4
39 El Trapiche C5
40 La Casa de Frida B5
41 La Chaya Maya D4
42 La Chaya Maya C4
43 La Socorrito D2
44 La Tradición D4
45 La Tratto D4
Lo Que Hay .... (see 31)
46 Manjar Blanco D2
Mercado Municipal Lucas de Gálvez .... (see 8)
47 Mercado Municipal No 2 .... A4
48 Pórtico del Peregrino D4
49 Rescoldo's D1

Drinking & Nightlife
50 La Fundación Mezcalería E4
51 La Negrita D2
52 Mayan Pub C4
53 Orgánico D3

Entertainment
Centro Cultural Olimpo .... (see 5)

Shopping
54 Artesanías Bazar García Rejón C6
55 Camisería Canul C4
56 Casa de las Artesanías B5
57 Guayaberas Jack C5
58 Hamacas Mérida C6
59 Librería Dante C5
Miniaturas .... (see 57)
60 Tejón Rojo D3

Mon-Sat) FREE The city tourist office runs free guided walking tours of the historic center departing daily from the Palacio Municipal. You can also rent audio guides here for M$80 if you prefer to go it alone.

Transportadora Turística Carnaval BUS TOUR
(☎999-927-61-19; carnavalito@turitransmerida.com.mx; Calle 55, btwn Calles 60 & 62; tour M$120; ⏰tours 10am, 1pm, 4pm & 7pm Mon-Sat, 1pm & 3pm Sun) Conducts two-hour guided tours of Mérida in English and Spanish on its Paseo Turístico bus departing from Parque Santa Lucía.

Regional

Nómadas Hostel TOUR
(☎999-924-52-23; www.nomadastravel.com; Calle 62 No 433; tours to Celestún/Chichén Itzá/Uxmal & Kabah M$695/475/475) Nómadas arranges a variety of tours, such as day trips including transportation and guide to the ecological reserve of Celestún and outings to the Maya ruins of Chichén Itzá and Uxmal. The hostel also provides DIY sheets with written instructions detailing costs and transportation tips for more than a dozen destinations in the region.

Turitransmérida TOUR
(☎999-924-11-99; www.turitransmerida.com.mx; Calle 55, btwn Calles 60 & 62; ⊙8am-7pm Mon-Fri, to 1pm Sat, to 10am Sun) Turitransmérida does group tours to sites around Mérida, including Celestún, Chichén Itzá, Uxmal and Kabah, the Ruta Puuc and Izamal.

Ruta Puuc Tour BUS TOUR
(☎999-924-08-30, ext 2909; tour M$179; ⊙tour 8am-4pm Sun) Bus line Oriente runs a day tour to Uxmal, Kabah and the Ruta Puuc sites, departing from the Terminal de Segunda Clase (2nd-class terminal) in Mérida on Sunday morning.

Ecoturismo Yucatán ECOTOUR
(☎999-920-27-72; www.ecoyuc.com.mx; Calle 3 No 235; day tours to Chichén Itzá/Uxmal & Kabah M$730/762; ⊙9am-6pm Mon-Fri, 9am-1pm Sat) The owners of reputable Ecoturismo Yucatán are passionate about both sharing and protecting the state's natural treasures. Trips focus on archaeology, birding, natural history, biking and kayaking. The price of one-day excursions to Chichén Itzá or Uxmal and Kabah include entrance fees, transportation and lunch.

Festivals & Events

Dates for events may vary from year to year. For more specific information, visit www.culturayucatan.com.

Mérida Fest CULTURAL
(www.merida.gob.mx/festival; ⊙Jan) This cultural event held throughout most of January celebrates the founding of the city with art exhibits, concerts, theater and book presentations at various venues.

Anniversary of the Universidad de Yucatán CULTURAL
(⊙Feb) During the last week of February the Universidad de Yucatán celebrates its anniversary with free performances by the Ballet Folklórico, concerts of classical music, *trova* (troubadors), *serenatas* (serenades) and other manifestations of Yucatán's cultural roots.

Carnaval RELIGIOUS
(⊙Feb/Mar) Prior to Lent, in February or March, Carnaval features colorful floats, dancers in costumes and nonstop festivities. It's celebrated with greater vigor in Mérida than anywhere else in Yucatán state.

Semana Santa RELIGIOUS
(Holy Week; ⊙Mar/Apr) A major celebration in Mérida over Easter week. The main feature of the celebrations is the city's Passion Plays.

Primavera Cultural MUSIC
(www.culturayucatan.com; ⊙May/Jun) A month-long event usually in May or June, it celebrates *trova* (troubadour-type folk music) and just about any other music genre you can imagine.

Otoño Cultural CULTURAL
(www.culturayucatan.com; ⊙Sep & Oct) Typically held in September and October, this three-week autumn fest stages more than 100 music, dance, visual art and theater events.

Exposición de Altares de los Muertos RELIGIOUS
(⊙Oct 31) A big religious tradition. Throughout Mexico families prepare shrines to welcome the spirits of loved ones back to earth for Day of the Dead. Many Maya prepare elaborate dinners outside their homes, and Mérida observes the occasion with festivities and displays in the town center, usually on October 31.

Toh Bird Festival FESTIVAL
(Festival de las Aves Toh; www.festivalavesyucatan.com; ⊙Nov) Holds various events throughout the year, culminating with a 'bird-a-thon' (bird-counting competition) in late November. Based in Mérida.

Sleeping

Budget rooms generally have fans; spending the extra money for air-con is well worth it in the hotter months.

Nómadas Hostel HOSTEL $
(☎999-924-52-23; www.nomadastravel.com; Calle 62 No 433; dm from M$169, d M$450, without bathroom M$390; P⊖✱@🛜≋) One of Mérida's best hostels, it has mixed and women's dorms, as well as private rooms. Guests have use of a fully equipped kitchen with fridge, as well as showers and hand-laundry facilities. It even has free salsa and cooking classes, and an amazing pool out back. See the hostel's website for various tours available to nearby ruins.

Hostal Zócalo HOSTEL $
(☎999-930 95 62; hostalzocalo@yahoo.com; Calle 63 No 508; dm M$175, r M$450, without bathroom M$350, incl breakfast; ⊖@🛜) A great location in a beautiful old colonial building makes

this hostel unique. It has firm beds and the big breakfast buffet gets rave reviews. The staff is friendly enough; however, the service comes up short at times.

Art Apart Hostel HOSTEL **$**
(999-923-24-63; www.artaparthostel.com; Calle 60 No 456A; dm with fan/air-con M$135/160, r with fan/air-con M$400/550;) It's like stepping into a museum at this funky hostel, where you'll find oddball art in every nook and cranny, including the gardens, hallways and pool area. Dorms and rooms vary; some are fairly simple, but all have original artwork. The previous owner was an eccentric collector who was much better at buying than selling the pieces.

Hotel Santa Lucía HOTEL **$**
(999-928-26-72; www.hotelsantalucia.com.mx; Calle 55 No 508; s/d/tr M$450/540/600;) Across from the park of the same name, this centrally located hotel is clean, secure and popular. The pool is small but clean, and the rooms have TV, phone and just so-so mattresses.

★**Luz en Yucatán** BOUTIQUE HOTEL **$$**
(999-924-00-35; www.luzenyucatan.com; Calle 55 No 499; r US$59-79, ste US$99, apt US$69-150;) While many much blander hotels are loudly claiming to be 'boutique,' this one is quietly ticking all the boxes – individually decorated rooms, fabulous common areas and a wonderful pool-patio area out back. The house it offers for rent across the road, which sleeps seven people and has a hot tub, is just as good, if not better.

Check out the spacious apartments here.

Hotel La Piazzetta HOTEL **$$**
(999-923-39-09; www.hotellapiazzettamerida.com; Calle 50A No 493, btwn Calles 57 & 59; d incl breakfast M$850;) Off a quiet side street overlooking Parque de la Mejorada, this friendly little place has just four rooms with views of the park or the pleasant patio area. Each of the well-appointed rooms contains memorabilia from the owners' world travels. Free bike loans are available and at last visit an onsite restaurant was being built.

Hotel del Peregrino HOTEL **$$**
(999-924-30-07; www.hoteldelperegrino.com; Calle 51 No 488, btwn Calles 54 & 56; r incl breakfast M$895;) After a recent colonial-style makeover the new-look Peregrino is sporting restored tile floors, Talavera tile sinks and some modern creature comforts, such as Netflix service (because cable TV is so '90s). Breakfast is served in a patio downstairs and upstairs you can relax in the hotel's rooftop hot tub.

62 St Guesthouse GUESTHOUSE **$$**
(999-924-30-60; www.casaalvarezguesthouse.com; Calle 62 No 448, btwn Calles 51 & 53; d with fan/air-con M$600/750;) Impeccably clean and about as tranquil as you can get, this old-school guesthouse offers a friendly, one-of-the-family ambience, along with nice showers, spotless bathrooms and in-room fridges. The house is full of antiques, including a cylinder-style gramophone player. Guests have use of a kitchen and small pool out back.

Hotel Julamis BOUTIQUE HOTEL **$$**
(999-924-18-18, cell 998-1885508; www.hoteljulamis.com; Calle 53 No 475B; r incl breakfast US$69-95;) Book well in advance if you expect to stay at this highly popular adults-only boutique hotel. Each room has unique design details, such as colorful murals and original tile floors. All rooms come with fridges stocked daily with free beverages.

Casa Ana B&B B&B **$$**
(999-924-00-05; www.casaana.com; Calle 52 No 469; r incl breakfast from US$50;) Casa Ana is an intimate escape and one of the best deals in town. It has a small natural-bottom pool and a cozy overgrown garden complete with Cuban tobacco plants (memories of home for the Cuban owners, no doubt). The rooms are spotless and have Mexican hammocks and (whew) mosquito screens.

Gran Hotel HOTEL **$$**
(999-923-69-63; www.granhoteldemerida.com; Calle 60 No 496; s/d M$695/925;) This was indeed a grand hotel when built in 1901. Most rooms in this old-timer got a recent makeover; several still have the same old period furnishings and faded carpets. Despite the wear, they retain many elegant and delightful decorative flourishes.

Hotel Dolores Alba HOTEL **$$**
(999-928-56-50; www.doloresalba.com; Calle 63 No 464, btwn Calles 52 & 54; d M$800-1000;) On a somewhat gritty side of town, this well-managed hotel is surprisingly quiet inside. Rooms surround two courtyards and have two price categories; those in the more expensive, modern wing

feature shiny new tile floors, flat-screen TVs and face the lovely pool.

★**Casa Isabel** B&B $$$

(999-286-73-16; robertdstix@gmail.com; Calle 54 No 476; r incl breakfast US$80-100;) The former residence and architectural work of Manuel Cantón (the architect who designed Mérida's iconic Palacio Cantón), this glorious porfiriato era mansion has been passionately restored to regain its splendor of old. On offer are just two rooms: one a cozy setup near the pool area, the other a street-facing room with high ceilings and pretty tile floors.

The hosts, an amiable American and Iranian couple, love animals so feel free to bring Fluffy. Formerly Casa Esperanza.

Hotel Medio Mundo HOTEL $$$

(999-924-54-72; www.hotelmediomundo.com; Calle 55 No 533; d incl breakfast US$80-90;) This former private residence has been completely remodeled and painted in lovely colors. Its ample, simply furnished rooms have super-comfortable beds, beautiful tiled sinks and plenty of natural light. One of the two courtyards has a swimming pool, the other a fountain, and there's a good onsite vegan restaurant. The well-traveled, charming hosts make their guests feel at home.

Los Arcos Bed & Breakfast B&B $$$

(999-928-02-14; www.losarcosmerida.com; Calle 66 No 448B; d incl breakfast US$85-95;) Certainly not for minimalists – there's art on every wall and in every corner – Los Arcos is a lovely, gay-friendly B&B with two guestrooms at the end of a drop-dead-gorgeous garden and pool area. Rooms have an eclectic assortment of art and antiques, excellent beds and bathrooms.

Hotel Casa del Balam HOTEL $$$

(999-924-88-44; www.casadelbalam.com; Calle 60 No 488, btwn Calles 55 & 57; d/ste from M$1200/1800;) This place is centrally located, has a great pool and large, quiet colonial-style rooms with firm beds. It often offers hefty discounts during quiet times.

Eating

Don't miss 'Mérida en Domingo,' an all-day food and crafts market on the main plaza every Sunday. It's a great place to try a wide variety of regional dishes, and it's cheap, too!

★**Wayan'e** TAQUERÍA $

(cnr Calles 59 & 46; tacos M$11-15, tortas M$18-25; 7am-2:30pm Mon-Sat;) Popular for its *castacan* (fried pork belly), Wayan'e (meaning 'here it is' in Maya) is one of Mérida's premier breakfast spots. Vegetarians will find options here, such as the *huevo con ixkatic* (egg with chili) taco and fresh juices. But if you eat meat, it's all about the greasy goodness of the *castacan torta* (sandwich).

Mercado Municipal Lucas de Gálvez MARKET $

(cnr Calles 56A & 67; mains & ceviche M$60; 6am-5pm;) Mérida's least expensive eateries. Upstairs joints have tables and chairs and more diverse menus offering main courses of beef, fish or chicken. Look for *recados* (spice pastes). Downstairs at the north end are some cheap *taquerías* (taco stalls), while near the south end are *coctelerías* – seafood stalls specializing in shellfish cocktails as well as ceviche (seafood marinated in lemon or lime juice, garlic and seasonings).

Mercado Municipal No 2 MARKET $

(Calle 70 s/n; mains M$30-50; 6am-2pm) Numero Dos is cheap, good and less crowded than some of the busier markets in town. On the north side of Parque de Santiago, it's packed with juice stalls and *loncherías* (economical eateries).

La Chaya Maya MEXICAN $$

(www.lachayamaya.com; Calle 55 No 510; mains M$67-178; 1-10pm Mon-Sat, 8am-10pm Sun;) Popular with locals and tourists alike, this restaurant opened a new location in a lovely downtown colonial building. Consider La Chaya your introduction to classic Yucatecan fare like *relleno negro* (black turkey stew) or *cochinita pibil* (slow-cooked pork). The **original location** (cnr Calles 62 & 57; from 7am daily) opens for breakfast.

Manjar Blanco MEXICAN $$

(Calle 47, btwn Calles 58 & 60; mains M$75-140; 8am-6pm; ; R-2) This family-run restaurant puts a gourmet twist on regional favorites. The *tortillitas tropicales* (fried plantains topped with smoked pork) are delicious, and sweet tooths will love the namesake *manjar blanco* (a coconut cream dessert).

Rescoldo's MEDITERRANEAN $$

(www.rescoldosbistro.com; Calle 62 No 366, btwn Calles 41 & 43; mains M$75-160; 6-10pm Tue-Fri, to 11pm Sat;) Offering up wood-fired pizzas

THE COCHINITA QUEST

It seems like just about everyone in Mérida has an opinion on where you can get the best *cochinita pibil* (slow-cooked pork marinated in citrus juice and annatto spice). *Cochinita* is prepared in tacos, *tortas* (sandwiches) or as a main dish and the best of the best is cooked in a pit, giving it a smoky flavor. Mérida has some very tasty options.

Taquería Nuevo San Fernando (Av Cupules s/n, btwn Calles 60 & 62; tortas M$24; 7am-1pm; R-2) Out-of-towners staying in the nearby business-class hotels have been known to buy kilos of this stuff to take back home with them. The freshmade bread, roasted habanero salsa and tender *cochinita* is *that* good.

La Socorrito (Calle 47, btwn Calles 58 & 60; tortas M$17; 7am-2pm; R-2) These old pros have been slow-cooking *cochinita* in underground pits for more than six decades. You'll find this delightful hole-in-the-wall on the plaza side of the Mercado de Santa Ana.

La Tradición (www.latradicionmerida.com; cnr Calles 60 & 25; mains M$85-195; noon-6pm;) For an upscale take on *cochinita* (cloth napkin and all), this popular restaurant serves a generous portion accompanied with pickled red onion, handmade tortillas and usually live *trova* music. There's a downtown branch near Parque Santa Lucía (Calle 60 No 468).

and calzones, yummy pastas and rounding it off with homemade gelato, this highly recommended Mediterranean restaurant is a great place to get a little variety in your diet.

Amaro INTERNATIONAL **$$**

(999-928-24-51; www.restauranteamaro.com; Calle 59 No 507; mains M$99-235; 11am-2am;) This romantic dining spot (especially at night, when there are performing *trova* acts) is in the courtyard of the house where Andrés Quintana Roo – poet, statesman and drafter of Mexico's Declaration of Independence – was born in 1787. The menu includes Yucatecan dishes, such as annatto-marinated chicken, and a variety of vegetarian and continental dishes.

La Casa de Frida MEXICAN **$$**

(999-928-23-11; www.lacasadefrida.com.mx; Calle 61 No 526A; mains M$130-190; 6-10pm Mon-Sat;) Go here for delicious duck in *mole* sauce or another well-prepared Mexican classic, *chile en nogada* (stuffed poblano chili). Don't be surprised if pet bunny Coco hops into the dining area to greet you. No rabbit on the menu here.

Pórtico del Peregrino MEXICAN **$$**

(999-928-61-63; www.porticodelperegrino.com; Calle 57 No 501, btwn Calles 60 & 62; mains M$85-210; noon-midnight;) There are several pleasant, traditional-style dining rooms surrounding a small courtyard in this upscale eatery. Yucatecan dishes such as *pollo pibil* (chicken flavored with *achiote* – annatto spice – sauce and wrapped in banana leaves) are its forte, but you'll find many international dishes and a broad range of seafood and steaks, too. *Mole poblano,* a chocolate and chili sauce, is a house specialty.

El Trapiche MEXICAN **$$**

(Calle 62 No 491; mains M$48-120; 8am-11pm;) A great place close to the city centre, El Trapiche has cheap Mexican eats in a casual environment. It bills itself as the best pizza joint in town, but it's actually the Yucatecan dishes that stand out. The menu has a fair share of vegetarian options.

Cafetería Pop CAFE **$$**

(999-928-61-63; www.cafeteriapop.com; Calle 57 s/n, btwn Calles 60 & 62; breakfasts M$50-70, lunches M$60-115; 7am-midnight Mon-Sat, from 8am Sun;) There's an art deco bebop feel to this little cafeteria-style restaurant, which serves cheap breakfast combinations and a good variety of Mexican dishes; try the chicken in dark, rich *mole* sauce.

Lo Que Hay VEGAN **$$**

(www.hotelmediomundo.com; Calle 55 No 53; 3-course dinners M$160; 7-10pm;) Even non-vegans usually give an enthusiastic thumbs up to this dinner-only restaurant, where three-course vegan meals are served in a serene courtyard. The changing menu ranges from Mexican and international cuisine to raw vegan, and it includes a drink and dessert. Lo Que Hay is in the Hotel Medio Mundo and it welcomes nonguests.

Apoala MEXICAN $$$

(☎999-923 19-79; Calle 60 No 471, Parque Santa Lucía; mains M$135-260; ⊜ᯤ) Drawing on traditional recipes from Oaxaca, which much like the Yucatán is known for its extraordinary regional cuisine, Apoala reinvents popular dishes such as *enmoladas* (stuffed tortillas in a rich *mole* sauce) and *tlayudas* (a large folded tortilla with sliced beef, black beans and Oaxaca cheese).

Eureka ITALIAN $$$

(☎999-926-26-94; www.facebook.com/eurekacucinaitaliana; Av Rotary Internacional 117, cnr Calle 52; mains M$120-240; ⏲1-11pm Tue-Sat, to 6pm Sat; ⊜ᯤ✎) Many locals consider this to be the best Italian food in town – and that's no small feat in a city known for excellent *cucina italiana*. The signature dish of Chef Fabrizio Di Stazio is the *riccioli eureka,* freshmade pasta in white ragu sauce with mushrooms and an aromatic hint of truffle.

La Tratto ITALIAN $$$

(☎999-923-37-87; www.trottersmerida.com; Calle 60 s/n, btwn Calles 53 & 55; mains M$145-240, set menu M$195; ⏲1pm-2am; ⊜ᯤ) A bistro known for its gourmet pizzas, handmade pastas and excellent wine list, La Tratto opened a new downtown location on the renovated Parque Santa Lucía. The 'prix fix' (set menu) includes an appetizer and your choice of pasta, chicken or beef for the main dish.

Drinking & Nightlife

You need not look far to find a friendly neighborhood bar.

★La Fundación Mezcalería BAR

(www.facebook.com/lafundacion; Calle 56 No 465; ⏲8pm-3am Wed-Sat; ᯤ) A popular bicyclists' hangout, especially on Wednesday, this retro-styled bar with nightly live music has an excellent selection of organic mezcals and an atmosphere conducive to knocking 'em back. Careful though: this stuff packs a mean punch.

La Negrita DANCING

(www.lanegritacantina.com; Calle 62 s/n, cnr Calle 49; ⏲noon-10pm; ᯤ) If the live music here doesn't inspire you to get a tropical groove on, it's just a matter of time before the mojitos and mezcals have you dancing the night away. The rear garden makes a nice spot to catch a breather and chat with locals. Groups go on after 5pm from Wednesday to Sunday.

Orgánico CAFE

(Calle 53 No 502, btwn Calles 60 & 62; coffee M$20-42; ⏲8am-4pm Mon, to 11pm Tue-Sat; ᯤ) Java junkies will love this place's organic coffee, which is prepared with beans from the highlands of Chiapas, Veracruz and Guerrero. Hungry? You'll find good vegetarian options here.

Slavia BAR

(cnr Paseo de Montejo & Calle 29; ⏲7pm-2am Tue-Sat) Jam-packed with Indian knickknacks, Slavia serves up fusion food and drinks in a casual environment, while adjoining bar Cubaro does mojitos (rum and mint cocktails) and DJ sessions on a deck overlooking Mérida's iconic Monumento a la Patria.

Mayan Pub BAR

(www.mayanpub.com; Calle 62 s/n, btwn Calles 55 & 57; ⏲7pm-3am Wed-Sun; ᯤ) Live bands play rock, reggae, ska and jazz in this festive pub's rear beer garden. Inside there's a pool table if you're up for a game of stick.

☆ Entertainment

Mérida organizes many folkloric and musical events in parks and historic buildings, put on by local performers of considerable skill. Admission is mostly free.

Centro Cultural Olimpo CONCERT VENUE

(☎999-924-00-00, ext 80152; www.merida.gob.mx/capitalcultural; cnr Calles 62 & 61) Offers something nearly every night: films, concerts, art installations, you name it.

Shopping

Guayaberas Jack CLOTHING

(www.guayaberasjack.com.mx; Calle 59 No 507A; ⏲10am-8:30pm Mon-Sat, to 2:30pm Sun) The *guayabera* (embroidered dress shirt) is the classic Mérida shirt, but in buying the wrong one you run the risk of looking like a waiter. Drop into this famous shop to avoid getting asked for the bill.

Tejón Rojo SOUVENIRS

(www.tejonrojo.com; Calle 53 No 503; ⏲noon-9pm) A great little shop that sells trendy graphic T-shirts and an assortment of Mexican pop-culture souvenirs, including coffee mugs, jewelry, handbags and wrestling masks.

Casa de las Artesanías HANDICRAFTS
(☎999-928-66-76; www.artesanias.yucatan.gob.mx; Calle 63 s/n, btwn Calles 64 & 66; ⌚8:30am-9pm Mon-Sat, 10am-5pm Sun) One place to start looking for handicrafts is this government-supported market for local artisans. Prices are fixed.

Artesanías Bazar García Rejón HANDICRAFTS
(cnr Calles 60 & 65; ⌚10am-7pm) A wide variety of products (primarily handicrafts) concentrated into one area of shops.

Camisería Canul CLOTHING
(☎999-923-56-61; www.camiseriacanul.com.mx; Calle 62 No 484; ⌚9am-8pm Mon-Sat, 10am-2pm Sun) A good place for *guayaberas* (embroidered dress shirts) and *huipiles* (traditional blouses and dresses). It has been in business for years, offering fixed prices and custom tailoring.

Miniaturas HANDICRAFTS
(☎999-928-65-03; Calle 59 s/n, btwn Calles 60 & 62; ⌚10am-2pm & 5-10pm Mon-Sat) Here you'll find lots of small Día de Muertos (Day of the Dead) tableaux, tinwork and figurines, from ceramics to toy soldiers. They all have two things in common: they're easy to pack and have nothing to do with Yucatán artisan traditions.

Librería Dante BOOKS
(www.editorialdante.com; cnr Calles 61 & 62, Plaza Grande; ⌚8am-10.30pm) Shelves a selection of archaeology and regional history books in English and has good Yucatecan cookbooks, too. The bookstore has other branches throughout the city.

 Orientation

The Plaza Grande has been the city's heart since the time of the Maya. Though Mérida now sprawls many kilometers in all directions, most of the services and attractions for visitors are within 10 blocks of the Plaza Grande. Following the classic colonial plan, the square is ringed by several barrios (neighborhoods), each with its own park and church.

Odd-numbered streets run east–west; even-numbered streets run north–south. Addresses are usually given in this form: 'Calle 57 No 481 x 46 y 48' (between streets 46 and 48).

 Information

EMERGENCY

Emergency (☎066)
Fire (☎999-924-92-42)
Red Cross (☎999-924-98-13)
Tourist Police (☎999-942-00-60)

YUCATECAN HAMMOCKS: THE ONLY WAY TO SLEEP

Yucatecan hammocks are normally woven from strong nylon or cotton string and dyed in various colors. There are also natural, undyed cotton versions. Some sellers will try to pass these off as *henequén* or jute, telling you it's much more durable (and valuable) than cotton, and even that it repels mosquitoes. Don't be taken in; real *henequén* hammocks are very rough and not something you'd want near your skin. Silk hammocks are no longer made, but a silk-rayon blend has a similar feel.

Hammocks come in several widths, and though much is made of the quantity of pairs of end strings they possess, a better gauge of a hammock's size and quality is its weight. The heavier the better. A *sencilla* (for one person) should be about 500g and cost around M$300. The queen, at 1100g, runs about M$450, and a 1500g king usually starts at M$600. *De croché* (very tightly woven) hammocks can take several weeks to produce and cost double or triple the prices given here.

Mérida and its surrounding towns have some good spots for buying a hammock.

Tixkokob This weaving town about 20km east of Mérida on Hwy 80 is famous for its quality hammocks. Frequent *colectivos* (shared vans; M$15) to Tixkokob depart from the corner of Calles 54A and 65.

Hamacas El Aguacate (☎999-285-05-74; www.hamacaselaguacate.com.mx; Calle 58 No 604, cnr Calle 73; ⌚8:30am-7pm Mon-Fri, 9am-5:30pm Sat) Hamacas El Aguacate stocks quality hammocks at decent prices, and there's absolutely no hard sell.

Hamacas Mérida (☎999-924-04-40; www.hamacasmerida.com.mx; Calle 65 No 510, btwn Calles 62 & 64; ⌚9am-7pm Mon-Fri, to 2pm Sat) Has a large catalog with all kinds of sizes, shapes and colors, plus it ships worldwide.

CRAFTS & TRADITIONAL WEAR

The Yucatán is a fine place for buying handicrafts and traditional clothes. Purchases to consider include *guayaberas*, colorfully embroidered *huipiles* and of course wonderfully comfortable hammocks.

Women throughout the Yucatán Peninsula traditionally wear straight, white cotton dresses called *huipiles*, the bodices of which are embroidered. You'll come across these loose-fitting garments in many markets across the peninsula.

Men commonly wear *guayaberas* (light, elegant shirts, usually with four square pockets). They can be worn in both casual and formal settings, and the cotton and linen materials keep the body cool on warm, humid days.

You'll also find craft shops and street stalls selling wooden handicrafts of Spanish galleons and carvings of Maya deities. Campeche is the state most associated with such items, but they are made by accomplished artisans in the states of Yucatán and Quintana Roo as well.

For more on handicrafts, pick up a copy of *The Crafts of Mexico*, by Margarita de Orellana and Alberto Ruy Sánchez.

INTERNET ACCESS

Chandler's Internet (Calle 61 s/n, btwn Calles 60 & 62; per hr M$15; ⌚9am-10pm) is just off the Plaza Grande.

MEDIA

Yucatán Today (www.yucatantoday.com) is a free Spanish-English magazine devoted to tourism in Yucatán. Pick up a copy of the magazine in hotels or visit the website for great tips.

MEDICAL SERVICES

The website for the US consulate in Mérida (http://merida.usconsulate.gov) has a good list of doctors and hospitals, as does *Yucatán Today* (www.yucatantoday.com/en/topics/healthcare-merida-yucatan).

Clínica de Mérida (☎999-942-18-00; www.clinicademerida.com.mx; Av Itzáes 242, cnr Calle 25; ⌚24hr; 🚌R-49) Good private clinic with laboratory and 24-hour emergency service.

MONEY

Banks and ATMs are scattered throughout the city. There is a cluster of both along Calle 65 between Calles 60 and 62, one block south of the Plaza Grande. *Casas de cambio* (money exchange offices) have faster service and longer opening hours than banks, but often give poorer rates.

POST

Post Office (☎999-928-54-04; Calle 53 No 469, btwn Calles 52 & 54; ⌚8am-7pm Mon-Fri, to 3pm Sat)

TELEPHONE

Card phones can be found throughout the city. Internet cafes also offer VOIP–based phone services.

TOURIST INFORMATION

You'll find tourist information booths at the airport and in the main bus terminal. Three tourist offices downtown have brochures, bus schedules and maps.

City Tourist Office (☎999-942-00-00, ext 80119; www.merida.gob.mx/turismo; Calle 62, Plaza Grande; ⌚8am-8pm) Right on the main plaza, it is staffed with helpful English speakers. Here you can hook up free walking tours of the city, which depart daily at 9:30am, and you can rent audio guides for M$80.

State Tourist Office (☎999-930-31-01; www.yucatan.travel; Calle 61 s/n, Plaza Grande; ⌚8am-8pm) In the entrance to the Palacio de Gobierno. There's usually an English speaker on hand.

Tourist Information Center (☎999-924-92-90; cnr Calles 60 & 57A; ⌚8am-8pm) On the southwest edge of the Teatro Peón Contreras, this office always has an English speaker on hand.

ℹ Getting There & Away

AIR

Mérida's Aeropuerto Internacional de Mérida (Mérida International Airport; ☎999-940-60-90; www.asur.com.mx; Hwy 180 Km 4.5; 🚌R-79) is a 10km, 20-minute ride southwest of the Plaza Grande off Hwy 180 (Avenida de los Itzáes). It has car-rental desks, an ATM, currency-exchange service and a tourist information booth.

Most international flights to Mérida make connections through Mexico City. Nonstop international services are provided by Aeroméxico and United Airlines.

Low-cost airlines Interjet, VivaAerobus and Volaris serve Mexico City. Mayair operates prop planes to Cancún and Cozumel.

DAY TRIPS FROM MÉRIDA

Mérida makes a great base for day trips to all kinds of interesting destinations in the countryside, from quiet coastal towns and fun swimming holes to Maya ruins and excellent birding locations. Here are some worthwhile trips:

Cuzamá Three amazing cenotes (p169; limestone sinkholes) can be accessed by horse-drawn cart.

Ruta Puuc Ruin yourself by visiting all five sites (including megadraw Uxmal) in one day. Extend your trip by visiting Mayapán (p168) and the Grutas de Loltún (p168; Loltún Caverns).

Celestún Head out early to catch a mangrove birding boat tour (p174). With a bit more time, you can visit the ruined haciendas along the way.

Dzibilchaltún & Progreso Visit the ruins (p177) and cenote or extend your trip for an afternoon of beach time in Progreso (p178).

Sisal This Gulf-coast town, about 60km northwest of Mérida, doesn't see much tourist traffic. There's a foggy-bottomed reef here, as well as a little shipwreck that you can snorkel out to. Plus, sea turtles are released during the month of August. While in town, grab a bite at **Muelle de Sisal** (M$95-150; ⊙11:30am-6pm).

Aeroméxico (☎ toll-free 800-021-40-00; www.aeromexico.com) Flies direct from Miami.

Interjet (☎ in USA 866-285-9525, toll-free 800-011-23-45; www.interjet.com) Serves Mexico City, where you can catch connecting flights to New York, Miami and Houston.

Mayair (☎ toll-free 800-962-92-47; www.mayair.com.mx) Runs prop planes to Cancún that continue on to Cozumel.

VivaAerobus (☎ in USA 888-935-98-48, toll-free 818-215-01-50; www.vivaaerobus.com) Service to Mexico City and Monterrey.

Volaris (☎ in Mexico City 55-1102-8000, in USA 866-988-3527; www.volaris.com) Direct to Mexico City and Monterrey.

BUS

Mérida is the bus transportation hub of the Yucatán Peninsula. Take care with your bags on night buses and those serving popular tourist destinations (especially 2nd-class buses); there have been reports of theft on some routes.

There are a number of bus terminals, and some lines operate from (and stop at) more than one terminal. Tickets for departure from one terminal can often be bought at another, and destinations overlap greatly among bus lines. Check out www.ado.com.mx for ticket info on some of the lines.

CAME Bus Terminal (☎ 999-920-44-44; Calle 70 s/n, btwn Calles 69 & 71) Aka the 'Terminal de Primera Clase,' Mérida's main bus terminal has (mostly 1st-class) buses – including ADO, OCC and ADO GL – to points around the Yucatán Peninsula and faraway places such as Mexico City.

Fiesta Americana Bus Terminal (☎ 999-924-83-91; cnr Calle 60 & Av Colón; 🚌 R-2) A small 1st-class terminal on the west side of the Fiesta Americana hotel complex servicing guests of the luxury hotels on Avenida Colón, north of the city center. ADO buses run between here and Cancún, Playa del Carmen, Villahermosa and Ciudad del Carmen.

Noreste Bus Terminal (cnr Calles 67 & 50) Noreste, Sur and Oriente bus lines use this terminal. Destinations served from here include many small towns in the northeast part of the peninsula, including Tizimín and Río Lagartos; Cancún and points along the way; and small towns south and west of Mérida, such as Celestún, Ticul, Ruinas de Mayapán and Oxkutzcab

Some Oriente buses depart from Terminal de Segunda Clase and stop here.

Parque de San Juan (Calle 69, btwn Calles 62 & 64) From all around the square and church, combis (vans and minibuses) depart for Muna, Oxkutzcab, Tekax, Ticul and other points.

Progreso Bus Terminal (☎ 999-928-39-65; Calle 62 No 524) There's a separate terminal with buses leaving for the northern beach town of Progreso (M$19, every 10 minutes).

Terminal de Segunda Clase (TAME; Calle 69) Aka TAME (Terminal de Autobuses de Segunda Clase), this terminal is just around the corner from the CAME bus terminal. ADO, Mayab, Oriente, Sur, TRT and ATS run mostly 2nd-class buses to points in the state and around the peninsula, including Felipe Carrillo Puerto and Ticul.

CAR

The most flexible way to tour the many archaeological sites around Mérida is to travel with a rental car. Assume you will pay M$450 to

M$500 per day (tax and insurance included) for short-term rental of an economy-size vehicle. Getting around Mérida's sprawling tangle of one-way streets is better done on foot or bus.

Several agencies have branches at the airport and on Calle 60, between Calles 55 and 57. You'll get the best deal by booking online.

There is an expensive toll highway between Mérida and Cancún (M$414).

Easy Way (☎999-930-95-00; www.easyway rentacar-yucatan.com; Calle 60 No 484, btwn Calles 55 & 57; ⏰7am-11pm)

National (☎999-923-24-93; www.nationalcar.com; Calle 60 No 486F, btwn Calles 55 & 57; ⏰7am-10pm)

Getting Around

TO/FROM THE AIRPORT

Two taxi companies provide speedy service between the airport and downtown, charging M$200 per carload (same price for hotel pick-up). A street taxi from the city center to the airport should cost about M$100 to M$120. If you want to get this same price *from* the airport, you'll need to walk out to the main street and flag down a city cab.

A city bus labeled 'Aviación 79' (M$7) travels between the main road of the airport entrance (the bus does not enter the airport) and the city center every 15 to 30 minutes until 9pm, with occasional service until 11pm. The best place to catch the same bus to the airport is at Parque San Juan, from the corner of Calles 62 and 69.

ADO (☎999-940-03-00) Airport taxi service.

Transporte Terrestre (☎999-946-15-29; per car M$200) Service from airport.

BUS

Most parts of Mérida that you'll want to visit are within 10 blocks of the Plaza Grande. Given the slow speed of city traffic, particularly in the market areas, travel on foot is often the fastest way to get around.

City buses are cheap at M$7, but routes can be confusing. Some start in suburban neighborhoods, skirt the city center and terminate in another distant suburban neighborhood.

BUSES FROM MÉRIDA

DESTINATION	COST (M$)	DURATION (HRS)	FREQUENCY (DAILY)
Campeche	202-254	2½-3	frequent
Cancún	198-440	4½-6½	frequent; CAME and Terminal de Segunda Clase
Celestún	56	2½	frequent; Noreste bus terminal
Chetumal	444	6	4
Chichén Itzá	80-144	1½-2	frequent; CAME and Noreste bus terminals
Escárcega	258	4-4½	4; Terminal de Segunda Clase
Felipe Carrillo Puerto	200	6	frequent; Terminal de Segunda Clase
Izamal	27	1½	frequent; Noreste bus terminal
Mayapán	25	1½	hourly; Noreste bus terminal
Mexico City	1582-1882	20	7
Palenque	544-576	7½-10	4
Playa del Carmen	408-450	4-6	frequent
Progreso	19	1	frequent; Progreso bus terminal
Río Lagartos/San Felipe	142-196	3½	3; Noreste bus terminal
Ruta Puuc (round-trip; 30min at each site)	179	8-8½	8am; Terminal de Segunda Clase
Ticul	50-76	1¾	frequent; Terminal de Segunda Clase
Tizimín	105-110	2	frequent; Noreste bus terminal
Tulum	298	4	4
Uxmal	55	1½	5; Terminal de Segunda Clase
Valladolid	95-178	2½-3	frequent

Merida.transpublico.com provides detailed maps of all the routes.

To travel between the Plaza Grande and the upscale neighborhoods to the north along Paseo de Montejo, catch the R-2 'Hyatt' or 'Tecnológico' line along Calle 60. To return to the city center, catch any bus heading south on Paseo de Montejo displaying the same signs and/or 'Centro.'

TAXI

More and more taxis in town are using meters these days. If you get one with no meter, be sure to agree on a price before getting in. A cost of M$20 to M$50 is fair for getting around downtown and to the bus terminals. Taxi stands can be found at most of the barrio parks (dispatch fees may cost an additional M$10 to M$20).

Radio Taxímetro del Volante (☎999-928-30-35) is a 24-hour radio taxi service.

SOUTH OF MÉRIDA

There's a lot to do and see south of Mérida. The major draws are the old *henequén* plantations, some still used for cultivating leaves, and the well-preserved Maya ruins like Uxmal and the lesser-known sites along the Ruta Puuc. Beyond these tourist attractions you'll find seldom-visited cenotes and caves, and traditional villages where life moves at an agrarian pace: women wear *huipiles* and speak Maya, and men still bike out to cut firewood or shoot a pheasant for dinner. It's a rough-and-tumble landscape, and one of the few spots on the peninsula where you'll actually find a few hills.

Oxkintok

Archaeologists have been excited about the ruins of **Oxkintok** (www.inah.gob.mx; admission M$47, guides M$550; ⏲8am-5pm; P) for several years. Inscriptions found at the site contain some of the oldest known dates in the Yucatán, and indicate the city was inhabited from the Preclassic to the Postclassic period (300 BC to AD 1500), reaching its greatest importance between AD 475 and 860.

Three main groups of the approximately 8-sq-km site have been restored thus far, all near the site entrance. Though much of the rebuilding work looks like it was done with rubble, you can see examples of Oxkintok, Proto-Puuc and Puuc architecture. The highest structure (15m) is Ma-1, **La Pirámide**, in the Ah-May group, which provides good views of the area. Probably the most interesting structure is **Palacio Chich** (Estructura Ca-7), in the Ah-Canul group, for its original stonework and the two columns in front carved with human figures in elaborate dress. Researchers discovered a labyrinth beneath La Pirámide, though unfortunately it's closed to the public.

The ruins are reached via a west-leading fork off the road to the Grutas de Calcehtok, which is 75km southwest of Mérida off Hwy 184, a few kilometers south of the town of Calcehtok. The 4.5km dirt road to the ruins is in poor shape, so expect a slow bumpy ride.

Grutas de Calcehtok

The **Grutas de Calcehtok** (Grutas de X'Pukil; ☎cell 999-2627292; off Hwy 184; 1hr tour M$100; ⏲8am-8pm; P 👪), aka Grutas de X'Pukil, are said to comprise the longest dry-cave system on the Yucatán Peninsula. More than 4km have been explored so far, and two of the caves' 25 vaults exceed 100m in diameter (one has a 30m-high 'cupola'). The caves hold abundant and impressive natural formations; however, if you're claustrophobic, have a fear of dark spaces or don't like getting dirty, this definitely isn't for you.

Archaeologists have found and removed ceramic arrowheads, quartz hammers and other tools, and you can still see low fortifications built by the Maya who sheltered here during the Caste War.

All tours are guided and flashlights are provided. The opening of the main entrance is an impressive 30m in diameter and 40m deep, ringed by vegetation often buzzing with bees. It's about 1m deep in bat guano at the bottom. You can opt for a basic, intermediate or adventure tour – the latter involves belly-crawling, rope descents and possibly the 7m long by 20cm wide 'Pass of Death,' or 'El Parto' (The Birth: you figure it out). Tours last one to three hours.

The caves are 75km southwest of Mérida off Hwy 184, a few kilometers south of the town of Calcehtok. They are best reached by car.

Uxmal

Pronounced oosh-mahl, **Uxmal** (Hwy 261 Km 78; adult/child under 13yr M$203/free, light & sound show M$83, parking M$30, guides M$700; ⏲site 8am-5pm, light & sound show 8pm Apr-Oct & 7pm Nov-Mar; 👪) is an impressive set of ruins, easily ranking among the top (and unfortu-

Uxmal

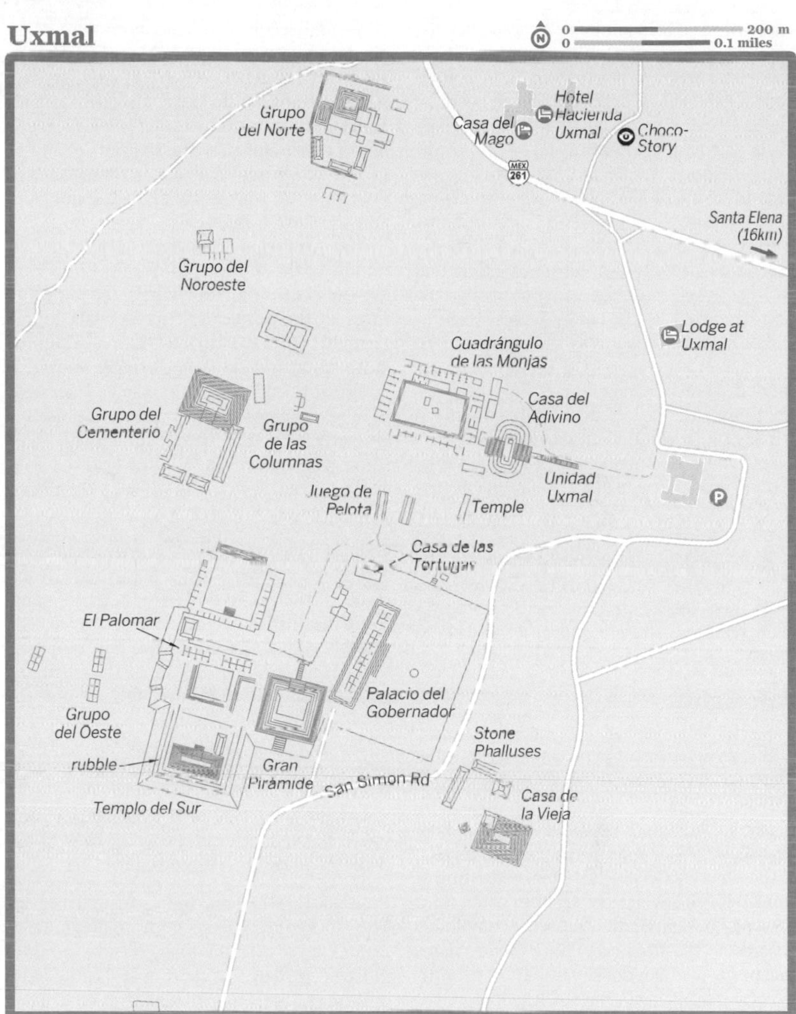

nately most crowded) Maya archaeological sites. It is a large site with some fascinating structures in good condition and bearing a riot of ornamentation. Adding to its appeal is Uxmal's setting near the hilly Puuc region, which lent its name to the architectural patterns in this area. *Puuc* means 'hills,' and these, rising up to about 100m, are the first relief from the flatness of the northern and western portions of the peninsula.

The site is entered through the modern Unidad Uxmal building, which has an air-conditioned restaurant, a small museum, shops selling souvenirs and crafts, a bookstore and an ATM. For an additional cost, Uxmal projects a nightly light-and-sound show. It's in Spanish but there are audio translators available for M$39.

History

Uxmal was an important city in a region that encompassed the satellite towns of Sayil, Kabah, Xlapak and Labná. Although Uxmal means 'Thrice Built' in Maya, it was actually constructed five times.

That a sizable population flourished in this dry area is yet more testimony to the engineering skills of the Maya, who built a series of reservoirs and *chultunes* (cisterns) lined with lime mortar to catch and hold water during the dry season. First settled about AD 600, Uxmal was influenced by highland Mexico in its architecture, most likely through contact fostered by trade. This influence is reflected in the town's serpent imagery, phallic symbols and columns. The well-proportioned Puuc architecture, with its intricate, geometric mosaics sweeping across the upper parts of elongated facades, was strongly influenced by the slightly earlier Río Bec and Chenes styles.

The scarcity of water in the region meant that Chaac, the rain god or sky serpent, carried a lot of weight here. His image is ubiquitous at the site in the form of stucco masks protruding from facades and cornices. There is much speculation as to why Uxmal was abandoned in about AD 900; a severe drought may have forced the inhabitants to relocate.

Rediscovered by archaeologists in the 19th century, Uxmal was first excavated in 1929 by Frans Blom. Although much has been restored, there is still a good deal to discover.

Sights

Casa del Adivino ARCHAEOLOGICAL SITE

(Pirámide del Adivino) As you approach Uxmal, the Casa del Adivino comes into view. This temple (the name translates as 'Magician's House'), 35m high, was built in an unusual oval shape. What you see is a restored version of the temple's fifth incarnation, consisting of round stones held rudely together with lots of cement. Four earlier temples were completely covered in the final rebuilding by the Maya, except for the high doorway on the west side, which remains from the fourth temple.

Decorated in elaborate Chenes style (a style that originated further south), the doorway proper forms the mouth of a gigantic Chaac mask.

Cuadrángulo de las Monjas ARCHAEOLOGICAL SITE

The 74-room, sprawling Nuns' Quadrangle is directly west of the Casa del Adivino. Archaeologists guess variously that it was a military academy, royal school or palace complex. The long-nosed face of Chaac appears everywhere on the facades of the four separate temples that form the quadrangle. The northern temple, the grandest of the four, was built first, followed by the southern, then the eastern and finally the western.

Several decorative elements on the exuberant facades show signs of Mexican, perhaps Totonac, influence. The feathered-serpent (Quetzalcóatl, or in Maya, Kukulcán) motif along the top of the west temple's facade is one of these. Note also the stylized depictions of the *na* (traditional Maya thatched hut) over some of the doorways in the northern and southern buildings.

Passing through the corbeled arch in the middle of the south building of the quadrangle and continuing down the slope takes you through the **Juego de Pelota** (Ball Court). From here you can turn left and head up the steep slope and stairs to the large terrace. If you've got time, you could instead turn right to explore the western **Grupo del Cementerio** (which, though largely unrestored, holds some interesting square blocks carved with skulls in the center of its plaza), then head for the stairs and terrace.

Casa de las Tortugas ARCHAEOLOGICAL SITE

The House of the Turtles, which you'll find south of the Juego de Pelota, takes its name from the turtles carved on the cornice. The Maya associated turtles with the rain god, Chaac. According to Maya myth, when the people suffered from drought, so did the turtles, and both prayed to Chaac to send rain.

The frieze of short columns, or 'rolled mats,' that runs around the temple below the turtles is characteristic of the Puuc style.

On the west side of the building a vault has collapsed, affording a good view of the corbeled arch that supported it.

Palacio del Gobernador ARCHAEOLOGICAL SITE

The Governor's Palace, with its magnificent facade nearly 100m long, is arguably the most impressive structure at Uxmal. The buildings have walls filled with rubble, faced with cement and then covered in a thin veneer of limestone squares; the lower part of the facade is plain, the upper part festooned with stylized Chaac faces and geometric designs, often lattice-like or fretted.

Other elements of Puuc style are decorated cornices, rows of half-columns (as in the Casa de las Tortugas) and round columns in doorways (as in the palace at Sayil).

Researchers recently discovered some 150 species of medicinal plants growing on the east side of the palace. Due to the high concentration of plants growing there it's believed they were cultivated by the Maya to treat stomach infections, snake bites and many other ailments.

Gran Pirámide ARCHAEOLOGICAL SITE

The 30m-high, nine-tiered pyramid has been restored only on its northern side. Archaeologists theorize that the quadrangle at its summit was largely destroyed in order to construct another pyramid above it. That work, for reasons unknown, was never completed. At the top are some stucco carvings of Chaac, birds and flowers.

El Palomar ARCHAEOLOGICAL SITE

West of the Gran Pirámide sits a structure whose roofcomb is latticed with a pattern reminiscent of the Moorish pigeon houses built into walls in Spain and northern Africa – hence the building's name, which means the Dovecote or Pigeon House. Honeycombed triangular 'belfries' sit on top of a building that was once part of a quadrangle.

Casa de la Vieja ARCHAEOLOGICAL SITE

Off the southeast corner of the Palacio del Gobernador's platform is a small complex, now largely rubble, known as the Casa de la Vieja (Old Woman's House). In front of it is a small *palapa* (thatch-roof shelter) that covers several large phalluses carved from stone.

Choco-Story MUSEUM

(www.choco-storymexico.com; Hwy 261 Km 78, near Hotel Hacienda Uxmal; adult/child 6-12yr M$120/90; 9am-7:30pm) You'll learn more than you ever wanted to know about chocolate at this interesting museum, and there's also interesting text about the nutritional and medicinal values of the flora in the surrounding botanical garden. The grounds are home to rescued jaguars and spider monkeys as well.

You cap off the visit tasting a bitter chocolate drink and then exit past, you guessed it, the gift shop. The museum is across the highway, next to Hotel Hacienda Uxmal.

Sleeping & Eating

There is no town at Uxmal, only several hotels, and there are no budget options. Cheaper lodgings can be found in Santa Elena, 16km away, or in Ticul, 30km to the east.

Casa del Mago HOTEL $$

(997-976-20-13; www.casadelmago.com; Hwy 261 Km 78; r incl breakfast US$57; P) The only midrange option in Uxmal, Casa del Mago consists of four basic rooms with red-tile floors and ceiling fans. Guests have use of the adjoining, sister property's pool. These are the cheapest rooms in town so book ahead.

Hotel Hacienda Uxmal HISTORIC HOTEL $$$

(in USA 877-240-58-64, toll-free 800-719-54-65; www.mayaland.com; Hwy 261 Km 78; r from US$104; P) This Mayaland Resort is 500m from the ruins. It housed the archaeologists who explored and restored Uxmal. Wide, tiled verandas, high ceilings, great bathrooms and a beautiful swimming pool make this a very comfortable place to stay. There are even rocking chairs to help you kick back after a hard day of exploring.

Lodge at Uxmal LUXURY HOTEL $$$

(in USA 877-240-5864, toll-free 800-719-54-65; www.mayaland.com; Hwy 261 Km 78; r from M$1600; P) Rooms could be nicer for the price, but you can't beat the easy access to the ruins and the pool certainly adds value. Some of the more expensive rooms have Jacuzzis. Don't suppose Stephens and Catherwood enjoyed such luxury when they passed through the area in the late 1830s.

Getting There & Away

Uxmal is 80km from Mérida. Departures (M$56, 1½ hours, four daily) on the Sur bus line leave from Mérida's 2nd-class terminal. But going back to Mérida, passing buses may be full. If you get stuck, a taxi to nearby Santa Elena costs M$150 to M$200.

Tours offered by Nómadas Hostel (p150) in Mérida are always a good option, or rent a car and visit other ruins in the area.

Santa Elena

Originally called Nohcacab, the town known as Santa Elena today was virtually razed in 1847 in the Caste War. '*Ele*-na' means burnt houses in Maya. The Mexican government changed the name to Santa Elena in a bold PR stunt.

If you're up for a little DIY adventure, head 4km outside of town to the Mulchic pyramid; locals can tell you how to get there.

Santa Elena makes a great base to explore the nearby ruins of Uxmal, Kabah and those along the Ruta Puuc.

Sights

Santa Elena Museum MUSEUM

(M$10; 9am-6:30pm) This small museum perched on a hill is dedicated to a gruesome find – 18th-century child mummies found buried beneath the adjoining cathedral. There are also some *henequén*-related exhibits.

Sleeping & Eating

★Pickled Onion B&B $$

(cell 997-1117922; www.thepickledonionyucatan.com; Hwy 261, Santa Elena; r incl breakfast from US$40; P) Offers the chance to stay in a modern adobe-walled hut with lovely tiled floors and bathrooms. The recently renovated rooms keep you cool with *palapa* roofs, and all come with coffee makers and mosquito netting. We love the pool and surrounding gardens, and the excellent restaurant does food to go if you want to picnic while visiting nearby ruins.

The Pickled Onion is on the south end of town, off Hwy 261.

Nueva Altia B&B $$

(cell 998-2190176; Hwy 261 Km 159; d incl breakfast US$49; P) If you're looking for some peace and quiet, this is *the* place. Geometrically designed to get nice cross breezes, the spiral-shaped bungalows were inspired by ancient Maya architecture. If you've got time, the caretaker will gladly show you around parts of the 13-hectare property and tell you about the unearthed Maya ruins tucked away on the wooded grounds.

The ecohotel runs on solar energy. The turnoff is 1km south of Santa Elena, then head 800m east down a dirt road.

Flycatcher Inn B&B $$

(997-978-53-50; www.flycatcherinn.com; off Hwy 261, Santa Elena; d incl breakfast from M$800, ste M$1200; P) Flycatcher Inn features seven squeaky-clean rooms, all with great porches, super-comfy imported beds, hammocks, excellent screenage and spiffy bathrooms. The owners have kept most of the land around the inn undeveloped, and a number of bird and animal species can be seen here, including the flycatchers that gave their name to the place.

The Flycatcher closes from mid-September to mid-October. The inn's driveway is less than 100m north of Santa Elena's southern entrance, near Restaurant El Chac-Mool.

Sacbe Boutique Inn BUNGALOW $$

(997-978-51-58; www.sacbebungalows.com.mx; bungalows from M$615; P) At last visit the Sacbe's new owners were building an onsite restaurant in the inn's garden area. All rooms have fans, good screens and decent beds, as well as excellent folders with information about local activities, flora and fauna. It's about 200m south of the town's southern entrance.

Restaurant El Chac-Mool MEXICAN $$

(997-978-51-17; www.facebook.com/chacmooluxmal; Calle 18 No 211B, Santa Elena; mains M$70-110; 9am-10pm;) Off Hwy 261 at the southern entrance to Santa Elena, Restaurant El Chac-Mool is a friendly place serving Yucatecan food that includes a hearty vegetarian plate of rice, beans and fried bananas. It doubles as a hotel, too.

Kabah

These often overlooked **ruins** (Hwy 261; M$47, guides M$450; 8am-5pm), 23km southeast of Uxmal, are right astride Hwy 261. The souvenir ticket office sells snacks and cold drinks. The bulk of the restored ruins are on the east side of the highway.

On entering, head right to climb the stairs of **El Palacio de los Mascarones** (Palace of the Masks). Standing in front of it is the Altar de los Glifos, whose immediate area is littered with many stones carved with glyphs. The palace's facade is an amazing sight, covered in nearly 300 masks of Chaac, the rain god or sky serpent. Most of their huge noses are broken off; the best intact beaks are at the building's south end.

These curled-up noses may have given the palace its modern Maya name, Codz Poop (Rolled Mat; it's pronounced more like 'Codes Pope' than some Elizabethan curse).

When you've had your fill of noses, head north and around to the back of the Poop to check out the two restored **atlantes** (an *atlas* – plural *'atlantes'* – is a male figure used as a supporting column). These are especially interesting, as they're some of the very few 3D human figures you'll see at the main Maya sites. One is headless and the other wears a jaguar mask atop his head.

Descend the steps near the *atlantes* and turn left, passing the small **Pirámide de los Mascarones**, to reach the plaza containing **El Palacio**. The palace's broad facade has several doorways, two of which have a column in the center. These columned doorways and the groups of decorative *columnillas* (little columns) on the upper part of the facade are characteristic of the Puuc architectural style.

Steps on the north side of El Palacio's plaza put you on a path leading about 200m through the jungle to the **Templo de las Columnas**, which has more rows of decorative columns on the upper part of its facade. At last visit, access to the temple was closed for restoration.

West of El Palacio, across the highway, a path leads up the slope and passes to the south of a high mound of stones that was once the **Gran Pirámide** (Great Pyramid). The path curves to the right and comes to a large restored **monumental arch**. It's said that the *sacbé*, or cobbled and elevated ceremonial road, leading from here goes through the jungle all the way to Uxmal, terminating at a smaller arch; in the other direction it goes to Labná. Once, all of the Yucatán Peninsula was connected by these marvelous 'white roads' of rough limestone.

At present nothing of the *sacbé* is visible, and the rest of the area west of the highway is a maze of unmarked, overgrown paths leading off into the jungle.

For good lodging, stay in Santa Elena, about 8km north of Kabah.

Getting There & Away

Kabah is 104km from Mérida. It's easiest to reach the site by car, or from Mérida you can take a weekly Oriente bus (M$170, 8am Sunday) that makes stops at Kabah, Uxmal and three Ruta Puuc ruins. The bus leaves from the Terminal de Segunda Clase (TAME) on Calle 69. **Turitransmérida** (p151) does Ruta Puuc tours on a more regular basis and **Nomadas Hostel** (p150) also runs tours to Kabah.

Ruta Puuc

The Ruta Puuc (Puuc Route) meanders through rolling hills dotted with seldom-visited Maya ruins sitting in dense forests. A road branches off to the east (5km south of Kabah) and winds past the ruins of Sayil, Xlapak and Labná, eventually leading to the Grutas de Loltún. The sites offer some marvelous architectural detail and a deeper acquaintance with the Puuc Maya civilization.

Sights

Sayil ARCHAEOLOGICAL SITE

(Ruta Puuc; M$47; 8am-5pm) Sayil is best known for El Palacio, the huge three-tiered building that has an 85m-long facade and is reminiscent of the Minoan palace on Crete. The distinctive columns of Puuc architecture are used here often, either as supports for the lintels, as decoration between doorways or as a frieze above them, alternating with stylized Chaac masks and 'descending gods.'

Taking the path south from the palace for about 400m and bearing left, you come to the temple named **El Mirador**, whose rooster-like roofcomb was once painted a bright red. About 100m beyond El Mirador, beneath a protective *palapa*, is a stela bearing the relief of a fertility god with an enormous phallus, now sadly weathered.

Grupo Sur is a bit further, and offers beautiful jungle-covered ruins with tree roots twisting through the walls.

The ruins of Sayil are 4.5km from the junction of the Ruta Puuc with Hwy 261.

Xlapak ARCHAEOLOGICAL SITE

(Ruta Puuc; 8am-5pm) FREE The ornate *palacio* at Xlapak (shla-pak), also spelled Xlapac, is quite a bit smaller than those at nearby Kabah and Sayil, measuring only about 20m in length. It's decorated with the inevitable Chaac masks, columns and colonnettes and fretted geometric latticework of the Puuc style. The building is interesting and on a bit of a lean.

Plenty of motmots brighten up the surrounding forests. The name Xlapak means 'Old Walls' in Maya and was a general term among local people for ancient ruins.

Xlapak is about 10km east of the Ruta Puuc junction with Hwy 261.

Labná ARCHAEOLOGICAL SITE

(Ruta Puuc; M$47; 8am-5pm; P) This is *the* Ruta Puuc site not to miss. Archaeologists believe that, at one point in the 9th century, some 3000 Maya lived at Labná. To support such numbers in these arid hills, water was collected in *chultunes* (cisterns); there were some 60 *chultunes* in and around the city; several are still visible. **El Palacio**, the first building you come to, is one of the longest in

PYRAMID SCHEME

It's tempting to skirt the (often unpoliced) signs that prohibit climbing, but please climb only where it's allowed – a million bootsteps can certainly take their toll. Be careful, and if you're worried about heights, give this surefire technique a try: zigzag up or down the steps, making diagonal passes to either side of the stairway. Once you master this style, you'll never descend again using the embarrassing sit-and-bump-down-on-your-butt method, or the painful trip-and-fall-to-your-near-death method, which is why most of the pyramids are closed to climbing in the first place.

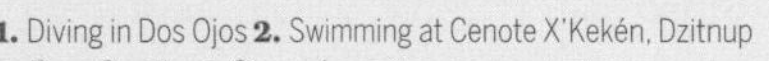

1. Diving in Dos Ojos **2.** Swimming at Cenote X'Kekén, Dzitnup
3. Gran Cenote **4.** Cuzamá

DAVID HISER / GETTY IMAGES ©

Yucatán Peninsula's Cenotes

One look and it's easy to see why the Maya thought cenotes (limestone sinkholes) were sacred: fathomless cerulean pools, dancing shafts of light, a darkened chamber. Even if you don't buy the spiritual aspects, they're still awe-inspiring examples of nature's beauty – and there are thousands of them dotting the peninsula. Here are our faves.

Dos Ojos (p112)

The cenotes at this Maya-run park on the Riviera Maya are part of one of the largest underwater cave systems on the planet. Experienced divers come from far and wide to plunge into **The Pit**, a 110m-deep cenote with ancient human and animal remains.

X'Kekén Jungle Park (Dzitnup)

You get two lovely cenotes at one location near Valladolid, both of which are great for swimming. At X'Kekén (p192) you'll see awe-inspiring stalactites hanging from the ceiling, while Samulá is a gorgeous cavern pool with *álamo* (poplar) roots. If Dzitnup is too crowded, hit nearby Hacienda San Lorenzo Oxman (p191), which sees fewer visitors.

Gran Cenote (p120)

Known for its large stalactites, stalagmites and columns, this 'grand' cenote appeals to divers, snorkelers and swimmers alike. It's 4km west of Tulum, making it a great little bike ride from town. The grounds are perfect for a picnic.

Cuzamá (p169)

A series of three cenotes reached by a horse-drawn rail cart near the town of Chunkanan, about 50km southeast of Mérida. Half the fun is getting there along tracks flanked by attractive agave fields. If you arrive early, before the crowds, you'll have a more pleasant experience in the crystal-clear blue waters.

the Puuc region, and much of its decorative carving is in good shape.

On the west corner of the main structure's facade, straight in from the big tree near the center of the complex, is a serpent's head with a human face peering out from between its jaws, the symbol of the planet Venus. Toward the hill from this is an impressive Chaac mask, and nearby is the lower half of a human figure (possibly a ballplayer) in loincloth and leggings.

The lower level has several more well-preserved Chaac masks, and the upper level contains a large *chultun* that still holds water. The view of the site and the hills beyond from there is impressive.

Labná is best known for **El Arco**, a magnificent arch once part of a building that separated two quadrangular courtyards. It now appears to be a gate joining two small plazas. The corbeled structure, 3m wide and 6m high, is well preserved, and the reliefs decorating its upper facade are exuberantly Puuc in style.

Flanking the west side of the arch are carved *na* with multitiered roofs. Also on these walls, the remains of the building that adjoined the arch, are lattice patterns atop a serpentine design. Archaeologists believe a high roofcomb once sat over the fine arch and its flanking rooms.

Standing on the opposite side of the arch and separated from it by the *sacbé* is a pyramid known as **El Mirador**, topped by a temple. The pyramid itself is largely stone rubble. The temple, with its 5m-high roofcomb, is well positioned to be a lookout, thus its name.

Labná is 14km east of the Ruta Puuc junction with Hwy 261.

Getting There & Away

To visit the Ruta Puuc sites, you can take a weekly Oriente bus (M$179, 8am Sunday) that makes stops at all three ruins, plus Kabah and Uxmal. The bus leaves from the Terminal de Segunda Clase (TAME) in Mérida on Calle 69.

Turitransmérida (p151) does Ruta Puuc tours on a more regular basis.

Grutas de Loltún

The **Grutas de Loltún** (Loltún Caverns; adult/child under 13yr M$117/free, parking M$22; ⏲tours 9:30am, 11am, 12:30pm, 2pm, 3pm & 4pm; 👪), one of the largest dry-cave systems on the Yucatán Peninsula, provided a treasure trove of data for archaeologists studying the Maya (Loltún means 'Stone Flower' in Maya). Carbon dating of artifacts found here reveals that the caves were used by humans 2200 years ago. Chest-high murals of hands, faces, animals and geometric motifs were apparent as recently as 25 years ago, but so many people have touched them that scarcely a trace remains, though some handprints have been restored.

A few pots are displayed in a niche, and an impressive bas-relief, El Guerrero, guards the entrance. Other than that, you'll mostly see illuminated limestone formations.

To explore the labyrinth, you must take a scheduled guided tour, usually in Spanish but sometimes in English if the group warrants it. The services of the guides are included in the admission price, though they expect a tip afterward (M$50 per person is fair). Tours last about one hour and 20 minutes, with lots of lengthy stops. Some guides' presentations are long on legends (and jokes about disappearing mothers-in-law) and short on geological and historical information.

Getting There & Away

About 15km north and east of Labná, a sign points left to the Grutas de Loltún, 5km further northeast. The road passes through lush orchards and some banana and palm groves, an agreeable sight in this dry region.

Colectivos (shared vans) to Oxkutzcab (osh-kootz-kahb; M$55, 1½ hours, frequent) depart from Calle 67A in Mérida, beside Parque San Juan. Loltún is 7km southwest of Oxkutzcab, where you can catch *colectivos* (M$15) to the caves from Calle 51 (in front of the market). A taxi costs about M$120.

Renting a car is the best option for reaching the Grutas, though; once you're out of Mérida it's easy going on pretty good roads.

Ruinas de Mayapán

Though far less impressive than many Maya sites, **Mayapán** (M$39; ⏲8am-5pm) is historically significant – it was one of the last major dynasties in the region and established itself as the center of Maya civilization from 1200 to 1440. The site's main attractions are clustered in a compact core, and visitors usually have the place to themselves. It is one of few sites where you can ascend to the top of the pyramid.

The city of Mayapán was large, with a population estimated to be around 12,000; it covered 4 sq km, all surrounded by a great defensive wall. More than 3500 buildings, 20 cenotes and traces of the city wall were mapped by archaeologists working in the 1950s and in 1962. The late-Postclassic craft is inferior to that of the great age of Maya art.

Among the structures that have been restored is the **Castillo de Kukulcán**, a climbable pyramid with fresco fragments around its base and, at its rear side, friezes depicting decapitated warriors. The reddish color is still faintly visible. The **Templo Redondo** (Round Temple) is vaguely reminiscent of El Caracol at Chichén Itzá.

These ruins are some 50km southeast of Mérida. Don't confuse the ruins of Mayapán with the Maya village of the same name, which is about 40km southeast of the ruins, past the town of Teabo.

Getting There & Away

The Ruinas de Mayapán are just off Hwy 184, a few kilometers southwest of the town of Telchaquillo. Second-class buses to Telchaquillo (M$25, 1½ hours, hourly) run from the Noreste bus terminal in Mérida. They'll let you off near the entrance to the ruins and pick you up on your way back.

Again, you may want to consider renting a car to get here.

Cenotes de Cuzamá

Three kilometers east of the town of Cuzamá, accessed from the small village of Chunkanan, are the **Cenotes de Cuzamá** (cell 999-9261577; admission 1-4 people M$300; 8am-4pm), a series of three amazing limestone sinkholes accessed by horse-drawn railcart in an old *henequén* hacienda. The fun horse-drawn ride will jar your fillings loose while showing you attractive scenes of the surrounding, overgrown agave fields.

Iguana sightings are a sure bet here, but keen eyes can also spot vultures or caracaras, as well as other birds, lizards and the occasional rabbit or two.

One of the cenotes is featured in much of Yucatán's tourist literature, and all three are spectacular, with rope-like roots descending along with ethereal shafts of light to the crystal-clear, deep-blue water. You'll likely find yourself sharing a dip with other bathers unless you get an early start. Several cenotes have steep stairways or ladders that are often slippery, so use caution at all times.

Getting There & Away

To get here by car, take Hwy 180 toward Cancún until you get to a turnoff for Ticopo on the right; after Akankeh (there's a small pyramid here), bear to the left to reach Cuzamá. From there, head east at the cathedral for 3km to the cenotes. Signs will lead the way. Follow the road all the way to the hacienda (some competitors along the way will try to offer their services, telling you the hacienda no longer exists – not true).

Buses leaves for Cuzamá (M$24, two hours) from the Noreste bus terminal in Mérida, or you can take *colectivos* (M$24) that depart from in front of the bus terminal.

Ticul

997 / POP 33,000

Ticul, 30km east of archaeological site Uxmal, is the largest town in this ruin-rich region. It's dusty and fairly quiet, with few signs of nightlife other than perhaps a few watering holes. But it has hotels, restaurants and transportation, so it's a good base for day trips to nearby ruins. (It's not as attractive a jumping-off point as nearby Santa Elena, though.) Ticul is also a center for fine *huipil* weaving, and ceramics made here from the local red clay are renowned throughout the Yucatán.

Ticul's main street is Calle 23, sometimes called 'Calle Principal,' starting from the highway and going past the *mercado* (market) to the main plaza, Plaza Mayor.

Sights

Iglesia de San Antonio de Padua CHURCH

(Calles 25 & 26) Because of the number of Maya ruins in the vicinity, from which building blocks could be acquired, and the number of Maya in the area 'needing' conversion to Christianity, Franciscan friars built many churches in the region, including this 16th-century church. Although looted on several occasions, the church has some original touches.

Among them are the stone statues of friars in primitive style flanking the side entrances and a Black Christ altarpiece ringed by crude medallions.

Plaza de la Cultura PLAZA

It's all cement and stone but nevertheless the Plaza de la Cultura is an agreeable place to take in the evening breeze, enjoy the view of the church and greet passing townspeople.

OFF THE BEATEN TRACK

DIY ADVENTURES IN YUCATÁN

There are so many great adventures to be had in this region. Here are some ideas to get you started as you leave the guidebook behind for a few days of DIY adventure.

- Just off the road to Mayapán, **Tekit** has a cenote worth visiting.
- Friar Diego de Landa burned 5000 idols, 13 altars, 27 religious and historic codices, and 197 ceremonial vases in an auto-da-fé in 1562 in the town of **Maní**. The town has a nice cathedral, and the Príncipe de Tutul-Xiu restaurant's *poc-chuc* (marinated, grilled pork) is so popular that families drive here from afar to delight in the famed dish.
- The rarely visited tourist route **La Ruta de los Conventos** takes you to colonial-era convents in the towns of Maní, Oxkutzcab, Teabo, Mama, Chumayel, Tekax and Yotholín.
- A Maya-run cenote and park in the seldom-visited town of **Yokdzonot**, west of Chichén Itzá on the old highway, makes a refrshing stop after a day at the sunbaked ruins.

Sleeping

Posada El Jardín INN $

(997-972-04-01; www.posadajardin.com; Calle 27 No 216C, btwn Calles 28 & 30; r from M$520; P) Pleasant rustic rooms surround a lush garden with a swimming pool and a *palapa*-covered lobby at this peaceful getaway. The hosts at this family-run inn have great tips on Ticul's best eating options and the nearby sights.

Hotel Villa Real HOTEL $

(997-972-28-28; restaurantevillareal@hotmail.com; Calle 23 s/n, btwn Calles 26A & 28; r M$400-500; P) Considered one of the nicest places in town, which isn't saying much for Ticul's hotel offerings. But rooms here are comfortable enough and they have balconies so that you can get some fresh air. There's a restaurant as well.

Hotel Plaza HOTEL $

(997-972-04-84; www.hotelplazayucatan.com; Calle 23 No 202, btwn Calles 26 & 26A; d/ste M$500/640; P) Spacious rooms with tiled floors and small but fun balconies make this a pretty good choice, though keep in mind that street-facing rooms may get noise. The old building adds character as does the hotel's location right off the town plaza.

Hotel San Antonio HOTEL $

(997-972-18-93; hotelsan-antonio@hotmail.com; Calle 25A No 202, btwn Calles 26 & 26A; d M$330-390; P) Some rooms have great views of the Plaza de la Cultura. The hotel lacks character, but here in Ticul that's kind of reassuring. All rooms have TV and air-con, and there's also a small parking lot and onsite restaurant.

Eating & Drinking

★**El Mirador** YUCATECAN $

(off Calle 42; mains M$65-90; 11am-7pm;) El Mirador means lookout in Spanish and, yes, you get an awesome view of Ticul and beyond from this large *palapa* restaurant. But it's the wonderful Yucatecan comfort food that makes this place truly special. Try the *relleno blanco,* a hearty turkey stew, or go with a local favorite, *frijol con puerco* (beans and pork).

You'll find El Mirador's dirt road turnoff heading south on Calle 42. A taxi from the city center costs about M$20.

Mercado MARKET $

(Calle 28A, btwn Calles 21 & 23; snacks M$10, mains M$30-40; 8am-1:30pm) Ticul's lively Mercado provides all the ingredients for picnics and snacks, and offers nice photo ops, too. It also has lots of those wonderful eateries where the food is good, the portions generous and the prices low.

Bazar de Comidas MEXICAN $

(cnr Calles 25 & 22; mains M$25-50; 8am-5pm;) The friendly stalls here serve inexpensive regional food, such as *poc-chuc* (grilled pork) and *queso relleno* (stuffed cheese).

Super Willy's SUPERMARKET $

(Calle 23 s/n, btwn Calles 28 & 30; 7am-10pm) Across from the *mercado,* Super Willy's is a small supermarket with a big variety of groceries and household items.

Pizzería La Gondola PIZZA $$

(997-972-01-12; Calle 23 No 208, cnr Calle 26; pizzas M$85-135, sandwiches M$28-35; 5:30-11:30pm Mon-Fri, to midnight Sat & Sun;) Open late, this clean place has sandwiches and pizzas with the usual toppings. 'Order by number' options make it easy for non-Spanish speakers to get exactly what they want.

Flor del Campo JUICE BAR
(☎997-972-18-75; Calle 28, btwn Calles 23 & 25; juices M$8-14; ⏰6am-6pm Mon-Sat, to noon Sun) Juice up for the day at this tiny place, which just has chilled juices (no smoothies). It's near the *mercado*.

Information

You'll find banks with ATMs on Plaza Mayor. Several internet cafes and the **Post Office** (Calle 23 s/n, Plaza Mayor; ⏰8am-4:30pm Mon-Fri, to noon Sat) are in the area as well.

Getting There & Away

BUS

Ticul's 24-hour **Bus Terminal** (Calle 24 s/n, btwn Calles 25 & 25A) is behind the massive church. For most destinations, buses from Ticul make numerous stops along the way.

CAR

The quickest way to Uxmal, Kabah and the Ruta Puuc sites is via Santa Elena. From central Ticul, go west to Calle 34 and turn south; it heads straight to Santa Elena.

Those headed east to Quintana Roo and the Caribbean coast can take Hwy 184 from Ticul through Oxkutzcab to Tzucacab and José María Morelos (which has a gas station). At Polyuc, 130km from Ticul, a road turns left (east), ending after 80km in Felipe Carrillo Puerto. The right fork of the road goes south to Laguna Bacalar. Between Oxkutzcab and Felipe Carrillo Puerto or Bacalar there are few restaurants or gas stations.

COLECTIVO

Colectivos go direct to Mérida's Parque de San Juan (M$42, 1½ hours, 6am to 8:30pm) from the taxi terminal on Calle 24. There, you can also catch a *colectivo* to Tekax (M$25, one hour).

Combis for Oxkutzcab (M$16, 30 minutes, 6am to 8pm) leave from Calle 25A, on the south side of the church.

Colectivos to Santa Elena (M$15, 6:50am to 8pm), which lies between the Maya sites of Uxmal and Kabah, depart from Calle 30, between Calles 25 and 25A. In Santa Elena, catch another bus northwest to Uxmal (15km) or south to Kabah (3.5km).

TAXI

Taxis in front of the *colectivo* terminal, on the corner of Calles 24 and 25, charge M$800 for a full day touring the Ruta Puuc ruins. You can ask to make stops at Grutas de Loltún, Labná, Sayil, Xlapak, Kabah, and Uxmal if time permits.

Ticul to Tihosuco

The route from Ticul to Tihosuco, in Quintana Roo, is seldom traveled by tourists. Some might say there's nothing to see. But others will welcome the opportunity to travel through farmland and jungle and see glimpses of Maya life that have remained the same for centuries. Part of the route is called La Ruta de los Conventos (The Route of the Convents), as each of these tiny villages has a cathedral or church, many in beautiful disrepair. Prepare to hear many folks speaking Maya, though most speak Spanish as well.

The towns of Oxkutzcab and Tekax offer budget accommodations. Beyond Oxkutzcab, the towns along this route are linked by combis (shared vans) and, less frequently, local buses; they may be hailed from the roadside.

Oxkutzcab

Oxkutzcab is renowned for its daily produce market and colonial church. Markets were the principal means of trade for the ancient Maya, and the peninsula's indigenous people still travel from the countryside to central communities to exchange produce at stalls beside a main square. Oxkutzcab is such a community. A mural in the plaza

BUSES FROM TICUL

DESTINATION	FARE (M$)	DURATION (HRS)	FREQUENCY (DAILY)
Cancún	263-296	8	frequent
Chetumal	220	6	5
Mérida	50-76	1½	frequent
Oxkutzcab	15	½	frequent
Playa del Carmen	240	7	frequent
Tulum	214	6	frequent

THE MODERN MAYA

The area between Ticul and Tihosuco is truly the Maya heartland. Indeed, the Maya in these parts continue to honor the gods of rain, wind and agriculture, just as their ancestors did before them.

Yucatán state has the fifth-highest percentage of indigenous-language speakers in Mexico, but the number of Maya speakers is rapidly declining. In 2005 about 34% of Yucatecans claimed to speak Maya; at last count, less than 30% said they spoke any type of indigenous language at all.

So where have all the Maya gone? Many have moved to big tourist cities like Cancún, while others have moved all the way up to the US. Many small Maya communities are beginning to welcome tourists in an effort to keep young folks from fleeing to the cities. It's ironic, but inviting foreigners in may prove the best way to maintain traditions.

The homes of today's rural Maya are still wood-framed huts with lean-to roofs of palm. The walls are made of bamboo poles or branches, and the spaces between the poles are often filled with mud to keep pests out. The Maya tend to prefer hammocks to beds.

Anywhere from a stone's throw to an hour's walk from a Maya hut is a *milpa* (cornfield). Corn tortillas remain a staple of the Maya diet, but the Maya also raise pigs and turkeys and produce honey, squash and other crops, which they sell at town markets. Many of the younger generation, particularly men, hitchhike out to work for a week in the larger towns such as Playa del Carmen or Cancún, returning for a day or two, or for long weekends or holidays. A *small* family will have about five children.

Many Yucatecan Maya prefer baseball to soccer. And on any given Sunday, you are likely to witness a down-home game played on the town square. It's a serious endeavor with hired hitters, uniforms and plenty of spectators.

across from the market depicts inquisitor Friar Diego de Landa's auto-da-fé in Maní, when he burnt thousands of idols.

Oxkutzcab, or 'osh,' as locals call it, makes for a good stopover if you want to visit the Grutas de Loltún or nearby towns. It can also serve as a base for visiting sites along the Ruta Puuc. You'll find good cheap eats at the market along the main strip (Calle 51).

Sights

Iglesia de San Francisco de Asis CHURCH

(Calle 51 s/n) Constructed at a snail's pace from 1640 to 1693, this Franciscan convent is remarkable for its ornamental facade, at the center of which is a stone statue of St Francis, the mission patron. It's also notable for its magnificent altarpiece, one of only a few baroque altarpieces in the Yucatán to survive the revolts that have occurred since its construction.

Sleeping & Eating

Hotel Puuc HOTEL $

(☎997-975-01-03; www.hotelpuuc.com.mx; Calle 55 No 80, cnr Calle 44; d with fan/air-con M$420/470, ste M$570; P❄📶🏊) Offers a good deal for the price, with your choice of air-con or fan in every business-hotel-style room. The beds are firm, there's a good restaurant downstairs and out back you'll find a large pool surrounded by a grassy garden. Rooms at the front of the property face a sometimes noisy parking lot; suites on the back lot are quieter.

El Príncipe Tutul-Xiu MEXICAN $

(Calle 45 No 102, btwn Calles 50 & 52; mains M$50-90; ⏰11am-7pm; 🚭) Famous for its *poc-chuc* (grilled pork), El Principe Tutul-Xiu has several other classic Yucatecan dishes and yummy desserts as well.

Getting There & Away

Oxkutzcab is 16km southeast of Ticul on Hwy 184, which becomes a two-lane road as its passes through the town center. Buses depart frequently to Oxkutzcab from the Ticul terminal.

Tekax

The church in Tekax has been looted a couple of times, initially during the Caste War and later during the Mexican Revolution.

The Tekax area is increasingly prosperous (due to a successful crop switch from corn to sugarcane and citrus), and its residents recently replaced the church's damaged floor with a beautiful tiled floor and added a lovely new stone altar. According to *Maya Missions: Exploring the Spanish Colonial Churches of Yucatán,* a fabulous book by Richard and Rosalind Perry, during construction of the church one of its belfries collapsed, burying (and presumably crushing) the many indigenous laborers under tons of rubble. Miraculously, as local legend has it, no one lost their life in the collapse.

Also noteworthy is the shape of the church, which undoubtedly was constructed of materials taken from nearby Maya temples. The general form of the church is that of a three-tiered pyramid. Possibly the architecture was based on the Maya structure from which the blocks were taken.

Shared vans run here from Ticul's *colectivo* terminal (M$25, one hour).

Tours

La Boca del Diablo TOUR
(☎cell 997-9797963; marionovelo25@outlook.com; Calle 50A s/n, just south of Calle 57; tours M$300-500) There are some very interesting caves near Tekax, including a beautiful crystalline number called La Boca del Diablo. Mario Alberto Novelo Dorantes is a knowledgeable local guide with equipment. He doesn't speak English but can arrange for a translator. Drop by his house (look for the light pink house) or call to arrange a by-the-seat-of-your-pants adventure.

Sleeping & Eating

Hotel Sultán de la Sierra HOTEL $
(☎997-974-21-69; hector_pduarte@hotmail.com; Calle 50A No 211, btwn Calles 55 & 57; d M$300; P ⊖ ❄ ☰ ≋) On the main square, the Sultán is a decent budget option with rooms that stay fairly cool during the day, and a swimming pool just off the lobby.

El Huinic YUCATECAN $$
(Calle 61 No 202B, cnr Calle 50; mains M$60-140; ⏱7am-2pm; ⊖ ☰) Arguably the best eats in town and it doubles as a karaoke bar at night for you wannabe crooners. The restaurant specializes in Yucatecan classics such as *papadzules* (diced egg enchiladas bathed in pumpkin-seed sauce), *longaniza asada* (grilled Mexican sausage) and *queso relleno* (stuffed cheese), but there are steak, chicken and seafood dishes on the menu as well.

Tihosuco

Located inside the state of Quintana Roo, Tihosuco was a major military outpost for the Spanish during the late 16th century and for 300 years thereafter. During this time the town came under numerous Maya assaults, and in 1686 it was attacked, though not sacked, by pirates led by legendary Dutch buccaneer Lorencillo.

During many of those attacks, the Spaniards retreated to the heavily fortified 17th-century church at the town center, which for much of its life served as a house of God, an arsenal and a stronghold. But the town and church fell to rebel hands in 1866 following a long siege, and much of the magnificent building was gutted. What remains of the once-great church is worth investigating. Services are still held inside, as in many other roofless churches in the region.

From Tihosuco, it's a fast ride up Hwy 295 to Valladolid. Going the other way, Hwy 295 goes south to Felipe Carrillo Puerto.

Sights

About 30 minutes outside of town by car is a ruined 16th-century **Franciscan church** worth visiting. The area is known locally as Lal-Ka or La Capilla Poza. And while many consider it a sacred – and possibly haunted – site, you can usually get a taxi to take you here (you won't find it on your own).

If you've got your own wheels, it's worth taking a drive through the nearby Maya villages of Ixcabil, Saban, Sacalaca and Huay-Max. Every town has a unique church, and many even have a nearby cenote or two that the locals can point out.

Museo de la Guerra de Castas MUSEUM
(Caste War Museum; www.museogc.com; cnr Calles 17 & 26; admission M$68.50; ⏱10am-6pm Tue-Sun) Housed in an 18th-century building, this museum does a good job of detailing the more than four centuries of oppression suffered by the Maya on the peninsula, with its main focus on the Caste War. Only a few explanations are translated into English. There's a small botanical garden here as well, and there are cotton weaving and traditional medicine workshops offered.

WEST & NORTH OF MÉRIDA

Celestún

988 / POP 6800

West of Mérida, Celestún is a sleepy sun-scorched fishing village that moves at a turtle's pace – and that's the way locals like it. There's a pretty little square in the center of the town and some nice beaches, but the real draw here is Reserva de la Biosfera Ría Celestún, a wildlife sanctuary abounding in waterfowl, with flamingos as the star attraction.

It makes a good beach-and-bird day trip from Mérida, and it's also a great place to kick back and do nothing for a few days, especially if you've become road weary. Fishing boats dot the appealing white-sand beach that stretches to the north for kilometers, and afternoon breezes cool the town on most days. Celestún is sheltered by the peninsula's southward curve, resulting in an abundance of marine life and less violent seas during the season of *nortes* (winds and rains arriving from the north).

Calle 11 is the road into town (it comes due west from Mérida), ending at Calle 12, the road paralleling the beach.

Sights

Reserva de la Biosfera Ría Celestún WILDLIFE RESERVE

The 591-sq-km Reserva de la Biosfera Ría Celestún is home to a huge variety of animals and birdlife, including a large flamingo colony. You can see flamingos (via boat tours) year-round in Celestún, but they're usually out in full force from November to mid-March

Morning is the best time of day, though from 5pm onward the birds tend to concentrate in one area after the day's feeding, which can make for good viewing.

Hacienda Real de Salinas HISTORIC BUILDING

This abandoned hacienda a few kilometers south and east of town once produced dyewood and salt, and served as a summer home for a Campeche family. It's 5km in from the mouth of the estuary. Out in the *ría* (estuary) you can see a cairn marking an *ojo de agua dulce* (freshwater spring) that once supplied the hacienda.

The buildings are decaying in a most scenic way; you can still see shells in the wall mixed into the building material, as well as pieces of French roof tiles that served as ballast in ships on the journey from Europe. Many intact tiles with the brickworks' name and location (Marseille) are still visible in what's left of the roofs.

The hacienda makes a good bicycle excursion from town. Coming south on Calle 4, go left at the Y junction (a dirt road that flanks Puerto Abrigo), then turn right to reach El Lastre (The Ballast), a peninsula between the estuary and its western arm. Flamingos, white pelicans and other birds are sometimes seen here. If the water is high enough, it's possible to ask your flamingo tour captain to try stopping here on the way back from the birds. You'll find bike rentals on the town square.

Activities

Inland from the stretches of beach north of town lies a large section of scrub stretching east to the estuary that also provides good **birding** opportunities.

South and east of town, toward the abandoned Hacienda Real de Salinas, is another good area for nature observation. Flamingos, white pelicans, cormorants, anhingas and many other species frequent the shores and waters of the *ría*.

Horseback Riding HORSEBACK RIDING

(cell 999-9691111; www.villasdelmar.com.mx; Calle 12 s/n; per person M$250) For a ride along the coast, Hotel Villas del Mar does morning and afternoon tours, but it has just two horses available so you should reserve ahead.

Tours

Flamingo tours are Celestún's main draw. Trips from the beach last 2½ hours and begin with a ride along the coast for several kilometers, during which you can expect to see egrets, herons, cormorants, sandpipers and many other bird species. The boat then turns into the mouth of the *ría*.

Continuing up the *ría* takes you under the highway bridge where other boat tours begin and beyond which lie the flamingos. Depending on the tide, the hour, the season and climate conditions, you may see hundreds or thousands of the colorful birds. Don't encourage your captain to approach them too closely; a startled flock taking wing can result in injuries and deaths (for the birds). In addition to taking you to the flamingos, the captain will wend through a 200m mangrove tunnel and visit freshwater springs welling into the saltwater of the es-

THE LOST HENEQUÉN HACIENDAS OF YUCATÁN

Yucatán state would have been little more than a provincial backwater if it weren't for a spiky son-of-a-bitch-of-a-plant named Agave Fourcroydes. Some call it *henequén*, others call it sisal; call it what you will, the lanced-leaved plant used to create strong maritime rope and twine was 'green gold' from the late 19th century to the end of WWII. It was during this time that the 'sisal barons' of Yucatán built their elaborate haciendas for the booming business. But the industry bottomed out post WWII with the advent of synthetic fibers.

Not only did the demise of *henequén* force the region's haciendas to shutter operations; it had a devastating economic impact on the town of Sisal, the main seaport for *henequén* exports back in the heyday.

Most of the area's *henequén* haciendas are now in ruins, but others have been restored to past glory and make for amazing upscale retreats or simply interesting places to visit.

Hacienda Xcanatún (toll-free 800-202 25 66; www.xcanatun.com; Calle 20 s/n, Hwy 261 Km 12; r/ste incl breakfast from M$4900/5650;) One of the finest haciendas, no doubt. Originally built in the 18th century for agricultural activities and later converted into a *henequén* plantation, Hacienda Xcanatún now houses a luxury hotel. A standard room here gets you an elegant setup with polished stone floors, high ceilings and exquisite rustic furnishings.

Even if you don't stay, you can drop by the hacienda's award-winning Casa de Piedra restaurant (mains M$110 to M$285) on your way to the beach or nearby Maya ruins. You'll find it off Hwy 261, heading north to Progreso.

Hacienda San Ildefonso Teya (999-988-08-03; www.haciendateya.com; Hwy 180 Km 12.5; noon-6pm;) Founded as a livestock ranch in 1683 and converted into a *henequén* plantation in the 19th century, today Hacienda Teya is a restaurant, hotel and popular wedding venue. The restaurant (mains M$130 to M$180), known for its quality Yucatecan cuisine, has live *trova* acts on Saturday and Sunday afternoons. Book ahead if you want to stay in one of the hacienda's five colonial-style rooms (M$1600 including breakfast). From Mérida, it's off Hwy 180 toward Chichén Itzá.

Hacienda Yaxcopoil (cell 999-9001193; www.yaxcopoil.com; Hwy 261 Km 186; museum admission M$75; 8am-6pm Mon-Sat, 9am-5pm Sun;) A vast estate that grew and processed *henequén;* many of its numerous French Renaissance–style buildings have undergone picturesque restorations. There's a small museum that offers glimpses at the giant rasping machines that turned the leaves into fiber. You can stay in a fairly affordable restored room with antique furniture (there's only one room so you'll have the hacienda to yourself; US$100 including breakfast). Frequent Mérida–Ticul buses pass Yaxcopoil, 33km southwest of Mérida off Hwy 261, but it's easiest to drive.

Hacienda San Pedro Ochil (999-924-74-65; www.haciendaochil.com; Hwy 261 Mérida–Muna Km 175; admission M$30; 10am-6pm;) There's no lodging here but it provides a fascinating look at how *henequén* was grown and processed. From the parking lot, follow the tracks once used by small wheeled carts to haul materials to and from the processing plant. You'll pass hemp and filigree workshops, and a small museum with exhibits illustrating the cultivating, harvesting and processing of the plant. The *casa de maquinas* (machine house) and smokestack still stand. Ochil also has a restaurant (mains M$92 to M$175), swimming pool and small cenote.

It's about 35km south of Mérida, off Hwy 261.

Hacienda Santa Rosa (999-923-19-23; www.thehaciendas.com; Carretera Mérida-Campeche, Maxcanú turnoff; r/ste from US$558/657;) The only hacienda that has been converted into a hotel along a ruined haciendas route. The rooms and suites show amazing variety; some have private walled gardens with bathtubs or plunge pools. The hacienda has a lovely botanical garden and a gourmet restaurant (nonguests are welcome), but it costs a pretty peso.

Starwood Resorts operates three converted haciendas in Yucatán state – Santa Rosa, Temozón and San José.

tuary, where you can take a refreshing dip. Tours from the bridge run 1½ hours.

Hiring a boat on the beach can be frustrating at times. Operators tend to try to collect as many people as possible, which sometimes means a lot of waiting around. Prices are often quoted based on six passengers, but if fewer people show up, the quoted price rises. You can avoid this problem by coming up with a group of six on your own. Expect to pay around M$210 to M$230 per passenger.

With either the bridge or beach option, your captain may or may not speak English.

★Nature Tour BOAT TOUR
(cell 999-2660422, cell 988-9676130; henrydzib @hotmail.com; per boat incl guide M$1910) Brothers and naturalists Alex and Henry Dzib, Celestún's foremost experts on the area's wildlife, offer custom-made tours to watch flamingos, crocodiles, dolphins and a variety of birds. They also do fly-fishing trips.

Flamingo Tour BIRDWATCHING
(Hwy 281 s/n; per boat M$1260, per person M$230) Motorboats for bird-watching tours depart from the beach at Calle 11 (outside Restaurant Celestún) and from a dock at the town's entrance, just under the bridge. Tours from the bridge are more organized and you'll have a better chance of finding a knowledgeable English-speaking guide there. During the trip, you'll see flamingos, Bird Island, a mangrove tunnel and a spring.

Manglares de Dzinitún ECOTOUR
(cell 999-6454310; dzinitun@gmail.com; per canoe M$700) About 1km inland you'll find an ecotour operator offering canoe tours that run through a mangrove tunnel and good birding spots, made all the better by the lack of engine noise. To get here from the beach, turn right on the street after the second transmission tower. It's about 300m ahead.

Sleeping

Most of Celestún's hotels are on Calle 12, within a short walk of one another. Book ahead for a sea view, especially on weekends.

Villas del Mar HOTEL $
(cell 999-9691111; www.villasdelmar.com.mx; Calle 12 s/n, btwn Calles 23 & 25; r with/without air-con M$600/500;) If you're looking for comfort, this hotel with modern colonial-style rooms clearly has the upper hand on the other budget hotels in town. An added plus are the free kayaks, and for an additional cost the hotel offers coastal horseback-riding tours. The drawbacks: there's no wi-fi and the beach is generally cleaner on the north side of town.

Hotel Gutiérrez HOTEL $
(988-916-26-48; hotelgutierrez@hotmail.com; Calle 12 No 107, cnr Calle 13; r with fan/air-con M$450/600;) A decent remodeled budget option right on the beach. Rooms recently got a fresh coat of paint and new bathroom tiling. It has a great restaurant, too.

Hotel Manglares HOTEL $$
(988-916-21-56; hmanglares@prodigy.net.mx; Calle 12; d/cabañas M$1100/1600;) Although the architecture doesn't blend perfectly with the laid-back town, this is a nice midrange choice. The rooms all have sea views and private balconies. The well-appointed *cabañas* come with mini-kitchens, Jacuzzis and a small common area. It's 1km north of Calle 11.

Hotel Flamingo Plaza HOTEL $$
(988-916-21-33; drivan2011@hotmail.com; Calle 12 No 67C; r M$700;) Family-run hotel on the beach with a pool overlooking the coast. Weathered sinks and showers could use some maintenance but the place is kept clean. It's 800m north of Calle 11.

★Casa de Celeste Vida GUESTHOUSE $$$
(988-916-25-36; www.hotelcelestevida.com; Calle 12 No 49E; r/apt US$95/130;) This friendly Canadian-owned place offers comfortably decked-out rooms with kitchens and an apartment that sleeps four – all with water views and the beach at your doorstep. Kayak and bike use are free for guests. The hosts are happy to arrange flamingo tours, or if you prefer, a nighttime crocodile excursion. It's 1.5km north of Calle 11.

Castillito Kin-Nah GUESTHOUSE $$$
(988-916-26-27; www.castillito-kin-nah.com; Calle 12 No 47; r from US$85;) Known by locals as the 'little castle,' the Castillito certainly feels grandiose in small-town Celestún. Behind the castle's gates await immaculate rooms and some pretty sweet amenities, including a nice pool and satellite

Eating

Keep in mind that many restaurants close around 7pm.

El Palmar TAQUERÍA $
(Calle 13 s/n; tacos M$10-15; ⌚7pm-3am; ⊖) The only eating option in town that keeps late hours. The spit-roasted *tacos al pastor* (marinated pork) and *arrachera* (flank steak) tacos provide a welcome break from the fish and seafood routine.

Dolphin BREAKFAST $$
(Calle 12 No 104, cnr Calle 13; mains M$50-98; ⌚8:30am-1pm Wed-Mon, 6-10pm Fri & Sat; ⊖) An excellent breakfast spot at Hotel Gutiérrez. Full breakfasts include coffee, juice, freshmade bread, marmalade and some mighty fine egg dishes. Dolphin opens on Friday and Saturday night for dinner with menu items such as curry dishes, salads and *tortas* (sandwiches).

Restaurant Los Pampanos SEAFOOD $$
(Calle 12 s/n; mains M$90-140, lobster M$250; ⌚11am-7pm; ⊖) A tranquil joint on the beach, north of Calle 11, this is a great spot for afternoon margaritas on the sand. Try the fresh lobster or a fish fillet stuffed to the brim with shellfish.

La Palapa SEAFOOD $$
(restaurant-lapalapa@hotmail.com; Calle 12 No 105; mains M$75-165; ⌚11am-7pm; ⊖) A cut above the other seaside joints, La Palapa has an expansive dining area looking down to the sea, attentive staff and savory seafood dishes, including coconut-coated shrimp served in a coconut shell.

La Playita SEAFOOD $$
(Calle 12 s/n; mains M$70-150; ⌚10am-6pm; ⊖) Of all the sandy-floored beachfront joints here, this one gets the thumbs-up from the locals. Fresh seafood and ceviche are its main draw.

Information

There are no banks in town. You'll find an ATM on the plaza and another one inside Super Willy's, also located on the plaza. The best bet is to bring cash in case the ATMs run out of money. Don't plan on using high-speed internet here.

Getting There & Away

Frequent buses head for Celestún (M$56, 2½ hours) from Mérida's Noreste bus terminal. The route terminates at Celestún's plaza, a block inland from Calle 12.

There are also *colectivos* on the plaza that will take you to downtown Mérida for M$40.

By car from Mérida, the best route to Celestún is via the new road out of Umán.

Ruined Haciendas Route

Still very much under the radar, this fascinating route allows you to appreciate some impressive old haciendas in rural Maya communities. If you're driving out of Celestún, turn south off Hwy 281 and head toward Chunchucmil, the name of both a ruined *henequén* hacienda and a nearby Maya archaeological site. A caretaker there will gladly show you around – just make sure to pay him a tip.

After Chunchucmil (look for the covered Maya mounds as you drive away), about every 5km you'll pass another ruined hacienda all the way to Hacienda Granada, shortly before the road hits old Hwy 180. Several of the buildings are hard to see from the road, so you'll need to stop frequently to really give them their due.

Hacienda Santa Rosa (p175) is the only hacienda along the route that has been converted into a hotel, and there's a gourmet restaurant there if you want to stop for lunch.

About 5km after Santa Rosa, you'll reach a fork in the road. Veer right to visit Granada, where you can visit two **talleres de arte popular** (artisan workshops) near the church. Drop by from 9am to 6pm Monday to Friday to watch local women create *jipijapa* (palm frond) hats and baskets as well as *henequén* crafts. They make a living doing this, so it's a nice gesture to buy something from them. Hwy 180 (the road to Mérida) is 1km east of Granada.

Dzibilchaltún

Lying about 17km due north of central Mérida, **Dzibilchaltún** (Place of Inscribed Flat Stones; adult/child under 12yr M$132/free, parking M$20; ⌚site 8am-5pm, museum 9am-4pm Tue-Sun; P) was the longest continuously utilized Maya administrative and ceremonial city, serving the Maya from around 1500 BC until the European conquest in the 1540s. At the height of its greatness, Dzibilchaltún covered 15 sq km. Some 8400 structures were mapped by archaeologists in the 1960s; few of these have been excavated. Aside from the ruins, the site offers a lovely, swimmable cenote and a Maya museum.

In some ways it's unimpressive if you've already seen larger places, such as Chichén Itzá or Uxmal, but twice a year humble

Dzibilchaltún shines. At sunrise on the equinoxes (approximately March 20 and September 22), the sun aligns directly with the main door of the **Templo de las Siete Muñecas** (Temple of the Seven Dolls), which got its name from seven grotesque dolls discovered here during excavations. As the sun rises, the temple doors glow, then 'light up' as the sun passes behind. It also casts a cool square beam on the crumbled wall behind. Many who have seen both feel the sunrise here is more spectacular than Chichén Itzá's famous snake, and is well worth getting up at the crack of dawn to witness.

Enter the site along a nature trail that terminates at the modern, air-conditioned **Museo del Pueblo Maya**, featuring artifacts from throughout the Maya regions of Mexico, including some superb colonial-era religious carvings and other pieces. Exhibits explaining both ancient and modern Maya daily life are labeled in Spanish and English. Beyond the museum, a path leads to the central plaza, where you'll find an open chapel that dates from early Spanish times (1590–1600).

The **Cenote Xlacah** is more than 40m deep and a fine spot for a swim after exploring the ruins. In 1958 a National Geographic Society diving expedition recovered more than 30,000 Maya artifacts, many of ritual significance, from the cenote. The most interesting of these are now on display in the site's museum. South of the cenote is **Estructura 44** – at 130m it's one of the longest Maya structures in existence.

Chablekal-bound *colectivos* depart frequently from Calle 58 (between Calles 57 and 59) in Mérida. They'll drop you about 750m from the site's entrance.

Progreso

☎969 / POP 37,000

If Mérida's heat has you dying for a quick beach fix, or if you want to see the longest pier (6.5km) in Mexico, head to Progreso (also known as Puerto Progreso). The beach is long and, as with other Gulf beaches, the water is murky; visibility even on calm days rarely exceeds 5m. Winds can hit here full force in the afternoon and can blow well into the night, especially from December to March when *los nortes* (northern winds) kick up. *Méridanos* come in droves on weekends, especially during the Mexican holiday period of July and August. During that time it can be difficult to find a room with a view and, sadly, you'll see more litter on the beach. Once or twice a week the streets flood with cruise-ship tourists, but the place can feel empty on off nights, which makes a refreshing change. Generally Progreso has a very relaxed beach-town vibe and it makes a pleasant getaway from the inland.

Activities

El Corchito SWIMMING

(Hwy 27 s/n, cnr Calle 46; M$25; 9am-5pm) Take a refreshing dip in one of three fresh-water swimming holes surrounded by mangroves at nature reserve El Corchito. Motorboats take visitors across a canal to the reserve. El Corchito is home to iguanas, boa constrictors, small crocs, raccoons and a band of coatis. The coons and coatis are skilled food thieves, something to consider if you bring lunch.

El Corchito sees a lot of visitors, especially on weekends, so get there early for a more peaceful swim.

'Tecnológico' buses departing from a bus station at Calles 82 and 29 will leave you a block and a half from El Corchito. If you're driving, take Calle 46 south to Hwy 27.

Sleeping & Eating

The majority of hotels and restaurants here are no more than 11 blocks north and east of the bus terminal. Head inland to get cheaper eats.

Hostal Zócalo Beach HOSTEL $

(☎969-103-02-94; www.facebook.com/hostalzocalobeach; Calle 21 s/n, cnr Calle 54; dm M$150, r M$400-450, incl breakfast;) This 1920s art deco mansion houses the most colorful lodging in town. Previously it served as a boarding house, and long before the building existed the property was a pirates' base camp. The eccentric owner insists that a pirate ghost roams the hallways and it has signaled to him that a booty is buried under the house.

At last visit, he was digging up the backyard and employing sophisticated metal detectors in hopes of finding the lost treasure. The two-story house is a real beauty; dorms and private rooms feature high ceilings and each is individually painted.

Playa Linda Hotel HOTEL $$

(☎969-103-92-14; www.playalindayucatan.com; Calle 76 s/n, btwn Calles 19 & 21; r/ste from

M$600/900;) Rooms go fast at this hotel on the boardwalk, so book ahead. Comfy standard rooms are decked out with contemporary dark-wood furnishings, while suites come with kitchenettes and beachfront balconies. Walls can be a bit thin in some rooms; avoid those near the staircase and upgrade to a 'studio.' The rooftop view of the pier and coastline is spectacular.

Hotel Yaxactún HOTEL **$$**
(969-103-93-26; yaxactun@outlook.com; Calle 66 No 129, btwn Calles 25 & 27; r from M$600;) After a recent makeover, the Yaxactún has earned bragging rights as one of the most modern hotels in town. Street-facing rooms get good natural light and have balconies. The hotel also has an onsite restaurant specializing in Yucatecan food, and there's a swimming pool with a kiddie corral. It's three blocks from the beach.

El Naranjo YUCATECAN **$**
(Calle 27 s/n, btwn Calles 78 & 80; tacos/tortas M$8/14; 6am-2pm) One of the best options in the market for *cochinita* (slow-cooked pork) – and it's spiffy clean.

Restaurant El Cordobes MEXICAN **$**
(969-935-26-21; cnr Calles 80 & 31; breakfast mains M$52-90, lunch & dinner mains M$50-130; 6am-midnight) This locals' joint is on the north side of the plaza in a 100-year-old building. Weak 'American' coffee is served quickly, with a warm smile, and it's a perfect place to relax for a bit, sluice down a *cerveza* and look out on the main plaza.

Flamingo's SEAFOOD **$$**
(Calle 19 s/n, cnr Calle 72; mains M$95-200; 7:30am-midnight;) A longtime local favorite on the boardwalk, Flamingo's fries up a tasty *pescado boquinete al mojo de ajo* (whole hogfish cooked with garlic). Free snacks are served while you're waiting for the main dish.

Eladio's SEAFOOD **$$**
(www.eladios.com.mx; cnr Calles 19 & 80; mains M$49-199; noon-9pm;) Some say the five complimentary sampler plates that come to the table before the main dish arrives are the real reason to eat here. We'll let you be the judge.

Elio al Mare ITALIAN **$$$**
(Calle 21 No 60, btwn Calles 38 & 40; mains M$150-300; 1-10pm;) Far removed from the cruise-ship crowd, this Italian-owned beachfront *ristorante* prepares fresh fish, seafood and pasta dishes and quite possibly the best bread in town. Cap off the meal with a glass of wine on the deck, which catches pleasant ocean breezes.

Orientation

Progreso's even-numbered streets run north–south; odd ones, east–west. The bus terminal on Calle 29 is five short blocks south of the waterfront *malecón* (the beach promenade along Calle 19) and *muelle* (dock).

Information

There are several banks with ATMs and money-exchange service along Calle 80.

Internet cafes are sprinkled everywhere, especially around the bus terminal.

Getting There & Away

Progreso is 33km north of Mérida along a fast four-lane highway that's basically a continuation of the Paseo de Montejo.

The bus station on Calle 29 has frequent Mérida-bound buses and there are also *colectivos* (M$16) to Mérida departing from the corner of Calles 80 and 29.

To get to Progreso from Mérida, go to the **Progreso bus terminal** (p158) or catch a *colectivo* one block east of the terminal on Calle 60.

Traveling to Mérida, frequent buses depart from Progreso's **bus terminal** (Calle 29 No 151, btwn Calles 80 & 82) for M$19.

East of Progreso

Heading east from Progreso, Hwy 27 parallels the coast for 70km, to Dzilam de Bravo, before turning inland. It's a beautiful drive, and you'll pass miles of mixed mangrove clumps and notice that on the right (south) the mud takes on a pink color. Unsurprisingly, this area is named the Laguna Rosada (Pink Lagoon).

On the seaward (north) side of the Rose Lagoon, things are less pristine, with a lot of new timeshares, condo-mondos and hotels. Local fishing communities are taking a big hit as land prices rise with the tourism and second-home boom. But things are still pretty laid-back here. It might even be a good spot to do a little guerrilla camping on the beach. Remember, the beach is public property in Mexico.

From a tall wooden observation tower at the edge of the lagoon at **Uaymitún**, you can watch flamingos, as well as ibis, herons, spoonbills and other waterfowl.

The buildings thin out beyond Uaymitún, and about 13km east of it, a road heads south from the coast some 3km across the bird-riddled lagoon to the turnoff for the Maya ruins of Xcambó. Following the road south beyond the ruins turnoff takes you into grassy marshland with cattails and scatterings of palm trees, a beautiful landscape providing ample opportunities for bird-spotting without even getting out of the car.

Back on Hwy 27 heading east, the next town you'll reach isTelchac Puerto,which has the most eating and sleeping options in the region. If you're up for roughing it, you'll find several *cabañas* (cabins) on a quiet palm-bordered beach in the sleepy fishing town of **San Crisanto**, east of Telchac, and farther east, there are two great places to stay in Santa Clara and Dzilam de Bravo.

If you don't have wheels, a bus in Progreso departs from Calles 29 and 82 at 7:30am and 2:30pm and goes as far east as Dzilam de Bravo before returning to Progreso.

Telchac Puerto & Around

There really isn't much to do in Telchac Puerto but sit on the beach, suck the briny air and wait for the earth to turn another rotation. There are no ATMs or banks here, and it's best to arrive by car. The town, about 9km east of the turnoff to Xcambó on the road to Dzilam de Bravo, is a good place to base yourself for adventures along this forgotten-but-not-totally-lost coast.

Sights

Xcambó ARCHAEOLOGICAL SITE
(Dzemul–Xtampú road; admission M$62; 8am-6pm) The two-lane road to Xcambó is flanked by gorgeous wetlands often inhabited by flamingos. The seldom-visited ruins, 3km south of Hwy 27, formed part of a Maya salt distribution center and the site was an important ceremonial center. The *petén*-style structures surrounding the plaza were built during the early classic period.

Sleeping & Eating

Paomar APARTMENT $
(991-917-40-65; Calle 23 No 235, cnr Calle 36; apt M$500;) Telchac's best budget option, the Paomar rents apartments with kitchenettes, cable TV and air-con, and they're just 50m from the beach. You'll find it along Hwy 27, aka Calle 23.

Hotel Reef Yucatán HOTEL $$$
(991-917-50-00, reservations 999-941-94-94; www.reefyucatan.com; Hwy 27 Km 35.6, Zona Hotelera Telchac Puerto; all-inclusive per person M$1295;) The monstro all-inclusive Hotel Reef Yucatán has 147 rooms and family-friendly facilities, such as a large swimming pool, a miniature golf course, a tennis court and kids club.

La Picuda SEAFOOD $$
(Calle 20 s/n; mains M$75-150; 10:30am-6pm;) Locals highly recommend this eatery just off the square and near the pier. The *filete al mojo de ajo* (fish sautéed with garlic) is really good, as are the free *botanas* (snacks) that come to the table before the main dish.

Dzilam de Bravo & Santa Clara

Time seems to stand still on these secluded, breezy beaches – escapists will love the solitude of Dzilam de Bravo and Santa Clara.

Sleeping

Hotel Kame House HOTEL $$
(cell 991-1066847, cell in USA 770-5400509; www.hotelkamehouse.com; Calle 15 No 16, Santa Clara; r M$550-750;) You can either stay in breezy rooms with ocean views in the main house, or just across the beach there's an unusual round building with two fan-cooled rooms, tasteful rustic decor and large showers built from recycled objects. You'll have to head into town for meals, but it's easily walkable. Kame rents bodyboards and snorkeling equipment.

It's on the east end of Santa Clara.

Perla Escondida CABIN $$
(cell 991-1079321; miriam_figueroa2@hotmail.com; Calle 11 Km 1, off Hwy 27, 1km west of Dzilam de Bravo; r M$600;) On a quiet white-sand coast just west of Dzilam de Bravo, the Perla Escondida (Hidden Pearl) truly lives up to its name. Rustic cabins sit right on the beach and your hosts can arrange various activities, such as birdwatching, a cenote outing or fishing trips. A sandbar about a half-kilometer offshore makes a relaxing spot to while away the day.

EASTERN YUCATÁN STATE

Scrub jungle, intact colonial cities, cenotes aplenty and Yucatán's largest coastal estuary are but a few of the attractions in the eastern portion of this state. There's also none other than one of the 'new wonders of the world,' Chichén Itzá, as well as a smattering of less-visited (but nonetheless impressive) Maya ruins.

Izamal

☎988 / POP 16,000

In ancient times Izamal was a center for the worship of the supreme Maya god, Itzamná, and the sun god, Kinich-Kakmó. A dozen temple pyramids were devoted to these or other gods. No doubt these bold expressions of Maya religiosity are why the Spanish colonists chose Izamal as the site for an enormous and impressive Franciscan monastery, which still stands at the heart of this town, located about 70km east of Mérida.

The Izamal of today is a quiet provincial town, nicknamed La Ciudad Amarilla (The Yellow City) for the traditional golden yellow buildings that spiral out from the center like a budding daisy. It's easily explored on foot, and horse-drawn carriages add to the city's charm.

Sights

It's worth taking the time to visit the **talleres de arte** (artisan workshops) found throughout the city. Most hotels and the Central Cultural y Artesanal have free tourist maps with the workshops' locations labeled.

Convento de San Antonio de Padua MONASTERY

(Calle 31 s/n; admission free, sound & light show adult/child under 13yr M$94/free, museum M$5; ⌚6am-8pm, sound & light show 8:30pm Mon-Sat, museum 9am-5pm Mon-Fri) When the Spaniards conquered Izamal, they destroyed the major Maya temple, the Ppapp-Hol-Chac pyramid, and in 1533 began to build from its stones one of the first monasteries in the western hemisphere. Work on Convento de San Antonio de Padua was finished in 1561. Under the monastery's arcades, look for building stones with an unmistakable maze-like design; these were clearly taken from the earlier Maya temple. There's a **sound-and-light show** here six nights a week.

The monastery's principal church is the **Santuario de la Virgen de Izamal**, approached by a ramp from the main square. The ramp leads into the **Atrium**, a huge arcaded courtyard in which the **fiesta of the Virgin of Izamal** takes place each August 15.

At some point the 16th-century **frescoes** beside the entrance of the sanctuary were completely painted over. For years they lay concealed under a thin layer of whitewash until a maintenance worker who was cleaning the walls discovered them.

The church's original altarpiece was destroyed by a fire believed to have been started by a fallen candle. Its replacement, impressively gilded, was built in the 1940s. In the niches at the stations of the cross are some superb small figures.

In the small courtyard to the left of the church, look up and toward the Atrium to see the original sundial projecting from the roof's edge. A small **museum** at the back commemorates Pope John Paul II's 1993 visit to the monastery. He brought with him a silver crown for the statue of the patron saint of Yucatán, the Virgin of Izamal.

The monastery's front entrance faces west; it's flanked by Calles 31 and 33 on the north and south, respectively, and Calles 28 and 30 on the east and west.

Kinich-Kakmó ARCHAEOLOGICAL SITE

(Calle 27 s/n, btwn Calles 26D & 28; ⌚8am-5pm) FREE Three of the town's original 12 Maya pyramids have been partially restored. The largest (and the third largest in Yucatán) is the 34m-high Kinich-Kakmó, three blocks north of the monastery. Legend has it that a deity in the form of a blazing macaw would swoop down from the heavens to collect offerings left here.

Centro Cultural y Artesanal MUSEUM

(www.centroculturalizamal.org.mx; Calle 31 No 201; admission M$25; ⌚9am-7pm Mon-Sat, 10am-5pm Sun) Southeast of the monastery, this cultural center and museum showcases popular art from around Mexico. It also rents bicycles (M$25 per hour) and has an excellent shop selling fair-trade-certified crafts made by artisans from 12 indigenous communities. Any purchase you make is a direct source of income for rural indigenous families.

Sleeping & Eating

Several *loncherías* occupy spaces in the market on the monastery's southwest side.

Hotel Casa Colonial HOTEL $
(☎988-954-02-72; hotelcasacolonial@hotmail.com; Calle 31 No 331, cnr Calle 36;) A clean and spacious option compared to some of the other more rundown and cramped budget hotels in town. Some rooms come with dining tables, microwaves and mini-fridges.

★**Hacienda Hotel Santo Domingo** HOTEL $$
(☎cell 988-9676136; www.izamalhotel.com; Calle 18, btwn Calles 33 & 35; campsites M$150-250, r M$900-1290, ste M$1390-1890; P) Set on a 13-hectare property with lush gardens, walking trails, a pool and *palapa* restaurant, this serene spot will most definitely win over nature lovers. It's also that rare place with accommodations for all budgets, from camping and midrange options to very attractive suites, some with natural stone sinks and showers. It's five blocks from the monastery.

San Miguel Arcangel HOTEL $$
(☎988-954-01-09; www.sanmiguelhotel.com.mx; Calle 31A No 308; r incl breakfast from M$653;) You have the main square right at the doorstep, while in the rear there's an amazing garden area with anicent ruins of a pyramid dedicated to Hun-Pic-Tok, the Maya God of War. Rooms are done up colonial style with a few modern creature comforts like cable TV and air-con. There's also a Jacuzzi upstairs.

Rinconada del Convento HOTEL $$
(☎988-954-01-51; www.hotelizamal.com; Calle 33 No 294; r from M$900;) A tiered garden affords views of Izamal's iconic monastery and Maya ruins four blocks north of the hotel. 'Premium' street-facing rooms overlook the convent, while 'standards' surround the garden and pool area. If you're looking for something more affordable, Rinconada recently launched new budget accommodation **Hotel Zamná** (Calle 22, btwn Calles 31 & 33; r from M$550), which offers spotless rooms with air-con and a large swimming pool.

Macan Ché B&B $$
(☎988-954-02-87; www.macanche.com; Calle 22 No 305, btwn Calles 33 & 35; r/ste incl breakfast from M$820/1000; P) It's about three long (yes, long!) blocks east of the monastery (take Calle 31 toward Cancún and turn right on Calle 22) to this very Zen hotel, which has a cluster of cottages and a small rock-bottom pool in a woodsy setting. Most of the rooms have air-con and some have kitchenettes.

★**Kinich** MEXICAN $$
(Calle 27 No 299, btwn Calles 28 & 30; mains M$65-190; 10am-10pm;) Sure, it's touristy, but this is fresh, handmade Yucatecan cuisine at its finest. The *papadzules kinich* – rolled tortillas stuffed with diced egg and topped with pumpkin-seed sauce and smoky sausage – is a delightful house specialty. Kinich is also famous for its *dzic de venado,* a shredded venison dish.

El Toro MEXICAN $$
(Calle 33 No 303; mains M$50-120; 8am-11pm Sun-Thu, to 1am Fri & Sat;) At the southeast corner of the roundabout in front of the monastery, this small family-run establishment specializes in Yucatecan fare (with some international favorites thrown in to keep the tourists happy). Try traditional classics like the *queso relleno* (stuffed cheese).

Information

Most restaurants and hotels here have a copy of the excellent free tourist map. The map is available in several languages and describes various walking tours and locations for handicraft workshops.

You'll find an ATM in Willy's supermarket at Calles 33 and 30.

Getting There & Around

Buses run out of Izamal's **Oriente bus terminal** (☎988-954-01-07; Calle 32 s/n, cnr Calle 31A) and the nearby **Terminal del Centro**

BUSES FROM IZAMAL

DESTINATION	FARE (M$)	DURATION (HRS)	FREQUENCY (DAILY)
Cancún	160	5	5
Chichén Itzá	67	1½-2	3; Terminal del Centro; transfer in Hoctún
Dzilam de Bravo	39	1½	2; Terminal del Centro
Mérida	27	1½	frequent
Tizimín	85	2½	3
Valladolid	59	2	3

(www.autobusescentro.com; Calle 33, cnr Calle 30).

Taxis around town charge M$15; a base is at Calles 32 and 31A.

Horse carriage rides cost M$250 per hour.

Chichén Itzá

985 / POP 5500

The most famous and best restored of the Yucatán Maya sites, **Chichén Itzá** (Mouth of the Well of the Itza; www.chichenitza.inah.gob.mx; off Hwy 180, Pisté; adult/child under 13yr M$220/free, guided tours M$750; 8am-5pm Tue-Sun; P), while tremendously overcrowded – every gawker and his or her grandmother is trying to check off the new seven wonders of the world – will still impress even the most jaded visitor. Many mysteries of the Maya astronomical calendar are made clear when one understands the design of the 'time temples' here. Other than a few minor passageways, climbing on the structures is not allowed.

At the vernal and autumnal equinoxes (around March 20 and September 22), the morning and afternoon sun produces a light-and-shadow illusion of the serpent ascending or descending the side of El Castillo's staircase. The site is mobbed on these dates, however, making it difficult to see, and after the spectacle, parts of the site are sometimes closed to the public. The illusion is almost as good in the week preceding and following each equinox (and draws much smaller crowds), and is re-created nightly in the light-and-sound show year-round. Some find the spectacle fascinating, others think it's overrated. Either way, if you're in the area around the equinox and you've got your own car, it's easy to wake up early for Dzibilchaltún's (a site north of Mérida) fiery sunrise and then make it to Chichén Itzá by midafternoon, catching both spectacles on the same day.

The heat, humidity and crowds in Chichén Itzá can be fierce; try to explore the site either early in the morning or late in the afternoon.

The 45-minute light-and-sound show begins each evening at 8pm in summer and 7pm in winter. At last visit, tickets were free, but the show was only open to guests of participating hotels registered at www.nochesdekukulkan.com. By the time you're reading this the show may be open to the general public at an additional cost.

OFF THE BEATEN TRACK

PUEBLOS & PLACES OFF THE MAP

There's a ton of good off-the-map adventures to be had in and around Izamal. Here are a few of our favorites:

Cuauhtémoc A small community 6km south of Izamal on an extension of Calle 24, with a 17th-century chapel.

Kimbilá Located 8km west of Izamal on an extension of Calle 31, this town is famous for its embroidery.

Itzamatul, Habuk, Chaltún Há & beyond Some 80 pre-Hispanic structures have been discovered within Izamal's city limits. Habuk, Itzamatul and Chaltún Há are just a few. They are all free to the public.

History

Most archaeologists agree that the first major settlement at Chichén Itzá, during the late Classic period, was pure Maya. In about the 9th century, the city was largely abandoned for reasons unknown.

It was resettled around the late 10th century, and shortly thereafter it is believed to have been invaded by the Toltecs, who had migrated from their central highlands capital of Tula, north of Mexico City. The bellicose Toltec culture was fused with that of the Maya, incorporating the cult of Quetzalcóatl (Kukulcán, in Maya). You will see images of both Chac-Mool, the Maya rain god, and Quetzalcóatl, the plumed serpent, throughout the city.

The substantial fusion of highland central Mexican and Puuc architectural styles makes Chichén unique among the Yucatán Peninsula's ruins. The fabulous El Castillo and the Plataforma de Venus are outstanding architectural works built during the height of Toltec cultural input.

The sanguinary Toltecs contributed more than their architectural skills to the Maya: they elevated human sacrifice to a near obsession, and there are numerous carvings of the bloody ritual in Chichén demonstrating this.

After a Maya leader moved his political capital to Mayapán while keeping Chichén as his religious capital, Chichén Itzá fell into decline. Why it was subsequently abandoned

Chichén Itzá

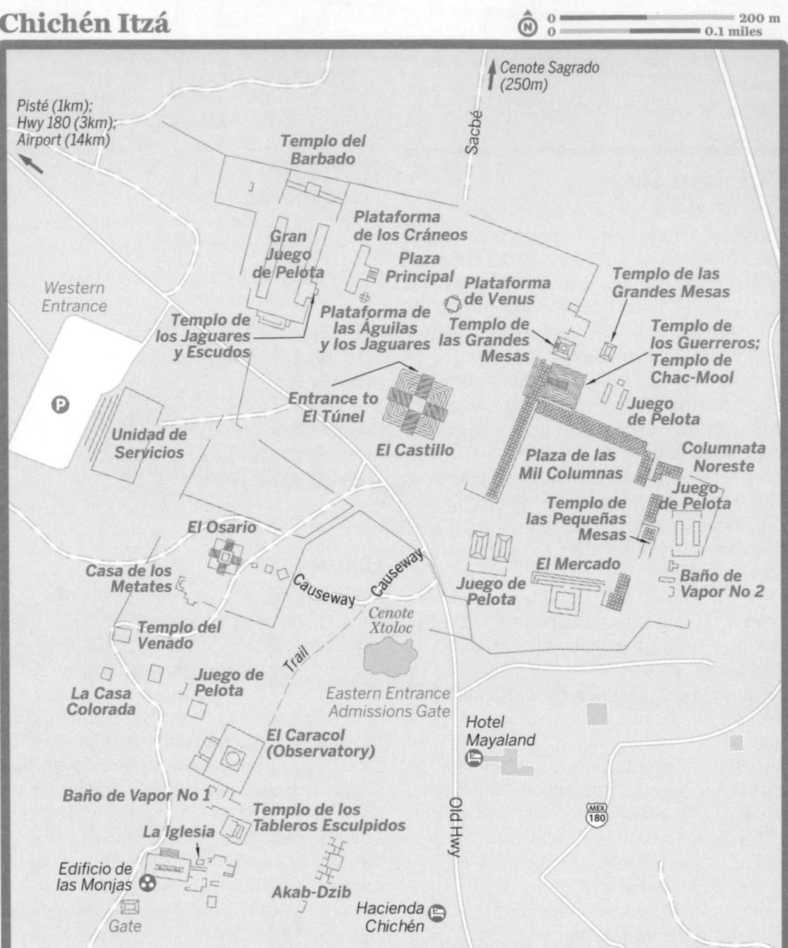

in the 14th century is a mystery, but the once great city remained the site of Maya pilgrimages for many years.

Sights

Visitors Center Museum MUSEUM
(8am-4pm) The visitors center has a small museum with exhibits providing explanations in Spanish, English and French.

El Castillo ARCHAEOLOGICAL SITE
Upon entering Chichén Itzá, El Castillo (aka the Pyramid of Kukulcán) rises before you in all its grandeur. The first temple here was pre-Toltec, built around AD 800, but the present 25m-high structure, built over the old one, has the plumed serpent sculpted along the stairways and Toltec warriors represented in the doorway carvings at the top of the temple. You won't see the carvings, however, as ascending the pyramid was prohibited after a woman fell to her death in 2006.

The structure is actually a massive Maya calendar formed in stone. Each of El Castillo's nine levels is divided in two by a staircase, making 18 separate terraces that commemorate the 18 20-day months of the Maya Vague Year. The four stairways have

91 steps each; add the top platform and the total is 365, the number of days in the year. On each facade of the pyramid are 52 flat panels, which are reminders of the 52 years in the Maya calendar round.

To top it off, during the spring and autumn equinoxes, light and shadow form a series of triangles on the side of the north staircase that mimic the creep of a serpent (note the carved serpent's heads flanking the bottom of the staircase).

The older pyramid inside El Castillo has a red jaguar throne with inlaid eyes and spots of jade; also lying behind the screen is a chac-mool (Maya sacrificial stone sculpture). The entrance to **El Túnel**, the passage up to the throne, is at the base of El Castillo's north side. You can't go in, though.

Researchers in 2015 learned that the pyramid most likely sits atop a 20m-deep cenote, which puts the structure at greater risk of collapsing.

Gran Juego de Pelota ARCHAEOLOGICAL SITE

The great ball court, the largest and most impressive in Mexico, is only one of the city's eight courts, indicative of the importance the games held here. The court, to the left of the visitors' center, is flanked by temples at either end and is bounded by towering parallel walls with stone rings cemented up high. Along the walls of the ball court are stone reliefs, including scenes of decapitations of players.

There is evidence that the ball game may have changed over the years. Some carvings show players with padding on their elbows and knees, and it is thought that they played a soccer-like game with a hard rubber ball, with the use of hands forbidden. Other carvings show players wielding bats; it appears that if a player hit the ball through one of the stone hoops, his team was declared the winner. It may be that during the Toltec period, the losing captain, and perhaps his teammates as well, were sacrificed (and you thought your dad was hard on you in Little League).

The court exhibits some interesting acoustics: a conversation at one end can be heard 135m away at the other, and a clap produces multiple loud echoes.

Templo del Barbado ARCHAEOLOGICAL SITE

The structure at the ball court's north end, called the Temple of the Bearded Man after a carving inside of it, has finely sculpted pillars and reliefs of flowers, birds and trees.

Templo de los Jaguares y Escudos ARCHAEOLOGICAL SITE

The Temple of the Jaguars and Shields, built atop the southeast corner of the ball court's wall, has some columns with carved rattlesnakes and tablets with etched jaguars. Inside are faded mural fragments depicting a battle.

Plataforma de los Cráneos ARCHAEOLOGICAL SITE

The Platform of Skulls (Tzompantli in Náhuatl, a Maya dialect) is between the Templo de los Jaguares y Escudos and El Castillo. You can't mistake it, because the T-shaped platform is festooned with carved skulls and eagles tearing open the chests of men to eat their hearts. In ancient days this platform was used to display the heads of sacrificial victims.

Plataforma de las Águilas y los Jaguares ARCHAEOLOGICAL SITE

Adjacent to the Platform of Skulls, the carvings on the Platform of the Eagles and Jaguars depict those animals gruesomely grabbing human hearts in their claws. It is thought that this platform was part of a temple dedicated to the military legions responsible for capturing sacrificial victims.

Cenote Sagrado ARCHAEOLOGICAL SITE

From the Platform of Skulls, a 400m rough stone *sacbé* (path) runs north (a five-minute walk) to the huge sunken well that gave this city its name. The Sacred Cenote is an awesome natural well, some 60m in diameter and 35m deep. The walls between the summit and the water's surface are ensnared in tangled vines and other vegetation.

There are ruins of a small steam bath next to the cenote.

Grupo de las Mil Columnas ARCHAEOLOGICAL SITE

This group east of El Castillo pyramid takes its name – which means 'Group of the Thousand Columns' – from the forest of pillars stretching south and east. The star attraction here is the **Templo de los Guerreros** (Temple of the Warriors), adorned with stucco and stone-carved animal deities. At the top of its steps is a classic reclining chac-mool figure, but ascending to it is no longer allowed.

Many of the columns in front of the temple are carved with figures of warriors. Archaeologists working in 1926 discovered a Temple of Chac-Mool lying beneath the Temple of the Warriors.

You can walk through the columns on its south side to reach the **Columnata Noreste**,

Chichén Itzá

It doesn't take long to realize why the Maya site of Chichén Itzá is one of Mexico's most popular tourist draws. Approaching the grounds from the main entrance, the striking castle pyramid **El Castillo** ❶ jumps right out at you – and the wow factor never lets up.

It's easy to tackle Chichén Itzá in one day. Within a stone's throw of the castle, you'll find the Maya world's largest **ball court** ❷ alongside eerie carvings of skulls and heart-devouring eagles at the Temple of Jaguars and the Platform of Skulls. On the other (eastern) side are the highly adorned **Group of a Thousand Columns** ❸ and the **Temple of Warriors** ❹. A short walk north of the castle leads to the gaping **Sacred Cenote** ❺, an important pilgrimage site. On the other side of El Castillo, you'll find giant stone serpents watching over the High Priest's Grave, aka El Osario. Further south, marvel at the spiral-domed **Observatory** ❻, the imposing Nunnery and Akab-Dzib, one of the oldest ruins.

Roaming the 47-hectare site, it's fun to consider that at its height Chichén Itzá was home to an estimated 90,000 inhabitants and spanned approximately 30 sq km. So essentially you're looking at just a small part of a once-great city.

THE LOWDOWN

» **Arrive** at 8am and you'll have a good three hours or so before the tour-bus madness begins. Early birds escape the merchants, too.

» **Remember** that Chichén Itzá is the name of the site; the actual town where it's located is called Pisté.

El Caracol
Observatory
Today they'd probably just use a website, but back in the day priests would announce the latest rituals and celebrations from the dome of the circular observatory.

Grupo de las Mil Columnas
Group of a Thousand Columns
Not unlike a hall of fame exhibit, the pillars surrounding the temple reveal carvings of gods, dignitaries and celebrated warriors.

LOLA L. FALANTES/GETTY IMAGES ©

ROSS BARNETT/GETTY IMAGES ©

El Castillo
The Castle

Even this mighty pyramid can't bear the stress of a million visitors ascending its stairs each year. No climbing allowed, but the ground-level view doesn't disappoint.

Gran Juego de Pelota
Great Ball Court

How is it possible to hear someone talk from one end of this long, open-air court to the other? To this day, the acoustics remain a mystery.

Entrance

Parking Lot

Visitors Center

Templo de los Jaguares (Temple of Jaguars)

Tumba del Gran Sacerdote (High Priest's Grave)

1

2

5

Plataforma de los Cráneos (Platform of Skulls)

3

4

Cenote Sagrado
Sacred Cenote

Diving expeditions have turned up hundreds of valuable artifacts dredged from the cenote (limestone sinkhole), not to mention human bones of sacrificial victims who were forced to jump into the eternal underworld.

Templo de los Guerreros
Temple of Warriors

The Maya associated warriors with eagles and jaguars, as depicted in the temple's friezes. The revered jaguar, in particular, was a symbol of strength and agility.

JUAN CARLOS MUNOZ/GETTY IMAGES ©

DREDGING CHICHÉN'S SACRED CENOTE

Around the year 1900, Edward Thompson, a Harvard professor and US consul to Yucatán, bought the hacienda that included Chichén Itzá for M$750. No doubt intrigued by local stories of female virgins being sacrificed to the Maya deities by being thrown into the site's cenote, Thompson resolved to have the cenote dredged.

He imported dredging equipment and set to work. Gold and jade jewelry from all parts of Mexico and as far away as Colombia was recovered, along with other artifacts and a variety of human bones. Many of the artifacts were shipped to Harvard's Peabody Museum, but some have since been returned to Mexico.

Subsequent diving expeditions in the 1920s and 1960s turned up hundreds of other valuable artifacts. It appears that all sorts of people – children and old people, the diseased and the injured, and the young and the vigorous – were forcibly obliged to take an eternal swim in Chichén's Cenote Sagrado.

The cenote is reached by walking about 400m north from the Plataforma de Venus.

notable for the 'big-nosed god' masks on its facade. Some have been reassembled on the ground around the statue. Just to the south are the remains of the **Baño de Vapor** (Steam Bath or Sweat House) with an underground oven and drains for the water. The sweat houses (there are two onsite) were regularly used for ritual purification.

El Osario ARCHAEOLOGICAL SITE

The Ossuary, otherwise known as the Bonehouse or the Tumba del Gran Sacerdote (High Priest's Grave), is a ruined pyramid to the southwest of El Castillo. As with most of the buildings in this southern section, the architecture is more Puuc than Toltec. It's notable for the beautiful serpent heads at the base of its staircases.

A square shaft at the top of the structure leads into a cave below that was used as a burial chamber; seven tombs with human remains were discovered inside.

El Caracol ARCHAEOLOGICAL SITE

Called El Caracol (The Snail) by the Spaniards for its interior spiral staircase, this observatory, to the south of the Ossuary, is one of the most fascinating and important of all Chichén Itzá's buildings (but, alas, you can't enter it). Its circular design resembles some central highlands structures, although, surprisingly, not those of Toltec Tula.

In a fusion of architectural styles and religious imagery, there are Maya Chaac rain-god masks over four external doors facing the cardinal points. The windows in the observatory's dome are aligned with the appearance of certain stars at specific dates. From the dome the priests decreed the times for rituals, celebrations, corn-planting and harvests.

Edificio de las Monjas ARCHAEOLOGICAL SITE

Thought by archaeologists to have been a palace for Maya royalty, the so-called Edificio de las Monjas (Nunnery), with its myriad rooms, resembled a European convent to the conquistadors, hence their name for the building. The building's dimensions are imposing: its base is 60m long, 30m wide and 20m high.

The construction is Maya rather than Toltec, although a Toltec sacrificial stone stands in front. A smaller adjoining building to the east, known as **La Iglesia** (The Church), is covered almost entirely with carvings. On the far side at the back there are some passageways that are still open, leading a short way into the labyrinth inside. They are dank and slippery, they smell of bat urine, and it's easy to twist an ankle as you go, but Indiana Jones wannabes will think it's totally cool.

Akab-Dzib ARCHAEOLOGICAL SITE

East of the Nunnery, the Puuc-style Akab-Dzib is thought by some archaeologists to be the most ancient structure excavated here. The central chambers date from the 2nd century. The name means 'Obscure Writing' in Maya and refers to the south-side annex door, whose lintel depicts a priest with a vase etched with hieroglyphics that have yet to be successfully translated.

Grutas de Balankanché CAVE

(Hwy 180 Km 126; adult/child under 13yr M$117/free; ⌚9am-4pm; P) In 1959 a guide to the Chichén Itzá ruins was exploring a cave on his day off when he came upon a narrow passageway. He followed the passageway for 300m, meandering through a series of caverns. In each, perched on mounds amid scores of glistening stalactites, were hundreds of ceremonial treasures the Maya had placed there 800 years earlier. Among the discovered objects were *ritual metates* and *manos* (grinding stones), incense burners and pots.

In the years following the discovery, the ancient ceremonial objects were removed and studied. Eventually most of them were returned to the caves, and placed exactly where they were found.

Outside the caves, you'll find a good botanical garden (displaying native flora with information on the medicinal and other uses of the trees and plants) and a tiny museum. The museum features large photographs taken during the exploration of the caves, and descriptions (in English, Spanish and French) of the Maya religion and the offerings found in the caves. Also on display is text about modern-day Maya ceremonies called Ch'a Chaac, which continue to be held in all the villages on the Yucatán Peninsula during times of drought, and consist mostly of praying and making numerous offerings of food to rain god Chaac.

Compulsory 45-minute tours (minimum six people, maximum 30) have melodramatic, not-very-informative recorded narration that is nearly impossible to make out, but if you'd like it in a particular language, English is at 11am, 1pm and 3pm; Spanish is at 9am, noon, 2pm and 4pm; and French is at 10am.

Be warned that the cave is unusually hot, and ventilation is poor in its further reaches. The lack of oxygen (especially after a few groups have already passed through) makes it difficult to draw a full breath until you're outside again.

The turnoff for the caverns is 6km east of Chichén Itzá on the highway to Valladolid. Second-class buses heading east from Pisté toward Valladolid will drop you at the Balankanché road. The entrance to the caves is 350m north of the highway.

Activities

Ik Kil Parque Eco-Arqueológico SWIMMING
(985-851-00-02; cenote_ikkil@hotmail.com; Hwy 180 Km 122; adult/child under 12yr M$70/35; 8am-5pm; P) About 2.5km east of the western entrance of the Chichén Itzá ruins, a cenote here has been developed into a divine swimming spot. Small cascades of water plunge from the high limestone roof, which is ringed by greenery. Arrive no later than 11am to beat the tour groups.

The onsite restaurant has a good lunch buffet (M$150), and there are also spacious *cabañas* (some sleep up to four and come with kitchens; double/quad M$1250/2500).

Sleeping

Most of Chichén Itzá's lodgings, restaurants and services are arranged along 1km of highway in the town of Pisté, to the western (Mérida) side of the ruins. It's about 1.5km from the ruins' main (west) entrance to the nearest hotel in Pisté, and 2.5km from the ruins to Pisté's town plaza.

On the eastern (Valladolid) side, it's 1.5km from the highway along the access road to the eastern entrance to the ruins; top-end hotels line the road, the closest being only about 100m from the entrance.

Don't hesitate to haggle for a bed in the low season (May through June and August to early December), when prices drop. Hwy 180 is known as Calle 15 on its way through Pisté.

Pirámide Inn HOTEL $
(985-851-01-15; www.piramideinn.com; Calle 15 No 30; campsites per person M$50, r M$500; P) Campers can pitch a tent or hang a hammock under a *palapa*, enjoy the inn's pool, have use of tepid showers and watch satellite TV in the lobby. Campers also have use of clean shared toilet facilities and a safe place to stow gear. The spacious rooms have decent bathrooms and two spring-me-to-the-moon double beds.

The hotel also has a book exchange and a Maya-style sweat lodge. Located on the main drag in Pisté, this place is as close as you can get to Chichén Itzá for cheap, though it's still a hike of about 1.5km. Animals are welcome.

Posada Olalde INN $
(985-851-00-86; cnr Calles 6 & 17; s/d M$250/350;) Two blocks south of the highway (heading east turn right just past Pollos Los Pajaros), this is the best of Pisté's several budget *posadas* (inns). It has clean, quiet rooms, a few twiddling parakeets and four decent-sized bungalows. Accommodations are fan-cooled, and the friendly manager speaks Spanish and English, as well as some Maya.

Hotel Chichén Itzá HOTEL $$
(985-851-00-22, in USA 800-235-4079; www.mayaland.com; Calle 15 No 45; r/ste M$980/1360; P) On the west side of Pisté, this hotel has 42 pleasant rooms with tiled floors and old-style brick-tiled ceilings. Rooms in the upper range face the pool and the landscaped grounds, and all have firm beds and minibars. Parents may bring two kids under 13 years old for free.

Hotel Dolores Alba HOTEL $$
(985-858-15-55; www.doloresalba.com; Hwy 180 Km 122; r incl breakfast M$1000; P)

This is a good midrange option with substantial online discounts, and kids will dig the hotel's two pools (one has a rock bottom). Semi-rustic rooms here won't wow you, but they're comfy enough. Dolores Alba offers transport to Chichén Itzá, but you're on your own getting back. It's 2.5km east of Chichén Itzá's eastern entrance and 5km from town.

Hacienda Chichén RESORT **$$$**
(999-920-84-07, in USA 877-631-00-45; www.haciendachichen.com; Zona Hotelera Km 120; d from M$2460;) About 300m from the Chichén Itzá entrance, this resort sits on the well-manicured grounds of a 16th-century hacienda with an elegant main house and towering ceiba trees. The archaeologists who excavated Chichén during the 1920s lived here in bungalows, which have been refurbished and augmented with new ones. Monthly activities on offer include Maya cooking classes and bird-watching.

Hotel Mayaland HOTEL **$$$**
(998-887-24-95, in USA 877-240-5864; www.mayaland.com; Zona Hotelera Km 120; d/ste from M$2100/3500;) The Mayaland is less than 100m from Chichén Itzá's eastern entrance: from the lobby and front rooms you can look out at the observatory, El Caracol. The rooms, pools and garden bungalows are nice and all, but when you're at El Caracol you'll wish the hotel hadn't cut an ugly swath through the jungle just so patrons could have a better view.

Eating

The highway (Calle 15) through Pisté is lined with dozens of eateries, large and small. The cheapest are clustered in a roadside market, known as Los Portales, on the west end of town.

Cocina Económica Fabiola MEXICAN **$**
(Calle 15 s/n; mains M$30-60; 7am-10pm;) For a good, honest, cheap meal hit this humble little place at the end of the strip of eateries opposite the church. The *sopa de lima* (lime soup) and *pollo yucateco* (Yucatecan chicken) come highly recommended.

Las Mestizas MEXICAN **$$**
(Calle 15 s/n; mains M$70-100; 8am-10pm;) *The* place to go in town if you're craving decent Yucatecan fare. There's indoor and outdoor seating – depending on the time of day, an outdoor table may mean you'll be getting tour-bus fumes to go along with that *cochinita* (slow-cooked pork).

Restaurant Hacienda Xaybe'h d'Camara MEXICAN **$$**
(985-851-00-39; buffet lunches M$120; 8:30am-5pm;) Set a block back from the highway opposite Hotel Chichén Itzá, this is a large place with attractive grounds. It's popular with tours and the food is a bit overpriced, but the selection of salads makes it a good option for vegetarians. Diners can use the swimming pool free of charge.

Information

Chichén Itzá's western entrance has a large parking lot and a big visitors center with an ATM and restaurant serving somewhat pricey food. You'll find other ATMs in the Oxxo store on Calle 15 and at Palacio Municipal, across from the church.

Getting There & Away

Oriente has ticket offices near the east and west sides of Pisté, and 2nd-class buses passing through town stop almost anywhere along the way. Many 1st-class buses only hit the ruins and the west side of town, close to the toll highway.

Shared vans to Valladolid (M$30, 40 minutes) pass through town regularly.

Getting Around

Buses to Pisté generally stop at the plaza; you can make the hot walk to and from the ruins in 20 to 30 minutes. There is a taxi stand near the west end of town; the prices are M$35 to the

BUSES FROM CHICHÉN ITZÁ

DESTINATION	COST (M$)	DURATION (HRS)	FREQUENCY (DAILY)
Cancún	137-258	3-4½	9
Cobá	69	2	1; 7:30am
Mérida	78-144	1¾-2½	frequent
Playa del Carmen	135-282	3½-4	2; 7:30am, 4:30pm
Tulum	100-190	2½-3	3
Valladolid	30	1	8

ruins, M$70 to Cenote Ik Kil and M$140 to Grutas de Balankanché.

During Chichén Itzá's opening hours, 1st- and 2nd-class buses serve the ruins (check with the driver), and they will take passengers from town when there's room. The 2nd-class buses will also leave you near Cenote Ik Kil and the Grutas de Balankanché. If you plan to see the ruins and then head directly to another city by 1st-class bus, buy your bus ticket at the visitors center before hitting the ruins, for a better chance of getting a seat.

Valladolid

985 / POP 49,000

Also known as the Sultaness of the East, Yucatán's third-largest city is known for its quiet streets and sun-splashed pastel walls. It's worth staying here for a few days or even a week, as the provincial town makes a great hub for visits to Río Lagartos, Chichén Itzá, Ek' Balam and a number of nearby cenotes. The city resides at that magic point where there's plenty to do, yet it still feels small, manageable and affordable.

History

Valladolid has seen its fair share of turmoil and revolt. The city was first founded in 1543 near the Chouac-Ha lagoon some 50km from the coast, but it was too hot and there were way too many mosquitoes for Francisco de Montejo, nephew of Montejo the Elder, and his merry band of conquerors. So they upped and moved the city to the Maya ceremonial center of Zací (sah-*see*), where they faced heavy resistance from the local Maya. Eventually the Elder's son – Montejo the Younger – took the town. The Spanish conquerors, in typical fashion, ripped down the town and laid out a new city following the classic colonial plan.

During much of the colonial era, Valladolid's physical isolation from Mérida kept it relatively autonomous from royal rule, and the Maya of the area suffered brutal exploitation, which continued after Mexican independence. Barred from entering many areas of the city, the Maya made Valladolid one of their first points of attack following the 1847 outbreak of the Caste War in Tepich. After a two-month siege, the city's occupiers were finally overcome. Many fled to the safety of Mérida; the rest were slaughtered.

Today Valladolid is a prosperous seat of agricultural commerce, augmented by some light industry and a growing tourist trade.

Sights & Activities

★Casa de los Venados MUSEUM

(985-856-22-89; www.casadelosvenados.com; Calle 40 No 204, btwn Calles 41 & 43, admission by donation; tours 10am or by appointment) Featuring over 3000 pieces of museum-quality Mexican folk art, this private collection is unique in that objects are presented in a house, in the context that they were originally designed for, instead of being roped off in glass cases. The tour (in English or Spanish) brushes on the origins of some of the more important pieces and the story of the award-winning restored colonial mansion that houses them.

Templo de San Bernardino CHURCH

(Church of San Bernardino; cnr Calles 49 & 51; Mon-Sat M$30, Sun free; 9am-7pm) The Templo de San Bernardino and the adjacent **Convento de Sisal** are about 700m southwest of the plaza. They were constructed between 1552 and 1560 to serve the dual functions of fortress and church. The church's charming decoration includes beautiful rose-colored walls, arches, some recently uncovered 16th century frescoes and a small image of the Virgin on the altar. These are about the only original items remaining; the grand wooden *retablo* (altarpiece) dates from the 19th century.

The convent's walled grounds hold a cenote with a vaulted dome over it and a system of channels that once irrigated the large garden.

Museo de San Roque MUSEUM

(Calle 41 s/n; 8am-8pm Mon-Fri, 9am-6pm Sat & Sun) FREE Previously a 16th-century convent, San Roque has models and exhibits relating the history of the city and the region. Other displays focus on various aspects of traditional Maya life.

Mercado Municipal MARKET

(Calle 32 s/n, btwn Calles 35 & 37; 6am-2pm) Locals come to this good, authentic Mexican market to shop for cheap clothing, produce and what-have-you, and to eat at inexpensive *taquerías*. The east side is the most colorful, with flowers and stacks of fruit and vegetables on offer.

★Hacienda San Lorenzo Oxman SWIMMING

(off Calle 54; M$30; 9am-6pm) Once a *henequén* plantation and a refuge for War of the Castes insurgents in the mid-19th

Valladolid

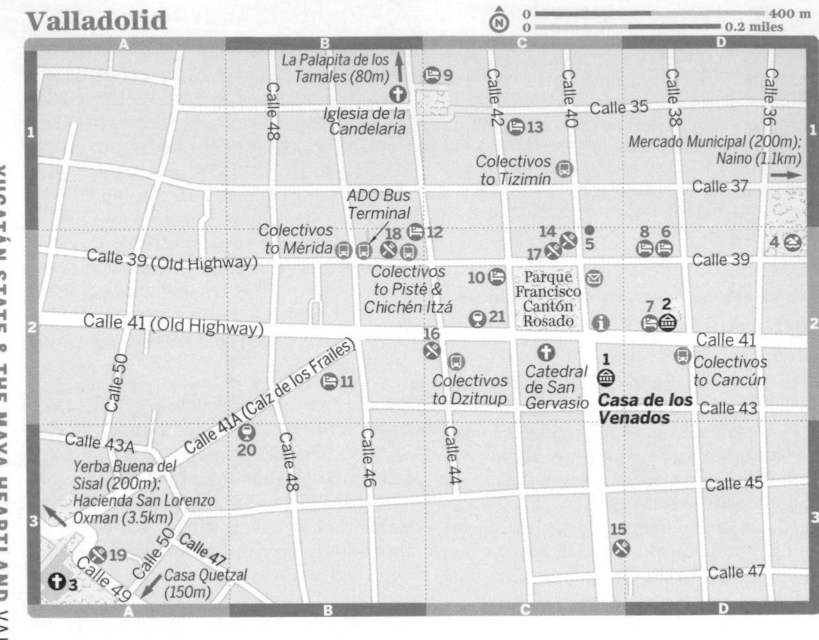

Valladolid

Top Sights
1 Casa de los Venados ... C2

Sights
Convento de Sisal ... (see 3)
2 Museo de San Roque ... D2
3 Templo de San Bernardino ... A3

Activities, Courses & Tours
4 Cenote Zací ... D2
5 Rudy Tours ... C2

Sleeping
6 Casa Marlene ... D2
7 Casa San Roque ... D2
8 Casa Tía Micha ... D2
9 Hostel La Candelaria ... C1
10 Hotel María de la Luz ... C2
11 Hotel Tunich-Beh ... B2
12 Hotel Zací ... B2
13 La Aurora ... C1

Eating
14 Bazar Municipal ... C2
15 Conato 1910 ... C3
16 El Tigrillo ... C2
17 Hostería del Marqués ... C2
18 Squimz ... B2
19 Taberna de los Frailes ... A3

Drinking & Nightlife
20 Cafeína Bistro Bar ... B3
21 La Chispa de 1910 ... C2

century, today the hacienda's main draw is a gorgeous cenote that's far less crowded than other sinkholes in and around Valladolid, especially if you visit Monday through Thursday.

To get there by bike or car, take Calle 41A (Calzada de los Frailes) past the Templo de San Bernardino along Calle 54A, turn right on Avenida de los Frailes, then hang a left on Calle 54 and head about 3km southwest. A taxi to the hacienda costs about M$70.

Cenote X'Kekén SWIMMING

(Cenote Dzitnup; 1/2 cenotes M$60/90; ⌚8:30am-5:20pm) One of two cenotes at Dzitnup (recently renamed X'Kekén Jungle Park), X'Kekén is a massive limestone formation with stalactites hanging from its ceiling. The pool is artificially lit and very swimmable. Here you can also take a dip in cenote Samulá, a lovely cavern pool with *álamo* roots stretching down many meters.

Pedaling a rented bicycle to the cenotes takes about 20 minutes. By bike from the town center take Calle 41A (Calzada de los Frailes), a street lined with colonial architecture. Go one block past the Templo de San Bernardino along Calle 54A, then make a right on Calle 49, which becomes Avenida de los Frailes and hits the old highway. Follow the *ciclopista* (bike path) paralleling the road to Mérida for about 3km, then turn left at the sign for Dzitnup and continue for just under 2km.

Sharod *colectivos* depart for Dzitnup (M$20) from Calle 44, between Calles 41 and 43.

Cenote Zací SWIMMING
(www.cenotezaci.com.mx; Calle 36 s/n, btwn Calles 37 & 39; adult/child 3-11yr M$25/20; ⏲9am-6pm; 📶) Among the region's several underground cenotes is Cenote Zací, set downtown in a park that also holds a restaurant and souvenir shops. People swim in this open-air swimming hole, and while it's pleasant enough, don't expect crystalline waters. Look in the water for catfish or overhead for a colony of bats.

Tours

Rudy Tours BICYCLE TOUR
(☎985-856-20-29, cell 985-1131565; roesro27@hotmail.com; Calle 40, btwn Calles 37 & 39; tours M$300, bike per hr M$20; ⏲10am-6pm) Rodolfo 'Rudy' Escalante, an experienced bilingual guide, offers two-hour bicycle tours to nearby cenotes. He also rents bikes if you want to explore on your own. Look for him in Relojería Cronos.

Sleeping

Most hotels are on or near the main plaza, Parque Francisco Cantón Rosado.

Hotel Zací HOTEL $
(☎985-856-21-67; www.hotelzaci.com.mx; Calle 44 No 191; d M$595; P⊖❄📶≋) Conveniently located one block west of the bus station and a block east of the main plaza, rooms here get the colonial treatment, as does the lobby with its handsome antique furniture. The Zací also runs a 'more austere' budget hotel across the street but we much prefer this one, where you get a pool out back.

Hostel La Candelaria HOSTEL $
(☎985-856-22-67; www.hostelvalladolidyucatan.com; Calle 35 No 201F; dm/r incl breakfast M$160/440; ⊖@📶) A friendly place right on a quiet little square, this hostel can get a little cramped and hot, but there are two kitchens, a cozy garden area complete with hammocks, a gals-only dorm, and plenty of hangout space, making it one of the best hostels in town. The hostel also rents bikes for M$15 per hour.

★**La Aurora** HOTEL $$
(☎985-856-12-19; www.hotellaaurora.com; Calle 42 No 192; d M$640; P⊖❄📶≋) If only more economical hotels were like the colonial style Aurora. Well-appointed rooms overlook a pretty courtyard with a pool and potted plants, and the kicker is the rooftop Jacuzzi and bar. If possible, avoid the noisier street-facing rooms.

Casa Quetzal BOUTIQUE HOTEL $$
(☎985-856-47-96; www.casa-quetzal.com; Calle 51 No 218; r M$900; P⊖❄📶≋) The spacious rooms here offer a good mix of modern comfort and colonial style. They're set around a lush patio with a decent-sized pool. Get a room upstairs for better ventilation and a private balcony. It's about 200m south of the Convento de Sisal.

Hotel Tunich-Beh B&B $$
(☎985-856-22-22; www.tunichbeh.com; Calle 41A, btwn Calles 46 & 48; d incl breakfast from M$950; P⊖❄📶≋) At this great old house lovingly converted into a hotel, well-equipped rooms surround a swimming pool and there are some nice *palapa*-shaded common areas for kicking back. The staff is very helpful and there are bikes available for riding to nearby cenotes.

Casa San Roque B&B $$
(☎985-856-26-42; www.casasanroquevalladolid.com; Calle 41 No 193B; r incl breakfast M$850; P⊖❄📶≋) With just six colonial rooms on offer you'll get more privacy and personalized attention here than at some of the larger hotels on the main plaza. The full breakfast and a pool with dual fountains in the rear garden are the clinchers.

Hotel María de la Luz HOTEL $$
(☎985-856-11-81; www.marialuzhotel.com.mx; Calle 42 No 193C; d M$780; P⊖❄📶≋) Rooms here got a recent makeover with new beds and upgraded furnishings, but not all have been renovated so check what you're getting beforehand. The airy lobby-restaurant overlooks the main plaza and there's a pool here, too.

Casa Tía Micha BOUTIQUE HOTEL $$$
(985-856-04-99; www.casatiamicha.com; Calle 39 No 197; r incl breakfast from US$115;) The corridor and rear garden are beautifully lit at night in this family-run boutique hotel just off the plaza. Some of the tastefully adorned colonial-style rooms have king-size beds, and the upstairs suite comes with a Jacuzzi. If the Tía is booked, on the same block you'll find sister property **Casa Marlene** (985-856-04-99; Calle 39 No 193).

Eating & Drinking

★Yerba Buena del Sisal MEXICAN $
(985-856-14-06; www.facebook.com/yerbabuenadelsisal; Calle 54A No 217; mains M$60-80; 8am-5pm Tue-Sun;) Wonderfully healthy and delicious dishes are served in a peaceful garden. Tortilla chips and three delectable salsas come to the table while you look over the menu, which offers many great vegetarian and mostly organic dishes, such as the delightful *tacos maculum* (made with handmade corn tortillas, beans, cheese and aromatic Mexican pepper leaf).

If you're craving meat, try the *tacos de carne ahumada* (smoked pork tacos).

La Palapita de los Tamales MEXICAN $
(Calle 42 s/n, cnr Calle 33; tamales M$25; 6-10:30pm Mon-Sat;) You've probably never had tamales like these before. The menu changes daily here. At last visit, which may or may not have been a Friday, the tamal of the day had a pork, egg and bean filling and it was lightly fried in *manteca* (lard) to give the exterior a hardened texture. Let's just say it was quite a snack.

Bazar Municipal MARKET $
(cnr Calles 39 & 40; breakfast M$30-50; 6am-10pm;) A collection of market-style eateries that are popular for their big, cheap breakfasts. At lunch and dinner some offer *comida corrida* (set meals of several courses). El Amigo Casiano, on the left side nearly at the back, is good and always crowded; it closes by 2pm.

El Tigrillo YUCATECAN $
(cnr Calles 41 & 44; tacos/tortas M$6/16; 11:30am-5pm;) Hit this popular street stand for some finger-licking-good *cochinita* (slow-cooked pork).

Conato 1910 MEXICAN $$
(Calle 40 No 226; mains M$60-130; 5pm-midnight Wed-Mon;) A meeting spot for revolutionaries in the early 20th century, this historic building now houses one of the best restaurants in town in an atmospheric setting with muraled walls. The vegetarian-friendly menu features a wide variety of options, such as salads and pastas, and there are also excellent chicken and beef dishes.

Naino INTERNATIONAL $$
(985-104-90-71; www.facebook.com/zentikproject; Calle 30, btwn Calles 27 & 29; mains M$80-150; 8am-10:30pm;) Aside from this hotel having an open-air restaurant serving good international food, there's also a lovely cave that has been converted into a heated underground swimming pool. The day pass for the pool (M$150; open from 8am to 6pm) includes a free beverage.

Hostería del Marqués MEXICAN $$
(985-856-20-73; www.mesondelmarques.com; El Mesón del Marqués, Calle 39 No 203; mains M$79-330; 7am-11pm;) Dine in a tranquil colonial courtyard with a bubbling fountain, or the air-con salon looking onto it. The restaurant specializes in Yucatecan fare, such as *longaniza Valladolid* (Valladolid-style sausage) and *cochinita pibil* (marinated pork), and there are also international dishes such as Angus beef cuts.

Squimz CAFE $$
(www.squimz.com.mx; Calle 39 No 219; mains M$47-125; 7am-11pm;) A delightful little cafe just a few doors east of the ADO bus terminal, Squimz offers cakes, pastries and good espresso drinks.

Taberna de los Frailes YUCATECAN $$$
(www.tabernadelosfrailes.com; Calle 49 s/n, cnr Calle 41A; mains M$110-300; 10am-10pm;) The new age music has gotta go, but the verdant garden and wonderfully prepared Yucatecan food make up for it. Try the signature Tikin Xic, a grilled *pibil*-style red snapper (marinated in citrus juice and annatto spice).

Cafeína Bistro Bar BAR
(Calle 41A s/n; 5pm-2am;) A nice little pub to catch a televised sporting event or chat over Mexican draft beer and well-made pizzas.

La Chispa de 1910 KARAOKE
(985-856-26-70; Calle 41 No 201, btwn Calles 42 & 44; 5pm-3am;) Sparks fly at this bar-restaurant that often features live music. Test your liquid courage at nightly karaoke sessions.

Entertainment

Following a centuries-old tradition, dances are held in the main plaza from 8pm to 10pm on Sunday, with music by local groups playing *cumbia* (dance music originating from Colombia), *danzón* (dance music originating from Cuba) and other danceable styles.

Information

Various banks (most with ATMs) near the town center are generally open 9am to 5pm Monday to Friday and to 1pm Saturday.

Grupo Médico del Centro (985-856-51-06; Calle 40 No 178B, btwn Calles 33 & 35; 7:30am-12:30pm & 5:30-7:30pm) A centrally located private medical clinic.

Main post office (Calle 40 s/n, btwn Calles 39 & 41; 8am-4:30pm Mon-Fri, to 1pm Sat)

Tourist Information Office (985-856-25-51, ext 114; cnr Calles 40 & 41; 9am-9pm Mon-Fri, to 7pm Sat & Sun) The staff could use training courses, but at least there's some useful tourist brochures.

Getting There & Away

BUS

Valladolid's main bus terminal is the convenient **ADO bus terminal** (www.ado.com.mx; cnr Calles 39 & 46). The main 1st-class services are ADO, ADO GL and OCC; Oriente and Mayab run 2nd-class buses.

Buses to Chichén Itzá/Pisté stop near the ruins during opening hours.

COLECTIVO

Often faster, more reliable and more comfortable than 2nd-class buses are the *colectivos* that depart as soon as their seats are filled. Most operate from 7am or 8am to about 7pm.

Direct services run to **Mérida** (near the ADO bus terminal; M$110, two hours) and **Cancún** (Calle 41, one block east of the plaza; M$170; two hours); confirm they're nonstop. *Colectivos* for **Pisté and Chichén Itzá** (M$30, one hour) leave north of the ADO bus terminal; for **Tizimín** (M$40, 40 minutes) from Calle 40 between Calles 35 and 37; and for **Ek' Balam** (M$50) take a 'Santa Rita' *colectivo* from Calle 44 between Calles 35 and 37.

Getting Around

The old highway passes through the town center, though most signs urge motorists toward the toll road north of town. To follow the old highway eastbound, take Calle 41; westbound, take Calle 39.

Bicycles are a great way to see the town and get out to the cenotes. You can rent them at **Hostel La Candelaria** (p193) or **Rudy Tours** (p193) for M$15 to M$20 per hour.

Ek' Balam

The town of Ek' Balam itself is worth a visit to see what a traditional Maya village looks like. There are several nice hotels, as well as a handful of artisan stands along the main plaza, which also serves as the town's soccer field.

Sights

Ek' Balam ARCHAEOLOGICAL SITE

(adult/child under 13yr M$181/free, guide M$600; 8am-5pm) The fascinating ruined city of Ek' Balam reached its peak in the 8th century, before being suddenly abandoned. Vegetation still covers much of the archaeological site, but excavations and restoration continue to add to the sights, including an interesting ziggurat-like structure near the entrance, as well as a fine arch and a ball court. Most impressive is the gargantuan Acrópolis, whose well-restored base is 160m

BUSES FROM VALLADOLID

DESTINATION	FARE (M$)	DURATION (HRS)	FREQUENCY (DAILY)
Cancún	102-186	2½-3½	frequent
Chichén Itzá/Pisté	27-84	¾	frequent
Chiquilá (for Isla Holbox)	105	4	1; 3am
Cobá	48-114	1	5
Izamal	55	2½	1; 12.50pm
Mérida	102-178	2-3½	frequent
Playa del Carmen	186	2½-3	frequent
Tizimín	27	1	frequent
Tulum	108	1½-2	9

long and holds a 'gallery' – actually a series of separate chambers.

Built atop the base of the Acrópolis is Ek' Balam's massive main pyramid, reaching a height of 32m and sporting a gaping jaguar mouth. Below the mouth are stucco skulls, while above and to the right sits an amazingly expressive figure. On the right side stand unusual winged human figures (some call them Maya angels, although a much more likely explanation is that they are shaman or medicine men).

The turnoff for the archaeological site is 17km north of Valladolid, and the ruins are another 6km east from the turnoff.

From the Ek' Balam entrance you can visit the **X'Canché Cenote** (admission M$30), a 1.5km walk – or you can rent a bicycle (M$70). Also available at this ecotourist center are zip-line tours and cabin rentals.

Sleeping & Eating

★Genesis Eco-Oasis GUESTHOUSE **$$**
(cell 985-1010277; www.genesisretreat.com; Ek' Balam pueblo; d from M$919, without bathroom M$685, incl breakfast;) The Genesis Eco-Retreat offers B&B intimacy in a quiet, ecofriendly setting. This is a true ecotel: gray water is used for landscaping, some rooms are naturally cooled and there's even an entire wall made out of plastic bottles. The place is postcard-beautiful – there's a chilling swimming pool and a temascal (pre-Hispanic steam bath) onsite – and it offers delicious veggie meals.

The hotel is sometimes closed between September and early October. Reservations required.

Dolce Vacanza HOTEL **$$**
(cell 999-1148517; vacanzadolce@gmail.com; Ek' Balam pueblo; d from M$650;) This Italian-run property has a fine collection of 15 super-clean fan-cooled and air-conditioned rooms. The yummy restaurant specializes in, as you might guess, Italian fare.

Getting There & Away

Colectivos (M$50) to Ek' Balam depart from Calle 44, between Calles 35 and 37, in Valladolid.

Tizimín

986 / POP 47,000

You won't find much in Tizimín that's designed with the tourist in mind; in fact, for most folks it serves as a mere stopover point en route to the coast. That said, some travelers may find the town a refreshing change if they've just come from Playa del Carmen or Cancún.

Two great colonial structures – **Parroquia Los Santos Reyes de Tizimín** (Church of the Three Wise Kings) and its former **Franciscan monastery** (the ex-*convento*) – are worth a look. They're on opposite sides of Calle 51, reached by walking two blocks south on Calle 48, which itself is a block west of the bus terminals.

The city fills with people from outlying ranches during its annual fair to celebrate **Día de los Reyes Magos** (Three Kings' Day; January 6).

The church fronts Tizimín's main plaza, the Parque Principal, which has an ATM and currency exchange on its southwest side.

Sleeping & Eating

Hotel San Carlos HOTEL **$**
(986-863-20-94; www.hotelsancarlostizimin.com; Calle 54 No 407, btwn Calles 51 & 53; r with fan/air-con M$350/450;) Two blocks west of the plaza, this is one of the nicest hotels in town. All the air-con rooms have private patios looking onto the shared garden area.

Hotel 49 HOTEL **$**
(986-863-21-36; contacto@hotel49.com; Calle 49 No 373, btwn Calles 46 & 48; r M$450-600;) A centrally located option with parking and super-clean rooms with air-con.

BUSES FROM TIZIMÍN

DESTINATION	FARE (M$)	DURATION (HRS)	FREQUENCY (DAILY)
Cancún	119-280	3½	3
Izamal	70-85	2½	3
Mérida	105	4	7; Noreste
Río Lagartos/San Felipe	36-46	1¼	5; Noreste
Valladolid	28	1	frequent

Ricardo's MEXICAN $

(Calle 48 No 371, btwn Calles 45 & 47; mains M$55-100; 7am-5:30pm;) Ricardo's is known for its affordable breakfast combos, hearty daily lunch specials and a wide variety of Yucatecan dishes.

Pizzería César's PIZZA $$

(Calle 50; mains M$63-130; 8am-1am;) A popular joint off the main plaza, it serves inexpensive pasta dishes, sandwiches and burgers in addition to pizzas.

Getting There & Away

Buses offering 2nd-class services share a **bus terminal** (Calle 47, btwn Calles 46 & 48) just east of the market. You'll find Mérida-bound *colectivos* (M$130) here, too. The **Noreste bus terminal** (Calle 46), with 1st- and 2nd-class services, is just around the corner. San Felipe–bound *colectivos* (M$40, five daily) depart from the market.

Río Lagartos

986 / POP 2200

On the windy northern shore of the peninsula, sleepy Río Lagartos (Alligator River) is a fishing village that also boasts the densest concentration of flamingos in Mexico, supposedly two or three flamingos per Mexican, if one believes the provided math. Lying within the **Reserva de la Biosfera Ría Lagartos**, this mangrove-lined estuary shelters bird species, including snowy egrets, red egrets, tiger herons and snowy white ibis, as well as the crocodiles that gave the town its name. It's a beautiful area. At the right time of year you can see numerous species of birds without even getting out of your vehicle.

The Maya knew the place as Holkobén and used it as a rest stop on their way to Las Coloradas, a shallow part of the vast estuary that stretches east almost to the border of Quintana Roo. There they extracted precious salt from the waters, a process that continues on a much vaster scale today. Spanish explorers mistook the narrowing of the *ría* (estuary) for a *río* (river) and the crocs for alligators, and the rest is history.

Less than 1km east of town, on the edge of the estuary, an *ojo de agua* (natural spring) has been developed into a swimming hole.

Most residents aren't sure of the town's street names, and signs are few. The road into town is the north–south Calle 10, which ends at the waterfront *malecón*.

FLAMINGO ETIQUETTE

Although the sight of flamingos taking to the wing is impressive, for the well-being of the birds, please ask your boat captain not to frighten the birds into flight. You can generally get to within 100m of the birds before they walk or fly away.

There are no banks or ATMs in town and many places do not accept plastic, so bring plenty of cash.

Sights

Isla Cerritos ISLAND

Just 5km from the nearby fishing village of San Felipe, tiny Isla Cerritos was an important Maya port city back in the day. And while the entire island was covered with buildings during this era – archaeological expeditions have turned up nearly 50,000 artifacts – it's virtually deserted today, and none of the buildings have been restored. You can get there with a tour or catch a motorboat on the east side of the San Felipe boardwalk for M$600 per boat.

Tours

The brilliant orange-red flamingos can turn the horizon fiery when they take wing. Depending on the time of year and the forces of nature, you'll see either hundreds or thousands of them. Normally the best months for viewing them are from April through September; March and October are not so great.

To see the flamingos, you'll need to rent a boat and driver. You'll see more birdlife if you head out at sunrise or around 5pm. Prices vary by boat, group size (maximum six), number of hours and destination. A two-hour trip costs around M$1000 to M$1200. Plan on packing something to eat the night before, as most restaurants open long after you'll be on the water. Ask to stop at the *arcilla* (mud bath) on the way back.

You can negotiate with one of the eager men along the boardwalk. They speak English and will connect you with a captain (who usually doesn't), but the best option is going with one of the knowlegable English-speaking guides operating out of restaurants Ria Maya and Balneario Chiquilá.

CELEBRATING LA FERIA DE SANTIAGO & DÍA DE LA MARINA

Río Lagartos knows how to party, and two festivals, La Feria de Santiago and Día de la Marina, are well worth checking out. **La Feria de Santiago**, the patron-saint festival of Río Lagartos, is usually held from July 20 to July 25. A bullfight (really bullplay) ring is erected in the middle of town during the event, and every afternoon anyone who wishes is able to enter it and play matador with a young bull. The animal is not killed or even injured, just made a little angry at times.

Another big annual event in Río Lagartos is **Día de la Marina** (Day of the Marine Force), which always falls on June 1. On this day, following a morning Mass, a crown of flowers is dedicated to the Virgin and carried from the church to a boat, where it is then taken 4km out to sea and placed in the water as an offering to all the fishermen who have perished at sea.

The boats, not incidentally, are heavily decorated on this day, and tourists are welcome to ride to the site for free. Just ask if you can go, and be friendly and respectful. A tip for their kindness, following the service, is always appreciated (M$50 to M$100 per visitor).

★Río Lagartos Adventures BOAT TOUR
(cell 986-1008390; www.riolagartosadventures.com; Calle 19 No 134; per boat 2hr M$1200, fly-fishing from M$2200) This outfit run by local expert Diego Núnez Martinez does various water and land expeditions, including flamingo- and crocodile-watching, snorkeling to Isla Cerritos, fly-fishing and excursions designed for photography. Diego is a licensed English-speaking guide with formal training as a naturalist and is up to date on the area's fauna and flora, which includes some 400 bird species.

He organizes the tours out of Ria Maya Restaurante.

Ismael Navarro BOAT TOUR
(986-862-00-00, cell 986-8665216; riolaga@hotmail.com; Calle 9; per boat 2hr M$1000, fly-fishing M$3500) A licensed naturalist worth seeking out for a tour of the local flora and fauna. Besides the flamingo and fly-fishing outings, Ismael takes shorebird tours along the mudflats in winter. You'll find him and his partner, captain 'Chino Mosca', at Balneario Chiquilá, a restaurant and swimming hole on the east end of Calle 9.

Sleeping & Eating

Punta Ponto Hotel HOTEL $
(986-862-05-09; www.hotelpuntaponto.com; Calle 9 No 140, cnr Calle 19; r incl breakfast M$450-700; P) One of the best deals in town and your kind host, Roger, is a great source of information. Two rooms have balconies with estuary views, and the breezy, open-air common spaces seal the deal.

El Perico Marinero HOTEL $$
(986-862-00-58; www.elpericomarinero.com; Calle 9, near Calle 19; d incl breakfast M$600-700;) Business must be booming at the Perico's waterfront seafood restaurant just down the road. Rio Lagarto's newest hotel offers seven pleasant rooms, some with estuary vistas, rocking chairs and handmade wood furnishings, and all come with excellent beds.

Hotel Villas de Pescadores HOTEL $$
(986-862-00-20; www.hotelriolagartos.com.mx; cnr Calles 14 & 9; d incl breakfast M$750; P) Near the water's edge, this nice hotel offers 12 very clean rooms, each with good cross-ventilation (all face the estuary), satellite TV and air-con. Upstairs rooms have balconies, and there's a rickety spiral staircase leading up to a rooftop lookout tower where guests can watch the sun set.

Restaurant y Posada Macumba SEAFOOD $$
(986-862-00-92; www.restaurantmacumba.com; Calle 16 No 102, cnr Calle 11; mains M$85-135; 8am-8pm;) One of the best restaurants in town specializing in fresh fish and seafood. Upstairs the waterfront Macumba has four smallish rooms (M$400 to M$500) with funky Caribbean design details. The panoramic view of the penthouse (M$700) makes it a screaming deal.

Ría Maya Restaurante SEAFOOD $$
(www.riolagartosrestaurante.com; Calle 19 No 134, cnr Calle 14; mains M$90-200, lobster M$250; 9am-9pm;) A popular two-story *palapa* with waterside sunset views, this is a

good place to meet other travelers and form groups for boat tours. Lobster, at market price, is a delicious seasonal specialty.

Getting There & Away

Several Noreste buses run daily between Tizimín (M$36 to M$46, one hour and 15 minutes), Mérida (M$142 to M$196, three to four hours) and San Felipe (M$8, 20 minutes). The bus terminal is on Calle 19, between Calles 6 and 8. Noreste serves Valladolid and Cancún, but you'll need to transfer in Tizimín.

East of Río Lagartos

The road between Río Lagartos and El Cuyo is truly a birder's delight. It's best to take the trip early in the morning, when you are likely to see egrets, blue heron, osprey and gaggles of pink flamingos. If you do stop to observe wildlife, be as quiet as possible and remember that there are crocodiles in the shallows, as well as venomous snakes: don't let that great-roseate-spoonbill photo opportunity send you to the hospital.

Start your trip by turning east at the junction about 2km south of Río Lagartos. About 8km from the junction, on the south side of the road, is the beginning of a 1km **interpretive trail** to Petén Tucha (a *petén* is a hummock or rise often forming around a spring).

Continuing east on the road 4km beyond the trailhead you'll reach a bridge over a very narrow part of the estuary. Fishers cast nets here, and you can sometimes see crocs lurking in the water (look for dead horseshoe crabs on the bridge). Another 6km beyond this is **Las Coloradas**, a small town housing workers who extract salt from the vast shallow lagoons of the same name; they stretch eastward for kilometers on the south side of the road. The salt is piled in gleaming mounds that look like icebergs, up to 15m high, and from a distance it appears oddly incongruous, as if you've arrived in the Arctic despite the blistering heat.

The road turns to sand after Las Coloradas, but you can still make it to El Cuyo most times of year. The unique roadside vegetation includes the century plant, an agave species that lives for decades before sending up a tall stalk that blossoms, in turn triggering the final demise of the plant. These are different from the *henequén* agaves that you see further south.

The road often washes out in rainy season, but it's normally passable in dry season (even with a non-4WD vehicle). Ask locally before you take the trip (you'll need your own wheels).

El Cuyo

El Cuyo has a clear white-sand beach, muddy waters and a windy coast, which makes for good kiteboarding. At the end of the road from Río Lagartos, the town sees a few local tourists looking for a short beach vacation, but not many foreigners visit here. Maybe this is the off-the-beaten-track spot you've been looking for.

At El Cuyo the road travels through broad expanses of grassy savanna with palms and some huge-trunked trees, passing the site of the original founding of Valladolid, in 1543. At Colonia Yucatán, 38km south of El Cuyo, you can head east to pick up the road to Chiquilá and Isla Holbox or west to Tizimín.

Sleeping & Eating

Posada El Faro HOTEL $
(986-853-40-15; Calle 40; d M$500; P ❄ wi-fi) Rooms here are comfortable enough and El Faro now has wi-fi! It's just south of the plaza.

Villas Chac Chi APARTMENT $$
(cell 998-5773380; www.facebook.com/villaschacchi; d M$1000) About 1km east of the plaza along the main dirt road are two ample apartments with full kitchen and air-con, and they're just a hop, skip and a jump to the beach. Reservations required.

Hotel Aida Luz HOTEL $$
(986-105-32-93, cell 986-8534088; www.hotelaidaluzelcuyo.com; Calle 40 No 3A; r M$600; P ❄) You can't miss this big orange-and-white building near the plaza. Rooms are nothing spectacular, but they're a block from the water.

Miramar SEAFOOD $$
(mains M$85-140; 7am-6pm) Try the delicious crispy shrimp served in a coconut at this large fan-cooled eatery on the plaza's west side.

Getting There & Away

The Noreste bus line has six daily departures to El Cuyo (M$60) from Tizimín; going the other way, buses head to Tizimín from the town plaza. Hitchhiking may be possible, but a rental car is by far the better way to go.

San Felipe

986 / POP 1800

About 12km west of Río Lagartos, San Felipe is a fishing village seldom visited by travelers. It's notable for its orderly streets, cheery Caribbean feel and painted wooden houses. With its laid-back air, this is a good alternative to staying in Río Lagartos. Getting there you'll pass primarily mangrove-dotted lagoons, and perhaps surprise a turtle or two crossing the road. Its beach lies across the mouth of the estuary, at Punta Holchit, and the mangroves there and on the western edge of town are a bird-watcher's paradise. Just looking out the windows of the town's main hotel you can see white and brown pelicans, terns, cormorants, great blue herons, magnificent frigate birds and jabirus (storks).

Buses from Tizimín pass through Río Lagartos and continue to San Felipe (M$46, one hour, five daily). The bus ride from Río Lagartos takes 20 minutes. San Felipe–bound *colectivos* (M$40, five daily) depart from the market in Tizimín.

Tours

Boat Tours BOAT TOUR

(Calle 9; bird-watching/fishing tours M$600/1500) *Lancheros* (boat owners) on the east end of waterfront Calle 9 charge M$125 to M$150 per boatload to take passengers across to Playa Bonita beach. They also do fishing excursions and birding expeditions to Isla Cerritos.

Sleeping

Hotel San Felipe de Jesús HOTEL **$$**

(986-862-20-27; hotelsfjesus@hotmail.com; Calle 9A, btwn Calles 14 & 16; d M$600-650, ste M$700) A friendly, clean and cleverly constructed hotel at the west edge of San Felipe's harbor, it's definitely worth a few extra pesos to get a room with a private balcony and water views. The restaurant offers good seafood at low prices. To get here, turn left at the water and proceed about 200m.

Campeche & Around

Includes ➡

Best Places to Eat

- ➡ Río Bec Dreams Restaurant (p224)
- ➡ Marganzo (p210)
- ➡ La Fuente (p220)

Best Places to Stay

- ➡ Hotel Las Villas (p220)
- ➡ Río Bec Dreams (p224)
- ➡ Hacienda Puerta Campeche (p209)

Why Go?

Tucked into the southwestern corner of the Yucatán Peninsula, Campeche state is home to serene villages, vast stretches of tangled jungle, bird-dotted mangroves and lagoons, and some of the region's most imposing Maya ruins – many of which you might have all to yourself. On deserted beaches endangered turtles lay their eggs, while offshore playful dolphins frolic in the surf. The walled capital city of Campeche is the region's cultural epicenter, providing a great jumping-off point for your adventures into this offbeat hinterland.

Campeche is the least visited of the Yucatán's states, laced through with lonely back roads, friendly people, quiet coastlines and a provincial, lost-land charm. It makes a welcome break from the tourist hordes that descend on the peninsula's more popular destinations; here you'll find peace and surprising attractions.

When to Go

➡ Visit Campeche city any time of year, though high season is from mid-December to Easter. Hotel prices are at their peak during this time, but there are also some merry festivities – especially Carnaval (late February to early March).

➡ The dry months of November through March are the most pleasant for visiting Calakmul and its nearby sites. During the rainy season access is often limited due to muddy roads.

➡ To set turtle hatchlings free in Sabancuy, be there from April to October (peak June to August).

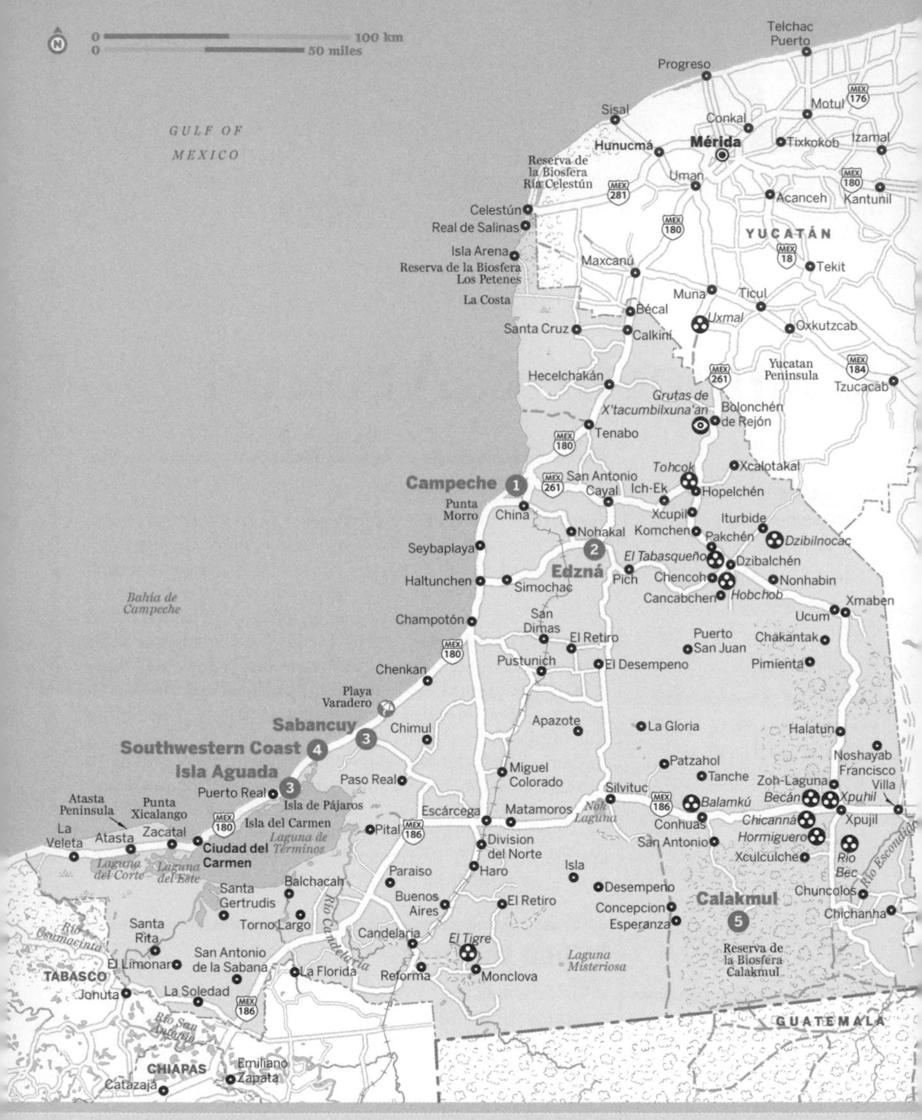

Campeche Highlights

1. Stroll through history along the colonial streets of **Campeche** (p203), lined with pastel-hued buildings and edged by stone ramparts.

2. Explore the large and impressive complexes of **Edzná** (p216), the most significant Maya ruins near Campeche.

3. Spot dolphins and seabirds from **Isla Aguada** (p218), or set turtle hatchlings free at **Sabancuy** (p218).

4. Eat fresh seafood or find yourself a little patch of deserted beach along the **southwestern coast** (p217).

5. Haul yourself up the massive pyramids of **Calakmul** (p221) while the calls of howler monkeys reverberate in the surrounding jungle.

CAMPECHE

981 / POP 220,000

Campeche is a colonial fairyland, its walled city center a tight enclave of perfectly restored pastel buildings, narrow cobblestone streets, fortified ramparts and well-preserved mansions. Added to Unesco's list of World Heritage sites in 1999, the state capital has been so painstakingly restored it almost doesn't seem like a real city. But leave the inner walls and you'll find a genuine Mexican provincial capital complete with a frenetic market, peaceful *malecón* (boardwalk) and old fishing docks.

Besides the walls and numerous mansions built by wealthy Spanish families during Campeche's heyday in the 18th and 19th centuries, no fewer than seven of the *baluartes* (bastions or bulwarks) have also survived. Additionally, two perfectly preserved colonial forts guard the city's outskirts, one of them housing the Museo de la Arquitectura Maya, an archaeological museum with many world-class pieces.

Relatively few tourists visit Campeche, and its citizens – the big-hearted and proud *campechanos* – are likely to show you an unobtrusive hospitality not seen in other regional capitals. The city's central location on the Gulf of Mexico also makes it the perfect base for day trips to Edzná, the Chenes sites and neighboring beaches. And at night, the gauzy lights on the illuminated church and other central landmarks add an almost magical atmosphere to this gem of a destination.

History

Once a Maya trading village called Ah Kim Pech (Lord Sun Sheep-Tick), Campeche was first briefly approached by the Spaniards in 1517. Resistance by the Maya prevented the Spaniards from fully conquering the region for nearly a quarter-century. Colonial Campeche was founded in 1531, but later abandoned due to Maya hostility. By 1540, however, the conquistadors had gained sufficient control, under the leadership of Francisco de Montejo (the Younger), to found a permanent settlement. They named the settlement Villa de San Francisco de Campeche.

The settlement soon flourished as the major port of the Yucatán Peninsula, but this made it subject to pirate attacks. After a particularly appalling attack in 1663 (p205) left the city in ruins, the king of Spain ordered construction of Campeche's famous bastions, putting an end to the periodic carnage.

Today the economy of the city is largely driven by fishing and, increasingly, tourism, which has helped fund the downtown area's renovation.

Sights & Activities

Plaza Principal & Around

Shaded by carob trees and ringed by tiled benches and broad footpaths radiating from a belle-epoque kiosk, Campeche's appealingly modest central square started life in 1531 as a military camp. Over the years it became the focus of the town's civic, political and religious activities and remains the core of public life. *Campechanos* come here to chat, smooch, have their shoes shined or cool off with an ice cream after the heat of the day. The plaza is at its best on weekend evenings, when it's closed to traffic and concerts are staged.

★Centro Cultural Casa Número 6 CULTURAL CENTER

(Calle 57 No 6; M$20, audio guide M$15; 9am-9pm) During the prerevolutionary era, when this mansion was occupied by an upper-class *campechano* family, Número 6 was a prestigious plaza address. Wandering the premises, you'll get an idea of how the city's high society lived back then. The front sitting room is furnished with Cuban-style pieces of the period. Inside are exhibition spaces, a pleasant back patio and a gift shop.

Catedral de Nuestra Señora de la Purísima Concepción CATHEDRAL

(Calle 55; 6:30am-9pm) FREE Dominating Plaza Principal's east side is the two-towered cathedral. The limestone structure has stood on this spot for more than three centuries, and it still fills beyond capacity most Sundays. Statues of Sts Peter and Paul occupy niches in the baroque facade; the sober, single-nave interior is lined with colonial-era paintings.

Biblioteca de Campeche LIBRARY

(State Library; 9am-8pm Mon-Fri, 9am-1pm Sat) On the northern (seaward) side of Plaza Principal stands a replica of the old government center, now housing the modern Biblioteca de Campeche. The impressive porticoed building on the opposite side housed an earlier version of the city hall; it is now occupied by shops and restaurants.

Mansión Carvajal HISTORIC BUILDING
(Calle 10 btwn Calles 51 & 53; ⌚8am-2:45pm Mon-Fri) FREE Once the mansion of wealthy landowner Fernando Carvajal, this beautiful building now houses state offices. Visitors are welcome to take a peek inside, however. Black-and-white tiled floors, Doric columns, elaborate archways and a dramatic marble and ironwork staircase are highlights. Note the historical plaque.

Museo del Archivo General de Estado MUSEUM
(☎981-816-09-39; Calle 12 No 159; ⌚8am-3pm Mon-Fri) FREE At this small museum, learn how Campeche came to be. It's free and air-conditioned, and you get to check out old documents and maps, and watch a video (in Spanish or English) that recounts the history of the state.

Casa del Arte ARTS CENTER
(Calle 55 btwn Calles 12 & 14; ⌚8am-3pm & 6-9pm Mon-Fri, 10am-3pm Sat) FREE Come here to see rotating art, photography and painting exhibits by local artists.

Ex-Templo de San José HISTORIC BUILDING
(former San José Church; cnr Calles 10 & 63; ⌚10am-8pm) Faced with blue-and-yellow tiles, the Ex-Templo de San José is a wonder to behold; note the lighthouse, complete with weather vane, atop the right spire. Built in the early 18th century by Jesuits who ran it as an institute of higher learning until they were booted out of Spanish domains in 1767, it now serves as an exhibition space.

Baluartes

After a particularly blistering pirate assault in 1663, the remaining inhabitants of Campeche set about erecting protective walls around their city. Built largely by indigenous labor with limestone extracted from nearby caves, the barrier took more than 50 years to complete. Stretching more than 2.5km around the urban core and rising to a height of 8m, the hexagonal wall was linked by eight bulwarks. The seven that remain display a treasure trove of historical paraphernalia, artifacts and indigenous handicrafts. You can climb atop the bulwarks and stroll sections of the wall for sweeping views of the port.

Two main entrances connected the walled compound with the outside world. The **Puerta del Mar** (Sea Gate; cnr Calles 8 & 59) FREE provided access from the sea, opening onto a wharf where small craft delivered goods from ships anchored further out. (The shallow waters were later reclaimed so the gate is now several blocks from the waterfront.) The **Puerta de Tierra** (Land Gate; Calle 18; M$15; ⌚9am-6pm), on the opposite side, was opened in 1732 as the principal ingress from the suburbs. It is now the venue for a sound-and-light show (p211).

★ **Museo de la Arquitectura Maya** MUSEUM
(Calle 8; M$39; ⌚9am-5:30pm Tue-Sun) The Baluarte de Nuestra Señora de la Soledad, designed to protect the Puerta del Mar, contains the fascinating Museo de la Arquitectura Maya, the one must-see museum in Campeche. It provides an excellent overview of the sites around Campeche state and the key architectural styles associated with them. Five halls display stelae taken from various sites, accompanied by graphic representations of their carved inscriptions with brief commentaries in flawless English.

Baluarte de Santiago GARDENS, HISTORIC BUILDING
(cnr Calles 8 & 49; adult/child 3-12 M$10/5; ⌚9am-9pm Mon-Sat, 9 to 4pm Sun) Completed in 1704 – the last of the bulwarks to be built – the Baluarte de Santiago houses the **Jardín Botánico Xmuch Haltún**, a botanical garden with numerous endemic and some non-native plants. It's not a huge place, but provides a green and peaceful spot to rest up for a bit.

Museo de la Ciudad MUSEUM
(Calle 8; M$35; ⌚9am-8pm) Named after Spain's King Carlos II, the Baluarte de San Carlos houses the Museo de la Ciudad. This small but worthwhile museum chronologically illustrates the city's tempestuous history via well-displayed objects: specimens of dyewood, muskets, a figurehead from a ship's prow and the like. The dungeon downstairs alludes to the building's use as a military prison during the 1700s.

Baluarte de San Pedro HISTORIC BUILDING
(cnr Avs Circuito Baluartes Este & Circuito Baluartes Nte; ⌚9am-9pm) FREE Directly behind Iglesia de San Juan de Dios, the Baluarte de San Pedro served a post-piracy defensive function when it repelled a punitive raid from Mérida in 1824. Carved in stone above the entry is the symbol of San Pedro: two keys to heaven and the papal tiara. Climb the steep ramp to the roof and look between the

RIBALD TALES: THE MARAUDING PIRATES OF CAMPECHE

Where there's wealth, there are pirates – this was truer in the 1500s than it is today. And Campeche, which was a thriving timber, chicle (gum) and logwood (a natural source of dye) port in the mid-16th century, was the wealthiest place around.

Pirates (or 'privateers', as some preferred to be called) terrorized Campeche for two centuries. Time and time again the port was invaded, ships sacked, citizens robbed and buildings burned – typical pirate stuff. The buccaneers' hall of shame included the infamous John Hawkins, Francis Drake, Henry Morgan and the notorious 'Peg-Leg' himself. In their most gruesome assault, in early 1663, the various pirate hordes set aside rivalries to converge as a single flotilla upon the city, massacring Campeche's citizens.

This tragedy finally spurred the Spanish monarchy to take preventive action, but it was another five years before work on the 3.5m-thick ramparts began. By 1686 a 2.5km hexagon incorporating eight strategically placed bastions surrounded the city. A segment of the ramparts extended out to sea so that ships literally sailed into a fortress to gain access to the city. With Campeche nearly impregnable, pirates turned to other ports and ships at sea. In 1717 the brilliant naval strategist Felipe de Aranda began a campaign against the buccaneers, and eventually made this area of the Gulf safe from piracy. Of course, all that wealth from chicle and timber was created using indigenous slaves, leading one to question: who were the real bad guys, anyway?

For a taste of the pirate life, take a 50-minute cruise on the **Lorencillo** (981-816-19-90; barcopiratalorencillo@hotmail.com; Av Resurgimiento No 120 , 4km south of Campeche city, near restaurant El Faro del Morro; adult/child M$130/70). This 'pirate ship' heads out Tuesday through Sunday at noon and 5pm (or noon and 6pm in warmer seasons). Get information at a kiosk near the *tranvía* kiosk, in the Plaza Principal.

battlements to see San Juan's cupola. Downstairs, the Galería y Museo de Arte Popular displays beautiful indigenous handicrafts.

Baluarte de San Francisco HISTORIC BUILDING
(Calle 18) FREE Once the primary defensive bastion for the adjacent Puerta de la Tierra, the Baluarte de San Francisco now houses a small cultural center.

Baluarte de San Juan HISTORIC BUILDING
(Calle 18; 8am-7:30pm Tue-Sun) FREE The Baluarte de San Juan is the smallest of the seven bulwarks. On its south side you can see the bell that was rung to alert the population in times of danger.

Baluarte de Santa Rosa HISTORIC BUILDING
(cnr Calle 14 & Av Circuito Baluartes Sur; 9am-3pm) FREE The Baluarte de Santa Rosa has some pirate-themed woodcuts and information on the city's forts.

Malecón

A popular path for joggers, cyclists, strolling friends and cooing sweethearts, the *malecón*, Campeche's 7km-long waterfront promenade, makes for a breezy sunrise ramble or sunset bike ride.

A series of monuments along a 2.5km stretch of the *malecón* allude to various personages and events in the city's history. Southwest of the Plaza Moch Couoh stands a statue of Campeche native **Justo Sierra Méndez**, a key player in the modernization of Mexico's educational system. Next to the plaza is a **monument** of the walled city's four gates. Three blocks up is a monumental sculpture of native son **Pedro Sáinz de Baranda**, who played a key role in defeating the Spanish at their last stronghold in Veracruz, thus ending the War of Independence.

Just beyond the Centro de Convenciones Campeche XXI, the girl gazing out to sea is the **Novia del Mar**. According to a poignant local legend, the *campechana* fell in love with a foreign pirate and awaits his return. About 1km further north, the **Plaza Cuatro de Octubre** (October 4 Plaza) commemorates the date of the city's 'founding,' depicting the fateful meeting of conquistador Francisco de Montejo, a priest and a Maya *cacique* (chief, who was evidently lost, since it took Montejo to 'found' the city).

At the *malecón*'s northern tip, 4.5km northeast from downtown, lies a cluster of seafood restaurants called Parador Gastronomico de Cocteleros. Good place for lunch, despite the waiters touting for customers.

Campeche

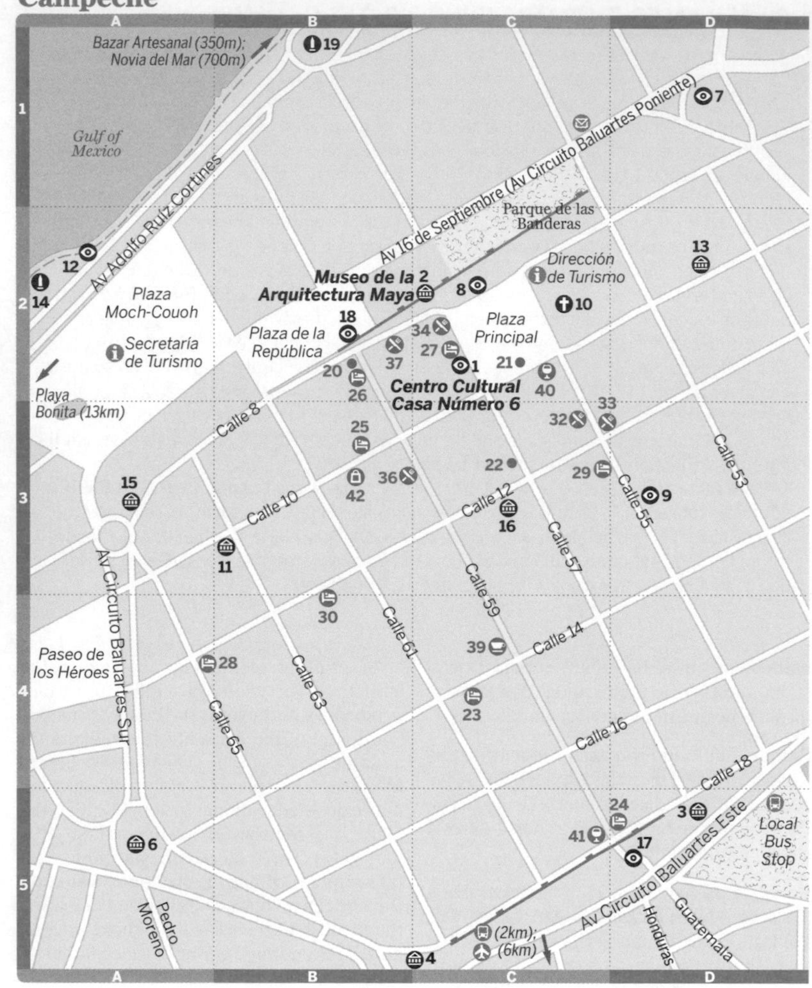

Outside the City Centre

Museo Arqueológico de Campeche & Fuerte de San Miguel MUSEUM, FORT

(Campeche Archaeological Museum; Av Escénica s/n; M$46; 8:30am-5pm Tue-Sun; P) Campeche's largest colonial fort, facing the Gulf of Mexico some 4km southwest of the city center, is now home to the excellent Museo Arqueológico de Campeche. Here you can admire findings from the sites of Calakmul and Edzná, and from Isla de Jaina, an island north of town once used as a burial site for Maya aristocracy.

To get here take a bus or combi (minibus; marked 'Lerma') from the market. Ask the driver to let you off at the access road (just say 'Fuerte de San Miguel), then hike 300m up the hill. Taxis cost M$50.

Stunning jade jewelry and exquisite vases, masks and plates are thematically arranged in 10 exhibit halls. The star attractions are the jade burial masks from Calakmul. Also displayed are stelae, seashell necklaces and clay figurines.

Equipped with a dry moat and working drawbridge, the fort itself is a thing of beauty. The roof deck, ringed by 20 cannons, affords wonderful harbor views.

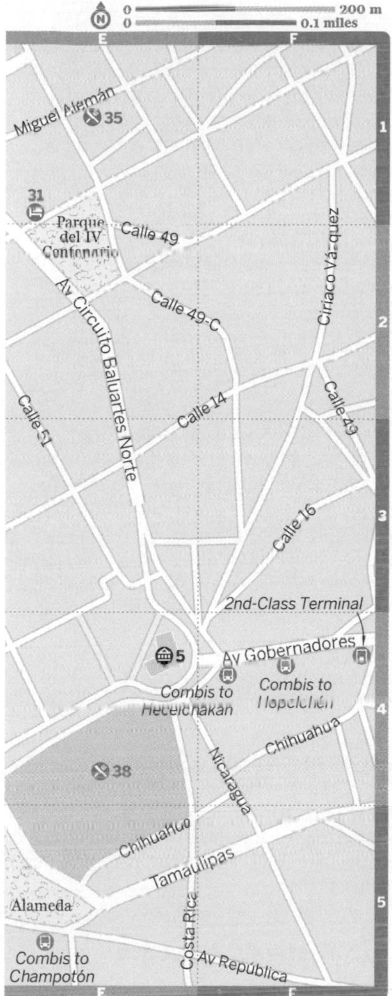

Fuerte Museo San José del Alto FORT

(Calle Francisco Morazán; M$43; ⏱8am-5pm Tue-Sun; 🅿) Built in the late 18th century, this neatly restored fort (with drawbridge and moat) sits atop Cerro de Bellavista. Inside, a **museum** illustrates the port's maritime history through models, weaponry and other paraphernalia, including a beautiful ebony rudder carved in the shape of a hound.

To get here, catch a 'Bellavista Josefa' or 'Morelos' bus from the market; some might also be marked 'San Jose del Alto'. You might have to walk a bit from where the bus drops you. Taxis cost around M$50.

Campeche

Top Sights
1 Centro Cultural Casa Número 6 .... C2
2 Museo de la Arquitectura Maya C2

Sights
3 Baluarte de San Francisco D5
4 Baluarte de San Juan C5
5 Baluarte de San Pedro E4
6 Baluarte de Santa Rosa A5
7 Baluarte de Santiago D1
8 Biblioteca de Campeche C2
9 Casa del Arte D3
10 Catedral de Nuestra Señora de la Purísima Concepción C2
11 Ex-Templo de San José B3
12 Malecón A2
13 Mansión Carvajal D2
14 Monument to the City Gates A2
15 Museo de la Ciudad A3
16 Museo del Archivo General de Estado C3
17 Puerta de Tierra D5
18 Puerta del Mar B2
19 Sculpture of Pedro Sáinz de Baranda B1

Activities, Courses & Tours
20 Kankabi' Ok B2
21 Tranvía de la Ciudad C2
22 Xtampak Tours C3

Sleeping
23 H177 Hotel C4
24 Hacienda Puerta Campeche D5
25 Hotel América B3
26 Hotel Boutique Casa Don Gustavo B2
27 Hotel Campeche C2
28 Hotel Francis Drake A4
29 Hotel Guarandocha Inn C3
30 Hotel López B4
31 Hotel Plaza Campeche E1

Eating
32 Café La Parroquia C3
33 Chef Color C3
34 El Bastión de Campeche C2
35 La Pigua E1
36 Luz de Luna B3
37 Marganzo B2
38 Mercado Principal E4

Drinking & Nightlife
39 Chocol Ha C4
40 La Casa Vieja C2
41 Salón Rincón Colonial C5

Entertainment
Puerta de Tierra .... (see 17)

Shopping
42 Casa de Artesanías Tukulna B3

THE MENNONITES OF CAMPECHE

Campeche is in the midst of a quiet arrival by an unlikely community – the Mennonites. Seeing them waiting in bus stations, hanging about the main plazas of villages or crowding a pickup, you may wonder if you've somehow stumbled onto the set of *Little House on the Prairie*. Clad in black coveralls and long-sleeved flannel shirts in the midday heat, the men tower over their Maya neighbors. The women wear dark floral-print dresses and straw hats with broad ribbons.

Tracing their origins to 16th-century Reformist Germany, the Mennonites have inhabited some northern Mexican states since the 1920s. Drawn by cheap land, they first migrated down to Hopelchén, Campeche, in 1983 and since then have established agricultural communities around Dzibalchén, Hecelchakán and Edzná. Once they've settled in, the Mennonites work relentlessly, growing corn, melons and other crops, raising cattle and producing cheese for the domestic market. They live in *campos* (self-contained communities with their own schools and churches), and speak among themselves in a form of Low German.

Mennonite men customarily fraternize and conduct business with the Mexicans and many converse fluently in colloquial Spanish (the women only speak with their own). Though they are generally accepted by the local community, some *campechanos* (residents of Campeche) have expressed resentment at the Mennonite presence, complaining that the 'Menonas' buy *ejido* (communal) lands for less than they're worth and have the capital to purchase expensive farm machinery while *campechanos* have to scrape by with lesser means.

The film *Luz silenciosa (Silent Light)* by Mexican director Carlos Reygadas looks at life in Mexico's Mennonite communities. It won the coveted Jury Prize at Cannes in 2007.

Playa Bonita BEACH
(pedestrians free, cars M$10; 8am-5pm; P) About 13km south of downtown, just past the port village of Lerma, Playa Bonita is the closest real beach to Campeche. Don't expect an isolated paradise though – this is a gated, developed resort with gritty sand and sandbagged swimming areas (to keep sand from washing away). Still, it's not unpleasant – plenty of *palapas* provide shade (M$25) and there's a restaurant and *fútbol* pitch. Come on weekdays to avoid the crowds.

To get here, take one of the frequent combis from the market (M$6, 20 minutes) and ask to be dropped at the beach entrance. Taxis cost around M$100.

Tours

Tranvía de la Ciudad TOUR
(tours adult/child 11yr & under M$100/30; hourly 9am-noon & 5-8pm) Daily bilingual tours by *tranvía* (trolley) depart from Calle 10 beside the Plaza Principal, lasting 45 minutes. They cover Campeche's historical center, traditional neighborhoods and part of the *malecón*. Occasionally, another trolley called *El Guapo* goes to Fuerte de San Miguel and Fuerte de San José, though they don't leave enough time to visit the forts' museums. Check schedules at the ticket kiosk in the Plaza Principal.

Kankabi' Ok TOUR
(981-811-27-92; www.kankabiok.com; Calle 59 No 3; 9am-8pm Mon-Sat, 10am-2pm Sun) Offers city tours, trips to archaeological sites such as Edzná, Chenes and the Ruta Puuc. Also rents bikes and does ecotourism and beach trips.

Festivals & Events

Carnaval CULTURAL
Campeche pulls out all the stops for Carnaval in February (date varies), with at least a week of festivities leading up to Sábado de Bando (Carnaval Saturday), when everyone dresses up in outrageous costumes and parades down the *malecón*. The official conclusion is a week later, when a pirate effigy is torched and hurled into the sea.

Feria de San Román RELIGIOUS
This festival on September 14 honors the beloved Cristo Negro (Black Christ) of the Iglesia de San Román. Fireworks and ferris wheels take over the zone just southwest of the center, along with beauty contests, boxing matches and a music-and-dance

competition that brings in traditional ensembles from around the peninsula.

Día de Nuestra Señora de Guadalupe RELIGIOUS
On December 12 pilgrims from throughout the peninsula travel to the Iglesia de Guadalupe, 1.5km east of the Plaza Principal, Mexico's second-most-visited shrine (after the Virgin of Guadalupe).

Sleeping

Campeche has some fine hotels but generally doesn't offer great-value accommodations. Note that during Christmas and Easter prices can skyrocket.

Hotel Guarandocha Inn HOTEL $
(981-811-66-58; rool_2111@hotmail.com; Calle 55, btwn Calles 12 & 14; incl breakfast d M$460-550, tr M$670;) One of the better options in town is at this modest but pleasant hotel. Rooms are nice and spacious, and the newer ones upstairs are brighter and more open (and cost a bit more). A very simple breakfast is included.

Hotel Campeche HOTEL $
(981-816-51-83; hotelcampeche@hotmail.com; Calle 57, btwn Calles 8 & 10; s/d with fan M$280/320, with air-con M$370/450;) Not much in the way of frills here, but the plaza-side location and big rooms in this classically crumbling building are about the best budget bet in town. A couple of rooms have little balconies looking out over the plaza.

★ **Hotel López** HOTEL $$
(981-816-33-44; www.hotellopezcampeche.com.mx; Calle 12 No 189; s/d/ste M$650/720/980;) This elegant hotel is one of Campeche's best midrange options. Small but modern and comfortably appointed rooms open onto curvy art-deco balconies around oval courtyards and pleasant greenery. Bring your swimsuit for the lovely pool out back.

H177 Hotel HOTEL $$
(981-816-44-63; Calle 14 No 177; s/d incl breakfast M$900/1250;) With its slick and trendy lines, this hotel is different from anything else in traditional Campeche. It boasts 24 spacious and modern-styled rooms decked out in strong natural colors, and the bathrooms have glass-walled showers. There's also a Jacuzzi. Ask for a discount in low season.

Hotel Francis Drake HOTEL $$
(981-811-56-26; www.hotelfrancisdrake.com; Calle 12 No 207; s/d M$860/950, ste from M$1050;) A somewhat baroque lobby leads to cool, fresh rooms with a sprinkling of tasteful decoration. Bathrooms and balconies are tiny, but the rooms are huge (other hotels would call them suites) with king-sized beds and separate sitting areas.

Hotel América HOTEL $$
(981-816-45-76; www.hotelamericacampeche.com; Calle 10 No 252; s/d M$550/680;) A large central hotel, the América is a good midrange choice. The highlight here is a pretty courtyard restaurant with tables and umbrellas – don't worry, the music dies down at night. Nearly 50 large, clean rooms are located in the surrounding arcaded corridors and can vary widely, so check out a few if you don't like what you first see.

★ **Hacienda Puerta Campeche** BOUTIQUE HOTEL $$$
(981-816-75-08; www.luxurycollection.com; Calle 59 No 71; r from M$4258;) This beautiful boutique hotel has 15 suites with high ceilings and separate lounges. Perfectly manicured gardens and grassy lawns offer peace, while the partly covered pool has nearby hammocks that are fit for a Maya king. It also runs a restored luxury hacienda 26km outside the city, on the way to the Edzná ruins.

Hotel Boutique Casa Don Gustavo BOUTIQUE HOTEL $$$
(981-816-80-90; www.casadongustavo.com; Calle 59 No 4; r/ste from M$2200/2600;) Just 10 rooms decorated with antique furniture (and huge modern bathrooms), though everything is so perfectly museumlike it's almost hard to relax. Give it a shot at the small pool with hammocks nearby, or try the rooftop jacuzzi. Colorful tiled hallways line an outdoor courtyard, and there's a restaurant too. Call or check the website for promotions.

Hotel Plaza Campeche HOTEL $$$
(981-811-99-00; www.hotelplazacampeche.com; cnr Calle 10 & Av Circuito Baluartes; r/ste M$1450/2400;) Just outside the historic center, on somewhat scruffy Parque del IV Centenario, the Plaza caters to business travelers and tour groups. It's elegant enough, with a sumptuous dining room, pleasant patio, fancy bar and attentive

DIG INTO TRADITIONAL CAMPECHANO CUISINE

On weekends look for *campechano* cuisine at Plaza Principal. Before sundown stalls set up and offer a few regional specialties such as *pibipollo* (chicken tamales traditionally cooked underground) and *brazo de reina* (tamales with chopped *chaya* – a spinachlike vegetable – mixed into the dough), plus various desserts and cold drinks. *Pan de Cazón* is another regional specialty, mostly available in restaurants, but note that these *tostadas* (fried tortillas) are made from small or baby shark meat and that sharks are becoming an endangered species worldwide.

Campeche's bustling **Mercado Principal** (Av Circuito Baluartes Este; ⏲7am-5pm) offers some good snacks – if you can handle the 'rustic hygiene.' At the Calle 53 entrance, regional-style tamales are dispensed from big pots in the morning. Inside, take a battered stool at Taquería El Amigo Carlos Ruelas and order a *tranca* – a baguette stuffed with *lechón* (roast pork) – and an ice-cold glass of *agua de lima* (sweet lemon drink). Nearby, a number of *cocina económica*s (basic eateries) cook up very affordable meals.

Parador Gastrónomico de Cocteleros (Av Costera; mains M$120-150; ⏲9am-6:30pm), 4.5km from Plaza Principal at the north end of the *malecón* (taxis from the city center cost around M$35), is a great place to sample the area's bountiful seafood. Over a dozen thatched-roof restaurants all serve pretty much the same thing: shrimp cocktails, fried fish and other seafood dishes. Competition between restaurants is lively and you'll no doubt be confronted by waiters trying to convince you to eat at their place. Just pick a spot that looks appealing, have a seat and enjoy the sea views.

bellhops. The 82 rooms come in four categories; all are comfortable and have flat TVs and safes, though they're not superluxurious.

Eating

Café La Parroquia MEXICAN **$**
(☎981-816-25-30; Calle 55 No 8; mains M$60-170, lunch specials M$80; ⏲24hr) Open 24 hours, this casual restaurant appeals to both locals and foreigners with its wide-ranging menu and attentive staff. Order everything from fried chicken to grilled pork to turkey soup, plus regional specialties and seafood dishes like ceviche. Tons of drinks make it all go down easy, and don't miss the creamy flan for dessert.

Chef Color MEXICAN **$**
(☎981-811-44-55; cnr Calles 55 & 12; half/full lunch platters M$35/60; ⏲11am-5pm Mon-Sat) This cafeteria-style eatery serves up large portions of tasty Central American–influenced Mexican dishes from behind a glass counter; just point at what you want. The menu changes daily but it's always good, cheap and filling.

★**Marganzo** MEXICAN **$$**
(☎981-811-38-98; Calle 8 No 267; mains M$120-200; ⏲7am-11pm) Marganzo is popular with tourists, for good reason – the food is great, the portions large and the complimentary appetizers numerous. An extensive menu offers everything from international fare to regional treats like *chochinita pibil* (roasted suckling pig). Service is attentive, and wandering musicians provide entertainment.

★**Luz de Luna** INTERNATIONAL **$$**
(☎981-811-06-24; Calle 59 No 6; mains M$90-150; ⏲8am-10pm Mon-Sat) Carved, painted tables and folksy decor add a creative atmosphere to this popular restaurant on a pedestrian street. The menu choices are equally interesting – try the shrimp salad, chicken fajitas, flank steak or vegetarian burritos. There are plenty of breakfast options as well, especially omelettes.

El Bastión de Campeche MEXICAN **$$**
(Calle 57 No 24; mains M$100-180; ⏲6:30pm-midnight) Don't let the drab exterior fool you – this plazaside stalwart serves up some good Campechano dishes. Cool off with a chaya (spinachlike vegetable) juice before tucking in to a chicken breast stuffed with *cochinita pibil* – as delicious and decadent as it sounds.

La Pigua SEAFOOD **$$$**
(☎981-811-33-65; Miguel Alemán 179A; mains M$200-310; ⏲1-9pm) Some of Campeche's finest meals are served at this upscale restaurant in a downscale neighborhood. But never mind the location – just enjoy the attentive service and seafood dishes like

camarones al coco (coconut shrimp), whole fish in cilantro sauce and grilled squid with ground almonds and paprika.

Drinking & Entertainment

There's invariably someone performing on the Plaza Principal every Saturday and Sunday evening from around 6:30pm, be it a rock-and-roll band, pop-star impersonator, traditional dance troupe or a folk trio. On Sunday, the Banda del Estado (State Band) kicks off the program, performing Campeche classics, show music, marches and other rousing fare. The tourist office puts out a weekly events booklet.

For Campeche's hottest nightlife, head 1km south from the center along the *malecón* past the Torres de Cristal, where you'll find a cluster of bars, cafes and discos.

Chocol-Ha CAFE

(☎981-811-78-93; Calle 59 No 30; drinks M$20-40, snacks M$50-60; ⌚5:30-11pm Mon-Thu, to 12:30am Fri & Sat) When that chocolate craving hits, head on over to this cute little cafe with a patio in front and grassy yard in back. Drinks include bittersweet hot chocolate with green tea or chile, and a chocolate frappé. Sweet treats such as chocolate cake, chocolate crepes and even chocolate tamales are also available.

La Casa Vieja BAR

(Calle 10 No 319A; ⌚8:30am-12:30am) There's no better setting for an evening cocktail than La Casa Vieja's colonnaded balcony overlooking the Plaza Principal. Look for the stairs next to the McDonald's ice-cream counter.

Salón Rincón Colonial BAR

(Calle 59 No 60; ⌚10am-6pm) With ceiling fans high over an airy hall and a solid wood bar amply stocked with rum, this Cuban-style drinking establishment appropriately served as a location for *Original Sin*, a 2001 movie with Antonio Banderas that was set in Havana. The *botanas* (appetizers) are exceptionally fine, and check out the little covered patio in back.

Puerta de Tierra LIGHT SHOW

(adult/child 4-10 yr M$50/25; ⌚8pm Thu-Sun) Incidents from Campeche's pirate past are re-enacted several nights a week at the Puerta de Tierra. It's a cheesy extravaganza with lots of cannon blasts and flashing lights; audio guides come in four languages.

Shopping

Bazar Artesanal HANDICRAFTS

(Plaza Ah Kim Pech; ⌚10am-8pm) The state-run Folk Art Bazaar, down by the *malecón* near the Centro de Convenciones Campeche XXI, offers one-stop shopping for regional crafts. One section of the market is reserved for demonstrations of traditional craft techniques.

Casa de Artesanías Tukulna HANDICRAFTS

(☎981-816-21-88; Calle 10 No 33; ⌚8:30am-8pm Mon-Sat) A central shop selling textiles, clothing, hats, hammocks, wood chairs, sweets and so on – all made in Campeche state.

LA LOTERÍA

'Twenty-three, *melónes*' (melons)...'47, *volcán*' (volcano)...'41, *mecedora*' (rocking chair)...'78, *rosa*' (rose)...'two, *paloma*' (dove).

It's Saturday night in Campeche, and the tables in front of the cathedral are already full for the ritual game of *la lotería*, held every Saturday and Sunday evening from 6pm to 11pm. The litany of icons is chanted through a microphone by a woman in a *huipil* (colorfully embroidered tunic), as she picks up numbered balls from the spinner cage and places them on a panel of 90 pictures.

A bingolike game of European origin that uses numbered images, *la lotería* has been played on the peninsula since the 19th century. John L Stephens' *Incidents of Travel in Yucatan* has a good description of the game as he observed it at a fiesta in Mérida in 1841. The action now may not be as heated as he describes, but some folks can get pretty excited when they finish a row.

At a peso per card, most anyone can afford to play. Players usually mark the images on their cards with bottle caps. A variation on bingo is that markers can be placed in a variety of patterns: in addition to the usual rows, players can arrange their five markers in the form of a 'V,' a pair of scissors, or several kinds of crosses. The first person to form one of these patterns takes the pot – and the bragging rights that come with it.

Information

Campeche has numerous banks with ATMs. For internet, there are several 'cybers' in the city center.

Central Post Office (cnr Av 16 de Septiembre & Calle 53; ⌚8:30am-4pm Mon-Fri, 8-11:30am Sat)

Cruz Roja (Red Cross; ☎981-815-24-11; cnr Av Las Palmas & Ah Kim Pech) Medical services; some 3km northeast of downtown.

Dirección de Turismo (☎981-811-39-89; Calle 55 No 3; ⌚8am-9pm Mon-Fri, 9am-9pm Sat & Sun) Basic information on Campeche city.

Emergency (☎066)

Hospital Dr Manuel Campos (☎981-811-17-09; Av Circuito Baluartes Nte, btwn Calles 14 & 16)

HSBC Bank (Calle 10 btwn Calles 53 & 55; ⌚9am-5pm Mon-Fri, 9am-3pm Sat) Campeche's only bank that is open Saturday.

Secretaría de Turismo (☎981-127-33-00; www.campeche.travel; Plaza Moch-Couoh; ⌚8am-9pm Mon-Fri, to 8pm Sat & Sun) Good information on the city and Campeche state.

Getting There & Away

AIR

Campeche's small but modern airport is 6km southeast of the center; it has a tourist office, car-rental offices and a tiny coffeeshop/snack bar. **Aeroméxico** (☎800-021-40-10; www.aeromexico.com) provides services.

BUS

Campeche's **main bus terminal** (☎981-811-99-10; Av Patricio Trueba 237), usually called the ADO or 1st-class terminal, is about 2.5km south of Plaza Principal via Av Central. Buses provide 1st-class services to destinations around the country, along with 2nd-class services to Sabancuy (M$102, two hours), Hecelchakán (M$62, one hour) and Candelaria (M$188, four hours).

The **2nd-class terminal** (☎981-811-99-10; Av Gobernadores 289), often referred to as the 'old ADO' station, is 600m east of the Mercado Principal. Second-class destinations include Bolonchén de Rejón (M$82, two hours), Hopelchén (M$62, 1½ hours), Bolonchén (M$81, two hours), Xpujil (M$193, four hours) and Bécal (M$61, 1¾ hours).

To get to the main bus terminal, catch any 'Las Flores,' 'Solidaridad' or 'Casa de Justicia' bus by the post office. To the 2nd-class terminal, catch a 'Terminal Sur' bus from the same point.

CAR

If you're arriving in Campeche from the south, via the *cuota* (toll road), turn left at the roundabout signed for the *universidad* and follow that road straight to the coast, then go north.

If you're heading to either Edzná, the long route to Mérida or the fast toll road going south, take Calle 61 to Av Central and follow signs for the airport and either Edzná or the *cuota*. For the non-toll route south, just head down the *malecón*. For the short route to Mérida go north on the *malecón*.

In addition to some outlets at the airport, several car-rental agencies can be found downtown including **Easy Way** (☎981-811-22-36; www.campechecarrental.com; Calle 59, btwn Calles 8 & 10; ⌚8:30am-9:30pm Mon-Sat). Rates run from M$680 per day.

Getting Around

Taxis from the airport to the center cost M$150 (shared taxis M$60 per person); buy tickets at the taxi booth inside the terminal. Going to the airport, some street taxis (ie not called from your hotel, which are more expensive) charge 'only' M$120; penny-pinchers can try taking the hourly bus to Chiná (a village outside Campeche; M$10) from the market, and getting off at the airport entrance, then walking 500m to the airport doors.

Within Campeche city, taxis charge M$30 to M$60; prices are 10% more after 10pm, and 20% more from midnight to 5am.

BUSES FROM CAMPECHE

DESTINATION	FARE (M$)	DURATION (HRS)	FREQUENCY (DAILY)
Cancún	578-698	7	7
Chetumal	440	6½	1-2
Ciudad del Carmen	192-300	3	hourly
Mérida	200-254	2½	hourly
Mérida (via Uxmal)	150-195	4½	5 from 2nd-class terminal
Mexico City	1444-1742	18	3
Palenque	384	5	5
San Cristóbal de las Casas	548	10	1 at 10.15pm
Villahermosa	356-572	6	every 2 hrs
Xpujil	314	5	2pm

Most local buses (M$6) have a stop at or near the Mercado Principal.

Consider pedaling along the *malecón*; get bike rentals at **Kankabi' Ok** (p208).

Drivers should note that even numbered streets in the *centro histórico* take priority, as indicated by the red (stop) or black (go) arrows at every intersection.

NORTH OF CAMPECHE

The northeast corner of Campeche state is rarely visited by foreigners, but Mexicans love it for the good food, traditional customs and laid-back rural charm.

Hecelchakán

996 / POP 10,300

Bicycle taxis with canvas canopies noiselessly navigate the tranquil central plazas of Hecelchakán, a pleasant town 60km northeast of Campeche known for its culinary pleasures and an excellent small museum. Hecelchakán's inhabitants, who include a Mennonite community, are primarily devoted to agriculture.

Sights

Iglesia de San Francisco de Asis CHURCH

Dating from the 16th century, the Iglesia de San Francisco de Asis (on the main plaza) is a former Franciscan monastery with woodbeam ceiling and striking altar; note the flaming hearts flanking a crucifix.

Museo Arqueológico del Camino Real MUSEUM

(Calle 18 s/n; admission M$37; 8.30am-5.30pm Tue-Sat) This museum, on the north corner of the plaza, contains a small but compelling collection of ceramic art excavated from Isla de Jaina, a tiny island due west of Hecelchakán that flourished as a commercial center during the 7th century. Portraying ballplayers, weavers, warriors and priests, the extraordinary figurines on display here paint a vivid portrait of ancient Maya life. There's also a collection of stelae in the courtyard. Look for the entrance to the left of the church and at the end of the yellow building.

Sleeping & Eating

Campechanos sometimes visit Hecelchakán just for its famous snacks. From 6am to 10am (!), outside the church, little pavilions serve up *cochinita pibil* (barbecued suckling pig wrapped in banana leaves) and *relleno negro* (turkey stuffed with chopped pork and laced with a rich, dark chili sauce) in tacos or baguettes, along with *horchata* (a rice-based drink) and *agua de cebada* (a barley beverage served with a spoon).

Hotel Margarita HOTEL $

(996-827-04-72; Calle 20 No 80; s/d with fan M$180-220, s/d with air-con M$280-320;) On the main drag about 200m from the plaza (look for the green building) is Hotel Margarita, a very basic place with budget rooms that are good enough for a night.

Chujuc Haa MEXICAN $

(996-827-07-07; Calle 20 s/n; mains M$65-80; 7am-midnight Mon-Sat, 11am-midnight Sun) This popular restaurant serves regional cuisine like *poc-chuc,* a flat but flavorful steak that comes with rice, beans and salad. A half order is plenty. Located four doors left of the ADO/ATS bus office.

Information

For tourist information there's the **Dirección de Turismo** (8am-3pm Mon-Fri, 9am-1pm Sat), in a building across from the ADO/ATS bus office and near the plaza. Head up the stairs just left of the Telecom office and it's the first door on your left.

Getting There & Away

The ADO/ATS bus office is across from the post office and just south of the plaza on Calle Principal. ATS buses from Campeche's 2nd-class terminal stop here en route to Mérida every half-hour till around 10pm (M$38 to M$62, one hour). In addition, frequent combis (M$32, one hour) shuttle passengers between Campeche's Mercado Principal (look for the 'El Cubano' sign) and Hecelchakán's plaza.

Bécal

POP 6500

Bécal, about 90km north of Campeche just before you enter the state of Yucatán, is a center of the Yucatán panama hat trade. Some inhabitants here make their living weaving *jipijapas,* as the soft, pliable hats are known locally. The finest hats are destined for export to connoisseurs in foreign cities. The tranquil town clearly identifies with its stock in trade, as is made obvious by the centerpiece of its plaza.

DISCOVER THE ROOTS OF THE JIPIJAPA HAT

While on the surface Bécal may look like a somnolent *campechano* town, underground are people laboring away at the traditional craft of hat making. Called *jipijapas* (or *jipis* for short), these soft, pliable hats have been woven by townsfolk from the fibers of the *huano* palm tree since the mid-19th century, when the plants were imported from Guatemala by a Catholic priest.

The stalk of the plant is cut into strands to make the fibers; the quality of the hat depends on the fineness of the cut. The work is done in humid limestone caves that provide just the right atmosphere for shaping the fibers, keeping them moist and pliable. These caves – often no bigger than a bedroom – are reached by a hole in the ground in someone's backyard. Once exposed to the relatively dry air outside, the panama hat is surprisingly resilient and resistant to crushing.

Today, Bécal's hat-making art is a dying industry due to cheap global competition. So if you want to shade your head in style while supporting a worthy cause, buy a handmade *jipi*. Prices range from around M$200 for coarsely woven hats made in a couple days, to nearly M$3000 for the finest hats that can take months to complete.

To find out where *jipijapas* are crafted and sold in town, hail a bicycle taxi (M$12) on Bécal's plaza and ask the rider for his recommendation. You'll likely be approached by a young guide (perhaps on a bicycle) - some who work on donation. A half-block from the plaza, on the road into town, is **Artesania Becaleña** (996-431-40-46; Calle 30 No 210; 8am-10pm), one of several shops where you can check out some hats.

In April the Fiesta de Flor del Jipi is celebrated with dancing and bullfights.

From Campeche's 2nd-class bus terminal, ATS buses bound for Mérida stop in Bécal's main plaza every half-hour (M$55, two hours).

EAST OF CAMPECHE

Along with a quaint town, there are plenty of archaeological destinations in this region. The Chenes sites are best visited with a private vehicle, though Edzná is easily reached by combi.

Hopelchén

996 / POP 7500

The municipal center for the Chenes region, Hopelchén (Maya for 'Place of the Five Wells') makes a pleasant base for visiting the various archaeological sites in the vicinity while also providing a glimpse of everyday life in a small Campeche town.

The **tourist information office** (Calle 20; 8am-3pm Mon-Sat) is in the Casa de Cultura, two blocks north of the main plaza.

On a typical morning here, Maya *campesinos* (agricultural workers) and Mennonites congregate under box-shaped laurels as bicycle taxis glide past. Opposite the central plaza, the 16th-century **Parroquia de San Antonio de Padua** church features an intricate *retablo* (altarpiece), with a gallery of saints and angels amid lavishly carved pillars.

Herbalists, midwives and shamans practice traditional Maya medicine at the **Consejo Local de Médicos Indígenas** (Colmich, Calle 8; 8am-5pm Tue & Thu), five blocks east of the plaza.

Hotel Los Arcos (996-822-01-23; Calle 23 s/n; s/d M$220/280;), at the plaza, is a convenient, no-frills option with an attached restaurant. The rooms are clean (though TV is an extra M$100) and have hammock hooks for sleeping extra people or just general hanging around.

For a good *caldo de pollo* (chicken soup), try the stalls on Plaza Chica, which are open from 7am to 3pm and 5pm to midnight.

Getting There & Away

Combis (located on the main road a half block toward the center from Campeche's 2nd-class bus terminal) run every half-hour from Campeche (M$60, 1½ hours) to Hopelchén's plaza, stopping at villages along the way.

Hopelchén's bus terminal is at the market on Calle 16 between Calles 17 and 19, behind the church. Get tickets at the first *'antojitos regionales'* counter you see. There are buses to Campeche (M$65, 1½ hours, hourly) and Mérida (M$102, two hours, six services).

Around Hopelchén

Tohcok (8am-5pm; spelled Tacob on signs) FREE is 3.5km northwest of Hopelchén. Of the 40-odd structures found at this Maya site, the only one that has been significantly excavated displays features of the Puuc and Chenes styles. The talkative custodian, Pepe, can point out a *chultún* (Maya underground cistern), one of around 45 in the zone.

You can walk to Tohcok from Hopelchén along the main 'highway', but there are also half-hourly white vans (marked 'Transporte Escolares'; M$7) that leave from the plaza and take kids to a nearby school; from here it's only a few hundred meters to the ruins.

The **Grutas de X'tacumbilxuna'an** (admission M$65; 10am-5pm Tue-Sun;), some of the most significant caves in the peninsula, are found 31km north of Hopelchén, shortly before you reach the town of Bolonchén de Rejón. The local Maya have long known of the existence of the Grutas de X'tacumbilxuna'an, a series of underground cenotes in this water-scarce region. In 1844 the caves were 'discovered' by the intrepid John L Stephens and Frederick Catherwood, who depicted the Maya descending an incredibly high rope-and log staircase to replenish their water supply.

Today the cenote is dry but X'tacumbilxuna'an (*shtaa*-koom-beel-shoo-*nahn*) is open for exploration and admiration of the vast caverns and incredible limestone formations within. A light-and-sound extravaganza accompanies the tour, and you can hear the sounds of motmots echoing off the walls as you descend.

Buses traveling between Hopelchén and Mérida will drop you at the cave entrance before Bolonchén (M$25, 25 minutes). In addition, combis depart for Bolonchén from Hopelchén's plaza, passing near the caves. Check with the driver for return times.

Chenes Sites

Northeastern Campeche state is dotted with more than 30 sites in the distinct Chenes style, recognizable by the monster motifs around doorways in the center of long, low buildings of three sections, and temples atop pyramidal bases. Most of the year you'll have these sites to yourself. The three small sites of El Tabasqueño, Hochob and Dzibilnocac make for an interesting single-day trip from Campeche if you have your own vehicle (or you can take a tour from Campeche with Kankabi' Ok Tours, p208).

El Tabasqueño ARCHAEOLOGICAL SITE

(8am-5pm) FREE Supposedly named after a local landowner from Tabasco, El Tabasqueño boasts a temple-palace (Estructura 1) with a striking monster-mouth doorway, flanked by stacks of eight Chac masks with hooked snouts. Estructura 2 is a solid free-standing tower, an oddity in Maya architecture. To reach El Tabasqueño, go 30km south from Hopelchén. Just beyond the village of Pakchén, there's an easy-to-miss sign at a turnoff on the right; follow this rock-and-gravel road 2km to the site.

Hochob ARCHAEOLOGICAL SITE

(admission M$36; 8am-5pm) About 60km south of Hopelchén, Hochob, 'the place where corn is harvested,' is among the most beautiful and terrifying of the Chenes-style sites. The Palacio Principal (Estructura 2, though signposted as 'Estructura 1') is on the north side of the main plaza, faced with an elaborate doorway representing Itzamná, creator of the ancient Maya, as a rattlesnake with open jaws. Facing it across the plaza, Estructura 5 has two raised temples on either end of a long series of rooms; the better preserved eastern temple retains part of its perforated roofcomb.

To reach Hochob, go 5km south from El Tabasqueño, then turn right just before the Pemex station at Dzilbalchén. Now go 7.5km to the Chencoh sign, turn left, then after 400m go left again. Drive another 3.5km to Hochob.

Dzibilnocac ARCHAEOLOGICAL SITE

(8am-5pm) FREE Though it only has one significant structure, Dzibilnocac possesses an eerie grandeur that merits a visit. Unlike the many hilltop sites chosen for Chenes structures, Dzibilnocac ('big painted turtle' is one translation) is on a flat plain, like a large open park. As Stephens and Catherwood observed back in 1842, the many scattered hillocks in the zone, still unexcavated today, attest to the presence of a large city.

The single, clearly discernible structure is A1, a palatial complex upon a 76m platform with a trio of raised temples atop rounded pyramidal bases. The best preserved of the three, on the east end, has fantastically elaborate monster-mask reliefs on each of its four sides and the typically piled-up Chac masks on three of the four corners.

Dzibilnocac is located beside the village of Iturbide (also called Vicente Guerrero), 20km northeast of Dzibalchén. From Campeche's 2nd-class bus terminal there are several buses daily to Iturbide via Hopelchén (M$86, three hours). There's no place to stay here so you'll need to make it back to Hopelchén by nightfall.

Edzná

If you only have the time or inclination to visit one archaeological site in northern Campeche, **Edzná** (admission M$48; ⏲8am-5pm) should be your top pick. It's located about 60km southeast of Campeche.

Edzná's massive complexes were built by a highly stratified society that flourished from about 600 BC to the dawn of the colonial era. During that period the people of Edzná built more than 20 complexes in a mélange of architectural styles, installing an ingenious network of water-collection and irrigation systems.

After its demise in the 15th century, the site remained unknown until its rediscovery by *campesinos* in 1906.

Edzná means 'House of the Itzá,' a reference to a predominant governing clan of Chontal Maya origin. Edzná's rulers recorded significant events on stone stelae. Around 30 stelae have been discovered adorning the site's principal temples; a handful are on display underneath a *palapa* just beyond the ticket office.

A path from the *palapa* leads about 400m through vegetation; follow the 'Gran Acropolis' sign. Soon, to your left, you'll come upon the **Plataforma de los Cuchillos** (Platform of the Knives), a residential complex highlighted by Puuc architectural features. The name is derived from an of-

Edzná

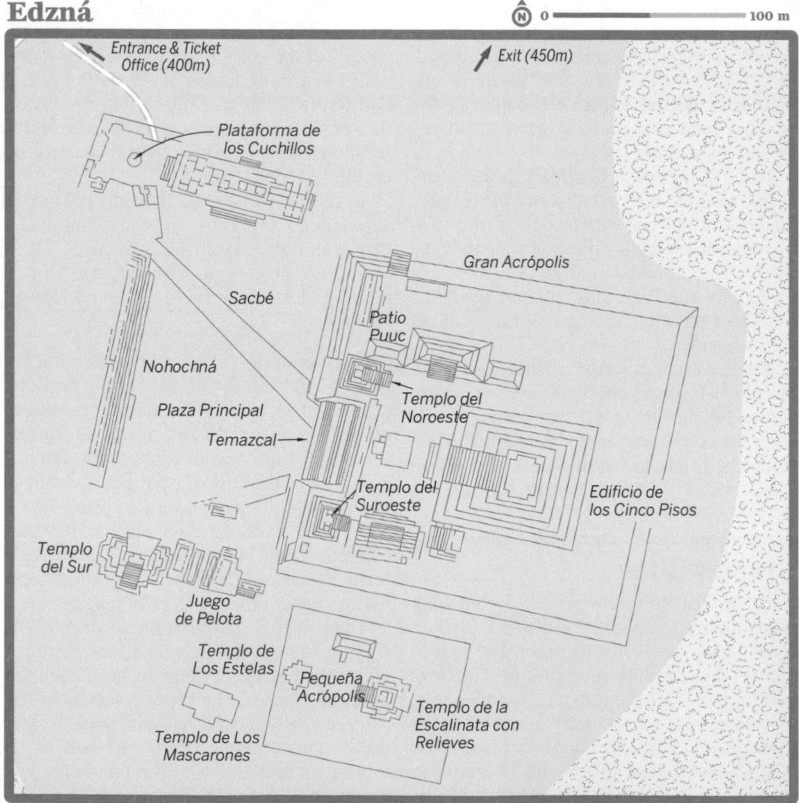

fering of silica knives that had been found within.

Crossing a *sacbé* (stone-lined, grass walkway), you arrive at the main attraction, the **Plaza Principal**. Measuring 160m long and 100m wide, the Plaza Principal is surrounded by temples. On your right is the **Nohochná** (Big House), a massive, elongated structure topped by four long halls likely used for administrative tasks, such as the collection of tributes and the dispensation of justice.

Across the plaza is the Gran Acrópolis, a raised platform holding several structures, including Edzná's major temple, the 31m-high **Edificio de los Cinco Pisos** (Five-Story Building). The current structure is the last of four remodels and was done primarily in the Puuc style. It rises five levels from its base to the roofcomb and contains many vaulted rooms. Note the well-preserved glyphs along the base of the central staircase.

South of Plaza Principal is the **Templo de los Mascarones** (Temple of the Masks), with a pair of reddish stucco masks underneath a protective *palapa*. Personifying the gods of the rising and setting sun, these extraordinarily well-preserved faces display dental mutilation, crossed eyes and huge earrings, features associated with the Maya aristocracy.

There's a fairly tasteful **sound-and-light show** (admission M$125; ⌚8pm Thu-Sun Apr to Oct, 7pm Nov to Mar) which can be cancelled in case of heavy rains. Get here a half-hour early to get good seats. Shows are daily during popular times such as Mexican holidays; contact Campeche's tourist office (p212) for details.

There are minimal services near Edzná, which is an easy day trip from Campeche. If you have the pesos, check out **Hacienda Uayamon** (☎981-813-05-30; www.haciendauayamon.com; Carr Uayamon-China-Edzna Km 20; rooms from M$4900; ❄📶🏊).

ℹ Getting There & Away

Combis (M$40, one hour) leave when full from Calle Chihuahua near Campeche's Mercado Principal. Most drop you 200m from the site entrance unless the driver is feeling generous. The last combi back is around 4pm, but ask the driver to make sure!

Kankabi' Ok (p208) in Campeche provides guided tours of Edzná (including transport) for M$820 per person.

SOUTHWESTERN COAST

This sparsely developed stretch of seafront is fringed with usually deserted beaches that are ideal for watching pelicans, going on shell-searching expeditions and taking an occasional dip in the shallow aquamarine waters. Heading south from Campeche, the coastal highway passes through the city of Champotón, along with small fishing towns and spots like Playa Varadero, where you can stop for a cold beer and hang your hammock in a thatched shelter. Then you'll hit Laguna de Términos, a vast mangrove-fringed lagoon home to riots of migratory birds and a prime sea-turtle nesting spot. After all this, the noise and bustle of Ciudad del Carmen will seem like a culture shock.

Champotón

POP 31,000

Champotón, at the mouth of the river of the same name, has great historical significance as the landing place of the first Spanish exploratory expedition from Cuba, led by Francisco Hernández de Córdoba, in 1517. Probably seeking a source of water along the river, the Spaniards were assailed by warriors under the command of the *cacique* Moch Couoh, forcing them to retreat. Hernández de Córdoba died shortly after his return to Cuba from wounds he received at Champotón, which from then on was known as the 'Bahía de la Mala Pelea' (Bay of the Bad Fight).

Now a pleasant enough city between Ciudad del Carmen and Campeche, Champotón sustains itself mainly on fishing, and perhaps the best reason to stop is to sample its abundant seafood. Try **Pelicano's** (Av Carlos Sansores Pérez , btwn Calles 11 & 13; mains M$90-160; ⌚8am-8pm), a clean, modern and family-friendly restaurant on the coastal road about 2km south of the colorful market (which also has cheap seafood eateries). There are also several *coctelerías* (seafood shacks, specializing in shellfish cocktails) under thatched roofs about 4.5km north of town, along the beach. If you want to stay overnight, head to **Posada La Regia** (☎982-828-15-52; Carretera Champoton-Isla Aguada 443; r from M$627; ❄📶), a good-value family-run setup with clean rooms and a pool; they also organize bird- and crocodile-watching river trips to a nearby mangrove.

The bus terminal is easy to find – it's on the coastal road into town, next to the market at the mouth of the river. Destinations include

Campeche (M$65 to M$88, one hour), Sabancuy (M$88, one hour), Ciudad del Carmen (M$144 to M$180, two hours) and Xpujil (M$250, four hours). From Campeche, frequent combis (M$40, 45 minutes) leave for Champotón from Av República near the Mercado Principal. If you're driving, note that two roads head south from Campeche to Champotón: a meandering coastal route (free) and a direct toll road (M$68).

Sabancuy

POP 7500

Sabancuy is a picturesque fishing town on the lower side of an estuary that branches off the northeastern end of Laguna de Términos. It's located 2km inland, connected via land bridge to the coast highway, where there's a **state tourist office** (⌚9am-4pm Mon-Fri, 9am-1pm Sat).

The beaches around Sabancuy are major nesting grounds for hawksbill and green sea turtles. Workers from a local university program called **Campamento Tortuguero La Escollera** (www.unacar.mx/psabancuy/tortuguero_campamento.html) gather up eggs from nests during the season, moving them to protected areas until they hatch. If you're here from April to October (peak season June to August), you can take part in liberating baby sea turtles; over 100,000 hatchlings are set free annually. To find out more about this free program, check out the website and contact **Alfonso Díaz Molina** (☎cell 938-1522883; amolina@pampano.unacar.mx), the program director who works at Escuela Preparatoria, which is at the edge of town.

Those really into crumbly buildings can visit the **ex-Hacienda de Tixchel**, 15km from town. This old cattle ranch and sugar plantation is from the late colonial period, constructed by the Spanish from nearby Maya ruins. The easiest way to get here is by boat (M$1350 for up to six people); ask for Marcos at a beach *palapa* just north of the state tourist office. **Dr José de Jesús Ambrosio Reyes** (☎982-825-01-28), who works at the Farmacia de Jesús, one block up from the plaza on the right side of the church, might also have information.

There's a cheap hotel next to the bus terminal, but for more comfortable accommodations walk to **Hotel Sabancuy Plaza** (☎982-825-00-81; hotelsabancuyplaza@hotmail.com; Calle Hidalgo s/n; r with fan/aircon M$280/400, ste M$710; P ❄), just a block west of the plaza. For good seafood with seaside setting, head to **Viaducto Playa** (☎982-731-55-74; Km 77.5; mains M$100-160; ⌚8am-8pm), on the beach about 500m south of the land bridge (mototaxi M$35).

The bus terminal is right on the village's cute little waterfront plaza, and there are a couple of ATMs nearby. Bus destinations include Campeche (M$128 to M$158, two hours), Champotón (M$47 to M$68, one hour), Isla Aguada (M$25, 30 minutes) and Ciudad del Carmen (M$66 to M$106, 1¼ hours). Folks get around via mototaxis; rides around town cost M$10.

Isla Aguada

Isla Aguada is a large fishing town, but not quite an island as its name implies. It's known for its pretty lighthouse, which is over 100 years old and was recently restored into a museum. Also popular here are boat tours. The standard excursion stops at **Isla de Pájaros**, where thousands of herons, gulls and magnificent frigate birds converge at sunset. You're almost guaranteed to see dolphins along the way, and most trips end with a cruise through the mangroves for more wildlife-spotting. Morning and dusk are the best times to take these trips, most of which run from April to July. One boat operator is **El Rey de Los Delfines** (☎938-400-62-85; Zapata s/n), which leaves from the muelle turístico (tourist dock); you can also inquire at the Comisaría near Parque Benito Juárez. A two-hour excursion for up to eight people costs around M$1200.

If you want to stick around, **Hotel Playa Punta Perla** (☎cell 938-1064955; r M$480; ❄ ≋ 👪) has plain rooms and could use a little upkeep – but at least it has a pool and is right at the beach.

Relatively frequent combis and buses connect Isla Aguada with nearby Sabancuy (M$25, 30 minutes) and Ciudad del Carmen (M$29, 40 minutes). If you're driving, the 3.2km Puente La Unidad (M$65 toll) spans the strait towards Ciudad del Carmen, 46km further west.

Laguna de Términos

The largest lagoon in the Gulf of Mexico area, the Laguna de Términos comprises a network of estuaries, swamps and ponds that together form a uniquely important coastal habitat.

Red, white and black mangroves fringe the lagoon, and the area is an important

TRADITIONAL HARVEST: THE SWEET HISTORY OF MAYA HONEY

The Yucatán's flowers yield a sweet, mollifluous harvest, and bees have held an exalted place throughout its honeyed history. Records show that at the time of the conquest, the Maya produced vast amounts of honey and Yucatecan villages paid tribute to the Spanish in honey, which was valued more for its curative properties than as a sweetener. Bees were important in the Maya pantheon: bee motifs appear in the surviving Maya codices, and the image of Ah Mucenkab, god of bees, is carved into the friezes of Chichén Itzá, Tulum and Sayil.

Mexico remains the world's number-four producer of honey, and the nectar of the Yucatán is especially coveted for its blend of flavors and aromas, a result of the diversity of the region's flowers. Many *campesinos* (agricultural workers) keep bees to supplement their agricultural output. However, the stingless variety known to the ancient Maya has long since been supplanted by European bees, which in turn are being pushed aside by the more aggressive African bees, notorious among handlers for their nasty sting.

Koolel Kab (Women Who Work With Bees; ☎996-822-00-73; www.koolelkab.wordpress.com; Domicilio Conocido s/n) is a Maya women's cooperative in the village of Ich-Ek, near Hopelchén that wants to preserve the ancient heritage. They produce honey with indigenous *melipona* bees, which take up residence in hollow trees. Using techniques much like those of their ancestors, the women place sections of tree trunk under a shelter, capping each end of the trunk with mud. An average trunk yields 12L of honey, which is marketed chiefly for its medicinal properties as throat lozenges, eye drops, soaps and skin creams. If you're in the area you can pay Koolel Kab a visit, and buy honey, soaps and farm produce from their small store.

nesting ground for several species of marine turtle and numerous migratory birds. As well as encompassing wildlife habitat, the Laguna de Términos is home to the state's second-largest city and Mexico's principal oil-production center. The lagoon's ecosystem remains threatened by various environmental dangers – including oil spills and overfishing – despite being designated a Flora and Fauna Protected Area in 1994.

Hemmed in by a narrow strip of land that is traversed by Hwy 180, the lagoon can be explored from various points along the way.

Ciudad del Carmen

☎938 / POP 170,000

Campeche state's second-biggest city occupies the western end of a 40km-long, narrow island between the Gulf of Mexico and the Laguna de Términos. Ciudad del Carmen was once dependent on jumbo shrimp, dyewood and chicle (gum) for its livelihood, but in the late 1970s oil was discovered. Investment poured in and the population swelled. The 3.8km Puente Zacatal (Zacatal Bridge) was completed in 1994, linking the city with the rest of Mexico; unfortunately most of the city's streets remained narrow, and horrific traffic jams are now a daily part of life.

Sights & Activities

Parque Zaragoza SQUARE

(Central Plaza) Parque Zaragoza has a handsome 19th-century kiosk and is one the city's most pleasant areas to hang out, especially in the evenings. On its north side is the 1856 **Santuario de la Virgen del Carmen**, which pays homage to the patron saint of sailors. Vestiges of Carmen's earlier prosperity remain in the *centro histórico,* where chicle barons' 19th-century mansions run along Calles 22 and 24, south of the plaza.

Museo Victoriano Nieves MUSEUM

(cnr Calles 22 & 41; adult/child M$5/2.50; ⏰8am-8pm Mon-Fri, 9am-4pm Sat & Sun) The city's decent history museum is located in an interesting old hospital building. Inside are archaeological relics (including stelae from Xpujil), a petroleum exhibition and information on the region's pirate history – plus a kids pirate ship, complete with plank.

Playa Norte BEACH

Playa Norte, on the Gulf of Mexico, is Carmen's beach area. It's rather bleak-looking, with wide expanses of coarse sand, murky green water, parking areas and the occasional *palapa* restaurant. Development is coming fast, however, in the form of shiny new hotels, restaurants and other services.

To get here, take a bus from center marked 'Playa Norte' or 'zoológico'.

Festivals & Events

Ciudad del Carmen has a renowned and colorful **Carnaval** celebration, with locals wearing elaborate costumes and dancing in the streets for four days. Another exciting event is the **Fiesta de la Virgen del Carmen**, which kicks off two weeks of festivities on July 16, when the port's patron saint is taken on a cruise around the harbor. There are also many exhibits of art, culture and local industries.

Sleeping

Because of the oil industry, there aren't any real bargains in town.

Hotel Zacarías HOTEL $

(938-382-35-06; www.hotelzacarias.com; Calle 24 No 58; d with fan/air-con M$350/500;) Boasting a good, central location and basic, somewhat overpriced rooms, this is about as good as it gets for budget travelers here in oil town.

★**Hotel Las Villas** HOTEL $$

(938-382-99-16; Calle 28 No 116; s/d M$616/693;) The center's best hotel, with just 10 spacious, modern and tasteful rooms surrounding a leafy patio area. It's a peaceful little paradise in a bustling city; room 10 has its own spiral staircase. Look for it just behind the plaza's church.

Hacienda Real HOTEL $$$

(938-381-17-00; www.hotelhaciendareal.com.mx; Calle 31 No 106; r from M$1620;) Big and brassy, the Hacienda lays it all out with king-sized beds, a top-notch restaurant, great balcony views and a surprisingly tasteful mosaic-inlaid pool.

Eating

El Último Recurso MEXICAN $

(Calle 28 No 118; set lunch M$50; 7am-9pm) Located behind the central plaza's church, this no-frills lunch hall has daily stick-to-your-ribs specials, such as chicken in green sauce (Mondays) and pork in *adobo* (Thursdays).

★**La Fuente** MEXICAN $$

(Calle 20 No 203; snacks M$45-60, mains M$80-150; 7am-midnight;) This classic, open-fronted waterfront cafe is a busy gathering place for families and friends. It's an excellent spot to sample treats such as *pibipollo* (chicken tamales traditionally cooked underground) and *arrachera encebollado* (marinated flank steak with onions and chilies). Don't come starving – the food tends to take a while. On the upside, there are some play structures nearby that should keep the kids happy for a while.

Callejón 6 MEXICAN $$

(Calle 27 No 6; mains M$100-210; 5pm-1am) There's always something going on at this bar/restaurant: live *trova* music Thursdays to Saturdays, random performers and DJs other nights and, if all else fails, football on the big screen. The food's fairly standard Mexican seafood but the atmosphere makes the place.

Information

There are banks with ATMs near the plaza.

The **Municipal Tourist Office** (938-286-09-54; Calle 20 s/n, cnr Calle 31; 8am-4pm Mon-Fri) is inside the city hall with a few brochures.

Getting There & Away

Interjet (866-285-95-25; www.interjet.com.mx) has daily flights to/from Mexico City.

Both 1st-class ADO and 2nd-class Sur buses use Ciudad del Carmen's modern **bus terminal** (Av Periférico s/n), a 15-minute drive east of the main plaza. A *taxi-colectivo* (shared taxi) from the terminal to the plaza should cost M$25 (M$30 after 10pm). You can check schedules and buy tickets at the **ADO Ticket Office** (Calle 24) located next to the Hotel Zacarías. Destinations include Campeche (M$192 to M$216, three hours, hourly buses), Mérida (M$460 to M$512, five hours, hourly buses) and Villahermos (M$170 to M$252, three hours, every 45 minutes).

Combis run to/from Isla Aguada (M$30, 40 minutes); the stop is three blocks northeast of the plaza at the corner of Calles 32 and 35.

Atasta Peninsula

West of Ciudad del Carmen across the Puente Zacatal is the lush, tropical Atasta Peninsula. A scarcely visited ecological wonderland, it stretches along a thin strip between the Gulf and a network of small mangrove-fringed lagoons that feed into the Laguna de Términos. Various waterfront seafood shacks prepare crab and shrimp pulled out of the lagoon. **Atasta Mangle Tours** (938-286-70-26), in the village of Atasta, offers two-hour boat excursions for up to eight people for around M$2100 (Saturday and Sundays from 1pm to 5pm only). Howler monkeys, manatees and river turtles may be spotted along the journey through the estuarine waterway. They also rent two-person kayaks for M$120 per hour.

ESCÁRCEGA TO RÍO BEC

The southern peninsular region from Escárcega to Río Bec, which borders modern-day Guatemala, was the earliest established, longest inhabited and most densely populated region in the Maya world. Here you'll find the most elaborate archaeological sites on the Yucatán Peninsula.

Hwy 186 heads east across Campeche state, climbing gradually from the unappealing town of Escárcega to a broad, jungle plateau and then down to Chetumal, in Quintana Roo. The highway passes near several fascinating Maya sites including historically significant Calakmul and through the ecologically diverse Reserva de la Biosfera Calakmul. The largest settlement between Escárcega and Chetumal is the town of Xpujil, where there are three gas stations.

Calakmul and most of the other Maya sites in this area are best visited by private vehicle. If you're on public transport, plan on hiring taxis or taking a tour. Tour companies can be found in either Xpujil or Campeche (reserve tours ahead of time).

Among the region's archaeological sites, the Río Bec architectural style dominates. It is actually a hybrid of styles fusing elements from the Chenes region to the north and Petén to the south. Río Bec structures are characterized by long, low buildings divided into three sections, with a huge 'monster' mouth glaring from a central doorway. The facades are decorated with smaller masks and geometric designs. At each end are tall, smoothly rounded towers with banded tiers supporting small false temples flanked by extremely steep, nonfunctional steps.

Balamkú

'Discovered' only in 1990, **Balamkú** (Temple of the Jaguar; admission M$36; ⌚8am-5pm) boasts a remarkably ornate, stuccoed frieze that bears little resemblance to any of the known decorative elements in the Chenes or Río Bec styles. Well preserved, with traces of its original red paint, the frieze is a richly symbolic tableau that has been interpreted as showing the complementary relationship between our world and the underworld.

Along the base of the scene, stylized seated jaguars (referred to in the temple's Maya name) represent the earth's abundance. These figures alternate with several grotesque fanged masks, upon which stand amphibianlike creatures (toads or crocodiles?) that in turn support some royal personages with fantastically elaborate headdresses. Readers of Spanish can find more details in the explanatory diagrams that front the frieze.

The solid stone that hid the frieze for centuries has been replaced by a protective canopy with slit windows that let in a little light. The door is kept locked, but the site custodian will usually appear to open it and give you a tour (no flash photography allowed).

Balamkú is 91km east of Escárcega and 60km west of Xpujil (2km past the Calakmul turnoff), then about 3km north of the highway along a fissured road.

Calakmul

Possibly the largest city during Maya times, **Calakmul** (admission M$48, road maintance fee per car M$50 plus per person M$30, park fee M$56; ⌚8am-5pm) was 'discovered' in 1931 by American botanist Cyrus Lundell. The site bears comparison in size and historical significance to Tikal in Guatemala, its chief rival for hegemony over the southern lowlands during the Classic Maya era. It boasts the largest and tallest known pyramid in Yucatán, and was once home to over 50,000 people.

A central chunk of the 72-sq-km expanse has been restored, but most of the city's approximately 7000 structures lie covered in jungle. Exploration and restoration are ongoing, however, and occasionally something very special comes along. In 2004, amazingly well-preserved painted murals were discovered at the Chiik Naab acropolis of Estructura 1. They depicted something never before seen in Maya murals – the typical daily activities of ordinary Mayans (as opposed to the usual political, ceremonial or religious themes). A few years before that, a significant 20m-long, 4m high stucco frieze was uncovered at Estructura II, whose features seemed to mark a transition between Olmec and Maya architecture.

The murals and frieze are not currently open to the public, but hopefully will be in the years to come. Their reproductions can be seen at Calakmul's modern **Museo de Naturaleza y Arqueología** (⌚7am-3pm) FREE, at Km 20 on the 60km side road to Calakmul. This worthwhile museum also

OFF THE BEATEN TRACK

EL TIGRE & CENOTES MIGUEL COLORADO

Off Hwy 186, heading southwest from Escárcega, **El Tigre** (M$36; 8am-5pm) is one of Campeche's most recently uncovered Maya sites, El Tigre. Archaeologists are almost certain it is none other than Itzamkanac, the legendary capital of the Itzá. This is supposedly the place where Hernan Córtes executed Cuauhtémoc, the last Aztec ruler of Tenochtitlán.

Unlike other Campeche sites, El Tigre occupies a wetlands environment crisscrossed by rivers, with two excavated pyramids amid swaying palms and diverse birdlife. From Candelaria take the road towards Monclova; a short distance beyond the village of Estado de México is the turnoff to the site.

Cenotes Miguel Colorado (cell 982-1085669; village of Miguel Colorado; admission M$120; 8am-5pm) has two large scenic cenotes (limestone sinkholes). The price of admission includes kayak rental and a couple of very high zip-lines that go over one of cenotes. You can hike along hilly, rocky trails to each cenote, keeping an eye out for spider and howler monkeys. Swimming is currently not allowed but might be in the future; there may also be rappelling opportunities.

It's possible to visit a bat cave in the area and a lake called **Laguna de Mokú** (home to crocodiles), but you'll need a guide (M$30 extra for each).

To get to the cenotes, drive 60km south of Champotón on Hwy 261, then take a 10km potholed side road to the village of Miguel Colorado. Turn left at the village and go 3km more.

has geological, archaeological and natural-history exhibits.

Visiting Calakmul is not just a historical experience, it's also an ecological one. Lying at the heart of the vast, untrammeled **Reserva de la Biosfera Calakmul** (which covers close to 15% of the state's total territory), the ruins are surrounded by rainforest, with cedar, mahogany and rubber trees dotting a seemingly endless canopy of vegetation. While wandering amid the ruins, you might glimpse ocellated turkeys, parrots and toucans among the over 350 bird species that reside or fly through here. It's also possible to see or hear spider and howler monkeys, but much less likely to spot a jaguar - one of five kinds of wildcat in the area. There are also many other mammal, reptile and amphibian species that call this biosphere home. Animals are most active during the mornings and evenings.

Calakmul is 60km south of Hwy 186 at the end of a good paved road (the turnoff is 56km west of Xpujil). Give yourself at least a full day (or two) not only to get to Calakmul, but also to visit the extensive ruins - both driving and walking distances are great. Just the 60km side road in from Hwy 186 to the ruins takes an hour. For an online map of the ruins, see http://mayaruins.com/calakmul/calakmul_map.html.

History

From about AD 250 to 695, Calakmul was the leading city in a vast region known as the Kingdom of the Serpent's Head. Its decline began with the power struggles and internal conflicts that followed the defeat of Calakmul's King Garra de Jaguar (Jaguar Claw) by Tikal. Calakmul flourished again in the late Classic period by forming alliances with the Río Bec powers to the north.

As at Tikal, there are indications that construction occurred over a period of more than a millennium. Beneath Edificio VII, archaeologists discovered a burial crypt with some 2000 pieces of jade, and tombs continue to yield spectacular jade burial masks; some of these objects are on display in Campeche city's Fuerte de San Miguel (p206). The cleared area of Calakmul holds at least 120 carved stelae, the oldest dating from 435 BC, registering key events such as the ascent to power of kings and the outcome of conflicts with rival states.

Sights

It's about a 1km walk through the woods to the ruins from the ticket booth at the end of the road. Arrows point out three suggested walks - a long, medium and short route. The short route leads straight to the Gran Plaza; the long route directs you through the Gran Acrópolis before sending you to the main attractions.

The **Gran Plaza**, with loads of stelae in front of its buildings (Estructura V has the best ones), makes a good first stop.

Estructura II ARCHAEOLOGICAL SITE

Climbing the enormous Estructura II, at the south side of the Gran Plaza, is a must. Each of this pyramid's sides is 140m long, giving it a footprint of just under 2 hectares – the largest and tallest known Maya structure. After a good climb you'll come to what appears to be the top of the building, but go around to the left to reach the real apex.

From here, 45m above the forest floor, you'll have magnificent views of Estructura I to the southeast and Estructura VII to the north – as well as jungle canopy as far as you can see. Facing southwest, you'll be looking toward the Maya city El Mirador, in neighboring Guatemala, and with the aid of binoculars you may be able to spot that site's towering El Tigre pyramid.

Estructura III ARCHAEOLOGICAL SITE

A path on the left (east) side of Estructura II leads past the palatial Estructura III, with a dozen rooms atop a raised platform. Archaeologists found a tomb inside the 5th-century structure that contained the body of a male ruler of Calakmul surrounded by offerings of jade, ceramics and shell beads. He was wearing not one but three jade mosaic masks – one each on his face, chest and belt.

Estructura I ARCHAEOLOGICAL SITE

Walking south from Estructura III you come to Estructura I, Calakmul's second great pyramid, which is nearly as big as Estructura II. (American botanist Cyrus Lundell named the site Calakmul, Maya for 'two adjacent mounds,' in reference to the pair of then-unexcavated pyramids that dominated the site.) The steep climb pays off handsomely with top-of-the-world views.

Gran Acrópolis ARCHAEOLOGICAL SITE

A trail leading west from Estructura I around the back of Estructura II takes you to the Gran Acrópolis, a labyrinthine residential zone with a ceremonial sector containing a ball court. From the northern perimeter of this zone, you head east and follow the path back to the entrance.

Tours

Ka'an Expeditions and Campeche's **Xtampak Tours** (981-811-64 73; Calle 57 No 14; 8am-8pm Mon-Sat, to 2pm Sun) run tours to Calakmul. Río Bec Dreams (p224) offers tours by native English speakers, but these are only available to their guests. You can also hire a taxi from Escárcega or Xpujil (M$900 to M$1000 with a three-hour wait).

Ka'an Expeditions TOUR

(983-871-60-00; www.kaanexpeditions.com; 4-hr tour per person M$400) Good tours by nature specialists. Book two days in advance for an English guide. Three people minimum; must have private vehicle. Tours leave from Calakmul's museum. If you don't have a private vehicle, eight-hour tours from Xpujil are available (M$990 per person); these include transport, food and entrance fees. It also does multiday tours of the region.

Sleeping & Eating

Bring food and drinks with you when visiting Calakmul – there are sandwiches and snacks sold at the museum, but no services at the site itself.

Comedor & Cabañas La Selva CABIN $

(983-733-87-06; Hwy 186 Km 95; campsite M$50, cabins M$300-600; restaurant 6am-10pm) A simple, friendly, open *palapa* restaurant (set meals M$90) with nearby grassy camping sites. Ask about its very basic and rustic *cabañas* (cabins), within the nearby village of Conhuás. Look for the restaurant near the entrance to Balamkú ruins.

THE ROAD TO RUINS

Maya sites around Xpujil are most conveniently reached by private vehicle. If you're on public transportation, either book a tour or hire a **taxi** (983-871-61-01). The taxi stop is at the Xpujil junction (with the stoplight).

Typical round-trip fares:

- Balamkú & Calakmul: M$1200 with a three- to four-hour wait.
- Becán & Chicanná: M$400 with one-hour wait at each.
- Hormiguero: M$420 with one-hour wait.

Hotel Puerta Calakmul HOTEL $$$
(998-892-26-24; www.puertacalakmul.com.mx; Hwy 186 Km 98; cabañas from M$2620;) This upscale jungle lodge is 700m from the highway turnoff. The 15 spacious bungalows are nice though not luxurious, and all come with mosquito nets and overhead fans. There's a decent, screened-in restaurant where you can dine from 7am to 9:30pm (mains M$120 to M$300), plus a small pool. Wi-fi in main building only.

Chicanná

Aptly named 'House of the Snake's Jaws,' **Chicanná** (admission M$43; 8am-5pm) is best known for one remarkably well-preserved doorway with a hideous fanged visage. Located 11km west of Xpujil and 400m south of Hwy 186, Chicanná is a mixture of Chenes and Río Bec architectural styles buried in the jungle. The city attained its peak during the late Classic period, from AD 550 to 700, as a sort of elite suburb of Becán.

Beyond the admission pavilion, follow the rock paths through the jungle to **Estructura XX**, which boasts not one but two monster-mouth doorways, one above the other. The top structure is impressively flanked by rounded stacks of crook-nosed Chac masks.

A five-minute walk along the jungle path brings you to **Estructura XI**, with what remains of some of the earliest buildings. Continue along the main path about 120m northeast to reach the **main plaza**. Standing on the east side is Chicanná's famous **Estructura II**, with its gigantic Chenes-style monster-mouth doorway, believed to depict the jaws of the god Itzamná – lord of the heavens and creator of all things. Note the painted glyphs to the right of the mask. A path leading from the right corner of Estructura II takes you to **Estructura VI**, which has a well-preserved roofcomb and some beautiful profile masks on its facade. Circle around back, noting the faded red-painted blocks of the west wing, then turn right to hike back to the main entrance.

Sleeping & Eating

★**Río Bec Dreams** CABIN $$
(www.riobecdreams.com; Hwy 186 Km 142; 2-person cabañas M$620-1300, extra person M$180;) This Canadian-run jungle lodge is a little paradise. Though it's located just off noisy highway 186, once you get here you'll be welcomed by tropical grounds, a lovely restaurant and a few pet dogs. Reception's at the bar. There are seven thatched-roofed *cabañas*, some small and simple and others with two bedrooms and a screened porch. Two have shared bathrooms. The friendly owners also do good tours of area ruins. Breakfast is extra; cash payment only.

The wonderful, open-air **restaurant** (mains M$85-150; 7:30am-9pm), set amid tropical plants, has the best home-made food in the area. The wide variety of main dishes includes roasted pork loin, Mediterranean pasta, Indian curry and chili con carne. Ingredients are high quality and fresh; note IVA and service taxes are added to the bill.

Río Bec Dreams is located 9km west of Xpujil and 2km west of Chicanná, officially at Km 142 (though marked at 145); look for the bus stop and flags.

Becán

The Maya word for 'canyon' or 'moat' is *becán*, and indeed a 2km moat snakes its way around the must-visit Maya site of **Becán** (admission M$48; 8am-5pm). Seven causeways provide access across the moat to the 12-hectare site, within which are the remains of three separate architectural complexes. A strategic crossroads between the Petenes civilization to the south and Chenes to the north, Becán displays architectural elements of both, with the resulting composite known as the Río Bec style.

The elaborate defenses surrounding the site alude to the militaristic nature of the city which, from around AD 600 to 1000, was a regional capital encompassing Xpujil and Chicanná.

Enter the complex via the western causeway, skirting Plaza del Este on your left. Proceed through a 66m-long arched passageway and you will emerge onto the **Plaza Central**, ringed by three monumental structures. The formidable 32m **Estructura IX**, on the plaza's north side, is Becán's tallest building – though the sign says not to climb it, a rope is provided! **Estructura VIII** is the huge temple on your right, with a pair of towers flanking a colonnaded facade at the top. It's a great vantage point for the area; with binoculars, you can make out Xpujil's ruins to the east. Across the plaza from VIII is **Estructura X**, with fragments of an Earth Monster mask still visible around the central doorway. The other side of X opens onto the west plaza, with a ritual

ball court. As you loop around Estructura X to the south, check out the encased stucco mask on display.

Follow around the right side of the mask to another massive edifice, **Estructura I**, which takes up one side of the eastern plaza. Its splendid south wall is flanked by a pair of amazing Río Bec towers rising 15m. Ascend the structure on the right side and follow the terrace alongside a series of vaulted rooms back to the other end, where a passage leads you into the **Plaza del Este**. The most significant structure here is **Estructura IV**, on the opposite side of the plaza; experts surmise it was a residence for Becán's aristocrats. A stairway leads to an upstairs courtyard ringed by seven rooms with cross motifs on either side of the doorways. Finally, go around Estructura IV to complete the circle.

Becán is located 8km west of Xpujil, 500m north of the highway.

Xpujil

☎983 / POP 4000

The unremarkable town of Xpujil (shpu-*heel*) is a good base for exploring the area's many ruins. It has a few hotels, some unexceptional eateries, two ATMs (one at supermarket Willy's), an exchange house (Elektra Dinero on Calle Chicanna near Xnantun), an internet cafe and a bus terminal. Most services are along the seven-block main drag, Av Calakmul (aka Hwy 186). There are three gas stations in the area.

Sights

Xpuhil ARCHAEOLOGICAL SITE
(M$13; 8am-5pm) On the west edge of town, the ruins of Xpuhil are a striking example of the Río Bec style. The three towers (rather than the usual two) of Estructura I rise above a dozen vaulted rooms. The 53m central tower is the best preserved. With its banded tiers and impractically steep stairways leading up to a temple that displays traces of a zoomorphic mask, it gives you a good idea of what the other two towers must have looked like in Xpuhil's 8th-century heyday. Go around back to see a fierce jaguar mask embedded in the wall below the temple.

Sleeping & Eating

All of Xpujil's sleeping options are along the main highway, which can be noisy. Around the bus terminal at the east end of town you'll find cheap hotels and restaurants; the nicer hotels (with nicer restaurants) are at the west end of town.

Hotel Victoria HOTEL $
(☎983-871-60-27; Hwy 186; r with fan/air-con M$250/350; P ❄ @) The best of a clutch of fairly nondescript hotels around the main intersection, this one has large, clean rooms and a reasonable on-site restaurant.

Hotel Calakmul HOTEL $$
(☎983-871-60-29; www.hotelcalakmul.com.mx; Av Calakmul No 70; cabañas M$400, r from M$650; P ❄ 🛜 ≋) At the west end of town, about 350m west of the stoplight, is this large hotel. It has 27 small, tiled rooms with tiny bathrooms and little sitting areas out front. The six so-called *cabañas*, near the parking lot, are tiny shacks set too close together and sharing outside bathrooms – a very odd combination with the more modern hotel. With luck they'll just tear them down to make more room around the new pool. There's a good restaurant on premises (open 6am to midnight, mains M$60 to M$120).

Getting There & Away

No buses originate in Xpujil, so you'll have to hope there's a vacant seat on one passing through. This usually isn't a problem outside holiday times. The **bus terminal** (☎983-871-65-11) is just east of the Xpujil stoplight next to the Victoria Hotel.

There are also taxi *colectivos* to Chetumal (M$115 per person, 1½ hours).

BUSES FROM XPUJIL

DESTINATION	FARE (M$)	DURATION (HRS)	FREQUENCY (DAILY)
Campeche	314	4 to 5	1 at 1.40pm
Cancún	290-514	8	3
Chetumal	86-140	2	5
Escarcega	100-166	2	6

Zoh-Laguna

POP 1500

The village of Zoh-Laguna, 9.5km north of Hwy 186 along the Hopelchén road, offers a pleasant alternative to staying in Xpujil. It's much more peaceful than Xpujil, but has only two simple places to stay and hardly any services.

Sights

Museo Deocundo Acopa Lezama MUSEUM
(cnr Calle Caoba & Zapote ; hrs vary, generally 5-10pm Mon-Fri) FREE Zoh-Laguna's interesting history is illustrated photographically in the small Zoh-Laguna Museum, situated on the same block as Cabañas El Viajero; look for the lime-green building. Conveniently enough, it's also a pizzeria with internet service.

Sleeping

★**Cabañas Mercedes** CABIN $
(cell 983-114-97-69; Calle Zapote s/n; cabañas s/d M$250/300) Fifteen basic bungalows with mosquito nets, ceiling fans and open-shower bathrooms can be found at this rustic place. Decent meals are served in the thatched-roof restaurant (mains from M$80). Don Antonio is the well-informed host who knows about the area's ruins.

Cabañas El Viajero HOTEL $
(983-163-96-13; Calle Caobas s/n; cabañas/d M$230/280; P ❄) Travelers can choose from two very basic *cabañas* with fan, or six more modern, air-conditioned rooms across the street. All meals are prepared in a simple restaurant (meals M$80).

Getting There & Away

Zoh-Laguna is best reached with your own vehicle. Taxis from Xpujil are around M$60.

Río Bec

A collection of small but significant structures in 74 groupings, Río Bec covers a 100-sq-km area southeast of Xpujil. The remoteness of this site and ongoing excavations give it a certain mystique that's lacking in more established sites. Couple this with the fact it's only accessible from February to mid-May (the dry season) and you have the makings of a real adventure.

Grupo B has some of the best-restored buildings, particularly the magnificent **Estructura I** (AD 700). 'Discovered' in 1907 by French archaeologist Maurice de Périgny, this palatial structure features a pair of typical tiered towers crowned by matching temples with cross motifs on their sides.

The main structure at Grupo A is a 15m-long **palace** with intact towers and unusual basrelief glyphs on the lower panels.

Getting here without a guide is nearly impossible – the very rough dirt road is accessible only via 4WD vehicle and it's unsigned, with many twists and turns that can change from year to year. It's best to go with either Ka'an Expeditions (p223), with tours at M$990 per person, or Río Bec Dreams (p224), if you're a guest with them. Reserve at least two to three days in advance for both.

Hormiguero

Though not easy to reach, **Hormiguero** (8am-5pm) FREE has two impressive and unique buildings that are worth the trek. Buildings date as far back as AD 50; the city (whose name is Spanish for 'anthill') flourished during the late Classic period.

As you enter you'll see the 50m-long **Estructura II**. The facade's chief feature is a very menacing Chenes-style monster-mouth doorway, jaws open wide, set back between a pair of Classic Río Bec tiered towers. Around the back is intact Maya stonework and the remains of several columns. Follow the arrows 60m north to reach **Estructura V**, with a much smaller but equally ornate open-jawed temple atop a pyramidal base. Climb the right side for a closer look at the incredibly detailed stonework, especially along the corner columns that flank the doorway.

This site is reached by heading 14km south from Xpujil's stoplight, then turning right and going 8km west on a very rough but (hopefully) improving dirt-sand road, passable except following heavy rains.

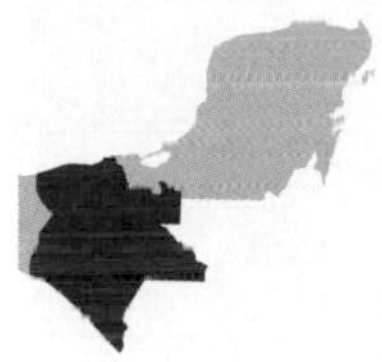

Chiapas & Tabasco

Includes ➡

Best Places to Eat

- Don Mucho's (p245)
- TierrAdentro (p236)
- Restaurante LUM (p236)
- Café Jade (p245)
- Trattoria La Nonna (p236)

Best Places to Stay

- Boutique Hotel Quinta Chanabnal (p245)
- La Joya Hotel (p235)
- Hotel b¨o (p235)

Why Go?

Chilly pine-forest highlands, wildlife-rich rainforest jungles and well-preserved colonial cities exist side by side within Mexico's southernmost state, a region awash with the legacy of Spanish rule and some fabulous remnants of ancient Maya civilization.

The state has the second-largest indigenous population in the country, and the modern Maya of Chiapas form a direct link to the past, with a traditional culture that persists to this day. The fine city of San Cristóbal de las Casas is at the heart of this region and was once the central bastion for the rebel group Zapatistas, now much less influential than in the 1990s.

Chiapas contains swathes of wild green landscape that have nourished its inhabitants for centuries. And nature lovers willing to venture off the beaten path will be rewarded with frothy cascades, exotic biosphere reserves and adventurous geological destinations.

When to Go

- The rainy season is from May to October, with the heaviest rainfall mostly in June, September and early October. Some of the less visited, more out-of-the-way Maya ruins are located on dirt roads which are impassable during the rainy season.
- The dry season is between November and April, when warm, sunny days are the norm.
- Temperatures don't vary much with the changing seasons – altitude is a much more influential factor. Lowland areas (such as Palenque and Villahermosa) are hot and sticky year round, with punishing humidity and daily highs above 86°F (30°C). In more elevated places (like San Cristóbal), the climate is fresher and nights get fairly cold in winter (November to March).

Chiapas & Tabasco Highlights

❶ Explore the extraordinary ruins of **Palenque** (p241), where jade masks and priceless jewels were found inside a ruler's sarcophagus, and the architecture boasts unique features.

❷ Wander around high-altitude **San Cristóbal de las Casas** (p230), home to charming cobblestone streets, pretty colonial buildings and colorfully dressed indigenous peoples.

❸ Ponder the mysterious sculptural art of the ancient Olmecs while wandering around the junglelike grounds of Villahermosa's **Parque-Museo La Venta** (p239) – a paradise within the bustling city.

❹ Visit the ancient cities of **Yaxchilán** (p247), reachable via an adventurous river-boat trip, and **Bonampak** (p247), which offers amazingly preserved painted murals.

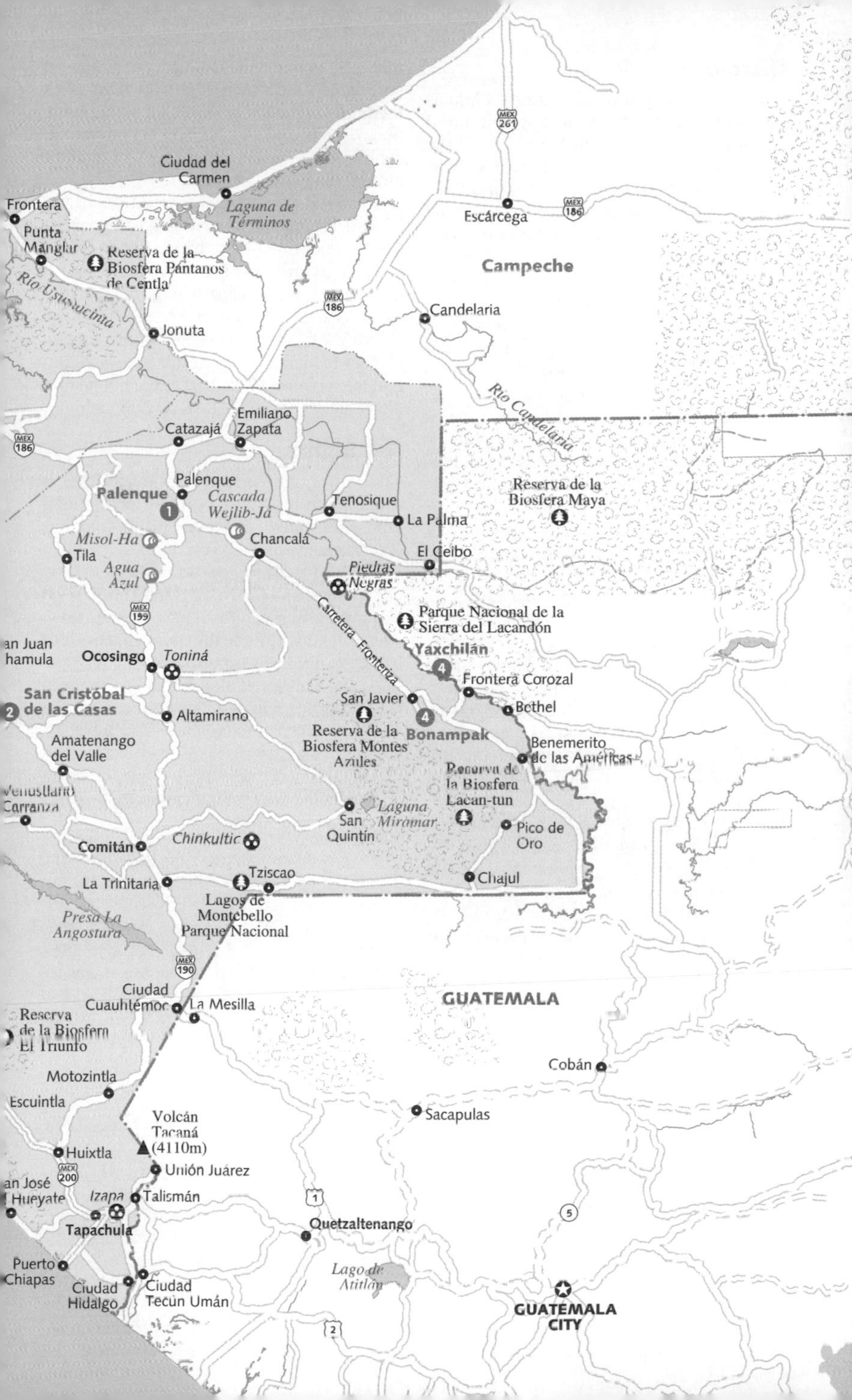

Ciudad del Carmen
Laguna de Términos
Frontera
Punta Manglar
Reserva de la Biosfera Pantanos de Centla
Río Usumacinta
Jonuta
Escárcega
Campeche
Candelaria
Río Candelaria
Emiliano Zapata
Catazajá
Palenque
Cascada Wejlib-Já
Tenosique
La Palma
Misol-Ha
Tila
Chancalá
Agua Azul
El Ceibo
Piedras Negras
Reserva de la Biosfera Maya
Parque Nacional de la Sierra del Lacandón
Yaxchilán
Carretera Fronteriza
Ocosingo
Toniná
Frontera Corozal
San Cristóbal de las Casas
San Javier
Bethel
Altamirano
Reserva de la Biosfera Montes Azules
Bonampak
Benemerito de las Américas
Amatenango del Valle
Reserva de la Biosfera Lacan-tun
Laguna Miramar
San Quintín
Pico de Oro
Comitán
Chinkultic
Chajul
La Trinitaria
Tziscao
Lagos de Montebello Parque Nacional
Presa La Angostura
Ciudad Cuauhtémoc
La Mesilla
GUATEMALA
Reserva de la Biosfera El Triunfo
Cobán
Motozintla
Escuintla
Sacapulas
Volcán Tacaná (4110m)
Huixtla
Unión Juárez
Izapa
Talismán
Tapachula
Quetzaltenango
Puerto Chiapas
Lago de Atitlán
Ciudad Hidalgo
Ciudad Tecun Umán
GUATEMALA CITY

History

Low-lying, jungle-covered eastern Chiapas gave rise to some of the most splendid and powerful city-states of the Maya during the Classic period (about AD 250 to 900), such as Palenque and Yaxchilán. But as Maya culture reached its peak of artistic and intellectual achievement, dozens of lesser powers also prospered here. After the Classic Maya collapse around AD 900, the ancestors of many distinctive indigenous groups of Chiapas appear to have migrated to the highlands.

Central Chiapas was brought under Spanish control by the 1528 expedition of Diego de Mazariegos, and most outlying areas were subdued in the 1530s and '40s. New diseases arrived with the Spaniards, and an epidemic in 1544 killed about half of Chiapas' indigenous population. Chiapas was ineffectively administered from Guatemala for most of the colonial era, with little check on the colonists' excesses against its indigenous people, though some church figures, particularly Bartolomé de las Casas (1474–1566), the first bishop of Chiapas, did fight for indigenous rights.

In 1824 Chiapas opted to join Mexico, rather than the United Provinces of Central America. From then on, a succession of governors appointed by Mexico City maintained control over Chiapas. Periodic uprisings bore witness to bad government, but the world took little notice until January 1, 1994, when Zapatista rebels suddenly and briefly occupied San Cristóbal de las Casas and nearby towns by military force. ('Zapatista' comes from the Mexican revolutionary Emiliano Zapata, whose followers during the Mexican Revolution in 1910 were known as Zapatistas.)

The rebel movement, with a firm and committed support base among disenchanted indigenous settlers, used remote jungle bases to campaign for democratic change and indigenous rights. The Zapatistas have failed to win any significant concessions at the national level, although increased government funding has resulted in improvements in the state's infrastructure, the development of tourist facilities and a growing urban middle class.

San Cristóbal de las Casas

☎967 / POP 171,400

Set in a gorgeous highland valley surrounded by pine forest, the colonial city of San Cristóbal (cris-*toh*-bal) has been a popular travelers destination for decades. It's a pleasure to explore the cobbled streets and markets, soaking up the unique ambience and wonderfully clear highland light. This medium-sized city also boasts a comfortable blend of city and countryside, with restored century-old houses giving way to grazing animals and fields of corn.

Surrounded by dozens of traditional Tzotzil and Tzeltal villages, San Cristóbal is at the heart of one of the most deeply rooted indigenous areas in Mexico. A great base for exploration, it's a place where ancient customs coexist with modern luxuries.

Bring a jacket in the cooler months of November to March – the altitude here is 2120m and nights can get downright chilly. Note that street names change at Real de Guadalupe.

Sights

The leafy main **Plaza 31 de Marzo** (📶) is a fine place to take in San Cristóbal's highland atmosphere. Its pretty bandstand has occasional live music. For the best views in town, head to **Cerro de Guadalupe** (off Real de Guadalupe) and **Cerro de San Cristóbal** (off Hermanos Dominguez). You'll have to work for it, because at this altitude the stairs up these hills can be punishing. Churches crown both lookouts, and the Iglesia de Guadalupe becomes a hot spot for religious devotees around the Día de la Virgen de Guadalupe (December 12). Cerro de San Cristóbal has a better view but should be avoided after dark (it's more isolated and there have been muggings in the past).

Catedral CATHEDRAL

(Plaza 31 de Marzo) On the north side of the plaza, the cathedral was begun in 1528 but wasn't completed until 1815 because of several natural disasters. Sure enough, new earthquakes struck in 1816 and also 1847, causing considerable damage, but it was restored again from 1920 to 1922. The gold-leaf interior has five gilded altarpieces featuring 18th-century paintings by Miguel Cabrera.

Templo & Ex-Convento de Santo Domingo de Guzmán CHURCH

(Utrilla; ⏰6:30am-2pm & 4-8pm) FREE Located just north of the center of town, the 16th-century Templo de Santo Domingo is San Cristóbal's most beautiful church, especially when its facade catches the late-afternoon sun. This baroque frontage, with outstanding filigree stucco work, was added in the 17th century and includes the double-headed Hapsburg eagle, then the symbol of the Spanish monarchy. The interior is lavishly gilded, especially the ornate pulpit.

On the western side, the attached former monastery contains a regional museum and an excellent Maya **textile museum** (Calz Lázaro Cárdenas; admission M$52; ⏲9am-6pm Tue-Sun). Around Santo Domingo and the neighboring **Templo de la Caridad** (built in 1712), Chamulan women and bohemian types from around Mexico conduct a colorful daily crafts market. The weavers showroom of **Sna Jolobil** (snajolobil@gmail.com; Calz Lázaro Cárdenas s/n; ⏲9am-2pm & 4-7pm Mon-Sat) is now in a separate light-filled building on the northwest section of the grounds.

Mercado Municipal MARKET

(⏲6am-6pm outside shops, 8am-3pm inside stalls) For a closer look at local life – and an assault on the senses – visit San Cristóbal's busy municipal market, eight blocks north of the main plaza between Utrilla and Belisario Domínguez.

Na Bolom HISTORIC BUILDING

(www.na-bolom.org; Guerrero 33; M$40, with tour M$50; ⏲7am-7pm) An atmospheric museum-research center, Na Bolom for many years was the home of Swiss anthropologist and photographer Gertrude Duby-Blom (Trudy Blom; 1901–93) and her Danish archaeologist husband Frans Blom (1893–1963). Na Bolom means 'Jaguar House' in the Tzotzil language (as well as being a play on its former owners' name). It's full of photographs, and archaeological and anthropological relics and books.

Museo del Ámbar de Chiapas MUSEUM

(www.museodelambar.com.mx; Plazuela de la Merced; M$20; ⏲10am-2pm & 4-8pm Tue-Sun) Chiapas amber – fossilized pine resin, around 30 million years old – is known for its clarity and diverse colors. Most is mined around Simojovel, north of San Cristóbal. This museum explains all things amber (with information sheets in English, French, German, Japanese and Italian), and displays and sells some exquisitely carved items and insect-embedded pieces. Note that a number of nearby jewelry shops have appropriated the museum's name, but this is the only place around that's housed in an ex-convent – you can't miss it.

Museo de la Medicina Maya MUSEUM

(Av Salomón González Blanco 10; M$20; ⏲10am-6pm Mon-Fri, to 4pm Sat & Sun) This award-winning museum on the northern edge of town introduces the system of traditional medicine used by many indigenous people in the Chiapas highlands. Exhibits include displays of a ritual scene inside a church and a midwife assisting at a birth, a dated video about the work of traditional midwives and a new display about the issue of native plants and corporate biopiracy.

Arco del Carmen GATE

The Arco del Carmen, at the southern end of the Andador Turístico on Hidalgo, dates from the late 17th century and was once the city's gateway.

Museo del Cacao MUSEUM

(☎967-631-79-95; www.kakaw.org; 1ro de Marzo 16; admission M$30; ⏲10am-7pm Mon-Sat, 11am-4pm Sun) This chocolate museum runs along an open upstairs balcony of a cafe. Learn about the history of chocolate and how it was used by the Maya. Also on display are modern chocolate drinking vessels and utensils, and the process to create the delicious substance. Includes a free sample.

Café Museo Café MUSEUM

(MA Flores 10; M$30; ⏲8am-10pm Mon-Sat, to 8pm Sat & Sun; 📶) This combined cafe and coffee museum is a venture of Coopcafé, a grouping of more than 17,000 small-scale, mainly indigenous, Chiapas coffee growers. The museum covers the history of coffee and its cultivation in Chiapas, from highly exploitative beginnings to the community-based indigenous coffee production that's increasingly well marketed today. The information is translated into English. You can taste some of that flavorful organic coffee in the cafe.

Museo Bichos e Insectos MUSEUM

(www.museodebichos.com; 16 de Sepiembre 23; admission M$35; ⏲10:30am-2pm & 4-8pm Mon-Fri, 11am-6pm Sat & Sun; 👪) A small museum but still home to over 2000 insects (only a few of them alive, and very few of the mounted ones are labeled). Check out old wasp nests, huge beetles, leaf insects, spiders, crickets, butterflies and dragonflies. Live insects and other creepy crawlies include scorpions, beetles and centipedes; you can hold a tarantula too.

 Courses

El Puente Spanish Language School LANGUAGE COURSE

(☎967-678-37-23; infoelpuente@gmail.com; Real de Guadalupe 55; individual/group classes per week $US160/140, with homestay & meals US$250/230) Housed in the Centro Cultural El Puente, which also has a vegetarian cafe, a cinema and a gallery. Classes are offered for any period, starting from one day.

San Cristóbal de las Casas

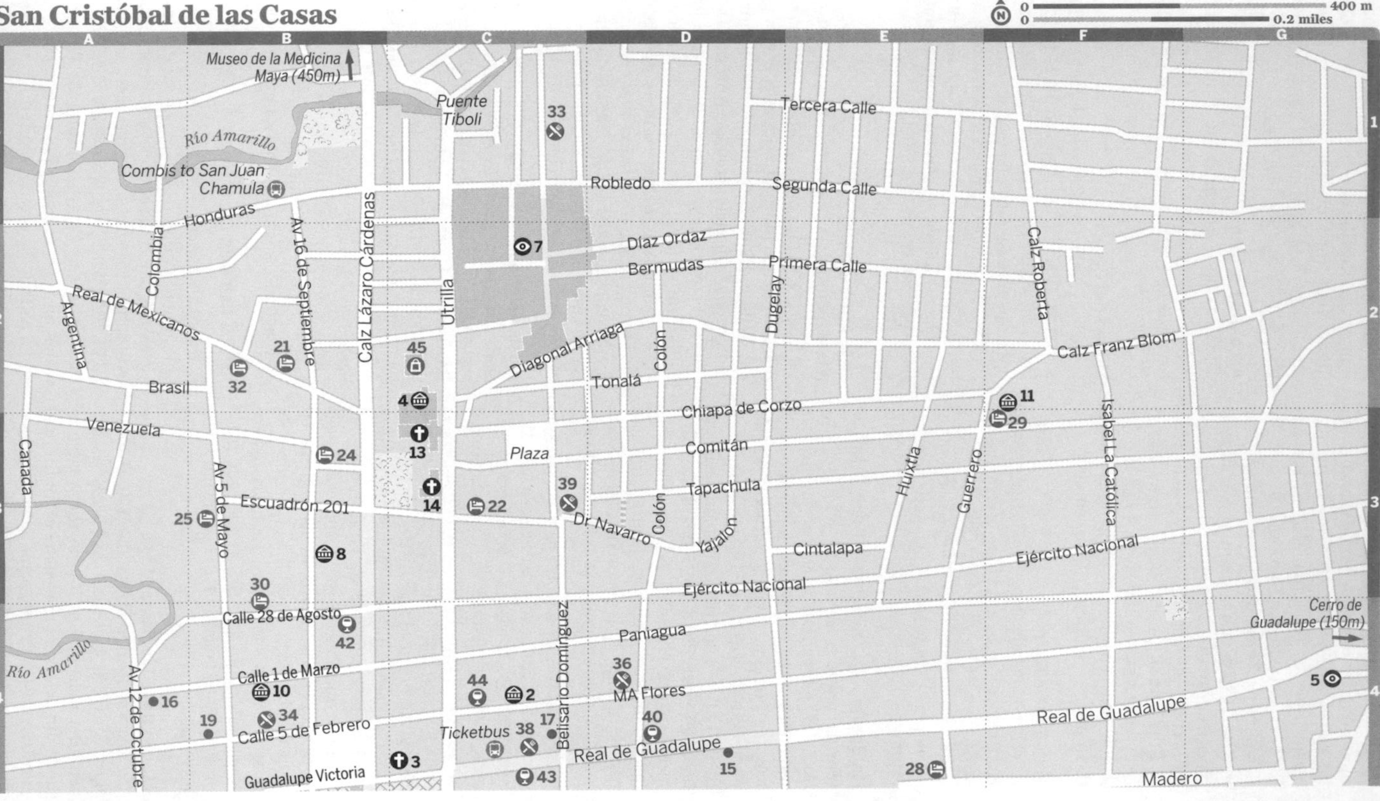

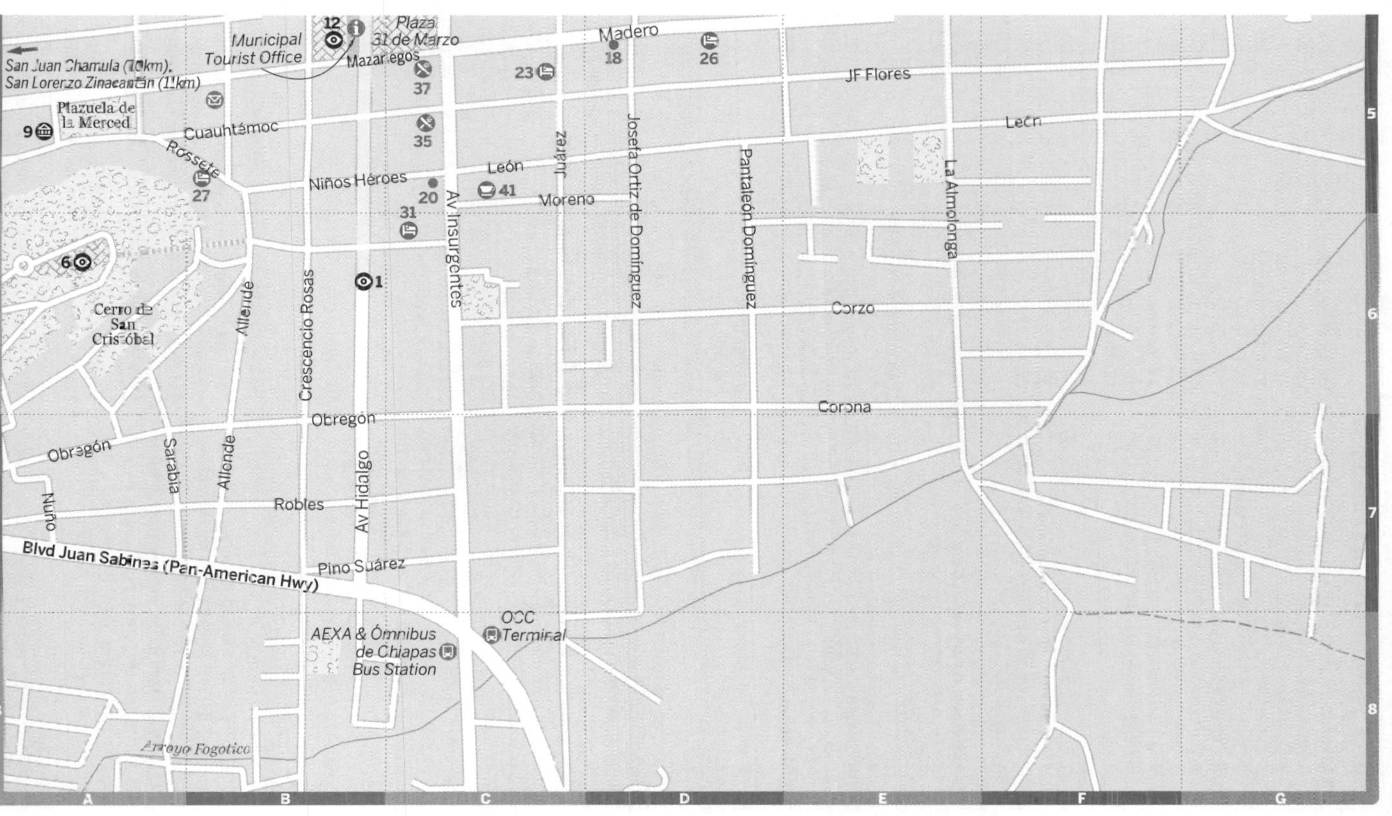
San Juan Chamula (10km), San Lorenzo Zinacantán (11km)
Municipal Tourist Office
Plaza 31 de Marzo
Mazariegos
Madero
JF Flores
Plazuela de la Merced
Cuauhtémoc
León
Rossete
Niños Héroes
León
Moreno
Juárez
Josefa Ortiz de Domínguez
Pantaleón Domínguez
La Almolonga
Av Insurgentes
Cerro de San Cristóbal
Allende
Crescencio Rosas
Corzo
Corona
Obregón
Obregón
Sarabia
Allende
Av Hidalgo
Nuño
Robles
Blvd Juan Sabines (Pan-American Hwy)
Pino Suárez
OCC Terminal
AEXA & Ómnibus de Chiapas Bus Station
Arroyo Fogotico
1
6
9
12
18
20
23
26
27
31
35
37
41

San Cristóbal de las Casas

Sights

1 Arco del Carmen ... B6
2 Café Museo Café ... C4
3 Catedral ... C4
4 Centro de Textiles del Mundo Maya ... C2
5 Cerro de Guadalupe ... G4
6 Cerro de San Cristóbal ... A6
7 Mercado Municipal ... C2
8 Museo Bichos e Insectos ... B3
9 Museo del Ámbar de Chiapas ... A5
10 Museo del Cacao ... B4
11 Na Bolom ... F2
12 Plaza 31 de Marzo ... B5
13 Templo & Ex-Convento de Santo Domingo de Guzmán ... C3
14 Templo de la Caridad ... C3

Activities, Courses & Tours

15 El Puente Spanish Language School ... D4
16 Explora ... A4
17 Jaguar Adventours ... C4
18 La Casa en el Árbol ... D5
19 SendaSur ... B4
20 Shaktipat Yoga ... C5

Sleeping

21 Anthara Hotel ... B2
22 Bela's B&B ... C3
23 Docecuartos ... C5
24 Hostal Akumal ... B3
25 Hotel b¨o ... B3
26 La Joya Hotel ... D5
27 Las Escaleras ... B5
28 Le Gite del Sol ... E4
29 Na Bolom ... F3
30 Posada Ganesha ... B3
31 Posada La Media Luna ... C6
32 Rossco Backpackers ... B2

Eating

33 Alebrije ... C1
34 El Eden ... B4
35 La Tertulia ... C5
36 Mumo ... D4
Restaurante LUM ... (see 25)
37 Sensaciones de Chiapas ... C5
38 TierrAdentro ... C4
39 Trattoria La Nonna ... C3

Drinking & Nightlife

40 Cocoliche ... D4
41 Kakao Natura ... C5
42 La Ruina ... B4
43 La Viña de Bacco ... C4
44 Mezcalería Gusana Grela ... C4

Shopping

45 Sna Jolobil ... C2

La Casa en el Árbol LANGUAGE COURSE
(☎967-674-52-72; www.lacasaenelarbol.org; Madero 29; classes per week from M$1200, homestay & meals per week M$1625) The 'Tree House' teaches Tseltal and Tsotsil. It offers lots of out-of-school activities and is also a base for volunteer programs. Mexican cooking classes are also available.

Shaktipat Yoga YOGA
(☎cell 967-130-33-66; http://shaktipatyoga.com.mx; Niños Héroes 2; class M$50) A studio in the healing arts complex of Casa Luz with multilingual vinyasa, ashtanga and hatha yoga classes. Multiclass discounts.

Tours

Jaguar Adventours BICYCLING
(☎967-631-50-62; www.adventours.mx; Belisario Domínguez 8A; bicycle rentals per hour/day M$40/M$200; ⏲9am-2:30pm & 3:30-8pm Mon-Sat, 9am-2:30pm Sun) Does bicycle tours to Chamula and Zincantán (M$700), plus longer expeditions. Prices start at M$450 per person. Also rents mountain bikes with helmet and lock.

Explora ADVENTURE TOUR
(☎967-631-74-98; www.ecochiapas.com; Calle 1 de Marzo 30; ⏲9:30am-2pm & 4-8pm Mon-Fri, 9:30am-2pm Sat) Adventure trips to the Lacandón Jungle, including multiday river kayaking and rafting.

Festivals & Events

Semana Santa RELIGIOUS
The crucifixion is acted out on Good Friday in the Barrio de Mexicanos, northwest of town.

Feria de la Primavera y de la Paz CULTURAL
(Spring & Peace Fair) Easter Sunday is the start of the week-long town fair, with parades, musical events and bullfights.

Festival de las Culturas CULTURAL
(www.conecultachiapas.gob.mx) In mid- to late October, this free, week-long cultural program keeps hopping with music, dance and theater.

Festival Cervantino Barroco CULTURAL
(Cervantes Festival) A fair with art, music, dance and theater in October or November.

Sleeping

High season is mid-December through March, with peak times (and prices) around Christmas and Easter. We list prices during high season; in low season prices drop by 20% or more.

Hostal Akumal HOSTEL $

(☎cell 967-1161120; Calle 16 de Sepiembre 33; dm/s/d incl breakfast M$120/210/420; 📶) Friendly, live-in owners, a decent location and a big free breakfast (a prominent sign quite rightly states "Continental breakfast is not real breakfast") are some of the winning points at this centrally located hostel. There's a roaring fireplace in the lounge for chilly nights, a funky courtyard hangout area and the rooms and dorms are adequate, if nothing exciting.

Le Gite del Sol HOTEL $

(☎967-631-60-12; www.legitedelsol.com; Madero 82; s/d M$340/440, without bathroom M$240/305; @📶) A bountiful breakfast complements simple rooms with floors of radiant sunflower yellow and bathrooms that look a bit like oversized shower stalls, or pleasant rooms with shared facilities in a newer location across the street. French and English spoken, and kitchen facilities available.

Rossco Backpackers HOSTEL $

(☎967-674-05-25; www.backpackershostel.com.mx; Real de Mexicanos 16; incl breakfast dm M$180-220, d/tr M$550/800; P⊖@📶) Backpackers is a friendly, sociable and well-run hostel with good dorm rooms (one for women only), a guest kitchen, a movie-watching loft and a grassy garden. Private upstairs rooms have nice skylights. A free night's stay if you arrive by bicycle or motorcycle!

Posada Ganesha GUESTHOUSE $

(☎967-678-02-12; www.posadaganesha.com; Calle 28 de Agosto 23; dm/s/d without bathroom incl breakfast M$190/320/500; ⊖📶) An incense-infused posada trimmed in Indian fabrics, this is a friendly and vibrant place to rest your head, with a simple guest kitchen and a pleasant lounge area. The free-standing *cabaña* (cabin) room is especially nice. Yoga sessions twice daily Monday to Friday.

Docecuartos HOTEL $$

(☎967-678-10-53; Benito Juárez 1; r from M$1250; 📶) Set around a charming courtyard, there are indeed only 12 rooms here, which adds to the intimate feel but makes booking a necessity pretty much any time of year. The rooms are gorgeously decked out, with just the right balance of colonial stateliness, indigenous color and modern amenity, and the super-central location gets a big thumbs up.

Posada La Media Luna HOTEL $$

(☎967-631-55-90; www.hotel-medialuna.com; Hermanos Domínguez 5; s/d with bathroom M$630/770, without bathroom M$420/600, apt M$1540; @📶) This friendly, Italian-owned place is great value. It's well maintained and offers comfortable and pretty rooms with cable TV, all set around a covered patio with potted plants. The one apartment has two rooms and a kitchen. But beware nearby church bells – especially on Sunday morning!

Anthara Hotel HOTEL $$

(☎967-674-77-32; www.antharahotel.com; Real de Mexicanos 7; d M$900-1000; ⊖📶) 🌿 Solar-heated hot water and heated floors distinguish this three-floor hotel centered around a small garden courtyard. Rooms have dark wood furniture and large closets, though bathrooms aren't particularly ample. Snag 301 for choice mountain views.

★**La Joya Hotel** B&B $$$

(☎967-631-48-32; www.lajoyahotelsancristobal.com; Madero 43A; r incl breakfast US$160-205; P⊖@📶) A visual feast, offering five rooms ripped from a high-end design magazine, with exquisite cabinetry, enormous bathrooms and antiques curated from the owners' world travels. Fireplace sitting areas and heaters grace each room, and a rooftop terrace beckons with hill views. Attentive service includes afternoon snacks, bedtime tea, and a specially prepared light dinner for late international arrivals.

Hotel b¨o BOUTIQUE HOTEL $$$

(☎967-678-15-15; www.hotelbo.mx; Av 5 de Mayo 38; r from M$3885, ste M$4965; P⊖@📶) 🌿 San Cristóbal meets Miami Beach in a boutique hotel that breaks the traditional colonial-architecture barrier with super-modern, trendy lines and unique, artsy touches. The large rooms and suites are very elegant and boast glass-tile bathrooms with ceiling showers, while the flowery gardens host fine water features.

Na Bolom HOTEL $$$

(☎967-678-14-18; www.nabolom.org; Guerrero 33; r/ste incl breakfast M$1395/2387; P⊖📶) This famous museum/research institute (p231), about 1km from Plaza 31 de Marzo, has 16 stylish (though not necessarily luxurious) guest rooms, all loaded with character and all but two with log fires. Meals are served in the house's stately dining room. Room rates include a house tour.

Bela's B&B B&B $$$

(☎967-678-92-92; www.belasbandb.com; Dr Navarro 2; incl breakfast s/d M$1280/1540, without bathroom M$770/1030; P⊖📶) A dreamy

DRINKS OF CHIAPAS

Comiteco A unique variant of mezcal (an alcoholic agave drink) made with *piloncillo* (cooked sugarcane). It's smoother and more syrupy than tequila, with a clear appearance or a greenish tint. Traditionally made in Comitán.

Pox Inexpensive grain alcohol made from sugarcane, it's pronounced (and sometimes spelled) 'posh.' The undisputed choice for those who want to pass out cold on the street, but not so deadly when mixed with lots of fruit juice.

Pozol A thick heavy mixture of *masa* (cornmeal dough) in water, it's often mixed with sugar and sometimes has chili or chocolate added. It's the equivalent of an energy drink, and you can see indigenous people everywhere carrying it around in reused plastic liter bottles. Travelers often take a ball of the *masa* and make some up when there's water available.

Tascalate A cold sweet concoction prepared from ground cacao, pine nuts, toasted corn, cinnamon and *achiote* (annatto). Very interesting and superdelicious!

oasis in the center of town, this tranquil dog-friendly B&B will seduce you with its lush garden, electric blankets, towel dryers and onsite massages. The five comfortable rooms are trimmed in traditional local fabrics and some have lovely mountain views. There's a three-day minimum stay.

Las Escaleras BOUTIQUE HOTEL **$$$**
(967-678-81-81; www.lasescalerashotel.com; Isauro Rossette 4; r M$1992-2816;) Sophisticated, charming and oozing with character, this hilltop retreat isn't for the leg-weary (there are even more stairs than the name implies) but if you're looking for style, it's one of the best options in town.

Eating

San Cristóbal has become a magnet for international immigrants, and with them comes a delicious variety of cuisines. You can find felafel, sushi, Thai, Indian, Italian, Argentine and Lebanese restaurants in town.

★TierrAdentro MEXICAN **$**
(Real de Guadalupe 24; set menu M$55-130; 8am-11pm;) A popular gathering center for political progressives and coffee-swigging, laptop-toting locals (not that they're mutually exclusive), this large indoor courtyard restaurant, cafe and pizzeria is a comfortable place to while away the hours. It's run by Zapatista supporters, who hold frequent cultural events and conferences on local issues.

La Tertulia CAFE **$**
(Cuathémoc 2; breakfasts around M$38; 9:30am-5pm Sun & Mon, to 10pm Tue-Sat) One of the coolest cafes in town also does great breakfasts, yummy salads and a passable pizza, all served up with ooh-la-la presentation in pleasingly boho surrounds. A little on-site gift store selling local produce and souvenirs rounds out the picture.

Alebrije MEXICAN **$**
(Caminero 4; mains M$35-70; 8am-6pm Mon-Sat) A fun, economical and busy *cocina popular* across from the Mercado Municipal, Alebrije serves freshly prepared food like *enfrijoladas con pollo* (tortillas with bean sauce, cheese and chicken), *chilaquiles* and *pollo con verduras* (chicken and vegetables) to a dedicated local clientele.

★Restaurante LUM MEXICAN **$$**
(Hotel Bo, Av 5 de Mayo 38; mains M$110-200; 7am-11pm) This swanky indoor-outdoor restaurant which serves up the regional cuisines of Chiapas, Veracruz and the Yucatán is in San Cristóbal's first designer hotel. Custom-made lamps, reflecting pools and walls of geometrically stacked firewood create a funky contemporary ambience.

Trattoria La Nonna ITALIAN **$$**
(Dr Navarro 10; mains M$135-180; 2-10pm Mon & Wed-Sat, 2-4:30pm Sun;) This mother-and-daughter-run Italian eatery specializes in ravioli, handmade fresh every day. Depending on what's in season, expect fillings of sea bass with eggplant, four cheese with walnut and arugula, or rabbit with rosemary and green olive. The sauces are divine – don't miss the mango, chipotle and gorgonzola if it's around.

Mumo INTERNATIONAL **$$**
(MA Flores 16; mains M$80-160; 12:30-11pm Tue-Sun) This tiny 10-seater is well-loved throughout the city, both for its eclectic decorations and the loving care that goes into each plate. Bread, salad dressings and ice cream are all made in-house and the build-

your-own salads (choose from 20 ingredients) are well worth a mention. Live music and guest chefs Thursday nights.

El Eden MEXICAN, INTERNATIONAL $$
(Hotel El Paraíso, Calle 5 de Febrero 19; mains M$82-180; ⏲7am-11pm;) This quality restaurant's tempting European and Mexican menu includes *fondue suiza* (Swiss fondue), *sopa azteca* (tortilla, chilli, onion and herb base topped with shredded chicken, fresh cheese, lime, avocado and coriander) and succulent meat dishes, all served around a cozy fireplace or out in the leafy courtyard. There's a good-sized wine list too, including French and Spanish vintages.

Sensaciones de Chiapas MEXICAN $$
(Plaza 31 de Marzo 10A; mains M$80-130; ⏲8am-midnight) Inside the Hotel Ciudad Real, this is a great place to try authentic Chiapas cuisine including *chipilin* soup, quesadilla de Cochinita, a great range of *mole* dishes and the house specialty – chicken thighs stuffed with cheese, ham and other goodies. Occasional live marimba bands accompany your meal.

Drinking & Nightlife

Cocoliche COCKTAIL BAR
(Colón 3; ⏲noon-midnight;) By day, a bohemian international restaurant (mains M$75 to M$120), in the evening Cocoliche's mismatched Chinese lanterns and wall of funky posters set the scene for hanging out with friends over boozy *licuados* (milkshakes). On chilly nights jostle for a sofa near the fireplace, and check out the nightly Latin jazz and salsa, and occasional theater events at 9pm.

La Viña de Bacco WINE BAR
(☎967-119-19-85; Real de Guadalupe 7; ⏲2pm-midnight Mon-Sat) At San Cristóbal's first wine bar, chatty patrons spill out onto the street, a pedestrian block off the main drag. It's a convivial place, pouring a large selection of Mexican options (among others), starting at a reasonable M$25 per glass. A free tapa with every glass of wine.

Mezcalería Gusana Grela MEZCALERÍA
(MA Flores 2; ⏲7pm-3am Mon-Sat) Wedge yourself in at one of a handful of tables and try some of the dozen or so artisanal mezcals (M$40 to M$50) from Oaxaca, many which are fruit-infused.

Kakao Natura CAFE
(Moreno 2A; ⏲8am-10pm) For something different, melt into a hot chocolate at this *chocolatería*. The dozen or so varieties of artisanal chocolates (M$9 each) make fine gifts – if you can resist eating them yourself.

La Ruina CLUB
(Calle 28 de Agosto 13; ⏲10pm-late Wed-Sat) Everyone drifts here after hours to dance the rest of the night away in a diminutive wooden building with full bar and cheap beer. Work it to a fun mix of *cumbia* (Colombian dance music), hip hop, dub step, reggae and salsa.

ℹ Information

There are many internet cafes around town, including a couple on Real de Guadalupe.

Banamex (Insurgentes btwn Niños Héroes & Cuauhtémoc; ⏲9am-4pm Mon-Sat) Has an ATM; exchanges dollars.

Hospital de la Mujer (☎967-678-07-70; Insurgentes 24) General hospital with emergency facilities.

Main Post Office (Allende 3; ⏲8am-4pm Mon-Fri, 8am-2pm Sat)

Municipal Tourist Office (☎967-678-06-65; Palacio Municipal, Plaza 31 de Marzo; ⏲9am-9pm) Staff are generally knowledgeable about the San Cristóbal area; English spoken.

ℹ Getting There & Away

AIR

San Cristóbal's airport, about 15km from town on the Palenque road, has no regular passenger flights; the main airport serving town is at Tuxtla

BUSES FROM SAN CRISTÓBAL DE LAS CASAS

DESTINATION	FARE (M$)	DURATION (HRS)	FREQUENCY (DAILY)
Campeche	548	11	1 at 6:20pm
Cancún	700-1242	18	4
Ciudad Cuauhtémoc (Guatemalan border)	132	3½	3
Mérida	778	14	1 at 6:20pm
Palenque	122-248	5	9
Villahermosa	402	6	1 at 10am

Gutiérrez. Five daily direct OCC minibuses (M$210, 1¼ hours) run between Tuxtla's airport and San Cristóbal's main bus terminal; book in advance.

BUS, COLECTIVO & VAN

The road between San Cristóbal and Palenque is long and most of it is very curvy; take medicine if you're prone to motion sickness.

The main bus terminal is the 1st-class **OCC terminal** (☎967-678-02-91; cnr Pan-American Hwy & Insurgentes). Bus tickets are also sold in the center of town at **Boletotal** (☎967-678-85-03; Real de Guadalupe 16; ⏰7:30am-10pm).

First-class **AEXA** (☎967-678-61-78; www.autobusesaexa.com.mx) and 2nd-class **Ómnibus de Chiapas** (☎967-678-84-62; Insurgentes 89) share a **terminal** on the south side of the highway. Also, various combi and *colectivo taxi* companies to Ocosingo, Tuxtla and Comitán have depots on the highway in the same area (it's a frenzied madhouse with shouting operators competing for passengers).

For Guatemala, most agencies offer daily van service to Quetzaltenango (M$390, eight hours), Panajachel (M$390, nine hours) and Antigua (M$500, 11 hours).

CAR

A fast toll *autopista* (M$56) zips towards Chiapa de Corzo.

San Cristóbal's only car-rental company, **Optima** (☎967-674-54-09; optimacar1@hotmail.com; Mazariegos 39), has manual transmission cars. Rates vary wildly depending on the season and demand. Sizable discounts are given for payment in cash. Drivers must be 25 or older and have a credit card.

Getting Around

Combis (M$8) go up Crescencio Rosas from the Pan-American Hwy to the town center. Taxis cost around M$30 within town and M$35 at night.

Croozy Scooters (☎cell 967-683-22-23; Belisario Domínguez 7; scooters per 3hr/day M$300/450, motorcycles per 3hr/day M$400/540; ⏰10am-6pm) rents well-maintained Italika CS 125cc scooters, plus 150cc motorcycles and bicycles. **Jaguar Adventours** (p234) rents bicycles.

BUS TRAVEL WARNING

Be careful on overnight buses to or from San Cristóbal, especially to Palenque. Use a lock on baggage stored in the hold below, and keep your personal hand luggage close by – even sleeping on it at night. Thefts have occurred in the past.

Around San Cristóbal

The inhabitants of the beautiful Chiapas highlands are descended from the ancient Maya and maintain some unique customs, costumes and beliefs, and some of their villages are worth visiting. In addition to San Juan Chamula, there's San Lorenzo Zinacantán (notable for its old church) and Amatenango del Valle (famous for pottery). Those into natural wonders should head to **Las Grutas de Rancho Nuevo** (a long cavern).

If you'd like a guide to the villages, contact **Alex & Raúl Tours** (☎967-678-91-41; www.alexyraultours.wordpress.com; per person M$240) in San Cristóbal. It conducts tours to Chamula and Zinacantán daily; simply meet your guide at 9:30am at the cross in front of San Cristóbal's cathedral. Trips to other surrounding villages can also be arranged.

San Juan Chamula

POP 3330

The Chamulans are a fiercely independent Tzotzil group, more than 80,000 strong. Their principal village is San Juan Chamula, located 10km northwest of San Cristóbal. There's a weekly market on Sunday, when people from the hills stream into the village to shop, trade and visit the main church. Many tour buses also visit on Sunday, so expect crowds then.

The white **Templo de San Juan**, Chamula's pretty main church, is vividly accented in green and blue. Step inside and you'll instantly notice hundreds of flickering candles, clouds of copal incense and worshippers kneeling with their faces to the pine needle–carpeted floor. Chanting medicine men or women may be rubbing patients' bodies with eggs or bones, and you might even see a chicken or two being sacrificed. As you can imagine, it all makes for a powerful impression.

As on outsider, you must obtain a ticket (M$20) before entering the church. There's usually someone selling them at the door, or you can get one at the **tourist office** (⏰7am-6pm) in the orange building in front of (and to the side of) the church's front courtyard.

Be warned: absolutely NO photography is allowed inside the church. However tempting, *do not* ignore this restriction as the community takes it very seriously.

Three blocks back up the hill from the church, toward San Cristóbal (and off a side street), is the town's **graveyard**. Black crosses are for people who died old, white for young, and blue for others.

To get to Chamula, take a combi from Calle Honduras in San Cristóbal. They leave frequently from 4am to 6:30pm (M$16, 30 minutes).

Tabasco

They say that Tabasco has more water than land, and if you look at the lagoons, rivers and wetlands on a map you can see why – especially during the rainy season. It's always hot and sweaty, marginally less so when you catch a breeze along the Gulf of Mexico or if you venture into the southern hills. Few travelers linger in Tabasco longer than it takes to see the outstanding Olmec stone sculpture in Villahermosa's Parque-Museo La Venta, but it can be an interesting slice of Mexico, with some intriguing pre-Hispanic sites (both the Olmecs and the Maya flourished here), a large capital city, a beautiful natural environment and a relaxed populace.

Villahermosa

POP 650,000

This sprawling, flat, hot and humid city is home to over a quarter of Tabasco's population and was never the 'beautiful town' its name implies. Settled on the winding Río Grijalva, the city's most attractive attribute became its worst enemy when the river burst its banks and engulfed the city in 2007. Villahermosa still struggles to control its surging waterway.

The tourism information kiosk at the ADO bus terminal has maps and can book hotels.

Sights

Parque-Museo La Venta PARK, MUSEUM

(Av Ruíz Cortines; M$47; 8am-4pm; P) This fascinating outdoor park, zoo and museum was created in 1958, when petroleum exploration threatened the highly important ancient Olmec settlement of La Venta in western Tabasco. Archaeologists moved the site's most significant finds, including three colossal stone heads, to Villahermosa.

Plan two to three hours for your visit, and take mosquito repellent (the park is set in humid tropical woodland). Parque-Museo La Venta lies 2km northwest of the Zona Luz, beside Avenida Ruiz Cortines, the main east–west highway crossing the city. It's M$30 via *colectivo*.

Inside, you first come to a zoo devoted to animals from Tabasco and nearby regions: cats include jaguars, ocelots and jaguarundi, and there are white-tailed deer, spider monkeys, crocodiles, boa constrictors, peccaries and plenty of colorful birds, including scarlet macaws and keel-billed toucans.

There's an informative display in English and Spanish on Olmec archaeology as you pass through to the sculpture trail, the start of which is marked by a giant ceiba (the sacred tree of the Olmec and Maya). This 1km walk is lined with finds from La Venta. Among the most impressive, in the order you come to them, are Stele 3, which depicts a bearded man with a headdress; Altar 5, depicting a figure carrying a child; Monument 77, 'El Gobernante,' a very sour-looking seated ruler; the monkey-faced Monument 56; Monument 1, the colossal head of a helmet-wearing warrior; and Stele 1, showing a young goddess (a rare Olmec representation of anything female). Animals that pose no danger (such as coatis, squirrels and black agoutis) roam freely around the park.

Museo de Historia Natural MUSEUM

(Av Ruíz Cortines; admission M$24; 8am-5pm Tue-Sun, last admission 4pm; P) Just outside the Parque-Museo La Venta entrance, the small Museo de Historia Natural has good displays on dinosaurs, space, early humanity and Tabascan ecosystems (all in Spanish).

Museo Regional de Antropología MUSEUM

(http://iec.tabasco.gob.mx; Periférico Carlos Pellicer; M$60; 9am-4:30pm Tue-Sun; P) Villahermosa's shiny, recently rebuilt regional anthropology museum holds some excellent exhibits on Olmec, Maya, Nahua and Zoque cultures in Tabasco – including Tortuguero #6, the infamous tablet *solely* responsible for the dire 'end of world' predictions forecast for December 21, 2012. It's in the CICOM complex, a 15-minute walk from Zona Luz and just south of the Paseo Tabasco bridge.

Sleeping & Eating

Hotel Oriente HOTEL $

(993-312-01-21; hotel-oriente@hotmail.com; Madero 425; d with fan M$270-350, with air-con M$400-490;) The Oriente is a friendly and well-run downtown hotel with simple budget rooms, all with TV. Rooms overlooking the main street are bright, but bring earplugs for noise. It's small, so reserve two days in advance.

Hotel Provincia Express HOTEL $$

(993-314-53-78; www.hotelesprovinciaexpress.infored.mx; Lerdo de Tejada 303; r incl breakfast from M$860; P) Excellent value in a central location, this hotel has small but

INDIGENOUS PEOPLES OF CHIAPAS

Of the nearly 5 million people of Chiapas, approximately a quarter are indigenous, with language being the key ethnic identifier. Each of the eight principal groups has its own language, beliefs and customs, a cultural variety that makes Chiapas one of the most fascinating states in Mexico.

Travelers to the area around San Cristóbal are most likely to encounter the **Tzotziles** and the **Tzeltales**. Their traditional religious life is nominally Catholic, but integrates pre-Hispanic elements. Most people live in the hills outside the villages, which are primarily market and ceremonial centers.

Tzotzil and Tzeltal clothing is among the most varied, colorful and elaborately worked in Mexico. It not only identifies wearers' villages but also continues ancient Maya traditions. Many of the seemingly abstract designs on these costumes are in fact stylized snakes, frogs, butterflies, birds, saints and other beings. Some motifs have religious-magical functions: scorpions, for example, can be a symbolic request for rain, since they are believed to attract lightning.

The **lacandones** dwelled deep in the Lacandón Jungle and largely avoided contact with the outside world until the 1950s. They now number less than 1000 and mostly live in three main settlements in that same region (Lacanjá Chansayab, Metzabok and Nahá), with low-key tourism being one of their major means of support. Lacandones are readily recognizable in their white tunics and long black hair cut in a fringe. Most lacandones have now abandoned their traditional animist religion in favor of Presbyterian or evangelical forms of Christianity.

Traditionally treated as second-class citizens, indigenous groups mostly live on the least productive land in the state, with the least amount of government services or infrastructure. Many indigenous communities rely on subsistence farming and have no running water or electricity, and it was frustration over lack of political power and their historical mistreatment that fueled the Zapatista rebellion, putting a spotlight on the region's distinct inequities.

Today, long-standing indigenous ways of life are challenged both by evangelical Christianity – opposed to many traditional animist-Catholic practices and the abuse of alcohol in religious rituals – and by the Zapatista movement, which rejects traditional leadership hierarchies and is raising the rights and profile of women. Many highland indigenous people have emigrated to the Lacandón Jungle to clear new land, or to Mexican and US cities in search of work.

Despite all obstacles, indigenous identities and self-respect survive. Indigenous people may be suspicious of outsiders, and may resent interference in their religious observances or other aspects of their life, but if treated with due respect they are likely to respond in kind.

tidy and pleasant rooms and a homey yellow color scheme. It's on a pedestrian street, so get a window if possible; avoid the windowless rooms. There's a cafe in the lobby.

Café Punta del Cielo CAFE **$**

(Plaza de Armas; coffee M$27-45; ⏲7am-10pm;) A respite from the raging heat and humidity, this small air-conditioned glass box next to the Torre del Caballero footbridge is a dream come true. Primarily a cafe, it serves premium hot and cold coffee drinks (some organic), as well as panini and light snacks. Go for brain freeze with an arctic frappé.

Rock & Roll Cocktelería SEAFOOD **$$**

(Reforma 307; mains M$140-220; ⏲10am-10pm;) A maelstrom of heat, swirling fans and blaring TVs. Everyone's here for the seafood cocktails (though they also have good ceviche and seafood stew) and cheap beer. It's on a pedestrian street across from the Miraflores Hotel, and has 60 years under its belt.

ℹ Getting There & Around

Villahermosa's **Aeropuerto Rovirosa** (☎993-356-01-57; Carretera Villahermosa-Macuspana Km 13) is 13km east of the town center, off Hwy 186. It's serviced by Aeroméxico and United Airlines. A taxi from the airport to the center costs M$240 and takes about 20 minutes. You can also walk 600m to the suburb of Dos Montes, where *colectivo* (shared) taxis cost M$25 per person and leave you at a market about 1km north of Zona Luz (on Amado Nervo between Piño Suárez and Constitución). Taxis from the center to the airport cost from M$180, or you can take the Dos Montes *colectivo* taxi from that same market.

The first-class **ADO bus station** (993-312-84-22; Mina 297) is 750m north of the Zona Luz. It's a busy place and long lines can form, so get here early if you're on a schedule. Second-class bus terminals include **Cardesa** (cnr Hermanos Bastar Zozaya & Castillo) and the **Central de Autobuses de Tabasco** (CAT; 993-312-29-77; cnr Av Ruíz Cortines & Castillo); these terminals are within walking distance of the ADO station. Destinations from Villahermosa include Campeche (M$356 to M$572, six to seven hours, 15 daily), Cancún (M$550 to M$1134, 12 to 16 hours, 20 daily), Mérida (M$430 to M$960, nine to 10 hours, 28 daily), Palenque (M$85 to M$164, 2½ hours, 22 daily) and San Cristóbal de las Casas (M$402, six hours, 11:40pm only).

Most taxis in town are *colectivo,* and most of these shared rides within the center cost M$25. Just flag down a taxi and the driver will ask which direction you're going.

Comalcalco

Comalcalco, 51km northwest of Villahermosa, is typical of the medium-sized towns of western Tabasco – hot, bustling, quite prosperous and spread around a broad, open central plaza (Parque Juárez).

What makes it especially worth visiting are the impressive ruins of **ancient Comalcalco** (M$48; 8am-4pm), 2km north of the city limits. This Maya site is unique because many of its buildings are constructed of bricks and/or mortar made from oyster shells. The museum at the entrance has a fine array of sculptures and engravings of human heads, deities, glyphs and animals such as crocodiles and pelicans. There is also an interesting exhibit explaining how Comalcalco's dead were buried under giant jugs. Bring mosquito repellent for your visit.

The site is about 1km (signposted) off the main road. Combis to the turnoff run north along López Mateos, two blocks east of the Comalli bus depot (M$10, 10 minutes). A taxi to the site costs M$50; either negotiate a roundtrip with waiting time or take a combi back, which requires walking 1km to the main road, going under the overpass and flagging one down.

In Villahermosa, the Comalli bus depot is near the corner of Gil y Saénz and Aberlardo Reyes, a block northwest of the ADO terminal. Buses to Comalcalco leave from Villahermosa every 15 minutes from 5am to 10:30pm (M$34, one hour).

Palenque

916 / POP 43,000

Deservedly one of the top destinations of Chiapas, the soaring jungle-swathed temples of ancient Palenque are a national treasure and one of the best examples of Maya architecture in Mexico. Modern Palenque town, 8km to the east, is a sweaty place with little appeal except as a hub for many services, and as a jumping-off point for the ruins.

History

The name Palenque (Palisade) is Spanish and has no relation to the city's ancient name, which may have been Lakamha (Big Water). Palenque was first occupied around 100 BC, and flourished from around AD 630 to around 740. The city rose to prominence under the ruler Pakal, who reigned from AD 615 to 683. Archaeologists have determined that Pakal is represented by hieroglyphics of sun and shield, and he is also referred to as Sun Shield (Escudo Solar). He lived to the then-incredible age of 80.

Pakal's son Kan B'alam II (r 684–702), who is represented in hieroglyphics by the jaguar and the serpent (and is also called Jaguar Serpent II), continued Palenque's expansion and artistic development. During Kan B'alam II's reign, Palenque extended its zone of control to the Río Usumacinta, but was challenged by the rival Maya city of Toniná, 65km south. Kan B'alam's brother and successor, K'an Joy Chitam II (Precious Peccary), was captured by forces from Toniná in 711, and probably executed there. Palenque enjoyed a resurgence between 722 and 736, however, under Ahkal Mo' Nahb' III (Turtle Macaw Lake), who added many substantial buildings. After AD 900 Palenque was largely abandoned.

Sights

Palenque Ruins RUINS

(M$51; 8am-5pm, last entry 4:30pm) Just 8km from Palenque city, the ruins of ancient Palenque stand at the precise point where the first hills rise out of the Gulf Coast plain. The dense jungle covering these hills forms an evocative backdrop to Palenque's exquisite Maya architecture. Hundreds of ruined buildings are spread over 15 sq km, but only a fairly compact central area has been excavated. The forest around these temples is home to howler monkeys, toucans and ocelots.

The ruins and surrounding forests form a national park, the **Parque Nacional**

Palenque Ruins

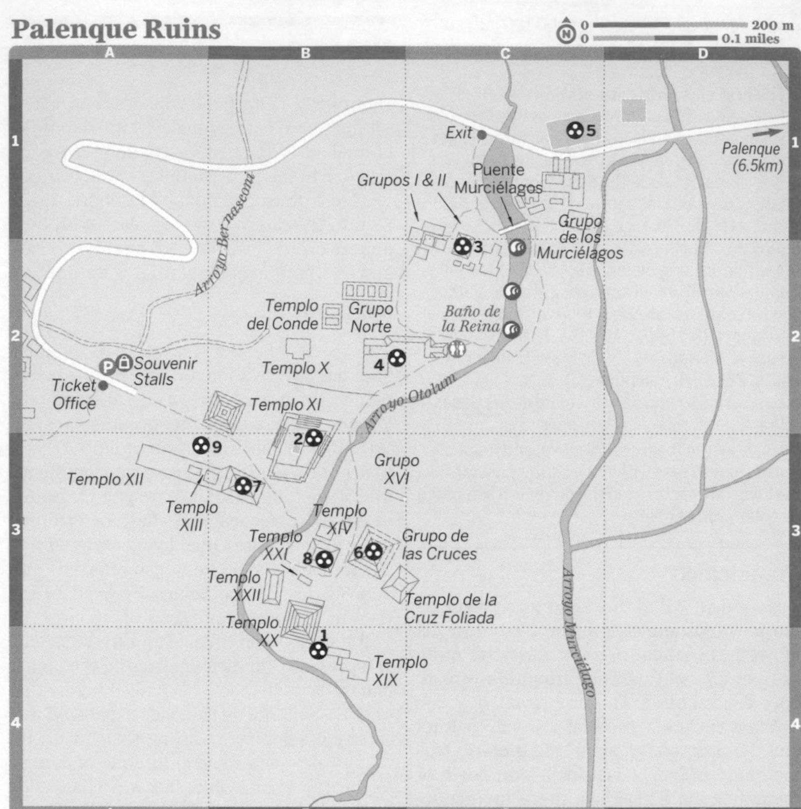

Palenque Ruins

Sights

Palenque, for which you must pay a separate M$27 admission fee at Km 4.5 on the road to the ruins. Plan on staying at the ruins at least three hours; the last entry is at 4:30pm.

Don't miss Palenque's extraordinary **Museo de Sitio** (Carretera Palenque-Ruinas Km 7; with ruins ticket free; ⏲9am-4:30pm Tue-Sun), which displays finds from the site and interprets, in English and Spanish, Palenque's history. The highlight here is the life-size reproduction of Pakal's (Palenque's greatest leader) carved stone sarcophagus lid.

Official site **guides** (2-hr tour for up to 7 people in English/Spanish M$1020/880) hang out near the entrance and can be identified by their neck badges. Unofficial guides are also around and charge less. Food and beverages are available, and there are plenty of souvenir vendors both inside and outside the site.

Combis run to and from the ruins about every 15 minutes from 6am to 6pm daily (M$24 each way). They will pick you up or drop you off anywhere along the town-to-ruins road.

Exploring the Site

As you enter the site, a line of temples rises in front of the jungle on your right, culminating about 100m ahead at the **Templo de las Inscripciones** (Temple of the Inscriptions), the tallest and most stately of Palenque's buildings. From the top, interior stairs lead down into the tomb of Pakal (closed indefinitely to avoid further damage from the humidity exuded by visitors). This is where, in 1952, Pakal's jewel-bedecked skeleton and jade mosaic death mask were uncovered by Alberto Ruz Lhuillier (whose **tomb** is in front of Templo XIII). It was one of the greatest Maya archeological finds in history. The site museum has a reproduction of Pakal's sarcophagus lid; the real lid remains down in the closed tomb.

Diagonally opposite the Templo de las Inscripciones is **El Palacio** (The Palace), a large structure divided into four main courtyards, with a maze of corridors and rooms. Keep following the path over a bridge and up some stairs; go left at the 'Y' and you'll soon reach the **Grupo de las Cruces** (Group of the Crosses). Soon after the death of his father, Pakal's son Kan B'alam II (r 684–702) started designing the temples here. The **Templo del Sol** (Temple of the Sun), to the west, has the best-preserved roofcomb at Palenque. Nearby, steep steps climb to the **Templo de la Cruz** (Temple of the Cross), the most impressive in this group.

South of the Grupo de las Cruces is the **Acrópolis Sur**, where archaeologists have recovered some terrific finds in recent excavations. It appears to have been constructed as an extension of the Grupo de las Cruces, but this area was closed at research time and unfortunately will probably remain closed for a few more years.

Follow the path north and back down to the river; you'll eventually reach the **Juego de Pelota** (Ball Court) and, behind it, the handsome and blissfully souvenir-free buildings of **Grupo Norte** (Northern Group). After a visit here you can follow a steep path down to mildly interesting **Grupo II**, but better yet double back to the original path and take it across the river again and down a series of steep stairs, eventually reaching the **Grupo de los Murciélagos** (Bat Group). You'll then cross a pretty bridge with a view of a small waterfall – now head up a short way to Grupo II if you'd like, and finally exit via the back way (this exit is open until 4pm only). Be sure to give yourself enough time to visit the site museum; from here you can easily flag a transport van back to the entrance, or to Palenque city.

Sleeping

It's very convenient to stay in Palenque town, where most services are located. However, if you'd rather have jungly peace, and especially if you have your own wheels, consider sleeping at one of several accommodations along the 8km road to Palenque ruins. Frequent combis (M$10) run between town and the ruins, so getting back and forth is easy.

The hippie-bohemian jungle enclave of El Panchán is a good middle ground (if you can handle 'backpacker rustic'). It's located halfway between town and the ruins, and offers a few accommodation choices, a couple of restaurants and a tour agency.

Palenque town has its own version of a 'jungle' neighborhood, called La Cañada. It's very leafy and more peaceful than staying in the center, which is only a few blocks away.

Prices are for high season, which is around Christmas, Easter, July and August. Rates drop 20% to 50% outside these times.

In Palenque Town

Yaxkin HOSTEL $

(916-345-01-02; www.hostalyaxkin.com; Prolongación Hidalgo 1; dm M$162, d with/without bathroom M$472/342, r with air-con & bathroom M$586; P ⊖ ❄ @ ≈) Channeling laid-back El Panchán from pretty La Cañada, this former disco has been revamped into a modern hostel with a guest kitchen, ping-pong table, multiple lounges and a swank restaurant/bar and cafe. Rooms without air-con are monastic but funky. The fan-cooled dorms (one for women only) and private rooms with air-con feel more pleasant and comfortable.

Hostal San Miguel HOTEL $

(916-345-01-52; hostalmiguel1@hotmail.com; Hidalgo 43; dm M$150, s/d with fan M$250/380, with air-con M$380/510; ⊖ ❄ ≈) Who doesn't love a hotel with towel animals? A quiet and clean economical choice; rooms have good light and views from the upper floors. Dark two- and four-bed dorms don't have hot water or air-con, and all air-con rooms have two queen beds.

Hotel Lacandonia HOTEL $$

(916-345-00-57; Allende 77; s/d/tr/q M$550/620/750/810; P ❄ ≈) A modern hotel with a subtle splash of style. Tasteful airy rooms all have wrought-iron beds, reading lights and cable TV, and there's a good restaurant. The upstairs rooms facing the street have cute balconies and the best light.

Hotel Maya Rue HOTEL $$

(916-345-07-43; www.hotelmayaruepalenque.com; Aldama s/n; r/tr M$750/900; ❄ @ ≈) Tree-trunk beams and dramatic lighting add unexpected style to this 12-room offering combining traditional materials and industrial chic. Some rooms have shaded private balconies, but all are spacious and come with cable TV. Cafe on premises.

Hotel Maya Tulipanes HOTEL $$$
(☎916-345-02-01, 800-714-47-10; www.mayatulipanes.com.mx; Cañada 6, La Cañada; r/tr M$1450/1600; P ⊖ ❄ @ ≋ ≋) Entered through a muraled foyer, this La Cañada hotel has large, comfortable, air-conditioned rooms with two wrought-iron double beds and minimalist decor. It's designed around a pretty garden with a small pool and a restaurant. Contact for discounts.

Outside Palenque Town

Margarita & Ed Cabañas GUESTHOUSE $
(☎916-348-69-90; www.margaritaandedcabanas.blogspot.com; Carreterra Palenque-Ruinas Km 4.5, El Panchán; cabañas M$285, r with fan M$320-410, s/d with air-con M$480/570; P ❄) With the most spotless digs in the jungle, Margarita has welcomed travelers to her exceptionally homey place for decades. Bright, clean and cheerful rooms have good mosquito netting, and the more rustic screened *cabañas* are well kept too, with reading lights and private bathrooms. There's free drinking water, a book exchange, and a lovely newer building with super-spacious rooms.

Mayabell HOTEL, CAMPGROUND $$
(☎916-341-69-77; www.mayabell.com.mx; Carretera Palenque-Ruinas Km 6; campsites per person M$75, vehicle site with hookups M$210, cabañas without bathroom M$320, r with fan/air-con M$820/1100; P ❄ ≋ ≋) With a sprawling jungle-side pool frequented by monkeys, this spacious grassy campground has tons of clean and comfortable sleeping options, plus an enjoyable restaurant. Rooms with air-con are very homey and comfortable; those with fan are more basic, as are the shared bathrooms.

EXPLORE MORE OF CHIAPAS

For more information on Chiapas, check out our comprehensive coverage in the *Mexico* guidebook or download a PDF copy at www.shop.lonelyplanet.com. Here are some of our DIY adventures:

- A respite from both the steamy lowland jungle and the chilly highlands, the bustling market town of **Ocosingo** sits in a gorgeous and broad temperate valley midway between San Cristóbal and Palenque. The impressive Maya ruins of **Toniná** are just a few kilometers away.
- Two spectacular water attractions – the thundering cascades of **Agua Azul** and the 35m jungle waterfall of **Misol-Ha** – are both short detours off the Ocosingo–Palenque road.
- The largest Lacandón Maya village, **Lacanjá Chansayab**, is 12km from Bonampak. Its family compounds are scattered around a wide area, many of them with creeks or even the Río Lacanjá flowing past their grassy grounds. Check www.ecochiapas.com/lacanja for details on visiting the region.
- The temperate pine and oak forest along the Guatemalan border east of Chinkultic is dotted with over 50 small lakes of varied hues, called the **Lagos de Montebello**. The nearby **Chinkultic ruins** add to the mystery.
- Ringed by rainforest 140km southeast of Ocosingo in the Reserva de la Biosfera Montes Azules, **Laguna Miramar** is one of Mexico's most remote and exquisite lakes. Rock ledges on small islands make blissful wading spots, while petroglyphs and a sea-turtle cave are reachable by canoe, which you can rent from the community tourism project in **Emiliano Zapata**.
- The luxuriant cloud forests of **Reserva de la Biosfera El Triunfo**, high in the remote Sierra Madre de Chiapas, are a bird-lover's paradise.
- The large **Reserva de la Biosfera La Encrucijada** protects a 1448-sq-km strip of coastal lagoons, sand bars and wetlands.
- Set 12km east of Tuxtla Gutiérrez on the way to San Cristóbal, **Chiapa de Corzo** is a small and attractive colonial town with an easygoing, provincial air. Set on the north bank of the broad Río Grijalva, it's the main starting point for trips into the **Cañón del Sumidero**.
- The dramatic sinkhole **Sima de Las Cotorras** punches 160m wide and 140m deep into the earth. It's about 1½ hours from Tuxtla Gutiérrez.

★Boutique Hotel Quinta Chanabnal BOUTIQUE HOTEL $$$
(☎916-345-53-20; www.quintachanabnal.com; Carretera Palenque-Ruinas Km 2.2; r US$210, ste US$340-462; P❄☎≋) The Maya-inspired architecture and impeccable service at this decadent boutique hotel will leave you swooning. Enter through heavy wood doors carved by local artisans into spacious stone-floor suites that contain majestically draped four-poster beds and cavernous bathrooms. Water features on the premises include a creek, a small lagoon and a multitiered swimming pool.

Jardines La Aldea HOTEL $$$
(☎916-345-16-93; www.hotellaaldea.net; Carretera Palenque-Ruinas Km 2.8; r M$1300-1500; P❄☎≋) The four-star Aldea has 33 large, beautiful and bright *palapa*-roofed rooms set amidst lovely grounds. Each room has an outside terrace with hammock. It's a stylish place, with a peaceful hilltop restaurant and a wonderful pool area. There are no TVs, making it an ideal place to get away from it all.

Eating

In Palenque Town

Café Jade MEXICAN, CHIAPANECO $
(Prolongación Hidalgo 1; breakfast M$42-68, mains M$53-90; ⏲7am-11pm; ☎) A chill indoor/outdoor spot on the ground floor of the Yaxkin hostel, with long sofa seating at tree plank tables. Good for breakfast, Chiapan specialities and chicken dishes.

★Restaurant Las Tinajas MEXICAN $$
(cnr Av 20 de Noviembre & Abasolo; mains M$85-130; ⏲7am-11pm;) It doesn't take long to figure out why this place is always busy. It slings enormous portions of excellent home-style food – enough to keep you (and possibly another person) fueled up for hours. *Pollo a la veracruzana* (chicken in a tomato/olives/onion sauce) and *camarones al guajillo* (shrimp with a not-too-hot type of chili) are both delicious, as is the house salsa.

El Huachinango Feliz SEAFOOD $$
(Hidalgo s/n; mains M$90-160; ⏲9am-11pm) Popular, atmospheric restaurant in the leafy La Cañada neighborhood. It has an attractive front patio with tables and umbrellas, and there's also an upstairs covered terrace. Seafood is the specialty here – order seafood soup, seafood cocktails, grilled fish or shrimp served 10 different ways. The service is slooow but the food is worth the wait.

La Selva MEXICAN $$
(☎916-345-03-63; Hwy 199; mains M$85-220; ⏲11:30am-11pm;) Palenque's most upscale restaurant serves up well prepared steaks, seafood, salads and *antojitos* (typical Mexican snacks) under an enormous *palapa* roof, with jungle-themed stained-glass panels brightening one wall. Try the *pigua* (freshwater lobster) when it's available in the fall. Reserve ahead in high season.

Outside Palenque Town

★Don Mucho's MEXICAN, INTERNATIONAL $
(Carretera Palenque-Ruinas Km 4.5, El Panchán; mains M$60-150; ⏲7am-11pm) The hot spot of El Panchán, popular Don Mucho's provides great-value meals in a jungly setting, with a candlelit ambience at night. Busy waiters bring pasta, fish, meat, plenty of *antojitos,* and pizzas (cooked in a purpose-built Italian-designed wood-fired oven) that are some of the finest this side of Naples.

Information

There are several internet cafes and banks with ATMs in Palenque town center.

Clínica Palenque (Velasco Suárez 33; ⏲8:30am-1:30pm & 5-9pm) Dr Alfonso Martínez speaks English.

Post Office (Independencia s/n; ⏲8am-8:30pm Mon-Fri, to noon Sat)

Municipal tourist information kiosk (El Parque; ⏲9am-2pm & 6-9pm Mon-Fri)

Getting There & Away

Highway holdups are more a thing of the past, but it's still best not to travel Hwy 199 between Palenque and San Cristóbal at night.

Palenque's airport has no commercial flights. The closest major airport is in Villahermosa.

ADO (☎916-345-13-44) has the main bus terminal, with deluxe and 1st-class services, an ATM and left-luggage facilities; it's also used by **OCC** (☎916-345-13-44) (1st-class) and TRT (2nd-class). **AEXA** (☎916-345-26-30; www.autobusesaexa.com.mx; Av Juárez 159), with 1st-class buses, and **Cardesa** (☎no tel; Av Juárez 159) (2nd-class) are 1½ blocks east.

Transportes Palenque (cnr Allende & Av 20 de Noviembre) runs vans to Tenosique, which has onward connections to Guatemala.

Getting Around

Taxis charge M$55 (up to M$70 at night) to El Panchán and M$60 to the ruins. Combis (M$24) head to the ruins from 6am to 6pm. You can also get picked up along the west half of Av Juarez as the combis drive their way out of town.

Bonampak & Yaxchilán

The ancient Maya cities of Bonampak and Yaxchilán, southeast of Palenque, are easily accessible thanks to the Carretera Fronteriza. This good, paved road runs parallel to the Mexico–Guatemala border all the way from Palenque to the Lagos de Montebello, and goes around the fringe of the Lacandón Jungle.

Bonampak, famous for its frescoes, is 152km by road from Palenque. The bigger and more important Yaxchilán, with a peerless jungle setting beside the broad and swift Río Usumacinta, is 173km by road, then about 22km by boat. Both can be visited in one long day.

The **Mesoamerican Ecotourism Alliance** (www.travelwithmea.org) and San Cristóbal–based **SendaSur** (☎967-678-39-09; www.sendasur.com.mx; 5 de Febrero 29; ⏲9am-2pm & 4-7pm Mon-Fri, 9am-noon Sat) organize multiday excursions to the region, including visits to several Lacandón villages.

Getting There & Away

PUBLIC TRANSPORTATION

To reach Bonampak from Palenque via public transportation, take an hourly combi bound for either Frontera Corozal or Benemerito and ask to be let out at San Javier (M$73, two hours). This is the 12km turnoff for Bonampak; from here you'll have to take a Lacandón vehicle to the ruins (M$180 per person roundtrip with two hours waiting time).

The combis that drop you at San Javier leave from a small van depot just south of the Maya Head statue at the entrance to Palenque; look for the black grate fence next to the 'Carne Suprema' sign. They also leave from the Transportes Montebello bus terminal, which is a few blocks northwest of Palenque's center, on Velasco Suárez near the corner of Calle 4a Poniente Norte.

To reach Yaxchilán from Palenque, take an hourly combi bound for Frontera Corozal (M$94, 2¾ hours), where you'll have to pay a M$20-per-person charge to enter the *embarcadero* (dock) area. From here it's a 40-minute *lancha* (motorboat) ride to the ruins. All boat operators charge M$900 for a roundtrip transporting one to three people with 2½ hours waiting time; four people costs M$1050; five to seven people is $1450; eight to 10 people is M$1800. *Lanchas* normally leave relatively frequently from 7am until 1:30pm or so, and it's sometimes possible to hook up with other travelers or a tour group to share costs.

It's possible to take a combi between the two ruins. Visit Yaxchilán first, then wait for a combi heading back to Palenque and ask to be let off at San Javier.

Always check when the last combi back to Palenque is; usually it's at 4pm or 5pm, depending on the season.

TOURS & PRIVATE VEHICLES

If you don't have a private vehicle, the easiest way to see both Bonampak and Yaxchilán is by taking a tour from Palenque. This is more much time efficient, less stressful and actually cheaper than dealing with public transportation – and allows enough time at each site for most people. Various tour agencies in Palenque organize this tour, and each charge the same amount: M$750 to M$1000 per person, depending on the season. Entry fees, two meals and all transportation (except a M$20 dock fee at Yaxchilán) are included, but there's no tour guide (these can be hired at each site).

Be aware that a cooperative requires ALL travelers to take a Lacandón van through their jungle to Bonampak. This happens about 3km into the side road towards the ruins; all travelers must stop at a checkpoint (whether they're in private vehicles or tour vans) and switch into a Lacandón van. The charge is high – M$180 per person for essentially a 19km roundtrip ride. This charge is *already included* in the price for travelers taking the day tour from Palenque.

There's a Pemex gas station at Chancalá and another at Benemerito on the Carretera Fronteriza. Because of its location near Guatemala, self-drivers should expect to stop at a few military checkpoints where you'll be checked to ensure you are not transporting illegal immigrants or drugs. It's best not to drive this road at night.

BUSES FROM PALENQUE

DESTINATION	FARE (M$)	DURATION (HRS)	FREQUENCY (DAILY)
Campeche	382	5	5 ADO
Cancún	630-1040	13	6 ADO
Mérida	576	8	5 ADO
San Cristóbal de las Casas	122-206	5	12 ADO, 5 AEXA
Villahermosa	150-174	2½	frequent ADO & AEXA

TRAVELING SAFELY IN CHIAPAS

In general, Chiapas is a safe place to travel. Many people associate the state with the Zapatistas, but this revolutionary organization has become less influential in the last decade and their main significant uprising occurred in 1994. In any case, tourists are not targeted by the Zapatistas.

Drug trafficking and illicit immigration are concerns along the border regions with Guatemala, and military checkpoints are frequent on the Carretera Fronteriza along the Guatemalan border from Palenque to the Lagos de Montebello. These checkpoints generally increase security for travelers, though it's best to be off the Carretera Fronteriza before dark. For similar reasons all border crossings with Guatemala are places you should aim to get through early in the day.

Indigenous villages are often extremely close-knit, and their people can be suspicious of outsiders and particularly sensitive about having their photos taken. In some villages cameras are, at best, tolerated – and sometimes not even that. You may put yourself in physical danger by taking photos without permission. Always ask first.

Travelers to Villahermosa should note the region is subject to seasonal floods.

Bonampak

The site of **Bonampak** (M$55; ⊙8am-5pm) spreads over 2.4 sq km, but all the main ruins stand around the rectangular Gran Plaza. Never a major city, Bonampak spent most of the Classic period in Yaxchilán's sphere of influence. The most impressive surviving monuments were built under Chan Muwan II, a nephew of Yaxchilán's Itzamnaaj B'alam II, who acceded to Bonampak's throne in AD 776. The 6m-high **Stele 1** in the **Gran Plaza** depicts Chan Muwan holding a ceremonial staff at the height of his reign. He also features in **Stele 2** and **Stele 3** on the **Acrópolis**, which rises from the south end of the plaza.

However, it's the vivid frescoes inside the modest-looking **Templo de las Pinturas** (Edificio 1) that have given Bonampak its fame – and its name, which means 'Painted Walls' in Yucatec Maya. The Bonampak site abuts the Reserva de la Biosfera Montes Azules, and is rich in wildlife.

Yaxchilán

Jungle-shrouded **Yaxchilán** (M$55; ⊙8am-5pm, last entry 4pm) has a terrific setting above a horseshoe loop in the Río Usumacinta. The control this location gave it over river commerce, plus a series of successful alliances and conquests, made Yaxchilán one of the most important Classic Maya cities in the Usumacinta region. Archaeologically, Yaxchilán is famed for its ornamented facades and roofcombs, and its impressive stone lintels carved with conquest and ceremonial scenes. A flashlight (and insect repellent) are helpful for exploring some parts of the site.

Yaxchilán peaked in power and splendor between AD 681 and 800 under the rulers Itzamnaaj B'alam II (Shield Jaguar II, 681–742), Yaxun B'alam IV (Bird Jaguar IV, 752–68) and Itzamnaaj B'alam III (Shield Jaguar III, 769–800). The city was abandoned around AD 810. Inscriptions here tell more about its 'Jaguar' dynasty than is known of almost any other Maya ruling clan. The shield-and-jaguar symbol appears on many buildings and steles; Yaxun B'alam IV's hieroglyph is a small jungle cat with feathers on its back and a bird superimposed on its head.

As you walk toward the ruins, a signed path to the right leads up to the **Pequeña Acrópolis**, a group of ruins on a small hilltop – to save sweat, visit this later. Staying on the main path, you soon reach the mazy passages of **El Laberinto** (Edificio 19), built between AD 742 and 752, during the interregnum between Itzamnaaj B'alam II and Yaxun B'alam IV. A few bats shelter under the structure's roof today. From this complicated two-level building you emerge at the northwest end of the extensive **Gran Plaza**.

Though it's difficult to imagine anyone here ever wanting to be any hotter than they already were, **Edificio 17** was apparently a sweat house. About halfway along the plaza, **Stele 1**, under a tarp and flanked by weathered sculptures of a crocodile and a jaguar, shows Yaxun B'alam IV in a ceremony that took place in AD 761.

The four-ton, **Stele 11**, under a *palapa* at the northeast corner of the Gran Plaza, was originally found in front of Edificio 40.

THE LACANDÓN JUNGLE

The Selva Lacandona (Lacandón Jungle), in eastern Chiapas, occupies just one-quarter of 1% of Mexico. Yet it contains more than 4300 plant species (about 17% of Mexico's total), 450 butterfly species (42% of the total), at least 340 bird species (32% of the total) and 163 mammal species (30% of the total). Among these are such emblematic creatures as the jaguar, the red macaw, the white turtle, the tapir and the harpy eagle.

This great fund of natural resources and genetic diversity is the southwest end of the Selva Maya, a 30,000-sq-km corridor of tropical rainforest stretching from Chiapas across northern Guatemala into Belize and the southern Yucatán. But the Lacandón Jungle is shrinking fast, under pressure from ranchers, loggers, oil prospectors, and farmers desperate for land. From around 15,000 sq km in the 1950s, an estimated 3000 to 4500 sq km of jungle remains today. Waves of land-hungry settlers deforested the northern third of the Lacandón Jungle by about 1960. Also badly deforested are the far eastern Marqués de Comillas area (settled since the 1970s) and La Cañada, between Ocosingo and Montes Azules. Most of what's left is in the Reserva de la Biosfera Montes Azules and the neighboring Reserva de la Biosfera Lacan-tun.

Not surprisingly, property rights within the region have been incredibly contested. In 1971, the Mexican government deeded a large section of land to 66 Lacandón 'guardian' families, ostensibly to protect the forest from over-exploitation. This, however, created tensions with other indigenous communities who were forced off their lands and whose own claims were put aside. It also helped create the Zapatista movement, since they saw the Lacandón Jungle as land that belonged to various indigenous communities – and not just the lacandones.

The lacandones argued that they were defending their property against invasive settlers, and have used it wisely for ecotourism projects. Other communities within the reserve, however, viewed it as an obfuscated land grab and pretext for eviction under the guise of environmental protection. They claim that new settlers were also using the forests in sustainable ways and that research companies were seeking to utilize the forests for bioprospecting (patenting) traditional plants, thus benefiting everyone.

Due to ongoing, and sometimes violent, conflicts since that fateful land deed over 40 years ago, the Mexican government has not been able to clearly demarcate land borders to this day. A carbon-sequestration program, along with economic development projects for the area, are the newest strategies for 'saving' this region, but only time will tell whether this is likely to make life any better for those living there.

A documentary film called *Keepers of the Earth* chronicles the environmental fight in the Lacandón Jungle.

The bigger of the two figures visible on it is Yaxun B'alam IV. Up the hill, **Edificio 20**, from the time of Itzamnaaj B'alam III, was the last significant structure built at Yaxchilán; its lintels are now in Mexico City.

An imposing stairway climbs from Stele 1 to **Edificio 33**, the best-preserved temple at Yaxchilán, with about half of its roofcomb intact. The final step in front of the building is carved with ball-game scenes, and relief carvings embellish the undersides of the lintels. Inside is a statue of Yaxun B'alam IV, minus his head, which is nearby (looters sought treasure inside his body).

From the clearing behind Edificio 33, a path leads into the trees. About 20m along this, fork left uphill (signed); go left at another fork after about 80m, and after a kilometer or so of uphill, you'll reach three buildings on a hilltop: **Edificio 39**, **Edificio 40** and **Edificio 41**.

Go back down the same way, then left at the sign to Pequeño Acropolis; after a few minutes you'll arrive there, then exit down the main stairs you passed on your way in.

Howler monkeys *(saraguates)* inhabit the tall trees at Yaxchilán, and are an evocative highlight. You'll almost certainly hear their roars, and you stand a good chance of seeing some. Spider monkeys, and occasionally red macaws, are also spotted here at times.

Drinks and snacks are available at the *embarcadero*. On your boat ride in, keep your eyes peeled for crocodiles sunning on the river banks. Also note that the land on other side of the river is Guatemala.

Understand Cancún, Cozumel & the Yucatán

The Yucatán Peninsula Today

Tourism is one of the driving forces behind life in the Yucatán, Mexico's most visited destination. For better or worse, the industry helps shape politics, economics and many of the region's important social and environmental issues. And because the peninsula is unquestionably one of the safest and most visitor-friendly places in all of Mexico, the tourism economy is thriving like never before.

Best on Film

Alamar (To the Sea; 2009) Moving docudrama about a Maya father–son relationship; Mexican filmmaker Pedro González-Rubio shot it at Banco Chinchorro, off the Mahahual coast.

Before Night Falls (2000) Partially filmed in Mérida, this Oscar–nominated biography of Cuban poet Reinaldo Arenas, played by Javier Bardem.

Che! El Argentino (2009) Campeche city stood in as Santa Clara, Cuba, for Steven Soderbergh's biopic about Argentine Ernesto 'Che' Guevara.

Toro Negro (Black Bull; 2005) Produced by Oscar winner Alejandro González Iñarritu, this Mexican documentary about a self-destructive amateur bullfighter was filmed in several Yucatán Maya communities.

Best in Print

Time Among the Maya (Ronald Wright; 1989) A travel memoir that explores past and present-day Maya culture and identity.

Incidents of Travel in Yucatán (John Lloyd Stephens; 1848) American writer Stephens recounts his adventures with English artist Frederick Catherwood in this classic travel book.

The Art of Mexican Cooking (Diana Kennedy; 1989) Food expert Diana Kennedy's definitive cookbook features mouth-watering recipes from the Yucatán and other Mexican regions.

The Yucatán Perserveres

The Yucatán has proved time and again that it can resist even the mightiest of blows to its flourishing tourism economy. In recent times, the peninsula has seen category 5 hurricanes raze entire cities, a massive viral outbreak and a crippling economic crisis.

In 2005, the northern parts of the Quintana Roo coast, including Cancún, Isla Mujeres and Isla Holbox, were dealt a devastating one-two punch by Hurricanes Emily and Wilma (the latter is the most intense Atlantic hurricane on record). In addition to leaving behind billions of dollars' worth of property damage, the storms wiped out Cancún's pristine white beaches and left much of Holbox under water. Dozens of lives were lost and it took years to rebuild many towns.

Another major crisis struck the peninsula in 2009, when the swine-flu outbreak drastically affected visit numbers to the Yucatán's resort areas. That, coupled with a worldwide economic crisis, made life extremely difficult for tourism-dependent communities throughout the region.

Around the same time as the swine-flu epidemic, the industry was facing another huge problem: drug-related violence, or, better said, misconstrued perceptions of the violence. Mexico's decade-long drug war has claimed more than 100,000 lives, but throughout it all the peninsular region has remained a safe haven. The Yucatán is actually safer than most US cities, but news of the drug war continues to scare away potential visitors. The truth is drug gangs rarely target tourists, not just in the Yucatán but in Mexico in general.

Tale of Two Economies

Yes, tourism is alive and well in the Yucatán: the peninsula's busiest gateway cities, Cancún and Mérida, both saw double-digit growth in international arrivals in 2015.

While that may be great for hotels, restaurants and tour operators, sadly, most folks in the region are not reaping the benefits of the tourism boom. In fact, a broad segment of the population continues to live in poverty.

Poverty in Mexico is defined as living on less than M$2542 a month in cities and less than M$1615 a month in rural areas (where jobs are extremely hard to come by nowadays). Here's a breakdown of poverty rates in states in and around the peninsula.

STATE	POVERTY RATE
Campeche	44%
Chiapas	76%
Tabasco	50%
Quintana Roo	36%
Yucatán state	46%

Progress at a Cost

There's no denying that tourism continues to generate many jobs across the peninsula, as does the manufacturing industry in and around Mérida. But locals worry that all the rapid development is causing long-lasting environmental and cultural degradation.

Sure, the peninsula has some of the largest protected areas in Mexico, such as the biosphere reserves of Calakmul, Sian Ka'an, Ría Lagartos and Ría Celestún, but now more than ever there's a serious need for sustainable development programs in the region's fast-growing cities, where water demand and waste management have become pressing concerns.

Another cause for concern on the peninsula is the gradual disappearance of indigenous languages. As more and more hotels and restaurants seek English speakers, new generations of workers are choosing to learn English over Maya as a second language. It's a decision usually based on sheer economic necessity. In Quintana Roo, for instance, only 16% of state residents speak an indigenous language; in Campeche it's just 12%; and in Yucatán state, which has Mexico's largest Maya-speaking population, the number of indigenous-language speakers has dwindled to 30%.

POPULATION (PENINSULAR STATES): **4.1 MILLION**

AREA: **148,961 SQ KM**

PENINSULA COASTLINE: **1764KM**

PERCENTAGE OF NATIONAL POPULATION: **CAMPECHE 0.7%, QUINTANA ROO 1.2%, YUCATÁN 1.7%**

if Mexico were 100 people

62 would be mixed ancestry (mestizo)
28 would be indigenous ancestry
10 would be mostly European ancestry

belief systems

(% of population)

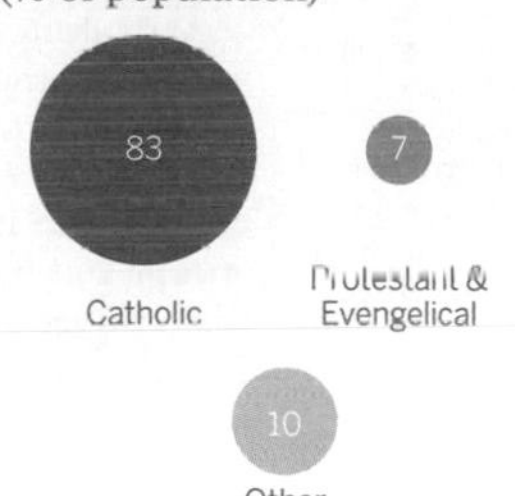

population per sq km

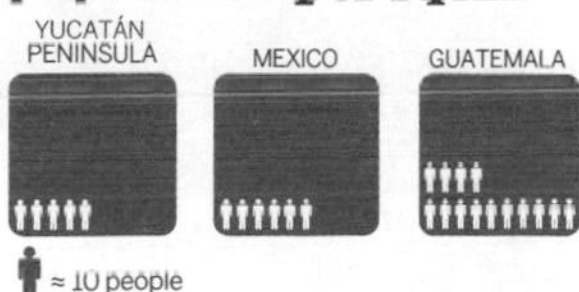

History

Reminders of the Yucatán's storied past are just about everywhere you turn on the peninsula: from extraordinary ancient Maya ruins and old-world colonial cities to Caste War battleground sites and crumbling *henequén* (sisal) haciendas. Even the relatively new kid on the block, the glitzy resort city of Cancún, has left an indelible mark on history as the region's cradle of mass tourism.

Legend has it the peninsula got its name when the Spanish conquistadors asked the indigenous locals what they called their land. The response was 'Yucatán' – Maya for 'We don't understand you.'

The Olmec Influence

Mexico's ancestral civilization arose near the Gulf coast, in the lowlands of southern Veracruz and neighboring Tabasco. These were the Olmecs, who invented a hieroglyphic writing system and erected ceremonial centers for the practice of religious rituals. Best known for the colossal heads they carved from basalt slabs, the Olmecs developed an artistic style, highlighted by jaguar motifs.

Even after their demise, aspects of Olmec culture lived on among their neighbors, paving the way for the later accomplishments of Maya art, architecture and science. Borrowing significantly from the Olmecs, the Zapotec culture arose in the highlands of Oaxaca at Monte Albán, and subsequent civilizations at Teotihuacán (near current-day Mexico City) and at El Tajín in Veracruz also show Olmec influence.

The Maya

Archaeologists believe Maya-speaking people first appeared in the highlands of Guatemala around 2500 BC, and in the following century groups of Maya relocated to the lowlands of the Yucatán Peninsula.

For a concise but complete account of the ancient cultures of southern Mexico and Guatemala, read *The Maya*, by Michael D Coe.

Agriculture played an important role in Maya life. Watching the skies and noting the movements of the planets and stars, the Maya were able to correlate their astronomical observations with the rains and agricultural cycles. As the Maya improved their agricultural skills, their society stratified into various classes. Villages sprang up beneath the jungle canopy and temples were constructed from the abundant limestone. An easily carved substance, limestone allowed the builders to demonstrate a high degree of artistic expression. The material could also be made into plaster, upon which artists painted murals to chronicle events.

TIMELINE

3114 BC

Our current universe is created – at least according to Maya mythology. Archaeologists have even been able to pin down a specific date for the creation: August 13, 3114 BC.

2400 BC

Maya-speaking farmers arrive in the Yucatán Peninsula. The Olmec culture creates a system of writing. Olmec culture later influences the Zapotec culture.

1000 BC–AD 250

Pre-Classic period. Maya villages appear in Yucatán, Chiapas and Guatemala. The Maya become adept farmers and astronomers. The Izapan civilization creates a calendar and writing system, and massive pyramids are built.

Local potentates were buried beneath these elaborate temples. As each successive leader had to have a bigger temple, larger platforms were placed upon earlier ones, forming gigantic step pyramids with a thatched shelter on top. Often these temple-pyramids were decorated with huge stylized masks. More and more pyramids were built around large plazas, much in the same manner that common people built their thatched houses facing a common open space. This heralded the flourishing of the Classic Maya civilization.

Mundo Maya online (www.mayadiscovery.com) features articles on Maya cosmology, navigation and agriculture, among other aspects of this incredible ancient civilization.

The Golden Age

Over the nearly seven centuries of the Classic Maya period (AD 250 to 925), the Maya made spectacular intellectual and artistic strides, a legacy that can still be admired today throughout the peninsula and beyond.

The great ceremonial centers at Copán, Tikal, Yaxchilán, Palenque, and especially Kaminaljuyú (near present-day Guatemala City), flourished during the early phase of this period. Around AD 400 armies from Teotihuacán invaded the Maya highlands, imposing their rule and their culture for a time, though they were eventually absorbed into the daily life of the Maya.

After AD 600, at the height of the late Classic period, Maya lands were ruled not as an empire but as a collection of independent – but also interdependent – city-states. Each of these had its noble house, headed by a king who was the social, political and religious focus of the city's life. This ruler propitiated the gods by shedding his blood in ceremonies where he pierced his tongue or penis with a sharp instrument, and he led his soldiers into battle against rival cities, capturing prisoners for use in human sacrifices.

YUCATÁN'S DINOSAUR-KILLING METEORITE?

Most scientists agree that a meteorite slammed into the Yucatán about 65 million years ago, triggering a series of events that may have caused the dinosaurs and other species to go extinct.

Using seismic monitoring equipment, geologists have found evidence for the existence of such an enormous crater (estimated to be around 200km wide) off the northern coast of the Yucatán, near the port of Chicxulub.

Scientists have theorized that the impact event kicked up enough debris to block out the sun for a decade, which either sparked a global freeze or made the air unbreathable. And now there's new research suggesting that the colossal impact also may have caused a worldwide surge in volcanic activity, which in turn blanketed the Earth's atmosphere with ashes and toxic fumes.

An international research team plans to drill 1500m below the seabed to extract geological samples from the crater. They hope the results of the investigation will once and for all reveal the mystery of why the dinosaurs disappeared from the Earth.

AD 250–925

Classic period. It's a time of high society, marked by the invasion of Teotihuacán, the rise of the Puuc, and the eventual collapse of the Classic Maya and the ascendancy of the Toltec.

925–1530

Post-Classic period. The Toltecs of central Mexico establish their domain at Chichén Itzá then the Itzá form the League of Mayapán, which dominates politics in northern Yucatán for 200 years.

late 1400s

Beginning of the end of the post-Classic period. Maya decline hits full tilt, as fractious city-states replace Mayapán rule. Until the coming of the conquistadors, northern Yucatán is riddled with battles and power struggles.

1492

Spanish arrive in the Caribbean, settling momentarily on Hispañola and Cuba, but it will be several hundred years before they truly 'conquer' the region. European diseases will eventually kill 90% of indigenous inhabitants.

Toward the end of the Classic period, the focus of Maya civilization shifted northward to Yucatán, where new nuclei developed at what is now called Chichén Itzá, Uxmal and Calakmul, giving us the artistic styles known as Puuc, Chenes and Río Bec.

Post-Classic Period

The Toltecs

The collapse of Classic Maya civilization is as surprising as it was sudden. It seems as though the upper classes demanded ever more servants, acolytes and laborers, and though the Maya population was expanding rapidly, it did not produce enough farmers to feed everyone in the region. Thus weakened, the Maya were effectively prey to the next wave of invaders from central Mexico.

The elite of the Classic Maya often received enemas of a sweet mead named *balché*. They also thought being cross-eyed was particularly beautiful.

In the wake of Teotihuacán's demise, the Toltec people emerged as Mexico's new boss, establishing their capital at Tula (north of present-day Mexico City). According to most historians, a Toltec faction, led by a fair-haired king named Topiltzin – the self-proclaimed heir to the title of Quetzalcóatl (Plumed Serpent) – was forced to leave its native land by hostile warrior clans. Quetzalcóatl and his followers retreated to the Gulf coast and sailed eastward to Yucatán, establishing their new base at Uucil-abnal – which would later be renamed Chichén Itzá. The culture at this Toltec-dominated center flourished after the late 10th century, when all of the great buildings were constructed, but by 1200 the city was abandoned. Many Mexicans believed, however, that the Plumed Serpent king would some day return from the direction of the rising sun to reclaim his domain at Tula.

The Itzá

Chronicle of the Maya Kings and Queens, by Simon Martin and Nikolai Grube, tells in superbly illustrated detail the histories of 11 of the most important Maya city-states and their rulers.

Forced by invaders to leave their traditional homeland on the Yucatán's Gulf coast, a group called the Itzá headed southeast into northeastern Guatemala. Some continued to Belize, later making their way north along the coast and into northern Yucatán, where they settled at the abandoned Uucil-abnal around AD 1220. The Itzá leader proclaimed himself Kukulcán (the Maya name for Quetzalcóatl), as had the city's Toltec founder, and recycled lots of other Toltec lore as well. The Itzá strengthened the belief in the sacred nature of cenotes (limestone sinkholes that provided the Maya with their water supply), and they even named their new home Chichén Itzá (Mouth of the Well of the Itzá).

From Chichén Itzá, the ruling Itzá traveled westward and founded a new capital city at Mayapán, which dominated the political life of northern Yucatán for several centuries. From Mayapán, the Cocom lineage of the Itzá ruled a fractious collection of Yucatecan city-states until the mid-15th century, when a subject people from Uxmal, the Xiú, overthrew

1519–21

Hernán Cortés, first landing on Isla Cozumel, begins making his way along the Gulf coast toward central Mexico, home of the Aztec empire. He captures the Aztec ruler Moctezuma II and conquers Tenochtitlán.

1527

Francisco de Montejo and his son (the Younger) land in Cozumel and then in Xel-Há with the idea of conquering the region. Eventually they return to Mexico City in defeat.

1530–1821

The *encomienda* system basically enslaves the indigenous populations, and friars begin to convert the population in earnest. The Maya blend Christian teachings with their own beliefs, creating a unique belief system.

1542

Francisco de Montejo (the Younger) avenges his father's legacy, establishing the colonial capital at Mérida upon the ruins of the Maya city of T'ho.

Cocom power. Mayapán was pillaged, ruined and never repopulated. For the next century, until the coming of the conquistadors, northern Yucatán was alive with battles among its city-states.

The New World Order

Led by Christopher Columbus, the Spanish arrived in the Caribbean in 1492 and proceeded to seek a westward passage to Asia. They staged exploratory expeditions to the Yucatán in 1517 and 1518, but hostile locals fiercely resisted their attempts to penetrate Mexico's Gulf coast.

Then Diego Velázquez, the Spanish governor of Cuba, asked his young personal secretary, Hernán Cortés, to lead a new expedition westward. Even though Velázquez subsequently tried to cancel the voyage, Cortés set sail on February 15, 1519, with 11 ships, 550 men and 16 horses.

Landing first at the isle of Cozumel off the Yucatán, the Spaniards were joined by Jerónimo de Aguilar, a Spanish priest who had been shipwrecked there several years earlier. With Aguilar acting as translator and guide, Cortés' force moved around the coastline to Tabasco. After defeating the inhabitants there, the expedition headed inland, winning more battles and some converts to Catholicism in the process.

Central Mexico was then dominated by the Aztec empire from its capital of Tenochtitlán (now Mexico City). The Aztecs, like many other cultures in the area, believed that Quetzalcóatl would one day return from the east, according to most historians, and – conveniently for him – Cortés' arrival coincided with their prophecies of the Plumed Serpent's return. The Aztecs allowed the small Spanish force into the capital, perhaps fearful of angering these strangers who might be gods.

By this time thousands of members of the Aztecs' subject peoples had allied with Cortés, eager to throw off the harsh rule imposed by their overlords. Many Aztecs died of smallpox introduced by the Spanish, and by the time they resolved to make war against Cortés and their subjects, they found themselves outnumbered, though they put up a tremendous fight.

Cortés then conquered central Mexico, after which he turned his attentions to the Yucatán.

Check www.sacred-texts.com for good translations of two sacred Maya books, the *Popol Vuh* and *Chilam Balam of Chumayel*.

Conquest & the Colonial Period

Despite political infighting among the Yucatecan Maya, conquest by the Spaniards was not easy. The Spanish monarch commissioned Francisco de Montejo (El Adelantado, or the Pioneer) with the task, and he set out from Spain in 1527 accompanied by his son, also named Francisco de Montejo (El Mozo, or the Lad) and a band of men. Landing first at Cozumel, then at Xel-Há on the mainland, the Montejos discovered that the local people wanted nothing to do with them.

When the indigenous Xiú leader was baptized, he was made to take a Christian name, so he chose what must have appeared to him to be the most popular name of the entire 16th century – and became Francisco de Montejo Xiú.

1562
Franciscan Friar Diego de Landa orders the destruction of 27 codices and more than 5000 idols in Maní, essentially cutting the historic record of the Maya at the root.

1761
Maya Jacinto Canek leads an armed insurrection against the Spanish colonial government; the so-called Canek Rebellion was short-lived but inspires the Maya revolutionary movement in the 19th century.

1810–41
Beginning of the War of Independence from Spain. Yucatán state joins the newly independent Mexican republic. Yucatán will declare independence from Mexico in 1841.

1847–48
The Caste War erupts. The Maya are whipped solidly at first, retreating to Quintana Roo. They continue to revolt for another 100 years, though an official surrender is signed in 1936.

The father-and-son team then sailed around the peninsula, quelled unrest in Tabasco in 1530 and established their base near Campeche. They pushed inland to conquer, but after four long, difficult years they were forced to return to Mexico City in defeat.

Back in the 1500s traveling Maya merchants would burn incense nightly on their journeys as an offering to the god Ek-Chuah for safe passage.

The younger Montejo took up the cause again, with his father's support, and in 1540 returned to Campeche with his cousin named... Francisco de Montejo. The two Montejos pressed inland with speed and success, allying themselves with the Xiú against the Cocomes, defeating the Cocomes and converting the Xiú to Catholicism.

The Montejos founded Mérida in 1542 and within four years subjugated almost all of Yucatán to Spanish rule. The once proud and independent Maya became peons working for Spanish masters without hope of deliverance except in heaven. The conquerors' attitude toward the indigenous people is graphically depicted in the reliefs on the facade of the Montejo mansion in Mérida, which portrays armor-clad conquistadors standing on the heads of generic barbarians that are not Maya, but the association is inescapable.

The Maya lands were divided into large fiefdoms of sorts, called *encomiendas*, and the Maya living on the lands were mercilessly exploited

FRIAR DIEGO DE LANDA

The Maya recorded information about their history, customs and ceremonies in beautifully painted picture books made of beaten-bark paper coated with fine lime plaster. These codices, as they are known, must have numbered in the hundreds when the conquistadors and missionary friars first arrived in the Maya lands. But because the ancient rites of the Maya were seen as a threat to the adoption and retention of Catholicism, the priceless books were set aflame upon the orders of the Franciscans. Only four of the painted books survive today, but these provide much insight into ancient Maya life.

Among those Franciscans directly responsible for the burning of the Maya books was the inquisitor Friar Diego de Landa, who, in July 1562 in Maní (near present-day Ticul), ordered the destruction of 27 'hieroglyphic rolls' and 5000 idols. He also had a few Maya burned to death for good measure.

Though he was despised by the Maya for destroying their cultural records, it was Friar de Landa who wrote the most important existing book on Maya customs and practices – the source for much of what we know about the Maya. Recalled to Spain for displaying a degree of zeal that even the clerical authorities found unwarranted, he was put on trial for his excesses, but was absolved by the Council of the Indies. But the governing body ordered him to jot down everything he knew about the Maya. These scribblings resulted in a book, *Relación de las Cosas de Yucatán* (An Account of the Things of Yucatán), which covers virtually every aspect of Maya life in the 1560s, from Maya houses and funeral customs to the calendar and counting system.

1850–93

An independent Maya republic is established with its capital at Chan Santa Cruz. The war rages on, with the Maya (getting arms from the British) winning key victories. Britain stops arming the Maya in 1893.

1876–1911

The Porfiriato period – the name given to the era of Porfirio Díaz' 35-year rule as president-dictator, preceding the Mexican Revolution. Under Díaz, the country is brought into the industrial age.

1901

The Mexican army, under Porfirio Díaz, recaptures the Maya-controlled territory, executing many Maya leaders and destroying the shrine of the talking cross in Chan Santa Cruz.

1910–20

Almost two million people die and the economy is shattered during the Mexican Revolution. Eventual agrarian reform gives much of the Yucatán back to local cooperatives called *ejidos*.

by the land owners. With the coming of Dominican friar Bartolomé de las Casas and Franciscan and Augustinian friars, things improved slightly for the Maya. In many cases the clergymen were able to protect the local people from the worst abuses, but exploitation was still the general rule.

Of the illustrated Maya books called codices, only four survive to the present day: *Dresden Codex*, *Madrid Codex*, *Paris Codex* and *Grolier Codex*.

Independence for Some

During the colonial period, Spain's New World was a highly stratified society, and nowhere was that more evident than on the peninsula, which operated under a repressive caste system. Native Spaniards were making the big decisions at the very top; next were the criollos, people born in the New World of Spanish stock; below them were the mestizos or *ladinos*, people of mixed Spanish and indigenous blood; and at the bottom were the pure-race indigenous people and black people. Only the native Spaniards had real power, a fact deeply resented by the criollos.

The harshness of Spanish rule resulted in frequent revolts, none of them successful for long, or at least not until the War of Independence. After Mexico proclaimed its independence from Spain in 1821, the state of Yucatán, which at that time encompassed the entire peninsula, joined the Mexican federation as a semi-autonomous entity called the Federated Republic of Yucatán.

Though independence brought new prosperity to the criollos of the Yucatán, it worsened the lot of the Maya. The end of Spanish rule meant that the Crown's few liberal safeguards, which had afforded the Maya minimal protection from extreme forms of exploitation, were abandoned. The new powers that be stole the Maya's land and forced them to work under miserable conditions. Eventually, things would come to a head in the Caste War.

One of the forgotten victims of the Caste War is the Maya calendar: shamans were too busy with war to keep track of the days, thus losing count. Luckily, Maya priests in the Guatemalan highlands still maintain an accurate Maya calendar.

The Caste War

Just 20 years after Mexico's independence from Spain, Yucatán's local government voted to break away from the Mexican federation in order to establish a fully sovereign republic that would guarantee individual rights and freedom of religion. Mexican president Santa Anna sent in troops in 1843, but Yucatán's forces managed to stave them off. Economic isolation proved to be a more powerful incentive to return to the fold, however, and a treaty was signed with Mexico that same year. But Yucatán again declared independence in 1846.

For the Yucatecan Maya, independence from Mexico made little difference – they remained subordinate to a white elite. In January 1847 indigenous rebels attacked Valladolid, rampaging through the city, killing and looting. Now alerted, federal authorities caught a Maya *batab* (community leader) with a letter detailing a plot to attack the town of Tihosuco (in present-day Quintana Roo). He was shot at Valladolid. Undaunted, the plotters attacked the town of Tepich, south of Tihosuco, and killed a

1940s

The Yucatán's once-booming *henequén* (sisal) industry collapses due to the advent of cheaper synthetic fibers.

1970s

Mexico's oil boom: widespread extraction and exploration begins in the Gulf; environmental problems go widely unchecked. In Quintana Roo another boom is taking hold with the development of Cancún.

1976

Yucatán state elects Francisco Luna Kan, its first governor of pure Maya descent. After his term ends in 1982, it becomes more common to see high-ranking Maya politicians in Yucatán.

1988

Chichén Itzá, home to the Yucatán's most-visited Maya ruins, is named a Unesco World Heritage Site for its 'outstanding universal value.'

The Caste War of Yucatán, by Nelson Reed, is a page-turning account of the modern Maya's insurrection against the criollo elite and the establishment of an independent state.

number of criollo families. Thus began the Caste War, which spread relentlessly across the Yucatán region and raged on in some parts until the turn of the 20th century. An estimated 40,000 men joined the insurrection.

In little more than a year after the Valladolid uprising, Maya revolutionaries had driven their oppressors from every part of the Yucatán except Mérida and Campeche. But then the rebels suddenly abandoned the attack and went home to plant the corn they would need to carry on the fight. This gave the criollos and mestizos a chance to regroup. Yucatán's governor appealed to England, Spain and the US for protection from the indigenous rebels, in exchange for annexation to any of those countries, but all three nations refused to help. Finally, in a desperate move to strengthen its military and economic position, Yucatán rejoined the Mexican federation in 1848, receiving aid from its former adversary and effectively regaining the upper hand against most of the insurgent forces.

But the Maya continued the fight in southern Quintana Roo, where they overwhelmed the Mexican garrison in Bacalar's San Felipe fortress in 1858. By about 1866 the governments in Mexico City and Mérida gave up on the area and the British in Belize recognized an independent Maya republic, which remained virtually sovereign for the latter half of the 19th century.

Revolution, Rope & Reform

Porfirio Díaz, who definitively reclaimed current-day Quintana Roo for Mexico, ruled the country from 1876 to 1911 as a dictator, banning political opposition and free press. During this period, Díaz brought the country into the industrial age, and passed laws that created an even larger class of landless peasants and concentrated wealth in the hands of an ever-smaller elite.

THE TALKING CROSS

Tucked away off a quiet backstreet in the small town of Felipe Carrillo Puerto, about 95km south of Tulum, you'll find one of the most important Maya shrines at the Santuario de la Cruz Parlante. The history of the shrine is legendary, to say the least.

During the Caste War, some Maya combatants sought refuge in the jungles of what is now southern Quintana Roo. There, they were inspired to continue fighting by a religious leader believed to be working with a ventriloquist, who, in 1850 at Chan Santa Cruz (present-day Felipe Carrillo Puerto), made a sacred cross 'talk.' The talking cross convinced the Maya that their gods had made them invincible, and it guided them in a decades-long struggle to maintain their independence. Even after the federal government had captured and executed the last of the rebel chiefs in 1901, local Maya kept alive a guerrilla-style resistance movement until they officially surrendered in 1936. To this day, the cross remains a tremendous source of pride for the Maya, especially on May 3 (Day of the Holy Cross), when you can see various Maya communities paying their respects in religious ceremonies.

1989

To the delight of nature conservationists, the federal government establishes Calakmul (in Campeche) as a biosphere reserve, making it one of the largest protected areas in Mexico.

1994

The Zapatista uprising starts in Chiapas when rebels take over San Cristóbal de las Casas. They later retreat but continue to fight to overturn the oligarchy's centuries-old hold on land, resources and power.

2000–1

Vicente Fox of Partido Acción Nacional (PAN) is elected president of Mexico, ending seven decades of uninterrupted autocratic rule by the Partido Revolucionario Institucional (PRI). Yucatán elects PAN governor Patricio Patrón.

2005

Hurricane Wilma, the most intense Atlantic hurricane on record, does wide-scale damage to the tourist centers of Cancún, Cozumel, Isla Mujeres and Isla Holbox, with billions of dollars in damage to Cancún alone.

In the Yucatán, enormous fortunes were made by the owners of haciendas producing *henequén*, then a lucrative plant for making into rope and other products.

Díaz was brought down by the Mexican Revolution, a major war that erupted in 1910 and plunged the country into chaos for the next 10 years. The revolution pitted Diaz' military against the forces of revolutionary leaders such as Francisco Madero, Emiliano Zapata and Pancho Villa. In the decades following the revolution, agrarian reforms redistributed much of the peninsula's agricultural land, including many of the haciendas, into the hands of peasant cooperatives called *ejidos*.

Oil Production & Rising Tourism

In the 1970s an Organization of the Petroleum Exporting Countries (OPEC) embargo sent world oil prices soaring, around the same time that vast oil reserves were discovered in the Gulf of Mexico. Mexico became the darling of international investors, who loaned the country billions. With its newly borrowed wealth, Mexico invested heavily in infrastructure, including the installation of the Cantarell complex in the Bay of Campeche, which, by 1981, was producing over a million barrels of crude oil a day. The Cantarell field now produces about a third of that.

A world oil glut caused prices to plummet in 1982, leading to a serious debt crisis. As a result, the government restructured the legal framework of the *ejido* system to allow outside investment as well as privatization and sales of cooperative land.

During the 1970s window of prosperity, investment also poured into Quintana Roo for the development of Cancún, igniting the peninsula's tourism industry and radically transforming the economic panorama. As tourism grew, many of the region's Maya left their villages to find work in Cancún, Cozumel, Playa del Carmen and other tourist haunts. The rise of tourism is thought by many scholars to be the single greatest threat to the culture and language of the Maya.

But at the same time tourism also represents a very important source of income for many locals and any issues that affect it have a serious impact on the economy. Hurricane Wilma, for instance, left behind billions of dollars in damage to hotels and restaurants after it ripped through Quintana Roo, plus the economy suffered a significant loss of tourist dollars when visitors stayed away from the area in the aftermath. On the flipside, in 2012, as the Maya Long Count calendar was nearing completion, the peninsula benefited from a spike in tourism as mass media hyped it as the coming of the apocalypse.

Even without the benefit of gimmicky events, the Yucatán tourism sector seems to be doing just fine, as Cancún and Mérida consistently rank among Mexico's top 10 busiest airports for national and international arrivals.

The website of the Foundation for the Advancement of Mesoamerican Studies (www.famsi.org) contains numerous resources for broadening your understanding of Maya history.

2006–07

The PAN party's Felipe Calderón holds off leftist Andres Manuel López Obrador in the 2006 election. The next year, Hurricane Dean rolls over the peninsula, leveling the Quintana Roo town of Mahahual.

2009

The misperceived dangers of swine flu and the drug war, plus the global economic crisis, trigger a 30% drop in tourist visitation.

2012

On December 21, 2012, the Maya Long Count reached completion, signaling the dawn of a new cycle – and not the end of the world as some media outlets were suggesting.

2015

The entire Caribbean coast is hit by an influx of Sargassum seaweed. The government spends millions in cleanup efforts to rid the white-sand beaches of the mounds of brown algae.

Yucatecan Way of Life

Drawing from a mix of ancient Maya and Spanish colonial-era influences, many aspects of domestic and social life on the Yucatán Peninsula remain very much steeped in tradition. Whether you find yourself in a Maya village, a small fishing town or a bustling colonial city, folks in these parts will gladly share with you their passion for song, dance, art and all things uniquely Yucatecan.

Mesoweb (www.mesoweb.com) and Maya Exploration Center (www.mayaexploration.org) are fabulous resources on the Maya, past and present.

The Everyday Reality

Travelers often comment on the open, gentle and gregarious nature of the people of the Yucatán, especially the Maya. Here, more than elsewhere in Mexico, it seems, you find a willingness to converse and a genuine interest in outsiders. This openness is all the more remarkable when you consider that the people of the Yucatán Peninsula have fended off domination by outsiders for so long. The situation persists today – much of the land is foreign owned and the Maya generally aren't making the big decisions when it comes to large-scale development and infrastructure.

Maya culture is facing some difficult challenges moving forward in the 21st century as more and more young Maya people gradually abandon their language and traditions (highly rooted in an agrarian way of life) and head to Cancún or Playa del Carmen to work as busboys, waiters, maids and construction workers. But survival has always been at a premium here, and the Maya (and the region's poor) are finding ways to endure, be it by working in the service and manufacturing industries in big cities or moving to the US to work. In 2014, families in five states in and around the peninsula received more than US$950 million in remittances sent from Mexican workers abroad.

Others are staying home and turning to community-based tourism as a means to bring in income – artisan workshops, Maya-owned tour operators and local cooperatives all have had varying degrees of success. It always helps anytime that you purchase crafts or hire the services on offer from the local community.

Despite the winds of progress and modernization, many of the age-old traditions remain. Yucatecans highly value family bonds, and are only truly themselves within the context of the family – and though they are

SPELLING OUT OUR STYLE

While Lonely Planet tries its darndest to keep up with linguistic trends, we've decided (purposely) to skip the latest trend in Maya orthography: adding an apostrophe to indicate a glottal stop. The apostrophe was adopted by Maya linguists and historians in 1989 as a vehicle to standardize and legitimize the language. The Maya glottal stop (most often used between two vowels) closely resembles the cockney double 't,' as used in the cockney English pronunciation of bottle. Thus, if we were following the new system, Tikal would be spelled Tik'al, and Chichén Itzá would be spelled Chich'en Itza. It was a tough decision, but in the end we decided to balance the needs of travelers (signs have yet to be converted to the new orthography) with the need to accurately document language.

THE BEEKEEPERS' STRUGGLE

Honey production, an ancient practice on the peninsula dating back to the pre-Hispanic era, is facing challenging times due to the prevalence of genetically modified crops. How? For years, agribusiness giants have been allowed to cultivate fields of genetically modified soybeans on a commercial scale. The controversial practice has spurred protests in the states of Yucatán, Quintana Roo and Campeche, where apiarists claim that transgenic herbicide-resistant crops affect honey production – and that's no small problem in a region that produces about 40% of Mexico's honey.

The problem, say researchers, is that bees in the region are collecting a genetically modified pollen that makes its way into the honey, making it more difficult to export honey from the Yucatán to foreign markets because of health concerns. Mexico is one of the world's top honey exporters.

Some locals also blame GM crops on the disappearance of entire colonies of bees in certain areas, saying the so-called Frankenstein crops are either killing off the bees or forcing them to look for pollen elsewhere.

Court cases to determine whether Mexico should ban transgenic crops are ongoing, so the bee farmers' battle appears to be far from over.

hardworking, the people of the region still like to enjoy leisure pursuits to the fullest. They are also deeply religious; their faith is a mélange of pre-Hispanic beliefs and Catholicism. As elsewhere in Mexico, traditional gender roles may seem exaggerated to the outsider, though the level of machismo on the peninsula is somewhat less pronounced.

Life in Rural Yucatán

Perhaps more than elsewhere in Mexico, ancient rhythms and customs form part of everyday life in the Yucatán. In rural areas this is apparent on the surface. Women wear colorfully embroidered, loose-fitting *huipiles* (long, woven, white sleeveless tunics, from the Maya regions, with intricate, colorful embroidery) as they slap out tortillas in the yard, families live in traditional oval thatched houses, rest in hammocks after a day's work, and consume a diet of corn, beans and chilies.

Various forms of Maya are widely spoken, and pre-Hispanic religious rituals are still observed and forms of social organization followed. In some parts of the region, Maya languages prevail over Spanish, or Spanish may not be spoken at all. More than 30 Maya dialects exist, spoken by up to three million people in southern Mexico and northern Central America. Yucatec Maya is the dialect spoken on the Yucatán Peninsula. Eight Maya languages are spoken in Chiapas; Tzeltal, Tzotzil and Chol are the most widely used, the latter believed to most closely resemble the one spoken by the Classic Maya.

Many youngsters are now choosing to leave their rural roots, heading to the *maquiladoras* (factories) of Mérida, to the megaresorts of Quintana Roo or even to the US. Rather than study Yucatec Maya, many are learning English instead. But still, there remains a broad, ubiquitous undercurrent of pride in Maya culture – a hopeful sign that the culture will endure.

In *The Modern Maya: A Culture in Transition*, Macduff Everton documents the period from 1967 to 1990 among the Yucatecan Maya with superb black-and-white photos, while reflecting on the impact of modern influences on this resilient culture.

Popuation at a Glance

For more than a millennium the Maya of the Yucatán have intermarried with neighboring and invading peoples. Most of Mexico's population is mestizo (a mixture of indigenous and Spanish blood), but the Yucatán has an especially high proportion of pure-blooded Maya, about four times the national average. There are around 1.5 million Maya in southern Mexico, with more than 800,000 Maya speakers. Of the peninsular

GAME OF DEATH

Probably all pre-Hispanic Mexican cultures played some version of a Mesoamerican ritual ball game, perhaps the world's first-ever team sport. Over 500 ball courts have survived at archaeological sites around Mexico and Central America. The game varied from place to place and era to era but had certain lasting features. It seems to have been played between two teams, and its essence was to keep a rubber ball off the ground by flicking it with hips, thighs, knees or elbows. The vertical or sloping walls alongside the courts were most likely part of the playing area. The game had (at least sometimes) deep religious significance, serving as an oracle, with the result indicating which of two courses of action should be taken. Games could be followed by the sacrifice of one or more of the players – whether winners or losers, no one is sure.

states, the bulk of Maya speakers (around 538,000) reside in the state of Yucatán.

Overall in Mexico, only 6% of the population (approximately 6.7 million people) speaks an indigenous language.

There are 4.1 million people living in the peninsular states. Not surprisingly, Quintana Roo (home to tourist centers Cancún and the Riviera Maya) has the highest population-growth rate at around 16%, followed by Campeche and Yucatán, at 9% and 7%, respectively.

Passion for Sports

As in most Caribbean destinations, *béisbol* (baseball) is very popular in these parts. In fact, in some towns in the states of Yucatán and Campeche you'll see more action around the baseball diamond than the soccer field.

On the semi-professional level, the quality of play is quite high, equivalent at least to AAA ball in the US. The Mexican League season runs from March through August; among its teams in the region are the Piratas de Campeche (Campeche Pirates), Delfines de Ciudad del Carmen (Ciudad del Carmen Dolphins), Olmecas de Tabasco (Tabasco Olmecs), Leones de Yucatán (Mérida Lions) and Tigres de Quintana Roo (Quintana Roo Tigers), the latter having enjoyed recent success with multiple national championships.

Mexico Online (www.mexonline.com) has good history and culture links, and information about destinations in the Yucatán and elsewhere in Mexico.

As elsewhere in Mexico, *fútbol* (soccer) is always present around schoolyards and playing fields on the peninsula. Fans are customarily glued to their TV sets to watch matches of the region's two professional teams: Chiapas' Jaguares and Cancún's Atlante; the latter was demoted to the second-tier league following the 2014 season. The season is divided into two big tournaments: Torneo Apertura (August to December) and Torneo Clausura (January to May). Games are played over the weekend; check newspapers for details.

Yucatecans are also passionate about *charreadas* (rodeos), which you'll usually find at ferias (fairs) around the peninsula.

Hybrid Religion

Among the region's indigenous populations, ancient Maya beliefs blend nearly seamlessly with contemporary Catholic traditions – the values and rituals of the two religions are often quite similar. Today's Maya identify themselves as Catholic, but they practice a Catholicism that is a fusion of shamanist-animist and Catholic ritual. The traditional religious ways are so important that often a Maya will try to recover from a malady by seeking the advice of a religious shaman rather than a medical doctor. Use of folk remedies linked with animist tradition is widespread in Maya areas.

Mestizos and criollos (Creoles; born in Latin America of Spanish parentage) are more likely to follow strict Catholic doctrine, although here, like nearly everywhere else in Latin America, Catholicism has been losing ground to fast-growing evangelical sects.

Roman Catholicism accounts for the religious orientation of around 80% of residents in Yucatán state, and 63% of those living in Quintana Roo and Campeche. In Yucatán state and Campeche, a growing segment of the population identifies itself with Pentecostalism. Congregations affiliated with churches such as the Assemblies of God, the Seventh-Day Adventists, the Church of Jesus Christ of Latter-day Saints and Jehovah's Witnesses can be found throughout the Yucatán.

Arts & Traditional Dress

The Yucatán's cultural scene is enormously rich and varied. The influence of the Maya or Spanish cultures (or both) appears in almost every facet of Yucatecan art, from literature and dance to music and fashion.

Tales from the Yucatan Jungle: Life in a Mayan Village, by Kristine Ellingson, is the story of an American expat who discovers a whole new world while living in the Maya community of Santa Elena.

Literature

For some cultural and historical context, here are just some of the many Yucatán-themed books that you can read before (or during) your visit.

- *Chilam Balam of Chumayel* One of Yucatán's earliest-known literary works. Written in Maya after the conquest, it is a compendium of Maya history, prophecy and mythology collected by priests from the northern Yucatán town of Chumayel. It has been translated into English.
- *Relación de las Cosas de Yucatán* (An Account of the Things of Yucatán) Diego de Landa, the Spanish friar, could be said to have produced the first literary work from the Yucatán in Spanish, in which he relates his biased perception of the Maya's ceremonies, daily life and traditions, even as he engineered their eradication.
- *La Hija del Judio* (The Jew's Daughter) Aside from (unsuccessfully) seeking US intervention against the Maya during the Caste War, Justo Sierra O'Reilly is credited with writing what is possibly the first Mexican novel, a story about the ill-fated romance of a Jewish merchant's daughter in colonial Mexico.
- *Canek: History and Legend of a Maya Hero* Yucatecan author Ermilo Abreu Gómez synthesized the peninsula's Maya heritage in various fictional works such as this novel, which centers on an indigenous laborer's struggle against injustice.
- *Imagen Primera* (First Image) and *La Noche* (The Night) Novelist, playwright and art critic Juan García Ponce, who died in 2003, is perhaps the Yucatán's best-known modern literary figure. These two titles, which make good starting points for exploring his work, are collections of his short stories.

Music

Two styles of music are traditionally associated with the Yucatán: *jarana* and *trova yucateca*.

A type of festive dance music, a *jarana* is generally performed by a large ensemble consisting of two trumpets, two clarinets, one trombone, a tenor sax, timbales and a güiro (percussion instrument made from a grooved gourd). The music pauses for the singers to deliver *bombas* – improvised verses, usually with a humorous double meaning, that are aimed at the object of their affections. A *jarana* orchestra always ends its performances with the traditional *torito,* a vivacious song that evokes the fervor of a bullfight.

In a visit to the church at the Tzotzil village of San Juan Chamula, you may see chanting *curanderos* (healers) carrying out shamanic rites, such as rubbing patients' bodies with eggs and bones.

A hybrid of Cuban, Spanish, Colombian and homegrown influences, *trova yucateca* is a catchall term for romantic ballads, Cuban claves, tangos, boleros, Yucatecan folk songs and other tunes that can be strummed on a guitar by a *trovador* (troubador). The style is often played by the guitar trios who roam the squares of Mérida seeking an audience to serenade. In a *trova,* as with *jaranas,* the subject matter is usually a suitor's paean of love to an unattainable sweetheart.

MIND YOUR MANNERS

Some indigenous people adopt a cool attitude toward visitors: they have come to mistrust outsiders after five centuries of rough treatment. They don't like being gawked at by tourists and can be very sensitive about cameras. Always ask for permission before taking a photo or shooting video.

A more contemporary figure of Yucatecan song is Armando Manzanero, a singer and composer from Ticul, in Yucatán state. Though Manzanero speaks to an older generation, his songs have been covered by contemporary pop stars such as Luis Miguel and Alejandro Sanz.

On the Caribbean coast, electronic music gets top billing in the party towns of Cancún, Playa del Carmen and Tulum, and you'll also find a fair share of establishments staging Cuban-style salsa acts.

Music festivals abound on the peninsula, particularly in Mérida, Playa del Carmen and Campeche. Annual fests feature traditional and contemporary performers from Mexico and abroad. The Mérida government's website (www.merida.gob.mx/cultura) is a great source of information for music festivals and live events.

Lively Dance

The Spanish influence on Maya culture is abundantly clear in the *jarana*, a dance Yucatecans have been performing for centuries. The dance bears more than a passing resemblance to the *jota,* performed in Spain's Alto Aragón region. The movements of the dancers, with their torsos held rigid and a formal distance separating men from women, are nearly identical; however, whereas the Spanish punctuate elegant turns of their wrists with clicks of their castanets, Maya women snap their fingers.

The best place to see dancers perform to the accompaniment of *jarana* is at *vaquerías* – homegrown fiestas held in the atriums of town halls or on haciendas. The women wear their best embroidered *huipiles,* flowers in their hair and white heels; men wear a simple white cotton outfit with a red bandanna tucked into the waist. In Mérida, you can catch traditional dance performances at Plaza Grande on Sunday afternoon.

Guty Cárdenas, un Siglo del Ruiseñor, produced by the prestigious Mexican record label Discos Corasón (www.corason.com), includes a CD and DVD covering the musical career of seminal Yucatecan composer-performer Guty Cárdenas.

Traditional Attire

Women throughout the Yucatán Peninsula traditionally wear *huipiles,* the bodices of which are always embroidered. The tunic generally falls to just below the knee; on formal occasions it is worn with a lacy white underskirt that reaches the ankle. The *huipil* never has a belt, which would defeat its airy, cool design. Light and loose fitting, these garments are ideally suited for the tropics. Maya women have been wearing *huipiles* for centuries.

Similar to the *huipil* in appearance is the *gala terno*, a straight, white, square-necked dress with an embroidered overyoke and hem, worn over an underskirt with an embroidered strip near the bottom. The *gala terno* is a bit fancier than the *huipil* and is often accompanied by a hand-knitted shawl.

Men commonly wear *guayaberas* (light, elegant shirts, some made with four square pockets). They can be worn in both casual and formal settings (they're often worn at weddings), and the cotton and linen materials keep the wearer cool on warm, humid days.

Yucatecan Cuisine

We hope you're good and hungry because on the Yucatán Peninsula you're in for a real feast. Yucatecans are enormously proud of their history and cultural background, and they love sharing it with you at the table. The relative geographic isolation from the rest of the country, together with a strong Maya influence, have made *la cocina yucateca* the Mexican regional cuisine with the most distinctive personality, and as you travel around the region you'll find dishes using ingredients and techniques unheard of anywhere else in Mexico. At first some will resemble specialties that you can find elsewhere in the country, such as tacos or tamales, but soon you will discover that in the Yucatecan kitchen these Mexican-food staples have been transformed with a Maya and Caribbean flair.

On the Table

The staples of Mexican food – corn, and an array of dry and fresh chilies and beans – are also basic ingredients in the Yucatán. *Achiote* (the seeds from the annatto flower), *epazote* (a herb called pigweed or Jerusalem oak in the US), *chaya* (a shrub also known as tree spinach), *cat* (a variety of cucumber) and the habanero chili are some of the regional ingredients that are building blocks of Yucatecan cuisine.

Archaeologists in the Yucatán have detected chocolate residue on plate fragments believed to be about 2500 years old, meaning the ancient Maya may have used it as a spice or cacao sauce similar to *mole*.

Getting Started

On the Yucatán Peninsula you will find an array of typical *antojitos* using corn as the base. The word *antojitos* translates as 'little whims, a sudden craving.' But as any Mexican will quickly point out, it is not just a snack. You can have an entire meal of *antojitos*, or have a couple as appetizers. A classic Yucatecan *antojito* is *panuchos*, lightly fried, thin-layered tortillas topped with meat, shredded poultry or *cazón* (dogfish). In Maya, *kots* refer to small stuffed tacos, and that is exactly what minced-pork *codzitos* are. *Papadzules* are tortillas filled with diced hard-boiled egg and bathed in pumpkin-seed sauce, along with a few drops of pumpkin-seed oil.

The peninsula is also distinguished for its variety of tamales. Tamales are made with *masa* (dough) mixed with lard; they are stuffed with stewed meat, fish or vegetables, then wrapped and steamed. The word *tamal* comes from the Nahuatl word *tamalli* and refers to anything wrapped up. *Tamalitos al vapor* are small tamales filled with pork and a sauce made from tomatoes, *epazote* and *achiote*, and wrapped in banana leaves. The *muc bil pollo* is a tamal prepared traditionally on Día de Muertos (Day of the Dead). *El brazo de indio* (Indian Arm) is a large tamal that can be 28cm long and 10cm wide. It is made by rolling layers of *masa* and *chaya* leaves.

TIPPING & TAXES

A mandatory *impuesto de valor agregado* (IVA, or value-added tax; 16%) is added to restaurant checks in Mexico, but the *propina* (gratuity) is not. The average tip is 10% to 15%, or 20% for excellent service. Remember that the check is brought to your table only if you ask for it; it's considered rude in Mexico to leave a check while people are still eating.

SAVOR THE RECADO FLAVOR

Recado is the generic name used for the local rubs or marinades that combine dry chilies, spices, herbs and vinegar, and are applied to meats and poultry. The Maya called the *recados* '*kuux*,' and they are essential to preparing an array of dishes on the peninsula. Not so long ago you could find *recauderías* (spice stores) in most towns and cities. Today this name is only used to designate some market stalls dedicated to selling spices and dry chilies. Some popular *recados* are *recado blanco* (white), which contains oregano, garlic, cloves, cinnamon, salt, pepper and sour oranges. It's also known as *recado de puchero* because it is used for cooking *puchero*, a hearty beef and vegetable stew. *Recado negro* (black) consists of corn tortillas and local chilies that are charred (hence the color) with an array of spices. It's the foundation of one of the region's classic dishes: *relleno negro* (turkey stuffed with minced pork, dry fruits, tomatoes and *epazote*). But the most famous of all is *recado rojo* (red), which contains black and red pepper, oregano, cloves, cinnamon, salt, water and the *achiote* (annatto) seeds that infuse an intense red color and flavor to *cochinita pibil* (slow-roasted pork) and other regional favorites. *Recado rojo* is sometimes simply called *achiote*, but this refers to the prepared paste and not to the *achiote* flower.

Caldo de pavo (turkey soup) is also popular, but *sopa de lima* is the favorite Yucatecan soup, a local version of chicken soup using tomatoes, sweet chili, chopped onion, lightly fried tortilla strips and lime.

Main Dishes

Some Yucatecan dishes take the name of the cities and towns in which they were created. Motul is the birthplace of *huevos motuleños* (fried eggs and beans on a tortilla topped with tomato sauce, cheese, ham and green peas). *Longaniza de Valladolid* is a chorizo sausage that has been smoked for up to 12 hours, and *pollo ticuleño* (chicken rubbed with *recado rojo*) hails from Ticul.

Cochinita pibil is the region's most famous dish. In Maya *'pib'* means a hole in the ground, and *'al pibil'* is a centuries-old regional technique for cooking all kinds of meats. Originally *pibil keh* (venison) was all the rage. Today *lechón* (piglet) is the meat of choice, hence the name *cochinita*, meaning little pig, although many places use meat from adult pigs. It's prepared by rubbing the meat with *recado rojo*, which is thinned using the juice of sour oranges. The meat is then wrapped in banana leaves and cooked underground or in an oven for up to eight hours. It is usually served shredded and topped with pickled red onions. You can make *tacos de cochinita pibil* with corn tortillas or use it for *tortas* (sandwiches).

With the Caribbean Sea to the east and the Gulf of Mexico to the north and west, you can expect an incredible array of fish and seafood dishes on the Yucatán Peninsula. *Mariscos* (shellfish) and *pescado* (fish) are prepared *al ajillo* (in garlic and *guajillo* chili sauce), *a la plancha* (grilled) or *a la diabla* (with garlic, tomato and *cascabel* chili). *Achiote* is used in dishes like *tikin-xit* (fish wrapped in banana leaves and then grilled). Crab is famous in the coastal lagoons of the Gulf, such as Celestún and Laguna de Términos, and is served in many forms, especially in *chilpachole* (crab soup with *epazote*, tomatoes and smoky chili chipotle).

¡Salud!

Alcoholic Drinks

As elsewhere in Mexico, on the peninsula you will find the popular tequila and its cousin mezcal. Both spirits are distilled from the agave plant; one difference is that tequila comes from blue agave in the central state of Jalisco and is protected with Denomination of Origin status.

Cerveza (beer) is also widely available; the most popular mass-produced brew is Montejo. There is a growing number of breweries producing craft beers, such as Tulum, which makes a fine IPA, and Ceiba.

Balché is a Maya spirit that was offered to the gods during special ceremonies. It is fermented inside the hollow trunk of the *balché* tree with water and honey. In Valladolid, during indigenous weddings, the bride is sprayed with *balché* as a sign of abundance. *Balché* is not commercially available, but another Maya spirit, *xtabentún*, is easy to find in the region. *Xtabentún* is an anise-flavored liqueur that, when authentic, is made by fermenting honey.

Nonalcoholic Drinks

The great variety of fruits, plants and herbs that grow in the Yucatán Peninsula are a perfect fit for the kinds of nonalcoholic drinks Mexicans love. *Juguerías* (small establishments selling fresh-squeezed juices) are widely available. In some cases they will serve local fruits, like mangos, *cayumito* (a purple plumlike fruit), *zapote negro* (a black fruit with a pearlike consistency) and *marañón* (cashew fruit). *Juguerías* also sell *licuados*, a Mexican version of a milkshake that normally includes banana, milk, honey and fruit.

Aguas frescas (fresh drinks made with fruit, herbs or flowers) are standard Mexican refreshments. Some of them resemble iced teas. In *agua de tamarindo* the tamarind pods are boiled and then mixed with sugar before being chilled; *agua de jamaica* is made with dried hibiscus leaves. Others like *horchata* are made with melon seeds and/or rice.

Two local favorites are *agua de chia* (a plant from the salvia family), which is typical during Holy Week celebrations in Chiapas, and *agua de chaya*, enjoyed throughout the peninsula, in which the leaves of the native shrub *chaya* are mixed with lime, honey and pineapple.

A regular weekly dish in many Yucatecan homes is *frijol con puerco*, a local version of pork and beans. Pork cooked with black beans is served with rice and garnished with radish, cilantro and onion.

Fiestas

Food and fiestas go hand in hand. During the spring *ch'a chaak* ceremony, which takes place in agricultural villages around the peninsula, tortillas and turkey are traditionally offered up to the rain gods and then eaten. The tortillas are made into 'layered cakes,' with ground squash seeds, beans and other vegetables, wrapped in banana leaves and buried to be cooked over charcoals. Turkey and other wild game is cooked in *kol* (a broth thickened with corn dough). Men drink *balché*.

During the Day of the Dead in early November it is traditional in many areas of the peninsula to eat a special tamal called *muc bil pollo*. In Maya

A BOOZEY LOVE STORY

According to legend, *balché* was created as an act of love between a beautiful Maya girl, Sak-Nicté (White Flower), and a brave young warrior. As the story goes, the young couple fled their tribe when a powerful *cacique* (indigenous chief) also declared his love to Sak-Nicté. After days of wandering in the Maya forest, the lovebirds found a honeycomb. Sak-Nicté and the warrior had a feast with the sweet honey, and decided to save some inside the trunk of a *balché* tree. That night brought rain and thunder, and the water blended with the honey inside the tree, creating a luscious beverage.

When the *cacique* found them, he ordered Sak-Nicté to return to her tribe. The young warrior was devastated and, in a desperate attempt to keep his lover at his side, he offered to cook a fantastic meal for the *cacique*. The *cacique* accepted and the couple served him a banquet, crowned with the sweet drink they had discovered. The *cacique* was so impressed with the *balché* that he let the two lovers go, on condition that they share with him how to prepare it.

H IS FOR HOT, HABANERO & HELP!

That's right, the habanero, one of the hottest chilies grown on our planet, finds its home in Yucatán, and it's a foundation of its cuisine. Does this mean that everything you're going to eat will burn your mouth? No.

Despite the fierce reputation of the habanero chili, Yucatecan food is not as spicy as you might think. The habanero is most commonly found in table salsas, and it's up to you how much to add to the dish. The habanero grown in Yucatán has an international reputation for being a high-quality pepper with a bright-orange color, and one of the highest numbers of Scoville heat units found in any pepper.

This method, developed by American scientist Wilbur Scoville to measure the piquancy in chilies, quantifies the amount of the chemical compound capsaicin found in chilies. The habanero can have between 100,000 and 500,000 units. In comparison, a jalapeño chili has between 5000 and 15,000 units.

The heat of the habanero is relentless and will spread quickly throughout your mouth. No matter what your instincts tell you, don't drink water. Any liquid will spread the flames deeper into your mouth. Instead, eat something that will neutralize the capsaicin: bread, beans or rice are good options. Chocolate is by far the best antidote to cut the burning sensation caused by a hot pepper.

mukbil means buried, and this is how the tamales are made. Corn dough is mixed with beef broth and placed inside a container covered with banana leaves. The dough is stuffed with chicken and pork that has been cooked with *achiote, chile dulce, epazote,* onion and habanero chili, and it's wrapped with more banana leaves and tied. The tamal is buried and covered with charcoal and sand.

When & Where

Meal times in Mexico are different from those in other countries; restaurants close early in small towns.

Desayuno (breakfast) Served in restaurants and cafeterias from 8am to 11am.
Almuerzo (a type of brunch) Those who skip breakfast can have an *antojito*. *Loncherías* (places that serve light meals) are good options for an *almuerzo*.
Comida Main meal between 2pm and 5pm. *Fondas* (family-run eateries) serve *comida corrida*, an inexpensive set menu of three or four courses.
Cena (dinner) Served any time after 7pm at restaurants and taco shops.

Vegetarians & Vegans

Mexicans think of a vegetarian as a person who doesn't eat red meat. Many have never heard the term *vegano* (Spanish for vegan). The good news is that almost every city, large or small, has real vegetarian restaurants, and their popularity is increasing. Also, many traditional Mexican and Yucatecan dishes are naturally vegetarian.

Be aware that some dishes are prepared using chicken or beef broth, or possibly with some kind of animal fat, such as *manteca* (lard). Most waiters will be happy to help you in choosing vegetarians or vegan dishes, but you have to make your requirements clear.

Keep in mind that if you have a delicate constitution, only eat unpeeled fruit and uncooked veggies in higher-end restaurants.

Food & Drink Glossary

MEAT & POULTRY

a la parilla	a la pa·*ree*·ya	grilled
a la plancha	a la *plan*·cha	pan-broiled
albóndigas	al·*bon*·dee·gas	meatballs
aves	*a*·ves	poultry
bistec	*bis*·tek	steak
borrego	bo·*re*·ga	sheep
carne (asada)	*kar*·ne (a·*sa*·da)	meat (grilled beef)
carne de puerco	*kar*·ne de *pwer*·ko	pork
carne de res	*kar*·ne de res	beef
chicharrones	chee·cha·*ro*·nes	deep-fried pork skin
chorizo	cho·*ree*·so	Mexican-style sausage made with chili and vinegar
frijol con puerco	fri·*khol* kon *pwer*·ko	*Yucateco*-style pork and beans, topped with a sauce made with grilled tomatoes, and decorated with garnishes; served with rice
jamón	kha·*mon*	ham
lechón	le·*chon*	suckling pig
milanesa	mee·la·*ne*·sa	breaded beef cutlet
pavo	*pa*·vo	turkey
pibil	pee·*beel*	meat wrapped in banana leaves, flavored with *achiote*, garlic, sour orange, salt and pepper, and baked in a pit oven; the two main varieties are *cochinita pibil* (suckling pig) and *pollo pibil* (chicken)
picadillo	pee·ka·*dee*·yo	a ground beef filling that often includes fruit and nuts
poc-chuc	pok·chook	tender pork strips marinated in sour orange juice, grilled and served topped with a spicy onion relish
pollo	*po*·yo	chicken
puchero	pu·*che*·ro	a stew of pork, chicken, carrots, squash, potatoes, plantains and *chayote* (vegetable pear), spiced with radish, fresh cilantro and sour orange
tocino	to·*see*·no	bacon
venado	ve·*na*·do	venison, a popular traditional dish

SEAFOOD

calamar	ka·la·*mar*	squid
camarones	ka·ma·*ro*·nes	shrimp
cangrejo	kan·*gre*·kho	large crab
ceviche	se·*vee*·che	raw fish, marinated in lime juice
filete	fee·*le*·te	fillet
langosta	lan·*gos*·ta	lobster
mariscos	ma·*rees*·kos	shellfish
ostiones	os·*tyo*·nes	oysters
pescado	pes·*ka*·do	fish as food
pulpo	*pool*·po	octopus

EGGS

(huevos) estrellados	*(hwe*·vos) es·tre·*ya*·dos	fried (eggs)
huevos motuleños	*hwe*·vos mo·too·*le*·nyos	'eggs in the style of Motul'; fried eggs atop a tortilla, garnished with beans, peas, chopped ham, sausage, grated cheese and a certain amount of spicy chili
huevos rancheros	*hwe*·vos ran·*che*·ros	fried eggs served on a corn tortilla, topped with a sauce of tomato, chilies and onions
huevos revueltos	*hwe*·vos re·*vwel*·tos	scrambled eggs

SOUP

caldo	*kal*·do	broth or soup
consomé	con·so·*may*	broth made from chicken or mutton base
sopa	*so*·pa	soup, either 'wet' or 'dry' as in rice and pasta
sopa de lima	*so*·pa de *lee*·ma	'lime soup'; chicken broth with bits of shredded chicken, tortilla strips, lime juice and chopped lime

SNACKS

antojitos	an·to·*khee*·tos	'little whims,' corn- and tortilla-based snacks, such as tacos and *gorditas*
empanada	em·pa·*na*·da	pastry turnover filled with meat, cheese or fruits
enchiladas	en·chee·*la*·das	corn tortillas dipped in chili sauce, wrapped around meat or poultry and garnished with cheese
gordita	gor·*dee*·ta	thick, fried tortilla, sliced open and stuffed with eggs, sausage etc, and topped with lettuce and cheese
panuchos	pa·*noo*·chos	Yucatán's favorite snack: a handmade tortilla stuffed with mashed black beans, fried till it puffs up, then topped with shredded turkey or chicken, onion and slices of avocado
papadzules	pa·pad·*zoo*·les	tortillas stuffed with chopped hard-boiled eggs and topped with a sauce of marrow squash (zucchini) or cucumber seeds
papas fritas	*pa*·pas *free*·tas	french fries
quesadilla	ke·sa·*dee*·ya	cheese and other items folded inside a tortilla and fried or grilled
relleno negro	re·*ye*·no *ne*·gro	turkey stuffed with chopped, spiced pork and served in a rich, dark sauce
(queso) relleno	(*ke*·so) re·*le*·no	stuffed (cheese), Dutch edam filled with minced meat and spices
salbutes	sal·*boo*·tes	same as *panuchos* but without the bean stuffing
sope	*so*·pe	thick corn-dough patty lightly grilled, served with salsa, beans, onions and cheese
torta	*tor*·ta	sandwich in a roll, often spread with beans and garnished with avocado slices

DESSERTS

helado	e·*la*·do	ice cream
nieve	*nye*·ve	sorbet
paleta	pa·*le*·ta	popsicle
pastel	pas·*tel*	cake
postre	*pos*·tre	dessert

FRUIT & VEGETABLES

aceituna	a·say·*too*·na	olive
calabacita	ka·la·ba·*see*·ta	squash
cebolla	se·*bo*·lya	onion
champiñones	sham·pee·*nyo*·nes	mushrooms
coco	*ko*·ko	coconut
elote	o·*lo*·te	corn on the cob
ensalada	en·sa·*la*·da	salad
fresa	*fre*·sa	strawberry
frijoles	fri·*kho*·les	beans
guayaba	gwa·*ya*·ba	guava
jícama	*khee*·ka·ma	turniplike tuber, often sliced and garnished with chili and lime; sweet, crunchy and refreshing
jitomate	khee·to·*ma*·te	tomato
lechuga	le·*choo*·ga	lettuce
limón	lee·*mon*	lemon
maíz	mai·*ees*	corn
papas	*pa*·pas	potatoes
piña	*pee*·nya	pineapple
plátano macho	*pla*·ta·no *ma*·cho	plantain
plátano	*pla*·ta·no	banana
toronja	to·*ron*·kha	grapefruit
verduras	ver·*doo*·ras	vegetables

CONDIMENTS & OTHER FOODS

achiote	a·*cho*·te	reddish paste obtained from annatto seeds
arroz	a·*roz*	rice
azúcar	a·soo·*kar*	sugar
mantequilla	man·te·*kee*·ya	butter
mole	*mo*·le	a handmade chocolate and chili sauce
pan	pan	bread
sal	sal	salt

DRINKS

agua mineral	*a*·gwa mee·ne·*ral*	mineral water or club soda
agua purificada	*a*·gwa poo·ree·fee·*ka*·da	bottled uncarbonated water
atole	a·*to*·le	corn-based hot drink flavored with cinnamon or fruit
café (con leche/ lechero)	ka·*fe* (kon *le*·che/le·*che*·ro)	coffee (with hot milk)
café americano	ka·*fe* a·me·ree·*ka*·no	black coffee
caguama	ka·*gwa*·ma	liter bottle of beer
horchata	hor·*cha*·ta	rice drink
jamaica	kha·*may*·ka	hibiscus flower, chief ingredient of *agua de Jamaica*, a cold tangy tea
jugo de naranja	*khoo*·go de na·*ran*·kha	orange juice
leche	*le*·che	milk
té negro	te *ne*·gro	black tea

The Ancient Maya

Not only did the ancient Maya leave behind absolutely stunning architectural monuments, but their vision of the world and beyond remains a source of mystery and intrigue to this day. In fact, all across the peninsula ancient Maya culture and knowledge live on – most certainly a testament to a wondrous past.

Maya pyramids were painted in brilliant red, green, yellow and white colors, and the people of the region often painted their bodies red.

Religion & Spirituality

The Sacred Tree of Life & Xibalbá

For the Maya, the world, the heavens and the mysterious 'unseen world' or underworld, called Xibalbá (shi-bahl-*bah*), were all one great, unified structure that operated according to laws of astrology and ancestor worship. The towering ceiba tree was considered sacred. It symbolized the Wakah-Chan (Yaxché; Tree of Life), which united the 13 heavens, the surface of the earth and the nine levels of the underworld of Xibalbá.

Compass Cosmology

In Maya cosmology, each point of the compass had special religious significance. East was most important, as it was where the sun was reborn each day; its color was red. West was black because it represented where the sun disappeared. North was white and was the direction from which the all-important rains came, beginning in May. South was yellow because it was the sunniest point of the compass.

Everything in the Maya world was seen in relation to these cardinal points (eg the direction in which a building faced), with the Tree of Life at the center, and they were the base for the all-important astronomical and astrological observations that determined fate.

Bloodletting & Piercing

Just as the great cosmic dragon (the upper world) shed its blood, which fell to the earth as rain, so humans had to shed blood to link themselves with the underworld of Xibalbá.

As illustrated in various Maya stone carvings and painted pottery, the nobility customarily drew their own blood on special occasions, such as royal births or deaths, crop plantings, victories on the battlefield or accession to the throne. Blood represented royal lineage, and so the blood of kings granted legitimacy to these events. Often using the spine of a manta ray as a lancet, a noble would pierce his or her cheek, lower lip, tongue or genitalia and pull a piece of rope or straw through the resulting orifice to extract the sacred substance. Performed for lower-ranking members of the nobility or occasionally before dumbstruck commoners, the excruciating ritual served not only to sanctify the event but also to appease the gods, as well as to communicate with them through the hallucinogenic visions that often resulted from such self-mutilation.

Sacred Places

Maya ceremonies were performed in natural sacred places as well as in their artificial equivalents. Mountains, caves, lakes, cenotes (limestone sinkholes), rivers and fields were all sacred. Pyramids and temples were thought of as stylized mountains; sometimes they had secret chambers within them, like the caves in a mountain. A cave was the mouth of the creature that represented Xibalbá, and to enter it was to enter the spirit of the secret world. This is why you'll see that some Maya temples have doorways surrounded by huge masks: as you enter the door of this 'cave,' you are entering the mouth of Xibalbá.

The plazas around which the pyramids were placed symbolized the open fields or the flat land of the tropical forest. What we call stelae were to the Maya 'tree-stones'; that is, tree effigies echoing the sacredness of the Tree of Life. These tree-stones were often carved with the figures of great Maya kings, for the king was the tree of Maya society.

As these places were sacred, it made sense for succeeding Maya kings to build new and ever grander temples directly over older temples, enhancing the sacred character of a location. The temple being covered over was preserved, as it remained a sacred artifact. Certain features of these older temples, such as the large masks on the facades, were carefully padded and protected before the new construction was placed over them.

Ancestor worship and genealogy were very important to the Maya, and when they buried a king beneath a pyramid, or a commoner beneath the floor or courtyard of his or her *na* (thatched hut), the sanctity of the location was elevated.

Ah Tz'ib (scribes) wrote the sacred texts of the Maya, including the *Chilam Balam of Chumayel*. *H menoh* (shamans) and *Ah Tz'ib* still practice their craft throughout the peninsula.

Similarities with Christianity

The Tree of Life had a sort of cruciform shape and when in the 16th century the Franciscan friars required the indigenous population to venerate the cross, this Christian symbolism meshed easily with established Maya beliefs.

The ceiba tree's cruciform shape was not the only correspondence the Maya found between their animist beliefs and Christianity. Both traditional Maya animism and Catholicism have rites of baptism and confession, days of fasting and other forms of abstinence, religious partaking of alcoholic beverages, burning of incense and the use of altars.

MAYA 'BIBLE': UNRAVELING THE SECRETS OF POPOL VUH

The history, prophecies, legends and religious rites of the Maya were preserved on painted codices and through oral traditions. Nearly all of these codices were destroyed during the time of the conquest (only four survive today), effectively cutting the historic record of the Maya. Lucky for Mayanologists, the *Popol Vuh*, known to many as the Maya Bible, recaptured these myths and sacred stories.

The *Popol Vuh* is said to have been written by the Quiché Maya of Guatemala, who had learned Spanish and the Latin alphabet from the Dominican friars – the text was written in Latin characters rather than hieroglyphics. The authors showed their book to Francisco Ximénez, a Dominican who lived and worked in Chichicastenango, in Guatemala, from 1701 to 1703. Friar Ximénez copied the Maya book word for word and then translated it into Spanish. Both his copy and the Spanish translation survive, but the original has been lost.

According to the *Popol Vuh*, the great god K'ucumatz created humankind first from mud. But these 'earthlings' were weak and dissolved in water, so K'ucumatz tried again using wood. The wood people had no hearts or minds and could not praise their creator, so they were destroyed, all except the monkeys who lived in the forest, who are the descendants of the wood people. The creator tried once again, this time successfully, using substances recommended by four animals – the gray fox, the coyote, the parrot and the crow. White and yellow corn were ground into meal to form the flesh, and stirred into water to make the blood.

SWEATING OUT EVIL SPIRITS IN A MAYA TEMASCAL

The temascal (sweat lodge) has always been a cornerstone of indigenous American spiritual life. The Maya, like their brothers and sisters to the north, were no different, using the temascal for both ceremonial and curative purposes.

The word temascal derives from the Aztec word *teme* (to bathe) and *calli* (house). The Maya people used these bathhouses not just to keep clean but also to heal any number of ailments. Most scholars say they were most likely used during childbirth as well. Large bath complexes have been discovered at several Maya archaeological sites. Ironically, the hygienically challenged conquistadors considered temascals dirty places and strongholds of sin. To this day, they are used by the Maya (and tourists) to bathe and keep the evil spirits away.

The *Popol Vuh* legends include some elements that made it easier for the Maya to understand certain aspects of Christian belief, such as the virgin birth. As the story goes, a virgin underworld princess named Xquic was impregnated with the seed of a calabash fruit and gave birth to a pair of Maya hero twins.

Amazing Architecture

Maya architecture is famous for its exquisitely beautiful temples and stone sculptures. Some of the most stunning structures were built during the early and late Classic periods, many of which stand remarkably well preserved today.

Ixchel, the moon goddess, was the principal female deity of the Maya pantheon. Today she is linked with the Virgin Mary.

Back-Breaking Work

The achievements in Maya architecture are astounding in and of themselves – and even more so when one stops to think about how the architects and laborers went about their work.

For starters, Maya architects never seem to have used the true arch (a rounded arch with a keystone). The arch used in most Maya buildings is the corbeled arch (or, when used for an entire room rather than a doorway, corbeled vault). In this technique, large flat stones on either side of the opening are set progressively inward as they rise. The two sides nearly meet at the top, and this 'arch' is then topped by capstones. Though they served the purpose, the corbeled arches severely limited the amount of open space beneath them. In effect, Maya architects were limited to long, narrow vaulted rooms.

And consider this: boxes used to move around tons of construction materials did not have wheels. The Maya also lacked draft animals (horses, donkeys, mules or oxen). All the work had to be done by humans, on their feet, with their arms and backs.

What's more, they had no metal tools, yet could build breathtaking temple complexes and align them so precisely that windows and doors were used as celestial observatories with great accuracy.

Lavishly illustrated with sections of friezes, sculpted figurines, painted pottery and other fine specimens of Maya art, *The Blood of Kings*, by Linda Schele and Mary Ellen Miller, deciphers glyphs and pictographs to explore recurring themes of Classic Maya civilization.

The Styles

Maya architecture's storied history saw a fascinating progression of styles. Styles changed not just with the times but with the particular geographic area of Mesoamerica in which the architects worked. The Classic Maya, at their cultural height from about AD 250 to 900, were perhaps ancient Mexico's most artistic people. They left countless beautiful stone sculptures, of complicated design and meaning but possessing an easily appreciated touch of delicacy – a talent expressed in their unique architecture. Typical styles in the Yucatán include Esperanza, Puuc, Chenes and Río Bec.

Early Classic (AD 250–600)

The Esperanza culture typifies this phase. In Esperanza-style temples, the king was buried in a wooden chamber beneath the main staircase of the temple; successive kings were buried in similar positions in pyramids built on top of the original.

A good example of the early Classic style is La Pirámide at the Oxkintok site (south of Mérida), where a labyrinth inside the structure leads to a burial chamber.

Late Classic (AD 600–900)

The most important Classic sites flourished during the latter part of the period. By this time the Maya temple pyramid had a stone building on top, replacing the *na* of wooden poles and thatch. Numbers of pyramids were built close together, sometimes forming contiguous or even continuous structures. Near them, different structures, now called palaces, were built; they sat on lower platforms and held many more rooms, perhaps a dozen or more.

The Art of Mesoamerica, by Mary Ellen Miller, is an excellent overview of pre-Hispanic art and architecture.

In addition to pyramids and palaces, Classic sites have carved stelae and round 'altar stones' set in the plaza in front of the pyramids. Another feature of the Classic and later periods is the ball court, with the sloping playing surfaces of stone covered in stucco.

Of all the Classic sites, one of the most impressive is Uxmal, which stands out for its fascinating blend of Puuc, Chenes and Río Bec architectural styles. Equally impressive is Palenque, especially the towering Templo de las Inscripciones (Temple of the Inscriptions).

Puuc, Chenes & Río Bec (AD 600–800)

Among the most distinctive of the late-Classic Maya architectural styles are those that flourished in the western and southern regions of the Yucatán Peninsula. These styles valued exuberant display and architectural bravado more than they did proportion and harmony – think of it as Maya baroque.

The Puuc style, named for the hills surrounding Uxmal, used facings of thin limestone 'tiles' to cover the rough stone walls of buildings. The tiles were worked into geometric designs and stylized figures of monsters and serpents. Minoan-style columns and rows of engaged columns (half-round cylinders partly embedded in a wall) were also a feature of the style; they were used to good effect on the facades of buildings at Uxmal and at the Puuc sites of Kabah, Sayil, Xlapak and Labná. Every Puuc temple features the face of Chaac, the rain god. At Kabah, the facade of the Palacio de los Mascarones (Palace of the Masks) is covered in Chaac masks.

Joyce Kelly's *An Archaeological Guide to Mexico's Yucatán Peninsula* gives visitors both practical and background information on 91 sites.

The Chenes style, prevalent in areas of Campeche south of the Puuc region, is similar to the Puuc style, but Chenes architects seem to have enjoyed putting huge masks as well as smaller ones on their facades.

The Río Bec style, epitomized in the richly decorated temples at the archaeological sites between Escárcega and Chetumal, used lavish decoration, as in the Puuc and Chenes styles, but added huge towers to the corners of its low buildings, just for show. Adorned with stylized Chaac faces, the Palacio del Gobernador (Governor's Palace) of Uxmal is a fine example of a Río Bec building.

Early Post-Classic (AD 1000–1250)

The collapse of Classic Maya civilization around AD 1000 created a power vacuum that was filled by the invasion of the Toltecs from central Mexico. The Toltecs brought with them their own architectural ideas, and in the process of conquest these ideas were assimilated and merged with those of the Puuc style.

THE CELESTIAL PLAN

Every major work of Maya architecture had a celestial plan. Temples were aligned so as to enhance celestial observation of the sun, moon, certain stars or planets, especially Venus. The alignment might not be apparent except at certain conjunctions of the celestial bodies (eg an eclipse), but the Maya knew that each building was properly 'placed' and that this enhanced its sacred character.

Temples usually had other features that linked them to the stars. The doors and windows might frame a celestial body at an exact point in its course on a certain day of a certain year. This is the case with the Palacio del Gobernador (Governor's Palace) at Uxmal, which is aligned in such a way that, from the main doorway, Venus would have been visible exactly on top of a small mound some 3.5km away, in the year AD 750. At Chichén Itzá, the observatory building El Caracol was aligned in order to sight Venus exactly in the year AD 1000.

Other features might relate to the numbers of the calendar round, as at Chichén Itzá's El Castillo. This pyramid has 364 stairs to the top; with the top platform, this makes 365, the number of days in the Maya vague year. (The vague year corresponds to our 365-day solar year, with the difference that it is not adjusted every four years by adding an additional day. Therefore, the seasons do not occur at the same time each year but vary slightly from year to year. For that reason, the Maya solar year is characterized as 'vague.') On the sides of the pyramid are 52 panels, signifying the 52-year cycle of the calendar round. The terraces on each side of each stairway total 18 (nine on either side), signifying the 18 'months' of the solar vague year. The alignment of El Castillo catches the sun and makes a shadow of the sacred sky-serpent ascending or descending the side of El Castillo's staircase on the vernal and autumnal equinoxes (usually around March 20 and September 22) each year.

The foremost example of what might be called the Toltec-Maya style is Chichén Itzá. Elements of Puuc style – the large masks and decorative friezes – coexist with Toltec warrior *atlantes* (male figures used as supporting columns) and chac-mools, odd reclining statues that are purely Toltec and have nothing to do with Maya art.

Platform pyramids with broad bases and spacious top platforms, such as Chichén Itzá's Templo de los Guerreros (Temple of the Warriors), look as though they might have been imported from the ancient Toltec capital of Tula (near Mexico City) or by way of Teotihuacán (the Aztec capital also near Mexico City), with its broad-based pyramids of the sun and moon. Because Quetzalcóatl (a feathered serpent deity) was so important to the Toltecs, feathered serpents are used extensively as architectural decoration.

Late Post-Classic (AD 1250–1530)

After the Toltecs came the Cocomes, who established their capital at Mayapán, south of Mérida, and ruled a confederation of Yucatecan states during this period. After the golden age of Palenque, even after the martial architecture of Chichén Itzá, the architecture of Mayapán is a disappointment. The pyramids and temples are small and crude compared with the glorious Classic structures. Mayapán's only architectural distinction comes from its vast defensive city wall, one of the few such walls ever discovered in a Maya city. The fact that the wall exists testifies to the weakness of the Cocom rulers and the unhappiness of their subject peoples.

Tulum, another walled city, is also a product of this time. The columns of the Puuc style are used here, and the painted decoration on the temples must have been colorful. But there's nothing here to rival Classic architecture.

Cobá has the finest architecture of this period, when the building of monumental constructions had ceased. The stately pyramids here had new little temples built atop them in the style of Tulum's two-story Templo de las Pinturas (Temple of the Paintings).

Land & Wildlife

Sitting pretty between two seas in Mexico's easternmost corner, the Yucatán Peninsula has an insular character, in both its physical isolation from the Mexican interior and its distinct topography and wildlife.

Land & Geology

Separated from the bulk of Mexico by the Gulf of Mexico, and from the Greater Antilles by the Caribbean Sea, the Yucatán Peninsula is a vast, low limestone shelf extending under the sea for more than 100km to the north and west. The eastern (Caribbean) side drops off much more precipitously. This underwater shelf keeps Yucatán's coastline waters warm and the marine life abundant.

The peninsula is divided into three states in a 'Y' shape, with the state of Yucatán occupying the upper portion, flanked to the west by the state of Campeche and to the east by Quintana Roo. Note that Tabasco and Chiapas are not actually part of the Yucatán Peninsula.

Unlike much of Mexico, the Yucatán remains unobstructed by mountains. It rises no more than a dozen meters above sea level in its northern section and, at its steepest, in the southern interior of Campeche state, only reaches about 300m. About 60km south of Mérida, near Ticul, the Yucatán plain gives way to the rolling hills of the Puuc ('hill' in Maya) region. South of the peninsula, in Chiapas, it's one extreme to the other – from steamy lowlands to chilly pine-covered highlands. To the east, in southern Quintana Roo, swaths of jungle meet the Caribbean coast.

More than 6000 cenotes (limestone sinkholes – natural underground pools and caves) dot the Yucatán Peninsula. And that's a moderate estimate!

Barrier Reef

Approaching by air, you can easily make out the barrier reef that runs parallel to the Caribbean coastline at a distance of a few hundred meters to about 1.5km. Known variously as the Great Maya, Mesoamerican or Belize Barrier Reef, it's the longest of its kind in the northern hemisphere – and the second largest in the world – extending from southern Belize to Isla Mujeres off the northern coast of Quintana Roo. On the landward side of the reef, the water is usually no more than 5m to 10m deep; on the seaward side it plummets to depths of more than 2000m in the Yucatán Channel that runs between the peninsula and Cuba.

Agriculture

Capped by a razor-thin crust of soil, the peninsula is less productive agriculturally than elsewhere in Mexico. Formed by cretaceous-era sediments, its porous limestone bedrock does not allow rivers to flow on its surface, except in short stretches near the sea where its roof has collapsed and in the southernmost reaches of the region where the peninsula joins the rest of Mexico (and Guatemala). Some underground streams don't release their water until well offshore, while others empty into lagoons near the sea, such as the lovely Laguna Bacalar, in southern Quintana Roo.

HURRICANE ALLEY

Hurricanes have always walloped the Yucatán, and the peninsula has certainly experienced some big ones. Blame global warming, blame regularly shifting climate patterns; whatever you decide to blame, the real loser has been the region's people, plants and animals.

For a while there, Yucatecans just couldn't catch a break. In 2005, Hurricane Wilma (a category-5 storm) pounded the Yucatán's northeast coast for more than 30 hours, causing more than 60 deaths and over US$29 billion in damage and leaving many visitors stranded in shelters. Two years later Dean struck with so much force that it leveled the beach town of Mahahual and mowed down thousands of trees along the Costa Maya, in southern Quintana Roo.

Fortunately, recent hurricane seasons have shown some mercy. In 2011, Hurricane Rina was bearing down on the peninsula, prompting mass evacuations of tourists staying in Cancún and along the Riviera Maya. But before making landfall, Rina was downgraded to a tropical storm, and most importantly, no deaths or major damage were reported. A similar situation occurred in 2012 when Hurricane Ernesto had many people running for cover, but it weakened before hitting land. Once again, locals and visitors skirted a potential catastrophe.

The Atlantic hurricane season runs from June 1 to November 30. Every time a storm pounds the Caribbean coast, it causes massive erosion of the white-sand beaches. Much to the chagrin of area environmentalists, the quick-fix solution is to restore the beaches by bringing in sand from other areas, such as the channel between Cancún and Isla Mujeres.

Cenotes

A uniquely Yucatecan geological feature, cenotes (pronounced *seh-noh-tays*) – from the Maya word *d'zonot,* meaning 'water-filled cavern' – are limestone sinkholes formed by the erosive effects of rainwater drilling down through the porous limestone. Thousands of cenotes, both wet and dry, can be found throughout the peninsular landscape. Yucatecans have traditionally gotten their fresh water from these natural cisterns, while modern visitors favor their crystalline waters for swimming and snorkeling. South of the Puuc region, the inhabitants draw water from the *chenes* (limestone pools), more than 100m below ground.

Into the Wild

The isolation of the Yucatán Peninsula and its array of ecosystems results in an extraordinary variety of plant and animal life, including a number of species that are unique to the region. Whether you like watching birds, following the progress of sea turtles as they nest on the beach, swimming next to manta rays and schools of iridescent fish, or spying wildcats through your binoculars, you'll have plenty of nature activities to do here.

Birders should carry *Mexican Birds* by Roger Tory Peterson and Edward L Chalif, or *Birds of Mexico & Adjacent Areas* by Ernest Preston Edwards.

Animals

Birds of the Yucatán

For bird-watchers, the Yucatán is indeed a banquet. Over 500 bird species – about half of those found in all of Mexico – inhabit or regularly visit the peninsula. These include dozens of regional endemics; the island of Cozumel alone boasts three unique species.

Most of the peninsula's birds are represented in the various parks and biosphere reserves, and serious birders should make for at least a few of these. Numerous coastal species can be spotted at the Reserva de la Biosfera Ría Celestún and Reserva de la Biosfera Ría Lagartos, on the western and eastern ends, respectively, of Yucatán state's coast. The varied panorama is due to a highly productive ecosystem where substantial freshwater sources empty into the Gulf of Mexico. A similarly diverse coastal habitat can be found at the Laguna de Términos in western Campeche. Parque Nacional Isla Contoy, off the northeastern coast of Quintana Roo, is a haven for olive cormorants, brown boobies and many other seabirds. It's home to 173 bird species.

Moving inland, the panorama shifts. The low, dry forests of the Puuc region contain two species of motmot, which nest in ruined temples. In the denser forests of the Reserva de la Biosfera Calakmul, train your binoculars on harpy eagles, ocellated turkeys and king vultures.

The Yucatán Peninsula is along the central migratory flyway, and between November and February hundreds of thousands of birds migrate here from harsher northern climes. The region's proximity to the Caribbean Sea also means it receives island species not seen elsewhere in Mexico.

In November NGO Pronatura hosts the Toh Festival (www.festivalavesyucatan.com), an annual event that attracts bird enthusiasts from far and wide. The festival culminates in a birding marathon called Xoc Ch'ich, a Maya term meaning bird count. The event is organized out of Mérida.

The Spanish-language monthly magazine *México Desconocido* (www.mexicodesconocido.com.mx) points out off-the-beaten-track destinations and wildlife-watching spots with copious color photos and maps. Check its website for details.

Forest & Mangrove Dwellers

Around a quarter of the mammal species that exist in Mexico roam the Yucatán Peninsula. Some are the last of their breed.

There are jaguars in the forests, although, despite the Maya's traditional fascination with the New World's largest cat, poaching has all but wiped them out in southeastern Mexico. Of Mexico's estimated jaguar population of 4000, half are found on the peninsula. Your best chances of spotting one in the wild are probably in the Reserva de la Biosfera Calakmul in Campeche state. The peninsula's other native wildcat, the jaguarundi, is also at risk, as are the margay, ocelot and puma, though sightings of the latter aren't all that unusual in southern Yucatán.

The agile spider monkey also inhabits some forested areas of the region. It looks something like a smaller, long-tailed version of the gibbon (an ape native to southwest Asia). Another elusive primate, the howler monkey, frequents the forest around the ruins of Calakmul and isolated pockets elsewhere. Howlers are more often heard than seen, but you have a fair chance of seeing both them and spider monkeys at Punta Laguna.

Hiking around the forest, you may run into tapirs and piglike peccaries (javelinas), as well as armor-plated armadillos. There are several species of anteater, all with very long, flexible snouts and sharp-clawed, shovel-like front paws – the two tools needed to seek out and enjoy feeding on ants and other insects. The animal's slow gait and poor eyesight make it a common roadkill victim. Besides the *tepezcuintle* (paca) and *sereque* (agouti) – large, tailless rodents – a few species of deer can be found as well, including the smallest variety in North America.

To see recently snapped photos of jaguars, crocs, whale sharks and other Yucatán fauna in their habitat, go to the website of the environmental group Pronatura (www.pronatura-ppy.org.mx).

Crocodiles still ply the mangroves in Yucatán state and Quintana Roo. Since 1970 the government has prohibited the hunting of crocodiles and the population has recovered as a result. You can see plenty of the amphibious reptiles in biosphere reserves at Río Lagartos, Celestún and Sian Ka'an, while smaller numbers lurk up and down the Caribbean coast, including at Laguna Nichupté, which backs onto Cancún's Zona Hotelera.

Sea Creatures

The Great Maya Barrier Reef, which parallels the length of Quintana Roo's coast, is home to a tremendous variety of colorful marine life. The coney grouper, for example, stands out for its bright-yellow suit (it varies in color from reddish brown to sun yellow). The redband parrotfish is easy to recognize by the striking red circle around its eyes and the red band that runs from the eyes to the gills. Butterflyfish are as flamboyant as their name suggests (there are six species in the area), and the yellow stingray has spots that closely resemble the rosettes of a golden jaguar.

Providing an extraordinary backdrop to these brilliant stars of the sea is a vast array of coral. It comes in two varieties: hard coral, such as the great star coral, the boulder coral and numerous types of brain coral; and soft coral, such as sea fans and sea plumes, which are particularly delicate and sway with the current. Successive generations of coral form a skin of living organisms over the limestone reef.

The Selva Maya, which spans northern Guatemala and Belize and the southern part of the Yucatán Peninsula (including the Reserva de la Biosfera Calakmul), is the world's second-largest tropical forest after the Amazon.

But there's trouble in the waters of the Mexican Caribbean – invasive lionfish, which are native to the Indo-Pacific region but were introduced to Atlantic waters in the early 1990s, are reproducing at an alarming rate and that's bad news for indigenous fish species. Protected by venomous spines and with no known predators in the Atlantic, lionfish have a fierce appetite, making them a serious threat to the balance of reef ecosystems.

In an effort to control the population explosion, fishers are being encouraged to catch lionfish for human consumption. Also, many dive shops now offer lionfish-hunting expeditions, which is capped off with a feast of lionfish ceviche at the end of the day.

Endangered Species

Pollution, poaching, illegal traffic of rare species and the filling in of coastal areas for yet more resorts are taking an enormous toll on the Yucatán's wildlife. Deforestation is also a major threat.

Some of the species on the peninsula that are threatened with extinction or are protected include five species of cat (jaguar, puma, ocelot, margay and jaguarundi), four species of sea turtle, the manatee, the tapir and hundreds of bird species, including the harpy eagle, the red flamingo and the jabiru stork.

Efforts are being made to save these and other endangered creatures from extinction, chiefly by environmental NGOs, such as The Nature Conservancy (www.nature.org) and its local partner Pronatura (www.pronatura-ppy.org.mx). This group focuses on preservation of wildlife habitats, particularly in the biosphere reserves of Ría Celestún, Ría Lagartos and Calakmul. It's also a big promoter of ecotourism. In particular, Pronatura is working to recover jaguar habitat in the area between the Reserva de la Biosfera Ría Lagartos and Isla Holbox, where 120 to 200 of the big cats roam.

Tropical Mexico – The Ecotravellers' Wildlife Guide, by Les Beletsky, is a well-illustrated, informative guide to the land, air and sea life of southeastern Mexico.

Camps at Ría Lagartos, Laguna de Términos, Xcacel-Xcacelito, Akumal, Sisal and Isla Holbox have been established to promote the survival of the six species of marine turtle that nest on the Yucatán's shores. Volunteers collect turtle eggs and release hatchlings into the sea, and patrols prevent poachers from snatching eggs that are laid on the beaches. In Punta Laguna environmental groups are working with local agricultural workers to establish protection zones for endangered spider monkeys, which are closely monitored by researchers. The nutrient-rich waters around Isla Holbox attract whale sharks, which are threatened by commercial fishing, and environmentalists have succeeded in getting this area categorized as a protected zone.

Plants

Vegetation varies greatly on the peninsula, with plants falling into four main categories: aquatic and subaquatic vegetation, and humid and subhumid forest vegetation.

As you move inland from the coast, mangrove swamps are replaced first by a fairly dense forest of low deciduous trees, then by a more jungly zone with tall trees and climbing vegetation, and more than a few air plants (but without the soggy underbrush and multiple canopies you'd

SMALL FOOTPRINTS, LARGE IMPACT: TIPS FOR STAYING GREEN

Travelers can help protect the Yucatán's environment by taking the following steps.

➡ Hire local guides. Not only does this provide local communities with a more ecologically sound way of supporting themselves, it also attaches value to nature and wildlife.

➡ Pack a water purifier and/or a refillable container to avoid unnecessary waste of plastic bottles. Tourists the world over toss millions of plastic water bottles each day!

➡ Try to observe wildlife in its natural environment and do your best not to cause disturbances; avoid dive shops that feed sharks, which can be both dangerous for humans and harmful to sharks.

➡ Don't buy souvenirs made from endangered plants and animals that have been acquired illegally. By purchasing these items you aid wildlife extinction.

➡ Don't carry away anything that you pick up at the site of an ancient city or out on a coral reef. Don't buy these items if they're offered by locals.

➡ When snorkeling or scuba diving, be careful about what you touch and where you place your feet; not only can coral cut you, but it's extremely fragile and takes years to grow even a finger's length.

➡ Keep water use down, especially in areas that have signs requesting you to do so. Most of the Yucatán Peninsula has limited water reserves, and in times of drought the situation can become grave.

➡ Before plunging into a cenote make sure you're not using sunblock, lotions, perfumes, insect repellent or any other products that pollute the water system.

find further south). The taller trees of the peninsula's southern half harbor more than 100 species of orchid; for the really spectacular blooms, the avid orchid hunter will need to head into the highlands of Chiapas, where the exotic plants thrive at an elevation of about 1000m.

Dispersed among the mango and avocado trees are many annuals and perennials, such as the aptly named *flamboyán* (royal poinciana), which bursts into bloom like a red-orange umbrella, and the lavender-tinged jacaranda.

National Parks & Reserves

There are several national parks on the peninsula, some scarcely larger than the ancient Maya cities they contain – Parque Nacional Tulum is a good example of this. Others, such as Parque Nacional Isla Contoy, a bird sanctuary in northeastern Quintana Roo, are larger and have been designated to protect wildlife.

The fact that former president Ernesto Zedillo was an avid scuba diver was likely a factor in the creation of several *parques marinos nacionales* (national marine parks) off the coast of Quintana Roo: Arrecifes de Cozumel, Costa Occidental de Isla Mujeres, Punta Cancún y Nizuc and Arrecifes de Puerto Morelos.

Planeta.com (www.planeta.com) brims with information and links for those wanting to delve deeper into Mexico and the Yucatán's flora, fauna and environment.

Very large national biosphere reserves surround Río Lagartos, Celestún (both in Yucatán state) and Banco Chinchorro (Quintana Roo), spreading across thousands of hectares. The Reservas de la Biosfera Ría Lagartos and Ría Celestún are well known for their diversity of bird and animal species, including large colonies of flamingos, while Banco Chinchorro contains a massive coral atoll, many shipwrecks and a host of marine species.

Even more impressive are the two colossal Unesco-designated biosphere reserves found in the Yucatán: the Reserva de la Biosfera Calakmul and the Reserva de la Biosfera Sian Ka'an. Calakmul, covering more than

7230 sq km in Campeche, Quintana Roo and Chiapas, as well as parts of Belize and Guatemala, is home to more than 300 bird species, plus jaguars, pumas, tapirs, coatis, peccaries and many other animals. Sian Ka'an, beginning 150km south of Cancún, covers 6000 sq km, including 100 sq km of the Great Maya Barrier Reef. Its lifeforms include more than 70 species of coral, 350 species of bird (by comparison, there are 400 species of bird in all of Europe), crocodiles, pumas, jaguars and jabirus.

Environmental Issues

Large-scale tourism developments are affecting and sometimes erasing fragile ecosystems, especially along the 'Riviera Maya' south of Cancún. Many hectares of vital mangrove swamp have been bulldozed, and beaches where turtles once laid eggs are now occupied by resorts and condos. Ironically, tourism development is a major contributor to coastal erosion, as was made evident when 2005's Hurricane Wilma swept away the beaches (many artificial) that attract hordes of tourists annually. And with the proliferation of new hotels comes the need for freshwater sources, increasing the danger of salinization of the water table. As job-seekers converge on Quintana Roo's tourist zones, demand for building materials to construct housing for the burgeoning population is also a persistent issue.

The Yucatan Wildlife website (www.yucatanwildlife.com) provides a wealth of information about the region's animal and plant species, local ecotours and Yucatán-based nature organizations.

Another key problem is the fragmentation of habitat. As patches of jungle shrink with new settlement and the construction of highways, they become isolated and species become trapped in smaller areas. Animals' movements are restricted and the gene pool cannot flow beyond the borders of each piece of fragmented habitat.

Also of concern is the need for effective waste-management systems. Some places do not have water-treatment plants, which results in untreated sewage running through underground water systems and out to sea. The so-called *aguas negras* (black waters) contain nutrients that allow for mass algal growth. Unfortunately, these oxygen-depleting algae can have an asphyxiating effect on various forms of marine life, such as coral.

Mexico's largest oil field, the Cantarell complex, is in the Bay of Campeche, 85km off the shore of Ciudad del Carmen. In 2007 there was an 11,700-barrel oil spill in the bay, adversely affecting the area's marine flora and fauna. The Cantarell field is also yielding less oil than it did in the past, leading the company to seek new sources in the Alacranes reef off the coast of Progreso, and at Laguna de Términos, where further habitat destruction is feared.

The good news is that the level of protection on reserves and other important natural habitats has continued on a constant basis over the years. In 2012, 380 sq km consisting of jungle area and coastline on Isla Cozumel's northern and eastern sides were given protected status, and in 2009 some 1460 sq km of waters where whale sharks congregate (off the Quintana Roo coast) was declared a protected area. And in 2004, 1497 sq km of threatened forest in the Reserva de la Biosfera Calakmul was permanently protected. In Chiapas, Parque Nacional Lagunas de Montebello was designated a Unesco biosphere reserve in 2009, adding to the conservancy potential of the area.

But Yucatán's protected zones and reserves encompass private *ejidos* (communally owned land) occupied by *campesinos* (agricultural workers) whose activities, particularly cattle raising and logging, may infringe upon the environment. Seeking a solution, some environmental organizations have begun training *ejido* inhabitants as guides for ecotourism activities, thus providing alternative livelihoods. Such programs are under way in the Reserva de la Biosfera Calakmul and on Isla Holbox, and locals say the programs have worked out well because they provide a viable source of income.

Survival Guide

Directory A–Z

Accommodations

Accommodations in the Yucatán range from hammocks and *cabañas* to hotels of every imaginable standard, including world-class luxury resorts. In popular destinations for high season (Christmas through Easter, plus most of July and August), it's best to book in advance.

➡ Outside peak season, many midrange and top-end establishments in tourist destinations cut their room prices by 20% to 50%. They may also have special online offers.

➡ Some places (mostly top-end hotels) do not include a 14% to 19% tax charge in quoted prices. When in doubt, you can ask *'¿Están incluidos los impuestos?'* (Are taxes included?).

➡ We refer to 'single' (abbreviated 's') for a room for one person, and 'double' ('d') for a room for two people. Mexicans sometimes use the phrase *'cuarto sencillo'* (literally, 'single room') to mean a room with one bed, which is often a *cama matrimonial* (double bed). A *cuarto doble* often means a room with two beds.

Price Categories

Room prices quoted are for high-season rates and subject to change. Rates do not reflect 'ultra' high-season prices that some midrange and top-end establishments charge from mid-December to early January, and during the two-week Easter vacation period. Budget accommodations usually keep prices the same year-round (bless their hearts!). Hotels in developed resort areas – such as Cancún and Playa del Carmen – may publish their rates in US dollars. Places that stick with the peso sometimes adjust their prices according to exchange-rate fluctuations.

BUDGET

The Yucatán offers a mixed bag of affordable sleeping options, including hostels, *cabañas* (cabins), campgrounds, guesthouses and economical hotels. Rooms in this category are assumed to have bathrooms, unless otherwise stated. Recommended accommodations in this range will be simple and without frills but generally clean.

MIDRANGE

Midrange accommodations are chiefly hotels, but you'll also find many appealing B&Bs, guesthouses and bungalows in this price bracket. In some areas of the Yucatán, M$700 can get you a very comfortable and atmospheric setup. Keep in mind that not all rooms are the same in many establishments (some are larger or have better views), so it's worth having a look at several options before settling in.

TOP END

Places in this category run from classy international hotels to deluxe all-inclusive resorts and smaller boutique hotels catering to travelers with a taste for comfort and design.

Types of Accommodations

APARTMENTS & B&BS

In some places you can find *departamentos* (apartments) for tourists with fully equipped kitchens. Some are very comfortable and they can be good value for three or more people. The website www.locogringo.com is a good source of information.

In the Yucatán, B&Bs are generally upmarket guesthouses, often aimed at foreign tourists.

BOOK YOUR STAY ONLINE

For more accommodations reviews by Lonely Planet authors, check out http://lonelyplanet.com/hotels/. You'll find independent reviews, as well as recommendations on the best places to stay. Best of all, you can book online.

SLEEPING PRICE RANGES

The following price ranges refer to accommodations for two people in high season, including any taxes charged.

$ less than M$600

$$ M$600–1200

$$$ more than M$1200

CABAÑAS

Cabañas are usually cabins or huts – of wood, brick, adobe or stone – with a palm-thatched roof. Some have dirt floors and nothing inside but a bed, others are deluxe, with electric light, mosquito net, air-con, fridge and bar. Prices vary widely depending on location and amenities provided.

CAMPING & TRAILER PARKS

Some campgrounds are actually trailer parks set up for people with camper vans and trailers (caravans) and are open to tent campers at lower rates. They're most common along the coast. Some restaurants and guesthouses in beach spots or rural areas will let you pitch a tent on their property for M$100 per person.

CASAS DE HUÉSPEDES & POSADAS

Casas de huéspedes (guesthouses) and *posadas* (inns) are normally inexpensive and congenial, family-run accommodations with a relaxed atmosphere. More often than not, a *casa de huéspedes* is a home converted into guest lodgings, so it allows for plenty of interaction with the host family.

HAMMOCKS

A hammock can be a very comfortable place to sleep in hot areas (but mosquito repellent or a net often comes in handy). You can rent a hammock and a place to hang it – usually under a palm roof outside a small guesthouse or beach restaurant – for M$50 to M$100. With your own hammock, the cost comes down a bit. It's easy to buy hammocks throughout the Yucatán.

HOSTELS

Hostels exist in nearly all of the region's most popular tourist destinations. They provide dorm accommodations (for about M$180 to M$220 per person), plus communal kitchens, bathrooms and living space, and often more expensive private rooms. Standards of hygiene and security vary. Always ask if the dorms come with air-con – you might need it on a hot day.

HOTELS

Yucatán has hotels in all price ranges, especially in developed areas. Before settling on a room, ask to see the range of options available. An additional M$200 or so in the budget and midrange categories may be the difference between a musty interior room and airy digs with a nice view. Top-end hotels offer rooms with varying degrees of luxury, depending on what you're willing to fork out.

Climate

Cancún

°C/°F Temp

Rainfall inches/mm

40/104 – 30/86 – 20/68 – 10/50 – 0/32

16/400 – 12/300 – 8/200 – 4/100 – 0

J F M A M J J A S O N D

Cozumel

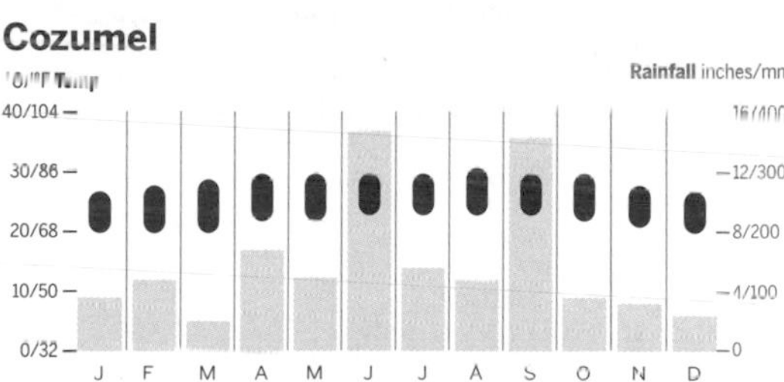

Mérida

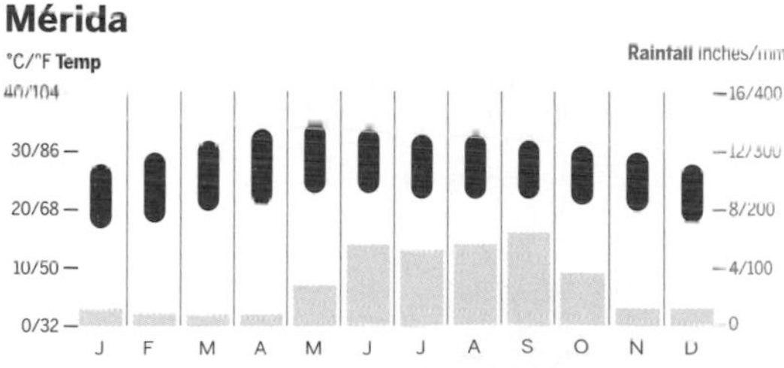

RESORTS

A popular option for families, particularly in Cancún and the Riviera Maya, these sprawling hotels usually offer all-inclusive packages and provide most of everything you'll need within the confines of the property. There are also adults-only resorts, which put a premium on luxury and comfort. Some resorts still promote cheaper European plans.

Activities

There's never a shortage of things to do on the Yucatán Peninsula, where you'll find some of the best scuba diving and snorkeling in the world, thousands of limestone swimming holes and ancient Maya ruins nearly everywhere you turn.

Resources

Planeta.com (www.planeta.com) Good resource on active and responsible tourism.

Mexico Online (www.mexonline.com) Includes listings of activities providers.

Amtave (Mexican Association of Adventure Travel & Ecotourism; toll-free 800-654-44-52; www.amtave.org) The Mexican Adventure Tourism & Ecotourism Association, with some 80 member organizations.

Courses

Taking classes can be a great way to meet people and get an inside angle on local life and culture. Mexican universities often offer classes. For long-term study in Mexico you'll need a student visa; contact a Mexican consulate for details. You can also arrange informal Spanish tutoring through some hostels. There are helpful links on the Lonely Planet (www.lonelyplanet.com) website.

- You can take language courses in Mérida, San Cristóbal de las Casas, Playa del Carmen and Puerto Morelos.
- For cooking courses you'll find good schools in culinary capital Mérida and beach town Puerto Morelos.

Customs Regulations

Visitors are allowed to bring the following items into Mexico duty-free:

- two cameras
- 10 packs of cigarettes
- 3L of alcohol
- medicine for personal use, with prescription in the case of psychotropic drugs
- one laptop computer
- one digital music player

See www.sat.gob.mx for more details.

After handing in your customs declaration form, an automated system will determine whether your luggage will be inspected. A green light means pass, a red light means your bags will be searched.

Discount Cards

Reduced prices for students and seniors on Mexican buses and at museums and archaeological sites are usually only for those with Mexican residence or education credentials, but the following cards will sometimes get you a reduction (the ISIC is the most widely recognized). They are also recognized for reduced-price air tickets at student- and youth-oriented travel agencies:

ISIC (www.isic.org) Student card.

IYTC (International Youth Travel Card) For those under 31 years.

ITIC (International Teacher Identity Card) For full-time teachers.

Electricity

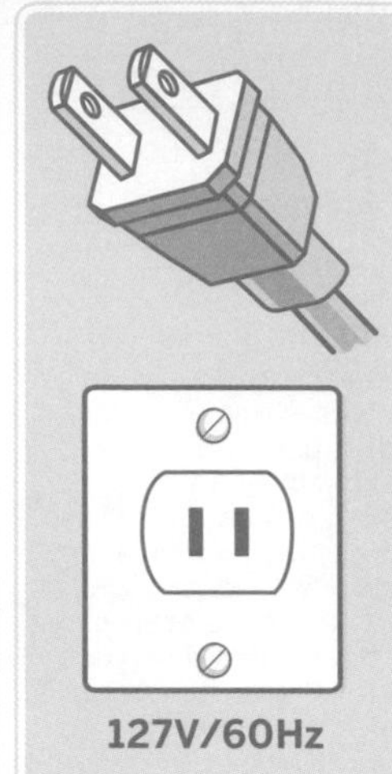

Embassies & Consulates

It's important to understand what your own embassy can and can't do to help you if you get into trouble. Generally speaking, it won't be much help in emergencies if the trouble you're in is remotely your own fault.

Remember that you are bound by the laws of the country you are in. In genuine emergencies you might get some assistance, such as a list of lawyers, but only if other channels have been exhausted.

Embassy details can be found at **Secretaría de Relaciones Exteriores** (www.sre.gob.mx) and **Embassyworld.org** (www.embassyworld.org).

Many embassies or their consular agencies are in Mexico City (including Australia, Ireland and New Zealand); Cancún is home to several consulates, and there are some diplomatic outposts elsewhere in the region as well.

Belizean Consulate Chetumal (☎983-129-3328; conbelizeqroo@gmail.com; Av Juárez 226B, btwn Avs Primo de Verdad & Carranza, Chetumal; ⊙9am-noon Mon-Fri)

Canadian Consulate Cancún (☎998-883-33-60; www.canadainternational.gc.ca; Blvd Kukulcán Km 12, Centro Empresarial Oficina E7; ⊙9:30am-1pm Mon-Fri); Playa del Carmen (☎984-803-24-11; www.canadainternational.gc.ca; Av 10 Sur, btwn Calles 3 & 5 Sur, in Plaza Paraíso Caribe; ⊙9am-1pm Mon-Fri)

Dutch Consulate Cancún (☎998-884-86-72; http://mexico.nlambassade.org; Av Nichupte s/n, in Pabellón Caribe, Cancún; ⊙9am-2pm Mon-Fri); Mérida (☎999-924-31-22; http://mexico.nlambassade.org; Calle 64 No 418; ⊙8am-2pm Mon-Fri)

French Consulate Mérida (☎999-930-15-00; Calle 60 No 385, Mérida; ⊙9am-5pm Mon-Fri)

German Consulate Cancún (☎998-884-15-98; Punta Conoca 36, SM24, Cancún); **Mérida** (☎999-944-32-52; Calle 49 No 212, Mérida)

Guatemalan Consulate Ciudad Hidalgo (☎962-698-01-84; 9a Calle Oriente 9, Colonia San José; ⊙9am-2pm & 3-5pm Mon-Fri); Comitán (☎963-110-68-16; www.minex.gob.gt; 1a Calle Sur Poniente 35, Int.3 4th fl, Comitán; ⊙9am-1pm & 2-5pm Mon-Fri); Tapachula (☎962-626-12-52; www.minex.gob.gt; Quinta Norte No 3, 3rd fl; ⊙9am-5pm Mon-Fri)

Italian Consulate Cancún (☎998-884-12-61; www.ambcittadelmessico.esteri.it; Alcatraces 39)

UK Consulate Cancún (☎998-881-01-00; Royal Sands, Blvd Kukulcán Km 13.5, Cancún; ⊙9am-2pm Mon-Fri)

US Consulate Cancún (☎998-883-02-72; Despacho 301, Torre La Europea, Blvd Kukulcán Km 13, Cancún; ⊙8am-1pm Mon-Fri); Mérida (☎999-942-57-77; http://merida.usconsulate.gov; Calle 60 No 338K, Mérida; ⊙9am-1pm Mon-Fri)

Food

For detailed information on eating in the Yucatán Peninsula, see Eat & Drink Like a Local (p45) and Yucatecan Cuisine (p265).

Gay & Lesbian Travelers

Mexico is more broad-minded about sexuality than you might expect. Gays and lesbians rarely attract open discrimination or violence. Discrimination based on sexual orientation has been illegal since 1999 and can be punished with up to three years in prison. Gay men have a more public profile than lesbians. Cancún has a small gay scene, and there are a number of gay-friendly establishments listed in Mérida at www.gaymexicomap.com.

Gay Mexico (www.gaymexico.com.mx) Useful online guide for gay tourism in Mexico.

International Gay & Lesbian Travel Association (www.iglta.org) Provides information on the major travel providers in the gay sector.

Out Traveler (www.outtraveler.com) Helpful general resource.

Health

Dr David Goldberg

Travelers to the Yucatán need to be careful chiefly about food- and water-borne diseases, though mosquito-borne infections can also be a problem. Most of these illnesses are not life threatening, but they can certainly impact on your trip. Besides getting the proper vaccinations, it's important that you bring a good insect repellent and exercise care in what you eat and drink.

Private hospitals give better care than public ones, but are more expensive.

Before You Go

RECOMMENDED VACCINATIONS

Make sure all routine vaccinations are up to date and check whether all vaccines are suitable for children and pregnant women at www.cdc.gov/travel. Since most vaccines don't produce immunity until at least two weeks after they're given, visit a physician four to eight weeks before departure.

Bring medications in their original containers, clearly labeled. A signed, dated letter from your physician describing all medical conditions and medications, including generic names, is also a good idea. If carrying syringes or needles, be sure to have a physician's letter documenting their necessity.

Hepatitis A All travelers (not recommended for pregnant women or children under two years); gamma globulin is the alternative.

Hepatitis B Long-term travelers in close contact with local population (requires three doses over a six-month period).

Rabies Recommended only for travelers who may have direct

PRACTICALITIES

Newspapers Mérida's *El Diario de Yucatán* (www.yucatan.com.mx) is one of the country's leading newspapers. *Yucatán Today* (www.yucatantoday.com) offers good English-language info on Yucatán state.

TV Local TV is dominated by Televisa, which runs four national channels; TV Azteca has the other two.

DVDs Mexico uses region 4. Many DVDs sold in Mexico are illegal copies.

Weights & Measures Mexico uses the metric system.

Smoking Mexico has a ban on smoking in public indoor spaces, except in designated areas. Enforcement, however, is inconsistent.

contact with stray dogs and cats, bats and wildlife.

Typhoid Recommended for all unvaccinated people, especially for those staying in small cities, villages and rural areas.

In the Yucatán

HEPATITIS A

➡ Hepatitis A occurs throughout Central America. It's a viral infection of the liver usually acquired by ingestion of contaminated water, food or ice, though it may also be acquired by direct contact with infected persons. Symptoms may include fever, malaise, jaundice, nausea, vomiting and abdominal pain. Most cases resolve uneventfully, though hepatitis A occasionally causes severe liver damage. There is no treatment.

➡ The vaccine for hepatitis A is extremely safe and highly effective. If you get a booster six to 12 months later, it lasts for at least 10 years. You should get it before you go to Mexico.

DENGUE FEVER & CHIKUNGUNYA VIRUS

Dengue fever is a viral infection found throughout Central America. In Mexico, the risk is greatest along the Gulf coast, especially from July to September. Dengue is transmitted by Aedes mosquitoes, which bite preferentially during the day and are usually found close to human habitations, often indoors. They breed primarily in artificial water containers, such as cisterns and discarded tires. As a result, dengue is especially common in urban environments.

➡ Dengue usually causes flu-like symptoms, including fever, muscle aches, joint pains, headache and nausea, and it's often followed by a rash.

➡ Expect similar symptoms if infected by the mosquito-transmitted chikungunya virus.

➡ There is no vaccine and no specific treatment for dengue and chikungunya, except analgesics. Severe cases may require hospitalization.

MALARIA

Occurs in Chiapas and in rare cases, Quintana Roo. It's transmitted by mosquito bites, usually between dusk and dawn. The main symptom is high spiking fevers, which may be accompanied by chills, sweats, headache, body aches, general weakness, vomiting or diarrhea.

➡ Taking malaria pills is strongly recommended when visiting rural areas. For Mexico, the first-choice malaria pill is chloroquine.

➡ Protecting yourself against mosquito bites is just as important as taking malaria pills, as no pills are 100% effective. If you develop a fever after returning home, see a physician, as malaria symptoms may not occur for months. It can be diagnosed by a simple blood test.

MOSQUITO BITES

➡ To prevent bites, wear long sleeves, long pants, hats and shoes (rather than sandals). In areas with *chaquistes* (gnatlike sand flies that can leave welts), avoid exposing your flesh at dusk and dawn when they're out in full force.

➡ Don't sleep with the window open unless there is a functional screen. Use a good insect repellent that should be applied to exposed skin and clothing, but don't use DEET-containing compounds on children under two years.

➡ Insect repellents containing certain botanical products, including eucalyptus oil and soybean oil, are effective but last only 1½ to two hours. Where there is a high risk of malaria, use DEET-containing repellents. Products based on citronella are not effective.

➡ If sleeping outdoors or in accommodations that allow entry of mosquitoes, use a mosquito coil.

TYPHOID FEVER

Typhoid fever is caused by ingestion of food or water contaminated by *Salmonella typhi*. Fever occurs in virtually all cases. Other symptoms may include headache, malaise, muscle aches, dizziness, loss of appetite, nausea and abdominal pain. Either diarrhea or constipation may occur.

➡ The drug of choice for typhoid fever is usually a quinolone antibiotic, such as ciprofloxacin (Cipro) or levofloxacin (Levaquin).

SNAKE & SCORPION BITES

Venomous snakes in the Yucatán generally do not attack without provocation, but may bite humans who accidentally come too close. Coral snakes are somewhat retiring and tend not to bite humans unless considerably provoked.

➡ In the event of a venomous snake or scorpion bite, place the victim at rest, keep the bitten area immobilized and move them immediately to the nearest medical facility. Avoid using tourniquets, which are no longer recommended.

➡ To prevent scorpion stings, be sure to inspect and shake out clothing, shoes and sleeping bags before use. If stung, apply ice or cold packs.

SUNBURN & HEAT EXHAUSTION

To protect yourself from excessive sun exposure, you should stay out of the midday sun, wear sunglasses and a wide-brimmed hat, and apply sunscreen with SPF 15 or higher, providing both UVA and UVB protection.

➡ Sunscreen should be applied to all exposed parts of the body approximately 30 minutes before sun exposure and be reapplied after swimming or vigorous activity.

➡ Do not apply sunscreen prior to swimming in cenotes (limestone sinkholes) – it pollutes the water!

➡ Drink plenty of fluids and avoid strenuous exercise when the temperature is high. Heat exhaustion is characterized by dizziness, weakness, headache, nausea or profuse sweating.

WATER

Tap water is generally not safe to drink.

➡ Vigorous boiling for several minutes is the most effective means of water purification.

➡ Another option is to disinfect water with iodine pills. Instructions are usually provided and should be carefully followed.

➡ Numerous water filters are on the market. Those with smaller pores (reverse osmosis filters) provide the best protection, but they are relatively large and readily plugged by debris. Those with somewhat larger pores (microstrainer filters) are ineffective against viruses, although they do remove other organisms.

Insurance

A travel-insurance policy to cover theft, loss and medical problems is a good idea. Some policies specifically exclude dangerous activities such as scuba diving and motorcycling.

Mexican medical treatment is generally inexpensive for common illnesses and minor treatment, but if you suffer some serious medical problem, you might want to find a private hospital or fly out for treatment. Travel insurance typically covers the costs but make sure the policy includes such things as ambulances and emergency flights home.

Some US health insurance policies stay in effect (at least for a limited time) if you travel abroad, but it's worth checking exactly what you'll be covered for in Mexico.

You might prefer a policy that pays medical costs directly rather than requiring you to pay on the spot and claim later. If you have to claim later, keep all documentation. There is a wide variety of policies; check the small print.

Worldwide medical insurance for travelers is available online at www.lonelyplanet.com/travel-insurance. You can buy, extend and claim online anytime – even if you're already on the road.

Internet Access

Internet cafes (which charge about M$10 per hour) abound in the Yucatán. Most computers have Skype installed.

Many places (hotels, bars and restaurants) have wi-fi available, but in some hotels the signal only reaches the lobby. We use the wi-fi icon (📶) in our reviews if the signal reaches at least some part of the premises; an internet icon (@) refers to establishments with internet-ready computers for guests.

Legal Matters

Mexican law presumes an accused person is guilty until proven innocent.

➡ As in most other countries, the purchase of controlled medication requires a doctor's prescription.

➡ It's against Mexican law to take firearms or ammunition into the country (even unintentionally).

➡ A law passed in 2009 decriminalized the possession of small amounts of certain drugs for personal use – including marijuana (up to 5g), cocaine (500mg), heroin (50mg) and methamphetamine (40mg). The law states that first-time offenders do not face criminal prosecution. Selling drugs remains illegal, and people found in possession may still have to appear before a prosecutor to prove that the drugs are truly for personal use. The easiest way to stay out of trouble is to avoid drugs all together.

Maps

➡ Free city and regional maps are available at tourist offices around the peninsula.

➡ Quality regional maps include the highly

detailed **ITMB** (www.itmb.ca) 1:500,000 *Yucatán Peninsula Travel Map* and **Guía Roji** (www.guiaroji.com.mx) 1:1,000,000-scale *Maya World* (M$90) showing all of the peninsula and parts of Tabasco and Chiapas.

➡ Guía Roji also publishes maps of each Mexican state and a national road atlas called *Por las Carreteras de Mexico* (M$220). It's widely available throughout Mexico and can be bought from the website.

➡ **Can-Do Maps** (MapChick; www.cancunmap.com) publishes various Yucatán maps that can be purchased online.

➡ A good internet source is **Maps of Mexico** (www.maps-of-mexico.com), with detailed maps of all the states.

Money

➡ Mexico's currency is the peso, usually denoted by the 'M$' sign. The peso is divided into 100 centavos. Coins come in denominations of five, 10, 20 and 50 centavos and one, two, five and 10 pesos; notes come in 20, 50, 100, 200, 500 and 1000 pesos.

➡ International credit cards are accepted for payment by most airlines, car-rental agencies, many midrange and upmarket hotels, and some restaurants, gas stations and shops; they can also be used to withdraw cash from ATMs. Visa is the most widely accepted card in the Yucatán.

➡ Many businesses take debit cards as well, but you'll usually wind up paying the card issuer a 3% international transaction fee. Some credit cards tack on international surcharges, too.

➡ As a backup to credit or debit cards, always carry cash, especially when visiting remote towns with few or no ATMs available. US dollars, euros, British pounds and Canadian dollars are the most easily exchangeable foreign currencies in Mexico. Some hotels offer discounts for cash-paying customers. Many restaurants outside tourist centers accept cash only.

ATMs

ATMs (*caja permanente* or *cajero automático*) are plentiful in the Yucatán and are the easiest source of cash. You can use major credit cards and some bank cards, such as those on the Cirrus and Plus systems, to withdraw pesos (or dollars) from ATMs. The exchange rate that banks use for ATM withdrawals is normally better than the 'tourist rate' – though that advantage is negated by transaction fees and other methods that banks have of taking your money. Use ATMs during daylight hours, and whenever possible, in secure indoor locations.

Banks & Casas de Cambio

You can change currency in banks or at *casas de cambio* (money-exchange offices). Banks have longer lines than *casas de cambio* and usually shorter hours. *Casas de cambio* can easily be found in just about every large or medium-size town and in some smaller ones. Some exchange offices will ask for your passport as a form of ID.

International Transfers

Should you need money wired to you in Mexico, an easy and quick method is through **Western Union** (☎USA toll-free 800-325-6000; www.westernunion.com). The service is offered by many bank branches and other businesses in the Yucatán, identified by black-and-yellow signs. Your sender pays the money online or at a Western Union branch, along with a fee, and gives the details on who is to receive it and where. When you pick it up, take along photo identification.

Tipping

Workers in tourism and service industries depend on tips to supplement miserable basic wages. Here's what you should leave:

Restaurants About 15% to 20% unless service comes included in the check.

Hotels From 5% to 10% of your room cost.

Taxis Drivers don't expect tips unless a special service is provided.

Gas station and parking attendants M$5 to M$10.

Baggers in supermarkets M$3 to M$5.

Hotel and airport porters M$20 per bag.

TAXES

Mexico's value-added tax (IVA) is levied at 16%. By law the tax must be included in prices quoted to you and should not be added afterward. Signs in shops and notices on restaurant menus often state '*IVA incluido.*' Occasionally they state instead that IVA must be added to the quoted prices.

Some hotels in the region do not include IVA and a 3% lodging tax in their published fares, so you might be paying an additional 19% in hidden fees.

Opening Hours

Standard hours are as follows:

Archaeological sites 8am–5pm.

Banks 9am–5pm Monday to Friday, 10am–2pm Saturday; some banks do not open Saturday; hours may vary.

Cafes 8am–9pm.

Casas de Cambio (Currency-exchange offices) 9am–7pm, usually daily.

Cenotes 9am–5pm.

Museums Many close on Monday.

Stores 9am–8pm Monday to Saturday; some close from 2pm–5pm.

Photography & Video

Keep in mind the following tips when shooting:

➡ Most Mexicans don't mind having their pictures taken but it's always a good idea to ask beforehand. Some indigenous people can be especially sensitive about this.

➡ Be forewarned that a M$45 fee for use of video cameras is charged at many archaeological sites.

➡ In large cities like Cancún and Mérida, you'll find shops selling everything from waterproof disposable cameras to camcorders and memory cards for digital cameras. Some even sell film (long live analog!).

➡ If your camera breaks down, you'll be able to find a repair shop in most sizable towns.

For more information on taking travel photographs, check out Lonely Planet's *Travel Photography*.

Post

➡ An airmail letter or postcard weighing up to 20g costs M$11.50 to send to the US or Canada, M$13.50 to Europe or South America, and M$15 to the rest of the world.

➡ Delivery takes 15 to 20 days, or five to to eight days if you pay for express service.

➡ If you're sending a package internationally from Mexico, be prepared to open it for inspection at the post office; take packing materials with you and don't seal it till you get there.

➡ For assured and speedy delivery, you can use one of the more expensive international courier services, such as **UPS** (toll-free 800-743-38-77; www.ups.com), **FedEx** (toll-free 800-900-11-00; www.fedex.com) or Mexico's **Estafeta** (toll-free 800 903-35-00; www.estafeta.com). A 1kg package typically costs about M$675 to the US and M$850 to Europe.

Public Holidays

Banks, post offices, government offices and many shops throughout Mexico are closed on the following national holidays:

Año Nuevo (New Year's Day) January 1

Día de la Constitución (Constitution Day) February 5

Día del Nacimiento de Benito Juárez (Anniversary of Benito Juárez' birth) March 21

Día del Trabajo (Labor Day) May 1

Día de la Independencia (Independence Day) September 16

Día de la Revolución (Revolution Day) November 20

Día de Navidad (Christmas Day) December 25

In addition, many offices and businesses close on the following optional holidays:

Día de la Bandera (National Flag Day) February 24

Viernes Santo (Good Friday) Two days before Easter Sunday

Cinco de Mayo (Commemorates Mexico's victory over French forces in Puebla) May 5

Día de la Raza (Columbus' 'discovery' of the New World) October 12

Día de Muertos (Day of the Dead) November 1 and 2

Día de Nuestra Señora de Guadalupe (Day of Our Lady of Guadalupe) December 12

Safe Travel

Despite all the grim news about Mexico's drug-related violence, the Yucatán Peninsula remains a safe haven. Most of the killings you hear about happen between rival drug gangs, so tourists are rarely caught up in the disputes – especially in the Yucatán, which keeps a safe distance from the turf wars occurring elsewhere in Mexico. Just to give you an idea of how safe it really is, major US cities such as New York and Chicago have higher murder rates than the entire state of Yucatán.

Foreign affairs departments can supply a variety of useful data about travel to Mexico.

Australia (outside Australia 612-6261-3305; www.dfat.gov.au)

Canada (in Canada 800-267-8376, outside Canada 1-613-944-4000; www.dfait-maeci.gc.ca)

UK (in UK 020-7008-1500; www.gov.uk/fco)

USA (in USA toll-free 808-407-4747, outside USA 1-202-501-4444; www.travel.state.gov)

Theft & Robbery

Pickpocketing and bag-snatching are relatively minor risks in the Yucatán, but it's a good idea to stay alert on buses and in crowded bus terminals and airports. Mugging is less common than purse snatching, but more serious: resistance may be met with violence (do *not* resist). Usually these robbers will not harm you: they just want your money, fast.

➡ Don't go where there are few other people in the vicinity; this includes camping in secluded places. A simple rule: if there are women and children around, you're probably safe.

➡ Don't leave any valuables unattended while you swim. Run-and-grab thefts by people lurking in the woods are a common occurrence.

➡ If your hotel has a safe, leave most of your money, important documents and smaller valuables there in a sealed, signed envelope. Leave valuables in a locker when staying at a hostel.

➡ Carry only a small amount of money – enough for an outing – in a pocket. If you do have to carry valuables, keep them hidden in a money belt underneath your clothing.

➡ Don't keep money, credit or debit cards, wallets or bags in open view any longer than you have to. At ticket counters, keep a hand or foot on your bag at all times.

➡ Do not leave anything valuable-looking in a parked vehicle.

➡ Be careful about accepting drinks from overly social characters in bars, especially in tourist-heavy zones; there have been cases of drugging followed by robbery and assault.

➡ Be wary of attempts at credit-card fraud. One method is when the cashier swipes your card twice (once for the transaction and once for nefarious purposes). Keep your card in sight at all times.

Telephone

Cell Phones

Using your own cell phone from home in Mexico can be extremely expensive due to high roaming fees. Roaming Zone (www.roamingzone.com) is a useful source on roaming arrangements. Alternatively, you can insert a Mexican SIM card into your phone, but your phone needs to be unlocked for international use. Some Mexican cell-phone companies will unlock it for you for a fee. The easiest option is to simply buy a new Mexican cell phone: they're inexpensive (a cheapo costs M$500 and comes with free credit). You'll often see cell phones on sale in convenience stores, where you can also buy more credit. Cell-phone service providers Telcel (www.telcel.com) and Movistar (www.movistar.com.mx) have the best coverage in the Yucatán region.

Like other Mexican phone numbers, every cell-phone number has an area code (usually the code of the city where the phone was bought). Here's how to make calls to and from Mexican cell phones.

➡ From local cell phone to cell phone, dial the 10-digit number.

➡ From cell phone to landline, dial the landline's area code and number.

➡ From landline to cell phone, dial ☎044 before the 10 digits for local cell phone calls, or ☎045 before the 10 digits for long-distance cell phone calls.

➡ From another country to a Mexican cell phone, dial your international access code, the Mexican country code (☎52), then ☎1 plus the 10-digit number.

Credit on Mexican cell phones or SIM cards burns fast, especially when making calls outside the phone's area code. How do you think Telcel boss Carlos Slim became one of the world's richest men?

Collect Calls

Una llamada por cobrar (a collect call) can cost the receiving party much more than if they call you, so you may prefer for the other party to call. You can make collect calls from card phones without a card. Call an operator at ☎020 for domestic calls, or ☎090 for international calls. The Mexican term for 'home country direct' is *país directo:* but don't count on Mexican international operators knowing the access codes for all countries.

Some call offices and hotels will make collect calls for you, but they usually charge for the service.

Landlines

Mexican landlines *(telefonos fijos)* have two- or three-digit area codes.

➡ From landline to another landline in the same town, dial the local number (seven or eight digits).

➡ From landline to landline in an other Mexican town, dial the long-distance prefix ☎01, the area code and the local number.

➡ To make an international call, dial the international prefix ☎00, the country code (☎1 for the US and Canada, ☎44 for the UK, etc), and the city area code and number.

USEFUL NUMBERS

Directory assistance ☎040

Domestic operator ☎020

Emergency ☎066

International operator ☎090

Mexican toll-free numbers ☎800 followed by seven digits; always require the 01 long-distance prefix

➡ To call a Mexican landline from another country, dial the international access code, followed by the Mexico country code ☎52, the area code and number.

Long-Distance Discount Cards

Available at many newspaper stands, usually in denominations of M$100 and M$200, *tarjetas telefónicas de descuento* (discount phone cards) offer substantial savings on long-distance calls from landlines. You can use them from most public card phones.

Public Card Phones

These are common in towns and cities; you'll usually find some at airports and bus stations. The most common are those of the country's biggest phone company, Telmex. To use a Telmex card phone you need a phone card known as a *tarjeta Ladatel*. These are sold at kiosks and shops everywhere in denominations of M$30, M$50 and M$100.

Calls from Telmex card phones cost M$3 per minute for local and national calls; M$1.50 per minute to cell phones; M$5 per minute to the continental US, Canada and Central America; and M$10 per minute to anywhere else.

VOIP

Voice Over Internet Protocol (VOIP) services such as Skype (www.skype.com) are a very economical option for travelers who have a computer and the required software. You can also use Skype at internet cafes.

Time

The states of Campeche, Chiapas, Tabasco and Yucatán observe the Hora del Centro, which is the same as US Central Time – GMT minus six hours in winter, and GMT minus five hours during daylight saving time (*horario de verano*, summer time), which runs from the first Sunday in April to the last Sunday in October. Clocks go forward one hour in April and back one hour in October. The state of Quintana Roo observes Eastern Standard Time, GMT minus five hours in winter.

Tourist Information

Just about every town of interest to tourists in the Yucatán has a state or municipal tourist office. They are generally helpful with maps, brochures and questions, and often some staff members speak English.

You can call the Mexico City office of the national tourism ministry **Sectur** (☎078; www.sectur.gob.mx) at any time – 24 hours a day, seven days a week – for information or help in English or Spanish.

Following are the contact details for the head tourism offices of each state:

Campeche (☎toll-free 800-900-22-67; www.campeche.travel)

Chiapas (☎961-617-05-50, toll-free 800-280-35-00; www.turismochiapas.gob.mx)

Quintana Roo (☎983-835-08-60, 998-881-90-00; sedetur.qroo.gob.mx)

Tabasco (☎993-352-36-02, toll-free 800-216-08-42; www.tabasco.gob.mx/turismo)

Yucatán state (☎999-930-37-60; www.yucatan.travel)

Travelers with Disabilities

Lodgings on the Yucatán Peninsula generally don't cater for travelers with disabilities, though some hotels and restaurants (mostly toward the top end of the market) and some public buildings now provide wheelchair access. The absence of institutionalized facilities, however, is largely compensated for by Mexicans' accommodating attitudes toward others, and special arrangements are gladly improvised.

Mobility is easiest in the major tourist resorts. Bus transportation can be difficult; flying or taking a taxi is easier.

Access-able Travel Source (www.access-able.com)

Mobility International USA (www.miusa.org)

Travel for All (lptravel.to/Travel-for-All) Lonely Planet's forum for travelers with disabilities

Visas

Every tourist must have a Mexican government tourist permit, which is easily obtainable. Some nationalities also need to obtain visas.

➡ Citizens of the US, Canada, EU countries, Australia, New Zealand, Iceland, Israel, Japan, Norway and Switzerland are among the dozens of countries whose citizens do not require visas to enter Mexico as tourists.

➡ The website of the **Instituto Nacional de Migración** (☎toll-free 800-004-62-64; www.inm.gob.mx) lists countries that must obtain a visa to travel to Mexico. If the purpose of your visit is to work (even as a volunteer), to report, to study, or to participate in humanitarian aid or human-rights observation, you may well need a visa whatever your nationality. Visa procedures can take several weeks and you may be required to apply in your country of citizenship or residence.

➡ US citizens traveling by land or sea can enter Mexico and return to the US with a passport card, but if traveling by air will need a passport. Non-US citizens passing (even in transit)

through the US on the way to or from Mexico should check well in advance on the US's complicated visa rules. Consult a US consulate, the **US State Department** (www.travel.state.gov), or **US Customs and Border Protection** (www.cbp.gov) websites.

➡ The regulations sometimes change. It's wise to confirm them with a Mexican embassy or consulate. Good sources for information on visa and similar matters are the **London consulate** (consulmex.sre.gob.mx/reinounido) and the **Washington consulate** (consulmex.sre.gob.mx/washington).

Tourist Permit & Fee

The Mexican tourist permit (tourist card; officially the *forma migratoria multiple* or FMM) is a brief paper document that you must fill out and get stamped by Mexican immigration when you enter Mexico and keep till you leave. It's available at official border crossings, international airports, ports, and often from airlines and Mexican consulates. At land borders you won't usually be given one automatically – you have to ask for it.

A tourist permit only permits you to engage in what are considered to be tourist activities (including sports, health, artistic and cultural activities).

➡ The maximum possible stay is 180 days for most nationalities but immigration officers will sometimes put a lower number unless you tell them specifically what you need.

➡ The fee for the tourist permit, called the *derecho para no inmigrante* (DNI; nonimmigrant fee), is M$332, but it's free for people entering by land who stay less than seven days. If you enter Mexico by air, however, the fee is usually included in your airfare.

➡ If you enter by land, you must pay the fee at a bank in Mexico at any time before you reenter the frontier zone on your way out of Mexico (or before you check-in at an airport to fly out of Mexico). Most Mexican border posts have on-the-spot bank offices where you can pay the DNI fee. When you pay at a bank, your tourist permit will be stamped to prove that you have paid.

➡ Look after your tourist permit because it may be checked when you leave the country. You can be fined for not having it.

LOST TOURIST PERMITS

If you lose your tourist permit, contact your nearest Instituto Nacional de Migración (National Immigration Institute; INM) office, which will issue a duplicate for M$332. All international airports have immigration offices.

Volunteering

Volunteering is a great way of giving back to local communities. In the Yucatán there are various organizations that welcome any help they can get, from environmental and wildlife-conservation NGOs to social programs. You can always look for opportunities at your local hostel or language school, some of which offer part-time volunteering opportunities. Most programs require a minimum commitment of at least a month, and some charge fees for room and board.

Volunteer Directories

Go Abroad (www.goabroad.com)

Go Overseas (www.gooverseas.com)

Idealist (www.idealist.org)

The Mexico Report (themexicoreport.com/non-profits-in-mexico)

Transitions Abroad (www.transitionsabroad.com)

Yucatán-based Programs

Centro Ecológico Akumal (www.ceakumal.org) Accepts volunteers for its environmental and protection programs.

Flora, Fauna y Cultura (☎984-871-52-44; www.florafaunaycultura.org; turtle observation tour US$25, volunteer program incl room & board M$1500) You can help with turtle conservation in Xcacel from June to October.

Junax (www.junax.org.mx) Works with indigenous communities in Chiapas; volunteers must speak Spanish.

Pronatura (www.pronatura-ppy.org.mx) Mérida-based environmental organization seeks volunteers to work on various projects in the Yucatán.

Women Travelers

Women can have a great time in the Yucatán, whether traveling with companions or traveling solo. Gender equality has come a long way in Mexico, and Yucatecans are generally a very polite people, but women traveling alone may still be subject to some whistles, loud comments and annoying attempts to chat them up.

Don't put yourself in peril by doing things that Mexican women would not do, such as drinking alone in a cantina, hitchhiking, walking alone through empty streets at night, or going alone to isolated places. Keep a clear head. Excessive alcohol will make you vulnerable. To keep yourself in company of other travelers, head for accommodations such as hostels and popular hotels where you're likely to join group excursions and activities.

On the streets of inland cities and towns, such as in Mérida and Valladolid, you'll notice that women cover up and don't display too much leg, midriff or even their shoulders. This also makes it easier to keep valuables out of sight.

Transportation

GETTING THERE & AWAY

Entering the Region

Immigration officers usually won't keep you waiting any longer than it takes to flick through your passport and enter your length of stay on your tourist permit. Anyone traveling to Mexico via the USA should be sure to check US visa and passport requirements. US citizens traveling by land or sea can enter Mexico and return to the US with a passport card, but when traveling by air will need a passport. Citizens of other countries need their passports to enter Mexico. Some nationalities also need a visa. Flights, cars and tours can be booked online at lonelyplanet.com/bookings.

Air

Most visitors to the Yucatán arrive by air. Direct flights normally originate from an airline's hub city and connecting flights often go through Mexico City.

Mexico's flagship airline is Aeroméxico. Its safety record is comparable to major US and European airlines. Domestic low-cost carriers provide service mostly from Mexico City. MayAir runs prop planes that stop in Cozumel, Cancún and Mérida.

Airports & Airlines

The majority of flights into the peninsula arrive in Cancún or Mérida. The Yucatán's major airports:

Aeropuerto Ángel Albino Corzo (☎961-153-60-68; www.chiapasaero.com; Sarabia s/n) Aka Tuxtla Gutiérrez; serves San Cristóbal de las Casas in Chiapas.

Aeropuerto Internacional de Cancún (☎998-848-72-00; www.asur.com.mx; Hwy 307 Km 22)

Aeropuerto Internacional de Mérida (Mérida International Airport; ☎999-940-60-90; www.asur.com.mx; Hwy 180 Km 4.5; R-79)

Cozumel Airport (☎987-872-20-81; www.asur.com.mx; cnr Av 65 & Blvd Aeropuerto;)

Other cities with airports include Campeche, Chetumal, Ciudad del Carmen, Palenque and Villahermosa.

DOMESTIC AIRLINES FLYING TO/FROM THE YUCATÁN

Aeroméxico (☎Mexico 55-5133-4000; www.aeromexico.com)

Interjet (☎Mexico 55-1102-5555, toll-free USA 866-285-9525; www.interjet.com)

Magnicharters (☎55-5141-1351; www.magnicharters.com.mx)

CLIMATE CHANGE & TRAVEL

Every form of transport that relies on carbon-based fuel generates CO_2, the main cause of human-induced climate change. Modern travel is dependent on airplanes, which might use less fuel per kilometers per person than most cars but travel much greater distances. The altitude at which aircraft emit gases (including CO_2) and particles also contributes to their climate change impact. Many websites offer 'carbon calculators' that allow people to estimate the carbon emissions generated by their journey and, for those who wish to do so, to offset the impact of the greenhouse gases emitted with contributions to portfolios of climate-friendly initiatives throughout the world. Lonely Planet offsets the carbon footprint of all staff and author travel.

MayAir (☎USA 414-755-2527, toll-free Mexico 800-962-92-47; www.mayair.com.mx)

VivaAerobus (☎Mexico 81-8215-0150, toll-free USA 888-935-9848; www.vivaaerobus.com)

Volaris (☎Mexico 55-1102-8000, toll-free USA 855-865-2747; www.volaris.com)

Land

Mexico

➡ Hwy 180 runs north from Villahermosa, the state capital of Tabasco, then it heads along the coast to Campeche and makes its way inland toward Mérida, where it veers east toward Cancún. You can either take the free highway to Cancún (Hwy 180) or a very expensive toll road (Hwy 180D).

➡ In Cancún, Hwy 180 connects with Hwy 307, which runs south along the Riviera Maya and Costa Maya to Chetumal, Quintana Roo's capital. From Chetumal, Hwy 186 takes you to Hwy 199, the turnoff for Palenque and San Cristóbal de las Casas, in Chiapas.

➡ Palenque is only about two hours from Villahermosa. If you'd like to explore more of Mexico beyond the peninsula, the continuation of Hwy 180 in Villahermosa goes west to the Gulf coast state of Veracruz.

Belize

➡ Crossing from Mexico into Belize, at the southern tip of Quintana Roo, is easy for most tourists and there are no special fees for such a visit.

➡ Each person leaving Belize for Mexico needs to pay a US$15 exit fee for visits less than 24 hours and US$19 for longer stays. All fees must be paid in cash, in Belizean or US currency – officials usually won't have change for US currency.

➡ Frequent buses run from Chetumal to the Belizean towns of Corozal (M$40 to M$50, one hour) and Orange Walk (M$75, two hours). The buses depart from the Nuevo Mercado Lázaro Cárdenas and some continue on to Belize City (M$150, four hours).

➡ Car-rental companies do not allow you to cross the Mexico–Belize border with their vehicles.

Guatemala

➡ The borders at La Mesilla/Ciudad Cuauhtémoc, Ciudad Tecún Umán/Ciudad Hidalgo and El Carmen/Talismán are all linked to Guatemala City, and nearby cities within Guatemala and Mexico, by plentiful buses and/or combis (minibuses).

➡ Agencies in San Cristóbal de las Casas offer daily van service to the Guatemalan cities of Quetzaltenango, Panajachel and Antigua.

➡ Additionally, there's a daily bus departing from the San Cristóbal de las Casas bus station that goes to the Ciudad Cuauhtémoc border, where you can catch Guatemalan buses on the other side in the border town of La Mesilla.

➡ **Transportes Palenque** (cnr Allende & Av 20 de Noviembre) runs vans out of Palenque to Tenosique (Tabasco), where you'll find onward connections to Guatemala.

➡ Travelers with their own vehicles can travel by road between Tenosique and Flores (Guatemala), via the border at El Ceibo.

➡ Car-rental companies do not allow you to cross the Mexico–Guatemala border with their vehicles.

Sea

Water taxis depart from Chetumal's *muelle fiscal* (dock) on Boulevard Bahía to San Pedro (Belize). Between the two companies operating water taxis, there's daily service to the island. See www.sanpedrowatertaxi.com and www.belizewatertaxi.com for more information.

You can also charter a boat to San Pedro at the **XTC Dive Center** (www.xtcdivecenter.com; Coast road Km 0.3; 2-tank dives to Banco Chinchorro US$110, snorkeling trips US$45-75, PADI certification US$529, r US$45-60) in Xcalak for US$300 (minimum of five passengers required).

Mahahual, Puerto Chiapas, Progreso and Isla Cozumel are ports of call for cruise ships. Many cruise-ship lines serve these ports.

Carnival Cruise Lines (☎toll-free USA 800-764-7419; www.carnival.com)

DEPARTURE TAXES

An airport departure tax is usually included in your ticket cost, but if it isn't you must pay in cash during airport check-in. It varies from airport to airport, but costs about US$26 (price fluctuates) for international flights departing from Cancún and less for domestic flights. This tax is separate from the fee for your tourist permit, which also is usually included in airfares.

There are two taxes on domestic flights: IVA, the value-added tax (16%), and TUA, an airport tax of about US$14. In Mexico, the taxes are normally included in quoted fares and paid when you buy the ticket. But if you bought a ticket outside Mexico, you will have to pay the TUA when you check-in in Mexico.

Crystal Cruises (☏toll-free USA 888-722-0021; www.crystalcruises.com)

Norwegian Cruise Lines (☏toll-free USA 866-234-7350; www.ncl.com)

P&O Cruises (☏UK 0843-374-0111; www.pocruises.com)

Princess Cruises (☏toll-free USA 866-758-4123; www.princess.com)

Royal Caribbean International (☏Mexico 55-5062-9200, toll-free USA 866-562-7625; www.royalcaribbean.com)

GETTING AROUND

Boat

Frequent ferries depart from Playa del Carmen to Isla Cozumel, Cancún to Isla Mujeres and Chiquilá to Isla Holbox. The following prices are one-way fares:

Isla Holbox M$80

Isla Cozumel M$135 to M$163

Isla Mujeres M$78 from Puerto Juárez, about M$230 from Zona Hotelera

Cancún and Chiquilá have long-term parking available near the terminals. For more information about schedules, points of departure and car ferries, see www.granpuerto.com.mx and www.transcaribe.net. The Holbox ferries do not have websites.

To reach the uninhabited island of Isla Contoy, you can hook up with tour operators with boats departing from **Cancún** (Map p58; ☏998-886-42-70; www.contoytours.com; Blvd Kukulcán Km 5.2; adult/child 5-12yr US$109/63; ⏲tours 9am-5pm Tue, Thu & Sat) and **Isla Mujeres** (Map p80; ☏cell 998-1534883; cnr Av Rueda Medina & Madero; snorkeling incl lunch M$350, Isla Contoy tours M$1000, whale-shark tour M$1400; ⏲office 8am-8pm).

Bus

The Yucatán Peninsula has a good road and bus network, and comfortable, frequent, reasonably priced bus services connect all cities. Most cities and towns have one main bus terminal where all long-distance buses arrive and depart. It may be called the Terminal de Autobuses, Central de Autobuses, Central Camionera or simply La Central (not to be confused with *el centro*, the city center). If there is no single main bus terminal, different bus companies will have separate terminals scattered around town. **Grupo ADO** (☏800-900-01-05; www.ado.com.mx) operates most of the bus lines that you'll be using.

Classes

DELUXE & EXECUTIVE

De lujo (deluxe) services, and the even more comfortable *ejecutivo* (executive), run mainly on the busy routes. They are swift, modern and comfortable, with reclining seats, adequate leg room, air-con, few or no stops, toilets on board (but not necessarily toilet paper), and sometimes drinks or snacks. Deluxe buses usually show movies on video screens and may offer headphones.

ADO Platino (☏toll-free 800-737-58-56; www.adoplatino.com.mx), **ADO GL** (☏toll-free 800-900-01-05; www.adogl.com.mx) and **OCC** (☏toll-free 800-900-01-05; www.occbus.com.mx) provide luxury services. You can buy tickets to these services in the bus terminal before boarding.

1ST CLASS

On *primera (1a) clase* (1st-class) buses, standards of comfort are adequate at the very least. The buses usually have air-con and a toilet, and they stop infrequently. They always show movies (often bad ones, unless Vin Diesel films are your idea of cinematic glory) for most of the trip.

Bring a sweater or jacket to combat over-zealous air-conditioning. As with deluxe buses, you buy your ticket in the bus terminal before boarding. ADO sets the 1st-class standard.

2ND CLASS

Segunda (2a) clase (2nd-class) buses serve small towns and villages, and provide cheaper, slower travel on some intercity routes. A few are almost as quick, comfortable and direct as 1st-class buses. Others are old, slow and shabby.

Many 2nd-class services have no ticket office; you just pay your fare to the conductor. These buses tend to take slow, non-toll roads in and out of big cities and will stop anywhere to pick up passengers: if you board midroute you might make some of the trip standing. The small amount of money you save by traveling 2nd class is not usually worth the discomfort or extra journey time entailed, though traveling on these buses is a great way to meet locals and see less-traveled parts of the countryside.

Second-class buses can also be less safe than 1st-class or deluxe buses, for reasons of maintenance, driver standards, or because they are more vulnerable to being boarded by bandits on quiet roads. In the remote areas, however, you'll often find that 2nd-class buses are the only transportation available.

The biggest 2nd-class companies are Mayab, Oriente and **Noreste** (☏toll-free 800-280-10-10; www.noreste.com.mx).

Microbuses or 'micros' are small, usually fairly new, 2nd-class buses with around 25 seats, often running short routes between nearby towns.

Costs

First-class buses typically cost around M$1 to M$1.50 per kilometer. Deluxe buses may cost just 10% or 20% more than 1st class, *ejecutivo* services can be as much as 50% more. Second-class buses cost about 20% less than 1st class.

Reservations

For trips of up to four or five hours on busy routes, you can usually just go to the bus terminal, buy a ticket and head out without much delay. For longer trips, or routes with infrequent services, buy a ticket a day or more in advance. Deluxe and 1st-class bus companies have computerized ticket systems that allow you to select your seat when you buy your ticket.

Seats on deluxe and 1st-class lines such as ADO and OCC can be booked through **Mi Escape** (toll-free 800-009-90-90; www.miescape.mx), a reservations service with offices in Mérida, Cancún, Cozumel, Campeche and San Cristóbal de las Casas. Mi Escape adds a 10% surcharge to the cost of the ticket so you can save a little money by simply purchasing tickets at the bus terminal.

ADO's website offers online discounts.

Car & Motorcycle

Driving in Mexico is not as easy as it is north of the border and rentals can get expensive for long visits, but having a vehicle gives you extra flexibility and freedom. To reach some of the peninsula's most remote beaches – such as faraway Punta Allen or the stretch of coast east of Progreso – having a car makes life much easier.

Drivers should know some Spanish, have reserves of patience and access to extra cash for emergencies. Very big cars are unwieldy on narrow roads, particularly in the peninsula's rural areas. A sedan with a trunk provides safer storage than a hatchback. Tires (including a spare), shock absorbers and suspension should be in good condition. For security, have something to immobilize the steering wheel.

Motorcycling around the Yucatán is not for the fainthearted. Roads and traffic can be rough, and parts and mechanics hard to come by. Scooters are a good option for getting around on the islands of Isla Mujeres and Cozumel. Helmets are required by Mexican law.

DRIVING TIPS IN THE YUCATÁN

Several things to consider when behind the wheel:

- Fast-approaching vehicles from behind will often shine their brights or use their left turn signal to indicate that you should change lanes and let them pass.
- Some streets may suddenly change direction without warning: pay close attention to the road or you may find yourself driving against the flow of traffic.
- Liability insurance does not include theft coverage: something to think about when parking your car overnight on the street.
- Spare tires sometimes get swiped in large cities: if you're going somewhere where you may need it, make sure it's still there before leaving.
- If you're pulled over at a military or police checkpoint, remain calm and courteous – they're usually just looking for vehicles transporting arms and drugs. You definitely don't want to be caught with either.

Bringing Your Own Car

Unless you're planning on spending a lot of time touring the Yucatán and other parts of Mexico, you're better off with a rental car. Of course, if you're bringing diving equipment or other cumbersome luggage, the long drive from the US or elsewhere may be worth your while.

You can check the full requirements for bringing a vehicle into Mexico with the **American Automobile Association** (AAA; www.aaa.com), a Mexican consulate or call **Mexican Tourist Information** (in US & Canada toll-free 866-640-0597).

DRIVER'S LICENSE

To drive a motor vehicle in Mexico you need a valid driver's license from your home country.

FUEL

All *gasolina* (gasoline) and diesel fuel in Mexico is sold by the government-owned Pemex (Petróleos Mexicanos). All major cities and most midsize towns in the Yucatán have gas stations. If you're heading to a remote coastal town or jungle region, you should fill up before leaving and wherever you can along the way.

The gasoline on sale is all *sin plomo* (unleaded). There are two varieties: *magna*, roughly equivalent to US regular unleaded, and premium, similar to US super unleaded. At last visit, *magna* cost M$13.57 per liter, and premium M$14.38. Diesel fuel is widely available at M$14.20 per liter.

Pump attendants at gas stations appreciate a tip of M$3 to M$5. Not all gas stations accept International credit and debit cards.

INSURANCE

It is very foolish to drive in Mexico without Mexican liability insurance. If you are involved in an accident, you can be jailed and have your vehicle impounded while responsibility and restitution is assessed.

If you are to blame for an accident causing injury or death, you may be detained until you guarantee restitution to the victims and payment of any fines. This could take weeks or months!

Adequate Mexican insurance coverage is the only real protection – it is regarded as a guarantee that restitution will be paid. Mexican law recognizes only Mexican motor insurance *(seguro)*, so a US or Canadian policy, even if it provides coverage, is not acceptable to Mexican officialdom. If you drive your own vehicle, you can buy Mexican motor insurance online through the well-established **Sanborn's** (☎in US toll-free 800-222-0158; www.sanbornsinsurance.com) and other companies.

Most visitors to the Yucatán rent vehicles, which come with optional insurance policies.

MAPS

Signposting can be poor, especially along the Yucatán's non-toll roads, and decent maps are essential. Regional road maps such as Guia Roji's *Mundo Maya* (M$90) or ITMB's *Yucatán Peninsula Travel Reference Map* (US$13) are good options, or if you plan on visiting other parts of Mexico, Guatemala or Belize, Guia Roji's *Por las Carreteras de México* (M$220) will serve you well. Guia Roji maps are sold at bookstores, Sanborns department stores, some newsstands and online at www.guiaroji.com.mx.

The alternative, of course, is Google Maps.

THE GREEN ANGELS

The Mexican tourism ministry, Sectur, maintains a network of Ángeles Verdes (Green Angels) – bilingual mechanics in green uniforms and green trucks who patrol 60,000km of major highways throughout the country daily during daylight hours looking for tourists in trouble. They make minor repairs, change tires, provide fuel and oil, and arrange towing and other assistance if necessary. Service is free; parts, gasoline and oil are provided at cost. If you have access to a telephone when your car has problems, you can call its **24-hour hotline** (☎078; av.sectur.gob.mx) or contact the network through the national **24-hour tourist-assistance service** (☎toll-free 800-006-88-39) based in Mexico City.

RENTALS

Auto rental in the Yucatán is fairly affordable and easy to organize. You can book by internet, phone or in person, and pick up cars at city offices, airports and many of the big hotels. You'll save money by booking ahead of time over the internet. Read the small print of the rental agreement.

- Renters must provide a valid driver's license (your home license is OK), passport and major credit card, and are usually required to be at least 21 years old (sometimes 25, or if you're aged 21 to 24 you may have to pay a surcharge).
- In addition to the basic rental rate, you pay tax and insurance to the rental company, and the full insurance that rental companies encourage can almost double the base cost. You'll usually have the option of taking liability-only insurance (called *daños a terceros*) at a lower rate. Ask exactly what the insurance options cover: theft and damage insurance may only cover a percentage of costs. It's best to have plenty of liability coverage; Mexican law permits the jailing of drivers after an accident until they have met their obligations to third parties.
- The complimentary car-rental insurance offered with some US credit cards does not always cover Mexico. Call your card company ahead of time to check.
- Most rental agencies offer unlimited kilometers. Local firms may or may not be cheaper than the big international ones. In most places the cheapest car available (often a Volkswagen Beetle) costs M$400 to M$500 a day, including unlimited kilometers, insurance and tax. If you rent by the week or month, the per-day cost can come down by 20% to 40%. You can also cut costs by avoiding airport pickups and drop-offs, for which 10% can be added to your total check. There's usually an extra charge for drop-off in another city.
- Remember that you cannot take a rental car out of Mexico unless you have obtained a special permit.

Alamo (☎toll-free 800-849-80-01; www.alamo.com)

Budget (☎toll-free 800-700-17-00; www.budget.com.mx)

Easy Way (☎toll-free 800-327-99-29; www.easywayrentacar.com)

Europcar (☎toll-free 800-201-20-84; www.europcar.com.mx)

Hertz (☎toll-free 800-709-50-00; www.hertz.com)

National (☎toll-free 800-716-66-25; www.nationalcar.com.mx)

Thrifty (☎toll-free 800-021-22-77; www.thrifty.com.mx)

ROAD CONDITIONS

There are several major toll roads (mostly four-lane) in the Yucatán that connect the big cities. They are generally in much better condition and a lot quicker than the alternative free roads.

Driving during the rainy season (usually from May to October) can be challenging to say the least, especially along bumpy dirt roads in rural and coastal areas.

Be especially wary of Alto (Stop) signs and speed bumps (called *topes, vibradores* or *reductores de velocidad*) and holes in the road. They are often not where you'd expect and missing one can cost you a traffic fine or car damage. Speed bumps are also used to slow traffic on highways that pass through built-up areas – they are not always signed and some of them are severe!

Driving on a dark night is best avoided – potential hazards include unlit vehicles, rocks, pedestrians and animals on the roads. Also, hijacks and robberies can occur (stay particularly alert while driving in the vicinity of the Mexico–Guatemala border).

Narrow two-lane roads, some with brush spreading onto the asphalt, are often plied by wide delivery trucks driving well over the speed limit. If you see one approaching, pull over to the side of the road (as much as you can) and let it pass rather than risking a head-on collision.

ROAD RULES

- Drive on the right-hand side of the road.
- One-way streets are common in many towns and cities. Signs with arrows usually indicate the direction of traffic; if the arrow points both ways, it's a two-way street.
- Speed limits range between 80km/h and 120km/h on open highways (less when highways pass through built-up areas), and between 30km/h and 50km/h in towns and cities. Traffic laws and speed limits rarely seem to be enforced on the highways.
- Seat belts are obligatory for all occupants of a car, and children under five years must be strapped into safety seats in the rear.
- Although less frequent in the Yucatán, there is always the chance that you will be pulled over by traffic police for an imaginary infraction. Remember that you don't have to pay a bribe, and corrupt cops would rather not work too hard to obtain one. You can also ask to see documentation about the law you have supposedly broken and always get the officer's name, badge number, vehicle number and department (federal, state or municipal). Pay any traffic fines at a police station and get a receipt, then if you wish to make a complaint head for a state tourist office.
- Street names are often difficult to find outside city centers. Some are labeled on telephone posts or walls of corner buildings.

Hitchhiking

Hitchhiking is never entirely safe in any country and even in Mexico's relatively safe Yucatán region it's best avoided. Travelers who decide to hitch should understand that they are taking a small, but potentially serious, risk. Keep in mind that kidnappings for ransom can – and do – still happen in Mexico. People who choose to hitch will be safer if they travel in pairs and let someone know where they are planning to go. A woman traveling alone certainly should not hitchhike in Mexico, and even two women together is not advisable, especially when traveling near the Mexico–Guatemala border.

However, some people do choose to hitchhike, and it's not an uncommon way of getting to some of the off-the-beaten-track archaeological sites and other places that are poorly served by bus. If you decide to do so, keep your wits about you and don't accept a lift if you have any misgivings.

In Mexico it's customary for the hitchhiker to offer to pay for the ride, especially if it's in a work or commercial vehicle. As a general rule, offer about M$30 to M$50 per person for fairly short rides and M$100 for longer trips.

If you're driving a vehicle through rural areas, it's not uncommon for Mexican townspeople to ask for a lift. Most folks in these parts are harmless and they are only asking for a ride because there is infrequent bus service, but by no means should you feel obligated, especially if the person gives off a strange vibe.

Local Transportation

Bus

Generally known as *camiones* or *autobuses*, local buses are a cheap way to get around any large city, such as Cancún or Mérida.

They usually stop at fixed *paradas* (bus stops), though in some places you can hold out your hand to stop one at any street corner. Most carry change.

Bicycle

Bicycling is becoming a more common mode of transportation in some cities. Having said that, never assume that motorists will give you the right of way and be particularly careful on narrow roads. A few areas, such as Valladolid, Tulum and Chetumal, now have bicycle paths. In Mérida, a main downtown street is closed to traffic on Sundays for morning rides and on Wednesday nights a group of bicycle activists organizes mass rides. You can rent bikes in many towns for about M$25 per hour or M$100 per day.

It's possible to purchase a bicycle in the Yucatán. Indeed, if you plan to stay on the peninsula for a few months and want to get around by bike or at least exercise on one, purchasing isn't a bad option, as there are many inexpensive models available in the big cities.

You're best off touring on bike from December through March, when the weather is cooler and it stays relatively dry.

Colectivos & Combis

On much of the peninsula, a variety of vehicles – often Volkswagen, Ford or Chevrolet vans – operate shared transportation services between towns or nearby neighborhoods. These vehicles usually leave whenever they are full. Fares are typically less than those of 1st-class buses. Combi is a term often used for the Volkswagen variety; *colectivo* refers to any van type. *Taxi colectivo* may mean either public or private transport, depending on the location.

Taxis

Taxis are common in towns and cities, and surprisingly economical. City rides usually cost around M$20 for a short trip. If a taxi has a meter, you can ask the driver if it's working (*'¿Funciona el taximetro?'*). If there's no meter, which is usually the case, agree on a price before getting in the cab.

Many airports and some bus terminals have a system of authorized taxis: you buy a fixed-price ticket to your destination from a booth and then hand it over to the driver instead of paying cash. Fares are higher than what you'd pay on the street but these cabs offer guaranteed safety.

In tourist centers you'll often find fares posted at taxi bases. If the driver does not respect the published fare, report it to a supervisor.

Renting a taxi for a daylong, out-of-town jaunt generally costs something similar to a rental car by the time you're done with gas – M$750 to M$1000.

Language

Although the predominant language of Mexico is Spanish, about 50 indigenous languages are spoken as a first language by more than seven million people throughout the country. There are more than 30 Maya languages still spoken today. In Chiapas the most widely spoken ones are Tzeltal, Tzotzil and Chol. Yucatec Maya is the most widely spoken indigenous language of the Yucatán.

SPANISH

Mexican Spanish pronunciation is easy, as most sounds have equivalents in English. Note that kh is a throaty sound (like the 'ch' in the Scottish *loch*), v and b are both pronounced like a soft English 'v' (between a 'v' and a 'b'), and r is strongly rolled. Also keep in mind that in some parts of Mexico the letters *ll* and *y* are pronounced like the 'll' in 'million', but in most areas they are pronounced like the 'y' in 'yes', and this is how they are represented in our pronunciation guides. If you read our colored pronunciation guides as if they were English, you'll be understood just fine. The stressed syllables are indicated with italics.

Where both polite and informal options are given in this chapter, they are indicated by the abbreviations 'pol' and 'inf'. Masculine and feminine forms of words are included where relevant and separated with a slash, eg *perdido/a* (m/f).

WANT MORE?

For in-depth language information and handy phrases, check out Lonely Planet's *Mexican Spanish Phrasebook*. You'll find it at **shop.lonelyplanet.com**, or you can buy Lonely Planet's iPhone phrasebooks at the Apple App Store.

Basics

Hello.	*Hola.*	*o*·la
Goodbye.	*Adiós.*	a·*dyos*
How are you?	*¿Qué tal?*	ke tal
Fine, thanks.	*Bien, gracias.*	byen *gra*·syas
Excuse me.	*Perdón.*	per·*don*
Sorry.	*Lo siento.*	lo *syen*·to
Please.	*Por favor.*	por fa·*vor*
Thank you.	*Gracias.*	*gra*·syas
You're welcome.	*De nada.*	de *na*·da
Yes./No.	*Sí./No.*	see/no

My name is ...
Me llamo ... — me *ya*·mo ...

What's your name?
¿Cómo se llama Usted? — *ko*·mo se *ya*·ma oo·*ste* (pol)
¿Cómo te llamas? — *ko*·mo te *ya*·mas (inf)

Do you speak English?
¿Habla inglés? — *a*·bla een·*gles* (pol)
¿Hablas inglés? — *a*·blas een·*gles* (inf)

I don't understand.
Yo no entiendo. — yo no en·*tyen*·do

Accommodations

I'd like a ... room.	*Quisiera una habitación ...*	kee·*sye*·ra *oo*·na a·bee·ta·*syon* ...
single	*individual*	een·dee·vee·*dwal*
double	*doble*	*do*·ble

How much is it per night/person?
¿Cuánto cuesta por noche/persona? — *kwan*·to *kwes*·ta por *no*·che/per·*so*·na

Does it include breakfast?
¿Incluye el desayuno? — een·*kloo*·ye el de·sa·*yoo*·no

air-con	*aire acondicionado*	ai·re a·kon·dee·syo·*na*·do
bathroom	*baño*	*ba*·nyo
bed	*cama*	*ka*·ma
campsite	*terreno de cámping*	te·*re*·no de *kam*·peeng
hotel	*hotel*	o·*tel*
guesthouse	*pensión*	pen·*syon*
window	*ventana*	ven·*ta*·na
youth hostel	*albergue juvenil*	al·*ber*·ge khoo·ve·*neel*

Directions

Where's ...?
¿Dónde está ...? — *don*·de es·*ta* ...

What's the address?
¿Cuál es la dirección? — kwal es la dee·rek·*syon*

Could you please write it down?
¿Puede escribirlo, por favor? — *pwe*·de es·kree·*beer*·lo por fa·*vor*

Can you show me (on the map)?
¿Me lo puede indicar (en el mapa)? — me lo *pwe*·de een·dee·*kar* (en el *ma*·pa)

at the corner	*en la esquina*	en la es·*kee*·na
at the traffic lights	*en el semáforo*	en el se·*ma*·fo·ro
behind ...	*detrás de ...*	de·*tras* de ...
far	*lejos*	*le*·khos
in front of ...	*enfrente de ...*	en·*fren*·te de ...
left	*izquierda*	ees·*kyer*·da
near	*cerca*	*ser*·ka
next to ...	*al lado de ...*	al *la*·do de ...
opposite ...	*frente a ...*	*fren*·te a ...
right	*derecha*	de·*re*·cha
straight ahead	*todo recto*	*to*·do *rek*·to

Eating & Drinking

Can I see the menu, please?
¿Puedo ver el menú, por favor? — *pwe*·do ver el me·*noo* por fa·*vor*

What would you recommend?
¿Qué recomienda? — ke re·ko·*myen*·da

I don't eat (meat).
No como (carne). — no *ko*·mo (*kar*·ne)

That was delicious!
¡Estaba buenísimo! — es·*ta*·ba bwe·*nee*·see·mo

Cheers!
¡Salud! — sa·*loo*

The bill, please.
La cuenta, por favor. — la *kwen*·ta por fa·*vor*

I'd like a table for ...	*Quisiera una mesa para ...*	kee·*sye*·ra *oo*·na *me*·sa *pa*·ra ...
(eight) o'clock	*las (ocho)*	las (*o*·cho)
(two) people	*(dos) personas*	(dos) per·*so*·nas

Key Words

bottle	*botella*	bo·*te*·ya
breakfast	*desayuno*	de·sa·*yoo*·no
cold	*frío*	*free*·o
dessert	*postre*	*pos*·tre
dinner	*cena*	*se*·na
fork	*tenedor*	te·ne·*dor*
glass	*vaso*	*va*·so
hot (warm)	*caliente*	kal·*yen*·te
knife	*cuchillo*	koo·*chee*·yo
lunch	*comida*	ko·*mee*·da
plate	*plato*	*pla*·to
restaurant	*restaurante*	res·tow·*ran*·te
spoon	*cuchara*	koo·*cha*·ra

Meat & Fish

beef	*carne de vaca*	*kar*·ne de *va*·ka
chicken	*pollo*	*po*·yo
crab	*cangrejo*	kan·*gre*·kho
lamb	*cordero*	kor·*de*·ro

Numbers

1	*uno*	*oo*·no
2	*dos*	dos
3	*tres*	tres
4	*cuatro*	*kwa*·tro
5	*cinco*	*seen*·ko
6	*seis*	seys
7	*siete*	*sye*·te
8	*ocho*	*o*·cho
9	*nueve*	*nwe*·ve
10	*diez*	dyes
20	*veinte*	*veyn*·te
30	*treinta*	*treyn*·ta
40	*cuarenta*	kwa·*ren*·ta
50	*cincuenta*	seen·*kwen*·ta
60	*sesenta*	se·*sen*·ta
70	*setenta*	se·*ten*·ta
80	*ochenta*	o·*chen*·ta
90	*noventa*	no·*ven*·ta
100	*cien*	syen
1000	*mil*	meel

Question Words

How?	*¿Cómo?*	*ko*·mo
What?	*¿Qué?*	ke
When?	*¿Cuándo?*	*kwan*·do
Where?	*¿Dónde?*	*don*·de
Who?	*¿Quién?*	kyen
Why?	*¿Por qué?*	por ke

lobster	*langosta*	lan·*gos*·ta
oysters	*ostras*	*os*·tras
pork	*cerdo*	*ser*·do
shrimp	*camarones*	ka·ma·*ro*·nes
squid	*calamar*	ka·la·*mar*
veal	*ternera*	ter·*ne*·ra

Fruit & Vegetables

apple	*manzana*	man·*sa*·na
apricot	*albaricoque*	al·ba·ree·*ko*·ke
banana	*plátano*	*pla*·ta·no
beans	*frijoles*	free·*kho*·les
cabbage	*col*	kol
capsicum	*pimiento*	pee·*myen*·to
carrot	*zanahoria*	sa·na·*o*·rya
cherry	*cereza*	se·*re*·sa
corn	*maíz*	ma·*ees*
cucumber	*pepino*	pe·*pee*·no
grape	*uvas*	*oo*·vas
lettuce	*lechuga*	le·*choo*·ga
mushroom	*champiñón*	cham·pee·*nyon*
nuts	*nueces*	*nwe*·ses
onion	*cebolla*	se·*bo*·ya
orange	*naranja*	na·*ran*·kha
peach	*melocotón*	me·lo·ko·*ton*
pineapple	*piña*	*pee*·nya
potato	*patata*	pa·*ta*·ta
spinach	*espinacas*	es·pee·*na*·kas
strawberry	*fresa*	*fre*·sa
tomato	*tomate*	to·*ma*·te
watermelon	*sandía*	san·*dee*·a

Other

bread	*pan*	pan
cake	*pastel*	pas·*tel*
cheese	*queso*	*ke*·so
eggs	*huevos*	*we*·vos
french fries	*papas fritas*	*pa*·pas *free*·tas
honey	*miel*	myel
ice cream	*helado*	e·*la*·do
jam	*mermelada*	mer·me·*la*·da
pepper	*pimienta*	pee·*myen*·ta
rice	*arroz*	a·*ros*
salad	*ensalada*	en·sa·*la*·da
salt	*sal*	sal
soup	*caldo/sopa*	*kal*·do/*so*·pa
sugar	*azúcar*	a·*soo*·kar

Drinks

beer	*cerveza*	ser·*ve*·sa
coffee	*café*	ka·*fe*
juice	*zumo*	*soo*·mo
milk	*leche*	*le*·che
smoothie	*licuado*	lee·*kwa*·do
tea	*té*	te
(mineral) water	*agua (mineral)*	*a*·gwa (mee·ne·*ral*)
(red/white) wine	*vino (tinto/ blanco)*	*vee*·no (*teen*·to/ *blan*·ko)

Emergencies

Help!	*¡Socorro!*	so·*ko*·ro
Go away!	*¡Vete!*	*ve*·te

Call ...!	*¡Llame a ...!*	*ya*·me a ...
a doctor	*un médico*	oon *me*·dee·ko
the police	*la policía*	la po·lee·*see*·a

I'm lost.
Estoy perdido/a. es·*toy* per·*dee*·do/a (m/f)

Where are the toilets?
¿Dónde están los baños? *don*·de es·*tan* los *ba*·nyos

I'm ill.
Estoy enfermo/a. es·*toy* en·*fer*·mo/a (m/f)

I'm allergic to (antibiotics).
Soy alérgico/a a (los antibióticos). soy a·*ler*·khee·ko/a a (los an·tee·*byo*·tee·kos) (m/f)

Shopping & Services

I'd like to buy ...
Quisiera comprar ... kee·*sye*·ra kom·*prar* ...

I'm just looking.
Sólo estoy mirando. *so*·lo es·*toy* mee·*ran*·do

Can I look at it?
¿Puedo verlo? *pwe*·do *ver*·lo

How much is it?
¿Cuánto cuesta? *kwan*·to *kwes*·ta

That's too expensive.
Es muy caro. es mooy *ka*·ro

There's a mistake in the bill.
Hay un error en la cuenta. ai oon e·*ror* en la *kwen*·ta

ATM	*cajero automático*	ka·*khe*·ro ow·to·*ma*·tee·ko
market	*mercado*	mer·*ka*·do
post office	*correos*	ko·*re*·os
tourist office	*oficina de turismo*	o·fee·*see*·na de too·*rees*·mo

Time & Dates

What time is it?	*¿Qué hora es?*	ke *o*·ra es
It's (10) o'clock.	*Son (las diez).*	son (las dyes)
It's half past (one).	*Es (la una) y media.*	es (la *oo*·na) ee *me*·dya

morning	*mañana*	ma·*nya*·na
afternoon	*tarde*	*tar*·de
evening	*noche*	*no*·che
yesterday	*ayer*	a·*yer*
today	*hoy*	oy
tomorrow	*mañana*	ma·*nya*·na

Monday	*lunes*	*loo*·nes
Tuesday	*martes*	*mar*·tes
Wednesday	*miércoles*	*myer*·ko·les
Thursday	*jueves*	*khwe*·ves
Friday	*viernes*	*vyer*·nes
Saturday	*sábado*	*sa*·ba·do
Sunday	*domingo*	do·*meen*·go

Transportation

boat	*barco*	*bar*·ko
bus	*autobús*	ow·to·*boos*
plane	*avión*	a·*vyon*
train	*tren*	tren

A ... ticket, please.	*Un billete de ..., por favor.*	oon bee·*ye*·te de ... por fa·*vor*
1st-class	*primera clase*	pree·*me*·ra *kla*·se
2nd-class	*segunda clase*	se·*goon*·da *kla*·se
one-way	*ida*	*ee*·da
return	*ida y vuelta*	*ee*·da ee *vwel*·ta

What time does it arrive/leave?
¿A qué hora llega/sale? a ke *o*·ra *ye*·ga/*sa*·le

Does it stop at ...?
¿Para en ...? *pa*·ra en ...

What stop is this?
¿Cuál es esta parada? kwal es es·ta pa·*ra*·da

Please tell me when we get to ...
¿Puede avisarme cuando lleguemos a ...? *pwe*·de a·vee·*sar*·me *kwan*·do ye·*ge*·mos a ...

I want to get off here.
Quiero bajarme aquí. *kye*·ro ba·*khar*·me a·*kee*

airport	*aeropuerto*	a·e·ro·*pwer*·to
bus stop	*parada de autobuses*	pa·*ra*·da de ow·to·*boo*·ses
ticket office	*taquilla*	ta·*kee*·ya
timetable	*horario*	o·*ra*·ryo
train station	*estación de trenes*	es·ta·*syon* de *tre*·nes

I'd like to hire a ...	*Quisiera alquilar ...*	kee·*sye*·ra al·kee·*lar* ...
bicycle	*una bicicleta*	*oo*·na bee·see·*kle*·ta
car	*un coche*	oon *ko*·che
motorcycle	*una moto*	*oo*·na *mo*·to

helmet	*casco*	*kas*·ko
mechanic	*mecánico*	me·*ka*·nee·ko
petrol/gas	*gasolina*	ga·so·*lee*·na
service station	*gasolinera*	ga·so·lee·*ne*·ra

Is this the road to ...?
¿Se va a ... por esta carretera? se va a ... por es·ta ka·re·*te*·ra

(How long) Can I park here?
¿(Cuánto tiempo) Puedo aparcar aquí? (*kwan*·to *tyem*·po) *pwe*·do a·par·*kar* a·*kee*

I've run out of petrol.
Me he quedado sin gasolina. me e ke·*da*·do seen ga·so·*lee*·na

I have a flat tyre.
Tengo un pinchazo. *ten*·go oon peen·*cha*·so

Signs

Abierto	Open
Cerrado	Closed
Entrada	Entrance
Hombres/Varones	Men
Mujeres/Damas	Women
Prohibido	Prohibited
Salida	Exit
Servicios/Baños	Toilets

YUCATEC MAYA

Yucatec Maya, spoken primarily in the Yucatán, Campeche and Quintana Roo, and in the northern and western parts of Belize, belongs to the Amerindian languages, spoken by Native American people across North America. This means that Yucatec Maya (commonly called 'Yucatec' by scholars and 'Maya' by local speakers) is related to many indigenous languages spoken in the southeastern United States, as well as far-off California and Oregon (eg Costanoan, Klamath and Tsimshian). Yucatec is just one of about 30 languages in the Maya family (together with Quiché, Mam, Kekchi and Cakchiquel), but it probably has the largest number of speakers, estimated at more than half a million people.

You can hear Yucatec spoken in the markets and occasionally by hotel staff in cities throughout the peninsula. To hear Yucatec spoken by monolingual Maya speakers, you must travel to some of the peninsula's more remote villages. Maya speakers will not assume that you know any of their language. If you attempt to say something in Maya, however, people will usually respond quite favorably.

Pronunciation

The principles of Maya pronunciation are similar to those found in Spanish. Just follow the colored pronunciation guides included next to the Maya phrases in this section and read them as if they were English.

Maya consonants followed by an apostrophe (b', ch', k', p', t') are similar to regular consonants, but they should be pronounced more forcefully and 'explosively'. On the other hand, an apostrophe following a vowel indicates a glottal stop (similar to the sound between the two syllables in 'uh-oh').

Maya is a tonal language, which means that some words have different meanings when pronounced with a high tone or a low tone. For example, *aak* said with a high tone means 'turtle', but when said with a low tone it means 'grass' or 'vine'.

In many Maya place names the word stress falls on the last syllable. In written language, Spanish rules for indicating word stress with accent marks are often followed for these words. This practice varies, however; in this book we have tried to include accent marks whenever possible. Note also that the stressed syllable is always indicated with italics in our pronunciation guides.

Note also that words borrowed from Spanish, even if they are common ones, tend to be stressed differently in Yucatec Maya, eg *amigo* (Spanish for 'friend') is pronounced 'a·*mee*·go' in Spanish and '*a*·mee·go' in Yucatec.

Basics

Note that Maya speakers often reiterate what is said to them, instead of saying 'yes'; eg 'Are you going to the store?' – 'I'm going'.

Hello.	*Hola.*	o·la
Good day.	*Buenos dias.*	*bwe*·nos *dee*·as
How are you?	*Bix a beel?*	beesh a bail
How are you? (less formal)	*Bix yanikech?*	beesh yaw·nee·*kech*
OK./Well.	*Maalob.*	*ma*·lobe
Bye./See you tomorrow.	*Hasta saamal.*	*as*·ta *sa*·mal
Goodbye.	*Pa'atik kin bin.*	*pa'a*·teek keen been
Thank you.	*Dios Bo'otik.*	dyos *boe'o*·teek
Yes.	*Haa./He'ele.*	haa/*he'e*·le
No.	*Ma'.*	ma'
expensive	*ko'o*	*ko'*·o
pretty	*ki'ichpam*	*kee'*·eech·pam

What's your name?
Bix a k'aaba? — beesh a *k'aa*·ba

My name is ...
In kaabae' ... — een ka·ba·*e'* ...

I don't speak Maya.
Ma tin na'atik mayat'aani. — ma' teen *na'*·a·teek ma·ya·*taa*·nee

Do you speak Spanish?
Teche', ka t'aanik wa castellano t'aan? — te·che' ka *t'a*·neek wa ka·stay·*ya*·no t'an

I want to drink water.
Tak in wukik ha'. — tak een woo·*keek* ha'

I'm hungry.
Wiihen. — wee·*hen*

It's (very) tasty.
(Hach) Ki'. — (hach) kee'

How much is that/this one?
Baux lelo'/lela'? — ba·*hoosh* le·*lo'*/le·*la'*

Where is the ...?	*Tu'ux yaan le ...?*	*too'*·oosh yan le ...
bathroom	*baño*	*ba'*·nyo
doctor	*médico*	*me*·dee·ko
hotel	*hotel*	o·*tel*
road to ...	*u be ti' ...*	u be tee ...

1	*un peel*	oom pail
2	*ka peel*	ka pail
3	*ox peel*	osh pail

When counting animate objects, such as people, replace *peel* with *tuul* (pronounced 'tool'). Beyond three, use Spanish numbers.

GLOSSARY

Words specific to food, restaurants and eating are listed on p305.

Ah Tz'ib – Maya scribes. They penned the Chilam Balam and still practice their craft today.

alux (s), **aluxes** (pl) – Maya 'leprechauns,' benevolent 'little people'

Ángeles Verdes – 'Green Angels;' bilingual mechanics in green trucks who patrol major highways, offering breakdown assistance

baluartes – bastions, bulwarks or ramparts

barrio – district, neighborhood

cacique – indigenous chief; also used to describe a provincial warlord or strongman

cafetería – literally 'coffee-shop,' it refers to any informal restaurant with waiter service; it is not usually a self-service restaurant

cajero automático – Automated Teller Machine (ATM)

camión (s), **camiones** (pl) – truck; bus

camioneta – pickup

campechanos – citizens of Campeche

campesinos – countryfolk, farm workers

casa de cambio – currency-exchange office

casetas de teléfono – call offices where an on-the-spot operator connects the call for you, often shortened to *casetas*

Caste War – bloody 19th-century Maya uprising in the Yucatán

cenote – a deep limestone sinkhole containing water

cerveza – beer

Chac – Maya god of rain

chac-mool – Maya sacrificial stone sculpture

chenes – name for cenotes in the Chenes region

chultún (s), **chultunes** (pl) – Maya cistern found at Puuc archaeological sites south of Mérida

coctelería – seafood shack specializing in shellfish cocktails as well as *ceviche*

cocina – cookshop (literally 'kitchen'), a small, basic restaurant usually run by one woman, often located in or near a municipal market; also seen as *cocina económica* (economical kitchen) or *cocina familiar* (family kitchen); see also *lonchería*

colectivo – literally, 'shared,' a car, van (VW combi, Ford or Chevrolet) or minibus that picks up and drops off passengers along its set route; also known as *taxi colectivo*

combi – a catch-all term used for taxi, van and minibus services regardless of vehicle type

comida corrida – set meal, meal of the day

conquistador – explorer-conqueror of Latin America from Spain

costera – waterfront avenue

criollo – a person of pure Spanish descent born in Spanish America

cuota – toll road

daños a terceros – third-party car insurance

de lujo – deluxe class of bus service

DNI – Derecho para No Inmigrante; nonimmigrant fee charged to all foreign tourists and business travelers visiting Mexico

ejido – communal landholding, though laws now allow sale of *ejido* land to outside individuals

encomienda – a grant made to a conquistador, consisting of labor by or tribute from a group of indigenous people; the conquistador was supposed to protect and convert them, but usually treated them as little more than slaves

feria – fair or carnival, typically occurring during a religious holiday

gringo/a – male/female US or Canadian visitor to Latin America (sometimes applied to any visitor of European heritage); can be used derogatorily but more often is a mere statement of fact

gruta – cave, grotto

guayabera – man's thin fabric shirt with pockets and appliquéd designs on the front, over the shoulders and down the back; often worn in place of a jacket and tie

hacienda – estate; Hacienda (capitalized) is the Treasury Department

henequén – agave fiber used to make rope, grown particularly around Mérida

h-menob – Maya shaman still practicing their trade in the Yucatán today

huipil (s), **huipiles** (pl) – indigenous women's sleeveless white tunic, usually intricately and colorfully embroidered

iglesia – church

INAH – Instituto Nacional de Arqueología e Historia; the body in charge of most ancient sites and some museums

INM – Instituto Nacional de Migración (National Immigration Institute)

Itzamná – lord of the heavens; a popular figure on the wooden panels of contemporary architecture

IVA – *Impuesto al valor agregado* or 'ee-bah,' a 15% value-added tax added to many items in Mexico

Ixchel – Maya goddess of the moon and fertility

jarana – a folkloric dance that has been performed by Yucatecans for centuries

jipijapa – an alternative name for panama hats (which are made from *jipijapa* palm fronds)

Kukulcán – Maya name for the Aztec-Toltec plumed serpent Quetzalcóatl

lagunas – small lakes, lagoons

lonchería – from English 'lunch'; a simple restaurant that may in fact serve meals all day (not just lunch); often seen near municipal markets. See also *cocina*.

lotería – Mexico's version of bingo

malecón – waterfront boulevard

mariachi – small ensemble of Mexican street musicians; strolling mariachi bands often perform in restaurants

méridanos – citizens of Mérida

mestizo – also known as *ladino*, a person of mixed indigenous and European blood; the word now more commonly means 'Mexican'

metate – flattish stone on which corn is ground with a cylindrical stone roller

mezcal – a distilled alcoholic drink made from the agave plant

na – thatched Maya hut

nortes – relatively cold storms bringing wind and rain from the north

Nte – abbreviation for *norte* (north), used in street names

Ote – abbreviation for *oriente* (east), used in street names

palapa – thatched, palm-leaf-roofed shelter usually with open sides

Popol Vuh – painted Maya book containing sacred legends and stories; equivalent to the Bible

porfiriato – the name given to the era of Porfirio Diaz's 35-year rule as president-dictator (1876–1911), preceding the Mexican Revolution

PRI – Partido Revolucionario Institucional (Institutional Revolutionary Party); the controlling force in Mexican politics for much of the 20th century

primera (1a) clase – 1st class of bus service

Quetzalcóatl – plumed serpent god of the Aztecs and Toltecs

retablo – altarpiece (usually an ornate gilded, carved wooden decoration in a church)

ría – estuary

roofcomb – a decorative stonework lattice atop a Maya pyramid or temple

sacbé (s), **sacbeob** (pl) – ceremonial limestone avenue or path between great Maya cities

segunda (2a) clase – 2nd class of bus service

Semana Santa – Holy Week, the week from Palm Sunday to Easter Sunday; Mexico's major holiday period

sur – south; often seen in street names

temazcal – bathhouse, sweat lodge

templo – in Mexico, a church; anything from a wayside chapel to a cathedral

tequila – clear, distilled liquor produced, like pulque and *mezcal*, from the maguey cactus

topes – speed bumps, sometimes indicated by a highway sign depicting a row of little bumps

torito – a vivacious song that evokes the fervor of a bullfight

tranvía – tram or motorized trolley

vaquería – a traditional Yucatecan party where couples dance in unison to a series of songs; the parties are often held in town halls or on haciendas

Xibalbá – in Maya religious belief, the secret world or underworld

xtabentún – a traditional Maya spirit in the Yucatán; an anise-flavored liqueur made by fermenting honey

yucateco – someone or something of the Yucatán Peninsula

Behind the Scenes

SEND US YOUR FEEDBACK

We love to hear from travelers – your comments keep us on our toes and help make our books better. Our well-traveled team reads every word on what you loved or loathed about this book. Although we cannot reply individually to your submissions, we always guarantee that your feedback goes straight to the appropriate authors, in time for the next edition. Each person who sends us information is thanked in the next edition – the most useful submissions are rewarded with a selection of digital PDF chapters.

Visit **lonelyplanet.com/contact** to submit your updates and suggestions or to ask for help. Our award-winning website also features inspirational travel stories, news and discussions.

Note: We may edit, reproduce and incorporate your comments in Lonely Planet products such as guidebooks, websites and digital products, so let us know if you don't want your comments reproduced or your name acknowledged. For a copy of our privacy policy visit lonelyplanet.com/privacy.

OUR READERS

Many thanks to the travelers who used the last edition and wrote to us with helpful hints, useful advice and interesting anecdotes:

Constantine Bogios, Jed Breed, Mara De Monte, Sylvie Gelinas, David Hixson, Max Holmberg, Patricia Kubala, Harriet Lawrence, Adrien Maggiora, Stephane Schockaert, Charles Silverman, Tomasz Smaczny, Felix Wagner, Estefania Welsh

AUTHOR THANKS

John Hecht

Thanks to the countless number of good people in the Yucatán who helped make this wonderful journey so special. Special gratitude goes out to commissioning editor Cliff Wilkinson, co-author Lucas Vidgen, the book's previous authors, Yurij Gabassi and my wife, Lau, who looked after two hyperactive kitties.

Lucas Vidgen

Thanks first and foremost to the Mexicans for making such an enjoyable country to travel and work in. Specifically, Andres and Sylvia were a huge help in San Cristóbal, and the Campeche section wouldn't have been the same without Alonso Escobar and his compadre César. And as always, thanks to América, Sofía and Teresa for being there, and being there when I got back.

ACKNOWLEDGEMENTS

Climate map data adapted from Peel MC, Finlayson BL & McMahon TA (2007) 'Updated World Map of the Köppen-Geiger Climate Classification', *Hydrology and Earth System Sciences*, 11, pp1633–44.

Chichén Itzá illustration pp186–7 by Michael Weldon

Cover photograph: Cenote at Dzitnup (X'Kekén), JoseIgnacioSoto/Getty Images ©.

THIS BOOK

This 7th edition of Lonely Planet's *Cancún, Cozumel & the Yucatán* guidebook was researched and written by John Hecht and Lucas Vidgen. The previous edition was written by John Hecht and Sandra Bao. The 'Yucatecan Cuisine' chapter was written by Mauricio Velázquez de León. This guidebook was produced by the following:

Destination Editor Clifton Wilkinson

Product Editors Kate Chapman, Saralinda Turner

Senior Cartographer Mark Griffiths

Book Designer Michael Buick

Assisting Editors Sarah Bailey, Melanie Dankel, Bruce Evans, Paul Harding, Lauren O'Connell, Kristin Odijk, Vicky Smith, Fionnuala Twomey

Assisting Cartographer Valentina Kremenchutskaya

Cover Researcher Naomi Parker

Thanks to Andi Jones, Karyn Noble, Lyahna Spencer, Tony Wheeler

Index

Map Pages **000**
Photo Pages **000**

Map Pages **000**
Photo Pages **000**

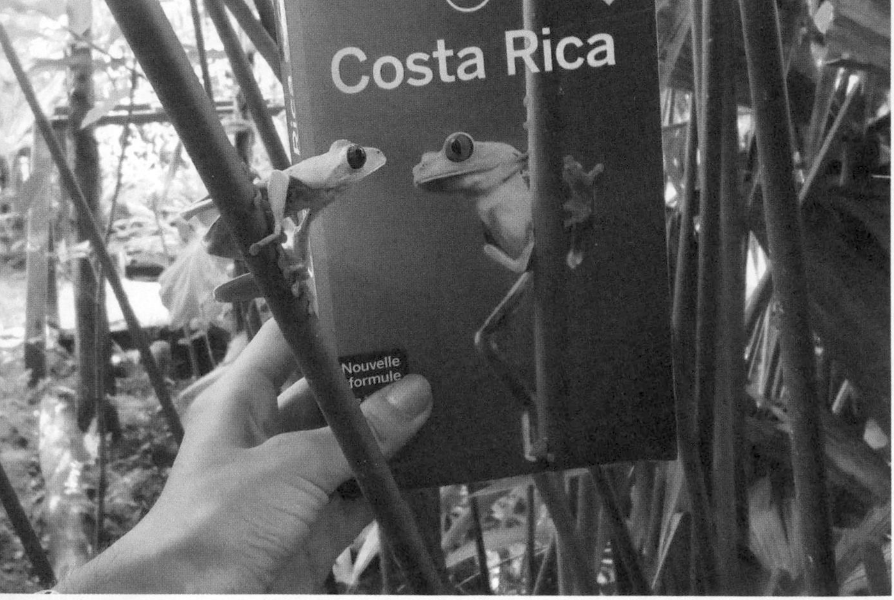

Map Legend

Sights

- Beach
- Bird Sanctuary
- Buddhist
- Castle/Palace
- Christian
- Confucian
- Hindu
- Islamic
- Jain
- Jewish
- Monument
- Museum/Gallery/Historic Building
- Ruin
- Shinto
- Sikh
- Taoist
- Winery/Vineyard
- Zoo/Wildlife Sanctuary
- Other Sight

Activities, Courses & Tours

- Bodysurfing
- Diving
- Canoeing/Kayaking
- Course/Tour
- Sento Hot Baths/Onsen
- Skiing
- Snorkeling
- Surfing
- Swimming/Pool
- Walking
- Windsurfing
- Other Activity

Sleeping

- Sleeping
- Camping

Eating

- Eating

Drinking & Nightlife

- Drinking & Nightlife
- Cafe

Entertainment

- Entertainment

Shopping

- Shopping

Information

- Bank
- Embassy/Consulate
- Hospital/Medical
- Internet
- Police
- Post Office
- Telephone
- Toilet
- Tourist Information
- Other Information

Geographic

- Beach
- Gate
- Hut/Shelter
- Lighthouse
- Lookout
- Mountain/Volcano
- Oasis
- Park
- Pass
- Picnic Area
- Waterfall

Population

- Capital (National)
- Capital (State/Province)
- City/Large Town
- Town/Village

Transport

- Airport
- Border crossing
- Bus
- Cable car/Funicular
- Cycling
- Ferry
- Metro station
- Monorail
- Parking
- Petrol station
- Subway/Subte station
- Taxi
- Train station/Railway
- Tram
- Underground station
- Other Transport

Note: Not all symbols displayed above appear on the maps in this book

Routes

- Tollway
- Freeway
- Primary
- Secondary
- Tertiary
- Lane
- Unsealed road
- Road under construction
- Plaza/Mall
- Steps
- Tunnel
- Pedestrian overpass
- Walking Tour
- Walking Tour detour
- Path/Walking Trail

Boundaries

- International
- State/Province
- Disputed
- Regional/Suburb
- Marine Park
- Cliff
- Wall

Hydrography

- River, Creek
- Intermittent River
- Canal
- Water
- Dry/Salt/Intermittent Lake
- Reef

Areas

- Airport/Runway
- Beach/Desert
- Cemetery (Christian)
- Cemetery (Other)
- Glacier
- Mudflat
- Park/Forest
- Sight (Building)
- Sportsground
- Swamp/Mangrove

OUR STORY

A beat-up old car, a few dollars in the pocket and a sense of adventure. In 1972 that's all Tony and Maureen Wheeler needed for the trip of a lifetime – across Europe and Asia overland to Australia. It took several months, and at the end – broke but inspired – they sat at their kitchen table writing and stapling together their first travel guide, *Across Asia on the Cheap*. Within a week they'd sold 1500 copies. Lonely Planet was born.

Today, Lonely Planet has offices in Dublin, Franklin, London, Melbourne, Oakland, Beijing and Delhi, with more than 600 staff and writers. We share Tony's belief that 'a great guidebook should do three things: inform, educate and amuse'.

OUR WRITERS

John Hecht

Cancún & Around, Isla Mujeres, Isla Cozumel, Riviera Maya, Costa Maya & the Southern Caribbean, Yucatán State & the Maya Heartland John has spent more than 20 years living in Mexico, during which time he has contributed to numerous editions of the Lonely Planet *Mexico* book. He was coordinating author on the previous edition of LP's *Cancún, Cozumel & the Yucatán* and he produced a series of short videos shot in the Yucatán region for Lonely Planet TV. He lives in Mexico City with his Mexican wife. Mom's still waiting for him to return to the good ole' USA. John also wrote the Plan Your Trip, Understand (except Yucatecan Cuisine), and Survival Guide chapters.

Lucas Vidgen

Campeche, Chiapas Lucas first visited Mexico back in 2002, breezing through the Yucatán long enough to be captivated by the lush scenery and irresistible food. Later he moved to Guatemala, which served as a good base for exploring Chiapas and the rest of the Mundo Maya. Lucas has contributed to a variety of Lonely Planet titles, mostly in Central and South America. Back home he publishes – and very occasionally works on – Quetzaltenango's leading nightlife magazine, XelaWho (www.xelawho.com).

Contributing Writer

Mauricio Velázquez de León was born in Mexico City, where he was given boiled chicken feet and toasted corn tortillas to sooth his teething pains. He is the author of *My Foodie ABC: A Little Gourmet's Guide* (Duo Press, 2010) and lives in Maryland with his wife and twin sons, whose teething pains were soothed with toasted corn tortillas. Mauricio wrote the Yucatecan Cuisine chapter in this book.

Published by Lonely Planet Global Ltd
CRN 554153
7th edition – September 2016
ISBN 978 1 78657 017 8

10 9 8 7 6 5 4
Printed in China